MW00397021

INDOMITABLE WILL

INDOMITABLE WILL

Turning defeat into victory from Pearl
Harbor to Midway

4/21/12

Charles Kupfer

To Mary & Jan,

w/love & thanks for

being mine.

continuum

Continuum International Publishing Group

The Tower Building
11 York Road
London SE1 7NX

80 Maiden Lane
Suite 704
New York, NY 10038

www.continuumbooks.com

© Charles Kupfer, 2012

All rights reserved. No part of this book may be reproduced, stored in a retrieval system, or transmitted, in any form or by any means, electronic, mechanical, photocopying, recording, or otherwise, without the written permission of the publishers.

ISBN: 978-0-8264-1068-9

Library of Congress Cataloging-in-Publication Data
Kupfer, Charles.
Indomitable will : turning defeat into victory from Pearl Harbor to Midway / Charles Kupfer.
    p. cm.
Includes bibliographical references and index.
ISBN-13: 978-0-8264-1068-9 (hardcover: alk. paper)
ISBN-10: 0-8264-1068-5 (hardcover : alk. paper) 1. World War, 1939–1945–Campaigns–
Pacific Area. 2. World War, 1939–1945–Naval operations, American. I. Title.
D767.K85 2012
940.54'26–dc23
2011048382

Typeset by Newgen Imaging Systems Pvt Ltd, Chennai, India
Printed in the United States of America

To Matthias Maass, Graduate School of International Studies,
Yonsei University
Scholar, Colleague, Friend
"Der Gute Kamerad . . . Einen bessern findst du nicht"

CONTENTS

FOREWORD AND ACKNOWLEDGMENTS

Take a look, and you will see the mind of America at work.
— BEPPE SEVERGNINI[1]

This book tells the story of what Americans knew and how they reacted during the six months after Japan's attack on Pearl Harbor. December 7, 1941 until mid-June, 1942 (when news of the Battle of Midway reached home) encompassed some of the worst military disasters in US history. Americans faced unremittingly bad news; daily stories of harrowing retreats and awful defeats. While there was shock and dismay, there was relatively little panic. Recriminations did crop up, but they were less prevalent than resolve. It is not always remembered that, early on, World War II was an experience of defeat on several fronts for the United States. The image of Britain standing alone against the Third Reich during the knife-edge days of 1940 is remembered, as it should be. But in the Winter of 1941 and Spring of 1942, the United States faced travails of its own. The war came with no guarantee of a positive outcome, which is sometimes overshadowed in memory by the magnitude of eventual victory. This book seeks to remind readers that defeat was an early and important part of the American war story, conditioning the nation, revealing much about the American attitude, and setting the stage for what came after.

Media necessarily plays a large role in this account. Radio, newspapers, and magazines contributed to the massive information flow Americans processed and interpreted. So, too, did literature, which limns patterns in American life. Certain writers and broadcasters played discernible roles, recapitulated here. The plentitude of accurate, balanced, and sober information and analysis available to Americans during the most dangerous phase of the war is still amazing. The overall performance of the American media during the time in question must be ranked as superb, and appropriately influential on the public.

This book is a work of American Studies in that it takes an interdisciplinary approach to studying the United States. It is a work of Intellectual History, in that it

---

[1] Beppe Severgnini, *Ciao, America! An Italian Discovers the US* (New York: Broadway Books, 2002 c1995), 175–6.

explores how certain ideas worked in the American mind to affect national policy. It is a work of Journalism History, in that it deals with media communications from the past. It is a work of International Relations, in that it delineates layered interactions between the United States and other nations. And it is a work of Military History in that it addresses war's vicissitudes. The hope here is that combining these methods lets them inform each other so readers can see parallel patterns across American life. My models are works by William H. Goetzmann, Robert A. Divine, and Robert Crunden, as well as recent historical/cultural studies such as Paul Lendvai's *The Hungarians: A Thousand Years of Victory in Defeat*. Two earlier books on 1942, John Toland's *But Not in Shame* and Henry H. Adams' *1942: The Year that Doomed the Axis*, enlivened my interest in the topic.

There are some "Big Ideas" in this book. Two predate the war, although the Pearl Harbor attack caused them to flourish and reach their mature state. These are navalism, or, "The Naval Idea," and Anglo-American Convergence. The Naval Idea is shorthand for reflexive acceptance of the proposition that American well-being requires a large, flexible navy to project and protect national interests. Anglo-American Convergence signifies the joining together of Great Britain and United States in an alliance propelled along by irresistible *cultural* influences as well as quotidian strategic considerations. Since I stress the cultural underpinnings of the "Special Relationship," there is discussion of Anglo-American literary and social bonds which might otherwise seem out of place in a war book. I contend that the cultural and military dimensions of the London–Washington alliance reaffirmed each other over decades, reflecting social developments in both nations. Another main idea is reflected in the title. "Indomitable Will" is a phrase used by Franklin Roosevelt in a cable to Douglas MacArthur on February 10, 1942. The President told the General that troops in the Philippines needed to reflect the indomitable will of the American people to win the war. It signified the insight that popular feelings affected the war's shape. "Turning Defeat into Victory" comes from the title of General William Slim's memoirs of the Burma campaign. Routed early, Slim fought on to see defeat turned into victory. The title signals the main finding of this book: Americans were steady and mature in their reaction to six months of military disaster. Their resolve informed military strategy. Because of their open media culture, they were well aware of battlefield setbacks. However, because they shared a set of common reference points and assumptions about the war and the world, Americans remained convinced that victory would come, albeit after years of struggle and loss. They did not waver in their commitment to victory. Half-a-year's worth of dire setbacks did not daunt The People.

Past teachers and professors at Sidwell Friends and Johns Hopkins, some now deceased, retain their motive power in my work, starting with Joe Wildermuth, Gertrude Guckenheimer, and Hall Katzenbach. Stephen Dixon, of the Hopkins Writing Seminars Department, still animates me when I recall his insistence on heedful prose. George Liska's insights on the warp and woof of international politics were revelatory. Elspeth Rostow, Terry and Jan Todd, Robert Abzug,

Richard Pells, and Mark Smith, of the University of Texas, were great teachers. Shelley Fishkin, now of Stanford University, roused my belief in using literature as a window into culture. At St. Catherine's and Nuffield colleges, Oxford University, Wilfrid Knapp, Brendan McLaughlin, and Keith Dowding taught me about Anglo-American similarities—and differences! Douglass Noverr and Larry Ziewacz, at Michigan State, fostered my early efforts on the project. At Penn State Harrisburg. American Studies Program Coordinator Simon Bronner was a steady source of moral and practical support. Michael Barton never stinted either as friend or mentor. John Haddad was a boon comrade. Anne Verplanck, too. Other helpful Penn Staters include Craig Haas (with special thanks for guidance on Paul Tillich), Greg Crawford, Henry Koretzky, Gary Cross, Irwin Richman, Rob Coffman, Jim Johnson, Paul Manlove, Yvonne Sims. Cheri Ross, Sam Winch, Matthew Wilson, Troy Thomas, David Witwer, Cat Rios, Glen Mazis, Meg Jaster, Patrick Burrowes, Amy Saeurteig, Erin Battat, and superb graduate assistant Claire Guest. Humanities School Director Kathryn Robinson merits special gratitude. Deans Marian Walters, Omid Ansary, and Chancellor Mukund Kulkarni lent Penn State support. Administrative experts Sue Etter, Jennie Adams, Cindy Leach, and Ella Dowell were fantastically helpful. A slew of energetic Penn State students—too numerous to name here—incited me with incessant questions about when the project would be finished. Master's graduates Cuc Nguyen, Jenny Bisht, Joe Martinak, and Erik Walker discussed international, cultural, and military affairs. Librarians at Penn State Harrisburg, Penn State Pattee Library, the Library of Congress, the National Archives, Johns Hopkins Milton Eisenhower Library, Yale's Sterling Library, and American University Library all assisted with kindness and can-do expertise. Rivendell Books, in Montpelier, Vermont, helped me track down a hard-to-find local text. It was a thrill to meet Pitt Professor Donald M. Goldstein on a Pennsylvania Cable Network program, and his encouragement of this project remains keenly appreciated. At Continuum, Marie-Claire Antoine keeps high standards while being patient and encouraging. She was the biggest help of all and my gratitude to her is maximal. Srikanth Srinivasan and the talented staff at Newgen were consummate professionals with whom it was a pleasure to work.

Personally, I thank friends and family, some of whom did not know they were helping. Kimberly Wolf Kupfer lives her own busy life, but many of her efforts advance the fortunes of our four children, so I am grateful to her. Willie, Teddy, Sandy, and Heidi Kupfer were my best sources of distraction and comic relief. Sarah Kupfer did triple-duty as a sister, Library of Congress Research Assistant, and Wodehouse consultant. Two fathers boosted my efforts. Although Carl Kupfer died before the book's completion, he tended my interest in the subject during childhood. Charles Jan Dyke read an early version of the manuscript, making sound suggestions. He also extracted Douglas MacArthur's gall bladder years ago at Walter Reed Hospital, which affords me a pleasing, if bilious, connection to the General. Lt. Col. Lester M. Dyke—"Uncle Robin"—and Aunt Mary Esther deserve thanks, as do my Texas cousins. Brothers Janny, Peter, and

Tommy Dyke and sister Abigail Dyke Klinect merit thanks. Barbara Wolf and Jerome Fine coaxed me along. Thanks to Anthony Pollina, Leo Sorokin, David Morgan, Kelly O'Neal, and their families. Mark Shaw, David Martin, Edward Meigs, Campbell McGrath, Michael Rossides, David Harding, Henry Steuart, and Will Rice contributed either specific ideas or general solidarity. In Camp Hill, Bob Charlton is my best discussion partner. Professionals whose assistance made progress possible were Vivian Blanc, Lawrence Altaker, Steve Schiffman, Ronald Barsanti, Scott Setzer, Ron Muroff, and Rick Weaver. In their own way, each put wind beneath my wings. No one helped more sincerely than Matthias Maass, to whom this book is affectionately dedicated. His solidarity, integrity, energy, and intelligence are unyielding; he embodies the best of scholarship and comradeship. This business can be lonely, yet it has given me such a fine friend, *mein guter kamerad*. I eagerly await future decades of lively collaboration and fun adventures. Live long, and prosper, Matti!

1 THROUGH DECEMBER 8

Infamy and Aftermath: Pearl Harbor, December 7–8, 1941

There Goes the Arizona!
> Mrs. Grace Earle, of Honolulu, to her neighbor, Fleet Commander Admiral Husband Kimmel, December 7, 1941, 7:53 a.m.[1]

Surprise Attack Successful!
> Message sent from Commander Mitsuo Fuchida to Akagi, forwarded to Japanese General Staff, Tokyo, December 7 (12/8 in Japan), 7:53 a.m.[2]

When Vice Admiral Chuichi Nagumo and Rear Admiral Ryunosuke Kusaka squinted into the bright Pacific sky shortly after 10:00 a.m. on December 7, they beheld a smattering of dark dots. These were Japanese planes fresh from Pearl Harbor. The dots grew, resolved into shapes, closed and landed on the flagship *Akagi* deck. Dive bombers disgorged excited crews, including Commander Mitsuo Fuchida. Three hours earlier, leading the first aerial wave, Fuchida plowed through 20-knot northeast winds and clouds before plunging into clearer skies.[3] Fuchida saw the white fringe of breaking surf below and the sunrise over Oahu. The resplendent orb's spreading rays looked benign, as omens went, since they resembled the Imperial Navy's own *Kyokujitsu-ki* Rising Sun ensign. He could believe that fate blessed Japan's gamble. His cry, *"Tora! Tora! Tora!"* opened the attack.[4]

Back on *Akagi*, Fuchida debriefed quickly since he expected to take off for the last lethal sortie. Leaving fiery confusion at the scene, Fuchida and his flyers were anxious to return to Pearl Harbor, strike with finality, and render the home port of the US Navy an unusable mess. Japanese attentions now fixed on fuel depots, air fields, repair docks, and ships in anchorage, all repairable or still unharmed.[5] One hundred and eighty-three airplanes—B5N2 "Kate" torpedo bombers, Aichi D3A1 "Val" dive bombers, and scores of the nimble Mitsubishi A6M2 "Zero" fighters[6]—all hit Pearl Harbor severely in their two-wave assault: 19 ships wrecked; 177 planes destroyed; 3,343 Americans killed or missing, 1,842 wounded.[7] But was it enough? Fuchida and his men wanted Pearl Harbor, strategic redoubt of the broad Pacific, to be the graveyard of American naval potentialities.

The power of command was Nagumo's; he had much on his mind. Foremost was the location of the American aircraft carriers which would have been the featured prize for his Combined Striking Force, *Kido Butai.* Still at large, the carriers loomed as a threat to his fleet of six carriers, two battleships, assorted cruisers, destroyers, supply ships, and tankers.[8] Moreover, the Americans still had flight-worthy planes. How long could the confusion last before vengeful American pilots took wing in search of his own task force? Lingering too long in the waters north of Hawaii might convert his victory into disaster. When Nagumo forbore to order the follow-up run which Fuchida expected, his reasons were cautious. The decision not to send another flight of bombers had merits and demerits in terms of naval tactics. But Nagumo's choice also ushered in the post-Pearl Harbor phase of the war. Borne of desperation, a gambler's hazard, Japan's surprise took months to plan and three hours to unfold. After 180 minutes of action, the process of clean-up and assessment started at Pearl Harbor and elsewhere. The belligerents needed to process the event. Bogged down in China, prodded by a dysfunctional congeries of army chauvinists enmeshed in the government, and chasing a delusory dominion over Asia, hard-pressed Tokyo saw few strategic options and a need to alter the Pacific situation. Now, they had done it. Washington would adjust to shock, assign blame, react according to its own lights. The United States was utterly in the war. Japan had changed the strategic calculus, but the shape of the change needed time to reveal itself.

*   *   *

It rained lightly at Pearl Harbor on the morning of December 8. But the scattered droplets hardly dampened the fires. Towering plumes of darkest smoke—choking, acrid, as oily as the slicks which fed the flames—wound heavenward above the double-line of ships moored off Ford Island. This was Battleship Row, once-proudest stretch of water in the world, whence sallied forth the battle wagons which were the joy of every navy sailor.

West Virginia, holed by torpedoes, rudder shorn, lay busted in the harbor mud. Destroyers *Townes* and *Cassin* were masses of twisted metal, aflame. Destroyer *Shaw*, blackened superstructure low in the water, rested hot in the ooze. *Maryland*, *Tennessee*, and *Pennsylvania* were hit, but lightly. Alongside *West Virginia* was the upturned *Oklahoma*. Minelayer *Oglala* capsized; *California* simmered in oil fires. Other ships—cruisers *Honolulu*, *Helena*, *Raleigh*, repair ship *Vestal*—struggled with damage containment. Aboard each, sweaty and exhausted men strove to save their ships while their mates lay around them burned, dying, or dead. *Nevada* had run for the open sea, almost making it before Japanese pilots noticed. Under attack, the ship beached so as not to block the harbor. *Nevada* now lolled aground in the shallows. *Arizona* listed more and more until capsizing, trapping hundreds of sailors in flooding darkness.[9] Their exits blocked by harbor waters, these crewmen were doomed.

The June 8 scene was in some ways worse than when the planes first hit. Oil, already burning or threatening to ignite, flowed across the harbor out to the ocean. So did torn and blackened bodies. They bobbed morbidly along until frenzied rescue crews could collect them. *Tern*, a minesweeper, floated by *West Virginia*, targeting its flames with hoses. On every damaged ship, crews buzzed, working beyond endurance. Small boats zipped around ferrying supplies and picking up cadavers.

Rescuers knew that men still fought for life in the upturned hulls of *Oklahoma* and *Arizona*. There might be time to save some, yet many must die trapped. Mere inches separated the trapped from their would-be saviors, but those were inches of steel. Cutting through a battleship took special equipment. Men from the Navy Yard crawled over the hulls like bugs on a carcass, trying to extricate comrades from the pitiless horror below. From within came a sound that stayed with all who heard it: "... TapTapTap ... Tap ... Tap ... Tap ... TapTapTap ..." Sailors inside had snaked through the blackness, rapping against the keel with whatever metal objects they could grasp, trying to guide their rescuers.[10] The rescuers knew their comrades were just a few feet away. A bare few survivors made it through hastily cut holes. Most on *Oklahoma* and *Arizona* tapped out their SOS until the flood silenced them. For those who heard, the taps never stopped, haunting them for life.

Washington, D.C.: Presidential messages

We await your commands.
David Sarnoff to Franklin Roosevelt, December 7, 1941[11]

Like prizefighters and thoroughbreds, Presidents depend upon a large supporting staff. But when the moment comes, they strive alone. Word of the attack, "AIR RAID PEARL HARBOR—THIS IS NO DRILL,"[12] came at 1:40 p.m. Franklin Delano Roosevelt was lunching in the Oval Office with *major domo* Harry Hopkins.[13] Hopkins was the President's most intimate advisor. For years, their chats were rife with worry about Japan's imitative Hitlerism: changing strategic problems through sudden moves. On December 6, they mused about British intelligence reports of Japanese troop transports steaming towards Thailand's Kra Peninsula. Thailand was weak, likely to comply with whatever Japan demanded.

Roosevelt and Hopkins knew the Japanese were stirring, with British Malaya and Dutch Java likely targets.[14]

As soon as Navy Secretary Frank Knox dropped off the radio report from Honolulu, it was clear that the President would shortly make the trip down Pennsylvania Avenue to address Congress. It was also apparent that anything he said would go beyond his congressional audience. The White House press corps went on highest alert, which made Press Secretary Steve Early a busy man. "I have a very important statement. It ought to go out verbatim," the President told Early, who hoped to spend the day golfing at Burning Tree.[15] Instead, Early spent the day as liaison between the White House and the press. "So far as known now, 4 attacks on Hon + Man wr md wholly wot warning when both nations at peace," read Early's note card when he first approached reporters.[16] This translated into the release he dictated by phone to the news wires: "The Japanese have attacked Pearl Harbor from the air and all naval and military activities on the island of Oahu, the principal American base in the Hawaiian Islands."[17] A second release went out a few minutes later. Thus did their elected leader let Americans know that the nation was no longer uneasily at peace.

Early was the one-man contact point between FDR and the mainstream press. But Roosevelt was too much the bet-hedger to delegate everything to one person. Early knew that his job was to handle the wholesale press. His next days would be full as he shuttled between the President, the White House switchboard, reporters, and his office.[18] But a retail approach was also a presidential specialty. During those quicksilver hours, Roosevelt brought Edward R. Murrow, America's most famous news gatherer into the White House. The key was to show that the White House was aware of events, in control of sources, and delivering usable information.

For years, FDR avoided unambiguous commitment to a single strategic policy. He saw Germany as the paramount international threat. But as long as the Third Reich followed its American appeasement, the President could not be sure of convincing the public that Berlin was a present danger. The popular Neutrality Act meant that Roosevelt could not tread too closely to Europe's conflict. He learned from experience. One presidential policy nostrum was too strong for American opinion. This was FDR's "Quarantine Speech," given in Chicago on October 5, 1937. It decried what Roosevelt labeled "a reign of terror and international lawlessness" around the world.[19] People knew that he referred to Japanese depredations in China and Hitler's moves in Europe. How individual Americans reacted to the speech depended upon how they felt about drawing the United States closer to conflict.[20] The main reaction was leeriness. Roosevelt tried to rally support for collective international action against tyrants abroad but succeeded mainly in angering isolationists at home. Having burned himself by getting ahead of the populace, Roosevelt would bob, weave, and recommit to neutrality with varying sincerity for four years. Well was it said by one wag that charismatic national leaders all had salutes: Mussolini, the fascist arm outstretched, palm out; Hitler, the grudging forearm wave; Churchill, the two-fingered V-for-Victory. FDR? A wet forefinger held aloft to feel prevailing winds.

This was the jape of a loser. Most who took on FDR lost. The Roosevelt administration was the first to make use of the emerging quasi-science of public opinion polling. The White House believed that, in a democracy, *vox populi* really was *vox dei*. While George Gallup and Elmo Roper developed their field in the private sector during the Depression, first-generation Finnish-American Emil Hurja introduced Trend Analysis to the Roosevelt campaign in 1932. Hurja served the White House during the early 1930s. He lent high-profile support to Finland when Stalin's Red Army attacked that Nordic country in 1939. By 1940, Hurja ran *Pathfinder Magazine*, while FDR used Hadley Quantril's issue-directed polling.[21] To the White House, using polling techniques was smart politics. To frustrated opponents, it seemed like political dark arts.

FDR's technical obedience of the Neutrality Act in the face of France's June 1940 collapse angered interventionists who wanted all aid to Britain short of war. Knowing that helping Britain was crucial, Roosevelt edged closer to the war, conjuring up Cash-and-Carry, Destroyers-for-Bases, and Lend-Lease. Each step eased the process of supplying Britain without running too far afoul of the Act. The Act was stretched beyond recognition, but Roosevelt could avoid junking it. At every step, isolationists from Washington and the America First Committee waved the bloody shirt of World War I. For them, FDR was pushing the naive public pell-mell to another war. Meanwhile, interventionists who gathered bundles for Britain lamented the meager commitment for embattled democracy abroad.

Laying a prewar course: navigating interventionist–isolationist shoals

We have only a one-ocean navy. Our army is still untrained and inadequately equipped for foreign war. Our air force is deplorably lacking in modern fighting planes because most of them have already been sent to Europe. When these facts are cited, the interventionists shout that we are defeatists, that we are undermining the principles of democracy, and that we are giving comfort to the enemy by talking about our military weakness. But everything I mention here has been published in our newspapers, and in the reports of congressional hearings in Washington. Our military position is well known to the governments of Europe and Asia. Why, then, should it not be brought to the attention of our own people? I say it is the interventionist in America, as it was in England and in France, who gives comfort to the enemy. I say it is they who are undermining the principles of democracy when they demand that we take a course to which 80 per cent of our citizens are opposed. I charge them with being the real defeatists, for their policy has led to the defeat of every country that followed their advice since the war began.

Charles A. Lindbergh, national radio speech, April 23, 1941[22]

You have seen the outpourings of Berlin in the last few days. You saw Lindbergh's statement last night. I think there is a striking similarity between the two.

Stephen T. Early, White House Press Secretary, September 12, 1941[23]

What isolationists and interventionists really argued about was the nature of World War II. Isolationists saw it as a case of the "toils of foreign caprice," which George Washington warned about in his admonitory Farewell Address. It was in 1796 that the Father of the Country asked what became isolationism's pointed query: "Why quit our own to stand on foreign ground?"[24] For a century, that question focused American strategy on securing hemispheric inviolability. It took Frederick Jackson Turner's 1894 Closing of the Frontier announcement to make Americans realize that North American control was theirs. From that point, outward thrust would reach other lands, placing Washington's question in a different context.

For interventionists, the Second World War was a global struggle with democracy at stake. If Britain fell, the United States would stand precariously in a world given over to tyranny. This prospect stoked the panic many onlookers felt when considering the energies harnessed in Germany, Spain, Italy, Japan, and the Soviet Union. Interventionists and isolationists each felt that American democracy could be protected only through adherence to their irreconcilable stances. The vitriolic argument pushed the two sides apart, polarizing national debate as factions intensified their rhetoric. Charles Lindbergh discerned conspiracies by internationalist bankers, arms merchants, and Jews conniving to maneuver the United States into a profitable war. He found support from conservative and progressive isolationists. Some of his followers muttered about London peddling subversive propaganda, abetted by puppets eager to conflate Britain's well-being with that of the United States.[25] Opposing suspicious isolationists was a spectrum of anti-Nazis, democratic idealists, and regular citizens who admired British pluck, especially during 1940s Battle of Britain. Prominent interventionists included Clare Booth Luce and Dorothy Thompson, who portrayed isolationists as shady, prisoners of obsolete Anglophobia, sympathizing with Hitler and indifferent to democracy's survival. For London's friends, heedlessness over Britain's fate automatically signaled ambivalence to freedom and attraction to fascism.

Whenever well-meaning isolationists tried to explain their position in fairer terms, they were tarred as clueless tyros or fascist sympathizers. Exactly that happened when Anne Murrow Lindbergh penned a slender but incendiary 1940 book, *Wave of the Future*. It posited that tired democracy needed a tune-up, while command-and-control regimes had mastered modern governance. Anne Morrow Lindbergh took real heat, even though her articulations were relatively mild. "A Prayer for Peace" was her 1940 *Reader's Digest* article, which supported American mediation to settle Europe's conflict, and hoped that Nazi Germany could be tamed by an international system of diplomatic and economic arrangements.[26] Her follow-up volume developed the argument. Hitler, Mussolini, and Stalin, were all of a type, she argued. Despite their unsavoriness, the tyrants had "felt the wave of the future and they have leapt upon it . . ."[27] In other words, change was coming, and Americans should get used to it. Morrow Lindbergh envisioned the slender volume laying out the "moral argument for isolationism."[28] It opened her up to the caustic irony of Clare Boothe Luce. In a book review, the playwright and wife of Henry Luce allowed that the aviatrix-author wrote "clear, chiseled, cadenced, almost classic" prose, and that she seemed "sweet." But Morrow Lindbergh was also a crypto-fascist, wrote Boothe Luce, and so was her pilot husband.[29]

Morrow Lindbergh expected to be violently criticized; her expectations were met in full. The only powerful figure with administration connections who took up her cause was Joseph Kennedy. He complained that Francis Biddle headed a cabal of interventionists pushing Roosevelt closer and closer to war. At a November 1940 meeting with the Lindberghs, the Kennedy *paterfamilias* predicted that the English were finished. They only wanted the United States involved to share the blame for the inevitable defeat when they finally negotiated a humbling peace treaty. Hitler was the coming man in Europe, argued the irascible Kennedy, expressing irritation with the President for being too pliant in the fact of interventionist pressures. But Kennedy declined to break publicly with the man who had appointed him, an Irish Catholic, as Ambassador to the Court of St. James.[30]

At the White House, attack dog Harold Ickes called *Wave of the Future* "the bible of every American Nazi, Fascist, and appeaser," adding that Anne's husband Charles was the nation's "number one Nazi fellow traveler," still earning the medal Luftwaffe chief Hermann Goering gave him years earlier.[31] Ickes and Boothe Luce made it plain that the war and one's attitude to it made for venomous discourse well before December 7, 1941. Isolationists stuck to their arguments no matter how ruthless the responses. There were some high-profile adherents to the "Stay Out" campaign, such as writer Oswald Garrison Villard and Socialist Party leader Norman Thomas. Isolationist ranks also included college presidents Phillips Bradley of Amherst, Robert Maynard Hutchins of Chicago, and Henry Noble MacCracken of Vassar.[32] The America First Committee organized across the nation, with scores of chapters on college campuses, lending isolationism a grass-roots framework around which to coalesce. Respectable figures lent credibility to the isolationist cause despite interventionist efforts to make the position disreputable. This helped to burnish a sheen that other sources of support tarnished. The Communist Party of the United States supported isolationism to back up 1939's Hitler–Stalin Pact. Obedient party members adopted the line that Britain and Germany were front/obverse sides of the imperialist coin. That pained some supporters, especially intellectuals with an ideological, ethnic, or religious aversion to Hitler's Reich.

Being an intellectual isolationist still carried risks to reputation, especially as the war went on. By arguing isolationism, Yale historian Charles Beard managed to transform from progressive academic darling into Roosevelt-hating crank.[33] The isolationist–interventionist dispute was vicious and widespread, and it took courage to make one's case on either side. This was the mood which moved E.B. White to opine that, for the whole country, the prewar phase was "like the time you put in a doctor's waiting room, years of fumbling with old magazines and unconfirmed suspicions, the ante years, the time of the moist palm and the irresolution."[34]

Through it all, the Man in the White House was cagey—not pushing isolationists too fast was as important as keeping the interventionists somewhat satisfied. Many people felt that genuine neutrality was increasingly an illusion, so the net effect of Roosevelt's back-and-forth foreign policy carried at least as much diffidence as cunning.[35] The overriding political element was that presidential initiative regarding security policy was severely limited. The White House was reactive: domestically, there was public and congressional opinion to worry about; overseas, the actions of other powers. By necessity, but not necessarily by preference, Roosevelt had to react to what Hitler, Stalin, Neville Chamberlain, or Hideki Tojo did. He could not drive the agenda himself as long as the United States stood outside the war.

*   *   *

A confused foreign policy suited a confused world, but did little to whittle down the presidential power base. No president generated more of a winner's aura than Roosevelt. To opponents and detractors alike, he was both Lion and Fox: formidable in direct combat, sly in backroom maneuvers, likely to win in the end. Blowing into Washington, D.C. in 1933, he remade the capital and its culture with assurance. In this, he was abetted by the larger and more slippery task of tackling the Great Depression. Fixing macroeconomic woes proved hard, but in building up the federal role, Roosevelt put into place the machinery which would make the capital city more central to American lives. Promising the American people that the only thing they had to fear was fear itself turned out to be dodgy as a fiscal proposition but perfect as rhetoric. It did not soothe abraded markets, but it calmed down an alarmed populace which wondered whether the American system faced a downturn or an existential crisis. This set an important Rooseveltian pattern, the ability to frame national discourse through his own rhetorical powers, which overwhelmed counter-narratives. *Fireside Chats* were more than radio balm. These and other speeches set the parameters within which the citizenry discussed and conceptualized political issues. Americans grew accustomed to hearing what their President had to say about each stage of the crisis. Radio was a huge help. The image of the family gathered around the console to hear the President's take became mythic because it mirrored truth.

Throughout the Depression, he exuded confidence, even complacence about the rightness of his power and policies. His words reflected presidential self-assurance, as did his demeanor. The cocksure angle of his cigarette holder was as much a part of his message tool-kit as his Appleknocker accent. By 1941, Washington was fully his city, thanks to two reelections, including 1940's trouncing of Wendell Willkie. Willkie, that bouncy Hoosier, briefly roused Republican supporters during the summer election months. Scrupling to adopt more than a mild anti-interventionist tone until the campaign's dying moments, Willkie made an unconvincing isolationist. His bipartisan approach to world events earned him plaudits for gentility, but did little to rouse isolationist fervor. Only in the autumn did he start warning that a vote for Roosevelt was a vote for war. Willkie's new tone helped cut into the President's lead, which stood at four points in a late October poll.[36] But Roosevelt, who earlier promised that only a direct enemy attack would prompt military action, counterpunched in a Boston speech on November 1, promising, "I have said it again and again and again: Your boys are not going to be sent to fight in any foreign wars."[37]

Willkie was too late and too obviously desperate in grasping for the anti-war vote. The election would not swivel on the interventionist–isolationist argument, which meant that isolationism as a movement was deprived of an outright champion at the top of the ticket. But that was exactly when AFC momentum might have made crucial impact upon the race. Being deprived of an ardent candidate was an awful handicap to the isolationist side.

Despite pepping up the sullen Grand Old Party for awhile, all the election excitement reenergized the White House occupant, who had made noises about heading home to Hyde Park before rounding into campaign shape.[38] By 1941, inaugurated for his unprecedented third term, FDR was without question America's man in charge. He still had to take Congress, with war powers of its own built into the Constitution, into account when it came to foreign affairs. His Democratic Party had loyal majorities in both houses. Post-December 7, it was Roosevelt's address to the legislative branch which all awaited breathlessly, for that would mark the formal American response to the attack. In the meantime, the President's cabinet and myriad assistants surrounded him as he readied for the occasion.

American attentions during the Depression understandably focused on problems at home. But the stereotype of willful isolationist blindness to foreign happenings was never wholly accurate. Even at the lowest points in those economic trough years, the wider world made itself known. News featured plenty of international coverage. Figures such as Hitler, Mussolini, or Edward VIII were instantly recognizable during the 1930s. Reporters were there when the Spanish Civil War broke out, while Japan's audacities in China also drew coverage.[39] The Quarantine Speech was ill-received enough that Secretary of State Cordell Hull pronounced himself stunned by the furor, which buttressed the very Neutrality Act the President was trying to loosen up.[40] Public disfavor for joining an international anti-dictator front was hardly born from unfamiliarity with the principals. Americans were not ignorant of the world, merely suspicious of it. Given the state of the world during the late 1930s, that was not irrational. It was their distrust of figures such as Hitler which accentuated their World War I and Versailles memories and made the American public leery of hasty or incremental foreign involvement.

When Germany invaded Poland on September 1, 1939, Americans certainly noticed, since war intensified the isolationist–interventionist debate. May 10, 1940, was when Hitler unleashed the *blitzkrieg* which shocked the world, conquering Luxembourg in a few hours, the Netherlands in five days, Belgium in 18, and France in 6 weeks. Americans realized how much "Europe's War" meant to them. World War II was the main news story in American media. Edward R. Murrow's masterful broadcasts from London shaped emotional coherence from chaotic events and gave Americans a narrative they internalized and understood. Meanwhile, correspondents in every wartime capital lent their voices to a sustained chorus of news which surrounded Americans at every turn. Murrow emblazoned London's fires onto the American mind, as poet, Librarian of Congress, and leader at the Office of Facts and Figures Archibald MacLeish put it at a 1941 awards banquet. "You burned the city of London in our houses and we felt the flames that burned it," MacLeish pointed out. "You laid the dead of London at our doors and we knew that the dead were our dead."[41]

People argued bitterly and long over how best to react to the war in those days—either through fortified isolationism or effective intervention—but few felt the conflict irrelevant to their lives. The Battle of Britain seemed to presage a German cross-channel invasion, which would mean a massive alteration in world balance of power. Meanwhile, the story of the enduring British, told so ably by Murrow and others, became more and more compelling to Americans. This was backed up in the Roper and Gallup polls.[42] From May 10, when Hitler's *blitzkrieg* in the west began, all the way through December 6, 1941, the war stayed subject number one in the American press. Being attacked by Japan was a very public trauma. But being drawn into the war was not in itself such a stunner. Americans had been fretting about that happening since Hitler invaded Poland.

"Blue of the Seven Seas, Gold of God's Great Sun!"[43]—the centrality of the naval idea in American leadership

Eternal Father strong to save/Whose arm hath bound the restless wave/Who bidd'st the mighty ocean deep/Its own appointed limits keep/Oh hear us when we cry to Thee/For those in peril on the sea!/O Christ! Whose voice the waters heard/And hushed their raging at Thy word/Who walked'st on the foaming deep/And calm amidst its rage didst sleep/O hear us when we cry to Thee/For those in peril on the sea!

> Rev. William Whiting, 1860. "Eternal Father Strong to Save," more commonly known as "The Navy Hymn"[44]

During the last two days, I have spent half my time, busy as I am, in reading your book. That I found it interesting is shown by the fact that, having taken it up, I have gone straight through and finished it. . . . It is a very good book—admirable; and I am greatly in error if it does not become a naval classic.

> Theodore Roosevelt to Alfred Thayer Mahan, May 12, 1890[45]

A British tar is a soaring soul/As free as a mountain bird/His energetic fist should be ready to resist/A dictatorial word./His nose should pant and his lip should curl/His cheeks should flame and his brow should furl/His bosom should heave and his heart should glow/And his fist be ever ready for a knock-down blow.

> Gilbert and Sullivan, "H.M.S. Pinafore"[46]

Isolationism was put to rest in the White House long before Pearl Harbor. The image of an administration removed from global currents was wrong. Since his Groton days, when "Cousin Theodore" enchanted schoolboy Franklin Roosevelt at Oyster Bay, FDR was profoundly aware of international affairs. Always at the heart of Theodore Roosevelt's presidency was the vital status of a robust navy capable of projecting power and protecting resultant American interests. This orientation is handily summed up as navalism, or "The Naval Idea."

The Naval Idea went back to the American dawn. Thomas Paine enthused, "No country on the globe is so happily situated, or so internally capable of raising a fleet as America."[47] But the quintessential theorist who foresaw the importance of a navy to a world power was Alfred Thayer Mahan. Born in 1840, son of a West Point professor, graduate of the Naval Academy, Mahan was a career naval officer who served in the Civil War, led the Naval War College, and became President of the American Historical Association in 1902. It was at the War College in

Newport that he formulated his seminal ideas about strategy. Like every military scholar of his day, Mahan studied the Napoleonic campaigns and understood historian-strategists such as Henri de Jomini. But it was the naval side of wars which focused Mahan's magnificent mind. As he saw it, history proved the central argument that economic and military power at sea made the difference when countries battled for supremacy.[48] In books such as *The Interest of America in Sea Power, Present and Future* (1897), and his justly honored *The Influence of Sea Power Upon History, 1660–1783* (1898), Mahan made the case that nations which saw the ocean as a path, not a barrier, and which managed their maritime interests accordingly, prospered in balance of power competition. His most important books coincided with the Spanish-American War, which vindicated his themes to readers. Mahan's was a conflict-based view of international relations articulated at the moment when prosperity, technological advances, and the realization of Manifest Destiny put the United States into position to actualize his vision. "The history of Sea Power is largely . . . a narrative of contests between nations, of mutual rivalries, of violence frequently culminating in war," he wrote, explaining how effective naval policy could ensure triumph.[49] Because of the clarity of his writing and the immediacy of his message, Mahan joined British geographer and theorist Halford Mackinder as one of two prime geostrategists of the twentieth century.[50] Whereas Mackinder became known as champion of the land-based strategic view, Mahan was the thinker associated with the blue parts of the globe. His was the moving spirit animating the US Navy.[51] From the presidency of Benjamin Harrison onward, keeping the navy large, visible, and aimed outward was American doctrine.[52]

Great Power positions shifted from decade to decade, so the navy adapted its outlook. Japan, seen hopefully in the mid-nineteenth century as a prosperous entrepot, then at the start of the twentieth century as a counterweight to Russia, Germany, and Britain, came to be viewed as a likely foe after World War I. Arguments and agreements over relative naval strength, hammered out with hurt feelings on the Japanese side in the Washington Naval Conferences and Treaties of 1921–1922, convinced the Japanese that Washington meant to check their naval progress.[53] But the US Navy never lost sight of Mahan's observation that its main duties were to deny any enemy its commercial and communication routes, while protecting critical American sea lanes.[54] Command of the seas became a basic twentieth century American strategic goal.[55]

In England, Rudyard Kipling understood that the Royal Navy incarnated Britain's Empire. Beholding cruisers sailing up the Thames, the author marveled at their latent power, considering that puissance his own, "by right of birth. Mine were the speed and power of the hulls, not here only but the world over." Always self-aware, Kipling realized that he was mentally adding up his "possessions with most sinful pride."[56] In the same vein, Winston Churchill, like every educated, patriotic Briton, knew precisely what Lord Horatio Nelson meant by, "England expects that every man shall do his duty," or, "Kiss me, Hardy."

But fulsome naval pride swelled in the United States, too. Young Franklin Roosevelt could thrill to immortal lines from American naval history: "I have not yet begun to fight," declared Captain John Paul Jones on board the *Bonhomme Richard*;[57] "We have met the enemy and they are ours," wrote Commodore Oliver Hazard Perry in his laconic dispatch to General William Henry Harrison[58]; "Damn the torpedoes! Full speed ahead!" shouted David Glasgow Farragut as the *Hartford* tore through Mobile Bay[59]; "You may fire when you are ready, Gridley," said George Dewey at Manila.[60] This aphoristic canon supported The Naval Idea in the national imagination. As President commanding the Great White Fleet, Theodore Roosevelt contributed his own immortal line in his 1902 message to Congress, "A good Navy is not a provocation to war. It is the surest guaranty of peace."[61] The elder Roosevelt was besotted with Mahan. Reading *The Influence of Sea Power Upon History, 1660–1783* changed TR's view of the world. "He was," one sharp historian later noted, "one of the few Americans in 1890 who understood the full significance of the book."[62]

Franklin understood the Naval Idea as he grew up. After Groton, the preparatory school which another cousin, journalist and fellow alum Joseph Alsop termed "a great ascendancy fortress,"[63] it was off to Harvard. Then Franklin worked for Woodrow Wilson, who appointed him Assistant Secretary of the Navy. Wilson supported the navy as the mainspring of American security. "A powerful Navy we have always regarded as our proper and natural means of defense," Wilson said in his 1914 message to Congress. "We shall take our leave to be strong upon the seas, in the future as in the past; and there will be no thought of offense or provocation in that. Our ships are our natural bulwarks."[64] The rising Franklin Roosevelt imbibed Mahan's tenets.

Mahan's forward-looking strategic advocacy did not convince every American to support an aggressive naval program. Many national leaders spent much of American history confident in a heartland strategy of their own, believing that North American continentalism, keeping strong in the home hemisphere while holding the rest of the world at bay, was the ordained American strategic posture. But there was room for the navy under these auspices, too, since it would keep the hostile world away. Navally oriented FDR never agreed that the navy was simply a deflector shield, but during his early White House tenure, he could be deferential to those advocating traditional isolationism while still supporting sea power.[65]

Mahan was no dogmatist. For him, the geographical and economic situation of a nation determined the suitability of a maritime or land-based strategy. Certain nations—the landlocked, or those with difficult access to the open sea—had few legitimate naval aspirations. There were a handful of defining characteristics which made the naval approach wise. Mahan saw that Britain and the United States both possessed these attributes. Colonies—useful as coaling and supply stations—were among the necessaries for any prospective maritime power.[66] The United States of the 1930s had territories in abundance, especially across the western Pacific, where possessions from Hawaii to the Philippines flew the Stars and Stripes. Wake Island came in handy as a stop-over for trans-oceanic aircraft. Other islands made useful navy bases. The Philippines served as frontispiece to the United States' Asia-facing exposure.

In the way he structured his thoughts about nations and their oceanic destinies, Mahan transcended military affairs, emerging as a distinctive American thinker whose ideas affected cultural discourse. Scholar Ralph Henry Gabriel made a point of including Mahan in his magisterial intellectual history, *The Course of American Democratic Thought* (1940). "His approach to his subject was as American as Conwell's 'Acres of Diamonds,' " wrote Gabriel. "Mahan's argument grew naturally out of those foundations of his thought, Protestant Orthodoxy and the gospel of wealth. The pattern of his philosophy was identical with that of the American democratic faith." [67] What Mahan understood, Gabriel argued, eluded progressives seeking international placidity through diplomatic covenants. Mahan recognized that law, "being artificial and often of long date . . . frequently is inapplicable to a present dispute; that is, its decision is incompatible with existing conditions, although it may rest on grounds legally unimpeachable."[68] Mahan pointed out the frequent discrepancy between legality and wisdom across corners of the world. The United States must will itself to international flexibility. Placing all strategic aspirations on signed agreements was noble in intention but disastrous in actuality. Instead, Mahan preached the need to accept "the concept of the equilibrium of natural forces in the society of nations."[69] Powers rose and fell, energies dissipated and gathered elsewhere; balance was always desired but ever-fleeting. The need was to harmonize naturally fluctuating forces with natural rights among nations. The Admiral was thinking specifically about Cuba in 1898, but such insights helped generations of American leaders to interpret international affairs. The result was an American foreign policy reflecting national impulses. The key was to have a realistic, systematic world view in place when strategic emergencies occurred.

The year 1940 took away the nation's European strategic props. The French Army was supposed to be the world's mightiest. The Royal Navy enforced Atlantic order. So long as Paris and London stayed democratic, these service branches functioned as *de facto* forward lines of American defense. But France fell and Britain's fate looked uncertain, so Americans could no longer take earlier assumptions for granted. The Pearl Harbor fiasco showed that North American heartland theories were obsolete. No credible voice advocated abandoning Hawaii; even a layman could see that the nation which controlled Hawaii controlled the Central Pacific. Americans did not want Seattle and San Francisco as their westerly trip-wire. Pearl Harbor vindicated Mahan in dreadful fashion.

Such was the argument of John Spykman, Professor at Yale's Institute of International Studies. Spykman was at work on a 1942 publication, *America's Strategy in World Politics.*[70] Arguing that the American continents were underpopulated in relation to Eurasia, Spykman tweaked Mackinder's ideas, making them compatible with Mahan. He reconciled land and sea strategies. Spykman knew that setting the two strategists up as pole stars was an oversimplification, especially for nations like the United States which needed to concern themselves with both land and sea operations. The gist of Spykman's explanation was that island nations—the United States so considered—needed to adopt effective policies far away before they grew grave enough to reach the homeland.[71] The idea received further development in Walter Lippmann's 1943 *Foreign Policy: Shield of the Republic.* Lippmann conceptualized a framework bearing Mahan's and Mackinder's imprints. He saw events in Eurasia as extremely relevant to American security. More nuanced than the old idea that the navy should fend off danger, the Strategic Shield notion posited a mighty maritime force and also advocated a strong army. Both should be used judiciously in foreign quarters before any power grew capable of attacking the United States. Running through this conception was the assumption that what happened in the rest of the world—even in quarters far off and little-known—could be central to American security. Spykman and Lippmann put forth important conceptions with major implications for the American world view. Their positions jibed with Roosevelt's.

FDR adopted views of world affairs from Wilson, who imagined international relations tamed and channeled by the League of Nations. Wilsonian diplomacy stood for a world society of countries bound up together, protected and restrained within an international web. Wilson wanted righteousness in diplomacy. His political science doctorate from Johns Hopkins bore out his conviction that understanding the mechanics of democracy was essential to statecraft. Democracy abroad strengthened the United States, he felt, and also reflected integrity back upon the republic. There was idealism within this proposition, but also self-serving circularity, since Wilson's pet diplomatic mission was to protect the United States through a values-based international outlook. The League of Nations was what he wanted; his beliefs supported membership. The Senate stayed unmoved. But Wilson, with Roosevelt looking on from a close vantage point, modernized the impulses that America should be "a light unto the nations," "a City Upon a Hill," "The last, best hope of earth." Wilson wanted an American foreign policy "more concerned about human rights than about property rights."[72] He connected the democratic American creed to foreign policy, while conducting massive foreign interventions.

The central conflict in Wilson's presidency was glaring. He campaigned in 1916 on staying out of war, then justified his 1917 change of heart, saying that protective self-interest supported American entry. His Presbyterian world view was sincere.

Like any good John Knox disciple, Wilson knew rectitude was hard won in the face of mighty sin. But like any progressive reared in the age of Social Darwinism, Wilson also believed in human improvement aided by correct governance.[73] Foreign policy was no morality-free zone, because that implied that God was not the author of history. But neither was cynicism an acceptable diplomatic outlook, since it denied the advent of human improvement. Wilson's holistic outlook united providentially inspired morality and humanly engineered social progress. It had internal tensions which could only be modulated by sacrifice.

Wilson could not casually cast aside his anti-war position. Instead, he arrived at the notion of fighting the war to end future wars, giving his administration and 1917s youth the job of using violence to secure a better world. The key was to win the war, then to shape the peace and the institutions arising out of it. There was no soft utopianism in his performance as commander-in-chief. Wilson oversaw the dispatch of the American Expeditionary Force. The infusion of fresh American men, materiel, and spirit boosted the Allies to victory. No less than competent command, belief that his ideals supported American strategic security permeated Wilson's war conduct. The 14 Points spelled everything out, supporting self-determination, freedom of the seas, and abjuring victor's justice.[74] They also represented Wilson's answer to a rising Bolshevik movement which contended that only violent revolution could fix what ailed the suffering world.[75] As a young politician, Franklin Roosevelt served a President whose administration operated under those notional commitments.

FDR learned how workaday Washington functioned during war and crisis. In his navy post, he enjoyed backing from Secretary Josephus Daniels, the wily North Carolinian for whom Washington held no secrets, and who guided the Assistant Navy Secretary though complications such as the resignation of Secretary of State William Jennings Bryan. Navy's blue and gold became as dear as Harvard's crimson or Groton's red–white–black to the impressionable Roosevelt. He received sustained instruction in operational maritime security issues while the navy battled German U-boats and kept the Atlantic sea lanes open.[76] On World War I's battle of the Atlantic hung the American plan to refresh Britain and France and break the stalemate. The German Navy was submarine-dependent, hoping its U-boats could break up the cross-Atlantic supply chain. Preventing that was the American Navy's main priority. Roosevelt mastered infighting against other branches of the government which coveted his authority while ensuring that the navy accomplished its goal.

As President in 1933, Roosevelt was stranger neither to his nation's byzantine capital nor to foreign policy. His training equipped him with a conviction that liberty tempered by social justice served peace and improvement. Some who knew him felt that polio, the effects of which he took pains to hide, toughened him. Roosevelt surprised many who expected that his rhetoric was merely political posing. His personal identification with American values and interests was profound.[77] Foreign observers found this sincerity fascinating, perplexing, or off-putting. Also confusing to them was Roosevelt's reluctance to place total trust or authority in his subordinates. He had favored advisors and sources of information, including William Bullitt, Ambassador in Paris, as well as Anthony Biddle, formerly Ambassador in Warsaw. Harry Hopkins held his confidence. He also utilized private intelligence channels from the French *Deuxieme Bureau* and the German opposition to broaden his perspective.[78] No organizational flow chart could capture the fragmented state of information movement in the White House. Everything depended upon the man at the top.

"Yesterday, December 7, 1941. . ." Roosevelt answers Japan

Once the fire is lighted under it, there is no limit to the power it can create.
> Edward Grey to Winston Churchill, likening the United States to "a gigantic boiler," 1911[79]

God damn Japan. We'll lick the hell out of those bastards now.
> Washington, D.C. taxi driver, overheard December 7, 1941.[80]

Cordell Hull may have been Secretary of State, but FDR ran his own foreign policy. The President was wont to negotiate directly with foreign leaders, to attend summits, to forge policy without consulting the State Department. To a real extent, Roosevelt acted as his own Secretary of State.[81] Hull's post, traditionally the foremost cabinet spot, presented problems which aggravated the proud Tennessean. Below Hull, the diplomatic old guard represented the striped-pants model of entanglement avoidance, which veered between long periods of somnolence and short fits of action intended to squelch crises wherever they arose with diplomatic bromides. Roosevelt made sure that the State Department knew it answered to him. Throughout State, he scattered reliable appointments answering to the Oval Office more than to their departmental superiors.[82] Divide and conquer was quintessential Rooseveltian management. He dominated cabinet departments by pitting subordinates against each other, making sure that White House loyalists provided communication pathways which ran around departmental channels. Undersecretary of State Sumner Welles was an FDR favorite. Another school chum, Welles felt secure enough in his White House channel to treat Hull with a distant formality bespeaking no respectful subordination.[83]

Hull knew it. He had to take it, but he hated it. Shrewd and patient, Hull's life journey took him from the rocky-topped Tennessee mountains to the judicial bench; to Congress and, in 1930, the Senate. As Secretary, he knew that Welles operated as a presidential instrument while Hopkins functioned openly as the President's preferred diplomatic agent. Hull countered by favoring Undersecretary Breckenridge Long, whom Dean Acheson described as "a gentleman of the old school," simpatico to Hull in return.[84] There was no question of revolt against the President. Welles would be protected as far as possible, while Hopkins was Roosevelt's vizier. But the White House still saw value in its Secretary of State, despite the opaque atmosphere. The President respected Hull, who had his own contacts around Washington and was a force not to be discounted. Between the two men there was nothing approaching friendship. Hull could not play courtier as Hopkins did. While Hopkins lived at the White House, Hull's position was more remote. "If the President wishes to speak to me," said the Secretary, "all he has to do is pick up the telephone and I'll come running."[85]

Some of Hull's duties were onerous. It was he who fielded the tardy December 7 presentation from Japanese Ambassador Kichisaburo Nomura and Special Emissary Saboro Kurusu. Tokyo, still mulling over the competing merits of peace and war, had tasked them with forging a Pacific *modus vivendi*. It fell to these two plenipotentiaries to inform Hull of what he already knew. Nomura was a retired admiral whose time in Washington went back to the days when, as naval attache, he knew Roosevelt as Assistant Secretary. Personal friends with American Ambassador to Japan, Joseph C. Grew, Nomura advocated Japanese–American understanding.[86] His career betokened the lost intimacies between Washington and Tokyo whose vestiges were now obliterated. Hull understood that it was demoralizing for Nomura to deliver the message. The Secretary was sorely tried, for, as Hopkins recalled, "Hull wanted peace above everything, because he had set his heart on making an adjustment with the Japanese and had worked on it night and day for weeks."[87] But diplomacy makes marionettes of the most independent men. Neither the crusty Hull nor the affable Nomura was an exception, so both had to endure the interview on December 7.

Hull expected the visit, having read the decoded intercept of the instructions sent from Foreign Minister Shigenori Togo to the Japanese diplomats. American decrypts were part of a long effort of stupendous difficulty in which a few dedicated intelligence officers let Washington know what its enemies said privately.[88] The two hapless emissaries came late to their appointment because Japan's embassy bungled in decoding and translating their instructions.[89] Upon their 2:05 p.m. arrival, Hull sent them into a waiting room, where they cooled their heels and grew more uncomfortable. It was hardly commensurate revenge for Pearl Harbor, but it gratified Hull. This was one of the rare occasions when Roosevelt picked up the telephone and called his Secretary of State. His advice to Hull was straightforward, "Receive their reply formally and coolly and bow them out."[90]

Hull stayed formal but not cool. This was Hull's office and his piece of the show, so he played things his way. At 2:20 p.m., he let Nomura and Kurusu in, not inviting them to sit. Taking their note, he pretended to read it, although, as he remembered, "I knew its contents already but naturally could give them no indication of this fact."[91] Nomura seemed especially abashed. Hull paused, in the process working up from cold hostility to fury—although he denied "cuss[ing] out the Japanese envoys in rich Tennessee mountain language," as rumor had it.[92] He cited their relationship and negotiations, reminding the diplomats that he was always honest with them. By association, he argued that the US had been honest with Japan. This made their paper of lies more damnable. It was "a document more crowded with infamous falsehoods and distortions—infamous falsehoods and distortions on a scale so huge that I never imagined . . . that any Government on this planet was capable of uttering them."[93] So Hull first injected the trope of "infamy" into America's reaction.

When Nomura, whom Hull discerned to be in a highly emotional state, seemed on the verge of speaking out, the Secretary—sparing the Japanese as well as himself the perils of an unscripted encounter—ushered the men out with a wave of his arm. That gesture of dismissal culminated a decades-long diplomatic conversation between Tokyo and Washington, which had see-sawed through years of conciliation and argument. The strategic visions of Washington and Tokyo proving irreconcilable, only war could resolve the differences.

Hull hustled to the White House, where FDR wanted to meet with his War Cabinet. This 3.00 p.m. gathering included Hull, Knox, Secretary of War Stimson, and General George C. Marshall. They reviewed the military situation, eyeing dispositions of American forces.[94] Also covered was the need to coordinate policies with Latin American nations and the British Commonwealth. Hitler's spies had worked South America for years. Axis infiltration was a staple American concern. Shoring up relations with fellow American republics would be a major project. Japan's official declaration of war arrived; the greatest example of closing the barn door after the cow's departure that Hull ever saw.[95] The assemblage addressed the need to warn American merchant ships that they were now targets. The cabinet agreed to pursue domestic information control, with details to be explored. That would devolve to Early, who would set up an effective news-management system within days.[96] FDR fielded a call from British Prime Minister Winston Churchill, already tending his personal relationship with Roosevelt under the guise of seeking confirmation about the news. For Churchill and the British, it was vital to ensure that the Americans did not lose sight of the point that Hitler's Germany remained the main strategic threat to western democracy.

Roosevelt told Churchill that the radio reports were "Quite true. They have attacked us at Pearl Harbor. We are all in the same boat now," explained the President. He would approach Congress the next day, Roosevelt said. Leaving aside the salient issue of Germany, Churchill took a supportive tack, noting that long-standing strategic ambiguity about war or peace was now at an end. Clarity was a virtue, in the eyes of the British leader. "This certainly simplifies things," he said.[97]

Matters of statecraft resolved, it was time for the full cabinet to meet. Roosevelt went over his plans for the speech to Congress, while the secretaries pitched in with suggestions. Hull advised a comprehensive review of Japanese–American diplomatic relations, firmly affixing blame on Tokyo. Others saw the moment as propitious for declaring war on Germany. These advocates argued that Japan was Hitler's cat's paw. The assumption was that US–German war was inevitable. Nevertheless, the question of which nation would formalize this was delicate. Roosevelt and his secretaries knew that Americans, many recently isolationist, would see vengeance against Japan as the main mission and object if it seemed that Tokyo was but a secondary target. Germany's place in the American war remained indeterminate. The fluid situation meant that Roosevelt preferred to move step by step. The Tripartite Pact binding Berlin, Rome, and Tokyo made it possible that Hitler would declare war first. Where Germany was concerned, Roosevelt would wait and see. Of immediate importance in the cabinet meeting was the need to keep supplies flowing to Britain and the Soviet Union, both of whom were likely to be American Allies very shortly.[98] They discussed Japan's attack on the Philippines. Roosevelt said that he had ordered General Douglass MacArthur to execute "all the necessary movement required in event of an outbreak of hostilities with Japan."[99] Given the gravity of the evening, congressional leaders came to meet the President. Titans from "the other end of the avenue" sifted into Roosevelt's study. From the House came Speaker Sam Rayburn (D-TX), Minority Leader Joseph Martin (R-MA), Representative Sol Bloom (D-NY); from the Senate came Tom Connally (D-TX), Alben Barkley (D-KY), and Hiram Johnson (R-CA). They listened to dickering over Roosevelt's speech, pitching in with questions of their own. Foremost on their minds—foreshadowing the hearings on the Hill that would cost Pacific Fleet Admiral Husband Kimmel his job—was the extent of the damage and the place for the blame at Pearl Harbor. On these matters Roosevelt stayed vague, since he had scanty information. He mentioned that Guam and Wake Island were also attacked, speculating that the Philippines was a target, too. But as to specifics from Honolulu, he could not satisfy. "I do not know what is happening at the present time, whether a night attack is on or not. It isn't quite dark yet in Hawaii. . . . The fact remains we have lost the majority of the battleships there."[100]

Roosevelt's information was too pessimistic, but nobody present knew that. Black news sobered the congressional visitors. "Didn't we do anything to get—nothing about casualties on their side?" one of the pols sputtered in frustration.[101] When the interrogators asked about Japanese losses, Roosevelt answered that, perhaps, some submarines were sunk. To Francis Biddle, the President seemed more downcast than ever before, his blithe self-confidence nowhere apparent.

Biddle was used to thinking about larger contexts. His speech to the California State Bar Association three months before won national attention. The gist of that address was that democracy was up to the world's challenges, and that influential citizens should fight off pessimism put forth by "timid souls who doubted that democracy could be made to work when disaster threatened." If ever the United States was attacked, Biddle had assured lawyers gathered at Yosemite National Park, the American military "must be ready at any hour, any day, to leap at the throat of the invader."[102] It cannot have pleased the Attorney General that the heretofore sanguine Roosevelt looked so depressed.

"They were all asleep?" thundered Connally. "Where were our patrols?"[103] To these and other queries, a shaken Roosevelt offered no concrete answers. His spirit only recovered when someone in the gathering remarked, "Well, Mr. President, the nation has got a job ahead of it, and what we have got to do is roll up our sleeves and win the war."[104] Blame would be affixed later. Now was a time for solidarity and fortitude.

That ended the meeting, sending Washington's leaders into the first night of the war. Cabinet deliberations were secret, but the thrust of the conversation would have encouraged Churchill, wondering about FDR's current feelings on the Germany-first plan agreed upon in August's Atlantic Charter. Once the cabinet meeting broke up, the President dictated to Grace Tully.[105] Tully's work was swift, since Roosevelt's speech would be a short one. He would not take the legalistic approach favored by Hull. Neither would he discuss Germany. Not yet. As rhetoritician-in-charge, the President would follow his own instincts.

All day long and into the night, Washingtonians gathered outside. The nation's capital was home to the powerful, but also to those people in whose interests the politicians supposedly worked; citizens whose sinews and blood war would demand. The people, known from the Constitution's Preamble, were recently in vogue thanks to populist currents in Depression culture. Throughout the 1930s, the people were the subject of Woody Guthrie's songs, Walker Evans' photographs, Carl Sandburg's poems, and Murrow's news. Murrow discovered a main truth of the war while he monitored the British during their Blitz peril. What he saw in London tube stations, serving as makeshift bomb-shelters, was a people's war, not in the marxist sense, but in the looser and more real sense of democracy battling dictatorships for life and a just world. The tyrannies presumed to lead the people in the name of race, nationality, and class. Who best represented a people was a bitter question. While leaders claimed to steer events, people were the determinants, Murrow decided. That attitude became the powerful theme of his newscasts.

While Murrow, Guthrie, Evans, Sandburg, and many other prominent creative intellectuals, invoked and chronicled the people's spirit, pollsters divined the popular will. That December 7, people milled outside the wrought-iron fence around the White House as news of Pearl Harbor clarified. Reporters and clerks mingled with workers, housewives, and children. The Pennsylvania Avenue trolley clattered back and forth, while the crowd peered in at the blazing lights of the White House, seeking illumination as they stood in the dark. Nervous, resolute, angry, hopeful; voices rose and fell as winter's chill wafted across the Potomac. Some sang "God Bless America."[106] To one reporter, everything seemed eerily familiar. Eric Sevareid, whose CBS report on France's capitulation in June 1940 was the biggest war news scoop yet, gazed over the milling Washingtonians. He had seen such faces around the Quai d'Orsay in Paris just two years prior.[107]

Sevareid made the comparison to his boss, Edward R. Murrow, when they met at the CBS office that night. Golfing at Burning Tree with his wife, Janet, when the news broke, Murrow spent the evening of December 8 at the White House. He saw Hull, Stimson, Knox, and other officials bustling by him as he sat on a corridor bench, smoking and noticing the "amazement and anger written large on most of the faces."[108] But Murrow was not in attendance as a reporter. He was there as a guest of the Roosevelts. Upon hearing of the bombing, he assumed their dinner date was off. Nonsense, replied First Lady Eleanor—"We still have to eat."[109]

While Franklin conducted business of state, Eleanor scrambled eggs to sustain America's preeminent newsman as he waited in the hall. At one juncture, Harry Hopkins saw the seated Murrow. "What in the hell are you doing here?" asked the right-hand man. "He told me to wait," Murrow explained.[110] Hopkins knew who "he" was, of course. Murrow was there at Roosevelt's call. The two bonded over their agreement that that isolationism was too dangerous to cosset as the war went on.[111] Murrow's presence later aroused suspicions among Anglophobes. They wondered if the reporter and President expected the Japanese attack. There was no conspiracy, but Murrow was the nation's foremost supporter of aid to Britain and a confirmed interventionist. Roosevelt knew it, and the two viewed each other with mutual regard. It was not odd that the President sought out the commentator's company, especially when Murrow's approval could be assumed, and his ability to affect public opinion was a proven fact.[112] Roosevelt had invited other media figures into the White House earlier for personal treatment. For example, he had Dorothy Thompson over twice in 1940 as her support for Wendell Wilkie wavered. Citing her devout commitment to anti-isolationism, which resulted in a prolonged feud with the Lindberghs, Thompson switched allegiances and backed FDR's bid for a third term, causing her critics to charge her with falling under the presidential spell.[113]

Murrow accompanied Hopkins to the latter's private quarters. The CBS broadcaster noted with concern that Hopkins, never robust, was more wan than usual. "His body was frail and he looked like a death's head," Murrow recalled.[114] Roosevelt's confidant did not conceal his frailness. Donning pajamas and contemplating the struggles ahead, Hopkins lamented his weakness: "Oh, God, if I only had more strength."[115] Murrow's Pearl Harbor memories would be haunted by the ill Hopkins in nightclothes, repining at events and the trials Roosevelt must now face.

When the meetings adjourned, Murrow moved in to his *tete-a-tete* with the President. Over sandwiches and beer, Roosevelt bemoaned the losses in Hawaii, the absence of air cover, the inability to fight back. "Our planes were destroyed on the ground, by God," he lamented, thinking of Hickham Field, the army air base knocked out early in the attack. His anguish was palpable.[116] Joining them after midnight was Colonel "Wild Bill" Donovan, soon to become Office of Strategic Services Director. Churchill called with an update on Japanese attacks against Britain's Asian possessions. The question of German–Japanese collusion came up. The idea that Germans must have been involved pointed to an illusion that Japanese fighters could not pull off such an attack on their own. Roosevelt expressed certitude that the Pearl Harbor attack would enrage Americans and put isolationism to rest. Murrow and Donovan agreed, betting that the citizenry would back a Declaration of War. Roosevelt—who rarely uttered a careless word and for whom media relations and politicking were one and the same[117]—asked CBS' top reporter if the attack was a surprise to him. When Murrow responded affirmatively, FDR, who knew that isolationist enemies like Beard and *Chicago Tribune* publisher Robert McCormick would suspect that the President provoked Japan's attack as a ruse, made it plain that the White House was also surprised. When that matter came up later, Murrow was straightforward. "I believed him," he said, citing his first-hand observations as evidence against the conspiracy theorists.[118]

Back at CBS, Murrow and Sevareid reminisced. The former had hired the young Sevareid to cover the war in Paris; Sevareid's stellar performance proved Murrow's perspicacity as a judge of reportorial talent. But now, fresh from the White House on the eve of a war declaration, Murrow had the goods for a story surpassing Sevareid's armistice scoop. He could have gone on the air that very morning, before Roosevelt's speech to Congress. No journalistic rule stopped Murrow. Instead, his reticence was a function of custom and shared conviction. The fact that Murrow never broke the story spoke volumes about the nature of media relations in FDR's White House. Murrow—probably the most prominent reporter of the entire war—was unsure just why he had been brought to the White House, and where the line lay between discretion and the public's right to know. "It's pretty bad," was all he said to Sevareid about Pearl Harbor.[119]

Roosevelt, Churchill, and the Japanese were not wrong in expecting that Pearl Harbor would have a clarifying effect. Evidence for this appeared before sunrise. Around the United States, young men awoke on December 8 eager to volunteer for military service. To accommodate those lining up before dawn, recruiting stations in major cities stayed open around the clock.[120] Roosevelt knew intuitively how enraged the populace was, and spent the morning readying for the Joint Session of Congress. Just past noon, the President spoke. Reporters, dignitaries, and citizens crowded the galleries. Vice President Henry Wallace and Speaker Rayburn sat on risers behind Roosevelt. "CBS," "NBC," "MBS" read the microphones ringing the podium, which had 11 electrical cables running down its front.[121] Of all the speeches in Roosevelt's talkative career, this would be the most widely heard and best-remembered.

What he said was memorable for its plainness, brevity, and force. People knew already that his highbrowed tone could be vehement. The unadorned speech was deceptively simple, laying out facts and letting these provide narrative power for 12 brief paragraphs. "Yesterday, December 7, 1941—a date which will live in infamy—the United States of America was suddenly and deliberately attacked by naval and air forces of the Empire of Japan."[122] So much hung between those dashes. While Hull first characterized Japan's attack as infamous, FDR's construction imprinted the date with a context that applied ever after. The emphasis tucked between the chronological marker and the respectful proper name of the new adversary sizzled through the message's formality. It was pure astringence.

The short and artful introduction segued into a reminder that the United States had still been "at peace with that Nation," that it was Japan which sought out negotiations pursuant to Emperor Hirohito's stated goal of maintaining Pacific peace. FDR mentioned Japan's note to Hull, which came an hour after the attack was underway and "contained no threat or hint of war or armed attack." The Japanese were not only late, they were liars. Underscoring geographic and tactical realities, the President observed that the vast distance between Japan and Hawaii meant that the attack had been planned "many days or weeks ago." Cynicism, thus adduced, was added to the list of Japanese crimes.

As to damage, Roosevelt was somehow up-front yet indefinite. "The attack yesterday on the Hawaiian Islands has caused severe damage to American naval and military forces. Very many American lives have been lost." Reinforcing rumor, he cited reports that American ships had been "torpedoed on the high seas between San Francisco and Honolulu," connecting the attack to the mainland. He also indirectly connected this speech to Woodrow Wilson's Declaration of War in 1917, which pinioned upon the American strategic imperative of maritime rights.

Then came six other Japanese targets: Malaya, Hong Kong, Guam, the Philippines, Wake Island, and Midway. Japan's offensive, Roosevelt explained, was a trans-Pacific operation. "The facts of yesterday speak for themselves," he opined. "The people of the United States have already formed their opinions and well understand the implications to the very life and safety of our Nation." Here, the presidential message adroitly linked what happened in Hawaii to what happened elsewhere, attaching the American military situation to the British. Linked thus to Britain, the United States was, by inference, involved with Britain's war in Europe—even though this speech would not confirm the "Europe First" plan.

He was in firm control as Commander-in-Chief, Roosevelt assured all, having taken measures for national defense. Returning to moral opprobrium and popular opinion, he was direct and prescriptive. "Always," he promised, "Will we remember the character of the onslaught against us." That did not equate to quick and satisfying vengeance, but it did posit the idea that America would survive, triumph, and remember. Again, FDR implied that the challenges ahead would be arduous. "No matter how long it may take us to overcome this premeditated invasion, the American people in their righteous might will win through to absolute victory."

Of all the sentences in the speech, that was the most predictive, terrible in its accuracy, actualized in August 1945 with fire and light at Hiroshima and Nagasaki. The war would last a long time. "Righteous might" was not inserted by happenstance. American might was supposed to be righteous—as in the Civil War, when Julia Ward Howe saw by Union Army campfires the coming of the Lord. She read God's "righteous sentence by the dim and flaring lamps."[123] Embedded in the Battle Hymn of the Republic was an understanding that carnage was bloody, but that a righteous cause could purify a struggle.[124] The Union seized control of the Civil War only after it became a moral crusade, which was the central truth Howe spied in the Union Army encampment. FDR intended World War II to be a moral crusade, something more profound than a contest with ships and guns for mastery of the globe. Roosevelt understood what predecessor Abraham Lincoln knew: a successful American war must be something more than a conflict between enemy interests. This essential American idealism was articulated at the birth of the nation by Thomas Paine. Like the Revolution, which Paine said heralded "the birthday of a new world,"[125] like the Civil War for Howe and Lincoln, like World War I for Wilson, World War II must be Roosevelt's crusade. Murrow saw a new world rising out of London's smoke. Roosevelt laid out the same image.

"Hostilities exist," continued the President. Two words wrapped up years of wrangling over war, peace, and neutrality. Strategic scholasticism was finished. "There is no blinking at the fact that our people, our territory, and our interests are in grave danger." Pragmatic Americans were supposed to face facts. The fact was that war was underway. FDR argued that war commenced with the attack; he wanted Congress to ratify that fact.

FDR's penultimate paragraph, another example of the parenthetical construction which allowed him to slip charged context into a thought, explained the war befalling the nation. "With confidence in our armed forces—with the unbounded determination of our people—we will gain the inevitable triumph—so help us God." He invoked the divine by swearing an oath. Moreover, he underpinned the democratic essence of America at war. It was a democratic speech, without the vainglorious "I" overused by Hitler and other totalitarians conflating their will with that of their people. "We" was FDR's preference. Roosevelt included himself among the people to whose unbounded determination he referred. It was to be a people's war, and he would serve as the people's leader because they—not destiny or history's material forces—had chosen him for the job.[126]

In reviewing the speech, presidential amanuensis Robert Sherwood noted that it lacked Churchill's signature defiance as well as Hitler's hysterical bombast.[127] This was entirely to the writer's satisfaction. It met the mood of the public, Sherwood believed, more than any talk Roosevelt ever delivered. The average citizen, like the President, saw Pearl Harbor as "a tragedy and a disgrace," which nonetheless served as "a boost to national pride" which would lead to "tremendous accomplishment" in the fighting to come.[128]

As The People's house, Congress had to affirm its answer, and did so with alacrity. Speech and Declaration took about 30 min. In one of the accidents of history, Representative Jeanette Rankin (R-MT) cast the sole vote against war. Her opposition to Wilson's call for a Declaration of War in 1917 angered her Montana constituents, who turned her out in 1918. Rankin's comeback took 22 years, and now, by voting "No," she ensured that her second stay in the House would be as brief as her first.[129]

Isolationism vaporized: the advantages of clarity and the end of *Dementia Praecox*

Conditioned by the stresses which inform the modern world, we . . . try to reconstruct the past.

Ralph Henry Gabriel 1940[130]

Rankin was not the only American misled by what she thought she knew. American isolationists learned from World War I. The tricky question was what the old war had to teach. Among the first casualties of Pearl Harbor was what Thorstein Veblen identified in 1922 as an aftereffect from an overdose of interventionism: a national case of "*dementia praecox*" which rendered Americans susceptible to foolish theories about the World War I experience. For Veblen, it was axiomatic that intervention in World War I had been a mistake. "It is evident now, beyond cavil," he argued, "that no part of Europe is better off for America's having taken part in the great war. So also is it evident that the Americans are all the worse for it."[131] But what alarmed the social critic was overreaction. Post-World War I America reminded Veblen of a "psychiactrical clinic" in which an entire citizenry was unbalanced by regret. "They are predisposed to believe in footless outrages and odious plots and machinations," he warned, pointing out that the determination to learn from World War I might lead them to absorb the wrong lessons.[132] Veblen's acuity came from his interdisciplinary methodology: economic analysis enlivened by history, anthropology, philosophy, and psychology.[133] His willingness to cross-pollinate information from different fields not only afforded him the luxury of multiple insights, it made Veblen sensitive to the ironies of conflicting impulses within the nation. American attitudes towards the foreign world were rife with cross purposes.

Veblen's concerns should not have been restricted to the United States. French generals Maurice Gamelin and Maxime Weygand learned their commitment to defensive attrition at venues such as Verdun and Passchendaele. Those lessons underpinned France's World War II effort, epitomized by the useless Maginot Line. Their German counterparts, *panzer* generals Heinz Guderian, Walther von Reichenau, and Erwin Rommel instead sought to alter what led to Germany's 1918 defeat. They learned the merits of speed, surprise, and infantry–air–armor coordination, the essentials for *blitzkrieg*. The lighting-quick demolition of French defenses in 1940 showed who learned properly.

In the United States, anti-war sentiment was stoked by lingering hunches that a cabal of arms merchants and unscrupulous politicians hoodwinked naive Americans, herding them to combat like swineherds driving pigs to the abattoir. When the gossamer Wilsonian dream of ending war and reinventing the international system was shredded by real diplomacy, progressive Senator Gerald P. Nye (R-ND) passionately argued that American boys had gone to war upon the command of Wall Street, gold, and "merchants of death." Nye did much to popularize this position during his high-profile Senate Committee for Investigating the Munitions Industry, which sat from 1934–1936.[134]

This became a widespread fixation. The retroactive anti-war movement attracted peace advocates, nationalists who wanted American purity preserved from foreign entanglements, and Anglophobes, like Baltimore's crotchety but trenchant H.L Mencken. Mencken detected media bias in Murrow's war coverage. "Virtually all of the men who have served as London correspondents are now conscientious Anglomaniacs," he complained in 1940.[135] The complaint did nothing to stem rising respect Americans felt for the British war effort. Mencken's temperament was conservative, but his passions were aesthetic more than political. All his life, the Bard of Baltimore championed culture at its highbrow best, advocating modernism and the *avant-garde,* loathing populism and bad taste, which he considered synonymous. Old and splenetic whenever the subject of FDR was at hand—which it always was—Mencken was ill-suited to serve as spokesman for any movement. Heartland progressives such as Nye represented the "booboisie" Mencken long derided, cousins to his old foil, William Jennings Bryan. Their position and his own were incompatible, which deprived isolationists of a potentially valuable intellectual ally and pointed to the fissures within the movement. Mencken's grudge against pro-British media stemmed from his commitment to continental cultural influences, rather than knock-off Anglicisms beloved by WASP elites.

Never one to ape the English, Mencken disparaged the old money class which conflated sophistication with Anglophilia. He was the product of a singular cultural environment, in New York's literary swirl but not of it. His Baltimore grounds were atypical—Southern, industrial, and German in the pre-Nazi cultural sense. Mencken was a creature of Baltimore's paradoxical milieu, which saw a vibrant German–American bourgeoisie, dependent upon Jewish leadership, working alongside the cosmopolitan Catholic community led by James Cardinal Gibbons, making for a uniquely fertile growth matrix for arts and letters. This incubator also birthed Gertrude Stein, but could not serve as model for another place.[136] There was nowhere in 1941 America for admiration of German culture. Mencken's animus for Roosevelt made him insensate to Roosevelt's own Anglophobic shades. Roosevelt believed that an insidious "Cliveden Set" of Nazi-loving English aristocrats headquartered at the Astor country demesne might seize power and cut a deal with Hitler.[137] This was mostly nonsense, but it took FDR years to get past the belief. In any event, it was hard to dent the already-widespread realization that Britain, admired since 1940 for standing fast against totalitarianism, was an ally.

The war's emergence as a democracy-versus-totalitarianism fight had frustrated the isolationist movement ever since the Summer of 1940. The Battle of Britain sparked new organizations such as Bundles for Britain and William Allen White's Committee to Defend America by Aiding the Allies, but it also spawned the America First Committee. Isolationists defied easy liberal/conservative categorization, since theirs was a national movement with real grass roots. AFC-friendly activity came from the traditionalist right and the Party left. Conservative spokesmen included radio commentator and retired General Hugh Johnson, former New Dealer and head of the National Recovery Act who later turned on Roosevelt and advocated a pro-preparedness, hands-off-Europe stance which was the standard AFC approach. Johnson launched the movement with a national broadcast in 1940.[138] "There is a committee in this country called Defend America by Aiding the Allies," he said. "Since there are no longer any Allies, that means defend America by defending England. There is another committee called Defend America First. That is my ticket."[139] The mainstream AFC position appealed to Americans who simply did not want a war. Less balanced was the posturing of fellow radio analyst Boake Carter, who grew convinced that London meant to drag in the United States.[140] The highest profile isolationist was Charles Lindbergh, also the most controversial. Long interested in the Third Reich and hostile to the Soviet Union, Lindbergh made remarks which drew concern and applause. He penned a November 1939 *Reader's Digest* article, in which he feared the war would "reduce the strength and destroy the treasures of the White Race," supposedly beset by a "pressing sea of Yellow, Black, and Brown."[141] Lindbergh veered into foul airwave space on September 11, 1941, with a speech in Des Moines, "Who Are the

War Agitators?" He took issue with Roosevelt's aggressive naval positioning in the North Atlantic, laying the blame for the sinking of the destroyer *Greer* upon the White House. Calling for "frankness," Lindbergh said that three main groups drew the country closer to war. These were "the British, the Jewish, and the Roosevelt Administration." They exploited propaganda to generate war-fever among the decent citizens, while smearing isolationism.[142] Although Lindbergh took pains to oppose Hitler's anti-Jewish persecutions, the reaction to his speech was ferocious. Opponents included some in the isolationist movement, like Senator Robert A. Taft (R-OH), who took exception to speaking as if "the Jews were some kind of foreign race and not American at all."[143] The White House counterattacked with vigor, Early and Ickes in the vanguard. Lindbergh also had defenders, such as MBS commentator Fulton Lewis and North Dakota's Nye.[144] But so toxic were his anti-Semitic utterances that the rest of his speech in Des Moines was overlooked. Lindbergh was not wrong in contending that there was an effective British campaign to present their case before the American people.[145]

The radical left saw the Communist Party of the United States of America hop aboard the cause. The Party shouted "The Yanks are Not Coming!" until the Nazi attack on Russia, June 22, 1941. But the AFC was avowedly anti-Communist, so collaboration between two such disparate groups was hard. The CPUSA's staunch Moscow orientation alienated the homegrown AFC. From the right and left fringes inward, however, anti-war voices coalesced into an anti-Roosevelt chorus which the White House scorned but feared. The mainstream AFC stuck to its non-involvement policy until December 7. But the group recognized that the anti-war cause was moot once news of Pearl Harbor came over the radio. The AFC had 450 branch units by December 1, 1941, with membership of 250,000.[146] In one week, it vaporized. On December 8, national committeeman William R. Castle wrote dejectedly to R. Douglas Stuart, Jr., one of the student founders along with Potter Stewart and Gerald Ford. Castle sadly predicted more Anglophilia. But he threw up his hands in the face of the Pearl Harbor attack: "I don't like the outlook, but there seems nothing at the moment for us to do but fight."[147]

This echoed the outlook of Jeanette Rankin's Montana political colleague, Senator Burton K. Wheeler (D-MT). Wheeler had battled interventionism with gumption as a true isolationist leader. His isolationism gave way to political necessity. Whereas Rankin could not approve the Declaration of War, Wheeler did not want to make a futile gesture. He patched things up with FDR at the White House with his "The only thing to do now is to lick the hell out of them," observation.[148] Rankin and Wheeler were two Montanans who represented an isolationist movement with an illustrious past but no future. Isolationism was suddenly defunct. Rankin's act of political suicide notwithstanding, the text of Congress' near-unanimous answer echoed Roosevelt. The brief response anchored in place the Rooseveltian interpretation of December 7. Unprovoked, war had "been thrust upon the United States" by Japan's attack. The onus was on Tokyo, war was declared because of Japan's actions, and the President had constitutional authorization and congressional direction to "carry on war against the Imperial Government of Japan; and to bring the conflict to a successful termination," with "all the resources of the country" pledged to that end.[149]

Fitfulness was the great vice of democracy, Anne Morrow Lindbergh had fretted. The twentieth century demanded more efficient government. Certainly, during the long build-up to outright American participation in World War II, the back and forth of public argument, political maneuvering, and diplomatic hairsplitting over how much intervention it took to abrogate neutrality frustrated those who considered speed as governmental virtues. Before December 8, democracy moved slowly. It heaved and whined but seemed not to advance. Doubters would now see how swiftly and irreversibly the American systems could shift into forward gear. The great federal machine was slow no more.

Within 48 hours, the nation adjusted to being at war. Plans large and small changed across American life, altering fates. Max Lerner's "The Sun Will Soon Be Setting on the Land of the Rising Sun" went to print on December 8, first in a slew of articles forecasting Japanese doom.[150] "You're a Sap, Mr. Jap," published by Mills Music Incorporated, was the first Pearl Harbor-related song.[151] In the Maine home of E.B. White, wife Katharine, fetching a hot water bottle, lost the stopper down the toilet, "beyond recall." Her essayist husband saw her discomfiture with bemusement, considering it disproportionate. Not until Katharine explained to him that "she felt that, now that the war had begun in earnest, there was no excuse for any clumsiness in home nursing" did he comprehend her frustration. At the White's home, "The loss of the stopper suddenly seemed as severe a blow as the loss of a battleship." What White considered the dreamlike quality of pre-war life ended abruptly. The picayune bathroom mishap brought new reality into focus: "The time for losing hot water bottle stoppers was over and gone."[152] But E.B. White's geniality meant that even the war news could not stop him from some positive observations. "The mechanics and spirit of a capitalistic press and radio are both comic and beautiful today," he observed. "The first words I heard after the news came of Japan's attack in Hawaii were: 'Give Mother foot comfort for Christmas.'" Meditating on the announcer's voice, White realized that "it had that thoroughly cockeyed quality for which in the long run we are fighting. It makes a man suddenly realize his strange and wonderful indebtedness to the cosmetic industry and the tobacco trade and all the rest which are supplying with capsules of news every few moments."[153]

Franchise owners in baseball's American League were to meet on December 8. The agenda included shifting Donald Barnes' St. Louis Browns to Los Angeles.[154] It was a rare ingenious idea for the usually unenterprising Major League owners. Barnes' Browns played second banana to the National League Cardinals in

St. Louis. Browns' 1941 attendance was a dismal 175,000, far behind Redbirds' healthy 600,000. Paltry gate receipts irritated visiting teams. The disparity was as bad in the standings; the 70-84 Browns tied with the equally lowly Washington Senators for sixth place in 1941, while the Cardinals battled the Brooklyn Dodgers to the end of the season, finishing second at 97-56.[155] 1942 promised no change.

Los Angeles had a lively baseball tradition. Fans rooted for the Pacific Coast League's Hollywood Stars, owned by Brown Derby restauranteur Robert H. Cobb—his eponymous salad was Cobb's most famous legacy—and the Los Angeles Angels. Celebrity fans visited Gilmore Field, on Beverly Boulevard, making it a festive spot filled with stars such as Gene Autry, George Burns, Gracie Allen, Cecil B. DeMille, George Raft, and William Powell. They made games into glittering occasions. Some owned shares in the team, and watching the actors root and kibitz was a part of the gate attraction. The rival Angels played in larger Wrigley Field, already up to major league specifications, at 42nd Place and Avalon Boulevard in south-central Los Angeles.[156]

The prospect of major league baseball piqued Angelenos. Local power-brokers guaranteed attendance of 500,000, with the Browns to take over Wrigley Field since Gilmore was too small.[157] Bing Crosby, who would sport a Browns jacket on his way to a Best Actor Oscar as Father O'Malley in 1944s *Going My Way*, was one high-profile booster of the move, so the allure of star power mingled with the scent of dollars. Major league owners were intrigued by the possibilities, but worried that travel to the West Coast would be prohibitive. To set their minds at ease, Barnes had priced air and rail fares for each team, working out schedules showing that moving to California was logistically feasible and definitely more lucrative than remaining in St. Louis.[158] Cardinals' boss Sam Breardon supported the idea, since he chafed at paying rent to the Browns, who owned the last segregated stadium in the majors.[159] The Los Angeles shift seemed to promise the Browns a brighter future, but the attack at Pearl Harbor cancelled the owners' meeting. Baseball's short-term prospects were suddenly obscure. Large gatherings on the West Coast were out; fuel and travel restrictions loomed. Roosevelt's famous "Green Light" letter permitted 1942s season to go ahead.[160] But the Browns went back to Sportsman's Park. Baseball's foray into the Golden State was an early war casualty.

Among the strategic questions on American minds were whether or not Nazi Germany was formally a foe. FDR's inner circle expected mainstream support for punishing Japan. Isolationism, they feared, might regroup around the idea of fighting Japan but not Germany. Entering Europe's war might prove tricky. With this concern, Roosevelt sought no declaration against Hitler's Reich. Instead, the White House would wait on events. He expected war with Germany, but the question was how it would happen.[161] In the meantime, the British, whose nightmare was an American Pacific war that left Germany out, worried. But FDR's next major address carried comforting hints. The Pearl Harbor Declaration speech was a masterpiece, but it was too short to satisfy an old campaigner like Roosevelt. The President needed more release and the public more information, so a Fireside Chat came on December 9. Not so well remembered as the congressional speech, it was actually more informative, spelling out the attack in larger context. The war against Japan was but one episode in the global struggle against totalitarianism— that was Roosevelt's essential message. And Hitler was still the epicenter of the global problem, he explained.

Americans had gathered by their radios for nine years for these Fireside Chats. The first came on March 12, 1933, one week after Roosevelt's first inauguration. December 9's was one of 11 FDR delivered during the war.[162] On this night, the major question was what Hitler would do. The applicability of the Tripartite Pact was hard to figure out, since Japan was the aggressor. Many Americans suspected that Berlin, having experienced American capabilities during World War I and having appeased the United States during the recent Battle of the Atlantic, still wanted to avoid war with Washington. Britain was not yet licked, while cold German soldiers were stuck short of Moscow. Why would Hitler want another enemy? But as listeners sat down to FDR's interpretation of the war, he delivered moral instruction, a jeremiad against world tyranny which made plain his view that Hitler's Germany was as bad as Japan.

His first sentence located the Pearl Harbor attack in a world context. Japan's criminal attacks were "the climax of a decade of international immorality."[163] Japan's leaders belonged to a global gang of "powerful and resourceful gangsters" warring "upon the whole human race." Besides decoupling aggressor states from the acceptable world community, this remark did double historical duty. It revived FDR's Quarantine thesis, and returned to the gangster motif he used in June 1940, when Mussolini declared war on France, an act Roosevelt termed as the hand holding a dagger sticking it in a neighbor's back. Now, the treachery was Japan's, which the United States would punish. The Tripartite Pact came off as a dictators' racket, an international Murder, Incorporated.

The issue went beyond punishing Japan. "Together with other free peoples," he explained, introducing the message of alliances, "We are now fighting to maintain our right to live among our world neighbors in freedom, in common decency, without fear of assault." Looking backward to establish the justice of the cause, FDR announced that he would submit the entire record of Japanese–American relations to Congress, from Commodore Perry's 1853 visit to December 7, 1941. The story would end with Imperial emissaries presuming to negotiate while their planes bombed Pearl Harbor.[164] Here was the historical survey Hull wanted the day before.

Roosevelt argued that the patience the United States displayed—and, by logical inference, the fact that Americans were surprised by the attack—was no shame, but a point of pride, proving the sincerity of "our efforts through all the years toward achieving a peace in the Pacific which would be honorable to every nation, large or small." Japan was bent on war because they were part of an international criminal conspiracy. Their policy "paralleled the course of Hitler and Mussolini in Europe and in Africa. Today, it has become far more than a parallel. It is a collaboration, actual collaboration." Since pernicious racial views made many Americans skeptical of Japanese abilities, there were rumors of German assistance at Pearl Harbor. These were bunk; the canard that Japan's military capabilities were sub-par was arrant foolishness, but the hint of collusion with Nazi Germany helped reinforce the connection the President wanted to make. Roosevelt stressed the war's indivisibility—Britain's struggle in Libya and Egypt, Russia's struggle before Moscow, America's struggle with Japan, formed a whole, so "all the continents of the world, and all the oceans, are now considered by the Axis strategists as one gigantic battlefield."[165]

Nobody could miss the point that the United States faced more than just Japan. Returning to his laundry list approach of the day before, Roosevelt took listeners through a review of the 1930s. He commenced with Japan's 1931 invasion of Manchuria, included Italy's 1935 invasion of Ethiopia, Germany's 1938 *Anschluss* and 1939 occupation of Czechoslovakia, along with the 1939 invasion of Poland and the conquests of 1940. He mentioned Italy's 1940 attacks against France and Greece, Germany's 1941 invasion of Yugoslavia and Russia. He stressed that these blows fell "without warning," just like Pearl Harbor. "It is all of one pattern," he insisted.[166] Left off the depredations list was the Soviet Union's 1939 onslaught against Finland. Russian troops under General Georgi Zhukov were now hitting Germans along a 600-mile front from Leningrad to Kursk, and the war's shift meant that the Red Army was a strategic asset, part of the Grand Alliance. This Fireside Chat was not the time for painful honesty about America's new ally. Stalin was not lumped in with the other tyrants. Explaining Stalin and the Soviets as fellow fighters against global tyranny was a conceptual challenge which lasted the length of the war. But it was not mentioned on December 9. Roosevelt left ambiguities out. The Fireside Chat was hardly the last time Roosevelt elided the Soviet angle.

Having reminded listeners of the degraded world situation, with tyranny on the move and diffident democracies disorganized, the President promised that things would improve. Of national unity, there was no doubt. Of Allied unity, none either. "We are all in it—all the way. Every single man, woman, and child is a partner in the most tremendous undertaking of our American history." By association, Americans could assume that they were matched with plucky Britons who made worthy partners, plain brave folk deserving admiration and trust.[167] The transitive property meant Americans could calculate that they were in the same fight as Britain, which made Britain's foes their own. That meant Germany.

"So far, the news has been all bad," FDR admitted. Hawaii was a setback; in the Philippines, forces including the "brave people of that commonwealth" were bombed, but "defending themselves vigorously." At Guam, Wake, and Midway, reports were "confused," but FDR did not wax cavalier: "We must be prepared for the announcements that all these three outposts have been seized." He promised listeners a full accounting, but warned against rumors. Rumors, he reminded, were part of the Nazi tool kit, used to demoralize. Roosevelt was right; *schrecklichkeit,* terror war, was the term for propaganda focused against enemy morale intended to spread fear and confusion. "Our government will not be caught in this obvious trap—and neither will the people of the United States."[168]

"It will not only be a long war, it will be a hard war," he said, making one promise sure to come true. All economic plans would be implemented on that assumption. The President explained his reluctance refusal to call for "sacrifice." "The United States does not consider it a sacrifice to do all one can, to give one's best to our nation, when the nation is fighting for its existence and its future life." Nor was it a sacrifice to serve in the armed forces. That was "a privilege." Likewise, industrialists, wage earners, farmers, and shopkeepers, trainmen, or doctors would be privileged to "forego extra profits, to work longer or harder at the task." There would be no curtailment plans right away, but Roosevelt made it apparent that Americans should expect national abundance to be diverted towards victory, not personal consumption. This was no time for individual complaints against pressures to serve the greater good. He vowed that whatever mischief led up to Pearl Harbor would be dispelled. The first item was to sweep away remaining isolationist distractions: "We must begin the great task that is before us by abandoning once and for all the illusion that we can ever again isolate ourselves from the rest of humanity." This speech marked the practical beginning of an American posture of world engagement that supported creation of the United Nations and shaped the postwar world. At the outset of his war Presidency, Roosevelt foreshadowed how he would complete a task dreamt of by Wilson, even if he did not make that plain.

Isolationism taught terrible lessons, he pointed out. It misconstrued the forces at work in the world; it endangered the nation. A world dominated by gangsterism made all Americans unsafe. Turning navy man for a moment, Roosevelt said that "Our ocean-girt hemisphere is not immune from severe attack." Lest anyone mistake Japan's malevolent surprise, which he acknowledged was "a brilliant feat of deception, perfectly timed and executed with great skill," as a lucky stroke, he laid it off to "modern warfare as conducted in the Nazi manner . . . a dirty business." Promising to punish the perpetrators, Roosevelt pointedly included Germany, which, he alleged, "has been telling Japan that if Japan did not attack the United States, Japan would not share in dividing the spoils with Germany when peace came." Even as a creative summary of German–Japanese relations this was far-fetched, but the President liked the message. He used such logic in 1940 to explain Italy's entry into the war, and now Japan got the same treatment. "We know also that Germany and Japan are conducting their military and naval operations in accordance with a joint plan. That plan considers all peoples and nations which are not helping the Axis powers as common enemies of each." In fact, the German–Japanese alliance was marked by grave lack of coordination, but that was not apparent at the time.

Only in his finale did FDR dwell upon the Russian connection. As he covered various theaters, he explained that guerrilla warfare in Serbia or Norway was helpful to Americans, "that a successful Russian offensive against the Germans helps us," as did any British successes. Germans and Italians—he did not list the Japanese, who were not fighting the Soviets—"consider themselves at war with the United States at this moment just as much as they consider themselves at war with Britain or Russia." Roosevelt made it clear that, regardless of attitudes towards Moscow, or war in Europe, the issue of American involvement had been decided elsewhere. Concluding, he referenced the world after war. "We are going to win the war and we are going to win the peace that follows."[169] On that forward-gazing note, Roosevelt sent Americans to bed on December 9. The chat included all the methods he used to establish broadcast intimacy. He spoke as a friend, aiming at unity of spirit in response.[170] But the low-key salesmanship covered much implicit and explicit information which listeners could assess. Everything Americans needed to know about how Roosevelt saw the war reverberated in the Fireside Chat.

The two days after Pearl Harbor set the tone for the rest of the war. The major notes were sounded, but there were stray intonations. The disposition of Germany still jangled. In one of the major decisions of the entire war, Hitler put things to rest by declaring war on the United States on December 11. Junior Axis partner Benito Mussolini followed suit. The President asked Congress for a matching declaration, which came immediately. His brief appeal was on-message. "The forces endeavoring to enslave the entire world now are moving toward this hemisphere," he warned, terming the Tripartite threat the greatest challenge ever to life, liberty, and civilization.[171] Montana's Rankin still could not vote "Yes," but neither did she oppose. Her abstention made the count in the House 393-0 for war with the Third Reich. In the Senate, the tally was 88-0.[172]

Washington, D.C. moved into wartime mode. The organs and acronyms of war were in place, established when the nation shifted to a preparedness economy in 1940. For example, William S. Knudsen's and Sidney Hillman's jointly led Office of Personnel Management, or OPM, already operated as subsidiary of the Office for Emergency Management. OEM was Executive branch authority. The Supply, Priorities and Allocations Board, SPAB, ran alongside, headed by Donald M. Nelson, similarly answering to the President. The Army and Navy Mutions Board, ANMB, answered to cabinet secretaries, who in turn answered to the President.[173] More such organizations were to come. Nobody knew exactly how they would work together, but everybody knew who was in charge.

Roosevelt spent the next two weeks on administration, having given Americans the language and ideas they needed to interpret events and understand what their nation was about to do. In the first week after December 7, Congress passed a supplemental defense bill of over $8 billion, which press accounts called a "huge sum," but which would not fund even the first year of fighting.[174] $1 billion from the initial outlay went to the navy, the rest to the army. On tap were new ships and planes, authorization to process 2 million new uniformed personnel, hundreds of thousands of trucks, jeeps, and assorted pieces of equipment.[175] Out went orders specifying air raid procedures, measures for defense of homeland installations, blackout plans, and the first of many rules dictating the position of workers, whose labor would be a vital factor in the wartime economy. United Mine Workers leader John L. Lewis angled for union shop rules in steel companies, and an arbitration board agreed, much to the chagrin of those who saw the ruling as against the presidential message of burden-sharing.[176] Congress would parry and the executive branch thrust as labor-related abstractions hardened into disputes. Factory owners and workers had just begun to fight, and the government would become embroiled. Home front battles lay ahead.

The federal government started implementing measures brought into being less by constitutional intricacy than by the animating spirit of Roosevelt. His main ideas about the war were easily summed up. First, vengeance: Japan must pay for Pearl Harbor. The attack was Japan's fault, hence the talk of "treachery." All shame lay with Tokyo. The fact that the United States was caught off-guard should be interpreted not as an unforgivable national security bungle, but as corroborative evidence of America's peaceable intentions. By acting treacherously, Japan made itself an outlaw, while the United States stood on the side of international morality. Second, the linkage between assailant Japan and supposed Axis enablers Germany and Italy. This gave support to the Europe-first plan which the Department of War would follow. It preemptively undercut armchair generals, or colonels, like Chicago's McCormick, who might call Japan the only priority. There should be no dividing up the enemy, which was one complex with three main appendages. The monstrous entity's brains were in Berlin. Third was Roosevelt's admission that the war would be difficult. But, like all American wars, it had to be something greater than a cynical fight for national interest. The war would be discussed in ennobled terms, as in FDR's Fireside Chat, with its higher purpose rhetoric about rising "far above and beyond the ugly field of battle."[177] American history was a passion of the President's. He knew that, ever since the Puritans, who saw their errand into the wilderness as part their covenant with God, Americans needed to see their own struggles as pieces in a morality play which put heavenly concerns at stake on earth.

Every time they fought, Americans considered armed struggle in moralistic terms. "Thou shouldst be a special people, an only people, none like thee on earth," instructed Puritan forefather Peter Bulkeley in 1646,[178] echoing the instructions to build the City upon a Hill given by Jonathan Winthrop in 1630.

For centuries, Americans internalized that message. If smallpox-decimated Narragansetts or Pequots lost their territories, it was a matter of providential action. That was how Winthrop saw things on May 22, 1634, when he wrote, "For the natives, they are neere all dead of small Poxe, so as the Lord hathe cleared our title to what we possess."[179] During the eighteenth century, the Revolution was a war to affirm the cause of Liberty, which Thomas Paine laid out as a matter of logic and ethics in *Common Sense* and *The Crisis*. The War of 1812 became something finer than breaking the British stranglehold on the Ohio Valley. Americans defined it as a necessary defense against the former master's threats against their Liberty.

Even wars of territorial conquest received the higher purpose treatment. A civilization seeing itself as blessed with divine favor thus resolved inner conflicts about land-grabbing, endowing the settlement of North America with spiritual dimensions lifting the settlement process above worldliness. Manifest Destiny was imbued with the transcendence of heroic fate. Taking tribal lands meant acting as vanguard for civilization's spread. War with Mexico stood for more than nabbing Texas and California—it meant actualizing a romantic vision, spreading the American eagle's wings across the romantic, ineffably desirable horizon.[180] The Civil War came to be understood as a fight about something greater than a sectional power-struggle. In the South, the war was rarely seen—by the master class—as inspired by slavery, but as a reaction against northern encroachments on southern freedoms. "And when our rights were threatened, the cry rose near and far/Hurrah for the Bonnie Blue Flag, that bears a single star!" sang Johnny Reb. In the North, battlefield success came only after the Emancipation Proclamation lifted the struggle to a higher plane. War with Spain in 1898 handed the United States new and enticing lands such as the Philippines, but the rationalization to intervene in Cuba was rife with idealistic talk about helping fellow Americans cast off their European imperial yoke. And while the maritime rights lent Wilson his strategic impetus in 1917, that paragon of presidential rectitude did not ask for war as a matter of commerce. Instead, Wilson's was a message of sacrifice to make a better world.

Roosevelt understood that the present war must fit into the pattern woven over centuries. Moreover, he could not lead Americans where they did not want to go, even with the most artful phraseology. The relationship between President and Public must be symbiotic in order to be successful. Roosevelt always intuited what Americans needed him to tell them. It was not enough to swear that the Japs would get theirs. Even vengeance-minded Americans needed to know that they would fight, suffer, and die in pursuit of worthier principles. There was plenty of passion about Japan's fate. But there were also other predictions. These were the cultural messages in Roosevelt's post-Pearl Harbor speeches. These were the emotional themes which emanated through the collective American unconscious, which a people understood viscerally. Having spoken in anticipation of the American reaction, Roosevelt went on to manage the federal colossus already growing so vast. He guided Americans through their feelings and provided context for what they were thinking, but the President did not implant or create those emotions and ideas. Instead, he cultivated them. It was less a matter of telling Americans what to say or showing them how to feel than of striking the proper pitch. Like a conductor with a tuning fork, Roosevelt delivered the right note. The constituent parts of the nation tuned up in harmony with the key he struck. After the Fireside Chat, he had two weeks before the start of the Christmas Season, which required another evocative performance from the Oval Office. Then, Roosevelt would have a performing partner, a man who considered Pearl Harbor a joyous occasion. That was Winston Churchill, who apotheosized the now intricate Anglo-American connection.

Their American cousin, after all—how currents of culture and strategy brought the United States and Great Britain together

The long and the short of the matter is that if I am satisfied with your answer, I am ready to drink a glass with you and be friends. If not, you and I will be two, I guess, Johnny.
                Brother Jonathan to John Bull, from The Diverting History of John Bull and
                                    Brother Jonathan, James Kirke Paulding, 1812[181]

English snobberies, English religion, English literary styles, English literary references and canons, English ethics, English superiorities, have been the cultural food that we have drunk in from our mothers' breasts.
                                    Randolph Bourne, "Trans-national America" 1916[182]

No American will think it wrong of me if I proclaim that to have the United States at our side was to me the greatest joy. I could not foretell the course of events. I do not pretend to have measured accurately the martial might of Japan, but now at this very moment I knew the United States was in the war, up to the neck and in to the death. So we had won after all!
                                    Winston Churchill[183]

There were many reasons for high emotions as three powerful men listened to the wireless at Chequers, the British Prime Minister's country retreat in Buckinghamshire.

With Churchill were Averell Harriman and American Ambassador John G. Winant, successor to isolationist Joseph Kennedy. Harriman was Roosevelt's Special Envoy to Europe and all-around diplomatic fixer. He helped to arrange the August 1941 meeting between the President and Prime Minister in August at Placentia Bay, Newfoundland. There, the two leaders forged the Atlantic Charter, codifying the convergence between Great Britain and the United States. None who saw Churchill and Roosevelt worshiping side by side on deck could doubt that the American establishment, of which FDR was a born member, was bound to the mother country by mystic cords. The hymn they sang together limned shared values:

Onward, Christian soldiers/marching as to war.
With the Cross of Jesus/Going on before.
Christ the royal Master/Leads against the foe;
Forward into battle/See his banners go!
At the sign of triumph/Satan's host doth flee,
Onward Christian soldiers/On to victory.
Hell's foundations quiver/At the shout of praise;
Brothers, lift your voices/Loud your anthems raise.[184]

No other 1941 world leaders could have played the scene. Stalin was too paranoid. His red church had room for one cleric; the Marshal presided alone with Lenin and Marx as saints. Hitler was too morbid and malevolent to understand religion. His faith was a witch's brew of virulent ethnocentrism, with the destiny of his people made immanent in his own person. Mussolini was as close as the *Fuhrer* got to a real partner. But Germany and Italy were not coeval powers, and the histrionic *Duce* was apposite for Roman mobs yet ridiculed elsewhere. Theirs was an imbalanced pairing. Hirohito, being a god, could have no human peers. His generals bowed down to him while bullying everyone else. But Roosevelt and Churchill, which is to say the United States and Britain, forged a true partnership. The friendship between the 'Former Naval Person' and the President was never problem-free, but the two statesmen were nothing but cousinly.

Roosevelt's name bespoke Dutch, not British, ancestry. He was no comprehensive Anglophile. His skepticism of British imperialism strained the alliance. Nor had he always found Churchill endearing. Roosevelt considered Churchill a stuck-up "stinker" at their only pre-war meeting, in 1918, when the bright young American spoke at Gray's Inn, London.[185] John Colville, Private Secretary to the Prime Minister, recalled Churchillian bitterness during May 1940. With the French Army reeling in disorder before German *panzers* and the British extricating their troops at Dunkerque, Roosevelt's bland sympathy rankled. France and Britain wanted planes, tanks, guns, but Roosevelt offered bromides. Churchill spat to his secretary, "Here's a telegram for those bloody Yankees. Send it off tonight."[186]

The President and Prime Minister were temperamental statesmen, not saints. Each had divergent strategic concerns. But there was enough overlap to nurture a relationship both affectionate and productive. 1940s *blitzkrieg* dangers led to Roosevelt's more aggressive assistance packages for Britain. The national interests ran mostly in sync, so the connection between 10 Downing Street and the White House hummed warmly.

This marked a major change. The British were the original enemy, and United States culture took many years to process the American prodigality at the heart of their relations. In 1812, James Kirke Paulding of the Knickerbocker literary set, collaborator with Washington Irving on *Salamagundi*, published *The Diverting History of John Bull and Brother Jonathan*.[187] Paulding's satire played with the enmeshed nature of John Bull, England's stock character, and Brother Jonathan, the wayward American son. Paulding, Secretary of the Navy under Martin van Buren, enjoyed stereotypes. John Bull was "a choleric old fellow who had a good manor in the middle of a great mill-pond . . . surrounded by water." He was "a good, hearty fellow, excellent bottle companion, generous, brave hearty old lad." But Bull had his faults—"a devilish quarrelsome, overbearing disposition which was always getting him into some scrape or another." Brother Jonathan, meanwhile, was a headstrong youth, "hard as a pine and tough as leather," who escaped his father's control— "taking his gun and his axe, he put himself in a boat and paddled over the mill pond to new some lands belonging to his father." His surroundings were in "quite a state of nature, covered with wood and inhabited by nobody but wild beasts." The satire jested as the "lad of mettle" and his crochety father jousted. At the end of the story, stubborn father accepts his son's independence, partly because nefarious Beau Napperty—symbolizing France—emerges as a more dangerous villain.[188] Paulding used a thick brush to paint respective national characters. England had good points but poked its nose in others' business. The United States was impetuous and headstrong. France was sly and opportunistic.

Connections between the United States and the parent nation grew more fraught with complexes during the nineteenth century. Much of the tension was cultural. Americans determined to stand on native grounds and develop their own modes of expression. At the same time, they were competitive and insecure when facing Britain's cultural superiority. Sometimes, this led to bizarre arguments, as when James Fenimore Cooper lauded Shakespeare as "the great author of America."[189] Cooper was not crazy—the Bard of Avon was popular across all boundaries of class and geography, which was why Alexis de Tocqueville found that there was "hardly a pioneer's hut that does not contain a few odd volumes. . . . I remember that I read the feudal drama *Henry V* for the first time in a log cabin."[190] Fifty years later, German traveler Karl Knortz echoed Tocqueville, writing "If you were to enter an isolated log cabin in the Far West, and even if its inhabitant were to exhibit many of the traces of backwoods living, he will most likely have one small room nicely furnished . . . in which you will certainly find the Bible and in most cases also some cheap edition of the works of Shakespeare."[191] The merit behind these observations can be seen in Mark Twain's *Huckleberry Finn*. Twain's adroit use of the Duke and the Dolphin, actors and con men who hilariously butcher Shakespeare, depended upon the assumption that Americans loved "their" Bard, even if they mixed up Hamlet's words with Macbeth's. British high culture was democratized to humorous effect.

American founders grew up in a world imbued with British culture. Thomas Jefferson called *King Lear* the best text for teaching filial piety. Abraham Lincoln thought *Macbeth* a perfect training book for lawyers who needed to know "the problems of tyranny and murder."[192] During the Great Awakening, Jonathan Edwards supported the French and Indian Wars, not because of religious affinity, but because a developing a sense of proto-nationalism made him see the American experience as extending the best traditions of English liberty.[193] Such claim to the fruits of English liberty were a main part of Revolution rhetoric, under the theory that George III traduced the noblest elements of British political evolution, which the New World preserved, untainted.

There were countervailing sentiments which manifested in the popular culture of their times. When Twain wrote *A Connecticut Yankee in King Arthur's Court*, he put the mercenary genius and democratic inclinations of his protagonist at odds with the Old World. The climactic Battle of the Sand-Belt devolves when the time-traveler attempts to import Republican virtue into Camelot. "The monarchy has lapsed, it no longer exists. By consequence, all political power has reverted to its original source, the people of the nation . . . there is no longer a nobility, no longer a privileged class, no longer an Established Church; all men are become exactly equal; they are upon one common level, and religion is free," reads his proclamation.[194] But mulish Britons remain insensate to these orders, so feudalism resists improvement in the novel.

There were also other European cultural influences at work in the nineteenth-century United States. George Bancroft attended Georg Friedrich Hegel's 1820 Berlin lectures leaving the American historian with an abiding respect for German intellectual prowess.[195] Immigrants brought with them German and continental philosophy. The heritage was expressed in such academic organs as the *Journal of Speculative Philosophy*, which counted among its readers and contributors George Sylvester Morris, Charles Sanders Peirce, William James, and John Dewey. It introduced Americans to Immanuel Kant, Hegel, Johann Gottlieb Fichte, and Friedrich W.J. Schelling.[196] Morris, especially, preached the virtues of adopting German intellectual heritage; academic institutions including Johns Hopkins, Michigan, and Harvard—which hired German-schooled, Johns Hopkins graduate Josiah Royce—created a Germanic-American intellectual legacy.[197] France always had its acolytes, from Thomas Jefferson through the Lost Generation. But differing linguistic convenience, political developments, and conflicting tides of strategic convergence and divergence, brought closer Anglo-American ties. There were fewer reasons for Americans to look towards Paris and Berlin than to London for cultural cues or a friend in a dangerous world. Most immigrants from Central Europe wanted to leave behind political violence and social oppression. German society and politics evolved in directions leading away from the United States. France was often in civil strife, bouncing between republican and monarchical restorations. The Anglo-American connection prospered.

Conflux was propelled by something which the upper classes of both nations admired: money. In the antebellum years, European capital midwifed American development, eased by legislation such as Henry Clay's American System. As the new nation built roads, canals, and railroads, it attracted Old World capital investment, with British interests at the head.[198] When British venture capitalists looked for attractive opportunities, they found them in North America, to the delight of American entrepreneurs. After the Civil War, the Trans-Mississippi West together with the rise of foreign markets for American resources made agriculture and cattle highly lucrative.[199] Also profitable were mining and steel. Investment came in from France and the Netherlands, but British firms supplied the lion's share of foreign funds.[200] The comprehensive involvement of London-based enterprise in developing the American West can be deduced from the fact that, between 1860 and 1901, 518 British limited-liability joint-stock companies registered to engage in mining enterprises, with a net capital amount of nearly 80 million pounds.[201] The trend was similar in other American industries, which meant that there were pecuniary reasons for British and American leaders to protect mutual interests.

Such cultural, political, and economic binding ties vexed Anglophobes such as Mencken. But to men like Harriman and Roosevelt, they constituted an immutable if sometimes unconscious element of lives marked by preparatory schools, Anglican communion, and other tropes. The American elite liked brokering deals with British counterparts. The former found in the latter not just investors, but role models. The ambivalent "emulative jealousy" which Malcolm Cowley identified within American attitudes towards Britain gave way to "pride of kindship." According to Cowley, even for non-English descendants, Britain became "our old home."[202] When *New York Tribune* correspondent Heywood Hale Broun landed in France with the A.E.F. in 1917, he lost his critical faculties in an unguarded moment. "Verdun and Joffre and 'they shall not pass,' and Napoleon's war tomb, and war bread and all the men with medals and everything," enthused the reporter. "There'll never be anything like it again. I tell you it's better than *Ivanhoe*. Everything's happening and I'm in it!"[203]

Long rivalrous Anglo-American strategic relations transformed into the "Special Relationship." International disputes were jointly resolved from 1895–1903—the Venezuela Boundary Dispute, the Anglo-Boer War, the Alaska-Yukon Boundary issue, and the Open Door Policy. Solving each in mutually beneficial ways helped Washington, anxious to project naval power in pursuit of foreign markets, and London, needful of protecting the Empire. When Venezuela challenged its frontier line with British Guyana, the United States helped to arbitrate. At first, there was American popular tension as the Monroe Doctrine reflex kicked in. Venezuela was a fellow American republic standing up to European tormentors. William James was swept up in the short spurt of anti-British jingoism. "It is instructive to find how near the surface in all of us the old fighting spirit lies and how slight an appeal will wake it up," he observed. "Once *really* waked, there is no retreat."[204] But Theodore Roosevelt's Corollary revealed a pragmatic statecraft friendly to Britain.[205] When Boers and Britons clashed in South Africa, the United States refrained from supporting the pioneers. Brahmin Senator Henry Cabot Lodge (R-MA) now saw the original enemy as an Anglo-Saxon partner in a world filled with alien races, nations, and values. "However much we sympathize with the Boers," he wrote to President Theodore Roosevelt, "the downfall of the British Empire is something no rational American could regard as anything but a misfortune to the United States."[206] London was pleased. A reliable United States was vastly preferable for British interests.[207] When the United States and Canada argued over the border between gold-rush Alaska and the Yukon, the British member of the international arbitration committee sided with the United States. It was bitter for Canadians, loyal to the Crown but weaker than their American neighbors.[208]

The Open Door Policy, under which the United States supported trading rights in China, blossomed after Anglo-American cooperation during the Boxer Rebellion. Rapprochement was best viewed through the lens of Mahan, since every issue dealt with the demands of power projection overseas. The United States and Britain shared complementary interests predicated on maritime trade. Neither navy feared the other. Since each wanted open sea lanes, the two navies could serve parallel missions. This was a long way from the Anglophobia of Commodore Matthew Perry, who focused on outstripping Britain at sea when his famous mission secured trading links with Japan. "When we look at the possessions on the east of our great maritime rival, England, and of the constant and rapid increase of their fortified ports, we should be admonished," he wrote. "Fortunately, the Japanese and many other islands of the Pacific are still left untouched . . . and some of them lay in the route of a great commerce which is destined to become of great importance to the United States."[209] The race for rich Eastern connections was a competition. But there was enough Asian lucre to satisfy more than one imperial urge. By the end of the nineteenth century, the links Perry wanted were in place. London was comfortable with American trans-Pacific connections, which did not impede Britain's imperial interests and added another power devoted to open seas. Theodore Roosevelt's Secretary of State, John Hay was annoyed by charges that TR's administration was too Anglophile. "These idiots say I'm not an American because I don't say, 'To Hell with the Queen,' at every breath," he complained.[210] But when it came to geopolitics, Hay was clear: "The one indispensable feature of our foreign policy should be a friendly understanding with England."[211]

Cultural similarity partnered with strategic confluence to build the new relationship. It was taken to with zest by the American WASP establishment. A wave of Anglo-Saxon solidarity helped to foster the notion that Britain and the United States were twins of global destiny. Senator Albert Beveridge's "March of the Flag" speech became the text of record for the American imperialist impulse. His outlook rendered the opportunism of the late 1800s divinely countenanced, because "God . . . has made us the master organizers of the world to establish system where chaos reigns. . . . He has marked the American people as His Chosen Race finally to lead in the regeneration of the world."[212] Beveridge might have prompted British eye-rolling, but London liked the equally forceful words of Josiah Strong, who wrote *Our Country* in 1885. Strong's vision of Anglo-Saxonism made plenty of room for sharing power with the British. "This race . . . having developed particularly aggressive traits calculated to impress its institutions upon mankind, will spread itself over the earth," Strong predicted.[213]

Actualizing such broad rhetoric was a raft of individual rediscoveries of the allures of British polite society. The phenomenon of upper-class attraction was well-painted by John Singer Sargent, well described by Henry James. Neither artist nor novelist lacked for real-life subjects. The convergence which brought together the richest Americans with English grandees set up a picturesque milieu within which two upper classes could be *entre nous*. An irony was that this late-nineteenth century vogue came after the most emotive expression of working-class solidarity between the two nations.

Once, the republican values of the United States inspired British radicals, like Chartists and Whigs, who saw their class system as ready for abolishment. The most stirring example of a populist connection occurred on New Year's Eve, 1862. For months, watching the American Civil War, Prime Minister Viscount Palmerston, and Foreign Secretary, Earl (later Lord) John Russell, corresponded about the merits of coercive "mediation to the United States Government, with a view to the recognition of the independence of the Confederates."[214] Cynical and strategic, the plan would have doomed the Union, perpetuated the American split, and enhanced Canada. Diplomats in London—including young Henry Adams, secretary to his ambassadorial father, Charles Francis Adams—realized that any such British maneuver meant defeat for the United States. The tantalizing chance prompted Chancellor of the Exchequer, William Ewart Gladstone, to his notorious claim at Newcastle that "Jefferson Davis and other leaders of the South have made an army; they are making, it appears, a navy; and they have made what is more than either, they have made a nation."[215]

Gladstone's overreach violated diplomatic etiquette, embarrassing London. It placed Anglo-American rivalry on the wrong side of history, since President Lincoln had just proclaimed Emancipation. While the *Times* dismissed Lincoln and his Emancipation Proclamation as a "pompous proclamation . . . more like a Chinaman beating his two swords together to frighten his enemy than like an earnest man pressing on his cause in steadfastness and truth,"[216] freeing Southern slaves fired admiration in humbler English circles. Any pro-Confederate intervention was nullified by the Workingmen of Manchester, who took diplomacy into their own hands. From their trade hall, they wrote to Lincoln on December 31, 1862, congratulating him for the Proclamation, ensuring that no British government would intervene on behalf of the Confederacy. The sincerity of their expression was proved by the fact that many were unemployed due to the war-induced cotton shortage. "We beg to express our fraternal sentiments toward you and your country. We rejoice in your greatness as an outgrowth of England, whose blood and language you share," went their salutation. The letter praised Lincoln for elevating the Civil War to a nobler plateau.

> Since we have discerned . . . that the victory of the North, in the war which has so sorely distressed us . . . will strike off the fetters of the slave, you have attracted our warm and earnest sympathy. We joyfully honor you, as the President and the Congress with you, for many decisive steps toward practically exemplifying your belief in the words of your great founders, "All men are created free and equal."[217]

In his response, Lincoln praised the workers for their "decisive utterance," which he termed "an instance of sublime Christian heroism."[218] This exchange epitomized a real connection between peoples. There would be no meretricious intervention, and British social notions looked due for a change.

But the Gilded Age extolled rather than modulated capitalism, and the United States came to be seen as the land of dollars, not of democratic checks on the upper classes.[219] Late nineteenth century prosperity put elitism more confidently in place. A throbbing mass of underlings, whose labor was plentiful and cheap, fought for self-protection through trade unions. But the working class in the United States and Britain were not about to seize power through revolution. Relationships between labor and capital in each country supported cultural convergence, according to Alfred North Whitehead. The former Cambridge don, who moved to Harvard after World War I, was also one of the better observers of social currents across the Atlantic. One evening in 1935, engaged in a *tete-a-tete* with friend and writer Lucien Price, Whitehead looked back over history. He observed that Oliver Cromwell's influence continued apace in the American colonies after Britain returned to its aristocratic, land-owning tradition in the later eighteenth century. The United States eventually married Cromwell's tradition to nineteenth century industrialism.[220]

"The Cromwellian revolution was undefeated in America, so the two countries have developed along quite different lines!" Whitehead explained: "In England, owing to the difficulty of individual talents finding their way up through class strata, people stay with their class, bring their class along, and we have a labor movement ably led by working class men."[221] Price demurred that, even with Franklin Roosevelt in office, American workers did not share high-level social power. "Yes, and isn't that one reason why your exceptional talents can rise as rapidly through the class strata? They rise, but they leave their class behind. Thus, English aristocracy is creating a genuine democracy, and American democracy is creating an aristocracy."[222]

Devotee of the American model for emergent elitism was Herbert Spencer, British prophet of Social Darwinism. He was a hero to the American industrialist class, led by Scotland native Andrew Carnegie, who invited him to New York for the celebrated Dinner at Delmonico's in 1882.[223] At that luxe banquet, wealth and ideology mingled. Outside the door of the New York restaurant seethed a slum city with many Irish who had no love for their historical oppressor. Nor did the Delmonico plutocrats love the urban masses. These people's gritty circumstances were the photographic focus of Jacob Riis, Danish immigrant bent on exposing inequities in a nation polarized along money lines. As Riis' Other Half teemed about questing after life's basics, the WASP upper crust had reason to feel pressured along ethnic and cultural lines.

Rapidly onrushing technology contributed to a sense of fast systemic change. Henry Adams saw it in the dynamo humming at the 1900 Great Paris Exposition: the end of the world he knew, the dawn of a fractured universe. In one of history's gloomy epiphanies, Adams realized that all he understood was obsolete. The dynamo flummoxed him. Adams interpreted the ultramodern device "as a moral force, much as the early Christians felt the cross . . .

> The planet itself seemed less impressive, in its old-fashioned, deliberate annual or daily revolution, than this huge wheel, revolving within arm's-length at some vertiginous speed, and barely murmuring—scarcely humming an audible warning to stand a hair's breadth further for respect of power—while it would not wake the baby lying close to its frame. Before the end, one began to pray to it . . .[224]

Education of Henry Adams painted a painfully brilliant awareness that a lifetime of learning had not equipped Adams for the future underway. He was prepared by heritage and training for a unitary world; he felt at odds with multiplicity. Immigrants frightened Adams, as they did Henry James. What James called "the dreadful chill of change"[225] seemed both unwelcome and unavoidable to Adams, wondering if his entire class was sentenced to obsolescence by a pitilessly moving world. Adams further developed this in a lugubrious book, *The Degradation of the Democratic Dogma*, articulating a dynamic theory of history in which reliability was out. Obsessed by thermodynamics, he posited that civilizations leached out energy. Fascinated by electricity and immaterial energy, Adams decided that human affairs were like matter—susceptible to pressure, attraction, repulsion, and resistance. He urged readers to admit that a phase of history was over, with astounding, and unsettling developments ahead.[226] Adams epitomized *fin-de-siecle* uneasiness. Brother Brooks Adams was less abstract, if just as pessimistic. In *The Law of Civilization and Decay* (1895), Brooks Adams picked up the theme of *translatio imperii*, the shift of influence and rule. He drew a westward-moving line of economic and strategic power. Rome was once the locus of world influence, then Madrid, then London. The good news for Americans was that New York would be the home of world financial and strategic might during the twentieth century. The bad news was that the line never stopped moving. Tokyo and Peking were next.[227] The Adams brothers' ambivalence about the end of the familiar world did not pester every well-to-do American. But there was a pervasive sense in privileged circles that Anglo-Saxon leadership was coveted by a jealous underclass. Charles Eliot Norton, Harvard Professor and colleague of William James, epitomized genteel declinism. A Radcliffe student took note of her professor, "so happy and benignant . . . while he gently tells us it were better for us had we never been born in this degenerate and unhappy age."[228]

Social Darwinism offered comfort to the wealthy. If one was destined to be rich, then there was no need for guilt. Those who understood Darwin realized that Social Darwinism bastardized the biologist's theories. Darwin's central thesis was that nothing lasted forever, that change was constant. He wrote about barnacles and finches, not social conditions. Nevertheless, a mania for competition-based social interpretations burst forth. William Graham Sumner wrote *What Social Classes Owe to Each Other* in 1883. Influenced by Spencer, he saw social welfare as misguided sentimentalism and individualism as the evolutionary American ideal. Sumner's vision of a world of groups in perpetual conflict was honest, if not charitable. He maintained that society's lower rungs owed no more to the prosperous than they were owed in return. "Certain ills belong to the hardships of nature," he explained, using the naturalistic argument so much in vogue in western intellectual circles of the day. "They are natural. They are part of the struggle with Nature for existence. We cannot blame our fellow-men for our share of these."[229]

Sumner explicated an American doctrine of permanent class conflict that chilled the comfortable. They feared progressivism, not to mention anarchism and bolshevism. Sumner's message was that those on top were not necessarily destined to stay there. An arch cultural pessimist, Sumner insisted that groups of people must contend against each other. The only binding ties in a society Sumner admitted were contractual. Only contracts between those free enough to enter into them served the cause of dignity and liberty. "It follows," he argued, "that one man, in a free state, cannot claim help from, and cannot be charged to give help to, another."[230]

This intensified the social unease which led American grandees to seek out English gentility. Their own homeland was the epicenter of worrisome flux, while, in Britain, the *haute monde* seemed at ease. Well-off Americans sought out the upper English crust, so confident and undaunted. The *Debrett's Peerage* crowd could not welcome well-bankrolled Americans unreservedly. But at least the British gentry did not castigate rich Americans for being well-off. Staid complacency proved steadying. Mutual discovery by elites was, as Henry James explained from London, a mixed experience. "In one sense, I feel intimately at home here, and in another sense—as an American may be on the whole very willing, at times, very glad to feel—like a complete outsider." James added, "There are some English institutions and idiosyncrasies that it is certainly a great blessing to be outside of." Then again, he admitted, he understood English manners and habits of mind so well, that "There are times indeed when I seem to myself to carry all England in my breeches pocket."[231]

British blue bloods were hard to copy. Their codes and behaviors were deceptively complicated. Rich Americans trying to pass came off as parvenus. This was always a problem when the adolescent republic sought to impress its former master. There was deep desire to avoid rejection by the parent culture.[232] Sometimes, Americans copied nobility's appurtenances with ridiculous family embellishments. "The young learn quickly, intuitively, spontaneously," observed Booth Tarkington, laughing at Midwesterners affecting pseudo-English haughtiness. "They perceive the obligations of *noblesse oblige*. They begin to comprehend the necessity of caste and its requirements. They learn what birth means—ah,—that is, they learn what it means to be well-born."[233]

Tarkington was a product of the Hoosier School, writers convinced that the Midwest, that "Valley of Democracy," was the best incubator of American virtues.[234] He considered fancy airs demeaning. But the match between American wealth and British social elegance remained attractive to those coveting hauteur. They were fit partners for the British ruling class of Lord Salisbury's day, dominated by landholders accustomed to govern by right, viewing politics as the gentleman's purview, seeing themselves just as Sargent painted them, oozing "natural arrogance, elegance, and self-confidence."[235]

Rich Americans could be accommodated. Most Yanks never rode to hounds with the Quorn. But Hugh Lowther, 5th Earl of Lonsdale and Master of that foxhunting outfit, contentedly hosted exceptional American visitors, like John Pierpoint Morgan. They played cards at the National Sporting Club.[236]

What brought Morgan, topmost corsair of American finance, to a card table with the Earl? Shared financial and social interests. Both men were mighty, both were rich, both looked at the world as their domain and its resources and inhabitants as fodder for their enterprises. J.P. Morgan was Junius Spencer Morgan's son. The elder Morgan, an American, was one of London's foremost bankers.[237] J.S.

Morgan & Company allied itself with Baring Brothers, so the younger Morgan was at home in London's halls of power. He refinanced the American railroad industry, cooperating with the world's largest banks, underwriting the US dollar during the Gold Scare of 1895. When President Grover Cleveland asked him in wonder how Morgan knew that European banks would help, the millionaire explained, "I simply told them that this was necessary for the maintenance of the public credit and the promotion of industrial peace, and they did it."[238] Morgan was accustomed to being taken seriously by Britain's most powerful men. That was how he and the Earl came together at the National Sporting Club.

Gambling, the Earl and the financier created Gilded Age folklore. The two made a famous wager which sent deadbeat playboy Harry Bensley circumnavigating the globe.[239] Bensley was a gambler whose debts were in the club book. But he went bust during the game, a potential disgrace. Morgan and the Earl let Bensley off the hook, issuing a challenge. To set aside the scandal, Bensley would travel the world incognito, in wacky costume. Bensley's travels were covered in the press, while Morgan and Lonsdale's sporting blood helped their public relations, finishing the popular image of Anglo-American comity.

Anglo-American links spanned the world, demonstrated by Henry Morton Stanley. Born illegitimate in Wales in 1841, Henry Rowlands grew up in and out of the workhouse before emigrating to the United States, where he adopted the name of a New Orleans benefactor who took him in as a teenager. An improbable career saw him fight for both sides during the Civil War before he became a *New York Herald* correspondent, protégé of publisher James Gordon Bennet. Bennet sent Stanley on the much-ballyhooed trek to find David Livingstone in the wilds of Central Africa. When Stanley found the missing missionary-explorer author at Ujiji, on the shores of Lake Tangyanika, on November 10, 1871, he may or may not have delivered the famous greeting, "Dr. Livingstone, I presume." But he did add another plank to the burgeoning platform of Anglo-American cultural intercourse. Florence Nightingale called Stanley's account of the discovery, *How I Found Livingstone*, "the worst possible book on the best possible subject,"[240] and Stanley's treatment of natives throughout his African journeys was brutal. But Bennet knew a good story. Stanley's fame and wealth conquered the circumstances of his birth. Knighthood and a seat in Parliament followed, while books like *In Darkest Africa* (1890) and *Through South Africa* (1898) thrilled American and British readers in equal measure.[241]

Less reckless, peregrinating wealthy Americans and Englishmen criss-crossed the Atlantic so often that the voyage became an extension of their pleasure pursuits. The tourism industry revealed its Anglo-American connections when Thomas Cook advertised western package tours in the *Trans-Continental Tourist Guide* during the late nineteenth century. Western travel impresario George Croffut assured readers that "Thomas Cook is an enterprising Englishman with Yankee ingenuity!"[242] That combination sounded formidable.

Shared popular culture brought the two national reading publics into close and intimate contact. Bright young things, goofy clubmen, and fancy swells like Bertram Wooster, Hildebrand Glossop, and Reginald Twistelton-Twistleton—beloved by millions of Americans thanks to regular serialization of P.G. Wodehouse's works in *The Saturday Evening Post*—made New York a second home during the Jazz Age. Well born and party focused, these fictional characters were innocents abroad in their own comfortable manner. Bertie, Tuppy, and Pongo wooed and were wooed by lissome, rich, athletic American beauties like Pauline Stoker. Pauline epitomized the spirit which caused Lord Ickenham—another Wodehouse creation, a mischief-bent Earl with an American wife, the only person who could tame him—to observe matter-of-factly: "American girls try to boss you. It's part of their charm."[243]

Wodehouse was a major Anglo-American literary phenomenon, and the comedic potentialities latent in trans-Atlantic social interactions formed a consistent background for his writing. Sometimes, his characters reversed the formula, with earnest Americans trying to figure out life and love in England.

New York lost a great baseball fan when Hugo Percy de Wynter Framlinghame, sixth Earl of Carricksteed, married Mae Elinor, only daughter of Mr. and Mrs. J. Wilmot Birdsey of East Seventy-Third Street; for scarcely had that internationally important event taken place when Mrs. Birdsey, announcing that, for the future, the home would be in England, as near as possible to dear Mae and dear Hugo, scooped J. Wilmot out of his comfortable morris chair as if he had been a clam, corked him up in a swift taxicab, and decanted him into a Deck B stateroom on the "Olympic." And there he was, an exile. . . . The crushing blow had been the sentence of exile. He loved base-ball with a love passing the love of women, and the prospect of never seeing a game again in his life appalled him. And then, one morning, like a voice from another world, had come the news that the White Sox and the Giants were to give an exhibition in London at the Chelsea Football Ground. He had counted the days like a child before Christmas.[244]

Wodehouse was prolific and his formula never changed. Starting before World War I, his books and stories piled up in their hundreds. Any story guaranteed a successful run for any magazine. Any book sold well. Wodehouse was the genial interpreter of British–American silliness. His characters cavorted in a lovely and gentle world, equal parts Edwardian and Roaring Twenties. Gentry folk chatted with Brooklyn burglars. East End prizefighters advised millionaires on romance. The stories were immune from current events and steeped in references which readers in the United States loved. Wodehouse's heroes, clueless and amusing, danced on the *soiree* circuit from London to their country homes; from Manhattan to Hollywood. His villains were never wicked, just overprotective fathers or con artists with hearts of gold. They were necessitarian students of human frailty more than dark-hearted baddies. If a marriage-minded young woman thought she could improve Bertie's vacuous mind by making him read philosophy, there was always the enterprising and sagacious *vade mecum*, valet Reginald Jeeves, to extricate his charge from fell clutches. Jeeves always found a way, and readers of the *Saturday Evening Post*, which thrived on Wodehouse's prolific output and became his American house organ, loved it. Wodehouse helped to forge Anglo-American comity. British-born public school product whose life included a youthful stint in a Hong Kong bank, Wodehouse sat astride the "Anglo-American" hyphen. He wrote musical comedies with Jerome Kern and Guy Bolton,[245] knew Hollywood, and lived on Long Island. When the war began, he was the most popular interpreter of English mores for any American audience. This continued during the war, despite the fact that Wodehouse was caught up in the invasion of France and interned by the Germans.

Wodehouse was in 1941 but the latest iteration in a series of shared literary figures who brought the two nations closer together. Charles Dickens' 1842 voyage resulted in *American Notes*, fixing his standing in the United States. Dickens found Americans loud, rude, and too familiar. All their talk of liberty struck him as disingenuous, given slavery. He hated it when American men spit tobacco juice.[246] Dickens' complaints mirrored the self-aware jokes by James Fenimore Cooper. Leatherstocking, the frontiersman, was his most famous character. But Cooper, a sailor who wrote the history of the US Navy in 1839,[247] also created comic masterpiece Aristobulus Bragg. Bragg's thoroughly American character was endowed with inalienable characteristics, "a compound of shrewdness, impulsive, common sense, pretension, humility, cleverness, vulgarity, kindheartedness, duplicity, selfishness, law honest, moral fraud, and mother wit."[248] For emphasis, Cooper made sure to put Bragg in contact with English high society, where his "go-aheadism" clashed with English impeccability. When Bragg attacks a trans-Atlantic shipboard buffet, he disregards "quiet manners" and plunges in, efficiently loading up his plate with every dish. No glutton, Bragg lacked polish. This Jacksonian "had never before sat down to so brilliant a table," but "was not a man to be disconcerted at a novelty."[249] American and British readers alike got Cooper's "go-aheadism" joke, and laughed at it.

Anglo-American comparisons were also institutional, pointing out differences as well as predicting convergence. Traveling to the United States garnering observations for *American Commonwealth*, Lord James Bryce was frequently asked "What do you think of our institutions?"[250] His analysis of what he called "an experiment in the rule of the multitudes" led him to conclude that each American felt "that the government is his own, and he individually responsible for its conduct."[251] Bryce drew contrast to continental Europe, where Germans saw their governmental regime as a machine operating above them. Only in Britain, which he put decades behind in the democratic impulse, did Bryce see movement towards the view that government ought to belong to the people.

Arthur Conan Doyle's Sherlock Holmes stories had abundant American references, thanks to the peripatetic author's travels. Several of the mysteries which Dr. John Watson and Holmes plunged into had American angles. Doyle brought the Utah frontier into "The Sign of the Four," Pennsylvania's Molly Maguires into "The Valley of Fear." American readers appreciated these connections. Christopher Morley remembered waiting eagerly for each new title to arrive at his local public library. "When one found at the library a Conan Doyle he had not read, he began it at once on the walk home. . . . It was quite a long trudge . . . and the tragedy often was that, loitering like a snail, almost like the locomotion of a slowed moving picture, the book was actually finished by the time one got home."[252] When Holmes and archenemy Professor Moriarity tumbled over Reichenbach Falls, American as well as British readers refused to accept their hero's demise. His authorial hand forced, Conan Doyle's resurrected Holmes, whose rebirth ran in *Collier's* in 1903 causing rejoicing in the United States.[253]

The first English-language writer to win the Nobel Prize in Literature was Rudyard Kipling, in 1907. That brought pride to the United States, since he married an American woman, Carrie Balestier, sister of a writer and publisher with whom Kipling collaborated.[254] The young couple embarked on a honeymoon in the United States, then settled in Brattleboro, Vermont, naming their home "Bliss Cottage." A local noted that Carrie clung to British ways more stoutly than her husband.[255] The effect of Brattleboro upon the author was profound. His sense of local light and color was stimulated as intensely by Fall in the Green Mountains as by childhood summers in the cool Indian hill station of Simla:

> A little maple began it, flaming blood-red of a sudden where he stood against the dark green of a pine-belt. Next morning there was an answering signal from the swamp where the sumacs grow. Three days later, the hill-sides as fast as the eye could range were afire, and the roads paved, with crimson and gold. Then a wet wind blew, and ruined all the uniforms of that gorgeous army; and the oaks, who had held themselves in reserve, buckled on their dull and bronzed cuirasses and stood it out stiffly to the last blown leaf, till nothing remained but pencil-shadings of bare boughs, one could see into the most private heart of the woods.[256]

It was in Brattleboro that Kipling wrote *The Jungle Books* (1894–1895), *Captain's Courageous* (1897), and *Kim* (1901).[257] An in-laws dispute, coupled with jingoism over the Venezuela Boundary Dispute, prompted the Kiplings to return to England.[258] His tales had a second incarnation in the movies before World War II, affording lustrous roles to stars such as Cary Grant, Spencer Tracy, Shirley Temple, and Lionel Barrymore.

Robert Louis Stevenson and D.H. Lawrence made their way through the United States, while Henry James and T.S. Eliot, decamped to England. Abetted by the trans-oceanic cable and reliably scheduled steamships, ties sundered by revolution reconstituted themselves in variant form. The prodigal and parent nation found each other again. Each national press increased coverage of each respective country. People consciously and unconsciously took in the idea that Britain and America were culturally connected. It worried Ralph Waldo Emerson—"Let us not europize—neither by travel nor by reading," he urged, "now that steam has narrowed the Atlantic to a strait, the nervous rocky West is intruding a new and continental element into our national mind."[259] But Anglo-American differences only accentuated the mutual interest.

It was left to Irish-Americans to tend the sputtering fires of Anglophobia. But even that ancient dynamic was finite. When Irish independence fighters rose in Dublin on Easter Sunday, 1916, they issued the Proclamation of the Republic, aimed not just at Ireland, but at "her exiled children in America."[260] The American sons and daughters to whom they appealed cheered when Eamon De Valera made his tour of the United States three years later. De Valera's American birth—in New York—saved him from the firing squad after the Easter Rising. But the aftermath, when 15 British executions created 15 new martyrs, was overshadowed in American attentions by the Great War. Public opinion in the United States supported the negotiations which led to end of the Anglo-Irish war and the establishment of the Irish Free State, in 1921.[261] At that point, the long cause of Irish independence was won, shriveling active Anglophobia all the more.

By World War II, hating Britain seemed an eccentricity rather than proof of patriotism. Isolationist Senator Peter Gerry (R-RI)—of Puritan vintage—resisted the urge to support Britain against Germany. Gerry was chastised by a young interventionist woman in 1941, who demanded, "How can someone with your background feel as you do about this war . . . when Britain is in such danger?" She assumed that the Senator should admire the British. "Well, madame," sneered the Brahmin relic, harkening to revolutionary times, "*You* perhaps won't understand; but in families *like mine* we still remember the lobsterbacks!" To Joe Alsop, Gerry's answer showed bad manners and irrelevance.[262]

Institutional mirroring by Alsop's "WASP Ascendancy" meant that top-level northeastern establishmentarians strove to be "more English than the English and more European than the Europeans," striking a frosty social pose to freeze out arrivistes.[263] The establishment mimicked English aristocratic behaviors in what American historian R.H. Tawney called "the functional view of class organization," the habitual revival of snooty attitudes which dated to Virginia settlement days.[264] So profound could be the identification that King George V called John W. Davis, Wilson's choice to serve as American ambassador to Great Britain from 1918 to 1921, "the most perfect gentleman I have ever met."[265]

Schools were one twentieth century venue where American imitation was most obvious. Copying Oxford and Cambridge, boat races became popular. Dining and social clubs sprouted across American campuses. F. Scott Fitzgerald knew how to apply a coat of Oxbrite gloss to Jay Gatsby. Showing mixed feelings, Fitzgerald mocked it with shady Mr. Wolfsheim. Wolfsheim was certain he had discovered a man of breeding after talking with Gatsby for an hour—"He's an Oggsford man." "Oh!" "He went to Oggsford College. You know Oggsford College?" "I've heard of it." "It's one of the most famous colleges in the world."[266]

Properly tapped Yale or Harvard men—Skull-and-Bones or Porcellian—were not as purebred as Oxonians or Cantabrigians. Few Americans attended such schools, but movies filled the experiential gap. Thrust ahead by Lionel Barrymore as the rich father, Robert Taylor plays the pushy American in 1938's *A Yank at Oxford*. There followed *A Yank at Eton* in 1942, Mickey Rooney's reprise. Best was Laurel and Hardy's *A Chump at Oxford* (1940), in which a blow to the head from a loose window knocked Stan Laurel into delusion, causing him to act like Lord Paddington. Merriment ensues before another smack on Laurel's dome brings reunion with Ollie. Half a century's collaboration between high-class Britons and their American counterparts made the joke easy to catch.

One of the signature signs of convergence was the dynastic marriage, which served both sides. The wealthy American young woman made the Grand Tour with an eye towards an alliance with a young European gentleman. English was easiest—fewer linguistic complications. All the connections buzzed and crackled from the 1890s onward, as two rising world powers gazed at each other through the new lens of mutual respect. Anglo-American rapprochement was going strong in 1941.

Churchill and Harriman could have a functional working relationship because they were not strange to each other. Son of Union Pacific Railroad owner Edward Henry Harriman, Averell was a Groton man, Skull-and-Bones at Yale, thoroughbred enthusiast, polo star, steamship executive, and Union Pacific Railroad Board member. His biographical details and bank balance allowed him to mix with England's best. His prosperity during the Depression inspired Franklin Roosevelt to name him Chairman of the Department of Commerce's Business Advisory Council in 1937. When war came to Europe, it was Harriman who supervised the Lend-Lease Administration, and coordinated aid to the British and Soviets.[267]

The proximate occasion for his weekend invitation to Chequers was daughter Kathleen's birthday. She was friend and roommate of Pamela Churchill, wife of the Prime Minister's son, Randolph.[268] Like his eponymous grandfather, Randolph was no stranger to fast living. Nor was Pamela, who became Mrs. Randolph Churchill while still a teenager. She proved only slightly less provocative to the British gossip press than Wallis Simpson, the Baltimore *femme fatale* who lured Edward VIII away from the throne. The day following Randolph and Pamela's marriage, one article labeled her "the red-headed tart of England."[269] Giving birth to "Young Winston," in October 1940, she, Randolph, and the newest Winston Churchill appeared on the cover of *Life*.[270]

At dinner, Churchill toasted Kathleen, presenting her with an autographed copy of his 1899 book on the Sudan War.[271] It was a lovely evening which served the purposes of statecraft. It might have been complicated by the fact that Harriman and Pamela were involved in a torrid love affair.[272] She was three decades his junior, but both lovers were flexible in romance. Powerful, rich, and hungry, Averell earned the nickname Alsop later appended to him, "The Old Crocodile."[273] With Randolph serving in Egypt and the second Mrs. Harriman in New York, Pamela and Averell drew close.[274]

Later, the rumor arose that Churchill knew his daughter-in-law was cuckolding his son. The claim was that the Prime Minister put Anglo-American intimacy ahead of familial seemliness. Colville emphatically denied it, pointing out that it would have horrified Lady Churchill and offended the Prime Minister's sense of honor.[275] More likely, the liaison between Harriman and Pamela Churchill was the product of mutual attraction spiced up by self-entitlement and distilled by the conditions of a blitz-riven nation, in which couples separated often and death was a possibility. War bent basic rules of romantic comportment beyond recognition. Harriman was never past noticing a younger woman's beauty, whatever his age or matrimonial situation. For her part, the energetic Pamela would eventually divorce Randolph, fall in love with Murrow, then with Harriman before war's end.[276] Pamela and Averell did find each other years later, at Winston Churchill's 1965 funeral. They wed in 1971, consummating one of World War II's longest episodes. Pamela reinvented herself as a Georgetown doyenne and Democratic power-broker.[277] The men twiddling dials on the Prime Minister's radio set were bound up tightly by ties of class, professional interest, and diplomacy.

Not every American in England in 1941 shared the same conditioning. Murrow was born to North Carolina Dixie Quakers and raised on the Washington Palouse. He rose through skill and vision, not pedigree. It showed in his reportage, which intimated that the war should usher in a new egalitarian era. Suffusing Murrow's coverage was faith that the fires of London would burn away the inequities of the past. "If the people who rule Britain are made of the same stuff as the little people I have seen today," he would tell CBS listeners during the Blitz, "If they understand the stuff of which people who work with their hands are made, and if they trust them, then the defense of Britain will be something of which men will speak with awe and admiration as long as the English language survives."[278] Always, he stressed the everyday courage of Londoners. Murrow reversed the old Whig polarity, looking to England for democratic equality.

Murrow was devoid of deference for *noblesse oblige*. He fit the trend which extolled plain people eager to stand against tyranny and make a better world.[279]

He also reawakened the old Wilsonian sacrifice message, reformatted by 1930s populism. Looking at the Battle of Britain, trying to figure out an answer to the question asked so fiercely by colleague Vincent Sheean—"Do you know what that *means?* London burning?"[280]—Murrow and his CBS partner Sevareid saw a people's war against Hitler, but also against inherited privilege. This set up a counterbalance against American copycats who acted English. Ninety years before Murrow made it to London, Emerson grumbled, "I do not wish to be mistaken for an Englishman, more than I wish Monadnock or Nahant or Nantucket to be mistaken for Wales or the Isle of Wight."[281] Murrow was always himself; Emerson would have approved. But Murrow also loved Britain deeply, working hard to ensure that American sympathies translated into pro-British policies.

When word of the Pearl Harbor attack reached Chequers on December 7, there sat Churchill, Harrimann, and Winant; three *gentlemen*, trying to decipher the news. It took Sawyers, the butler, to explain. "It's quite true," Sawyers told them with butlerine assurance. "We heard it ourselves outside. The Japanese have attacked the Americans."[282] Churchill needed a boost. Two days before, he endured an obnoxious duty, declaring war on Finland. Churchill admired the Finns for fighting off the Red Army in 1939–1940. But in 1941, co-belligerent with Germany, Finland fought to restore lost territories. Stalin expected British cooperation, so on December 5, Churchill declared war on a nation he esteemed in order to placate an ally he needed. He restricted Britain to symbolic bombing in the Gulf of Bothnia.[283]

His reaction to Pearl Harbor had deeply personal layers. He was half-American. His father was Lord Randolph Churchill, his mother Jeannette Jerome, daughter of Wall Street millionaire Leonard Jerome, owner of the *New York Times*, founder of the New York Jockey Club, consul at Trieste, and entrepreneur. Randolph met "Jennie" in 1873 at the Isle of Wight resort of Cowes, where she was ensconced with her sisters, angling for suitors. The rakish Lord was smitten by the dark beauty, whose poise and irreverence prompted Sargent to draw her as archly alluring, with the barest smile and a dab of cruelty in those saucer eyes, her fetching coronet of black hair on top.[284] The bijou heiress was a perfect match for any nobleman daring enough to win her. Jennie accepted the proposal from the Duke of Marlborough's descendent. His lineage, estate, and dash were impeccable, but the Spencer–Churchill family could stand pecuniary enrichment, which the Jeromes provided in gobs. Lord Randolph Churchill and Jennie Jerome epitomized the stereotype of the morganatic Anglo-American marriage. Marriage failed to temper Randolph's amatory spark; Jennie never lost her skillful coquetry. Philandering was mutual, since neither was suited to play the lovelorn homebody. Syphilis was one dark consequence of Randolph's carnal adventurism, while far into the future, Jennie remained attractive to men, and not in an abstract way. Her admirers included His Royal Highness, Prince Edward, whom Kipling called "a corpulent voluptuary."

Jennie and Randolph married on April 15, 1874 making their honeymoon way to his ancestral spread, Woodstock's Blenheim Palace. "This is the finest view in England," a proud Randolph told his bride upon showing her the magnificent park grounds. She agreed, but her "American pride forbade the admission."[285]

Winston, was born that November 30. High-level politics was Randolph's life, high-level society Jennie's. Parenthood was neither's occupation. Through the expected nursery-then-boarding-school childhood, young Winston loved his parents with the kind of fervor that a neglected romantic soul can muster up. The headwaters of his birth were refulgent yet turbulent, and while life's flow carried Winston far, he never lost his sense of those beginnings. On December 7, 1941, Winston Churchill sat with Harriman and Winant, craving accurate bearings on the relationship between his mother's homeland and his father's. A phone call came from Roosevelt. "It's quite true," said the President. "We're all in the same boat now."[286] "This certainly simplifies things," replied the Prime Minister. "God be with you."[287] Harnessed to the war effort, the industrial abundance of the United States would provide the Allies a definitive advantage. On the linchpin of American response hung strategic superiority over the Axis. Churchill noted that Harriman and Winant "took the shock with admirable fortitude."[288]

Churchill feared Japan-first pressures on Roosevelt. The Prime Minister knew that the President was calculating. Churchill wanted to inject his own factors into Roosevelt's equations. Roosevelt's language in their brief phone call gave him a rhetorical opening. "Now that we are as you say 'in the same boat' would it not be wise for us to have another conference? We could review the whole war plan in the light of reality and new facts, as well as the problems of production and distribution," he cabled on December 9.[289] He offered to "start from here in a day or two and come by warship to Baltimore or Annapolis."[290] The Prime Minister would drop whatever he was doing in order to take care of his new priority, ensuring that the United States did not veer from the Atlantic Charter. Christmas would be spent in Washington.

Most of Churchill's linguistic power aimed at the President over the next two weeks. Always, the message was the same: the need for consultation, cooperation, exchange of views, and solidarity in war planning. He addressed his own nation on December 8. Hong Kong, Malaya, and Singapore all faced Japanese attack; Hong Kong was already doomed. Churchill led off his parliamentary address by admitting that Britain and the United States faced the same dangers. "The enemy has attacked with an audacity which may spring from recklessness, but which may also spring from a conviction of strength," he warned.[291] Taking care to praise the "heroic Russian allies," and including India and China in his statements, Churchill pointed out that "at least four-fifths of the population of the globe" was on Britain's side.[292] With the full strength of the Allies, he promised, fortune's flickering light would soon "shine over land and sea."[293] The houses of Lords and Commons supported war with Japan. Having informed the Japanese Ambassador, Churchill appointed Duff Cooper Resident Minister for Far Eastern Affairs, as the British set about arranging their own Pacific campaign.[294]

Before sailing, Churchill pushed Eamon de Valera to abandon Irish neutrality. "Now is your chance. Now or never,"[295] urged the PM. Eire's Taioseach declined the invitation. Churchill also wrote to Chiang Kai-Shek, South Africa's Jan Christian Smuts, generals Claude Auchinleck, in North Africa, Archibald Wavell in Burma, and a host of politicians, including Anthony Eden. None of the communications mattered more to Churchill than his December 8 note to King George VI. "I have formed the conviction that it is my duty to visit Washington without delay," he explained. "The whole plan of Anlgo-American defence and attack has to be concerted in the light of reality."[296]

A last-minute complication was the news that *Prince of Wales* and *Repulse* had been sunk by Japanese planes. The King expressed consternation on December 10, also worrying about Australia. "I thought I was getting immune to hearing bad news, but this has affected me deeply," the monarch admitted. "There is something particularly 'alive' about a big ship."[297] The naval disaster occasioned more domestic duties for the Prime Minister, including a December 11 House of Commons to shore up support and morale.

In that speech, Churchill placed Pearl Harbor in the context of the European war. "It seems to me quite certain that Japan, when she struck her treacherous and dastardly blow at the United States, counted on the active support of the German Nazis and of the Italian Fascists," he reasoned. "It is, therefore, very likely that the United States will be faced with the open hostility of Germany, Italy, and Japan. We are in all this too." "The destruction of the English-speaking world and all it stands for" was the enemy's goal, but Churchill promised that Anglophone nations would be "the supreme barrier against their designs."[298] Once his tasks were done, the Prime Minister left London. He boarded a train at Euston Station on December 12, setting sail on the *Duke of York* hours later.

2 DECEMBER 9–31, 1941

Charles de Gaulle, "The Man Who Didn't Quit"

The man who didn't quit has a closely cropped mustache . . . and he is tall and straight. When he speaks, the words come out sharply, and when he talks of the betrayal of his country the words are bits of rounded hail on a tin roof.

Quentin Reynolds[1]

The position of France in December 1941 remained ambiguous. The Fall of France was the astonishing event which made Americans pay attention to the war. When France sought armistice terms, Americans faced the reality that the French Army was finished. It looked like the Royal Navy might fall into German hands, if Hitler could pull off an invasion. It was then that CBS became required listening. Murrow in London, Sevareid in France, and William L. Shirer in Germany, covered the war with unparalleled accuracy. They had the two most important scoops of the war's early phase. It was Sevareid who reported that France would seek terms from Hitler. It was Shirer, in tandem with NBC's Wayne Kerker, who broadcasted from Compiegne, where the armistice talks took place. Shirer thrilled listeners with an up-to-the-second relation of prostrate France's moment of humiliation.

France had its own special relationship with the United States. General John Pershing reminded everyone of that in World War I, with his statement, "Lafayette, we are here!" France had an air of indomitability and glamor. To young Americans like Sevareid, growing up in North Dakota, or Shirer, in Iowa, Paris represented liberation from Babbitry. Not for nothing did the Lost Generation find itself in Paris. Many young women tried to dress and love like Lady Brett Ashley; many young men affected terse, direct manners after reading *The Sun Also Rises*. Literary and artistic Americans were mesmerized by the glow from the City of Lights. To go there, or to read and fantasize about Parisian life, was to realize that the wider world was attainable, that love and culture thrived on the Seine. For Shirer, Paris offered everything he dreamt of while stuck in Cedar Rapids, straining against the "puritan, bourgeois, restraints that stifled a young American at home."[2] Kate Smith meant that when she sang Oscar Hammerstein and Jerome Kern's song:

A lady known as Paris, romantic and charming,
Has left her old companions, and faded from view.
Lonely men with lonely hearts are seeking her in vain,
Her streets are where they were/But there's no sign of her,
She has left the Seine.
The last time I saw Paris, her heart war young and gay,
No matter how they change her/I'll remember her that way.[3]

The expatriate world in Paris made the French capital the central spot for Americans in search of freedom and sophistication. By 1941, the Lost Generation was home, still in love with the France of its memory. Members populated the media, like Shirer, or *The New Yorker* writer A.J. Liebling. Some worked for Roosevelt, like Malcolm Cowley and Archibald MacLeish. The 1940 capitulation wrecked illusions about another Miracle on the Marne.[4] France in 1941 was perplexing.

There was a French government with which the United States kept diplomatic relations. Its capital was at Vichy, not Paris. This rump state kept alive the figment of French independence under Marshall Henri-Philippe Petain, octogenarian World War I hero. Petain's bag man was Pierre Laval, who crouched atop of a writhing pile of collaborationists, lending Vichy a noxious aspect. Laval tried to manipulate events by currying favor with Hitler, spitting bile at the British, preserving control over French colonies, and attacking whoever resisted. Not least because the French fleet remained in port did Roosevelt and Hull make the decision to dispatch Admiral William D. Leahy as Ambassador to Vichy.[5] The concern that French warships might sail into the Atlantic was sharp. The decision to treat with Vichy appalled Francophiles like MacLeish. The Librarian of Congress wept openly at his desk when France capitulated. To MacLeish, the prospect of the *Wehrmacht* marching through Paris was like William Butler Yeats' rough beast slouching towards Bethlehem. He told Ickes that day how much he wanted an immediate declaration of war.[6] MacLeish's response spoke to the emotive power of a French cultural ideal still operative among the American intelligentsia.

Recognizing Vichy was pure diplomatic calculation. Laval comprehended Allied fears about the French Navy. France *outremer* included places like St. Pierre and Miquelon, the Lesser Antilles and French Guyana, New Caledonia, the Society and

Marquesas island chains, Indochina, Algeria, and Senegal, all vitally located. The United States wanted France quiescent and worked to ensure that. Because Vichy might control these places, it seemed important to keep them inactive. There was logic to keeping the Vichy connection open. But it enraged those who saw it as a betrayal of Free France.

Leahy's job was to circulate and conciliate with figures like General Maxime Weygand and to counter pressures for Vichy to become a fighting German ally. This pitted Roosevelt's administration against those who supported *La Resistance*. That was how A.J. Liebling found solace. The *New Yorker* columnist, his magazine's top Paris writer before the German triumph, could no longer write his "Letter from Paris" columns. Instead, Liebling covered the rise of the resistance, as a way of reminding readers that the France worth loving was not dead. He could no longer extol eternal Paris, with its bookstalls and anglers along the Seine, its cafes, its "Girl operators in beauty parlors, bookkeepers in offices, boys delivering fancy cakes for first-Communion parties, and waiters solicitous of favorite clients."[7] The French establishment failed him and the plain folk he loved suffered under German dominion, so Liebling looked for the soul of France in its exiled ranks.[8] By December 1941, that meant Charles De Gaulle.

De Gaulle's radio calls for resistance commenced on June 18, 1940, when he challenged the armistice's legitimacy. "But has the last word been said? Must we abandon all hope? Is our defeat final and irremediable? To these questions, I answer—No!"[9] It was one of the most important speeches of the war. He regularly spoke on the BBC, reiterating his core messages: France was unbeaten, those saying otherwise were traitors, France remained one of the Allies, Vichy was dastardly. *Collier's* correspondent Quentin Reynolds interviewed the exiled general in London. Reynolds was taken by De Gaulle's demeanor and tough talk. "Only De Gaulle saw the handwriting on the wall," the American writer explained, contending that failure to heed De Gaulle's warnings about how to fight the Germans caused the Third Republic to fall.[10] De Gaulle showed a paper trail dating back to the early 1930s, when he wrote a book on tanks in modern warfare. The implication was that the German generals whose *panzers* smashed through French gaps, avoided strong points, and slaughtered the *poilus* learned from him. In a way, went this argument, German success was a result of De Gaulle's own military perspicacity, coupled with the obdurate inertia of the Third French Republic. Reynolds called De Gaulle a prophet, preaching French salvation, beset by venal enemies. The story explained that French soldiers, sailors, and airmen were fighting their way to the only leader they trusted. Only De Gaulle could create Free French forces of value to the Allies. To look at De Gaulle tall and unbowed; to hear De Gaulle speaking sharply and clearly, was to recognize a French fighting man who would resuscitate his poor country. Reynolds told his readers not to bet against De Gaulle.

Just before Pearl Harbor, De Gaulle kept up his vigorous speaking calendar. He understood what American entry into the war would mean. At a luncheon of London's Foreign Press Association, filled with American correspondents, he contended that, despite the seeming desperation of the moment, in fact "The scales of victory are trembling in the balance."[11] Running through production figures that counted on contributions from France's colonies, he argued that, even without taking American numbers into account, the Allies could outdo the Germans in creating the materials of war. On Armistice Day, November 11, 1941, he invoked the spirit of Georges Clemenceau, making sure to mention that, once again, grateful France saw "America advancing step by step towards the theater of war."[12] Three days later, speaking about Free France, he made another stirring reference to the once and future Ally—"We unreservedly associate ourselves with the moral and material action of the United States, without which there can be no victory."[13] His address to the Oxford French Club on November 25 concentrated on the twin contributions of Britain and France in western culture. To those wondering where America stood in this story, he was lavish. "So saturated has America become with this civilization of ours," he claimed, "That it may truthfully be said to have reached its fullest expression beyond the Atlantic."[14] The effect of those words on the American intelligentsia which still adored France had to be flattering.

In his first speech after Pearl Harbor, De Gaulle spelled out what American entry meant for the Allies. Leading off by noting the German policy of executing French civilian hostages to punish sabotage, excoriating Vichy for not preventing sanctioned murder, he promised that France would never beg for mercy. France would have vengeance in the end because France was an Ally, and the Allies would win the war. Axis confidence was self-delusion. Germans were "caught in their own bluff, and refuse to believe they are heading for defeat."[15] German soldiers retreating in Russia, or Italians on the run in Ethiopia, no longer looked invincible. The Axis was doomed and De Gaulle explained why: "The entry of our American Ally into the war on the side of Great Britain, Russia, and France is, quite simply, tantamount to victory."[16]

He liked citing production figures. In a post-Pearl Harbor talk, De Gaulle made a big point. "The fact is, in this war of machines, the potential output of America alone equals the total resources of all the other belligerent countries."[17] Venturing a prediction for 1942, he promised that the Allied edge would improve. He found the numbers comforting, but he guessed that Hitler would "have to weep ere long for his criminal insolence. The day is already appointed when we shall find ourselves both victors and avengers!"[18] Americans looking for a French leader to believe in had their man. When the General's colorful personality later annoyed Roosevelt, the President would find that De Gaulle already had an American fan club.

Berlin—the Fuhrer's malign blind spot: how Hitler misunderstood the United States

In North America, where the population is prevalently Teutonic, and where those elements intermingled with the inferior race only to a very small degree, we have a quality of mankind and a civilization which are different from those of Central and South America. . . . In North America the Teutonic element, which has kept its racial stock pure and did not mix it with any other racial stock, has come to dominate the American Continent and will remain master of it as long as that element does not fall a victim to the habit of adulterating the blood.

Adolf Hitler, Mein Kampf, 1924.[19]

The Leader is convinced that the prophecy he made then in the Reichstag, that if Jewry succeeded again in provoking a world war, it would end with the annihilation of the Jews, is confirming itself. It is becoming true in these weeks and months with certainty that seems almost uncanny. The Jews are having to pay the price in the east; it has to a degree already been paid in Germany, and they will have to pay it still more in the future. Their last refuge remains North America, and there in the long or short run they will one day have to pay it too.

Joseph Goebbels, Diary entry, August 19, 1942[20]

Commentators portrayed Germany's *fuhrer* as a mysterious character—brooding, cunning, sinister. This inscrutable Hitler pondered in solitude, conjuring up stratagems, hatching devices, then springing them upon an unsuspecting world. This image propped up the *fuhrerprizip*, touting the magic link between *volk* and leader. Actually, Hitler was usually surrounded by yes-men, careerists, office-seekers, and courtiers who fed his ego and kept him company in his hideouts. Besides the lonely leader, there were other Hitler images. These included the fulminating orator, the bullying boss, the conniving salesman, and the guardian of Germanic spirit. None captured the essence of the architect of World War II. There were enormous parts of his make-up which image-makers failed to relate. One overlooked aspect of Hitler's character was obtuseness. For all of his supposed strategic sense, there was wilful ignorance in the *weltanschauung* of the *Reichsfuhrer*. One fateful zone of ignorance in December 1941 was his benightedness regarding the United States.

The essential factor in Hitler's world view was race. For Hitler, race was not ethnicity, citizenship, or skin color. It paralleled national identity. National identity could be, but need not be, the same as political identity. There was much conflating of terms like "race," "people," and "nation" in the nineteenth and early twentieth centuries. Since European political frontiers did not always reflect the borders of identity, these labels helped to group humanity in different ways than citizenship might. On a continent where national boundaries changed but people lived in their homelands, identity might not appear reliably on a map, but in the language and culture of a folk community.

Hitler saw races locked in mortal combat. Whereas Marx saw social class as history's determinant, Hitler saw race as the marker. States were justifiable so far as they represented race. If they did not, they were abominations. Likewise, since not all races were equal, not all states had the same rights. There was no possibility of cohabitation between races fated to be enemies. This attitude made Hitler's treatment of Jews fearsomely logical. Jews, he fancied, were the Aryans' eternal enemy. Survival of one meant destruction of the other. Every aspect of race culture was channeled to advancement at the expense of the arch enemy. In cases where other forces shaped affiliations, such as religion, Hitler was dismissive. People foolish enough to believe that worshiping together perpetuated meaningful connections were dupes or liars. Hitler denied the religious tradition of Judaism, a mental contortion allowing him to ignore millennia of meticulously charted theological doctrine and practice. He preferred fake historicizing, which supported outlandish *Mein Kampf* observations like, "One of the most ingenious tricks ever devised has been that of sailing the Jewish ship-of-state under the flag of Religion and thus securing that tolerance which Aryans are always ready to grant to different religious faith. . . . But the Mosaic Law is really nothing else than the doctrine of the preservation of the Jewish race."[21]

Hitler complained that transnational Judaism inserted an alien presence in any nation. The Jew, he claimed, "Can live among other nations and States only as long as he succeeds in persuading them that the Jews are not a distinct people, but the representatives of a religious faith." Having thus fooled their naive hosts, Jews would always act "as a parasite among the nations,"[22] he wrote. Hitler denigrated socialists and communists for opening their doors to Jewish influence. Political parties—socialists or communists—and socioeconomic arrangements—democratic capitalism—were camouflage behind which Jews operated in their own interest. This trick of interpretation meant that in Hitler's scheme, Jews could be both the directors of capitalism and the leaders of communism; they could rule openly or in secret. Soviet communism was a Jewish ruse to fool the working class; American capitalism afforded Jews the chance to steer world powers.[23] According to Hitler, Jews ran the United States and the Soviet Union. If millions of Jews were indigent and powerless, so much the better for the smokescreen. *Shtetl* poverty also proved Jewish foulness. Anti-Semitism, for Hitler, was ever-fungible, and thus could never be disproved. It shaped to fit any space in his outlook. Any evidence against his pathological fixation merely convinced Hitler of fiendish Jewish genius. Hitler came to believe that he alone could discern the weave of the conspiratorial web.

That race emerged as history's moving force had to do with the timing of Hitler's life and the era in which he cobbled together his outlook. During the Industrial Revolution, old identity affiliations dissolved in the solvent of modernity. As in the United States, misunderstandings about Darwinism propagated. Darwin was zoologically oriented. He did notice differences between peoples as he sailed the world. But Darwin's focus on species led him to conclude that, no matter how different they seemed, peoples were fundamentally linked. "Although the existing races of man differ in many respects," he wrote in *The Origin of Species*, "yet if their whole structure be taken into consideration they are found to resemble each other closely in a multitude of points."[24] Extrapolating based upon his close observation during the *H.M.S. Beagle* voyage, Darwin concluded, "I was incessantly struck, whilst living with the Fuegians on board . . . with the many little traits of character, shewing how similar their minds were to ours; and so it was with a full-blooded negro with whom I happened once to be intimate."[25]

Many theorists used biology as a matrix within which to analyze race. A wave of scientists, chauvinists, and political hustlers distorted Darwin to support the idea of competition between races. In continental Europe, these ideas cross-pollinated with romanticism and nationalism. Germany's loss in World War I made Hitler's need to cast blame overwhelming. The Russian front of that war put Germany into sustained contact with the variegated peoples of Eastern Europe. From the Baltic to the Balkans, the German Army found itself immersed in a bewildering hodgepodge of ethnic confusion, familiar to the Hapsburgs but alien to the Teutonic *Heimat*.[26] World War I's eastern front was a scene of victory and empire-building for the German Army, thanks to 1918's Treaty of Brest-Litovsk. Lenin signed it, expecting revolutions in Central Europe to render it obsolete. Neither he nor German generals expected the appearance of a strong Poland, so the murky Soviet–German relationship got off to a fittingly jumbled start.[27] Hitler considered contact between German and eastern peoples as a hygienic threat to racial integrity. Anti-Semitism became his cosmogony, the way he made sense of the universe.

His complex was not tethered to empirical observation. Hitler habitually inserted himself into causality: seeing himself as a decisive historical factor. When events came to pass which he hoped for, it was thanks to his will. The remilitarization of the Saar, the reoccupation of the Rhineland, the *Anschluss*, and the Munich Pact convinced him that he could change world conditions. His generals went along when Hitler waved realities like the Russian weather aside. There were no checks on his imagination. If Hitler wanted to invade Russia, or declare war on the United States, he insisted that these were wise moves, and nobody dared correct him. Abdicating from the obligations of their consciences, subordinating to their master, became Germans' act of fealty. This left Hitler alone. When he looked at the world, he saw a mirror reflecting his own projections.

Given the nature of his early years, marked by indifferent academic performance, unmet artistic ambitions, transience, and an unstable personal trajectory, Hitler's adoption of racial determinism made sense. Race let him see his disappointments as the torments of a victim. He saw Germans cheated out of their due. Destiny became his solace. The first sentence of *Mein Kampf* made it clear that his birth near the Austrian-German frontier was supporting evidence: "It has turned out fortunate for me today that destiny appointed Braunau-on-the-Inn to be my birthplace."[28] Hitler wanted to unite Germany with Austria because Germans needed to live in one nation. For Hitler, the state was a racial organism mutilated by division into component parts.

Such thoughts concretized during his Vienna days. He arrived there at 16.[29] Hitler explored the streets of the metropolis epitomizing the polyglot Austro-Hungarian Empire. He lived alongside Czechs, Slovaks, Ruthenians, Bosniaks, Croats, Serbs, and Slovenes, all in full-throated protest against dominance by Austrians and Hungarians. Political talk about a federalized United States of Austria failed to overcome splenetic nationalism.[30] Hitler was disoriented by the political intensity and disgusted by the competition for power. For social democracy and the lifestyles of the working class, he felt contempt. Class-consciousness he considered a distraction from race-awareness. Popular habits convinced him venality was the hallmark of the masses; that people wanted to be handled by a proper leader.[31] Hitler read widely but erratically. He seethed as formerly subject nations chipped away at the Germanic foundation of the Austrian empire.

His prejudices grew florid when he discovered the pamphlet press.[32] Street literature pointed to the influx of subordinate peoples as an insuperable defilement of the German ethnic strain, meant to rule. Jews were the main villains in such tracts. Vienna was the miasma where anti-Semites congealed as they bemoaned the moribund realm. War seemed to offer release from slow decay. The confused, frustrated young Hitler breathed deep drafts from the atmosphere of a dying empire,[33] which, going to war in 1914, "committed suicide from fear of death."[34] Hitler decided that Jewish forces invented and used Marxism as a tool to control revolutionary energies and subvert nations. If the masses were moved towards communism, it had to be because they demonstrated a false consciousness due to Jewish influences. He also subscribed to the proposition that Germans lived under constant existential threat. During the Third Reich, this kind of language increased as the campaign against Judaism moved from persecution to extermination. As the final solution emerged, the Nazi press stepped up its argument that Jews endangered Germans.

The Third Reich applied Hitler's racial ideas to the larger world. Being racially singular did not guarantee a nation Hitler's acceptance, since races were presumably hierarchical. Predatory enemies like France needed to be punished, while contemptible countries like Poland were suited for slavery. But the main danger to his idealized Aryan state came from within, through contamination by Jews. That way lay racial doom, Hitler argued. "All the great civilizations of the past became decadent because the originally creative race died out, as a result of contamination of the blood."[35]

After the Fall of France, Hitler wanted the racially acceptable English to make terms, keep their maritime Empire, and give him a free hand in Europe. Their refusal to do so he attributed to Churchillian perversity and a ruling class ruined through soft living. Hitler divined the hidden hand of Jewish influence over London. His racial approach could have made the Tripartite Pact awkward. He explained it by praising the Italians and Japanese as fellow "warrior races," who embraced their own racial distinctiveness. In the case of two world powers not formed on racial lines, the Soviet Union and the United States, Hitler's approach varied. With the USSR, he blended hostility to communism with scorn for Soviet peoples. Hitler's approach to the United States tended to a different extreme. Obsessed with the USSR, which controlled lands he meant to acquire, Hitler alternately ignored or misunderstood the United States.

The absence of sustained comment on the United States in *Mein Kampf* is one of the prolix book's major lacunae. His volume deals with the United States in three ways. The first was his observation that the United States enjoyed enviable geography, what Hitler called "the incomparable inner strength of the USA."[36] Hitler appreciated the strategic advantage of a continental nation shielded by distance.[37] He made a racial–cultural argument that the United States remained linked to the British Empire by Anglo-Saxon ties: "England's position cannot be compared with that of any other state in Europe, since it forms a vast community of language and culture together with the USA."[38] He praised American immigration restrictions of the 1920s. "At present," he wrote, "there exists one State which manifests at least some modest attempts that show a better appreciation of how things ought to be done. It is not, however, in our model German Republic, but in the USA. . . . By refusing immigrants to enter there if they are in a bad state of health, and by excluding certain races from the right to become nationalized as citizens, they have begun to introduce principles similar to those on which we wish to ground the People's state."[39]

His unpublished *Zweite Buch*, or *Second Book* was not known to Americans in 1941. It featured more treatment of the United States. Hitler nodded at the American automobile industry, calling for protectionism to shelter German car manufacturing. He hoped Great Britain might drop its American alliance and partner with Germany. He also interpreted World War I, complaining about Wilson and Versailles. Again, Hitler alluded favorably to the 1924 Immigration Restriction Act, as well as Southern racial segregation.[40] Otherwise, he avoided the

American factor. His thrust was how nations should embody the *volk*. Since the United States did not, he concentrated elsewhere.

His view of international power drew inspiration from some theorists, but never from Mahan. Hitler viewed water as land's end. Mahan spoke to those who saw the oceans as highways. Karl Haushofer, University of Munich Geography Professor, articulated the notions of a heartland-based interpretation of world affairs. Haushofer become an imperial German staff officer and *geopolitik* expert. He derived central ideas from predecessors, such as Friedrich Ratzell, who viewed nation–states as quasi-organisms, and Rudolf Kjellen, Swedish political theorist who took that notion a step further, arguing that as organic entities, healthy states needed sufficient room to grow—*lebensraum*. Haushofer served as advisor to the Japanese Army from 1908 to 1910, studying problems that island nation faced in its attempts to expand overseas, and leaving imprints on the officers he trained.[41]

Haushofer believed that a nation's fate was geographically determined. He understood Mahan's pragmatic geography—not every country needed a mighty fleet. Imperial Germany should have learned that lesson, Haushofer decided. It squandered money on building a navy to little advantage. Kaiser Wilhelm's dreams of glory at sea took no notice of the fact that Germany's home fleet could always be bottled up in the Baltic. Germany's pre-World War I colonial designs were an outgrowth of a wrong-headed desire to convert a land-oriented nation into a maritime power.[42] Looking at the map made Japan's situation plain to Haushofer, too. Since island Japan must be a maritime power, Haushofer covered its obstacles and opportunities in *Geopolitics of the Pacific Oceans*, published in 1924.[43] He was then in contact with National Socialist Party leadership, including Hitler and Rudolf Hess.[44] This was one year after Hitler's Beer Hall Putsch, which landed him in Landsberg Prison, where he wrote *Mein Kampf*. The Nazi leader was still open to ideas which met his agenda. Haushofer visited Hitler in prison to explain his ideas. Hitler latched on to what he decided was relevant for Germany, which cinched the future dictator's interest in the Heartland Theory. During Hitler's 1940 bid for a settlement with Britain, he dispatched Hess to solicit Haushofer's advice. One idea was that Haushofer should use his contacts with British academics to push a settlement, which Haushofer considered unrealistic.[45] In 1941, Haushofer was featured in a *Life* article which introduced him to Americans as a Svengali whose books explained how Germany wanted to achieve world domination through control of Eurasia. But the idea that Eurasian hegemony would deliver world mastery, Haushofer admitted, was not his own. That came from an Englishman, Halford Mackinder. The tortuous intellectual thread was unspooled during the war by Dorothy Thompson, who went on to interview the retired Mackinder, a most unlikely candidate for inspiring Hitler.[46]

Haushofer, whose son Albrecht would be executed for his role in anti-Hitler plotting, was not the dictator's wizard. Neither was Mackinder. A patriotic

Englishman concerned about his nation's position in the world, Mackinder was a geographer made famous by a pivotal academic paper he published in the *Geographical Journal* in 1904. "The Geographic Pivot of History" laid out the possibility that Eurasia might come under the sway of a single power, which could use its mastery of that landmass, what the scholar called "the world island"—to dominate the world.[47] This broadened the ancient British strategic imperative obeyed since 1066—opposing Europe's domination by any single power. Mackinder ripened his thesis in a book, *Democratic Ideals and Reality*, published in 1919. What he earlier called the "pivot" Mackinder renamed the "heartland," and it was in this book that he delivered a famous caution: "Who rules East Europe commands the Heartland: Who rules the Heartland commands the World-Island: Who rules the World-Island commands the World."[48]

Mackinder's insights made sense for a British Empire guarding approaches to India. His view of World War I concentrated carefully on the Bosporus, where Europe and Asia come together, scene of the Battle of Gallipoli. Another bottleneck he scrutinized was the Baltic. In Turkey, the British could not pass the Dardanelles Straits. In the seas around Denmark, the trapped German fleet made the Skagerrak and Kattegat too dangerous for the Royal Navy to force. Realizing that his interpretation stressed the limits of naval power, his homeland's best strategic capability, Mackinder supported Wilson's plans to create a number of independent Central and Eastern European nations out of the Hapsburg imperial conglomeration.[49] In this collection of states, he saw a structural impediment to singular domination.

It was at this juncture that Haushofer picked up Mackinder's prospect and spun it into advice for Germany. In Haushofer's reformulation, a renewed German state could someday incorporate all German peoples scattered across Europe. Hitler liked this intellectual exercise in world rearrangement. As always, Hitler cherry-picked. He and Haushofer disagreed on the advisability of making an enemy of the Soviet Union. Despite his 1939 pact with Stalin, Hitler never let go of his eastward land hunger. The Professor had conflicting notions about the Soviets. On the one hand, he believed that Britain was Germany's best global partner.[50] On the other hand, cognizant of the USSR's gargantuan size, Haushofer hoped an understanding with Moscow could allow Berlin to gain *lebensraum* up to, but not across, Russia's doorstep. Haushofer saw danger in war against the Russians.[51] Laying nuance aside, Hitler grabbed onto the Big Idea: geography shaped history. Geography as destiny allowed him to keep Germany's focus on land expansion, to the exclusion of gazing across the world's waters. The ocean, being outside his interest, was dismissed. "I am water-shy," he said. "On land I am a lion, but on the water I don't know where to begin."[52]

As the world waited to see what Hitler would do after December 7, 1941, the nautically minded could not fathom that Germany might welcome war with the United States. Why would Hitler risk seeing American industrial power set against Germany again? But to Hitler, the United States remained *terra incognita*. By the time of Pearl Harbor, his preconceptions about the United States were encrusted. He considered the United States dominated by Jews. He ignored American dynamism or saw it as disorderly; he impugned democracy as decadent. While some saw a huge industrialized nation lifting itself out of the Depression, Hitler claimed that economic drive belonged to his Reich. "This is no longer the American tempo; it has become the German tempo," he said at a public ceremony to praise German workers when they finished the new Chancellery Building ahead of schedule.[53] He disparaged American soldiers as deficient in spirit due to their blended racial composition. Nazi production chief Albert Speer characterized Hitler's attitude, "No such thing as an American people existed as a unit; they were nothing but a mass of immigrants from many nations and races."[54] When adjutant Fritz Weidemann argued that settling with Washington would advance Berlin's diplomatic goals, the exasperated dictator sent him to San Francisco to serve as Consul General, with an insulting farewell: "Let him be cured of his notions there."[55]

The fact that Hitler never left Europe and was bound up inside his own world with ideas which made him comfortable gave him the unwarranted confidence to draw inane conclusions about the United States. He stayed immune to better points of view, since these interrupted the closed-circuit idea loop which kept his world view intact. One upshot was that the *Kriegsmarine* bore the brunt of Hitler's pre-Pearl Harbor decision to treat the United States with circumspection. Breaches of neutrality by the increasingly aggressive US Navy in 1941 were, for U-boat commanders, a series of vexations subordinated to land-based strategy.[56]

The cautious *Wilhelmstrasse* sent warnings about American strength, public patriotism, and problems for Berlin in case of war with Washington. Acting Chief of the German Mission in Washington, D.C. was Dr. Hans Thomsen. Long aware of Hitler's disinterest in the United States, he recalled serving as translator for a Hitler–Mussolini meeting in 1937. The topic of the United States never came up.[57] When ambassadors were withdrawn due to *Kristallnacht* in November 1938, Thomsen was left to man the Washington mission. He took a sober view of each downward tick in relations. Cables on questions such as the control of Iceland, which the United States assumed in 1941 to deny Germany its harbors, showed a realist who understood scale of the nation's preparedness campaign. Thomsen was handsome and polite. He and his wife, Bebe, gained traction in D.C. social circles, aided by their willingness to speak critically—in private—about the Nazis back home. This was diplomatic tradecraft, because the frank responses their behaviors evoked at those off-the-record parties went into the nightly dispatches by the *charge d'affaires*.[58] Thomsen worried about negotiations between Washington and Tokyo. His anxieties ranged from the chance that Japan might drag Germany into war with the United States, to the proposition that Roosevelt might buy off Japan with economic concessions. Thomsen's was a voice concerned about German–American war,[59] but Hitler largely ignored him.

While Thomsen played Cassandra, German Military Attache Friedrich von Boetticher played Pollyanna. Boetticher looked at the United States and saw a nation torn by division between Jewish-led interests maneuvering for war, and patriotic citizens fond of Germany and opposed to war.[60] The Pacific, said Boetticher, was America's area of legitimate concern, and preparations there precluded involvement in Europe. He saw powerful opposition to war with Germany on Capitol Hill and in the military. Boetticher admitted that the State Department was under the sway of interventionists, but promised that the US Army would not countenance a European war. Short and plump, his red hair cut in an old-fashioned brush, Boetticher wore a monocle and strolled Washington's streets in uniform, Nazi decorations pinned to his coat. The reliability of his reports can be adduced by the fact that he informed Berlin that Henry Stimson and Frank Knox were Jewish, which was untrue.[61] Boetticher had his own direct channels to Berlin and his interpretations of American opinion met with approval even though they were insupportable.[62]

After the Fall of France, Elmo Roper surveyed the data and said that

The US is fearful of the outcome of the European war, is willing, as never before since the First World War, to throw its resources (but not its men) into the scales to help the Allies win, and meanwhile is grimly determined to prepare for the worst by arming.[63]

Preparedness was the word of the day. Virtually nobody wanted Germany to win. Roper's findings were echoed by Hadley Cantril, whose American Institute of Public Opinion chose the moment to issue a special report entitled "America Faces the War: A Study in Public Opinion." Cantril, too, found that Americans, while not eager to send their young men into the fray, were strongly supportive of the British. Hitler's Germany received almost no measurable sympathy from any poll.[64] But none of that fazed Hitler. However, Pearl Harbor presented Germany with problems. It took Berlin by surprise, hardly a good sign for German–Japanese military integration. It cast into glare a strange alliance with an Asian power antipathetic to European arrogance.

Hitler liked creating crises, not reacting to them. He had avoided harsh responses to US Naval provocations in the Atlantic. He knew what a two-front war did to Germany in the last war. Hitler also believed that Roosevelt was an irreconcilable adversary waiting to intervene against the Third Reich.[65] But Hitler still hoped for a short European war; still intended his kick against the USSR to knock down the Soviet structure. What Hitler most wanted from Japan, his anti-Comintern partner, was an attack on the Soviet Union, which would put Stalin in the two-front position. Japan and Russia distrusted and spied on each other. Their armies fought battles along the Manchukuo frontier during the 1930's. Red Army successes made the Imperial Army itch for revenge.[66] Japan's Army, embroiled in its "China Incident," hated the communist threat on its northern flank. Unlike Japan's navy, which aimed at the United States, its army considered the Soviets an enemy. But Pearl Harbor meant that the Soviets were not Japan's first target.

For three days after Pearl Harbor, all of Washington waited to find out what the German situation would be. The volume and tenor of messages to the White House showed that most Americans already considered Germany and the Japanese to be partners.[67] Roosevelt's team felt relief that the feared public swell for ignoring Germany and concentrating on Japan looked overblown. But when news arrived on December 10 about the sinking of *Prince of Wales* and *Repulse*, the administration caught its breath. War planes had now destroyed capital ships. As much as Pearl Harbor, this event inaugurated a new era in naval combat, and forced sudden strategic recalculations. Churchill later called the shock the worst he experienced in the entire war.[68] Suddenly, one could imagine Isolationist arguments against dividing American naval strength across two oceans, if surface ships were inherently at risk against already-proven Japanese aerial capabilities. Roosevelt's dismay was not much less than Churchill's.[69]

December 4 MAGIC intercepts were part of American intelligence decryption efforts. Roosevelt knew that these contained German assurances that Berlin would join a fight against the United States.[70] This gave White House insiders some reassurance that maintaining the Tripartite Pact might trump avoiding an American conflict in Hitler's estimation. But these decrypts were secret, impossible to cite in justifying a declaration of war against the Nazi regime. Germany had committed no *casus belli* against the United States. On December 11, the *Fuhrer* plucked the President off the hook. Hitler's speech declaring war on the United States, delivered before to *Reichstag* members, took place in the Kroll Opera House.[71] Perhaps because of his surroundings, the leader was at his most melodramatic. His speech concentrated on Roosevelt, personifying the President as a one-man concentration of everything wrong with democracy and the United States. Hitler was angry over the latest embarrassment of Germany: a December 4 *Chicago Tribune* story in which isolationist Senator Wheeler described "Rainbow Five," the military approach prioritizing Germany's defeat and codifying the Europe-first strategy.[72] Wheeler and kindred isolationist, publisher McCormick, wanted to blow the secrecy of what the headline called "FDR'S WAR PLANS! GOAL IS 10 MILLION ARMED MEN; HALF TO FIGHT IN AEF."[73] The story went on to cite "a confidential report prepared by the joint Army and Navy high command by direction of President Roosevelt."[74] The story did not prompt much anti-Roosevelt sentiment. Instead, public reaction seemed to consider it evidence of McCormick's own obsessive need to smack at the President and his own press rivals.[75] The report did, however, come to Berlin's notice, increasing Hitler's personalized rage at his American rival.

Hitler had to contend with the question of what a German non-response would mean for Tokyo. "For the first time we have on our side a first-rate military power,"[76] he commented, showing approval for Japanese fighting qualities. There were intriguing aspects to Japan's assault on the United States. Japan would have a free hand in Asia, but Germany had no colonies there. The Japanese could battle the United States for years. Hitler appreciated the end of strategic ambiguity. His feelings upon hearing about the attack were "deliverance" and "vast relief."[77] This permeated his Declaration of War. He unburdened himself in public and focused invective on Roosevelt. For weeks, Josef Goebbels had upped the intensity of anti-Roosevelt propaganda. On October 28, 1941, the *Volkischer Beobachter* reacted to the President's Navy Day speech, in which he promised vigilance at sea, calling Roosevelt "not crazy, but simply a political counterfeiter and shameless gangster." "Until now," said the Nazi newspaper, "We were not quite certain whether the subterfuges of Roosevelt's policy and his ever-increasingly hysterical outpourings of hate against the new Europe could be attributed to psychopathic grounds."[78] In his declaration, Hitler attacked Roosevelt for delivering fireside chats, "while our soldiers are fighting in snow and ice."[79] Terming his newest adversary "the man who is the main culprit of this war," Hitler mentioned "insulting attacks made by this so-called President against me."[80] He mocked Roosevelt for calling him "a gangster," because "this expression was not coined in Europe, but in America, no doubt because such gangsters are lacking here."[81] For good measure, Hitler added that Roosevelt was insane, like Woodrow Wilson in 1917. He rolled out a counterfactual historical account to support his view of Germany-as-victim. "First he incites war, then falsifies the causes, then odiously wraps himself in a cloak of Christian hypocrisy and slowly but surely leads mankind to war, not without calling God to witness the honesty of his attack—in the approved manner of an old Freemason."[82]

Hitler developed the theme that Roosevelt served international Jewry. In five years, Hitler bragged, he ended German unemployment, while, "during the same period, Roosevelt has succeeded in undermining the American economy, in devaluing the dollar, and in keeping up the figure of unemployed. Jews, of course, have flourished."[83] Hitler mentioned that Germany, "never possessed any colonies whatsoever on the soil of the North American continent." The only German contribution to American history, he argued, was positive: "Germans who emigrated gave their blood fighting for the liberty of the United States." Hitler explained that Wilson's reasons for entering the war in 1917 were now "proved to be entirely spurious . . . by an investigation committee set up by none other than President Roosevelt himself." Hitler talked up Jewish influence in Washington. "We all know the intention of the Jews to rule all civilized states in Europe and America," said the *Reichsfuhrer* to his deputies. "We know this is a time when for nations it is the question of 'to be or not to be.'"[84] After this most unlikely Shakespearean reference in history, Hitler taunted the American President. "When President Roosevelt sees fit to give me good advice, he is like the bald hairdresser recommending a famous hair tonic to his clients."[85]

Hitler spoke as one experiencing catharsis. Contradictory American behaviors puzzled and thus angered him. Knowing little about the United States, Hitler could not interpret ambivalent American policy as reflecting popular ambivalence about war and crisis. Instead, to Hitler, American leadership was coy. For years, the United States edged closer to war without crossing the combat line; never hiding its disdain for the Reich; maintaining diplomatic relations; scolding Europe's belligerents to stop fighting; finding ways to support the British. There was no longer any need to conciliate a President he hated and a nation that defied his views of what a nation should be.

Hitler concentrated on Roosevelt's plutocratic background, contrasting it with his own humbler origins.[86] Here a major part of Hitler's constructed self-image: the tenacious riser, a man who cared for basics. "A world-wide distance separates Roosevelt's ideas and my ideas," Hitler explained. "Roosevelt comes from a rich family and belongs to the class whose path is smoothed in the democracies. I was the only child of a small, poor family, and had to fight my way by work and industry."[87] Hitler listed the contrasts: he was a front soldier in World War I, Roosevelt sat at a desk. The war improved Roosevelt's bank balance, while peace brought Hitler poverty. Roosevelt failed to improve American life, Hitler built a new Germany. Most damning, Roosevelt was controlled by a powerful coterie of Jews. Not a thousand Roosevelts and Churchills could stop him from securing German leadership in the new world order, he vowed. Hitler could not finish his next sentence: "I have therefore arranged for passports to be handed to the American *charge d'affaires* today. . ."[88] That was the signal for *Reichstag* puppets to bellow approval for war. Italy followed suit after Germany; the American Congress then declared war on both without a single "no" vote.

His declaration intermeshed with Hitler's army moves. He had just taken over control of the Russian front after firing Walther von Brauchtisch, a general of the old school. Declaring war against the United States liberated Hitler by removing the last strategic equivocalness from the war. The United States completed his roster of foes. Hitler now had no world opinion to palliate. Freed of any need to modify his desires, Hitler could try to actualize the prospects which had long bewitched him. Among his fondest initiatives was the eradication of Judaism. His twin fixations, eastern *lebensraum* and anti-Semitism, fused apocalyptically.[89] His regime turned away from emigration or deportation and fully committed to the Final Solution. Extermination of the main enemy to German survival was always the logical extension of his race-based explanation of history. Now, there was no need to pretend otherwise. The United States, that multi-ethnic vortex of ideas, peoples, and institutions which Hitler deplored, fit perfectly into the world situation he contemplated. The exact framework of Hitler's discussion with senior officials on

December 12, just hours after his anti-Roosevelt screed, remains obscure, but the gist was the need to move forward towards the Final Solution.[90]

There was a flurry of activity aimed that way over the next several days. Hans Frank, leader of the General Government in conquered Poland, gave a speech four days after attending Hitler's talk. "We must put an end to the Jews," Frank explained, "That I want to say quite openly."[91] Frank reminded the assembled governors and district leaders of Hitler's promise to put an end to Jews should they "once more succeed in unleashing a world war."[92] The arrival of war with the United States made the conflict a world war, while advances deep into the USSR put millions more Jews under direct Nazi control. The conditions set by Hitler for eliminating Jews and the opportunity to do so now intersected. Frank continued: "But what is to happen to the Jews? Do you believe they will be lodged in settlement in the Ostland?" he asked sarcastically. "In Berlin we were told: why all this trouble? . . . liquidate them yourselves!"[93] Articulating the Nazi argument that mercy for non-Aryans harmed the health of the Reich, Frank reminded them that total racial competition remained the moving force in the world. Helpful to this contention was the argument that Germans were in mortal danger from foes whose survival meant racial death for Germany. "We want," he explained, "to have compassion only for the German people, otherwise for no one in the whole world. Others have had no compassion for us."[94]

On December 14, Reich security chief Heinrich Himmler consulted with Viktor Brack, one of the designers of the euthanasia-for-the-handicapped scheme, now consulting on construction of concentration camps. Himmler was mildly indistinct, as judged by his warning, "One must work as quickly as possible if only for reasons of camouflage."[95] Four days later, Hitler met with his Gestapo chief in person. Himmler made a fateful note in his appointment diary after that December 18 confab: "Jewish question/to be exterminated as partisans."[96] Given upcoming developments, the Reich security head's notation was less cryptic than it might appear in isolation. The following day, Jewish policy specialist Bernhard Losener met with his boss at the Interior Ministry, State Secretary Wilhelm Stuckart.[97] Himmler intended to ensure that his SS and Gestapo claimed primacy over rival government branches whenever possible, especially on the ultra-sensitive matter of the Final Solution. "Jewish questions belong to me," Himmler made clear to Stuckart at a November 24 meeting.[98] Stuckart soon explained the facts to Losener. Among the items considered was the need to ship *Mischlinge*, or partly Jewish people, to the camps. Losener explained the newfound clarity on all matters Jewish to a hesitant colleague. "The proceedings against the evacuated Jews are based on a decision from the highest authority," he pointed out. "You must come to terms with it."[99] With all impediments removed, Final Solution planning could accelerate. Himmler's top assistant, Reinhard Heydrich, began planning to coordinate bureaucratic tasks and finalize Himmler's grab at administrative control over the Final Solution.

It says much about Hitler's pathological ability to avoid uncomfortable contemplation that, in the evenings following his announcement of war against the United States, the subject rarely came up during the lengthy hours of table talk that were an inescapable part of his mealtimes. Supper was when the *fuhrer* held forth on what interested him. His talks at table side revolved around happy memories of the old street-fighting days or lectures on the Jewish threat. Quotidian events ran through Nazi abstraction. In the nights following Pearl Harbor and his December 11 Declaration of War, Hitler roamed over favorite topics—Jesus Christ was really an Aryan, St. Paul was anti-Bolshevist, clergy should stay out of politics. Japan rated praise for fusing religion with the state: "One can envy the Japanese. They have a religion which is very simple and brings them into contact with nature. They've succeeded even in taking Christianity and turning it into a religion that's less shocking to the intellect."[100] Occasionally, in between lengthy "what-if" discussions about German politics and Jewish conspiracies, Hitler held forth on the war in the Far East. The actual flow of events in the Pacific was barely covered. Abstraction had free rein. Over lunch on December 18, Hitler and Himmler discussed the Dutch East Indies. Now was the end of an era in world history, the finale to European domination of Asia. Hitler blamed Britain. "For years I never stopped telling all the English I met that they'd lose the Far East if they entered into a war with Europe. They didn't answer, but they assumed a superior air. They're masters in the art of being arrogant!"[101] Himmler viewed the collapse of the Dutch in Asia as a racial boon for the Netherlands. "This way, the Dutch people will maintain its integrity, while before, it was running the risk of contaminating itself with Malayan blood."[102] Hitler prophesied that Japan would drive whites out of Asia and Australia. It was a topic to which he returned on New Year's Eve, praising Japan for racial homogeneity, lack of landed gentry, and middle-class values. In Japan, social class was moot, he said, obviating the need for a revolution to tame capital and bring it in service of the state.[103] Warming to his new allies, Hitler reported the words of Japanese Ambassador Hiroshi Oshima, who predicted that the Russian spaces being conquered by Germany, having a wild and rough climate, would toughen the German population, while the sunny archipelagoes of the Pacific might have a softening effect upon Japanese.[104]

Lorient, Brittany—Kriegsmarine dreams of an "Atlantic Pearl Harbor"

The lifting of all restrictions regarding USA ships and the so-called Pan-American Safety Zone has been ordered by the Fuhrer. Therefore the whole area of the American coasts will become open for operations by U-boats, an area in which the assembly of ships takes place in single traffic at the few points of departure for American convoys. There is an opportunity here, therefore, of intercepting enemy merchant ships under conditions which have ceased almost completely for some time. Further, there will be hardly any question of an efficient patrol in the American coastal area, at least of a patrol used to U-boats. Attempts must be made to utilize as quickly as possible these advantages, which will disappear very shortly, and to achieve a 'spectacular success' on the American coast.

War Diary of German Admiral Karl Donitz, December 7, 1941.[105]

The hour has come, Britain's power fades./U-Boat men's boldness, builds Germany's strength./U-Boats sail, far out into the sea! U-Boats hunt, torpedoes out of the tubes!/ Hunt England, unto death!/Bursting, creaking the steamer's hull breaks!/ The last trip down, isn't that certain death?

"U-Boat Lied," Song of the U-Boats[106]

There were powerful Germans in the navy who wanted an Atlantic counterpart to Pearl Harbor. Their weapon of choice, by necessity, was the U-boat. Whatever their weaknesses, the British still ruled the eastern Atlantic. French battleships might have balanced things out, but the British bombed the fleet at Oran lest it come under Nazi command. In 1939, *Graf Spee* attacked merchant shipping to great publicity, but wound up scuttled at Montevideo, Uruguay. *Bismark* enjoyed dramatic success before it was sunk. Other capital ships, like *Tirpitz*, were deemed too vulnerable to risk in action. *Tirpitz* sat out the war in a Norwegian fjord, pestered by Allied bombing. Submarines constituted the shank of effective German naval strength.

U-boat arm was supposed to disrupt Allied shipping. American naval cover for British convoys before December 1941 was increasingly aggressive. Roosevelt's September 13, 1941 order to shoot German subs on sight was by any fair definition a war-time measure. The resultant *Greer* incident, in which an American destroyer attacked a U-boat, showed how far Roosevelt's navy would go under a quasi-war situation.[107] U-boat captains knew that the US Navy was a foe. One was Reinhard Hardegen. He was among a handful of officers called to meet *Kriegsmarine* chief, Admiral Karl Donitz, one week after Hitler declared war. Hardegen hoped Germany would finally unleash the full brunt of U-boat power against the American enemy.[108]

Hardegen and his fellow commanders rode across the Ter River, down to the water's edge at Lorient, the French port commandeered as fleet headquarters. He reflected upon recent frustrations. "Two patrols ago, I was off the coast of

Africa, and the Americans with their hypocritical claims of neutrality made a fool of me. Time and time again, I would sight smoke clouds and mast tops on the horizon only to close with them and see that they belonged to ships with large painted American flags on their hulls."[109] Confident that American ships carried contraband, Hardegen and his fellows "couldn't touch them." "But," he considered cheerfully, "We can touch those guys now."[110]

Their mission remained unclear when they walked into the situation room. While Donitz walked his dog outside, his right-hand-man *Kapitan-zu-Zee* Eberhardt Godt readied the briefing. The Germans had their successes decrypting Allied orders, which helped them put together the up-to-date convoy map that dominated the room. Donitz had the benefit of recent intelligence to supplement his sharp awareness of nearly a half-century's worth of German naval contemplation about war with the United States.[111] In 1899, the Staff of the German Admiralty prepared a contingency plan for invading America. The main stroke was to be a direct attack on New York Harbor, with troop landings on Long Island. Land and sea attacks on Boston and Norfolk would follow. The plan, a war-game exercise, assumed that any success required absolute surprise and overall naval superiority of at least 1/3.[112] Other plans, such as seizing Puerto Rico or landing troops near Cape Cod while twin armadas hit New York and Boston, were just as far-fetched. None of the conditions for success were reasonable, so the schemes remained hypothetical.[113] In 1937, Hitler himself suggested occupying the Azores, using the Portuguese islands as a base for bombers operating against the American east coast.[114] He reiterated the idea in 1940, and talked up the *Amerikabomber*, a plane meant to reach New York. In February 1941, Hitler discussed a more feasible idea with his navy. The Naval Staff wanted a coordinated U-boat attack up and down the American east coast, from Boston to Hampton Roads. While Hitler concluded that such an attack was too difficult, Donitz and Godt vigorously supported the idea.[115] They were skeptical that American harbors were prepared to repel attackers. It took the British years to adapt to the U-boat menace, leading to the "Happy Time" for submarines. Moreover, Doentiz saw keenly how devastating such a coordinated blow might be to a nation operating under the auspices of Rainbow Five, which bound the United States to supply Britain and the USSR. A coordinated surprise attack up and down the Eastern Seaboard would be a maritime *blitzkrieg*. In that way, it fit into the German pattern. But maritime schemes were never Hitler's favorite.

Donitz wanted to use the element of surprise.[116] He could not help thinking big. But in order to make *Paukenschlag*, or Operation Drumbeat, a strategic success instead of a tactical irritant, it would be necessary to have sufficient U-boats operating synchronously. Donitz did not have enough submarines. He could only wonder about the psychological and economic effect of a vast submarine fleet sinking ships, shelling cities, strewing chaos across the main seaboard of a country waking up to war. Pearl Harbor, the main base of the Pacific Fleet, was caught unawares. How well-prepared would the East Coast be?

Donitz explained to his U-boat captains that they were to sail for the American coast even though their numbers were not as high as wished. Three hundred submarines was the number he asked for, 57 was how many he had at the war's 1939 outset. In December 1941, his fleet comprised 91 operational U-boats, with nearly a third allocated to the Mediterranean.[117] Improved Anglo-American defensive measures such as convoy tactics, ASDIC, and air reconnaissance cut short the U-boats' season of impunity by late 1941. But an unprepared enemy offered ample chances "to beat the drum along the American coast."[118] The Admiral knew that he must fight with what he had. Hardegen happily heard the orders sending him to patrol Newfoundland's approaches, from St. John's to Cape Race. He and four colleagues would command five U-boats of Operation Drumbeat, commencing when they reached their target areas and received their coded go-ahead on January 13, 1942.[119] They meant to live up to the U-boat motto: *"Angriefen! Ran! Versenken!*; "Attack! Advance! Sink Them!"[120]

Washington, D.C., departments of the Army and Navy—military brass gets to work

The United States can only inadequately defend its coast against air raids, hold Hawaii, the Panama Canal and other existing bases, gradually complete the relief of the British in Iceland, reinforce the Philippines or Dutch East Indies, occupy Natal, and possibly occupy some other base not seriously defended by Axis forces or sympathizers (Cape Verdes or Azores). It will be practicable and may be of some assistance to send some armored or infantry division to the British Isles in the winter or spring. . . . The shortage of U. S. flag shipping precludes the possibility of executing more than one, or at most two, or these operations concurrently.

War Plans Division Memo, "Immediate Military Measures,"
December 21, 1941.[121]

Preparedness was well underway before the Japanese strike. Rearmament started gaining pace in 1940. During that same year, the armored training maneuvers across the South brought new military names to public and press attention, including that of George S. Patton, Jr. In the Louisiana war games, Patton grabbed battlefield initiative with surprise and speed, moving his tanks in a style German *panzer* commanders would recognize. Wartime's demand for bravado launched his rise.[122] The pattern which moved battle-worthy leaders up military ranks occurred across the armed forces. Top brass like General George Marshall, who often visited Patton's staging base at Fort Benning, where Omar Bradley was commandant, kept a careful eye out for officers who could command.[123] The army also studied the ongoing war with utmost detail. When the Germans successfully assaulted Crete with parachutists in May 1941, taking a major step towards Suez, the War Department took notes. Their thinking about the possibilities of airborne strength grew far more expansive, much to Bradley's delight. Bradley was tabbed for command of the 82nd airborne just days after Pearl Harbor.[124]

Bradley's task in reviving the 82nd, born during World War I where it fought at St. Mihiel and the Meuse-Argonne, was not just to reawaken memories of glories past—this was Sergeant Alvin C. York's division—but to conduct a successful experiment in mass mobilization.[125] In the past, conscripts went to preexisting divisions and integrated therein. The 82nd came into being all at once, with a 10 percent core of experienced soldiers (700 officers and 1,200 enlisted men) surrounded by a mass of 16,000 raw draftees.[126] The challenge for leaders like Bradley was to transmit the needed knowledge to the new men, while simultaneously building unit cohesion. Because the challenges were immediate, there was some room for creative thinking. Bradley believed that rigorous training standards could be maintained while soldiers were made to feel at home in their division, serving under officers who cared about their welfare.[127] Bradley was an exceptional officer, yet his vision proved compelling across the army. It was a startlingly humane vision, and showed the pragmatism embedded in the goal-oriented American military establishment. The army's main shock came when the post-Pearl Harbor influx of new soldiers showed up unfit—"soft as marshmallows," Bradley called them.[128] Training could fix that.

General Marshall was not notified about the Pearl Harbor attack on the morning of December 7 while he ate breakfast in his Virginia home. He went for his Sunday morning horseback ride and had to be tracked down on the trail.[129] Marshall was as surprised as anyone that morning. But two months prior to Pearl Harbor, Secretary Stimson and Marshall were informed by Roosevelt that, at the war's 1939 outset, a group of physicists was aiming at splitting the atom.[130] German scientists were at work on the same problem, the scientists told the President. October 1941 saw the creation of the Top Policy Committee, whose membership included Vice President Henry Wallace, Office of Scientific and Research and Development chief Vannevar Bush, National Defense Research Committee chief James B. Conant, and Marshall. They agreed that, once work reached the "full-scale construction" stage, the army would assume control of what became the Manhattan Project. Roosevelt accepted this proposal in March 1942.[131] Leslie Groves was the project leader. He met often with Marshall and the navy's Ernest J. King.[132] Roosevelt expected his army and navy to be to talk with each other.

As of December 7, 1941, the major war issue was to decide what the strategic priorities should be. Just as the New Deal offered opportunities for experts to tackle economic emergencies, the war did the same thing for military problems. There were many competing pressures. Friends of the Soviet Union wanted an immediate second front in Europe to relieve the Red Army. Friends of the Philippines wanted reinforcements there. Australia's supporters wanted that continent protected. New allies, like the Dutch, wanted the Dutch East Indies flooded with men and materiel. Wholesale thinking was required, which meant burnishing Rainbow Five and honestly assessing American capabilities.

Planning with Britain signaled the Europe-first approach. The Americans and British hammered out Grand Strategy during the two weeks after December 7. The initial meetings centered delivered the realization that, for the moment, all actions must be defensive.[133] In an honest admission of current strength ratios, planners foresaw that 1942 would not bring fast counteroffensives. Campaigns such as "a return to the Continent, across the Mediterranean, from Turkey into the Balkans, or by landings in Western Europe" could not be imagined until 1943 at the earliest.[134] The goal then would be "closing and tightening the ring around Germany."[135] Under the same purview was a diagnosis of current manpower and supply situations. Peacetime forecasts proved insufficient: "The forces that the Associated Powers now estimate as necessary to achieve victory and for which productive capacity must be provided, may not be adequate or appropriate."[136] The prescription was more of everything. At the heart of that first joint planning session was the most fundamental realization of all, the fact that the Axis powers would determine the shape of the war for months, at least. The United States and Britain would be purely reactive while the enemy decided where and when to fight. Uncertainty and reaction were unavoidable. "No one can predict the situation that will develop while the enemy retains the strategic initiative," warned the planners.[137]

The service branches looked for security where they could. At the Navy Department, some stability lay in the files of War Plan Orange. War Plan Orange envisioned a struggle for mastery of the Pacific between a Blue (American) and Orange (Japanese) side. One of the most prescient programs in American history, War Plan Orange had its genesis in the late nineteenth century, when the Spanish-American War brought United States title to the Philippines. Other islands, such as Guam, were part of the booty as well. On the heels of annexing Hawaii and buying Alaska, contemporaneous with construction of the Panama Canal, it became clear that American fortunes were at stake across the Pacific. That ocean could no longer be seen as the end point of continental settlement. It was a venue for American expansion.

From hopeful ally to embittered enemy: Japanese disillusionment and War Plan Orange

During the whole of my six years of service at Tokyo I never remember an interval of any long duration in the controversies between America and Japan.

Sir Conyngham Greene, British Ambassador to Japan, 1920[138]

The thrashing given by Japan to Russia in their 1904–1905 war was settled through negotiations at Portsmouth, New Hampshire. Host Theodore Roosevelt toasted the delegates, hoping for a "just and lasting peace"; while the dignitaries drank in silence. Their silence was the best augury of the one-sided settlement which wound up plunging Japan into Manchuria, giving Tokyo effective control over Northern Chinese ports, destroying Russian naval power in the Pacific.[139] As far as Japan was concerned, this was fair. Victory came thanks to surprise naval attacks on February 8, 1904, followed by tough fighting against Russian-held Port Arthur, seized in January 1905. Japanese advances were clinched by the destruction of Russia's Baltic Fleet, shattered off Tsushima in May 1905. Victory over Imperial Russia allowed Japan to consolidate what it captured from China in the previous 1895 war. The Sino-Japanese War was followed by the Triple Intervention of Russia, Britain, and France, who restricted Japanese claims. That diplomatic intervention was resented by Tokyo, sparking antipathy towards Russian expansion to the East symbolized by the Trans-Siberian Railroad. The Triple Intervention also bred Japanese suspicion that Western nations would cheat Tokyo at the bargaining table.[140] At Portsmouth, the Japanese would insist on what they wanted. It was then that Japan emerged into American consciousness a rival Pacific power.

This meant that the Navy Department had new ideas to mull over. France and Britain looked at the island nation as a potential counterweight in global balance-of-power machinations. In Washington, the main result was a 1906 request by President Roosevelt to draw up a plan in case of war with Japan.[141] That brought the first Orange plan. Roosevelt's request did not signal official animus towards Japan, which enjoyed some respect in high American circles, where sympathy for Russia was low. Admiral Dewey, hero of Manila, visited the Emperor and Empress in Tokyo, finding the Mikado scene charming.[142] Over the years, the Orange Plan was constantly updated.

Always wrapped up in War Plan Orange was the disposition of China. Americans considered themselves guarantors of Chinese sovereignty, with opportunities for commercial enrichment thrown into the bargain. American missionaries there generated affection for the China they described. Meanwhile, Japan saw the fractious Middle Kingdom as a potential economic hinterland. Japan's pressure on

China became increasingly naked. By the 1930s, the Japanese Army was embroiled in what they called the "China Incident," an escalating war for control of the Asian mainland.

Relations between Washington and Tokyo grew increasingly fraught. War Plan Orange's basic shape was understood decades before Pearl Harbor. If war broke out, the Philippines would be Japan's first target. Only the US Main Fleet could forestall an attack. Lines of communication between the fleet and homeland would be long and vulnerable, with Pearl Harbor as their nexus. If the American fleet could control Philippine waters and engage the enemy, then the army contingent there could be reinforced by a pipeline of men and supplies.[143] If those lines of communication and supply could not be secured, then the Philippines would fall. There were many implications inherent in this plan. The main issue was that fighting Japan was made more complicated by the need to defend the Philippines. But the Philippines had to be protected because the United States owned them.

Japan smarted at Versailles after President Wilson opposed awarding Tokyo control of German's Central Pacific island colonies. Wilson objected since that might threaten Hawaii and complicate the knotty problem of Philippine defense.[144] Wilson's nominal allies Britain and France ignored his complaints, in a rebuke more serious than most appreciated at the time. Formalizing Japan's presence in the Central Pacific made war with the United States more likely. One onlooker who understood just how dreadful an outcome this was for American strategy was navy planner Captain Harry E. Yarnell. In 1919, he was frank about the Versailles disaster. "At one time," he wrote, "it was the plan of the Navy Department to send a fleet to the Philippines on the outbreak of war. I am sure that this would not be done at the present time." Yarnell could see how islands awarded to Japan could serve as bases from which to attack American supply lines to the Philippines. The agitated navy officer went even further: "It seems certain that in the course of time the Philippines and whatever forces we may have there will be captured."[145] Over the next two decades, as Japan's military asserted control over its civilian government and foreign policy, it became increasingly common for farsighted American leaders to see Tokyo as tomorrow's enemy.

Full of vim after victory in World War I, Japan committed to naval strength commensurate with its position and ambitions. The first move was the 8-8 Program, proposed in 1914 but passed through governmental channels in 1920. 8-8 called for the construction of eight battleships and eight cruisers, which would constitute a new main fleet.[146] Washington blanched, and so began the "Number Wars," painful three-way negotiations in which Allied nations sought to codify a naval balance. Britain, exhausted from World War I, needed to protect its colonies and came to see Japan as dangerous. These contentious naval talks unfolded against the backdrop of arms control mania culminating in 1928s Kellogg-Briand Pact, signed by both Japan and the United States. Kellogg-Briand, outlawing war, was an exercise in wishful thinking, but the Washington Naval Conferences featured hard bargaining. The result was a four-nation dickering session begun in November 1921, with the United States and Japan joined by Britain and France.[147] The "Washington Conference System" provoked Japan's belief that the status quo in Asia and the Pacific discriminated against its just ambitions. Leaders in Tokyo came to see the region as theirs to exploit. At the same time, the United States, Britain, and France seemed determined to maintain the status quo. Comity between the former World War I Allies broke down, as Tokyo grew disenchanted with the West.[148] Japan intended to be a first-rank naval force. The Four-Power Treaty of December 13, 1921, served as a cover for Britain's refusal to extend the alliance between Tokyo and London. The main Japanese reaction was resentment and bruised pride.[149] A Nine-Power Treaty followed, including the Netherlands, Portugal, Belgium, Italy, and China. This tacked-on document echoed the Four-Power Treaty, supported Chinese sovereignty, and further abraded Japanese self-esteem.[150]

Here was an example of China's ability to use the international diplomatic system to protect its fraying grasp over its sovereign lands. Disorganized, China knew its own weakness and saw voracious Japan as its main danger. International accords aimed at protecting national rights were China's best method for holding Japan at bay.[151] The negotiations were complicated. When the naval formulae were finally arrived at, things looked far different from the 8-8 parity Tokyo wanted. Instead, a 5:5:3 ratio was put in place. At every turn, when Japan argued for a 10:10:7, or a flat 70 percent level *vis-a-vis* the United States and Britain, they met with irreconcilable American objections. Japan left the conferences feeling burned.[152] The only positive outcome from a Japanese perspective was that the resultant treaties gave them room to operate in China. But the suspicion that white powers wanted to freeze Japan out of Asian influence took firm hold in Tokyo power circles.

At the same time, Canada and Australia mulled over the Pacific situation. The two nations realized that American armed strength must now form part of their strategic considerations. Britain was no longer dominant. Australia was aware of the distance to London. Canada recognized that Japanese adventurism in the North Pacific threatened its own interests.[153] An anti-Japanese coalition was lining up.

The 1920s and 1930s saw deepening divisions. As Chiang Kai-Shek emerged in China, his Kuomintang Party argued for national unity and a strong stance against Japanese incursions.[154] Japan saw him as a threat, opposing his 1928 attempt to seize Peking. As their involvement in Chinese affairs deepened, the Japanese meddled so as to influence outcomes. One meddlesome act led to its sequel. Assassinating a Manchurian leader in 1928[155] led to the next crisis, the Manchurian Incident of September 18, 1931, which prompted occupation of Mukden.[156] In 1932, rioting by patriotic Chinese in Shanghai sparked fighting with Chiang's 19th Route Army. Behind each deeper thrust was Japan's Kwantung Army, with political goals of its own and support in Tokyo. Chiang's challenge was to secure himself as China's national leader while retreating before each Japanese advance. "Selling space to buy time," he called it.[157] As Chiang backed up, Japan followed him. At home, the Japanese Army was not hesitant to involve itself in politics. There was a cycle of revolts and assassinations by officers. This semi-official violence erased civilian governmental control over national policy. The army became synonymous with political power, and the government answered to the military.[158] Diplomacy also reflected changes in Tokyo. The hated 5:5:3 formula was reiterated at a London negotiation in 1930. In order to gain ratification of the treaty, which the navy opposed, the withering civilian government in Tokyo attached a domestic agreement that the only limits upon Japanese military plans would be those decided by themselves.[159]

It was no surprise during the 1920s and 1930s that War Plan Orange remained topical within American military circles. By 1921, an army-drawn "Preliminary Estimate of the Situation" stated bluntly: "It may safely be assumed that Japan is the most probable enemy."[160] The question of what to do with the Philippines, so far away, so expensive to maintain, remained tough. There was no voting percentage in Congressional budgeting for colonial maintenance. The army was the main advocate for Filipino support. Governor-General Leonard Wood, former army Chief of Staff, took the navy to task for assuming that the Philippines were a millstone best cut loose. Wood, who saw the islands as his responsibility, hated that viewpoint. Such an "assumption by the Navy that in case of war with Japan the Philippine Islands could not be defended must be abandoned," he insisted. It carried with it the companion notion that, after abandonment, "a long war waged to take them back and re-establish ourselves in the Far East" would be indicated.[161] Failure to defend a country under American sovereignty, home to a people dependent upon American assistance, would be dishonorable. Moreover, it would cause a "disintegrating and demoralizing effect upon our people."[162] Wood made his case to the Secretary of the Navy, asking that "steps . . . be taken at once to see that the army and navy assume that the Philippine Islands must not only be absolutely defended, but succored by the Fleet."[163]

The army adopted Wood's position. When Douglass MacArthur rose to power in Manila, the argument would be even more unabashed. As the Joint Planners kept modernizing the Orange plans, opposition to abandoning the Philippines when war broke out became nearly dishonorable in army circles. There were cultural reasons behind the army's position. It won the painful counterinsurgency which ensured United States control over the refractory colony, giving the army some moral claim over the islands' fate. But there was also a problem: the Jones Act, a 1916 piece of legislation passed by Congress which promised the islands eventual independence.[164] This put the Philippines in a strange position—on the road to independence, still ruled from Washington. In 1931 and 1934, Joint Board reviews echoed earlier conclusions that simply unloading the islands would be unfair to Filipinos.[165] The political situation remained confusing. A 1933 bill passed by Congress to allow independence but maintain American military bases was rejected in Manila. Another plan, to grant the islands liberty but to annex the Sulu Archipelago and parts of Mindanao went nowhere.[166] It was only in 1934 that the Tydings-McDuffie Act went through, promising independence with no restrictions by 1946.[167]

Through all the evolutions of this ambiguous colonial relationship, War Plan Orange retained its shape. It was accepted that war was likely to come as the result of Japanese actions, probably via surprise attack. No less an authority than Mahan himself noticed that the Japanese attack at Port Arthur in 1904 came without a war declaration.[168] It was further understood that Japanese movements to the south, towards the Philippines, British Malaya/Singapore and the Dutch East Indies, would be part of any Tokyo offensive. Like any sound military plan, Orange aimed for victory. Paramount in its considerations was the requirement to keep Japan from controlling the Central Pacific and Hawaii. During war games, Team Orange (Japan) did best when it seized enough of the Pacific to hold out against the eventual counterattacks by Team Blue (United States). Victory for Orange/Japan looked like a matter of outlasting Blue/United States.[169] Victory for Blue/United States implied a grueling war.

Occasionally, alternatives to this forbidding outlook challenged War Plan Orange. A movement for "Defensiveism" arose in the 1930s, as a result of scanty Depression resources and strong isolationism. Defensiveism called for a strategic triangle between Alaska–Oahu–Panama.[170] But as long as Mahan and the navy held influence in the leadership's consciousness, Defensiveism faced psychological as well as strategic hurdles. It had some favor within the army, where certain planners worried about what General Malin Craig called "adventure of any magnitude."[171] On the other hand, Craig allowed, "the Navy is practically ready for instant action at all times and accordingly looks far afield."[172] This was because Mahan's navy trained itself to look over the horizon. A Joint Planning compromise in 1938, brokered by then-Secretary of War Harry H. Woodring and Navy Secretary Charles Edison gave the army space to generate a Strategic Concentration Plan, while the navy whipped up a Strategic Operations Plan for areas west of the security triangle.[173] This was an FDR-style compromise, which allowed the army to concentrate on homeland defense, while leaving War Plan Orange essentially untouched. One implication was sketchy for pro-Filipinos like MacArthur. The army basically accepted a homeland defense plan behind the triangle, while the navy clung to War Plan Orange. Where this equivocality left the Philippines was uncertain. War gamers in 1939 had trouble imagining a trans-Atlantic threat from Germany. But they envisioned a "practically foot-loose" Japanese navy taking the Philippines, many Pacific islands, and parts of the Aleutians, preparatory to threatening Hawaii.[174] Within the navy—which still had a benefactor in the White House—these war games prompted abundant discussion about how best to tune up plans.

War Plan Orange fit well under the larger Rainbow Five Plan. Rainbow Five called for prioritizing the European theater, but did not deny the need to fight Japan. Elements of Plan Orange, which called for a long war in the Pacific, could be integrated with Rainbow Five. Victory for the American side, as American War Plan Orange experts saw it, must come about through a willingness to outlast Japan in a protracted campaign. The contest would test each nation's endurance. The Japanese were obedient and would fight as long as they were told, navy planners expected. There was question about whether or not the American populace would support a war long enough to eject Japan from its initial gains.[175] Newcomers to Washington imbibed the Plan's central precept for a drawn-out war between two potent antagonists that would cover the world's largest ocean and be fought on a scale unknown to history. War Plan Orange posited that the United States and Japan would fight a war with no quick resolution.

Tokyo—desperation leads to "Victory Disease"

The glorious tradition and mission of the Yamato people do not permit their country to remain under this . . . economic oppression. Especially so, when the situation threatens to force Japan to suffer from gradual economic strangulation. We say it with conviction that a resolute step forward is the only way left for us in order to safeguard our honored history.
> Major Kametaro Tominaga, War Ministry Press Bureau,
> September 18, 1941[176]

Do we have adequate resources for a long war or not? The government has presented its estimates, but I am still concerned about this problem.
> Wakatsuki Reijiro, Senior Statesman Conference, November 29, 1941

In attempting to prevent Japan from being gradually weakened and reduced to a minor power by embargoes, pressure to withdraw from China and so on, the government should be very careful that the result is not instead our rapid defeat and destruction.
> Yonai Mitsumasa, Senior Statesman Conference, November 29, 1941

Please trust the Government.
> Prime Minister Tojo, Senior Statesman Conference,
> November 29, 1941[177]

The Kuriles stretch from Hokkaido to Russia's Kamchatka Peninsula. They form a slender volcanic island chain, sub-arctic and wild, between the frigid Sea of Okhotsk and the stormy North Pacific. Their isolation made Hitokappu Bay, on Etorufu, a secure spot from which to launch the Pearl Harbor Strike Force. When the ships slipped their stays on November 26, 1941, they sailed forth as a testament to the tight straits from which Japanese leaders hoped to escape. Japan's decision for war was a gamble born of desperation; a long-shot which even its supporters felt could bring disaster. But it seemed the only move left for a country out of options.

By 1941, the Imperial Army was into the second decade of Chinese combat, against a shifting array of foes including Chiang's KMT and Mao Tse-Tung's Communists.[178] Simultaneous nation-building in Manchukuo further strained the army. Wishing to further control China's northern regions, as well as to stymie incursions from the Soviet-controlled Mongolia, the army also backed an Inner Mongolian puppet state in 1937.[179]

Ancient Chinese place names became redolent with associations of Japanese brutality. Such was the case in Nanking. Capital of Chiang's regime, the city on the Yangtze River controlled access to the heartland, region of the KMT's greatest support. It made a tempting target for Japanese military plotters aiming to decapitate Chiang's government. The attack on Nanking started on December 10, 1937, but it was the aftermath, in which troops marauded through the captured city, that the world called "The Rape of Nanking." Even Nazi Germans at the site were taken aback by the scope of the Rape.[180] Americans were aroused to ire by the sinking of the gunboat *Panay*, patrolling the Yangtze to protect US nationals and property. A Japanese apology for the *Panay* dive-bombing calmed relations for the moment, but American anger was clearly reflected in the diary of General Joseph W. Stilwell, military attache to Chiang's regime. "The bastards!" read Vinegar Joe's diary entry.[181] Chiang debouched to Hankow, which fell soon after. Chiang's government then moved further up the Yangtze to Chungking. Chunking became theater for aerial battles featuring the Flying Tigers, the American-piloted air wing under command of Claire Chennault. Chiang's friends in the United States—the fabled "China Lobby"—pushed for assistance and kept the Chinese Generalissimo in the forefront of sympathetic American news coverage. Japan became a pariah nation, making friendship with the Third Reich and Italy more enticing. Tokyo cultivated Chiang's rival, Wang Ching-wei, who set up his own Nanking regime under Japanese protection. Mao's Communist guerillas made Yenan their stronghold.[182] The China incident was now far beyond the ability of the Kwantung Army to control.

At the same time, the equipoise which balanced the contraption of Japanese government, with centers of gravity representing industry, the military, cultural elements, and civilian parties all revolving around the pivot point of the Emperor, was totally uneven. The army short-circuited dissent at home by equating disagreement with lack of loyalty to the Emperor. Controls and penalties grew more draconian until civil rights were defunct. Potential centers of alternate power and influence, such as labor unions, the independent press, and the universities lost their freedom. Assorted propaganda campaigns like "Purification of Thoughts" actualized a mobilized totalitarian state.[183]

Generals supporting the idea of a Japan-at-arms at the center of an Asian imperium were frustrated by their inability to bring it about. This accentuated their suspicion that Japanese influence was incommensurate with its strength. Especially nettlesome was attitude of the United States, which interfered with Japan's drive to gain the rubber and oil which the Dutch East Indies possessed in luscious abundance. The Netherlands was under German occupation, but its exiled government clung to the colonies with American approval. The Dutch East Indies, long exploited for the Netherlands' benefit, comprised hundreds of islands, large and small. The biggest were mini-continents, like Borneo, Java, Celebes, Sarawak, and New Guinea, their vast hinterlands barely explored, places where colonial writ ran faintly. Enormous plantations run by small numbers of Dutch planters shored up the mercantile system. Batavia, on Java, was where the Dutch merchant class concentrated, but even there, colonists were surrounded by large numbers of natives with independence aspirations. Rich in the substances which Japan's war machine sorely lacked—rubber and oil foremost—this colony seemed destined for Japanese domination.

But the Dutch Government-in-Exile promised to continue the war as a fighting ally. This meant that the DEI was committed to resisting Japan. In fact, the islands were too weak to impede a good invasion plan. Japanese leaders with an eye on history could take pleasure from the turning of historical fate. During the early 1600s, Tokugawa Ieyasu was cowed by the Dutch East India Company. The mighty Shogun allowed trading concessions near Nagasaki, despite misgivings. Limited interactions with the Dutch proved fateful, opening views of the west to Japanese scholars and helping to prepare the way for Japan's emergence as a modern state.[184] Now, three centuries later, the once-intimidating Dutch were revealed as a small country, conquered by Japan's friend, clinging preposterously to an Asian empire.

In Tokyo, the sight of a rickety colonial remnant sitting on top of the very resources they needed intensified latent resentment against western high-handedness. Each time Japan took a step to become regional hegemon, it ran into counter pressures. Mindful of history, Japan's rulers knew how western machinations negatively affected their national interest. For example, commercial treaties in the wake of Perry's visit led to an influx of foreign goods and an outflow of gold reserves, which destabilized Japan's economy, contributing to the downfall of the Shogunate.[185] Colonial powers seemed spent by 1941, especially the Netherlands and Vichy France. A puissant and confident Japan would not be bluffed by failed European states who refused to admit that their colonial domination was over. The fall of

France in June 1940 marked a sea change. Britain must fight for naval control in the nearby Atlantic and Mediterranean, as well as in the far-off Indian Ocean.[186] With a distracted Royal Navy, Japan became more aggressive. In July 1941, Japan moved against Indo-China. Supine Vichy looked on bleakly as Vietnam fell under Japanese control.

Predictably, the Dutch, British, and Americans made a countermove—total embargo of oil and petroleum supplies.[187] This put Japan in a real predicament. There were ongoing military operations which could not be stopped; exciting notions for future actions, too. All needed necessary supplies, with oil the most pressing requirement. At a series of liaison conferences between army, navy, and governmental ministries, Japan's leaders sat in conclave and presented their findings to the Emperor. It became obvious in these gatherings that Japan's expansion had landed it in a corner from which there was no easy escape. Despite its power, Japan was vulnerable. China was a quagmire, with each Japanese land grab necessitating further measures against an enemy fighting out of its vast interior. Troops in Indo-China would soon run out of fuel. Just across the South China sea lay the oil-rich Dutch East Indies, seductively weak. That way, too, lay the Philippines, which meant the Americans.

The crisis outlook was typified in the November 5, 1941 Imperial Conference, at which Prime Minister Tojo—the General in Japan's top political spot—had an audience with Emperor Hirohito. Tojo claimed that he was "praying to the Gods that somehow we will be able to get an agreement with the United States" so as to end the embargo and avoid war.[188] Despite Tojo's expressed hope, the committee, composed of cabinet Ministers who asked questions of the Privy Council while the Emperor maintained regal silence, was heavily weighted towards a military solution.

In a disquisition which revealed Japan's deep belief in its uniqueness as a civilization, Privy Council Yoshimichi Hara emphasized the racial and cultural conflicts which pushed Japan to the brink. "We have endured hardships for four years because we are a unified nation under an Imperial family with a history of 2,600 years," he argued, adding that Britain suffered from "war weariness." Meanwhile, contingent American demands for ending the embargo were "impossible, from the standpoint of our domestic political situation and of our self-preservation, to accept." At the heart of American stubbornness, Hara discerned, was determination to buck up Chiang. "There is suspicion that the United States is acting as spokesman for the Chungking regime."[189]

Hara advised that Japan make no improvident concessions to the Americans. He did not want Tokyo's diplomats to relax their stance and negotiate a Pacific compromise that would sacrifice the Greater East Asian Co-Prosperity Sphere. "On the other hand," he confessed, "We cannot let the present situation continue," due to limited resource reserves. The only way out Hara could see was to change the situation with a surprise move, to smash the stalemate and introduce a new dynamic into an equation which, as currently constituted, presented Japan no good outcomes. This was the animating impulse behind the Pearl Harbor attack. It should be the amazing stroke that created a new reality. However, Hara pointed out, time was not on Tokyo's side. Every day made Japan weaker, less able to alter the deadly situation. "If we miss the present opportunity to go to war, we will have to submit to American dictation. Therefore, I recognize that it is inevitable that we must decide to start a war with the United States."[190]

Speaking to Tojo, Hara provided a long list of justifications for the upcoming attack, most of which relied upon the ideal of Japan as a crusader expelling whites from Asia. Among the most astounding lines of reason he spelled out was nervousness that war-weariness might prompt Germany and Britain to call off their conflict. In that event, Hara fretted, natural racial alliances might assert themselves. Germany and Britain might settle, leaving Japan on the outside while European powers reinvigorated their Asian positions. This was how deeply race-based skepticism ran in Japan's most powerful class. The European war, Hara contended, accelerated the need for action. Hara plainly distrusted Germany. White races, he suggested, would eventually stick together. "We have come to where we are because of the war between Germany and Great Britain," the Privy Council Minister explained. "What we should always keep in mind here is what would happen to relations between Germany and Great Britain and Germany and the United States, all of them being countries whose population belongs to the white races, if Japan should enter the war."[191]

Hara's talk proved the sad truth that major wars are often the result of misperceptions by parochial national leaders.[192] Hara complained that Hitler considered the Japanese "a second-class race, and Germany has not declared war against the United States." Showing that both sides of the Axis wore racial blinkers which precluded understanding, Hara sketched out a white power settlement which might leave out Japan. He claimed that American "indignation against Japan will be stronger than their hatred of Hitler."[193] Building on the theme of innate American hostility to Japan, Hara built up a false correlative of American sympathy for Hitler, as if there was not enough room in the United States for two enemies. Eventually, Hara's theorizing drew the Prime Minister into the discussion. It was left for Tojo to assuage concerns about a white anti-Japan conspiracy. Tojo urged an attack, which would clear up the situation. For Tojo, the salient issue remained that "the government has not given up its earnest desire to break the impasse in our negotiations with the United States." He reminded everyone of his government's attempts to parley with Washington. Here, Tojo introduced a novel interpretation of Roosevelt's willingness to negotiate: the yen to talk came not from American peaceableness, but because the United States suffered from three main weaknesses: "(1) They are not prepared for operations in two oceans;

(2) They have not completed strengthening their diplomatic structure; (3) they are short of materials for national defense."[194] Here was a case of strategic projection, since these were the same problems faced by Japan.

Tojo emphasized that Japan was down to its last maneuver. Americans, he said, would be demoralized when they discovered Japanese determination on the battlefield. He ventured a prediction. "If we enter into a protracted war, there will be difficulties," he confessed. "The first stage of the war will not be difficult. We have some uneasiness about a protracted war." Tojo's argument, like Hara's, hinged on the principle that desperate times called for desperate measures. What if Japan failed to hit at her enemy soon enough? Then the Pacific would belong to the Americans. Japan's war machine would be a useless relic, her ambitions squelched by pusillanimity just when bold action was called for. "How can we let the United States continue to do as she pleases, even though there is some uneasiness? Two years from now we will have no petroleum for military use. Ships will stop moving. When I think of the strengthening of American defenses in the Southwest Pacific, the expansion of the American fleet, the unfinished China Incident, and so on, I see no end to difficulties. We can talk about austerity and suffering, but can our people endure such a life for a long time?" Tojo was not blasé about the ethical implications of a surprise attack. Covering "our moral basis for going to war," he saw "some merit in making it clear that Great Britain and the United States represent a strong threat to Japan's self-preservation." He wrapped up with a projection. "If we are fair in governing the occupied areas, attitudes towards us would probably relax. America may be enraged for a while, but later she will come to understand. In any case I will be careful to avoid the war's becoming a racial war."[195]

The chimera of gathering regional support for Japanese ambitions persisted. The platform of an October 23 Conference was approved by invited Asian conferees representing future allies within the Co-Prosperity Sphere. There was rhetoric about an East Asian future based upon respect for national sovereignty, and traditions. The topper was a promise aimed at Asian and world opinion to "maintain friendly relations with all nations, abolish systems of racial discrimination, undertake extensive cultural exchanges, voluntarily open up their resources, and thus contribute to the progress of the entire world."[196] This document was intended to be a Pacific match for the Atlantic Charter,[197] which cast the China Incident in ironic light.

On 15 November, a Conference approved a Draft Proposal aimed at "Hastening the End of the War Against the United States, Great Britain, the Netherlands, and Chiang." This document converted war against new enemies into peace-chasing measures. "Our Empire will engage in a quick war," declared the document, calling for the destruction of American and British bases in Eastern Asia and the Southwest Pacific, and the simultaneous construction of an impassable defensive cordon across thousands of miles of open sea. Foremost among the goals were annihilating the main American battle fleet, and cutting "the connection between

Australia and India and the British mother country." Pearl Harbor was the method for achieving the first goal. The second would be accomplished "by means of political pressure and the destruction of commerce," as well as by propping up independent regimes in Burma and India.[198] In meticulous outline format, the plan spelled out such steps as pressing Germany and Italy to ratchet up their war against Great Britain, preferably through invasion, avoiding war with the Soviet Union, and luring the US Navy into a climactic battle. One astounding action item figured that, having defeated the United States at sea, the next step would be "persuading Americans to reconsider their Far Eastern policy, and pointing out the uselessness of a Japanese-American war. American opinion will be directed toward opposition to war."[199]

The format of these meetings lent itself to strategic fogginess. Insularity became a fatal comfort as the participants contemplated an enemy they did not comprehend. Their own patterns of mind were unhelpful. What they feared, that the Japan they had built was dying and could not survive the conditions of a future with no war,[200] obscured more rational judgment. What they hoped, that a swift blow might prove lethal to American power without bringing vengeance, was a product of their delusions. Reiteration of the supposed dangers posed by peace accompanied rosy banalities about how the war might go well. By the time the strike fleet was near Pearl Harbor, such platitudes had displaced clear and honest forethought at the highest levels of Japan's power structure. In Washington, Roosevelt waited to be pushed into war. In Tokyo, Tojo argued for pushing.

For some Japanese war chiefs, what was about to happen was not mysterious. While Tojo and other army figures dominated the inner circle around Emperor Hirohito, most of the detail work preparatory to Pearl Harbor fell to the navy, in particular to Admiral Isoruku Yamamoto. Yamamoto knew the United States intimately. Posted there as Naval Attache, he studied at Harvard, traveled the country as a hitchhiker, and fell in love with baseball and football. He adored poker.[201] His pioneering mentality helped him to appreciate the implications of aircraft carriers during the 1920s,[202] which many battleship admirals refused to recognize. Yamamoto could see how faulty so many Japanese stereotypes about Americans were. "It is a mistake," he warned a group of schoolchildren in 1940, "to regard the Americans as luxury-loving and weak. I can tell you Americans are full of the spirit of justice, fight, and adventure."[203]

Yamamoto was gloomy in the face of Tojo's hopeful constructions regarding war with the United States. But however forlorn his outlook, it did not prevent the dutiful naval genius from planning the attack. To a large extent, Japan's navy was his. The Pearl Harbor plan was his, too. Yamamoto had helped Japan break away from the onerous ration system imposed by the Washington and London naval conferences. Promoted Vice-Admiral in 1936, Yamamoto headed up the navy's aviation department, backing the Zero and other superb planes.[204] The planning and training for the Hawaiian operation took place under his watchful guidance; the long-shot bid to present the United States with a sudden irrecoverable loss became the capstone of his naval career. Pearl Harbor became the highest stakes venue for what Yamamoto's closest staff officer called his "gambler's heart."[205] He knew the odds were long. Prime Minister Prince Fumimaro Konoe opposed the Pearl Harbor gambit[206] before being replaced by Tojo. Konoe asked Yamamoto how he thought war with Britain and the United States would go. Looking ahead, the admiral saw past Pearl Harbor. Yamamoto's divination was startling: "I can raise havoc with them for one year or at most eighteen months. After that I can give no one any guarantees."[207]

American news and national discourse in December

"These are times that try men's souls." So wrote Thomas Paine in the days of the early reverses of the American revolution. Lethargy and divided opinion at that time were obscuring the certainty of ultimate victory, and Thomas Paine rallied flagging spirits in the American Army and throughout the 13 states. Today, with opinion undivided, with no lethargy, with spirits unflagging, the United States is again sure of ultimate victory. But today the full power of the United States is held back by a drag unique to our times. It is that we have been the victims of certain illusions. We have been the safest-minded people on earth. We have been brought up ocean-conscious. We have an out-of-date measurement of distance. And we have indulged to the full the extravagances of under-estimating our opponents.
Raymond Gram Swing, Mutual Broadcasting System, December 10, 1941[208]

The first test has already been put upon us: it is whether we shall react to our first great defeat as men and women with clear eyes and stout heart, or as a frightened crowd, lashed into a frenzy of futility by panic-mongers, many of whom were assuring us less than a week ago that we could not and would not ever be attacked if only we did nothing.
Walter Lippmann, "Today & Tomorrow," New York Herald-Tribune, December 11, 1941[209]

If the Navy had read the newspapers, it might have been better prepared last Sunday.
Drew Pearson & Robert Kittner, "Washington Merry-Go-Round," December 11, 1941

From the morning of December 7 through the end of the conflict, war news dominated American attention. Anyone who addressed the public knew that. No one addressed the public with more confidence than Walter Lippmann. Serene atop the heap of American commentators, ensconced as wise man since his career began at the *New Republic* in 1914,[210] Lippmann took in the world from 1525 35th Street NW, his Georgetown address.[211] That desirable spot was verged on the west by Georgetown University. Three blocks east was busy Wisconsin Avenue, five blocks south, the Potomac waterfront. Georgetown's famous elms ran along Q Street, yards from his house. Montrose Park and Dumbarton Oaks, owned by Harvard, his alma mater, gave Lippmann's neighborhood its quiet and complacent feel. But the colonial homes and tidy sidewalks understated the fact that P and Q streets formed a power axis along which lived several of the capital city's most powerful figures. The neighborhood attracted the well placed and the ambitious in fields ranging from intelligence to the press to politics.[212]

Decades of assiduous networking made Lippmann the nation's best-connected journalist. He was certain before Pearl Harbor that events had reached a crucial stage. So he wrote to friend Lady Nancy Astor on December 3, apologizing for canceling his autumn trip to England, because "affairs here took a turn which convinced me that they were decisive, from the point of view of our part in the war."[213] With a sense of his own importance, Lippmann explained to the Viscountess at Cliveden that the capital could not be without him during a crisis.[214] Cliveden was epicenter of Roosevelt's worst suspicions about Britain. The place was shorthand for lingering fears that anti-democratic aristocrats might broker a deal with Hitler. But it held no terrors for the columnist comfortably in touch with Lady Astor.

Once the Pearl Harbor attack happened, he and other writers were pushed aside for a short while. Erudite explanations would have to wait as radio dominated mass communications, providing the immediate information Americans wanted. The medium was perfectly suited to deliver news. The country wanted plenty of information, fast.

The need for prompt news in the capital was borne out as December 7 wore on. Since it was Sunday, the city's beloved Washington Redskins had a game at Griffith Stadium, at Florida Avenue and 7th Street. Lacking a big-time college team, Washington doted on its professional football squad, led by quarterback Sammy Baugh. The Redskins were especially popular with the military. The opponent for the season finale was the Philadelphia Eagles. At 5-5, the Redskins could secure a winning record with a win. At 2-7-1, the Eagles would finish as losers no matter how the game turned out. The game was close and exciting. But much of the tension unfolded in the stands, among 27,102 fans. Kickoff was at 2.00 p.m., which was 9.00 a.m. Honolulu time. Bombs had been falling for almost two hours.[215] Into the press box came an ominous instructions for the sportswriters: "Keep it short!"[216] Networks worried that reporters in the stadium might tie up phone lines. From one fan to the next went word that something major was up. The public address announcer began paging people. A particular general should immediately report to work. An admiral must call his staff at once. The demand for officers to check in was unprecedented. Soon, the PA called for employees of *Times-Herald*, the *Post*, and the *Star*. Congressmen should head to the Capitol. Ambassadors and diplomats were next. The Filipino representative must get to his legation at once.[217] "We didn't know what the hell was going on," said a bewildered Baugh. "I had never heard that many announcements one right after the other. . . . We just kept playing."[218] Redskin President George Preston Marshall refused to allow any public Pearl Harbor update, ostensibly because he feared panicking the crowd. An enterprising wife sent her newsman husband a telegram by specifying his seat location: "DELIVER TO SECTION P, TOP ROW, SEAT 27, OPPOSITE 25-YARD LINE, EAST SIDE GRIFFITH STADIUM: WAR WITH JAPAN! GET TO OFFICE!"[219] The Redskins held on for a 20-14 win. Eagle Nick Basca kicked two extra points. Three days later, he enlisted in the army. In 1944, Basca was killed fighting in France.[220] At the final gun, some hardy fans rushed the goal posts in celebration, but most spectators were gone. To find out what was happening, they turned on their radios.

By 1940, the news business, long dominated by newspapers, had made peace with radio. With the end of the Press-Radio War of 1933–1935, which restricted broadcasts to 30 words or less and kept hot stories from the news wire off the air, broadcasters were free to use stories from the wire services.[221] The wire service companies, such as International News Service, Associated Press, and United Press, appreciated the chance to sell their information to new clients. Transradio Press Service, a radio-specific wire operation, came into being.[222] Newspaper publishers tried to coopt the new medium, purchasing interest in hundreds of stations. The year 1940 saw newspapers with controlling or part ownership in nearly 250 American radio stations, about one-third of the national total.[223] The overall number of stations rose, from nearly 600 in the mid-1930s[224] to over 900 by 1941.[225] The stations were divvied up by the networks, NBC, with Red and Blue divisions, CBS, and Mutual, or MBS. At NBC, David Sarnoff signed up top singers and comedians like Jack Benny and Fred Allen, who kept the network secure as the nation's home entertainment leader.[226]

CBS signed its own stars, like Bing Crosby, who competed in the same time slot as NBC's *Amos 'n' Andy*.[227] CBS wanted brand differentiation. Highbrow critics often complained that NBC sacrificed quality news and cultural programming for low-denominator public schlock. NBC's news division did have a much lower profile than its roster of funny actors.[228] CBS boss William Paley staked his network's reputation on its own news branch, built by Murrow and his recruits, who handled their beats in the world's major capital cities. The round-up style, with sequential reports integrated by Murrow, was the CBS signature. CBS also boasted domestic talents like Elmer Davis and Paul White. Mutual, which had its own national reach but which trailed NBC and CBS in budget and audience, concentrated on niche programming.[229] A clever move was MBS' deal to pick up British Broadcasting Company news bulletins, which gave the third-place network first-rate war coverage.[230] MBS also used British commentators, including J.B. Priestley, Wickham Steed, and Leslie Howard, (the movie star who played Ashley Wilkes in *Gone With the Wind*).[231] The BBC liked the arrangement, which allowed them to target Americans as part of the campaign to win popular support for Britain.[232] Two American scholars in 1940 considered the British broadcasts over Mutual very effective in that regard. "On the whole," wrote Harold Lavine and James Wechsler, "The broadcasts from London were permeated with that sweet, unyielding spirit of reason which the British customarily adopt in lecturing the world."[233]

No corner of the United States was beyond reach of the news. Even small towns had a newspaper, while radio was ubiquitous. In a 1939 speech at Princeton's American Institute for Public Opinion, pollster George Gallup excitedly described a nation linked by media. Out of 45 million voters in the 1936 elections, 40 million read their daily paper and listened to radio. Only 2 million had access to neither. "This means," enthused the public opinion expert, "That the nation is literally one great room."[234] From Honolulu, where NBC and CBS shared KGMB, to Bangor, where Downeasters tuned into Mutual's WLBZ and CBS' WABI, Americans listened to the radio to find out the news and to relax.[235] Therefore, nearly every American could would turn on the radio to find out what happened at Pearl Harbor.

"NBC Piano Trio" and "Fantasy in Melody," was on NBC's Blue Network, while organist Charles Courboin played on the Red, when December 7's flash reports came in from Hawaii.[236] Quiz shows like "Second Guessers" could not stay ahead of the special news bulletins. At CBS and MBS, the situation was the same: news reports, clarifications, follow-ups. By evening, the basic facts stood out: the Japanese had attacked Pearl Harbor, the Philippines, and British possessions. The extent of damage in Hawaii was unclear. The President would address Congress tomorrow. December 8 gave networks the chance to recover after the breathless day before. CBS carried reports from Honolulu's KGMB that hundreds of planes took part in the attack. Elmer Davis opined that Japan hoped to "restrict United States operations in the Far East" through surprise.[237]

Early analysis came from CBS' in-house military expert, Major George Fielding Eliot. Eliot's biography was fascinating. Born in Brooklyn, moving to Australia as a child, he served in the Australian and Canadian armies during World War I before returning to the United States and army intelligence. Eliot left the army in 1933, becoming an author specializing in pulp fiction and popular military analysis. Among his works were the 1938 book *The Ramparts We Watch*, which argued that military preparedness was no threat to American democratic institutions.[238]

Attempting to explain the "why" behind Pearl Harbor, Eliot put it this way. "Japan is cornered, surrounded by forces she cannot overcome, and to which, in the end, she must succumb," he pointed out astutely. To Eliot, December 7 marked not just the start of war for Americans, but "the beginning of the decline of the Japanese Empire."[239]

December 8 introduced many place names to Americans. They heard that Guam was in trouble, that Shanghai was defenseless with nearly 3,000 stranded Americans, that the Pan Am Clipper was in the war zone, west-bound to Wake Island and Midway. Many listeners checked their maps, which they would do for the rest of the war. General MacArthur issued reassurances from the Philippines: "My message is one of serenity and confidence." But follow-up stories observed that "Manila has not yet realized the portent of the news that we are at war," backed up with reports read by broadcaster Ford Wilkins that children still played in the Philippine capital's schoolyards while American planes patrolled overhead. The sense developed that no matter how relaxed MacArthur was, Manila was next.[240] John Daly reported from Manila, noting the geography lessons listeners faced. "Since early yesterday morning," he said, Americans were newly introduced to "such places as Mindanao, and Nichols Air Force Base."[241] Bob Trout handled the London report, noting how solemnly Members of Parliament received Churchill's description of the attack. "It was that kind of speech," Trout observed.[242] Raymond Clapper, Scripps-Howard columnist who did twice-a-week commentaries for Mutual, was proud that the United States "tried to the bitter end to avoid war." Clapper was far-sighted. "This is suicide for Japan. . . . Japan can only live by sea trade," he pointed out, "but she has chosen to war with the two other sea powers . . . Japan will be blasted, bombed, burned, starved. Her people will suffer ghastly tortures."[243]

How to report American losses presented a challenge. One way networks handled it was to avoid speculating on damage figures themselves, instead referring to enemy claims heard by short-wave monitoring systems. For example, John Daly at CBS relayed Japanese claims that the attack at Pearl constituted a "blow of annihilation," adding that Tokyo now claimed "our Pacific Fleet now consists of only two battleships, six cruisers, and one aircraft carrier."[244] These and other Japanese claims came not just from Tokyo stations, but from pickups of German broadcasts. German radio gave CBS the news that Japanese troops were moving through Thailand to attack Burma.

Covering Roosevelt's Day of Infamy speech, Albert Warner explained for CBS that White House rhetoric brought "Hitler squarely into the center of the picture of world aggression."[245] This was an important instance of how central Germany appeared even though Japan was the assailant. Broadcasts on CBS and NBC covered not just news from the Pacific, but from other fighting fronts, underscoring the notion of a world war and providing subliminal support for Roosevelt and Rainbow Five. In what presaged sad news to come, CBS reported on December 9 that enemy aliens, that is, Germans, Japanese, and Italian diplomats, were being rounded up for internment.[246] Soon, the definition of "enemy alien" was stretched much farther.

A common theme was the jumpy nerves of Americans. Pearl Harbor made it difficult to pooh-pooh the prospect that enemy planes might attack an American city. William Winter, CBS reporter in San Francisco, told of an air raid fright which alarmed the city, although "people talked proudly of how they had remained calm through the night." The mayor met with Civil Defense authorities to go over measures such as filling up bathtubs and improving the blackout. "Death and destruction at any moment is now a possibility as far as this coast is concerned," said Lieutenant General Dewitt, of the 4th Army, who added erroneously that "enemy planes were over this area last night and why they did not bomb San Francisco only God knows."[247] Such false alarms were not auspicious. Nor were reports like that of two Japanese arrested in Fresno with "elaborate motion picture equipment," the implication being that saboteurs were loose across the west. More reassuring was the anecdote Warner passed along for comic relief about a Chinese reporter in Washington who spent much of his time smiling and explaining to onlookers, "Not Japanese, Please!"[248]

CBS: Cecil Brown, Bob Trout, and John Raleigh

I happened to be walking along a part of the parade route this afternoon when my eye was caught by a poster on an office building. It pictured a battleship at sea, which is not unusual here, but the slogan underneath is something new. Gone was that familiar rhythmic slogan, "Lend to Defend!" In its place is a new motto, not quite so pleasing to the ear, but quite pleasing to the mind. . . "Lend to Attack!"

Bob Trout, CBS Radio, London [249]

One of the exotic locales under fire was the Dutch East Indies, where John M. Raleigh served as CBS' man in Batavia. Raleigh's reports were lengthy and literate; he was a superb stylist with a smooth delivery. When the CBS announcer uttered the signal, "Go ahead, Batavia . . . Go ahead, Batavia . . ." listeners hung in aural suspense for a few seconds while the signal transmitted. Then, Raleigh's story let them hear the latest from Holland's main Asian outpost. Raleigh made excellent use of local color, the staple put to great effect by Murrow, Sevareid, and the network's European reporters. On December 9, he had little hard news to report, aside from the fact that the NEI Army was calling up conscripts including natives. But his story bore the touches that made CBS News distinctive. Raleigh talked about driving during blackout, "a darkness filled with grim possibilities," adding that he had gotten "around to several Dutch clubs. I wanted to listen to what the Hollanders are saying and feeling." His club-hopping allowed him to report that the Dutch stood behind the war effort and were proud of their immediate declaration of war against Japan.[250]

Bob Trout remained the main CBS reporter from London, since Murrow was in the United States. Trout was a long-term CBS broadcaster whose tenure started during the 1930s, reading the spots for *Jack Armstrong, All-American Boy* during station breaks.[251] Now, Trout filled Murrow's chair. While he did not imitate Murrow, Trout delivered well-rounded dispatches. "London is not blinded by the fighting the Pacific sector to the fact that there are other sectors," Trout led off on December 9. Trout listed the latest claims made by Moscow, passed along news from the Libyan front, and cited a commando raid on the Dutch coast. He spent time describing how Pearl Harbor filled fellow American reporters in London with "a keen longing to be at home." Delicately, he mentioned the fact that to some reporters their work in Europe was a failure, because "They have told the story year after year, but their fellow Americans would not pay any attention."[252]

This was a sensitive issue. Trout was covering ground which caused Eric Sevareid and other correspondents agonized self-doubt. During the mid-1930s, when he graduated from the University of Minnesota, Sevareid was a committed isolationist. His stint in France showed him a demoralized and torpid republic unable to rouse itself from torpor in the face of attack. This convinced him that the war was vital to American interests. After France fell, Sevareid suffered from what he described "an incomprehensible trance." The momentum of events kept him going; "The gyroscopic motion of violent events has a way of keeping one upon one's feet."[253] Upon return to the United States, his inability to convince his fellow Americans that interventionism was necessary maddened him. In New York, he felt disoriented, in a cultural landscape "devoid of meaning."[254] Sevareid and other reporters formerly based in Europe worried that they had sounded the alarm and failed to rouse their listeners. Only a shift to Washington, which he called "the command post destined to rally the free men of earth," relieved his sense of anomie. Pearl Harbor abolished the national ambivalence Sevareid found so perplexing. Moreover, it filled him and his peers with a renewed sense of possibility for media. He came to appreciate "the importance and power of the 'observers,' all those who speak and write." Along with colleagues, Sevareid understood himself as playing a wartime role. "The nation had entered full into a war of words, and words were my business."[255]

Trout understood what Sevareid meant. On December 10, Trout mentioned that the British were fascinated by United States news. News in the United States was free and open, he pointed out, drawing a contrast to Britain, where the Ministry of Information kept its grip on the information outlet. Trout argued that Americans understood how freedom of information—which CBS wanted—benefitted the war effort. "This war is being fought with ideas, as well as bullets and bombs," he argued.[256] For balance, he pointed out that Americans should learn from British *sang-froid*. Trout described how they faced disaster with calmness. The sinking of *Repulse* and *Prince of Wales*, he noted, failed to cause panic. This story had special resonance since CBS Singapore correspondent Cecil Browne had sailed with *Repulse*. His status was uncertain. Browne's fate became clear the following day. He was alive and broadcasting. His dispatch was a dramatic account of his journey. He described the lack of British air cover, the onrush of Japanese torpedo-bombers. Amidst "flashes blinding, roars deafening," Browne endured three waves of torpedo attacks before abandoning ship. While in the water, he "saw the ships go down."[257] Browne later recapitulated the story in *Collier's*.

In Washington, Albert Warner covered domestic subjects, including political support for FDR, as well as accounts of sabotage and civil defense—the former all exaggerated, the latter general. President Roosevelt and the federal government were the focus of the capital beat. On December 13, mentioning that Bulgaria and Hungary followed Hitler and declared war on the United States, Warner quoted John Connally's explanation for American non-reciprocation. "Our declaration of war against Hitler includes all the little Hitlers who may echo his purpose," sneered the Texan. "What would Kossuth say if he could look down from his eminence . . . and witness the base servitude and foul ignominy in which Hungary has been engulfed?"[258] That was the same line taken by Representative Sol Bloom (D-NY). The New Yorker's dismissive response—"For the moment, we've got a job on our hands, but we'll get around to it"[259]—made it clear that the small fry in Hitler's alliance barely rated notice.

It rarely fell to studio-bound Warner to narrate a combat story. When it did, it was disturbing. On December 12, Warner covered the developing battle at Wake Island. He discussed presidential reaction to Wake's plight. The unfamiliar island was already doomed by superior Japanese numbers. Warner mentioned FDR's praise for Wake's defenders. The Marines, said the President, were doing "a perfectly magnificent job."[260] Warner added his own coda—"That small group of Marines holding out on Wake Island is likely to go down in history with the defenders of the Alamo, but, Washington hopes, with a happier ending."[261] Only now did Wake Island come to popular awareness. Roosevelt mentioned it in his Declaration speech, but the remote atoll was only known as a stopping-over point for Pan-Am's China Clipper passenger planes. Wake was an isolated, V-shaped speck of coral halfway between Honolulu and Japan.[262] Besides crabs, rats, seabirds, and fish, it was home to a garrison of Marines, sailors, pilots, and civilian contractors now under attack. The full story took two more weeks to disclose. On December 14, Warner said, he came to work in a taxi driven by a former Marine whose son was stationed at Wake. Warner said that the cabby had another son,

17, eager to join the Marines. In fact, said the taxi driver, he wanted to reenlist himself.[263] Warner's tale of familial devotion, tucked into a lengthy news report, functioned as a patriotic coda.

Meanwhile, John Raleigh was developing one of the more hopeful news angles of the early war. On December 14, the suave reporter played up the dangers Japan would face in tackling Java. The first was the Dutch Navy, Raleigh explained. Five days after the sinking of *Repulse* and *Prince of Wales*, Raleigh dwelt upon a different European naval tradition. "Again, the Royal Dutch Navy has struck, and struck well," began his upbeat report. Citing an official naval communique whose accuracy he assumed, Raleigh added the Dutch were racking up an impressive toll in the seas of Java, Celebes, and Banda, and the straits of Sunda and Makassar. Raleigh seconded Dutch claims sending six Japanese vessels—most recently, a tanker and cargo steamer—to the bottom. Dutch sub pens at Suribaya made that spot the busiest place on Java. Raleigh reminded listeners. "The Hollanders have always been seamen by nature. The wind and the waves are their natural element."[264] Careful listeners might have picked up the ominous admission from Batavia that Japanese vessels were active across the East Indies. Turning to land, Raleigh added that the Dutch were expert jungle fighters. "Fighting is all they know," Raleigh said of the Dutch Indian Army, a conglomeration of Dutch and local troops. He went on to point out that the steep mountains and forested canyons were infested with warrior tribes fond of "severing the enemy's head with a simple clean stroke."[265] Left begging was the question of how these tribal forces, headhunters or not, would react to an Asian assault on their colonial masters. Moreover, Raleigh's cheerful explanation that Batavia's many canals were a great help to local firefighters coping with bombing raids implied that Japan ruled the skies. Despite his upbeat tone, which made him sound as if he was narrating a spicy radio drama, Raleigh's broadcasts had implications to make listeners wonder how well the Dutch would fare against Japan.

NBC: H.V. Kaltenborn and Lowell Thomas

Not long ago, one irate customer asked, 'How in hell do you know all the answers?' My reply is that I don't know all the answers. I just do my best to supply answers to questions which puzzle or disturb millions of Americans.

H.V. Kaltenborn[266]

I have never heard anyone criticize Lowell Thomas for anything. If he has even one enemy in this world, I don't know who it is.

Dale Carnegie[267]

Sarnoff's network, while not lionized for its news, was nevertheless equipped to deliver comprehensive war coverage. Among its prime commentators were Baukhage,[268] H.V. Kaltenborn, and Lowell Thomas. Correspondents included specialists like Fred Bate, as well as print reporters like Robert St. John, who already had good reputations for war coverage.[269] Bate was Murrow's NBC counterpart in London, where he reported until injured by the bombing, prompting his return to New York.[270] St. John, who covered Al Capone and the Chicago mob during the 1930s, was in Hungary when Germany invaded Poland. His coverage of the early war culminated in a circuitous escape from the Balkans in 1941, which he chronicled in columns and a 1942 book. St. John went to London, filling the gap left by Bate's departure.[271] NBC used these professionals to make sense of reports, striving for the straightforward style the network called, "Unvarnished, untarnished, and true."[272]

Baukhage, 51, had studied at the Sorbonne and in Germany. His language skills aided him in his youthful reporting days, including a World War I stint as a *Stars & Stripes* staffer which he landed through the help of the assistant officer at the military paper, Steve Early.[273] When Early became Roosevelt's Press Secretary, Baukhage had a well-placed friend. December 7, 1941, gave Baukhage a claim to radio history, since he was the first to broadcast live from the White House. He described the scene. "Hardly more than minutes after news came . . . the first microphone ever set up in the White House press room was keeping me busy sending out the bulletins. Soon others were set up and the place was in bedlam."[274] Baukhage had reason to mull over the ironies. Just the day before, he visited the Japanese Embassy to chat with a fellow University of Chicago graduate. It was Kurusu, preparing for his visit to Cordell Hull. The two alumni discussed campus memories, while the Embassy buzzed around them. "There was great activity in the rooms I passed through," he recollected. "People hurrying about—stacks of paper in their hands. The next day I sat before a microphone in the White House press room reporting the attack on Pearl Harbor as those papers were being burned."[275]

Baukhage's NBC colleague, Kaltenborn, had a more colorful image. Born in Wisconsin in 1878, Kaltenborn grew up in a small lumber town. Volunteering for the Spanish-American War gave him his first overseas exposure. After Harvard, he commenced a newspaper career, dropping "Hans" and adopting "H.V." as more urbane and less German, an advantage during World War I.[276] Kaltenborn was present during radio's earliest days, making his debut broadcast in 1921.[277] Entranced, he started work for CBS in 1929, staying until 1940 when he decamped to NBC.[278] Control of his voice, along with an Old World enunciation, gave his tenor a vibrating quality when Kaltenborn was excited, which was often. When Frank Capra needed a radio commentator to make a cameo appearance in 1939's *Mr. Smith goes to Washington*, the director hired Kaltenborn. The same showy style made Kaltenborn a natural choice to deliver the voice-over for "The World of

Tomorrow" exhibit at New York's 1939 World's Fair.[279] A live battlefield broadcast during the Spanish Civil War brought him renown, along with his marathon coverage of the Munich negotiations in 1938.[280] By 1941, NBC was glad to have his reliable presence, as a trusted voice with credibility as a news analyst and years of experience covering Hitler and Europe.

Kaltenborn favored the Europe-first strategy. Even before the Pearl Harbor attack, he stressed the linkages between Japan and Germany. On November 28, he emphasized Mussolini's weakness, predicting that "at the first sign of a Hitler defeat, Italy will seek peace."[281] The Russian theater drew his attention. Kaltenborn argued that the Germans could be defeated if the United States kept the Red Army supplied. Kaltenborn predicted that setbacks in Russia could have a triggering effect in the Reich. "Germany will collapse from within just as soon as the German General Staff decides it cannot win the war," he argued. "Don't forget that a dictator always looks good up to the last five minutes."[282]

Kaltenborn adopted a reassuring note designed to counter hysteria. When *Repulse* and *Prince of Wales* provoked questions about the viability of capital ships, Kaltenborn discussed the relationship between naval and air power. "Battleships without control of the air have become a liability," he reported on December 12. "Air control, even without sea control, is an asset."[283] Kaltenborn went on to develop his theme that "bombers are more important than battleships." He kept concordance with the Mahan faith by interpreting Pacific air battles as adjuncts to naval strategy. "Sea power is still essential on the great ocean highways," he explained. "Air power is the dominant factor everywhere else."[284] Already, proposals for an Air Force separated from navy and army command were in discourse. Kaltenborn saw that as a negative. "Our Navy now has a first-class, well-rounded, well-integrated air force," he argued. "Our Army has made a magnificent beginning in the development of such a force."[285] An independent Air Force might harm morale and confuse logistics. Instead, Kaltenborn pointed to the merits of integrated air branches. "Every navy must have its own air force operating from ship and shore. Every army must have observation planes, interceptor planes, and dive bombers working in the closest coordination with ground forces."[286] Kaltenborn told listeners that Roosevelt understood air war. "Our Commander-in-Chief is air-minded," he promised. "He has just made Major General Arnold, chief of the Army's independent air arm, a lieutenant general. This and recent changes in the command at Hawaii recognize the growing importance of our air arm."[287]

Responding to popular jitters about the air raids on American cities, Kaltenborn called the idea that New York City could face a London-style blitz "absurd."[288] He reminded NBC listeners that the Luftwaffe had secure air bases scarcely 100 miles from the British capital, while "The Nazi airport nearest to New York is 3,000 miles distant." Only two kinds of raids against the Atlantic coast were feasible, Kaltenborn argued. The first would be what he termed "a long-distance stunt raid," in which bombers carrying a small payload ditched their craft since no plane had the fuel to return across the ocean. The second idea was that of a carrier-based raid. Theoretically, he admitted, a German surface ship could sneak through the British blockade to launch planes. But that was unlikely in the Atlantic. "This could be done much more easily by the Japs on the Pacific Coast than by the Nazis on the Atlantic Coast."[289] National polls placed Kaltenborn near the top of preferred radio pundits. A 1939 survey saw 20.8 percent of respondents choose him as their favorite, second only to another NBC figure, Lowell Thomas, who came in first with 24.8 percent.[290] Whereas Kaltenborn was verbose, Thomas was always brief and chipper. His audience appeal cut across all geographic regions and income levels, with the strongest favor in middle-class households.[291] A folk hero on his own merits, Thomas was a globetrotter linked to exciting people and places. He covered T.E. Lawrence and the Arab Revolt during World War I, popularizing "Lawrence of Arabia."[292] Cheerfulness was a part of his appeal, as was timing. Early in his career, Thomas was shared by CBS and NBC, before landing with Sarnoff's network for good during the early 1930s. He acknowledged his good luck in inheriting the slot made popular by his predecessor, Floyd Gibbons, which followed *Amos & Andy*.[293] Thomas' language was bouncy, his broadcasts sequential snippets of observation offered up while summarizing headlines. He viewed Hitler as the main world danger to freedom, arguing that patriotic Americans should vigorously oppose the *Fuhrer*. In 1940, Thomas co-authored a textbook called *Stand Fast for Freedom*, which featured numerous drawings of Uncle Sam staring down Hitler. Thomas asked pupils to imagine their feelings if a policeman knocked at their door. "Your mother," he explained, "in America, has no reason to fear a policeman. But in a dictatorship, she would be in a state of cold panic when she saw the officer outside the door."[294]

His support for Roosevelt in the wake of Pearl Harbor was unstinting. Thomas' first account, on December 8, described "the most momentous weekend in the history of our country."[295] Thomas recapped the Joint Session speech, mentioned Japanese moves in Thailand and Malaya, and stressed German news reports declaring that weather precluded Moscow's capture until spring. His first piece of "good news" was the tale of Colin Kelly, the American pilot credited with sinking the Japanese ship *Haruna* in what was supposedly a suicide attack. The truth behind this episode was uncertain, but Kelly became the first hero of the Pacific campaign.[296] Thomas was upbeat even when news was grim. He described MacArthur as having "cooped up the Japanese invaders of Luzon into three small areas,"[297] when in fact the Imperial Army was moving across the Philippine island with dispatch. In Malaya, where General Tomoyuki Yamashita's troops were earning him the sobriquet "Tiger of Malaya," Thomas admitted that the British were "having a tough time," but allowed that they were "holding their own."[298] Still, Thomas kept the trust of his listeners by adjusting his reports to meet the known facts, so when the front line in Malaya kept moving southward, he admitted that the British were losing ground, observing that Singapore was the ultimate goal. Days before Christmas, Thomas' attention went back to the Philippines. He announced the bombing of Manila on December 24, as well as the fall of the Wake Island garrison.[299] When describing the action at Wake, he said the news was "the same, heroically the same. The tiny garrison of Marines has sustained two more air attacks by the besieging Japanese. But," he added by way of finale, "They're fighting back."[300] That pugnacious touch was vintage Thomas.

MBS: Raymond Gram Swing

It is not to our reproach that we were caught by surprise. In one sense it is to our credit. For the only nations not caught by surprise are the military oligarchies, which are organized for attack. By its nature a democracy in peacetimes can think only of defense. And a nation that thinks in terms of defense is foredoomed to being taken by surprise. For that reason the price of democracy is high. But the price of utter safety is still higher. It is to be a nation of obedient soldiers whose lungs draw no breath of free air.

Raymond Gram Swing, December 10, 1941[301]

One radio analyst who enjoyed a reputation for being especially thoughtful and unusually accurate was Raymond Gram Swing. Although NBC picked up his WOR broadcasts, he belonged to Mutual and White Owl Cigars, his longtime sponsor. An admiring *Time* profile called him "MBS's one-man brain trust on world affairs," mentioning that Swing fans included Supreme Court Justice Felix Frankfurter, British Ambassador Lord Lothian, Tallulah Bankhead, and Nicholas Murray Butler.[302] Unusual among American broadcasters, he had numerous listeners in Britain,[303] thanks in part to the respect of the BBC's Sir John Reith. In May 1940, the British started targeting American audiences through directed programming on the BBC World Service.[304] "Britain Speaks," a short-wave series in which high-profile commentators chatted conversationally to Americans about the aiding the Allied war effort, was augmented when Mutual—anxious for a distinctive news source but up against budgetary constraints—agreed to broadcast BBC news twice a day.[305] This led the BBC to program Swing's broadcasts for its own home listeners.

Swing had a style all his own. Tall, slump-shouldered, given to tweed suits and tortoiseshell glasses, his on-air persona was devoid of gimmickry. As *Time* put it, Swing told "what's what simply, calmly, right, with no flash-flashes, no calamitous crescendos, no special hallmark of his own except a level, almost hushed, 'Good night.'"[306] But if his radio delivery was plain, his life was unusual. A minister's son who rebelled against his strict upbringing, Swing dropped out of Oberlin and took up newspapering in his teens, heading to Europe as a foreign correspondent. Marriage to a French bride during World War I produced two children, but also a divorce. World War I made him famous, when Rudyard Kipling picked up the story of how, sailing aboard a Turkish freighter during the Dardanelles campaign, the calm American took it upon himself to answer a British submarine commander's challenge, "Who are you? What ship?" with a surprising, "I am Raymond Swing of the *Chicago Daily News*."[307] His second wife, Betty Gram, was an ardent suffragette and aspiring singer when he met her performing in Berlin in 1919. Revealing his non-traditional streak, he took her name and she took his when they married.[308] After years as a foreign correspondent, Swing joined the staff of the left-leaning *Nation* in 1934, before becoming Washington correspondent for the *Economist*. His 1935 book, *Forerunners of American Fascism*, skewered figures such as racist Senator Theodore Bilbo (D-MS), megalomaniac publisher William Randolph Hearst, and radio demagogue Father Charles Coughlin. He even sounded warning bells about the New Deal, viewing concentration of economic power under federal auspices with alarm, but crediting Roosevelt's commitment to democracy as a saving factor.[309]

During the late 1930s, Swing emerged as an important explicator of American policy to the British. The twists and turns surrounding the Neutrality Acts bewildered and exasperated Britons, who viewed American policy as evasive. "Things American" was the name of his program, which he shared with Elmer Davis. "If I can have my moment of vanity," he said of the broadcasts to Britain, "I like to think that I have contributed to understanding between England and America."[310] On Mutual's 110 network stations, Anglophilia and support for Roosevelt were Swing hallmarks.

His first chance for sustained comment on attack came on December 8. Swing called Japan's blow an act of "perfidy." But typically, he made a careful distinction: "The perfidy was not the motive for the attack."[311] The motive, he said, was "Japan's knowledge that it could not wheedle the United States into sacrificing its principles in the Far East and Europe." His insightful analysis seconded points raised by Japanese leaders, although Swing could not have known that. Japan, he explained "Had only two choices, to recant its dream of conquest or to go to war. To recant was hard, if not politically impossible. To go to war was politically easier. And since the choice was for war, Japan struck first and with all the surprise it could conjure up."[312] Almost alone among American commentators, Swing was able to identify the reasoning behind the Japanese decision. He did not excuse it, but neither did he peddle the simplistic idea that the Japanese were nasty sneaks. Swing interpreted what happened as an affair between two antagonistic nations caught up in mutually annihilating courses of action. His cool-headed ability to pierce through the veil of heat which enveloped war events became the ongoing standard of Swing's commentary.

Taking Japanese attacks across the Western and Southern Pacific in account, Swing explained how much "prolonged and painstaking preparation" obviously went into Tokyo's plans. Swing identified Singapore as Japan's great priority, not because it was more important than Pearl Harbor, but because it could more easily be captured.[313] "Singapore is the key of the South West Pacific," he lectured, "and so long as it stands, Japan will not be able to hold the riches it is set on possessing in that region."[314] Almost alone, Swing foresaw an all-out Japanese attack on Singapore from the landward northern side. Next would come the Philippines. Already, he pointed out, American air bases were under bombardment, as were army posts on Luzon, Mindanao, and Baguio. Swing saw the line of attack pointing to Manila, MacArthur's HQ.[315]

When *Prince of Wales* and *Repulse* went down, Swing called the loss a turning point in the history of naval and air warfare. Among his major themes was the hard fact that the offensive belonged to Japan. "Before Pearl Harbor was attacked, we were already on the defensive," he pointed out. "That defeat made us more so." Subsequent disasters, like the sinking of the Royal Navy ships, the advance of Japan's army towards Singapore, or the retreat of American forces in the Philippines, only added to the defensive nature of the war's early phase.[316] Swing was sober about Japanese strength. "Japan has all the early advantages by air power," he said, adding that only immediate dispatch of American and British planes would tilt the balance. But since Swing kept his eyes on Europe as well, he saw such resupply an unlikely course, lest it denude air power in the Atlantic and Mediterranean, where the Allies could ill afford it.[317]

Swing came as close as anyone could to admitting that lands held by Americans in the far Pacific were in terminal shape. "The British have a better chance to hold Singapore than we have to keep the Philippines," he contended. He admitted, "Anything held in the immediate future in the western Pacific is held more by heroism than by weight of power."[318] These were potentially controversial points of view, which went against the sentiment that righteous anger would swiftly tame the enemy. Swing gave his listeners no false hopes for fast reversals of bad fortune. Instead, he gave them accuracy. When Americans began to put faith in the coalesced command with British and Dutch forces, Swing was mordant. Look to Crete, he urged listeners. There, the British had tried to hold off a German attack through mastery of the sea. But German air power—in support of paratroop attacks—meant that the Royal Navy's main task at Crete wound up being to evacuate British soldiers. The Dutch Indies, Swing said, promised the same result, because the Japanese possessed the combination of ships and planes in force.[319] Taking issue with the traditional Naval Idea, which Swing felt was ossified, he likened the oceans to America's Maginot Line. "As a nation," he reminded all, "we had pride in the fleet. We were going to blow Japan out of the water. Today, we are sorely wounded in the Pacific."[320] The only consolation Swing offered was dour. "There is, however, one mercy in this grievous situation. Our Maginot Line has fallen at the outset of our entry into the war. Our defeat has come at the beginning, and it is, in effect, only the loss of a great battle, not of the war. But it is a costly battle, more costly than may be realized."[321]

Swing was no defeatist. "The war will be won," he promised, "and for two fundamental reasons. We can outproduce the Axis. And we can out-will the Axis."[322] Again displaying his nose for essentials, Swing already interpreted the war as a showdown between competing economies, as well as competing militaries. He gave full attention to the ideological dimensions of the conflict. This gave the Allies an advantage, he felt. "Free men merged in a single endeavor are mightier than any combination of underlings."[323] For the rest of December, he stayed with the theme that wars were not won by machinery, but by spirit. "The spirit of free peoples, once they are aroused, and once they are sufficiently armed, will sweep away any foe."[324] That optimism line came with a caveat. Always, Swing added, it was necessary for those free peoples to cast aside the comfy but misleading myths of the past. "We must face reality, purge the illusions, and work," he said, in language that would have fit into a Roosevelt speech.[325] In short, Swing said, the war could be won if Americans admitted to themselves that their old solutions to world problems were outmoded, that their new enemy was formidable, and that only new approaches to the war's problems would suffice in the current crisis. There would be defeats and tragedies before the war turned in America's direction. The sooner listeners accustomed themselves to that, the better.[326]

Looking back at year's end, Swing felt that 1941s two major events were Hitler's attack on the Soviet Union and Japan's attack on the United States. "In these two events," he explained, "the war reached its destined proportions. It became global in fact, whereas before it had been only global potentially. Swing took special care to explain how the United States fit into the larger war puzzle. Swing told listeners that "only the swiftness" of the attack in Hawaii was a real surprise. He reminded Americans that they had debated the war for years, "from hamlet to metropolis," going over the cases for and against involvement. December 7 took them by surprise, he said, but the war was something they understood before that date. "Before they struck us, our ideas had become clear and steady. We knew what the war was about, what our contribution had to be at a minimum, and we knew we would make it a maximum contribution if the need became apparent."[327] Swing's main message to Americans in the first month after Pearl Harbor was that the defeat, though grave, was not irreversible.

CBS: Eric Sevareid

The stunned and anxious nation slept badly that night, I have no doubt. For me there was a feeling of enormous relief; the feeling that we had won, even before the fight began, had survived, even before the onslaught. I slept like a baby.

–Eric Sevareid, remembering December 7, 1941[328]

On November 10, 1941, Murrow returned to the United States. The Battle of Britain was over and London was no longer the pivotal war theater. Bob Trout could handle the beat while Murrow took on domestic duties, including a cross-country speaking tour. On December 2, at the Waldorf-Astoria in New York, CBS feted its hero with a star-spangled banquet. Attendees included boss William Paley, colleagues Elmer Davis, Paul White, and William Shirer, and Librarian of Congress Archibald MacLeish. MacLeish spoke memorably: "You burned the city of London in our houses and we felt the flames that burned it," he recalled. "You laid the dead of London at our doors and we knew that the dead were our dead, were mankind's dead."[329] His encomium credited Murrow with convincing Americans that the war was vital to their lives. MacLeish was ardently interventionist, but his was not the only voice raised in Murrow's honor. *Time* paid heed to Murrow's performance, at the same time taking a dig at competitor Dorothy Thompson. "No bunk, no journalese, no sentimentality," claimed the magazine. "When Dorothy Thompson was telling the British that the poets of the world were on their side, he spoke for the sweating people who doubted the poets' effectiveness."[330] The evening showed the rationale behind Murrow's return. At first, the idea was to use his talks to combat isolationism, as well as to let him recuperate and sell *This is London*. But Pearl Harbor saw Murrow camping out at the CBS Washington bureau. This was not the first time Murrow's presence interrupted the work of his protégé, Sevareid. That December, the junior CBS man was tucked into his Washington post. After leaving France in a hurry, barely ahead of the advancing Germans, Sevareid had tried to make a go of reporting in London. There, he found himself overshadowed by his superior. Now, in Washington, Severeid carved out space as a domestic commentator. Murrow, slated to be on the road for much of the winter, would report in occasionally.

It fell to Sevareid to draw sense from the first flood of Pearl Harbor news and rumor. His December 8 report covered the conflicting damage claims, which accurately noted the potency of aerial torpedoes while grossly overstating Japanese air losses. Sevareid exercised the artfulness which made him a Murrow favorite, and which distinguished him as a powerful broadcaster in his own right. The best Sevareid broadcasts from France, like the best Murrow reports from London, went beyond reportage. They were real aural literature in their command of language and mastery of setting. From Washington that December 8, Sevareid's talent showed itself again. "This is a cold, grey morning in the capital of the United States," he observed. "At six, I could see lights still blazing in the Embassies along Massachusetts Avenue, in the State and Treasury Department, and one solitary lighted window high in the corner of the White House."[331] Left unasked was the question of whose light that was. Hopkins? A clerk? Listeners could also imagine their President, up before the capital itself, working on his papers for the coming Congressional address. Sevareid continued his *mis-en-scene*.

Troops, in full kits, were guarding the bridges around the War and Navy Departments. . . . The President has had almost no sleep, but his friend said he was on top of his form last night, calm, cool-headed, working rapidly and precisely.[332]

Sevareid refrained from mentioning that the friend praising Roosevelt was Murrow. Later that day, Sevareid put forth more lush detail. "The Germans are still around, on their respective jobs. Kurt Sell, correspondent for the official German news agency was present as usual when I walked into Mr. Hull's press conference," he pointed out. "The Japanese reporters have disappeared. One of them, though born here and an American citizen, became panicky. He packed a bag and was caught as he boarded a train last night in Union Station. By now close to a thousand Japanese have been arrested in the country."[333]

One of Sevareid's main subjects that December was the transformation of Washington into a war capital. He chronicled: "soldiers with steel helmets and bayonets" around sensitive spots like the Munitions Building, noted the diligence with which guards in federal buildings checked passes. But occasionally, he let slip a small humanizing touch, finding humor in the capital's wartime reconfiguration. "In front of the new War Department building was an armored car with a machine gun mounted in it," he reported. "When I passed, the four soldiers manning the car were reading a newspaper."[334] With his eye for the clever feature, Sevareid headed for the Japanese Embassy, which had become "a dormitory" full of diplomats and journalists. "They passed the hat today to collect enough cash to buy an order of groceries—lamb, a crate of eggs and five hundred pounds of rice. The grocer refused to take their check."[335]

Sevareid returned to the "Washington at War" angle often, as a closer to his broadcasts. On December 10, he noted that "army and navy uniforms are sprinkled throughout the crowds in the streets, on the buses, in theaters and cafes. Military tailors are doing a land-office business." He mentioned guards on duty at the White House: "In the half light at six this morning, I could see them slowly patrolling in twos, their bayonets faintly gleaming."[336] Such touches of scenery were lovely and non-controversial. Harder to manage was the task of deciphering official military communiques. In his mid-day broadcast that same day, Sevareid announced the very first War Department communique, noting that "it announces a victory for the United States." Going on to describe the contents, he passed along the claim that, at Luzon, "Our army and navy have thrown the Japanese back into the sea."[337] Those claims were overblown, and Sevareid seemed to know it. Several times in this newscast, he stressed the opacity of the facts, noting that "the communique is based on reports received late last night from General Douglas MacArthur, Chief of the Far East Command." Even if the initially positive reports were accurate, Sevareid admitted, "This does not mean that all danger to the islands from the landing parties is ended—it does not even mean that other landing parties have not seized beaches since this attempt was repulsed."[338] Moving on to the loss of *Repulse* and *Prince of Wales*, he emphasized "extreme shock" and "stupefaction" in naval circles that the news engendered, going so far as to compare it to the surprise felt over Pearl Harbor.[339] Wrapping up, he mentioned alien round-ups, concentrating on Germans and Italians as much as Japanese, passing along procedural clarifications regarding internment protocols from Attorney General Francis Biddle.

This exposed a problem inherent in Sevareid's Washington position. While he was close to the epicenter of decision-making, his reportage could not go beyond reiterating official accounts gussied up with local color. For a professional whose life was marked by a zest for adventure—as a teenager, Sevareid canoed from his North Dakota home all the way to Hudson Bay simply to prove that the Vikings might have been able to explore the American interior—Washington was important but dull. His post-Pearl Harbor reports were delivered in a "calm, rather sad voice" encapsulating CBS' refusal to "sugar-coat bad news."[340] But in his heart, Sevareid confronted the same questions he struggled with in London. His place in the war remained provisional. Eventually, he would make a change. For the moment, he concentrated on Washington. On December 14, he noted "a spirit of high optimism today among Navy men here;" he duly recapped Congressional budgetary moves, an update by Maxim Litvinov on the Russian front; naval communiques regarding "the remarkable resistance of the small band of marines and sailors on Wake Island."[341]

His narrative style remained replete with little stories and interpretive accents which were more than news recaps. Cogitating about the "suddenness with which the political opponents here resolve bitter quarrels," he was moved to historical reminiscing. "This afternoon I was sitting at home reading a book," he explained. "It was written 400 years ago. You have heard of the author. His name is Machiavelli. It is a study of the naked mechanism of power and as men have pointed out before, Adolf Hitler seems to have memorized the precepts of the author," he intoned.

> But there is one lesson Hitler and the Japanese rulers apparently forgot: The Veienti thought that, by assailing the Romans a moment when they were divided by internal dissensions, they would have an easy victory over them; but their very attack restored union amongst the Romans, and that caused the defeat of the Veienti.

Dissensions in republics, he explained, Machiavelli saw as "generally the result of idleness and peace, whilst apprehension and war are productive of union."[342]

Historicizing was creative, but it was not active reporting. There were stories to ferret out, such as Secretary Knox's return from a fact-finding trip to Pearl

Harbor, part of the process that would tie blame for Pearl Harbor around the neck of Admiral Husband Kimmel and Lt. General Walter C. Short. But whether that played out in formal proceedings or backrooms, it would be a tale of government process. Sevareid needed a more active environment. In January, when the Third Pan American Conference convened, in Rio de Janeiro, with an eye towards coordinating hemispheric policies and short-circuiting Argentine sympathies for the Axis, Sevareid was the right candidate to cover the event.

Keeping up with the war: Walter Lippmann

My dear Mr. Lippmann: Sincere thanks for your kindly thought. I shall never forget our negotiations of the last days of December 1918 and your understanding and help given to our cause then and ever since, nor our more recent conversations in Geneva, either. With all my best wishes in return . . .
Letter to Walter Lippmann from Eduard Benes, President of Czechoslovakia, January 14, 1936[343]

I have admired tremendously the articles you have written lately. When you analyze a situation, complicated as it may be, you make it so clear and throw such an honest light on it, that the solution of the problem appears with an implacable logic to the reader, even when you don't formulate it yourself . . .
Letter to Walter Lippmann from Eve Curie, August 21, 1941[344]

Dear Walter, It is now time for the sword rather than the diplomat—and I note your preaching of a Unified Plan—so I send you and Helen for Christmas a General about Generals. We still think him a very good one. I wouldn't tell you what hope we build on comradeship now and after with the U.S. and how we count on your instruction. I hope we at this end will be wise about it, too. England—or perhaps only Whitehall—had a rather petulant, frustrated autumn. But I think we will throw it off!—From Nevile Butler
Christmas card from Nevile Butler, Counselor, British Embassy, to Walter & Helen Lippmann, December 19, 1941[345]

Walter Lippmann's contacts made up his greatest asset as a columnist. Every day, correspondence from the world's cognoscenti crossed his desk. Generals, authors, scientists, senators—anyone with a claim to importance was likely to be in some degree of touch with Washington's wise man. Probably the sincerest testament to Lippmann's importance as a nexus for information was the fact that Mary Price, his secretary, was a member of the KGB spy network run by Jacob Golos and Elizabeth

Bentley, an arm of the CPUSA's "secret party apparatus" designed to gather useful intelligence for the Cominform and Soviets.[346] Price, who worked for Lipppmann until 1943, was valuable to her spy masters because, as the nation's most prestigious expert on current affairs, Lippmann enjoyed access to the powerful. This made him a rich espionage target. His secretary's spy role was unknown to Lippmann, whose ideology was nuanced but who was not communist.[347]

That winter, Lippmann had two main professional tasks at hand: keeping up with his contacts and writing his "Today and Tomorrow" column for the *Herald-Tribune*. Lippmann was one of the rare breed who managed the transition from *wunderkind* to *eminence grise*. Even as a young man, he always seemed a graybeard. He was a member of Harvard's famous Class of 1910, which included H.V. Kaltenborn, Heywoud Broun, and T.S. Eliot. Kaltenborn remembered him as "an earnest hardworking intellectual who was well known in Cambridge respectfully as one of Harvard's bright young boys."[348] Another classmate, radical John Reed, was moved to poetry on the subject:

Lippmann,—calm, inscrutable,
Thinking and writing clearly, soundly, well;
All snarls of falseness swiftly piercing through,
His keen mind leaps like lightning to the True;
Our all unchallenged Chief! But . . . one
Who builds a world, and leaves out all the fun, —
Who dreams a pageant, gorgeous, infinite,
And then leaves all the color out of it, —
Who wants to make the human race and me,
March to a geometric Q.E.D.[349]

Lippmann's position as a rising Harvard intellectual was more complex than many understood. He was a highly assimilated Jew. In 1922, over his own objections and those of former president Charles W. Eliot, Harvard instituted the informal, inflexible quota on Jewish applicants. Lippmann took the university to task, writing that, "Harvard, with the prejudices of a summer hotel; Harvard, with the standards of a country club, is not the Harvard of her greatest sons."[350] The issue at stake was principle, not Lippmann's own move beyond the confines of his cultural heritage. That breakout was already accomplished; when it came to Judaism, Lippmann neither denied nor practiced.

Part of the *New Republic* founding editorial board under Herbert Croly, Lippmann analyzed World War I, its causes, and the prospects for improvements in the international system. In 1916, he summed up his attitude by summoning up the Naval Idea. "The outstanding fact of this war for America is our relation to the Power which controls the seas."[351] He explained that tensions with Germany were the "direct result of British naval policy," that American access to markets across the world depended upon coordination with Britain. "The supreme question of foreign policy is our relation to the British Empire," he insisted, "The supreme danger lies in ignoring it or challenging it; and the greatest hope, I believe, for western civilization lies in agreement with it."[352] Lippmann wrote out his vision of a world in which stable, strong, and open ties of trade and intercourse bound powerful nations together in collaborative prosperity, in his 1916 volume, *The Stakes of Diplomacy*.

It took faith in theory over practice to look at World War I as an opportunity for progress. Wilson, who saw the carnage as the bitter fruits of an old world order needing replacement, had such faith, but Lippmann could not sustain it. For him, the devastation of 1914–1918 wrought a permanently changed world view, in which the potential of rational improvement was always accompanied by danger from the irrational, violent side of humanity.[353] These included tribal nationalism and ideological rigidity, both of which led to competition and violence. Nationalism, he termed "the primitive stuff of which we are made, our first loyalties, our first aggressions, the type and image of the soul . . . fixed in the nursery."[354] Only through constant, unbiased examination could international relations be conducted without resultant chaos. "Unless our ideas are questioned," he wrote in *The Stakes of Diplomacy*, "They become part of the furniture of eternity. It is only by incessant criticism, by constant rubbing in of differences, that any of our ideas remain human and decent."[355]

Because he saw the association between nationalism and "the essence of our being,"[356] Lippmann interpreted postwar developments as proving the point. Accompanying Colonel Edward M. House to Europe as part of Wilson's support team, Lippmann had a close perch at the attempt to recalibrate international affairs. In subsequent books, such as *A Preface to Morals* and *Public Opinion*, Lippmann elaborated his themes, but never lost his conviction that disaster across the world was most likely when subrational political impulses intruded into affairs of state. This overall stance permeated his "Today and Tomorrow" columns for the *Herald-Tribune* as well.

"Public Opinion" became a recognizable term during Lippmann's career, synonymous with polling data culled by experts like Gallup and Roper.[357] Earlier, during the 1920s, Lippmann used the "phantom public" as a phrase, implying the changeable nature of the citizenry. Trained professionals in fields such as politics and journalism would need to explain and execute the proper policies as part of their leadership role in society, he believed. By the 1930s, as Gallup and peers made a new science of their field, polling experts added themselves to the list of leaders. The charts, graphs, and data which they generated lent attention to the idea that the public's wishes were more accessible than before.[358] Lippmann was willing to study the data, but he never abandoned his belief that the many-headed mass needed to be pointed or driven in the right direction.

By 1941, Lippmann was "columnist of record" when it came to serious analysis of politics and diplomacy. While his personal life entailed travails and drama, including global fame, a gruesome divorce, and a happier remarriage, Lippmann's public image was that of a calm sage who sat above the fray and proffered his wisdom to those willing to learn from it.

World War II only accentuated the pace of his correspondence. He cabled Ambassador to France William Bullit during the German 1940 *blitzkrieg* asking him to help the family of an émigré French friend, who were marooned without papers and fearful of falling into German clutches.[359] He and journalist William Henry Chamberlin waged an epistolary spat over whether Chamberlin unfairly impugned him in a book which claimed that Lippmann was part of a pro-war intellectual clique in 1917. Lippmann indignantly refused Chamberlin's qualified apology, demanding a full retraction.[360] Alistair Cooke sought Lippmann's input for a collected volume he wanted to assemble dealing with the politics of neutrality.[361] Bernard Baruch sent him a long letter describing his difficulties in rousing Washington officialdom to the dangers of war, "pounding away, under and over because I find that the most effective way, trying to make the Army, Navy, and all the authorities aware of what is taking place."[362] Lippmann and Van Wyck Brooks exchanged mutual expressions of pleasure at a recent meeting.[363] Max Ascoli wrote him in July 1941, importuning the columnist's help in refuting Congressional claims that Ascoli was a Communist.[364] James Byrne passed along his correspondence with Al Smith, in which he asked for help countering Irish-American isolationism.[365] Late in the summer of 1941, Eve Curie wrote from New York, accepting Lippmann's invitation to visit his vacation home at Mount Desert, Maine.[366] Towards the end of the summer, Lippmann received a long collection of transcribed German shortwave broadcasts.[367] Lippmann and Gaillard Lapsley exchanged thoughts on the current situation of mutual friend Bernard Berenson, whose fate in Italy was a source of concern.[368] In fact, Lippmann served as a sort of focal point for correspondence regarding Berenson's fate, as well as the status of his art collection.[369] Advertising titan Bruce Barton wrote to Lippmann during Fall 1941, exploring the question of munitions production quotas, paper shortages, and governmental handling of supplies.[370] After apologizing for his delay in responding to an earlier letter, Noel Coward expressed hopes that Lippmann would visit London.[371] Two days before the attack, Lippmann wrote to Giiti Imai, New York-based Staff Correspondent of Tokyo's *Ashahi Shimbun*, agreeing to an interview with Takatika Hosokawa, provided the Japanese reporter could make it to Washington.[372] On December 6, Brigadier General Mark Clark wrote to mention how much he enjoyed chatting with Lippmann at a recent cocktail party, inviting the columnist to visit him at the army's General Headquarters.[373] Two days after the attack, old Harvard friend William Henry Chadbourne, New York progressive Republican, praised Lippmann's first post-attack column, "Wake Up, America," as his best ever. Looking ahead, Chadbourne wondered to Lippmann: "Don't you think the historians of the future in looking back upon the Second World War may conclude that the Japanese attack was the most fortunate thing that could have come to America?"[374]

The column winning Chadbourne's praise was but the first in a series of *Herald-Tribune* pieces in which Lippmann stressed to readers that the formal onset of war demanded a new national attitudinal framework. In this call for a more ordered approach to the national emergency, Lippmann operated very much in his philosophical element. "The first test has already been put upon us: it is whether we shall meet our first great defeat as men and women with clear eyes and stout hearts, or as a frightened crowd lashed into a frenzy of futility by panic mongers," he wrote on December 11.[375]

Lippmann's readership included Washington's power elites, and it was to them he directed his warning against panicky or opportunistic reactions. "The clatter for hearings, debates, and scapegoats does not come from those upon whom the nation must rely—from those who have foreseen the peril and have sought against persistent organized obstruction to avert it and prepare for it."[376] While the call for hearings would not be quelled, Lippmann's point was twofold. First, he wanted to prevent isolationists from adopting an "I-Told-You-So" position and arguing that American moves away from strict neutrality did bring war. Second, he wanted to ensure that leadership's emphasis would be on planning for military contingencies, not on looking back to cast aspersions.

When potentially controversial issues arose, such as censorship, Lippmann explained them in basic terms. "Some Necessary Measures" was the title of his December 13 column. He admitted that "No war can be conducted without censorship . . . Let us stop doing badly what has to be done because we do not like to look at it directly"[377] Lippmann knew that censorship was inevitable. What he called for was censorship that worked well, keeping intelligence away from the enemy while providing the American people information they needed. He also urged free market-oriented readers put off by the term "price controls" to get over their aversion by accepting that "in a total mobilization, the use of all essential goods and scarce goods has to be rationed."[378] Lippmann worried most about repeating what he saw as an error of 1917, "fighting a separate war as an associate rather than as an ally. It was that mistake which destroyed our influence at the peace conference and robbed us of the fruits of victory."[379] Having seen at close hand the failure of Wilson's postwar planning, he now wrote in favor of close Anglo-American coordination. Lippmann already contemplated a more successful postwar outcome.

Lippmann chastised leaders who failed to live up to his standards. This included Roosevelt. When word came out that New York Mayor Fiorello LaGuardia and First Lady Eleanor Roosevelt would play leading roles in coordinating Civil Defense policy, the pundit was scathing, terming the idea "nonsense" and charging the President with failing to move beyond his opportunistic political style. What the situation—and Lippmann—demanded was nothing less than a wholesale reorganization of home defense, with proper military organization "concerned with service to the American forces and the men of the merchant fleet and the men in the war industries, with the training of nurses and nurses' aides and medical auxiliaries and with activities to keep civilians fit."[380] Lippmann derided the possibility that the First Lady or Mayor were up to the task. "How can the home front be organized properly when we find Mrs. Roosevelt talking about air raids in one breath and in the next about what kind of toys to give children for Christmas?"[381] This was Lippmann at his purest: it was time to shove the political appointees aside and make room for a qualified elite. He stuck to that message through the holidays. Before Christmas, he insisted that American intervention in Europe was not only necessary, but desired by smart Europeans. "They have always looked to us—even in the days when we were paralyzed by our debate,"[382] he said, with an eye still on the shape of the postwar world. After Christmas, he warned readers that the nation "was not doing all that it is capable of doing. It is not doing a third of what it can and should do."[383] At issue, Lippmann warned, was securing maximum effectiveness from national resources, including industry and agriculture. He was an unabashed command-and-control supporter. A rational allocation of resources by rational leaders was his goal. Until the entire national economy was channeled towards victory, Americans would simply "gaze fondly but ineffectively upon our superior resources" without harnessing those to defeat the Axis.[384] Here, Lippmann's ire was aimed at the American people. William Knudsen could not "be expected to think out just what war work a manufacturer of bronze grave markers in New Hampshire is fitted to do; that manufacturer himself should be sitting up nights and Sundays and holidays with the heads of other metal-working firms near him studying what they can do, singly or combined, that is useful to the war."[385] Always hostile to the specter of socioeconomic inefficiency, Lippmann was now propelled by the force of war to make ever more plain his belief that organization under effective leadership was the key to American success. "The only practical way to launch the all-out war program and mobilize at once the vast unused energies of the people," wrote the man who forged his notions under the old Progressive faith in marshaling human energies and targeting them towards worthy goals. "It will cause a great dislocation. But to be at war, not phony war but real war, is to be dislocated."[386]

Drew Pearson: The Washington Merry-Go-Round

When Hitler rose to power in Europe, a collection of un-American crackpot intellectuals, intrigue-lovers, revolutionaries and plain crooks saw an opportunity to get rich over here and at the same time build up their apparent importance. Pearson is just one example but we use him here because he worked out of Washington and we know him. And how.

Cissy Patterson, Publisher, Washington Times-Herald[387]

Washington wisdom holds that one can learn much about powerful figures by the enemies they make. The exercise of political power leads to rivalries and bad feelings, winners and losers. The pragmatic side of the capital city also prompts reconciliations, since shifting fortunes might require help tomorrow from the foe of today. One who never minded enemies was Drew Pearson. Many in the capital mounted encomia from the powerful on their office walls to show their own importance, but Pearson could have collected imprecations from those who hated him. "A chronic liar," complained President Roosevelt.[388] "A slippery, devious fellow, absolutely insensitive to the inhibitions of truth and ethics," charged Westbrook Pegler.[389] "He gathers slime, mud and slander from all parts of the earth and lets them ooze out through his radio broadcasts and through his daily contributions to . . . newspapers," railed Senator Theodore Bilbo (D-MS).[390] Pearson enjoyed such discomfiture. He liked Roosevelt personally, even if the feeling was unreciprocated. Pegler was a hated competitor, Bilbo a segregationist whose vituperation Pearson returned in kind.

Born in Evanston, Illinois, in 1897, Pearson moved to Pennsylvania when his father became a professor at Swarthmore. Upon joining the faculty of the Quaker college, Pearson's Methodist father—along with his Jewish wife and their four children—converted to Quakerism.[391] Growing up in that faith's pacifist tradition, Pearson joined his family on the Chatauqua circuit.[392] The experience lent young Drew a gathering sense for the theatrical. He attended Phillips Exeter Academy on scholarship, then graduated from Swarthmore before assisting Quaker war relief efforts for World War I refugees in the Balkans. He arrived in Washington, D.C., where, in 1921, he wooed Felicia Patterson, daughter of Eleanor "Cissy" Patterson. Felicia's father was an impecunious Polish count, long divorced from Cissy, who paid him a handsome settlement to be rid of him. Cissy was a publishing heiress, cousin of Colonel Robert McCormick, destined to become editor of Washington's *Times-Herald*. Cissy strongly supported the pairing when Pearson married Felicia.[393] Cissy presented the couple with a round-the-world honeymoon, which Pearson treated as a chance to jump-start his investigative reporting career.[394]

Neither Pearson's career nor his marriage was tranquil. He moved through several posts, serving as Foreign Editor for the *United States Daily* (which became *US News & World Report*), diplomatic correspondent for the *Baltimore Sun*, writer for the *Times-Herald*, and founding President of the State Department Correspondents Association. Pearson showed the tenacity common to the best reporters. Probably the most propitious connection he made was the friendship with Robert S. Allen, *Christian Science Monitor* Washington Bureau Chief. The two collaborated on a 1931 book, *Washington Merry-Go-Round*, which exposed ineptitude in Herbert Hoover's administration.[395]

Felicia remained a wanderer. Born in Austro-Hungarian Moravia in 1905, her mother took to London in 1907. Some called it kidnapping; Cissy tapped Washington connections and President Taft appealed to Czar Nicholas to prevent subject Count Gizycki from pursuing his ex-wife and daughter.[396] The pattern repeated itself when, amidst Felicia and Drew's divorce, she fled for Europe with daughter, Ellen. Doggedly, Drew chased them, using his own contacts and eventually gaining custody of Ellen.[397] He had the support of Cissy,[398] who was purchasing the *Times-Herald*.[399] In the early 1930s, she gained control over the Hearst chain's *Times* and the *Times-Herald*, merging the two under the *Times-Herald* banner.[400] *Washington Merry-Go-Round* became a hit column, syndicated in 620 papers. It featured Allen and Pearson in a good guy/bad guy routine. Tales of scandal and incompetence were the column's mainstay.[401] Adding to his life's melodrama, Pearson took a controversial and very lucrative position as Western Hemisphere director for the Irish Sweepstakes. Under his direction, the American division of the Lottery overtook the parent Irish branch in profitability.[402] Enemies screeched about Pearson's link to an illegal gambling operation, but he shrugged off the complaints.

Pearson married his second wife, Luvie, who became the *Times-Herald* movie reviewer with Cissy's assent.[403] His second marriage was tempestuous but durable. The Pearsons were one of the city's major power couples on their Potomac estate. Drew Pearson also moved into radio with Allen, doing the on-air version of the *Merry-Go-Round* for NBC's Blue Network starting in 1933. In 1941, as Allen went into military service, Pearson continued with his own program, *Drew Pearson Comments*. He drew comparisons to NBC colleague Walter Winchell, whose rapid-fire delivery he openly emulated. Naturally, he and Winchell became rivals.

While most powerful Washington figures picked up their copies of the *Merry-Go-Round* with an inward cringe, since appearing in Pearson's sights was usually bad news, there were some who benefited from his support. New Dealers like Rexford G. Tugwell appealed to Pearson's combative liberalism, as did Eleanor Roosevelt. Averell Harriman was a close friend. Among his designated villains was General Douglas MacArthur. Pearson often alienated those for whom he had sympathy. Narrating an internal White House spat between Ickes and Hopkins, Pearson wrote, "For Ickes, canals; for Hopkins, ditches; for Ickes, highways, for Hopkins, sidewalks; for Ickes, water systems, for Hopkins, reservoirs; for Ickes, public buildings; for Hopkins, landscaping; for Ickes, big dams; for Hopkins, little dams."[404] Humiliated, Hopkins disparaged the Pearson style of snickering over "fights in a harem," seething that the querulous Quaker had exposed rifts within the New Deal team. Pearson's ability to fill his column with leaks from the White

House prompted Cordell Hull to begin a staff meeting with the wisecrack, "Is this for the room or for Drew Pearson?"[405] The remark showed up in the next *Merry-Go-Round.*

MacArthur was an intractable enemy. Roosevelt, resentful at the columnist for cutting through White House confidentiality, used Pearson's feud with MacArthur to mount an indirect attack on the columnist. The President invited the General to the Oval Office, where their mutual antipathy for the writer came up.[406] MacArthur, whom Pearson skewered as a martinet, listened when Roosevelt said he would enjoy seeing anyone with a good case mount an anti-Pearson libel action. Taking the suggestion, the General slapped the columnist with a $1,175,000 suit, also naming Allen and the United Features syndicate. At issue were past columns, including ones in which Pearson mocked the General's mother. The result was one of Washington's most merciless brawls.[407]

Pearson's reaction was to counterattack, so he put his investigatory skills to work. Pearson uncovered Isabel Rosario Cooper, known to some as "Helen Robinson," beautiful daughter of a Scottish businessman and an Asian woman. Her liaison with MacArthur originated in Manila. Socialite Dorothy Detzer described her appeal. "I thought I had never seen anything as exquisite. She was wearing a lovely, obviously expensive chiffon tea gown, and she looked as if she were carved from the most delicate opaline."[408] Lonely, single, and awed by his indomitable mother, "Pinky," MacArthur rendezvoused with Cooper in San Francisco; she followed him to Washington where he ensconced her in a suite at the Hotel Chastleton, on 17th Street.[409] His position as Chief of Staff meant that MacArthur was busy. Cooper grew restless, dipping into Washington's straitlaced social life, flying to Havana for a gambling vacation.[410] MacArthur realized that his girlfriend was dangerous to his career. Attempting to end the relationship, he sent her tickets back to Manila, in September, 1934.[411] Enclosed with the train and ship tickets were "Help Wanted" ads and the advice that she look elsewhere for further financial support.[412] It was then that Pearson crossed her path.

She showed Pearson love letters in the General's own hand. Major Dwight Eisenhower, was deputed to find her in Washington, but Cooper was then under Pearson's protection. Pearson warned her that MacArthur might have her murdered; at the same time, he employed a detective to monitor her movements and find out what company she kept. The upshot was that MacArthur withdrew his suit and paid Pearson's legal fees. Pearson and Allen kept photostatic copies of the letters, lest the General change his mind.[413] When Fleet Admiral William Leahy heard the story, he told friends that MacArthur would have won the suit, if he was willing to "look everybody in the face and say: 'So what? Cunt can make you look awfully silly at times!'"[414] To Leahy, MacArthur withdrew because he feared maternal disapproval. "It was that old woman he lived with at Fort Myer," insisted Leahy. "He didn't want his *mother* to learn about the Eurasian girl!"[415]

In November 1941, Pearson threw a party honoring Patterson. By this time, their opposing political views on vital matters such as isolationism, which she supported and he abhorred, or the President, whom Pearson liked but Patterson loathed, strained their relationship. The *Times-Herald* often cut his column. Pearson dangled his services before the *Washington Post*. In the week before the Pearl Harbor attack, Pearson and Allen ran a note in the *Merry-Go-Round*, gleaned from a tip passed along by Undersecretary of State Sumner Welles, that the Japanese fleet had just sailed, destination unknown.[416] While Allen joined up after the attack, Pearson, as a Quaker, did not join the military. The *Merry-Go-Round* shifted to war coverage under his watch.

On December 10, the column's 9th anniversary, United Features sent out a press release praising "the consistent hard-hitting record of Drew Pearson and Robert S. Allen in trying to bolster the national defense of the country."[417] The syndicate continued, "As far as the Navy is concerned, perhaps it is not going too far to say that if the Administration had followed up some of their fearless reporting, the nation might not now be in its present position in the Pacific."[418] There followed a list of scoops, all of which established for the record that Pearson and Allen had warned about scandalous defense neglect. Included were stories such as the November 22, 1937 disclosure "that five Japanese spies had been operating on US warships disguised as Filipino mess boys."[419] It was a list of 17 stories about topics such as naval inefficiency, advancement within ranks based on social standing rather than merit, and Roosevelt's reluctance to clean out the navy's worst admirals. It rang a discordant note in the unity chorus emanating from the nation's editorial pages. For Pearson, there was blame to assign, and the *Merry-Go-Round* was on that job.

His first investigative piece after Pearl Harbor claimed "sensational evidence about huge profits being made by shipbuilders, aircraft manufacturers, and other defense firms" unearthed by the House Naval Affairs Committee.[420] Readers were told about profiteering by war contractors. There was a bit on isolationist Representative John M. Vorys, (R-OH), one of Roosevelt's most bitter enemies in the House. The piece concentrated on the Congressman's strange fitness regimen of climbing trees in Rock Creek Park every Sunday, making the White House opponent appear loony.[421]

The next day, the column led off with the story that Special Envoy Kurusu had behaved oddly in Honolulu's Royal Hawaiian Hotel on his way to Washington. Calling room service asking for pajamas, Kurusu had selected "a bright-colored silk pair," only to call back minutes later, enraged. According to a bellhop, "the eminent Japanese visitor was boiling mad," because the nightclothes bore an American insignia on the breast pocket. "Take them back at once," he roared. "And tell that store I've decided I don't want any of their merchandise!"[422]

Alongside the Kurusu pajama tantrum, the *Merry-Go-Round* for December 11 took Naval Intelligence to task for allowing the Pearl Harbor surprise. "Their only explanation so far is that the Pacific is a very wide ocean," was Pearson's acerbic verdict. Pearson returned to his long-standing argument that naval advancement depended too much upon social position. "Obviously, it is the man who can speak a few languages, is not afraid to get his hands dirty in close contact with life, and who is not too particular regarding the percentage of blue blood in his veins," whom the navy needed to promote.[423] Incidentally, those traits of merit described Pearson.

Pearson still found time to praise his friends. Eleanor Roosevelt won plaudits for her dignified rebuke to the Japanese ambassador. "The nerve of that man sitting with my husband in the White House while Japanese bombs were falling on our boys!"[424] Ickes, described as "the toe-stepping, hit-em-harder Secretary of the Interior," rated kudos for being "The one member of the Cabinet who had a consistently 100 per cent, though sometimes unpopular, batting record regarding the Japanese." To those he disliked, such as the America First Committee or some diplomats, Pearson was dismissive, lumping them together. "A fair analogy can be drawn between the gentlemen of the State Department and the America First Committee," he editorialized. "Both were sincere, and definitely felt that the best way to treat the dictators was to give them more room to expand. . . . Apparently they had their heads too far in the clouds or did not understand human nature sufficiently to realize that the thirst of a dictator is never quenched."[425]

Pearson was among the few writers who harped on political anger in the wake of Pearl Harbor. He cited a "storm of criticism over the Navy's tragic failure at Hawaii," describing the December 7 White House session between Roosevelt, Cabinet members, and congressional chiefs, in his December 12 column. Tom Connally's frustration came through as Pearson delivered an accurate version of the White House gathering. Pearson described the taut relationship between the Texas Senator and Navy Secretary Knox. Pearson often attacked the navy's habits, what a later column called "this rigidity of mind, this mixture of cocksureness and sleepiness toward the grim fate of the nation which caused the worst naval defeat by any nation since Trafalgar."[426] Knox and Roosevelt both had reason to fear that this might spark public recrimination against the navy, which they wished to avoid. Pearson's pressure helped to push the government's inquiries, and Knox was soon on his way to Hawaii. Pearson called for naval "house-cleaning . . . to ensure future success."[427] For the *Merry-Go-Round*, Pearl Harbor was not a "tragedy," but a "debacle."[428]

Pearson fell under the fearful trend about subversion. On December 13, he informed readers that Representative Martin Dies (D-TX), who co-chaired the House Committee Investigating Un-American Activities sniffed out suspicious Japanese activities along the West Coast during the previous summer. He was skeptical when Dies' target was communist influence, but this time Pearson sounded approving. Reminding readers that "Hitler had many agents planted through

Norway, France, and the Low countries when he attacked," Pearson cited Dies' information that the Japanese "start out with 150,000 of their countrymen in the United States." Pearson stressed that many remained Japanese citizens, and some had even been "decorated by the Emperor during the past two years." Additionally, many were "in close cooperation with the homeland through the Central Japanese Association," which Dies claimed was directed by Japanese government officials.[429] The Dies report, which Pearson claimed had was suppressed by the State Department, included photographs of "Japanese truck gardens operated alongside oil tanks and strategic railroads," "5,000 Japanese residing on terminal islands in Los Angeles harbor," and maps supposedly seized by Dies' agents showing "strategic points and fortifications."[430] Pearson went on to cite the committee's belief that Japanese agents knew about American Pacific Fleet formations and movements. Pearson made it clear that the committee faced interference, citing Dies' complaint that he "received a letter from Matthew Maguire, then acting Attorney General and now US Federal Judge, stating categorically that the State and Justice Department, together with the White House, were opposed to the inquiry."[431]

"State Department Sought Appeasement While Japs Prepared War," was one of the *Merry-Go-Round* headlines which made Pearson's anti-State Department attitude very clear.[432] Pearson disapproved of Hull, terming his negotiations with Japan a disastrous failure. Left unmentioned was the point that Roosevelt conducted the nation's foreign relations. At the heart of Pearson's rationale for refusing to abandon his aggressive approach was his contention that "fair criticism is healthy." Pearson put the argument in terms of obligation to his readers and to the public at large. "We have a responsibility to our readers to continue pointing to the inefficiency, stupidity, and corruption, in the same spirit that Winston Churchill has considered criticism healthy for his wartime government, and in the same manner that Mrs. Roosevelt . . . referred to the energizing effect of fair criticism in war time."[433] To those who objected that war required new standards, Pearson played the victory card. "We also feel that this war cannot be won without knowing what we face, and who is responsible for our losses, in order that these losses may not happen again."[434] When, on December 16, Pearson's column concentrated on the upcoming censorship regime to be run out of the White House—"President Plans Centralized Censorship for Military News"—it could be read as a statement of awareness on his part that the Department of Public Information was a factor he understood but did not fear.[435]

But Pearson knew that the surge of patriotism required gestures of loyalty and a win-the-war spirit. Before Christmas, United Features sent out an advertisement which editors could use at their discretion. Written by Pearson, "A Gift for Uncle Sam," it was a *"Merry-Go-Round* suggestion for a new type of Christmas present." In it, Pearson asked readers to help Uncle Sam, who was in more "dire straits . . . than most of us realize," by writing him a check and sending it to the United States

Treasury. To defense workers, Pearson suggested contributing to the war effort by volunteering to work either Christmas or New Year's Day.[436]

Perhaps the most surprising element of Pearson's commentary that December was the shift in his on-the-record opinion of MacArthur. By December 17, Manila was imperiled. Readers might have expected "fair criticism," Pearson-style, aimed at MacArthur. Instead, Pearson led off that day's *Merry-Go-Round* with an eyebrow-raiser. "Those who knew General MacArthur in France are not surprised at the superb job he is doing in defending the Philippines," he wrote.[437] What followed was a supportive account of MacArthur's World War I combat record, projected onto his current Filipino defense strategy. Pearson praised MacArthur's inter-war service: "As Chief of Staff in Washington during the Hoover Administration, MacArthur was an energetic go-getter for anything the army needed and a good organizer."[438] Citing the General's organization of American and Filipino forces as "one of his greatest assets," Pearson suggested that current difficulties on the battlefield were not MacArthur's fault, but caused by the difficulties "getting cooperation with the Army, the Air Corps, and the Marines."[439] Pearson concluded by noting that the General was proving himself a suitable successor to his father, General Arthur MacArthur, "who became famous for cleaning up the Philippines after the Spanish-American War."[440] Pearson chose not to renew or his feud. Instead, he lent the General support. Perhaps the columnist felt the Christmas spirit.

"We Will Not Hide Facts:" media adjusts to war

In the fifty years of the existence of this Quarterly, this is the third war it has witnessed. Again it will continue to publish the work of scholars, critics, and poets who, feeling the war intensely, are carrying on their high pursuits, preserving intact the sacred trust committed to democracies to keep open the channels of rich and ennobling communications with the past for the building of a more adequate future. Its patriotism is the patriotism of devotion to American political ideals and institutions, completely committed to the ardors and sacrifices of War and firm conviction that our Cause will and must win.

William Knickerbocker, Editor, Sewanee Review[441]

To all newspapers and radio stations—all those who reach the eyes and ears of the American people—I say this: You have a most grave responsibility to the nation now and for the duration of this war. If you feel that your Government is not disclosing enough of the truth, you have every right to say so. But—in the absence of all the facts, as revealed by official sources—you have no right in the ethics of patriotism to deal out unconfirmed reports in such as way as to make people believe they are gospel truth.

President Franklin D. Roosevelt, December 1941[442]

Magazines: news, interpretation, and opinion

American news magazines knew that their once-a-week issues could never keep pace with the speed of this war. This lesson became obvious when Hitler launched his Case Yellow blitzkrieg at 5:35 a.m. on May, 10, 1940. Within hours, German paratroopers and assault troops seized strategic objectives such as airfields, bridges, fortresses, and towns across Luxembourg, Belgium, and the Netherlands. Within days, the forward troops were joined by the main wave of the *Wehrmacht,* and the small western democracies fell in short order. No less a surprise than Pearl Harbor, the attack was the first stage of Germany's drive to the Channel coast.[443] British forces barely escaped at Dunkerque and the Allies saw that their old tactics were inadequate. But American news media also learned that speed made old news methods useless. To adapt, weekly periodicals shifted to a blend of news summary and analysis, ceding immediacy to newspapers and radio.

Time, Newsweek, US News, and *Collier's* were able to adjust to the surprise of Pearl Harbor. The magazines asserted their relevance by stressing their sober assessment. They promised to make sense of the war one week at a time. *US News* converted formal war entry into a sales pitch. "WAR NEWS" headlined of a two-page advertisement explaining the magazine's case for itself. "Washington is now the center of the World War," pointed out the ad. "Published in the national capital itself, the *United States News* is the only news weekly in the country devoted entirely to national affairs."[444] The copy boasted of the magazine's large Washington bureau of 50 reporters, arguing that war news was not "merely the dispatches from the naval and military front," which it called "spot news," but "news that affects everyday business, everyday manufacturing, and everyday distribution." The magazine pointed out that "*The United States News* makes an excellent gift for your friends for 1942." Subscriptions cost $8 per year.[445]

US News proffered "Spot Analysis" as its prime function. It defined Spot Analysis as "the meaning of the news, and the trends based up first-hand contact with those who shape governmental policies and legislation."[446] The argument depended upon the idea that the war's agenda would be set in Washington, not elsewhere. American news magazines said they could give readers access to the corridors of power where decisions would be made. Backroom information was a conceit which *US News* worked hard to cultivate. One of the distinctive features was the "Newsgram," which looked like a lengthy telegram in type font. The first Newsgram after Pearl Harbor looked to Singapore as Japan's target. "It's Japan's objective," went the explanation. "It dominates the riches of the Indies. *If held:* Japan can't win, can't get the oil she must have. *If lost:* It's more difficult to see an end to this war; it's a vital loss."[447] The Newsgram termed Singapore's outlook "uncertain," stating that only fast American assistance could save the British stronghold. Also, the Newsgram considered the prospects for the Philippines. "So long as they're held," it explained, "these islands threaten Japan's communication lines. *If held:* Japan may be strangled. *If lost:* Japan will hold a screen of protective islands reaching to the Indies. *The outlook:* None too good for the U.S. It will take a very hard fight."[448]Moving on, *US News* readers were told that Suez was the objective of the Germans in North Africa. Again, there was an explanation, and a calculation: "*The purpose:* To crash through to a juncture with Japan at Singapore, if Britain's fleet can be beaten or destroyed. *The outlook:* Uncertain, depending importantly on Turkey and France."[449]

The magazine paid plenty of attention to the position faced by American business in the war environment. Similar to the Newsgram was the "Plus and Minus" column, a pretend memo and balance sheet. Describing "what war will mean for U.S. industry," "Plus and Minus" saw advantages in the end to questions. It predicted "an immense flood of arms orders," but also "severe trouble for nondefense industries using materials that compete with government demand: a ruthless use of priorities and rationing."[450] These turned out to be excellent predictions. "Plus and Minus" stressed the necessity for businessmen to engage in long-term planning, "in terms of a war of three years at a minimum" warning that even a six- or ten-year war was not impossible.[451] There was no suggestion of any chance for a quick victory.

Readers of *Time*, Henry Luce's flagship, expected more textual explanation than the publisher's photograph-intensive *Life* could supply. *Time* promised readers judicious interpretation of events. The issue in readers' hands after Pearl Harbor featured German General Fedor von Bock on its cover, with lengthy coverage of the Russian front. It was not until December 15 that *Time* could weigh in on Pearl Harbor. Kimmel graced the cover, the last positive professional event of the Admiral's career. Within, readers of the article "Tragedy at Honolulu" could see that the Commander in Chief of the Pacific Fleet was in trouble. "The U.S. Navy was caught with its pants down. Within one tragic hour—before the war had really begun—the U.S. appeared to have suffered greater naval losses than in the whole of World War I."[452] The tone continued, mercilessly. "Although the Japanese certainly had been approaching for several days, the Navy apparently had no news of either airplane carriers sneaking up or of submarines fanning out around Hawaii. Not till the first bombs began to fall was an alarm given. And when the blow fell the air force at Pearl Harbor was apparently not ready to offer effective opposition to the attackers."[453]

Elsewhere that week, *Time* continued the pro-intervention tone that marked it as a Luce publication. "Japan Runs Amuck" part of the multi-feature "U.S. at War" section, noted acidly that "just ten years ago, the Japanese press went wild at a report that Secretary of State Henry L. Stimson had accused the Japanese Army of "running amuck."[454] In fact, recalled the article, Stimson never made such a remark, "but he had every right to."[455] What followed was a recitation of Japanese depredations, starting at Mukden in 1931, running through Kurusu's arrival in Washington days before. Other articles mentioned panic on the West Coast after San Francisco's false air raid alarm, as well as the dire observation that the supply lifeline to Australia was in jeopardy. The magazine found space for some high prose style in the meditative "State of the Nation" column, "Last Week of Peace," which ruminated on the waning days before December 7. "Although the whole nation had long had the sense that the war was approaching," went the piece, "the country discarded its pre-war preoccupations slowly, regretfully, in the way that travelers across the plains were finally forced to throw away the lovely walnut bureau, the framed motto, the pictures of the graduating class, the heirlooms and excess baggage, when the going got tough."[456] There was also some humor, as the magazine covered the arrival in San Francisco, via China Clipper of Soviet Foreign Minister Maxim Litvinoff (*sic*.). As he exited the plane after a very long and roundabout journey from Kuibyshev, "Comrade Litvinoff and his snowy-haired English wife looked like any bourgeois tourist who had not enough sleep."[457]

The next issue, December 22, featured Yamamoto on the cover. The picture was a yellow-hued caricature, the tint no accident. But the Japanese naval chief's features were not exaggerated as they would be on *Collier's* cover. The accompanying text made plain the fact that Yamamoto was the talented and devoted chief of a powerful naval enterprise.

Time had covered the war theatre by theater for months, so adjusting to American involvement meant no structural changes to the table of contents or the arrangement of articles. There were stories from each war zone—"World Battlefronts." One new addition was a section entitled "The U.S. at War," subdivided topically, with titles such as "First Jitters," "Doctrine and Covenants," and "Civilian Defense."[458] Each article addressed a different aspect of the new situation, such as the laws of war or the handling of enemy diplomats. The December 22 edition manifested a determined tone while not sugarcoating the Pearl Harbor defeat. "Havoc in Honolulu" read a one headline, with an article calling December 7 the first act in "The Battle of the Pacific."[459]

Articles featuring American grit included "The U.S. at War: Full Blast," which described bold and decisive White House leadership. The good news, according to the report, was that "in some ways the nation was much better prepared for World War II than it had dreamed."[460] For example, Hitler's 1940 *blitzkrieg* kicked off the preparedness campaign, which meant that "Planes, tanks, guns, ships were in production." The magazine seconded the President's admission that "The U.S. had suffered a serious defeat in the Pacific," as well as his call "on the people to prepare for a long war, which we are going to win."[461] Roosevelt warned against heeding wild claims and rumors, at the same time promising that the ongoing preparedness drive would increase in intensity and output. "We are now in this war. We are in it—all the way," said the President, explaining that no sector of national life could be considered exempt from exigencies or irrelevant to "the greatest undertaking in our American history." Most of all, Roosevelt said, speaking to the media pointedly, "We must share together the bad news and the good news. So far, the news has been all bad."[462]

"The Press: Censorship in Action," clued readers into the type of coverage they should expect. The gist interpreted an FDR radio speech one week after the attack, in which he spoke to the media very bluntly. "To all those who reach the eyes and ears of the American people—I say this: You have a most grave responsibility to the nation now and for the duration of this war."[463] Roosevelt stressed that the government would release reliable and timely information. "We will not hide facts," he promised. But he also "laid down two censorship musts: First, that the information has been definitely and officially confirmed; and second, that the release of the information at the time it is received will not prove valuable to the enemy directly or indirectly."[464] Luce's magazine hoped that the President envisioned "a censorship which stuck to its proper function in a democracy."[465] These were enumerated as locking up military secrets and verifying that such secrets were legitimate, not pretexts to obscure military or political ineptitude; focusing on denying news to the enemy, not the American citizenry; and eschewing the temptation to control "public morale" through "propaganda, which can be made excuses for concealing anything."[466]

Memories of the previous war underlay several other stories during late December. In "The U.S. at War: To the Last Ounce," *Time* wrote of a "tall, spare, silvered man with a back as straight as a poplar," currently boarding at Walter Reed Hospital. This man, having written to President Roosevelt to offer his services, "in any way in which my experience and my strength, to the last ounce, will be of help in the fight,"[467] was 81-year old John J. Pershing. The article noted that, in 1918, Pershing led 2 million U.S. soldiers in France, and that currently, "one of his boys, General Douglas MacArthur, was beating off Japanese attacks in the Philippines."[468] The article recollected the 1918 words of another of Pershing's boys, George Marshall, sending American soldiers into action against the

Germans at Picardy in 1918. "You are going to meet a savage enemy. Meet them like Americans," Marshall had said. The article suggested that these worlds were "still good in 1941."[469]

Actually, MacArthur was conducting a phased retreat. This did not come through at all in the December 22 article, "World Battlefronts: The Philippines Stand." The basic American assumption was that the Philippines would withstand the Japanese invasion, contain it, and beat it back. In fact, Japanese offensive actions there had defenders reeling. But the tenor of this was defiantly positive. "The Philippines were ready. For days before that war began, the guns had been manned and the planes had stood alert," it began, stating that defenders broke Japanese beachheads on Luzon and kept ships at bay with aerial attacks. Singled out for praise was the defense of Clark Field. In reality, the destruction of American planes on the ground at Clark was one of the war's early disasters. But this article described a heroic defense by young officers of the new Filipino Air Force.

Looking elsewhere, *Time* joined those correctly perceiving that Japanese moves were squarely aimed at Singapore. "At Singapore," promised the analysis, "The future of the Allies in Asia was at stake."[470] The text dwelt upon the peninsula's geography. On the east side, wrote the author, lay inhospitable conditions. "Its beaches are broad, but they lie behind treacherous offshore ledges, riparian sandbars, and extended shallows, which will soon be pounded by the terrible surf of the northeasterly monsoon."[471] Besides a topography and meteorological lesson, readers got a dose of zoology. "Behind the beaches, beyond a fringe of graceful, feathery casuarina trees, lie the swamps—great stinking pestholes which house most of nature's nightmares: crocodiles, pythons, cobras, and the nasty little Anopheles, the mosquito of malaria." There were also deep jungles, with "adders, tigers, and other Japanophobes."[472]

The other side of narrow Malaya was more friendly. In fact, "Paradise lay to the west. Across the mountains there is a rolling country of bamboo, rubber plantations, tin mines: a country divided up by a network of good roads, cut up by rice paddies, full of people and not beasts . . . washed by the quiet Malacca Strait, sheltered by the long Island of Sumatra."[473] There followed an extensive description of British attempts to hold the west, forcing the Japanese attackers to the eastern side. As it happened, Major General Percival's Anglo-Indian defenders faced a rapid retreat, with defensive lines constantly outflanked by Japanese advances unperturbed by whatever conditions. The Dutch, counted on by the writer and the British for robust resistance across the Malacca Strait, were painted in the story as on the counteroffensive, when in fact Japan was ready to move against Java. Neither *Time* nor the mainstream media quite grasped how far along the Japanese threat to Singapore really was. As even realistic reportage predicting sustained battles ahead did not anticipate the swift Japanese victories in the offing. If they had, the articles might have sounded less optimistic about halting Japan's multiple front offensive, nicknamed "The Octopus" because it resembled a centrally directed southward grasp by several tentacles. "Like some vast octopus," Samuel Eliot Morrison later wrote, "It relied on strangling many small points rather than concentrating on a vital organ."[474]

Looking back, British Field Marshall Lord William Slim, fighting a losing campaign in Burma, attributed the dire Allied circumstances to a loss of what he called "moral ascendancy" to the Japanese. "They bought that initiative fairly, fairly and inevitably, by paying for it with preparation."[475] Terming the Japanese "ruthless and bold as ants while their designs went well," he saw that only disrupting their plans could throw them into confusion. But Allied commanders, Slim acknowledged, were too narrow in their thinking, administratively bound, and prone to disastrous optimism about their capacity to resist this foe.[476] Assessing the reasons for poor British performance in the face of Japan's peninsular blitz, Slim found plenty to criticize, including "extremely bad" intelligence, poor training and equipment for jungle warfare, and divisions which looked strong on paper but were below strength in the field.[477] Slim's war would be a long one, ultimately triumphant, but these insights about the situation that December were correct. However, these realizations were years away. *Time* and the American media were not thinking about the Allies losing Singapore, the Dutch Indies, and the Philippines in one fell swoop. It was what the Japanese saw as an *Iai*, a disabling samurai sword blow struck without preliminary rituals and intended to preclude any chance of counterstroke.[478] Seeing the war so clearly at this time would have been terrifying, so perhaps the conventional illusions had some protective effect.

Time gave a hint of the fast-spreading canard that Americans of Japanese background carried latent, dangerous characteristics, which Pearl Harbor might spark into efflorescence. "Home Affairs: How to Tell Your Friends from the Japs," was meant to help readers separate Japanese from other "Orientals," especially Chinese. The piece repeated the anecdote of news correspondent Joseph Chiang wearing the badge, "Chinese Reporter—NOT Japanese—Please."[479] Alongside images of Chinese and Japanese males, the December 22 article made a detailed physiological comparison. "There is no infallible way of telling them apart, because the same racial strains are mixed in both," confessed the text. "Even an anthropologist, with calipers and plenty of time to measure heads, noses, shoulders, hips, is sometimes stumped."[480] The article carried hints, noting that some Chinese were taller than 5' 5", while most Japanese were shorter, stockier, broader in their hips. Japanese were seldom fat, because "they often dry up and grow lean as they age."[481] Against that trend was fashionable plumpness among Chinese, who esteemed the portly as solid and prosperous citizens. Chinese were described as less hairy, less likely to wear moustaches, less fond of horn-rimmed spectacles than Japanese. The epicanthic folds of the upper eyelids were analyzed, with the hint that Japanese eyes were set closer together. "Those who know them best often rely on facial expression to tell them apart," continued the field guide to Orientals. "The Chinese expression is likely to be more placid, kindly, open; the Japanese more positive, dogmatic, arrogant."[482]

If any reader felt equipped to begin the selection process, the magazine cautioned that there were still more differentiations. For example, "some aristocratic Japanese have thin, aquiline noses, narrow faces, and, except for their eyes, look like Caucasians." Furthermore, "Japanese are nervous in conversation, laugh loudly at the wrong time. Japanese walk stiffly erect, hard-heeled. Chinese, more relaxed, have an easy gait, sometimes shuffle."[483] In its own way, this article was more chilling even than pieces telling of battlefield setbacks. Anyone reading it and considering the implications might not have been surprised when the cords of federal control began to tighten around Americans of Japanese descent across the western states. This really was a convenient form of racial taxonomy in service to war objectives that came to dominate media accounts of the Pacific theater, in which different Asian races were classified negatively—the Japanese—or positively—the Chinese.[484] Long-simmering racial and cultural hostility was hard to miss.

Newsweek rivaled *Time*. This was natural, given its roots as a schismatic publication, founded by Thomas J.C. Martyn, one-time top staffer at *Time* before his 1925 resignation. Noting Luce's controversial stances on editorial style and anti-New Deal politics, Martyn started *Newsweek* in 1933.[485] Taking a dig at his former employers, whose magazine he called "too inaccurate, too superficial, too flippant, and imitative," Martyn promised that *Newsweek* would rely on "simple, unaffected English, a more significant format, a fundamentally sober attitude on all matters."[486] From that moment, *Newsweek* spurred *Time* through competition. This continued after Vincent Astor bought the feisty weekly in 1937.[487]

The first post-Pearl Harbor *Newsweek* cover, December 15, 1941, featured a close-up of naval guns, with the resolute caption: "War! The U.S. Fleet's Guns Blast."[488] The image was encouraging but wishful, since the US Navy was far from its counterattack. Editorial coverage within was more forthright than the cover indicated. "Blitz Chronology: Swift Stroke by Japanese Caught U.S. Forces Unawares," was one example, admitting that the attack on Pearl "painfully effective" and to which the United States had no riposte.[489] The magazine promised that, eventually, American response would be mammoth and that the war long. "Nation's Full Might Mustered for All Out War," and "Washington Banks on Long-Term Strategy" were typical headlines.[490] *Newsweek* also noted a degree of Congressional dissatisfaction with official explanations to date, in "Initial Reverse Stirs Demand for Investigation."[491]

Other magazines depended more upon analysis and opinion than the newsweeklies. *New Republic*, Lippmann's old organ, still projected calm, liberal interpretations of current events. Its editorial board included Bruce Bliven, Malcolm Cowley, George Soule, and Stark Young; contributing editors were

H.N. Brailsford, Van Wyck Brooks, Julian Huxley, Max Lerner, E.C. Lindeman, and Rexford Tugwell. "Our War," was the cover story on December 15. "The turn of events proves that the Axis powers regard the United States as their major enemy," went the article, stressing the unity of Germany, Italy, and Japan, arguing that Pearl Harbor was "part of a strategic unit in which the war in Europe plays an important role."[492] The reasoning lent comfort to readership whose sympathies were stirred by the Soviet Union's fight against the Reich. The point was the holistic nature of the war, meshing with Roosevelt's old argument against aggressor nations led by Germany. The tone was realistic, including the admission that "Already there is doubt about the superiority of the forces opposed to the Japanese in the Pacific area."[493] One of the first post-attack articles, by William Harlan Hale, was "After Pearl Harbor." Hale assessed the attack, exploring how the resultant war might develop. It urged readers not to underestimate the Japanese triumph. Hale also noted the failure of Japan's strike force to follow up with more assaults. He pointed to lengthy Japanese supply lines, which he said would be vulnerable so long as Pearl Harbor remained in American hands. He predicted the fall of Guam, Wake, and Midway islands, adding that such events would disrupt US lines to the Far East. But, he went on, "they would by no means stop us from using the southerly route to Australia and the Java Sea. They would accomplish much; but so long as the vast South Pacific was in Allied hands, they would prove little."[494] Espying the Japanese scheme to set up a defensive screen of occupied islands behind which to resist the eventual American counterattack, Hale called the 1,500 mile stretch of Japanese-mandated islands "a calculated deathtrap for our fleet. If Japan, behind cover of them, attempts to seize Borneo, Celebes, or New Guinea, there is probably not a great deal we can do to stop her."[495] Burma, too, looked vulnerable. But Hale still saw the United States with an undeniable strategic advantage. The Japanese, he pointed out, could dislodge American forces from various spots on the map. But they could never surround Allied forces dispersed as from Alaska to Australia. This meant that Japan's navy could neither contain nor destroy the American fleet, which would choose the time and place of its response. In writing this way, Hale set up the speculative model perfect for avoiding censorship while informing readers of the war situation. Relying on educated guesswork, supported by supposition, he revealed no secrets. But he did educate readers on the broad and detailed aspects of the Pacific war. Except for his prediction that the Soviets would help against Japan, all of Hale's predictions were correct.

The next week, Hale turned his attention to top naval brass. "Trouble for Admirals" let him survey the navies of the world. He found trouble at the top quite common. The Royal Navy, still shocked from the loss of *Prince of Wales* and *Repulse*, had no excuse for its dilatory Pacific performance. The British had shown their own aerial assault capacities at Taranto on November 11 of the previous year, when Swordfish torpedo aircraft from the carrier *Illustrious* sunk Italy's battleship *Dulio* and damaged *Cavour* and *Littorio*.[496] It was an operation studied with interest by the Japanese. Hale was unforgiving of the recent lapse which the two Royal Navy ships to sea bereft of air cover: "It should not have happened."[497] Losing the strongest part of the Singapore squadron spelled nothing but trouble for the entire Allied effort. Hale took the Japanese navy to task for exposing its ships needlessly during landing operations on Luzon. Since those landings worked, Hale's castigation of the Japanese was misdirected. Most of his spleen vented at the US Navy. He saw the roots of the Pearl Harbor fiasco stretching back decades, embedded in a naval culture which laughed off the idea that battleships might be sunk by planes. He invoked the spirit of Billy Mitchell, but said that "the trouble at Pearl Harbor had better be passed over in silence, until more facts are published."[498]

Elsewhere, *New Republic* probed China as an ally. In "China's Future—and Our Own," Nathaniel Peffer located China as the nugatory cause of Japanese-American conflict. "Through all modern Far Eastern history runs a single logical thread: the status of China," he observed.[499] Peffer argued that the central issue was whether China would exist as a vassal state to another power, or as a country wholly free and in charge of its affairs. American interests, not to mention international justice, demanded Chinese independence, he explained, which placed the United States on the right side of history and rendered the alliance between the United States and China appropriate. The magazine also assessed Japanese capabilities in "Japan's Strategy—and Resources," finding that a long war would necessitate Japan holding on to and exploiting its conquered regions. Failure to fully extract resources would doom Tokyo in the end, thought T.A. Bisson.[500] The lead editorial was "The Unity Bandwagon," a supportive case for integrating British and American commands, which was on Churchill's agenda. Elsewhere, *The New Republic* wrote about labor unions in a war economy. It also included the usual assortment of poems and book reviews, as well as a survey of French literature from Vichy. To ring out 1941, *The New Republic* connected its Anglo-American unity-of-command theme with the USSR. On its cover, the magazine ran the words, "Today's watchword for coordinated Allied strategy reads: Second fronts here, second fronts there, second fronts everywhere!"[501] Max Lerner surveyed travails faced by the Germans. He thought Hitler's assumption of direct command might show Germany cracking. Lerner said that the outcome of the Russian campaign might be at hand. Lerner excused Stalin's refusal to enter the war against Japan as sensible rather than "appeasement or Russian isolationism."[502] Lerner wanted the United States to take pressure off the Russians through immediate offensives. Left unexplained was how the United States might create a second front in Europe at that point. His article was part of a left-wing campaign to help Moscow by keeping up pressure for a second front and for including the Soviet Union in the trans-Atlantic supply chain.

The New Republic was not always solicitous of Soviet views. Malcolm Cowley fell out with former friend Edmund "Bunny" Wilson over the Soviet invasion of

Finland, which Cowley deplored and Wilson excused. Writing to Wilson, a bruised Cowley analyzed the rupture of their friendship. "I wonder how it happened," he asked after Wilson's *To the Finland Station* appeared in 1940. "As a sequel to your present book describing the moment of Lenin's arrival in the Finland Station," wrote Cowley, "You ought to write another describing the devolution of an idea from Marx to the *New Leader* and from Lenin to the latest editorial in *Pravda* on exterminating the Finnish bandits."[503] For Cowley, Stalin's performance was too much to bear in good faith. Cowley, along with MacLeish, Lewis Mumford, Waldo Frank, John Strachey, and others, respected the Soviet revolution as a step in the direction of worldwide social justice. In particular, the USSR's willingness to assist Spanish Republicans against Franco's Nationalists while others pursed their lips showed Soviet international activism. But by 1941, Cowley exemplified the liberal who parted faith with Moscow, pushed to break faith with the Soviets by such prompts as the Show Trials of the 1930s, the Hitler–Stalin Pact, and the war with Finland. Doctrinaire loyalists at the *New Masses* attacked Cowley for ignoring Marxian analysis and doubting Stalin's leadership. "The fight against fascism is the fight against the entire process of modern capitalism," *New Masses* declared in 1940, when the USSR and the Third Reich were still in collusion.[504]

The idea that Britain must be opposed while Hitler could be handled was too much for Cowley, MacLeish, and peers. They found the positions of Roosevelt and Murrow more realistic than the Marxist-isolationist line. *The New Republic*, always the voice of internationally minded, responsible liberalism, became even more the house organ of that position. Lippmann was the historical antecedent. MacLeish, and Cowley found themselves working for the federal government before the war was old.

At *The Nation*, more reliably left-wing than *The New Republic*, the rehabilitation of the Soviet Union came through its status as an Ally. Since its founding as a nineteenth century abolitionist publication, *The Nation* stood for critical inquiry "into the state of the Nation and the world at large."[505] Unavoidably, since Oswald Garrison Villard took over in 1918, the position of the left-leaning magazine meant that it needed to reckon with issues such as class struggle, labor movements, and social justice in domestic and international contexts. Villard sold the magazine in 1935, when Frieda Kirchwey became Editor and Publisher.[506]

Kirchwey managed *The Nation* in a way that allowed the magazine to keep its relevance while retaining a principled independence lacking at *New Masses*. *The Nation* developed into a supportive voice the New Deal, and a scourge to the Dies Committee. It drew flak for being solicitous of Moscow, but as the war went on, *The Nation* considered the conflict from many angles and was not doctrinaire. When MacLeish wrote his devastating 1940 attack, "The Irresponsibles," which savaged intellectual inertia in the face of Nazism, Kirchwey published it.[507] MacLeish took on academicians who refused to involve themselves with politics, isolationists too rigid to see that American freedom was under assault, and pro-Soviets who denied that Britain merited support against Hitler. To the last group were directed some of his most astringent words: "The great Revolution of the Masses of which generous men once dreamed," he argued, had turned into a "Revolution of negatives, a revolution of despair. . . . Created out of disorder by terror of disorder. A revolution of gangs, a revolution *against*."[508] Kirchwey also published a raft of responses in subsequent issues. She supported pro-British intervention. "Today, more than ever," she wrote, "Britain is fighting our battle. We know that we shall face Nazi aggression if Britain is defeated; we face it now in all its initial stages."[509]

Once Hitler unleashed *Barbarossa* offensive, Kirchwey's magazine figured that the eastern front was where Nazi arms were directed. Help for the Soviet Union became as important to *The Nation* as aid to Britain had been. Among the writers who made this point was I.F. Stone. Stone himself had a controversial public image, which he relished. In 1941, he published a book attacking the United States' dilatory preparedness campaign, *Business as Usual*. From his Washington, D.C. base, Stone examined Otto Knudsen's Office of Production Management, as well as relations between the federal government and its main industrial contractors.[510] Stone was well informed on the complexities of federal–industrial collaboration. No less an observer than Senator Harry S. Truman (D-MO) thought so. He praised *Business as Usual* for showing "the way in which monopoly practices and big business control hamper mobilization of America's resources for defense."[511] Decades later, there would be questions about Stone's relationships with Soviet intelligence. But in 1941, Stone's main reputation was that of a dogged muckraker. His first wartime contribution, dateline December 14, was "Rumors for Russia." It debunked rumors of a new Hitler–Stalin pact designed to free up the Reich for better cooperation with Japan. At some length, he laid out the reasons why such a truce might make sense for the Soviets, then credited Stalin's good faith for not letting it happen. Stone speculated that Spain might be the next German target, and blamed Stalin's reluctance to move against Japan on the United States and Britain's earlier support for Finland.[512] These interpretations were idiosyncratic at best.

Kirchwey's attentions went to Latin America, which she surveyed for signs of pro-Axis activity. Looking ahead to the inter-American Rio de Janeiro conference, she was skeptical about Argentina, where she saw a neo-fascist governmental line out of step with popular desires.[513] Elsewhere, *The Nation* carried an article by a correspondent describing conditions in Japan before the attack, as well as a survey by Donald W. Mitchell of the Pacific Fleet's options for recovery after the Pearl Harbor disaster. He called Japan's attack "unquestionably so brilliant a success as to invite repetition."[514] Mitchell continued his examination the following week, in a story dated December 20, which ran in the December 27th issue. He located Japan's early success in their use of air power, which he contrasted darkly with British failures. American air defenses to date Mitchell praised as "nothing short of brilliant," giving readers hope that the lessons of coordinating naval and air actions were understood in Washington, as well as in Tokyo.[515] In that same December 27 issue, Stone opined on the roots of international social revolution at work in the war, which led "a coalition of smaller, poorer, and hungrier powers to attack the British, French, Dutch, and American empires with such success."[516] On matters of production, he laid inefficiencies at the root of "the double standard which normally determines our attitude toward the rights of property on one hand and the rights of people on the other," warning that war conditions should not provide the Administration with an excuse to abuse labor.[517] In keeping with his antagonism towards J. Edgar Hoover, he wondered why, if Navy Secretary Knox was right about claims of a massive fifth column at work in the west, the F.B.I was "so ineffective at curbing it."[518] As for Kirchwey, she supported Roosevelt's rhetorical stress on the "incredible duplicity practiced by Japan's responsible officials, from the envoys in Washington to the Mikado in Tokyo," and also continued her warning that inattention to the Latin American nations could provide the Axis with an unexpected opening through which to harm the United States.[519]

There were some magazines, like *Life*, and *Collier's*, whose dependence upon photographs meant that, once suitable pictures became readily available, they could help to form the visual record of the war. The lag time between events and publication meant that there was often a significant delay between an occurrence and the story covering it. Therefore, these magazines relied upon dramatic retrospective. For example, Cecil Brown's story, "The Last of the *Repulse*," chronicled the newsman's harrowing experience aboard the doomed British cruiser on December 10. But his lengthy retrospective only appeared in *Collier's* in 1943. Photographs were much more timely, but all war pictures came from official providers, such as the navy, which controlled and disseminated the first pictures of Pearl Harbor under attack.[520] *Collier's*, *Life*, and others showed initiative in those early days, running multiple pictures of scenes such as soldiers dancing in a USO club, conscripts being sworn in at an induction center, blood donors at a Red Cross station, and construction work on the Alaska Highway.[521] The appeal of the photograph-dependent magazines did not lag. They reflected reader attention without disturbing censorship and photograph distribution systems just being formed. In fact, war spurred a vast public appetite for relevant visual imagery, so much so that by 1942, *Life* claimed that two out of every three Americans in the services read the magazine, with civilian circulation numbering in the tens of millions.[522] The Office of Censorship claimed control over those international communications not already covered by military censorship, which was itself quite comprehensive, as well as over information originating from militarily-significant domestic sources.[523] Battle fronts, of course, were subject to the closest controls. All of this was supplemented by a very effective policy of discretionary cooperation by publishers themselves.

Some images needed editorial explanation—which canny editors used to fill up column inches. When the *Baltimore Evening Sun* ran the "First Photo From Pearl Harbor," showing a Japanese midget sub run beached on Oahu, the picture was accompanied by a lengthy piece spelling out the vessel's measurements and capabilities: "Jap Suicide Subs 41 Feet Long and 5 Wide."[524] More valuable than long descriptions of the sub's dimensions was the "suicide angle" encapsulated by the headline, and spelled out in the story's concluding paragraph. Noting that the small vessels carried explosives which could detonate, along with the sub, the story quoted navy sources which already understood the degree of commitment the enemy would show. "There are indications that the personnel operating the submarine will go to any extreme, however desperate, even to self-sacrifice to carry out their objective."[525]

It took over a week for photographs to start showing up in newspapers and magazines, which in the interval relied upon stock images. Once the new pictures started appearing, Americans appreciated them despite their sobering aspect. Already, coverage stressed the broadly understood fact that the war would be hard and that the Japanese were serious opponents. Readers knew from the beginning that the photographs they were shown had a high degree of honesty, censorship notwithstanding. This mirrored the overall news situation. While information was not uncontrolled, there was plenty of it, and Americans could see right away how the war looked.

There were other magazines which, for reasons of specialization or editorial stance, found their coverage of the war focused in particular directions. Among these were academic and cultural publications, which took up the challenge of arguing the relevance of their scholarly or *belle-lettriste* orientations. For other publications, the war accentuated the ongoing need to define their editorial purpose. *American Mercury*, once Mencken's home publication, was by 1941 under the leadership of Lawrence Spivak. Spivak would find his greater fame after the war, as founder of *Meet the Press*. But in 1941, *American Mercury* was part of his publishing outfit which also put out *Ellery Queen's Mystery Magazine* and the *Magazine of Fantasy and Science Fiction*. By this point, *American Mercury* strongly resembled *Reader's Digest* and the *Saturday Evening Post*. Because it was a monthly, it waited weeks to make a direct editorial response to events in the Pacific. But some articles that December were noteworthy. One, "Our Trade Barriers With Canada," was by Oswald Garrison Villard, the former *Nation* chief now wandering the tall grass of freelance journalism. The piece symbolized how out-of-step the old anti-militarist now was. Another, "America's 150,000 Japanese," concerned itself with the plight faced by Americans of Japanese descent. By the time this issue hit the stores, Japanese-Americans already felt gathering hostility. Author Ernest O. Hauser was not unsympathetic. "Japanese-Americans are on the spot, that they know it," he began. "Suspicion, accusations, and open threats are closing in on them."[526] Hauser explained the generational differences between first generation Issei and second-generation Nisei, covering the historical outline of Japanese immigration, with its strong roots in agriculture. He noted cultural heritage among Japanese-American communities, as expressed by 248 Japanese-language schools in California. Hauser also informed readers that citizenship issues which anti-Japanese elements pointed to as evidence of disloyalty had their roots in restrictive American laws. Hauser acknowledged the possibility that some might feel the tug of ancestral loyalties, but also decried that "those Americans who see a spy in every Japanese barber, who take down the number of every Japanese car parked near a dam or a power house, who report every Japanese who takes a picture of Los Angeles from the top of Mount Whitney."[527] He warned readers that persecution of Japanese-Americans would award Tokyo a propaganda boon. He emphasized that the people he wrote about hoped that "the brave new world which is their country now will judge them by their deeds—not by the color of their skin."[528]

At *Harper's*, Frederick Lewis Allen, author of *Only Yesterday* (1931), *The Lords of Creation* (1935), and *Since Yesterday* (1940), had just replaced deceased Lee Foster Hartman as editor.[529] The monthly schedule meant that it would take the magazine until January to respond to Pearl Harbor. But the December 1941 issue did run a persuasive piece by Peter Drucker, "We Must Accept Rationing." Drucker, prolific and significant writer on management, argued the political and economic necessity for measures bound to come. His far-seeing eye encompassed several fields. The essence of his case was that an armaments economy required something more profound and comprehensive than a set of temporary expedients. Drucker was not sanguine about the ease with which the United States might outperform Germany when it came to arms production. Nor did he take it for granted that the Third Reich would come to grief in its war with the Soviets. Drucker low-balled inflation fears, speaking up for measures that others might consider too drastic by stating, "a drastic program is precisely what we need."[530] He called rationing inevitable, arguing that since it could not be avoided, "it must be made into a political and economic asset."[531] The way to do that was to assure just distribution of sacrifices between wealthy and poor; a shared commitment to winning the war. This would help to avoid ruinous social discord. Drucker cited the British example, where "It was not the government which imposed rationing upon an unwilling British people; it was the British people who forced rationing upon an unwilling government."[532] He praised Churchill's legitimacy as a wartime leader. Rationing enhanced it, preventing complaints from Labour over the Prime Minister's Tory outlook. Winning the war against a capable set of foes would require avoiding any perceptions that the well-off might evade their commitment, or profit through the wartime economy. All must be equally devoted. Thanks to British rationing, Drucker said, there was faith in the government's priorities, made palpable by measures the privileged could evade. Roosevelt and Knudsen might not have known it, but Drucker's philosophical piece in *Harper's* that December was one of the most intellectually perceptive arguments in favor of a regimen that Americans were about to face. Virtually every point Drucker made would be put forth again by the administration.

Until the Fall of France, A.J. Liebling provided the best war coverage in the *New Yorker*. His reports from Paris were long, literate essays, befitting not just the magazine for which he wrote but his own background as a Columbia graduate and student at the Sorbonne and *L'Ecole de Chartres* in the 1920s. Those student years in France were devoted more to honing his appreciation of French cuisine, wine, and culture than to his academic subjects, he liked to say.[533] He loved sports and France in equal measure; his columns often combined the two, informing American readers about the scene at l'Auteuil, Paris' main race track, where gamblers and judges of horseflesh included "majors or colonels of cavalry, wearing long red spahi capes and so many spurs and buckles that they sounded like Swiss bell-ringers."[534] His eye for slices of Parisian life included the Springtime ritual of which brought anglers to the Seine in their droves, unimpeded by war: "Every Frenchman not in uniform seems to be buying a reel, a bait pail, a landing net, or a bamboo pole," he wrote in April 1940, watching them "on the right bank of the Seine between the Louvre and the Samriatine." War or not, Parisian papers published photographs of the best catches, with captions like "Spring brings the fishermen and the book merchants back to the Seine."[535] Love for France and its people radiated from each "Letter from Paris," and Liebling kept up his hope for French military recovery to the very last, when he opined that General Maxime Weygand, who replaced Maurce Gamelin in army command in June, might turn around the fortunes on the battlefield. "Like a pitcher going in with the bases full, Weygand will have to start carefully" Liebling guessed, but his winning record showed that, if he could stave off the immediate crisis, "He may change the whole complexion of the war."[536]

The German occupation of France put an end to Liebling's Letters, so attention at *The New Yorker* shifted to "Letters from London," written by Mollie Panter-Downes. During the Summer of 1940 and through the Blitz, she crafted well-constructed essays interpreting Britain's climate of morale. Panter-Downes noted British attitudes towards the United States, as on May 19, 1940, when she wrote that "The British attitude toward the hope of American intervention is now one of weary but complete resignation that the Yanks will not be coming. 'Nothing will bring them in this time,' people say cynically."[537] Panter-Downes' marvelous epistles made *New Yorker* readers feel as if they had an insightful correspondent writing from London directly to them.

It was that way the week before Pearl Harbor, when, after covering the latest reports from Libya about Erwin Rommel's *Afrika Korps*, she observed that Churchill was blessing to a new Free-French periodical, *La France Libre*.

Contributors included many of the best voices from occupied Europe, including Czechoslovakia's Eduard Benes, General De Gaulle, and Poland's Radek Sikorski. No doubt comforting American friends of France, Panter-Downes promised that a New York edition was in the works.[538]

That was the kind of small cultural nugget Panter-Downes found amidst the rubble of war news. But in her first "Letter" after Pearl Harbor, she faced a different challenge—selecting what was vital from a week in which "events . . . have been so closely packed and the emotional pressure . . . so intense that items of news which at most times would have made headlines for days . . . were received with practically no comment."[539] Panter-Downes reminded Americans that December 7 brought Japanese attacks against British possessions. "Suddenly and soberly," she wrote,

> this little island was remembering its vast and sprawling possessions of Empire. It seemed as though every person one met had a son in Singapore or a daughter in Rangoon; every post office was jammed with anxious crowds finding out about cable rates to Hong Kong, Kuala Lumpur, or Penang.[540]

This exquisite bit of writing accomplished two things. It reminded readers that Britain was a partner in the Pacific war and it supported the Anglo-American alliance. Pearl Harbor sparked real anger in Britain, she maintained, followed by gloom over the loss of *Repulse* and *Prince of Wales* which, "for sheer mass misery," made for "England's blackest day since the collapse of France."[541] The overriding opinion was devoid of jubilation over the entrance of the United States, marked instead by conviction that long and brutal fighting lay ahead. "There was a feeling that the war was going to be tougher from now on," she contended, "and that this country and American may easily have to take some knocks which will make the loss of a couple of capital ships seem like chicken feed."[542]

All Panter-Downes columns that month stressed that Britain had been fighting for a long time, and was tired, yet determined. Very mildly, she expressed British vexation that the United States had not learned from the war to date. When Knox and Congress threw over Kimmell and rearranged the command structure of the Pacific Fleet, she observed that the "wholesale reshuffle . . . brought but slight comfort to the British, who, occupied as they have been with their own naval tragedy, could only feel that the neighbors were having their upsets, too."[543] In other words, December 7 started not one but several war narratives. The stories in London were complementary to those in Washington, D.C. Knowing that Pearl Harbor looked different seen from an English angle could only help broaden the dimensions of the Anglo-American joint venture.

In both capitals, Panter-Downes knew, it was an unusual Christmas season. Seasonal color accented her war letters. On December 21, she observed that, while it had not felt much like Christmas recently, "the familiar fever has got under way and the shopping streets have been crowded with people who, however much Singapore is graven on their hearts, carry on their brows the unmistakable lines of anguished worrying over what to give Aunt Ethel."[544] In a message to Americans about learning how to shop under rationing, she mentioned the lack of wrapping paper and gift bags, which "has made most shoppers look like harassed and cruelly overloaded camels. Enterprising gift hunters have been toting suitcases around with them, and the resulting casualties among the young in crowded stores prompted a *Times* reporter to remark, "Many people have discovered how large a proportion of children are in height just about suitcase level."[545]

To lend further depth of feeling to her portrayals of life in Britain at war, Panter-Downes supplemented her "Letters from London" with short stories, which also ran in *The New Yorker*. One of these, "Goodbye My Love," appeared one week after Pearl Harbor. One of 21 stories she wrote during the war, this was a heart-rending tragedy in miniature, concentrating on the crushing emotional pressures felt by a wife who welcomes her husband home for a short leave, maintains her composure through his brief visit, then breaks down when the couple finds that his leave is extended by ten days. "Goodbye, My Love," emphasized the grinding fear of those left at home. "God, what luck," says the exultant husband over the phone. "I'm going out to find a taxi. Darling, don't move until I get there." Receiving the call, the wife hangs up and sits quite still. "The clock on the table beside her sounded deafening again, beginning to mark off the ten days at the end of which terror was the red light at the end of the tunnel. Then, her face became drawn and, putting her hands over it, she burst into tears." Panter-Downes' sensitive explorations of humanity under duress lent *New Yorker* war coverage a remarkably effective aspect. "Goodbye, My Love" was a warning to every American reader who would find out that one of war's main challenges was learning how to bid farewell.

It was institutional lore at *The Saturday Evening Post* that the magazine could trace its origins to Benjamin Franklin. If the actual connection was somewhat tenuous, the claim nevertheless showed the publication's pride at its roots in American publishing history. Its most significant editor was George Horace Lorimer, who stewarded the magazine from 1899 until 1937.[546] Lorimer's main achievement was the formidable formula of current events, human interest stories, literary offerings, cartoons, and winsome illustrations which made the *Post* a magazine of record for middle America. Lorimer forged the relationship with Norman Rockwell that started in 1916. He also brought on board numerous writers, both popular and literary. One of these had already done more than any other figure except Winston Churchill to fix positive notions of British culture in the American mind. This was P.G. Wodehouse, whose first big American break came when Lorimer bought serial rights to the novel *Something New*, in 1915.[547] Until that point, Wodehouse said, he felt the wolf at his door. After, he counted on a regular American outlet. The *Post* loved its relationship with Americans' favorite British author, and each serialized novel drove Wodehouse-mania higher among his fanatical readership. Wodehouse was enthralled about Lorimer and the effect of the *Post* on his career. "I've always thought that his buying *Something Fresh* showed what a wonderful editor he was," the grateful author would recall decades later. "Here was a story by an unknown man, and a story, what is more, about life in England, a country he didn't like, but it amused him, and so he decided without any hesitation that the public of *The Saturday Evening Post* were jolly well going to be amused by it, too, and he didn't give a damn if they weren't."[548] Readers loved the first of the Blandings stories, set in a stately English manor home, replete with eccentric Lords, rascally relatives, daunting aunts.

Blandings was just one of the gentle, amusing gossamers which Wodehouse draped over the less-appealing real world; a trick with which he seduced and held his fans. Wodehouse's relationship with the *Post* outlived Lorimer. *The Code of the Woosters*, featured earnest but scatterbrained Bertie Wooster and his savior, butler Jeeves, appearing in 1937. Poor Bertie falls victim to "The Code that if a girl says to a man 'I'm going to marry you,' he can't say, 'Oh no, you're not!'"[549] Engaged accidentally to nightmarishly sweet Madeline Basset, who views stars as God's daisy chain and talks with bunnies in the garden, Bertie also copes with the pugnacity of Madeline's secret admirer, a British fascist named Roderick Spode. Spode is leader of the Black Shorts. Things work out for the best, as the fascist Spoke marries Madeline, while Bertie escapes on a round-the-world cruise arranged by Jeeves.[550] American readers loved the complicated plot, the mockery of European militants wearing foolish uniforms, and the fizzy word play.

Roderick Spode, "a man with an eye that could open an oyster at sixty paces,"[551] differed from every other Wodehouse character in that he was firmly attached to current events. The unexpected demise of an uncle landed him in the House of Lords as the Right Honorable Lord Sidcup—depoliticizing him in the process. But before being sanitized by nobility, he led the Black Shorts. "About seven feet in height, and swathed in a plaid ulster which made him look about six feet across," Spode looked "as if Nature had intended to make a gorilla and had changed its mind at the last moment."[552] Beholding the behemoth, Bertie was reminded of current headlines. "I don't know if you have even seen those pictures in the papers of Dictators with tilted chins and blazing eyes," he says to the reader, "inflaming the populace with fiery words on the occasion of the opening of a new skittle alley, but that was what he reminded me of."[553] Only the assistance of Jeeves, who informs his employer that Spode, would-be *fuhrer* of Britain, designs women's undergarments as a business. Armed with this intelligence, Bertie diverts Spode's aggression, for, as Jeeves explains, "The subject of Eulalie, sir, is one which the gentleman, occupying the position he does in the public eye, would . . . be most reluctant to have ventilated."[554] *The Code of the Woosters* is a frothy meringue of humor, so

Spode did not herald political realism on Wodehouse's part. At most, Wodehouse dipped into political satire.[555] But Spode, like Charlie Chaplin's Adenoid Hynkel in 1940s *The Great Dictator,* mocked posturing dictators as ridiculous. *The Code of the Woosters* serial ran 1938 in the *Saturday Evening Post.*

Wodehouse commenced another Blandings novel, *Uncle Fred in the Springtime,* with intertwined plot lines involving the incorrigible flim-flammer Uncle Fred—"one of the hottest earls that ever donned a coronet"—making a visit to Blandings, where Lord Emsworth's attentions are devoted to his prize-winning pig, The Empress. Tension ensues when an unwanted guest, a Duke, inveigles Lady Constance to cede control of the manor to him. Lord Emsworth, appalled, enlists Uncle Fred to topple the unwanted Duke.[556] Two more quick volumes, *Eggs, Beans, and Crumpets* (1940), and *Quick Service* (1940), kept Wodehouse on a roll. By December 1941, American readers were enjoying the serial version of *Money in the Bank.* Meanwhile, the author collected a 1939 honorary degree at Oxford, while Hilaire Belloc's announcement that Wodehouse was the "best writer of English now alive" met approval in the United States.[557]

Wodehouse was less perspicacious when it came to the war. For years, he lived a trans-Atlantic life. During the early 1930s, he worked in Hollywood, particularly with Metro-Goldwyn Studios.[558] When studio politics led to the establishment of the Screenwriters Guild, the rival Screen Playwrights, and a degree of bitter labor controversies, Wodehouse found the arguments distracting and left his California perch for Le Toquet, France. He and wife Ethel purchased a country home there in 1935.[559] At the same time, Wodehouse became embroiled in tax disputes with United States federal authorities.[560] "Wodehouse was one of the highest paid writers in the United States," Paul R. Reynolds said, "but he never understood the business side of his writing or the function of an agent. In 1939, the *Saturday Evening Post* offered $45,000 for a Wodehouse serial."[561] That sum, as it happened, was the same as editor Wesley Stout offered the year before, so Reynolds, who succeeded his father as Wodehouse's agent, journeyed to Philadelphia for a negotiating session. There, the younger Reynolds offered $50,000 for serial rights to *Money in the Bank,* warning that failure to meet the figure would push Wodehouse to competing magazines. Aghast at the notion of losing their most popular author, the *Post* agreed to the higher sum. When a triumphant Reynolds related the negotiation details to Wodehouse, he was rebuked. "When I told Wodehouse, he was delighted at what he called the *Post'*s generosity. When I told him of my statement to Stout that it had to be $50,000 or we would go elsewhere, Wodehouse reproved me. He said he would not think of leaving such a generous magazine, and that my father would not have acted that way."[562]

The Wodehouses were at Le Toquet when the Germans invaded France. Failing to reach Dunkerque for evacuation, the author and his wife returned to their house.[563] The Germans found themselves with an unusual war prize; one of the most popular English-language writers, who had a loyal American readership just when when Berlin wanted to appease the United States. Wodehouse was interned and Nazi propagandists decided to put him to use. He was invited to Berlin to deliver five radio broadcasts to the United States.[564] Wodehouse unwisely agreed to deliver comic monologues on his situation, such as "How to be an Internee—and Like It."[565] His broadcasts were funny. His observation about Tost, where his camp was located, was a small gem: "There is a flat dullness about the countryside which has led many a visitor to say, 'If this is Upper Silesia, what must Lower Silesia be like?'"[566] The mistake Wodehouse made was in thinking that there was room for apolitical comedy from a beloved writer in the hands of Hitler. At a time when *Luftwaffe* bombs ravaged Britain, nothing was devoid of political significance.

Outcry was instantaneous. Elmer Davis, CBS broadcaster who later headed up the Office of War Information, scourged the novelist. "Mr. Wodehouse's many friends here in the United States will be glad to know he is free and he is apparently comfortable and happy . . . and of course, he was only in an internment camp. . . . People who get out of concentration camps, such as Dachau, for instance—well, in the first place, not a great many of them get out, and when they do, they are seldom able to broadcast."[567] Davis, who amplified his venom in writing, charged that Wodehouse had bargained his way out of internment through collaboration. Davis had no evidence, but the charges rankled. CBS correspondent Harry Flannery interviewed Wodehouse in Berlin. The June 26, 1941 interview, for which Flannery wrote the script, did as much damage to Wodehouse's reputation as the German broadcasts. The British resented his answer to Flannery's last question: "Anything you'd like to say, Mr. Wodehouse, about the United States?" "Yes, I'd like to be back there again," replied Wodehouse. "You see, I've always thought of the United States as sort of my country—lived there almost all the time since 1909—and I long to get back there once more. But I guess there's nothing I can do about that now, except write stories for you people. I hope you continue to like them."[568]

Flannery's interview was a set-up, for, due to Davis' claims, the reporter thought the author was pro-German. By his own account, Flannery was unfamiliar with Wodehouse's style. Flannery's 1942 book, *Assignment to Berlin*, further developed the claim that Wodehouse bought his way out of the internment camp with propaganda speeches.[569] Wodehouse naively thought the Flannery interview offered him the chance to communicate to American fans, whose friendliness he took for granted, and whose appetite for his current book project was undiminished. To the Germans, the interview and talks let them show Americans that their treatment of a favorite author was benign.

In Britain, William Connor, who penned a *Daily Mail* column as "Cassandra," wrote that Wodehouse was a traitor, pawning his honor to the Nazis "for the price of a soft bed in a luxury hotel."[570] Without discussing the broadcasts themselves, Conner charged that "Bertie Wooster faded out and Dr. Goebbels hobbled on to the scene." He linked the author to Judas and Vidkun Quisling, claiming that Goebbels took Wodehouse "into a high mountain, showed him all the Kingdoms of the world . . . and said unto him: 'All this power will I give thee if thou wilt worship the Fuhrer.'"[571] The follow-up in Britain saw a sustained campaign by the BBC to drum up the story and a war of letters and articles between those opposing Wodehouse, like Colin Vincent, who despised fiction friendly to the ruling-class, and those who supporting him, like George Orwell, who wrote the essay, "In Defense of P.G. Wodehouse." Evelyn Waugh astutely noted that Wodehouse's characters, whom the class-conscious Vincent decried as "moneyed and bored—the breeding ground of Fascism," made easy targets.[572] This was because a major part of the fighting faith animating Britain was the strong sense upper-class privilege was over, with a more equitable social system on the way. Such political sentiments were mostly absent in the United States, where Wodehouse's characters seemed innocent examples of English eccentricity, without of political significance.

The most accurate take on the entire affair came from the *Daily Mail*, which diagnosed Wodehouse's misguided diversion into radio as "amiable and boneheaded."[573] In the *Daily Telegraph*, Ian Hay, one of Wodehouse's old co-authors in theater and musical comedy, said that all thinking Britons were "horrified" by the broadcasts, even if they gave Wodehouse the benefit of their doubts. "No broadcast from Berlin by a world famous Englishman, however 'neutral' in tone, can serve as anything but an advertisement for Hitler," Hay observed.[574] Calling the upshot "soothing syrup for America," Hay wrote that Wodehouse "was deliberately released" for propaganda purposes, and that he had fallen for it. Calling his old friend "beloved but misguided," Hay spoke for millions when he asked him to "lay off."[575]

The aftermath of Wodehouse's mistake lasted for years. The affair was, at best, a colossal mistake by an author who ought to have known better. Still, Wodehouse was a valuable literary property; he had a new novel for which the *Saturday Evening Post* owned serial rights; he remained the best-read Anglo-American author in the United States. The *Post* wondered if the serial rights to the book Wodehouse wrote in captivity would pay off. Stout cabled his author in Germany, agreeing to run the serialization as long as Wodehouse made no more stupid radio appearances. "*Money in the Bank* good. Eager to buy but can only on your explicit assurance you will not broadcast from Germany . . . or act publicly in manner which can be construed as serving Nazi ends," ran the editor's telegram, adding "Your article strongly resented by many."[576] Stout knew how profitable any Wodehouse release could be to the *Post*, but he had to minimize the chance that his best author might blow residual American goodwill. For his part, the customarily remote Wodehouse revealed painful awareness of his boner, and kept trying to leave Germany.[577] Berlin refused to let him depart.

Stout's conditions were met in part because Wodehouse's sensible wife, Ethel, interposed herself between her clueless husband and his German captors. With his wife conducting his public affairs,[578] Wodehouse shut up and the headlines followed larger developments. Whatever public relations problems the broadcast imbroglio uncorked, American readers still loved a Wodehouse comic novel. Even in Britain, he sold over 450,000 books from 1941 until the end of the war.[579] *Money in the Bank* was serialized in 1941, with the seventh of eight installations appearing in December.

The novel started with a promising set-up: Viscount Uffenham, absent-minded yet protective of his family's interests, stashes away his diamonds and jewels in secret hiding places around the grounds of Shipley Hall. He forgets where he hid the valuables, leaving the family short of funds. Cash is supplied by renting the manor to a vegetarian exercise colony led by big-game hunter's rich widow, Mrs. Cork. American crooks Soapy and Dolly Molloy insinuate themselves into the Cork Health Colony, as does their rival, burglar Chimp Twist. Meanwhile, Jeff Miller is mistaken for a detective and Uffenham contemplates marrying Mrs. Cork for her fortune, so as to provide a dowry for his dutiful and beautiful daughter, Anne. Jeff and Anne, fated for each other, are engaged to the wrong people—Jeff, to Myrtle Shoesmith, his boss' daughter, and Anne to Lionel Green, an interior decorator keenly appreciative of beauty, especially his own. Uffenham disguises himself as Cakebread the Butler, serving Mrs. Cork and searching for the diamonds. The many *Post* readers who recognized the Wodehouse formula that December knew that happy endings were in store. The suspense lay in finding out how the storylines would resolve. Seven installations into an eight-part serial meant that December 1941 readers were at the comic high point. The tangled loose ends suddenly unknotted; the romance between Jeff and Anne was about to click; Uffenham remembered that he had deposited the diamonds in the bank—of the estate's duck pond.

Money in the Bank was not a major artistic event. What mattered most about it was its typicality; how the novel displayed the usual which earned its author such loyal readers. By pure coincidence, the novel's best portion appeared when the Pearl Harbor attack occurred. There were other articles in that December 20 edition of the *Saturday Evening Post*: "Prisoners of War," which discussed Nazi treatment of prisoners; "Night Action," and "The Yorkshireman Flies Again," two war-themed short stories; "The Biggest High School in the World," about New York's James Monroe High School, as well as poems and other pieces.[580] But nothing mattered as much as *Money in the Bank*. The book proved how durable Wodehouse's appeal remained, and how profound were the depths of American readers' appreciation for romantic literary frivolity set in the English countryside. There could be few subjects more distant from military tidings. But the serial's appearance that December demonstrated that, even after the onset of war, American readers enjoyed the dreamy comedies which painted their English allies in such lovable light. This was the hidden side of American support for Great Britain. There was a comprehensive British effort to win American hearts and minds. Journalists, diplomats, and broadcasters all told the British story. But American feelings had been heading in a pro-British direction for many years. Wodehouse's latest novel supported the Washington–London alliance, albeit accidentally. Broadcasters like Murrow supported the British out of conviction that it was the only proper thing to do; British writers like Malcolm Muggeridge put the best face on their nation because they were part of a public relations push to ensure positive American opinion. But Wodehouse wrote, not on the basis of wartime exigency or as part of an official campaign, but as a function of Anglo-American cultural concurrence which predated World War II. The war-induced push for pro-British American opinion was a success—fortunately for both nations. But it rested on a sturdy and organic cultural foundation, exemplified by Wodehouse.

Newspapers: all the war that's fit to print

While magazines had their editorial reactions predetermined by their publication schedule, newspapers had to deliver readable reaction each day. For the first days after Pearl Harbor, it was easy to rely on official announcements and speeches. But there were many reporters who found themselves well situated to report from war theaters once the action unfolded on December 7. One of the more well respected was *New York Times* correspondent, Otto D. Tolischus. Tolischus won the 1940 Pulitzer Prize for his coverage of the Polish campaign—which also earned him expulsion from the Third Reich on Goebbels' direct order.[581] He shifted to Stockholm before taking up his station as Tokyo bureau chief for the *Times*. Upon returning to the United States, he wrote *They Wanted War*, which appeared in 1942 and recounted his adventures in the Nazi capital. On December 7, 1941, he was in Tokyo, at work on a sketch of American ambassador Donald Grew. The story began at the beginning of Japanese–American relations. "Four score and seven years ago," wrote Tolischus,

> the 'black ships' of Commodore Matthew Calbraith Perry came knocking at the barred doors of the little-known and self-isolated Japanese islands, and, giving the *coup de grace* to the tottering feudal regime of the 'Taikun,' opened the country up to modern ideas and world commerce.[582]

He said that the current crisis resulted from Tokyo's sense that Japan had no more lessons to learn from her one-time mentors. Japan's violence he attributed to a determination to dominate Asia. Tolischus, worried that his lead might be too pugnacious, showed it to Grew, who telephoned his approval. Both men expected the story to draw flak from their hosts. Tolischus was interned along with other American reporters, and eventually exchanged, an experience he chronicled in *Tokyo Record*, which he wrote upon being returned to the United States.[583]

A far easier beat to cover, and one which showed how a reporter with some imagination could write war stories without venturing far afield, was Phenix City, Alabama. There, according to newswriter Walter Bernstein, who wrote a syndicated article, "the principal industry . . . is sex, and its customer is the Army."[584] Bernstein's article described the sedate action at Frankie's, named for "the woman who owns the place, a determined and ageless female with red hair and a strong pioneer streak."[585] He described soldiers on leave on a Saturday night, eating, drinking, gambling, talking to women, and avoiding the MP's, all to the tune of songs like, "Good-bye Mama, I'm Off to Yokohama."[586] Bernstein was on to something which Americans already realized: more and more young men were heading off to war, and into the services. Not only would they leave familiar faces and places behind, they would adopt an entire new set of references, customs, and patterns of behavior.

One challenge faced by layout editors in mid-to-late December was deciding how to cover official dispatches. The meaning of banner headlines such as "HUGE JAP FORCE IN LUZON: Japs Sink 2 British Capital Ships" required explaining by writers and untangling by readers.[587] That December 10 *Detroit News* banner told the story of the *Repulse* and *Prince of Wales*, while alluding to Japanese landings in the Philippines. But details were scarce and action hard to follow. Such remained the case on December 22, when the *News* front page announced "80 SHIPLOADS OF JAPS ATTACK LUZON; US DEFENSES HOLD IN HEAVY BATTLE."[588] Others headlines were simple to understand: "GERMANY, ITALY, DECLARE WAR ON U.S." required very little instruction for the readers.[589] Also easy to grasp was "SURRENDER OF HONG KONG IS REPORTED," which ran on Christmas.[590]

Maps provided newspaper editors with the opportunity to fill space with information. Ten days after Pearl Harbor, Associated Press ran a geography story about Johnston Island. "Johnston Island, Discovered in 1807, Is Only a Tiny Speck," explained the helpful headline.[591] What followed was a mini-history lesson on the islet 700 miles southwest of Honolulu, home to a naval air station referred to in a nearby article headlined, "Johnston, Maui Islands Shelled by Jap Vessels.[592] Closer to home, Washington, D.C. provided news in more abundance, including the build-up to the post-Pearl Harbor inquest. "BOARD NAMED TO INVESTIGATE PEARL HARBOR" carried a sub-header, "Justice Roberts Heads Inquiry Into Why Hawaii Was Not On Alert; Group Will Visit Island Soon For Study Ordered By Roosevelt."[593] Supreme Court Justice Owen J. Roberts brought the judiciary branch into the war effort. Former military brass made up the Board of Inquiry membership. Their names were included in the story, with the accompanying message that their retired status afforded them a degree of critical detachment from ongoing military politics: Major General Frank R. McCoy, long stationed in the Philippines and currently head of the Foreign Policy Association;

Brigadier General Joseph T. McNarney, Air Corps officer recently returned from London; Admiral William H. Standley, retired Chief of Naval Operations; Rear Admiral Joseph M. Reeves, former Commander-in-Chief of the Fleet.[594] Also present at the meeting were Navy Secretary Knox, Army Secretary Stimson, Army Chief of Staff General Marshall, and Admiral Ernest J. King.[595] The White House's move somewhat forestalled intervening Congressional inquiries, which Roosevelt considered dangerous for wartime unity. Congressional support came through in a quote from the Chairman of the House Naval Affairs Subcommittee, David I. Walsh (D-MA), who warned colleagues against public posturing: "I think everything has been said that ought to be said at this time." Continuing the theme of party and national solidarity and deference to Presidential prerogatives, Walsh made an argument from precedent. "It is customary for the army and navy to make their own investigations first," Walsh explained. "Then Congress will have opportunity, if it desires, to investigate the investigation."[596] Whether and how Congress chose to "investigate the investigation" was part of the tug-of-war between the Capitol and White House for dominance in foreign affairs dating back to George Washington's complaints about Senatorial obstructionism with the Jay Treaty.[597] The President, with majorities in both houses and abundant experience in working with, or working over, Congress, was unlikely to give the legislative branch much chance to gnawing at his dominant position. This interested Japan's diplomat, Nomura, following the story from internment. In his diary for December 16, Nomura observed that newspapers carried full reprints of Roosevelt's report to Congress on the history of Japanese–American relations. Regarding White House attempts to exercise damage control after Pearl Harbor, Nomura wrote that,

> They are endeavoring to calm down public opinion by publishing yesterday's statements of Secretary of Navy Knox. The paragraph which disclosed that *the responsible officers were "not on the alert against a surprise attack"* is arresting public attention. It appears that the Navy and Army will start investigations first of all . . .

he added, wondering whether Congress would get involved.[598]

Signs that the White House meant business came on December 18, when the *New York Times* carried details of the post-Pearl Harbor defense shake-up. "Kimmel is Succeeded by Nimitz in Command of the Pacific Fleet; Gen. Short Also Goes; Emmons Replaces Him—Tinker Takes Martin's Post in Air Force," was the lengthy headline. The story which made clear how complete the sweep was. Knox had been in Hawaii for two days. His portfolio included the power to spearhead the reorganization.[599] Short, Kimmel, and Frederick L. Martin were all replaced by successors not tarred by Pearl Harbor's brush, such as Admiral Chester Nimitz. Pre

December 7 brass would henceforth face inquiries while post-December 7 brass would wage the war.

In terms of straight battlefront news, newspapers carried the largest amount. But the quantity was often circumscribed by censorship or the fog of battle. As December progressed, it became obvious that Japanese thrusts were cutting deep down the Malay Peninsula, closer to Singapore and that Japan had Wake Island in a naval grip precluding relief of the garrison.[600] The other tentacle of the Japanese octopus squeezed the Philippines and MacArthur. It was at Wake and the Philippines where the first sustained American defensive battles were fought. Remote Wake was cut off and thus not a source of on-site reportage. The Philippines, however, while under assault, were vast, with large areas under American control.

The Philippines, Wake Island, and China—altered expectations

ENEMY ON ISLAND X ISSUE IN DOUBT
> Cable sent by Commander Winfield S. Cunningham, Wake Island, to CINCPAC,[601] Honolulu, December 23, 1941[602]

This is it. Our order of business changes. Be ready for any eventuality.
> Claire B. Chennault to members of the Flying Tigers American Volunteer Group, December 8, 1941[603]

Our criticisms are not for the boxing commission that makes the matches, but for the man who sends us into the ring in a worn-out pair of shoes.
> Lieutenant Henry G. Lee, Headquarters, Philippine Division, (Platoon Leader, M.P. Company)[604]

As early as the spring of 1941, the expected fall of the Philippines was an anticipated fact to the man who "sent us into the ring in a worn-out pair of shoes." In March 1941 the policy of 'Europe first' became the object of our 'boxing commission,' namely, the U.S. War Department, Chief of Staff Marshall, and the President of the United States. Every effort was made to build up the British defenses against Hitler while merely giving lip service to us in the Philippines.
> Richard M. Gordon, M.P. Company, Philippine Division[605]

We hadn't long to wait, after Pearl Harbor.
> Carlos P. Romulo[606]

The Philippines: the far command

Sir John Robert Seeley attributed Britain's gaining of Empire to "absent-mindedness," meaning that disparate diplomatic crises and political objectives led to colonial acquisition; not a well-planned campaign. Such was the pattern at work when the United States went to war with Spain, too. Egregious diplomatic miscommunication hardened misunderstandings into diplomatic circumstances which were no less dangerous for being wrong. Unfortunately for international peace, there are few defenses against determined ignorance. "This problem of reliable perception is compounded by the fact that foreign policy decision-makers believe they have a largely realistic view of the world they face, and that they understand the other side's views and intentions," wrote a diplomatic historian examining the Spanish-American slide towards war.[607]

Bitter comedy mixed in with the tragic. This was manifested when a bemused President William L. McKinley, upon hearing of Commodore Dewey's May 1898 victory at Manila Bay, confessed that he could not have come within 2,000 miles of locating the Philippines without consulting a globe.[608] McKinley later amplified his ignorance of the islands. "The truth is I didn't want the Philippines," the President insisted, "And when they came to us as a gift from the gods, I did not know what to do with them."[609]

The entire archipelago presented an idyll of physical beauty: soaring interior mountains, forested valleys, white beaches with waving palm fronds. The civilization presented an intriguing cultural mixture; Ferdinand Magellan brought Christianity, Roman Catholic-based laws and Spanish culture. Chinese expatriates controlled much of the commerce, linking to Asian via trade. Islam predominated in the south.[610] There were independence advocates, led by Emiliano Aguinaldo, who viewed the Spanish exit as the opportunity for national freedom. Aguinaldo's views occasioned some American sympathy when Jacob Schurman, founding chair of the Philippines Commission, laid out official United States policy: "The destiny of the Philippine Islands is not to be a state or territory of the United States, but a daughter republic of ours—a new birth of liberty on the other side of the Pacific, which shall animate and energize those lovely islands of the tropical seas . . . as a monument of progress and a beacon to all the oppressed and benighted millions of the Asiatic continent."[611]

Dulcet words concentrated Progressive impulses which Kipling would recognize as White Man's Burden. Aguinaldo, ready for immediate independence, rejected American-aided uplift and took to the bush, leading a guerilla struggle. Among the American military leaders who fought Aguinaldo and the affiliated Moros, none was more skilled than General Arthur MacArthur. He followed his successful counterinsurgency with a stint as Military Governor, during which he instituted educational, legal, and economic reforms. These popular measures earned trust for American intentions even from former rebels.[612] Joining his father in Manila in 1903 was son Douglas, fresh from heading his West Point class. Douglas' poised self-confidence shone through when an admiring Manila woman asked him if he was the General's son. "General MacArthur has that proud distinction," cracked the younger soldier, who befriended Filipino leaders like Manuel Quezon, the former guerrilla who joined the American-fostered political system.[613]

Meanwhile, there were plenty of Americans who journeyed there to lift up their new brethren. Teachers, missionaries, doctors, and engineers all came. The most famous influx was the Thomasites, named after the USS Thomas, which brought them in 1901. Idealistic Americans full of conviction that they could make life better for Filipinos fanned out, founding schools and as directed by Education Act Number 34, a commission headed by William Howard Taft instituted to set up a national educational system along American lines.[614] Some arrivals were motivated by a yen for adventure as well as an urge to serve. Among these were Roy and Edna Bell, from Emporia, Kansas. One day, the young couple attended a lecture by a missionary who taught at the Silliman Institute, on Negros Island. Inspired, the Bells trained and were hired at Silliman in 1921. The school, founded by Presbyterians, evolved into a university, where Roy was both physics professor and athletics coach.[615] These were exciting times for Americans there. Young Filipino charges picked up American cultural patterns, speaking English, Pledging Allegiance, playing baseball and basketball. The new system accepted and integrated the existing Filipino-Spanish elites, who continued exercising cultural leadership.[616] Elinor Chamberlain, who arrived in the islands to teach English after graduating from the University of Michigan in 1922, reminisced about the appeal of the colonial lifestyle. Political and social conditions were peaceful, she stressed,

> But nature in the Far Eastern tropics has unusual diversions in store to keep life uncertain. I grew familiar with typhoons and earthquakes; I saw a cholera epidemic conquered by modern methods of prevention; I lived . . . only a few feet from the edge of a jungle in a house shared with two charming American women and a changing assortment of ants, cockroaches, spiders as big as saucers, house lizards of various kinds, and snakes.[617]

For three-and-a-half decades, the islands drifted as a semi-nation, affiliated with the United States, but with a degree of autonomy. Part of Washington's hesitation stemmed from a basic fact: administering the islands was expensive. Defending them would be even more so. During World War I, the military had more pressing concerns; the 1920s spawned no desire to address Asian complexities; the 1930s saw the Depression, when spending on a colony was hard to justify. Major moves included the navy's stationing of the Asiatic Fleet's Main Station to Manila, and the construction of forts to protect the Bay.

Tensions with Japan brought greater scrutiny. The 1936 Tydings-McDuffie Act clarified Filipino status.[618] Total independence was promised by 1946. MacArthur's friend Quezon was an early favorite for the future presidency. Their relationship became strained as each grew more powerful. During a 1934 Washington visit, Quezon asked the General if the archipelago could be defended, presumably from the Japanese. "I don't *think* the Philippines can defend themselves, I *know* they can," was MacArthur's response.[619] Such confidence won the General the position as Chief Military Advisor to Quezon, elected as President of the Philippine Commonwealth in 1936. Sensitive to appearances, the new leader of the Filipino military desired a residence on a par with the magnificent Malacanan Palace, home of the Governor-General. "We cannot build another Malacanan Palace," Quezon admitted. "But perhaps we can give you comparable accommodation."[620] Quezon delivered, and MacArthur moved into a lofty penthouse apartment newly built atop the Manila Hotel. Its opulence delighted him—and his new wife—so that an aide observed that the General "conducted almost as much business while walking up and down the terrace as he did at his office."[621]

Among the points MacArthur could ponder gazing down at Manila's harbor below was how to refurbish and reorganize Filipino defenses. War Plan Orange, later Rainbow Five, presented him with problems and opportunities. As long as the plan called for holding the Philippines, MacArthur viewed the strategy favorably. But, if it ever appeared that the islands were deemed expendable, then MacArthur's lifelong devotion to the islands' destiny, and his own, meant he would oppose the plan.

The pattern of army life in the Philippines was stately and antiquated. It was, said a visitor, "An army of polo ponies and long golf games, of cheap domestic help and shopping trips to Shanghai and Hong Kong."[622] No event was more riveting than the annual army–navy football game back in the United States. When the game kicked off, Manila's Army and Navy Club was the place to be. Radios tuned in and mascots were procured. "Officers gathered each year on the lawn to listen . . . during the early hours of the morning. When Army made a touchdown, a mule would be ceremoniously paraded around the lawn. When Navy scored, a goat was similarly honored."[623]

A major resupply program was underway in the Philippines and other Pacific outposts on December 7. Strengthening the Philippine Army, building new air strips, roads, and bridges, and shoring up Commonwealth war reserves were articulated in a $52 million estimate submitted to Washington by the army on June 12, 1941.[624] On December 7, a convoy laden with troops, airmen, and tons of materiel was headed for Manila.[625] Serious plans to reinforce potential Pacific battle stations had coalesced the preceding Spring, prompted by Japan's Indochina invasion. The American military establishment was aware that existing defense arrangements in the Pacific were inadequate. Hawaii was the first recipient of more men and arms, but by late summer, the Philippines received supplies. MacArthur was an able lobbyist for this resupply effort. From September through November, it involved task force convoys ferrying artillery and tank battalions, bomber squadrons, armaments and weapons systems of various sorts, and PT boats.[626] MacArthur liked PT Boats. He envisioned these small, lightly armored, but fast and nimble torpedo craft as the backbone of the Philippine Navy he intended to build.[627]

MacArthur was assembling a staff when, on July 26, 1941, Roosevelt appointed him Commanding General of all United States Forces in the Far East. This authorized him to mobilize the Philippine Army.[628] The challenge was herculean; MacArthur needed more supplies. He had to administer and train inexperienced Filipino divisions while integrating them with Americans already in place. The outbreak of war cut preparations short. Ten Philippine Army reserve divisions went into action in July, each intended to sport three infantry regiments, and single artillery, antitank, engineer, medical, and quartermaster battalions, along with divisional headquarters supported by signal, ordnance, and motor transport sections. Not one division had its units in place by December 8. Several units that were in place were undertrained.[629] On the other hand, the Japanese attack was not completely unexpected, since all units on fortified islands were in readiness at battle stations, "prepared for any emergency" eight days before the assault began.[630] The situation was mixed. Resupply and training efforts were underway, but more time was needed for these to bear fruit. The worry was that American attentions lavished on the Commonwealth were too sparse and too late. While MacArthur exuded optimism, other close observers were less sanguine. Major Eisenhower, already showing a genius for organizational thinking, knew that MacArthur's overall plan for a fully formed army of 40 divisions, with 400,000 trained soldiers, was a pipe dream even by the 1946 timetable. Doubtful in light of the logistics, Eisenhower foresaw "a skeleton force that someday might have flesh put on its bones."[631]

When word from Pearl Harbor came to Manila, the lead officers were asleep. Asiatic Fleet Commander-in-Chief Admiral Thomas C. Hart, awakened by the duty officer, got word at 3:00 a.m.; MacArthur was roused in his penthouse one hour later.[632] The message they read was the same sent by Kimmel to Washington: AIR RAID ON PEARL HARBOR. THIS IS NO DRILL.[633] Alerts to personnel at sea and on land went out. Air power, long a concern of MacArthur's, was on his mind. Months before, aware that the air arm was his weakest, he wanted to build a bomber/fighter force that would give him offensive punch. The idea was to construct airfields from lower Mindanao northwards through Luzon, not only protecting supply lines from the Dutch East Indies and Malaya, but giving

MacArthur the chance to conduct raids on Japanese shipping lanes and bases as far away as Formosa.[634] These plans came together by October, but constructing and equipping such an air force took time and funds. MacArthur considered Harold Ickes an impediment, claiming that the intrusive Secretary of the Interior was obstructionist.[635] Stymied, MacArthur arranged with the meager air assets at his disposal. Formosa on his mind, he moved B-17s from Clark Field on Luzon to Delmonte Field, on Mindanao, on November 21. Only half of his Flying Fortress fleet was on Mindanao by December 8, which later puzzled the General.[636] Seeing that orders are obeyed and not being puzzled was a main aspect of MacArthur's duty.[637] With news of the war's outbreak, whether and how to disperse planes from Clark was a hot topic. Some officers advocated a prompt attack on Formosa, others argued that sending out the bombers without proper escort would mean a suicide mission.[638] A false alert scrambled planes at Clark around 8:30 a.m. P-40s flew skyward, circled, and, finding no Japanese attackers, landed at 10 a.m. They were still on their hardstands when the Japanese did appear overhead. The bombing and strafing at Clark continued until a considerable portion of MacArthur's existing air strength was demolished.[639]

Historians and investigators debated this debacle for years. Some blamed General Lewis H. Brereton, MacArthur's air chief. Others laid it off on confusion between service branches. Some pointed to foggy weather. Still others faulted MacArthur. MacArthur himself made a pretense of standing by Brereton, but his support included an accusation that "the tactical handling of his command, including all necessaries for its protection against air attack of his planes on the ground, was entirely in his own hands."[640] MacArthur's enemies pounced on the loss of planes at Clark, along with other concurrent inaction, such as the failure to move food stocks to defensible positions. They argued that this inaction during those crucial first hours was a failure.[641] Was MacArthur panicked by the start of the campaign? Merely the question might have ended his career. But the fast rate of events meant that Clark Field was not to become a public issue interfering with MacArthur's defense of the Philippines. MacArthur tossed off the potential scandal as irrelevant. His aircraft were too few and too obsolete to have changed the final outcome, he said, adding that the scale of losses at Pearl Harbor "destroyed any possibility of future Philippine air power. Our sky defense died with our battleships in the waves off Ford Island," MacArthur declared. "It cancelled Rainbow 5 and sealed our doom."[642] General Masaharu Homma's Luzon invasion force landed almost unopposed; ill-trained Filipino units took to the forested hills, and Manila lay bare between Japanese pincers.[643]

It was at offices of the *Herald*, Manila's English-language newspaper, that Carlos Romulo watched the first raiders over the capital on their sinister way to Clark. Trained newsman, Romulo belonged to Manila's elite and was a friend to MacArthur. The General told him two weeks before that, once the war started,

Romulo would serve as Philippine Army Colonel and Press Relations aid to the General. "If war breaks," Romulo had answered, "There's no place I'd rather be."[644] Manila was vulnerable—Romulo called it "unprotected and unprepared."[645] Church bells tolling the noon hour accompanied air raid sirens, while citizens fled through the streets: bearded priests from the College of San Juan de Letran, carters holding their ponies' halters, women huddling in a park full of acacia trees, a newsboy straddling a wall shaking his fist at the planes and shouting in Tagalog, "You will pay, you will pay!"[646]

To Romulo, the Japan was helped by subversion. "In my travels in the Far East I had learned how skillful they were at learning the secrets of other countries," he claimed. "Every Japanese in Manila was ready to welcome his invading countrymen. He had his suitcase packed, a first-aid kit, and a Japanese flag!"[647] By December 17, Romulo was introduced to press correspondents as MacArthur's top press aide. "Keep 'em warned," the General instructed him, "but don't panic them."[648] Romulo served as MacArthur's interlocutor over the next hectic weeks. His duties involved issuing press releases, concocting headlines, conferencing with editors, setting up radio programs, and coordinating public information.[649] What lay ahead was the evacuation of Manila, the withdrawal to the Bataan Peninsula, and the last stand at Corregidor. These were the developments that would earn MacArthur the plaudits which allowed him to overcome a shaky start to the war.

Wake Island: Pacific Siege

It was far from everyplace, and, at 2.5 square miles, tiny even for a stepping-stone. But no bit of rock was really obscure in the Pacific Ocean, not with Japan and the United States sizing up each other's maritime positions. Wake Island sits in the mid-Pacific, 1,034 miles west of Midway Island, 2,004 miles west of Hawaii, 600 miles closer to Tokyo than Pearl Harbor.[650] All of this was known to Japanese strategists planning to seize it. Capturing Wake would preclude American use of the island as an air base for raids against the Marshall and Gilberts, threaten Philippine resupply, and support any drive against Midway and Hawaii. Defense resources included a detachment of about 400 Marines from the First Defense Battalion of the Fleet Marine Force, Pacific, commanded by Major John P.S. Devereux, as well as a squadron of fighter planes, assorted navy personnel, and some private construction contractors reinforcing the garrison's structures.[651] Conspicuously absent was a radar unit. Despite hopeful rumors, Wake never received the radar its defenders wanted, which meant that Marine lookouts atop the island's two 50-foot water towers were the warning system. The last Wake Island supply ship brought a garbage truck instead, a choice due either to superannuated priorities or the navy's fear that the island was so vulnerable a radar might be captured.[652] Wake hummed with activity from October on, as Devereux prodded his men preparing defenses. Newly arrived Marines were impressed by the urgency emanating from their leaders. "It seemed like before we opened our seabags, they'd . . . told us to go to work," muttered a Corporal.[653] The Marines toiled up to 16 hours per day from October onward, filling, digging, hauling, loading, filling sandbags, building platforms, fixing gun emplacements. They complained, but they complied. "At that time, we thought Devereux was plain horse shit working us around the clock," one admitted.[654] Gradually, from a nearly bare state, Wake came to resemble a defensive outpost.

Devereux knew that, to Japan's planners, Wake was a tempting plum within their grasp. Bombing began on Pearl Harbor day, December 8 on the island since it lay west of the International Date Line.[655] Among the first targets was the Pan American Airways site, including a hotel and landing strip. This was the stop-over point for the China Clipper. It became clear that Wake Island was expected to defend itself as long as possible without much hope for relief. Prospects for assistance became more remote in the darkness of early morning on December 11, when Japan's invasion force arrived offshore: cruisers *Yubari, Tatsuta,* and *Tenryu*, along with six destroyers, four converted transports, and two submarines.[656] Rear Admiral Sadamichi Kajioka was in command, his pennant fluttering on *Yubari*.[657] Kajioka's superior was Vice Admiral Shigeyoshi Inoue, Fourth Fleet Commander and one of the most air-oriented admirals in the Imperial Navy.[658] For that reason, Kajioka's decision to forego aircraft carrier support, depending on the efficacy of the June 8 raids, was a gamble.[659] The island garrison spotted the ships. "Something seems to be moving out on the water. I think maybe we saw a faint light out there, too," a lookout reported. Told of the call, Devereaux responded, "Yeah, I'm getting some other reports about movements at sea. I'm going out to take a look for myself."[660]

What the Marine major saw was the Japanese invasion flotilla. What he could not have known was that his contingent was about to write the first tale of American glory in the war. The battle at Wake was no victory, but it impressed Americans longing for their forces to fight back against Japan. Prior to his Wake posting, Devereux was known in the Corps as a stickler, but duty on the remote atoll softened his image among the men. They saw him less as a taskmaster and more as a concerned commander.[661] The Major and his garrison were about to become symbols in military lore.

After they spotted the fleet, the Grumman Wildcats which had escaped the December 8 attacks scrambled, and went after the Japanese. Ashore, men— including civilian workers who voluntarily served as ammunition handlers— worked the shore batteries and anti-aircraft guns. Devereux had his defenses in order. When the time was right, salvos from his batteries answered *Yubari*, forcing a stunned Kajioka to withdraw. Transports in the water took direct hits, retreating along with the flagship. Barely three days after Pearl Harbor, United States forces on a small Pacific island drove their attackers back. A flummoxed Kajioka sailed over the horizon to plot his next attempt. Invasion was postponed.[662]

There was no news reporting from Wake. At this point, Roosevelt began praising the island's defense as magnificent. Reporters and commentators picked up the thread, spinning it into stories which gave Americans swallowing hard after Pearl Harbor a degree of relief. Embedded in the accounts was the awareness that Wake's heroics lay holding off a superior foe. Like the Alamo, Wake Island was a heroic defense against the odds. But defense, for all its doggedness, could have only one outcome.

It took two weeks for the Japanese to plan their next landing. In the darkness of December 23, the Japanese put troops ashore. Japanese soldiers ensured that the Marines, sailors, and civilians fighting them off were too preoccupied to target the ships. The Americans gave up ground slowly and at great cost to the Japanese, but implacable daylight made the hopelessness of the situation clear. Flat and small, Wake offered no chance for guerilla defense. Small squads counterattacked, and amidst the agonies of combat there were scenes of heroism which Americans at home could only guess at. It was a last-stand battle.[663] At this moment, Wake's garrison sent a message that the enemy had landed and the issue was in doubt. The publicized message became famous as shorthand for dauntlessness. Cunningham and Devereux conferred. "Well," said the Navy commander to his Marine counterpart, "I guess we'd better give it to them."[664]

After Dunkerque, a dejected Churchill said that wars were not won by evacuations. Neither, Devereux and Cunningham might have thought, were they won by last stands. To the Japanese, Wake Island was a tactical victory. But the defense of Wake gave Americans a resolute story and a slate of new heroes to admire, between Pearl Harbor and Christmas. Media accounts of the battle stressed the sacrifice made by the defenders. While Americans could not yet savor victory, they took solace in the performance at Wake, where 124 Americans—49 military and 75 civilian—died.[665] Moreover, the battle's aftermath brought to world attention an important and bleak aspect of the war: that heavy-handed contempt which Japan showed for prisoners. Mistreatment began on the island and continued when, on January 20, many were evacuated to Japan. Casual cruelty and planned violence were part of what the captured experienced. When Japanese propaganda photographs of POW's began appearing from Tokyo's news services, care was taken to showcase the Wake defenders. *Freedom* was the grotesque title of the English-language Japanese magazine based in Shanghai which featured a photo of a wan-looking Devereux holding a prop radio given to him by his supposedly generous captors.[666] Another picture showed Wake Island defenders in the Zentsuji prison camp, washing over a common sink. A third showed a volleyball game.[667] Failure to crop out the bayonet-wielding guard gave the volleyball picture an unintendedly ominous aspect.

As a battle, Wake Island was self-contained, unique in that there were so few images or written accounts. But as a symbolic event, Wake Island became totemic. Americans who could not see, listen to, or read accounts of what happened there for years imagined full well. So did Hollywood. When *Wake Island,* starring William Bendix and Robert Preston, hit theaters in 1942, it was a box-office sensation, earning four Oscar nominations and providing audiences visual supplement for the battle waged on that small island and in the national imagination. The degree to which Wake Island's heroics penetrated American thoughts and the speed with which they did so was everywhere apparent. *Virginia Quarterly Review* devoted 14 pages of its Summer 1942 issue to "The Saga of Wake," a literary recounting of the battle: "It was hot, and in the tangled thickets of ten-foot bush the love birds courted," supplementing a day-by-day account of the actions of Devereux and Cunningham. The story ended with a reminder that, while Americans were singing "Silent Night, Holy Night," two nights before Christmas, the Marines of Wake were sending their last messages while the enemy came in "through the white surf of the broken reef, crawling out of the landing boats on to the white beaches, charging in the moonlight toward the machine gun nests in the scrub and the hardwood."[668]

China—Tigers in the sky

American fascination with China started in 1784, when *Empress of China* sailed from New York, kicking off the China trade. After that, "The dream that China was a romantic land of great beauty" never vanished from American culture.[669] Through centuries of commerce, missionary work, and immigration, China imprinted itself onto the American imagination. Cultural encounters kicked up charismatic characters, a process which World War II perpetuated. That the "China of the American Imagination" was not always the China of earthly actuality was not always important to Americans suffused by the romance of the world's oldest civilization. Before World War II, there were many common American associations regarding China: the dread fun of Buffalo Bill's Boxer Rebellion reenactments at the turn of the century, the much-lauded heroism of Christian missionaries working spreading hope in the land of Confucian fatalism, the stoic nobility of Pearl Buck's Chinese peasants, tilling the good earth through political and natural catastrophe. More delineative was the strategic role played by China. It was the world's most populous nation, engaged in war with Japan. The two strains, romantic and strategic, ran together in American media accounts of China at war. Contributing was Henry Luce's long-time proprietary interest in the nation. But war news from China played across the media landscape, not just in *Time* and *Life*.

China's leadership was dominated by people suitable for lavish media coverage. The retinue surrounding Chiang Kai-Shek, dominated by the amazing Soong clan, played the dominant role. Chiang's wife, May-Ling Soong, was daughter of Charlie Soong, who, as Han Chiao-Shun, made his way from Hainan Island to Java, then to Boston, in 1878.[670] He graduated from Vanderbilt in 1885, and went to work for the American Bible Society doing missionary work back in China. Charlie Soong settled in Shanghai with wife, Ni Kwei-tseng—herself descended from a Ming Dynasty minister. They raised six children, three boys and three girls.[671]

These children became a phenomenon, individually and as a set. May-ling went to Wellesley, eventually marrying Chiang in 1927. Their wedding made the front page of the *New York Times*.[672] Sister Ai-ling married H.H. Kung, 75th generation descendant of Confucius, who became Chiang's Finance Minister.[673] His duties included pressing the West for financial aid to buttress the fight against Japan. Sister Ching-ling married Sun Yat-Sen, father of the Chinese Republic. Brother T.V. Soong's accomplishments included organizing the national Central Bank, and—importantly in 1941–1942—organizing the Chinese Air Force. Among his American friends Soong counted top media figures, including *Chicago Daily News* reporter Edgar Ansell Mower and *New York Herald-Tribune* star Joseph Alsop.[674] All the Soongs moved easily and among the highest circles of American society, winning over presidents, publishers, and generals. Soong and Kung rotated in and out of favor with Chiang but neither was ever far from Kuomintang political and economic power. American friends included Thomas Corcoran, "Tommy the Cork." Vintage New Dealer, one of the "Gold Dust Twins" along with Benjamin V. Cohen, and part of the original Brains Trust, Corcoran was a titanic lobbyist; the fixer who guided through Washington's labyrinth. Corcoran helped Soong arrange China Defense Supplies, Inc., which channeled Lend-Lease materiel from the United States to Chiang's government in Chungking.[675] The coveted Lend-Lease link was not enough for Chiang, however. Getting the supplies to China, virtually cut off from the world now that Japan controlled its coastline and ports, emerged as a major challenge. Chiang and his entourage focused on defending Burma, since it was from that British colony that tenuous trans-Himalaya connections linked to the Allies. Chungking, provisional capital, received news of Pearl Harbor jubilantly. The Nationalist government was certain that the United States connection would strengthen chances against Japan.[676]

The KMT's best advocate was Henry Luce. *Time* and *Life* covered its leaders, with lavish attention for Chiang. Luce, son of China missionaries, spent as much time reckoning on that country's path as he did contemplating the American Century. For Luce, Chiang became history's indispensable man in Asia. But that came later in the war. In late 1941, the Generalissimo was not yet Luce's greatest hero. The Sinophile publisher's magazines did not cover and praise Chiang to the exclusion of other regional figures, partly because dubious Theodore White had influence over coverage.[677] White worried that Chiang's government rested on tottery foundations; that pusillanimity and corruption dogged its battlefield performance. He found efforts against Japan too fitful, seeing the KMT distracted by Mao's communists.

In December 1941, however, these were arguments yet to unfold. Many of the figures who shaped American involvement with China had yet to take up the challenges which made their legacies. Major General Joseph W. Stilwell, not yet famous as "Vinegar Joe," was not in Asia. Instead, as senior tactical commander, he manned a desk in San Bernadino, California, drawing up plans to defend the coastline from San Diego to Pismo Beach. He and his wife heard the news of Pearl Harbor at their Carmel home. Right away, Stilwell realized that there was too little of everything—men, guns, ammunition—to fight off Japanese landings. Since no one knew where the Japanese fleet was, his concern was intense. Southern California made a luscious target. Stilwell's acrid manner came through when he informed the War Department he could barely resist for a few hours. He demanded the necessaries, only to find himself put off over the phone by a nervous War Department staffer. When the Washington-based officer replied that Washington would do "the best we can" to meet his need for arms, Stilwell roared, "The best you can! Good God, what the hell am I supposed to do? Fight 'em off with oranges?"[678] On December 22, General Omar Bradley ordered him to Washington, where the Anglophobic Stilwell joined in the ARCADIA Conference synchronizing plans with the British, developing plans for the invasion of North Africa. Not until late January did Stilwell learn that his wartime fate lay deep in Asia.[679] In late 1941, what counted for Americans was fighting back against the Japanese. From China, intriguing combat stories appeared. The tales were unexpectedly upbeat.

The Flying Tiger tale began one year earlier, at an October 1940 Washington dinner at which Soong, Mowrer, and Alsop hosted a craggy-faced Army Air Corps veteran serving as Colonel in the Chinese Air Force, Claire Lee Chennault.[680] After that dinner, Chennault made the capital rounds. Chiang's idea was for his minions to lobby against the puppet government of Wang Ching-wei and to ask for assistance denying the Nanking collaborators any diplomatic legitimacy. But Chennault focused on preaching the dangers to American aviation posed by Japan's new Zero fighter. The message was counterintuitive, given the prejudice that Japanese industry lacked originality and could only build shoddy knock-offs. Among those hearing Chennault's warning was Corcoran, who later recalled, "If he had left in the first ten minutes, I would have written him off as a fanatic."[681] As it happened, Chennault took an hour to convert Tommy the Cork into a believer. Chennault thereafter got highest access on his 1940 trip, even speaking with George Marshall, while Corcoran recommended him to Roosevelt as a good asset for use against the Japanese.[682]

By the time he came to official Washington's attention in 1940, Chennault had been fighting the Japanese for three years, commanding Chinese fliers and piloting his Curtiss Hawk 75 as he led Chiang's Air Force.[683] So, perhaps the story of the Flying Tigers began in 1937. Or perhaps it began earlier, when Chennault—like General Billy Mitchell, one of those independent-minded agitators whom military bureaucracies loathe at first—opposed the bomber focus in the Air Corps. Chennault hailed from East Texas and was always a maverick. He entered Louisiana State University in 1909, dropping out to follow a teacher training course at the Normal School in Natchitoches, and joining the army when the United States entered World War I. Flying excited him, so he gained his coveted wings in 1919. Making his way upward through ranks, he was a captain in 1930, when he earned appointment to the Air Corps Tactical School.[684]

Certain doctrines had already found favor along the corridors through which strolled the War Department's brightest. To go against accepted notions was to court career trouble. Billy Mitchell, whose strong belief in the efficacy of airplanes as a wing of combat at sea ran afoul of navy principles, learned this. So did Chennault. The dogma Chennault challenged was laid out in *The Command of the Air*, the hugely influential 1921 book written by Italian aviation theorist Giulio Douhet. Douhet was the first systematic thinker to address air war. Using his own experience and data from World War I, Douhet articulated a martial vision which vibrated with possibilities. Airplanes, he argued, opened up combat into a new dimension, making the vastness of the sky a new theater of operations. "The speed and freedom of the airplane," as Douhet put it, lent the air arm a host of specific advantages over surface elements on land and at sea.[685] Here was the millennial quest of military thinkers: how to liberate earthbound forces from terrestrial strictures. But if Douhet's view of aviation carried with it elements of that dream, it also implied inescapable conclusions. Among those were the certainty that airplanes' speed suited them for attack, that their element must be the offensive, that bombers were the best aerial weapons. Douhet was the initial advocate of strategic bombing, which he foresaw could be used, not just to batter an enemy's airplanes, but to sap a citizenry's will to fight on. He understood bombing as part of war's "national totality," which he explained as the condition when an "entire population and all the resources of a nation are sucked into the maw of war."[686]

Douhet was the most important early air theorist. But there were developments he did not foresee. His followers adopted his arguments wholesale. But Chennault disagreed with the overemphasis on bombers, which he thought were not so invincible. In attacking the bomber's cachet, Chennault earned himself enemies among the highest Air Corps echelons. Bombers carried with them the imprimatur of assault. This was part of aviation's appeal, so many military leaders, including Hitler, emphasized the bomber as epitomizing the aggressive spirit which a successful air force must possess. But Chennault considered the vastness of the sky from a different vantage point than Douhet. The stubborn American felt that properly deployed fighters planes could thwart bombers. The key to Chennault's belief was pursuit—using fast planes as interceptors, putting aviation into a defensive role. Opponents gagged, but Chennault argued that pursuit planes working together from high altitude, with good intelligence allowing proper positioning along aerial assault routes, could intercept and destroy attacking bombers.[687] This was the concept which annoyed his superiors, but which attracted Madame Chiang Kai-Shek when she and Soong built an air force to resist the Japanese.[688] Either Chennault was a better salesman than earlier with the US Army or his Chinese hosts were better listeners. He started creating China's interceptor force in 1937.

The plane for the job was the Curtiss P-40 Tomahawk. Half as fast as a Zero in most positions and not as maneuverable, its sluggishness in the climb stemmed partly from its heavy armament. It carried four .30 caliber guns along the wings, and two half-inchers shooting through the propeller arc.[689] While heavily armed planes were the norm in Europe, the Japanese depended upon lighter craft with less armament. Japanese planes were marvelously nimble, but they did have vulnerabilities. The pragmatic Chennault took the Tomahawk's statuesque qualities and, through appropriate tactics, rendered them beautiful and deadly. When the first wave of American pilots—part of the All Volunteer Group, or AVG, authorized by Presidential order on April 15, 1941—arrived in China, Chennault told them to love their plane for what it could do, not to complain about what it could not. Dog fights with Zeros would be suicidal, but the P-40's weight meant that it could gain fantastic speeds in a dive. Moreover, its ruggedness meant that it could take more of a beating than the delicate enemy craft. "You can count on a higher top speed, faster dive, and superior fire power," he explained. "The Japanese fighters have a much faster rate of climb, higher ceiling, and better maneuverability. Use your speed and diving power to make a pass, shoot, and break away."[690]

Chennault's American AVG men heeded him, although they were wildly independent. A Chinese liaison officer wrote to Chennault complaining that "Some of the personnel . . . are always drunk in the city, so much so that one of them lost his head completely and caught hold of a cook's chopper . . . fortunately, he was prevented from doing any injury by another person."[691] Added to these complaints were the aggressive courting habits aimed at the women of Kunming, typical for free-booting American men of action, but unknown to their very formal neighbors. They played softball before amused onlookers, built an American-style movie theater, and kept pets.[692] But what made their reputation was the paint scheme for their planes, worked up by AVG-er Allen Burt Chapman, former Associated Press staff artist. Admiring a photo of British P-40s in North Africa, which had sharp teeth painted along the engine's edge, Chapman came up with the Tiger Shark look. His design adorned every AVG plane, with teeth, red tongue, and menacing eyes supporting the "Flying Tiger" image.[693] Pilot wing pins and insignia featured a winged tiger, which also became a beloved visual cue.

Far from Kumming, at a press briefing in Washington, D.C. soon after Pearl Harbor, General Marshal confided to reporters that mere defense was not the American plan. "We are preparing for an offensive war against Japan," he said.[694] But Philippine-based B-17s which Marshall envisioned for a bombing campaign were in no position to be "dispatched immediately to set the paper cities of Japan on fire."[695] The Japanese destroyed them. There was much wrangling about how aerial power could be brought to bear against the enemy, with Laughlin Currie urging Roosevelt to release bomber crews to the China theater.[696]

December 7, 1941, galvanized the AVG. "This is it," Chennault informed his men, who already knew it.[697] More P-40s arrived at Kunming's Wu Chia Ba airport on the 18th, and Chennault kept one squadron on constant alert, with reconnaissance patrols aloft.[698] On Saturday, December 20, at 9:45 a.m., word arrived from the code room. "Ten Japanese bombers crossed the Unnan border at Laokey heading northwest."[699] Giving their bearing, Tiger Wang—Chinese chief-of-staff for the AVG—informed Chennault that Kunming had to be the objective. Other spotter locations rang in, and the vector was confirmed. A yellow flare was the signal to warm up engines, then the alert signal—a red ball—ran up the air warning mast. Pilots scrambled from ready rooms. Two squadrons, "The Adam and Eves," and "The Pandas," took off in pursuit of the Ki-48 bombers, which American fliers called "Lillies."[700] What followed was a public vindication of Chennault's ideas. The 10 Lily bombers, flying in a "porcupine" cluster to maximize their firing power, saw their formation shredded by P-40s which dove, twisted, and arced, shooting all the while. Diving through, the Tomahawks climbed skyward and dove again. The Lily formation shuddered, three bombers went down, and the remnant retreated to their base in Hanoi. While two AVG pilots were killed, Kunming went unharmed. The Hanoi-based 21st Hikotai group never again attacked it.[701]

News of the action spread across China, and American officials released the information to a grateful public. Victory in an air skirmish was a small piece of good news from a war theater dominated in the headlines that week by the fall of Hong Kong. Reports from Chungking's Chinese Central News Agency held the air battle as antidote to bad news from the coast.[702] American news professionals noticed what they called "Chinese confidence in the completeness of the success," giving the reports credibility which Chinese sources sometimes lacked.[703] Ultimately, the performance of the P-40s and the dash of the pilots not only redeemed Chennault, but added that touch of charm which only victory can lend to a military account. The War Department saw wisdom in playing up the air group's glamor. Crack reporters, like Leland Stowe, made the Burma Road theater their beat, and the tenuous link between Kunming and Burma was etched into the consciousness of Americans following the war news. Stowe, a Chiang doubter, wrote frankly about the shortcomings of KMT military performance. But he acknowledged effective Sino-American cooperation against Japanese attacks on Mandalay, key point on the famous road. The overall tone of Stowe's coverage was the improvement in China's performance, of which the AVG was a symbol.[704] Field Marshal Slim, new to command in Burma, noted Chennault's "dynamic command," and praised AVG fliers for being "as good a collection of fighter pilots as could be found anywhere."[705]

At Christmas, the AVG tackled Japanese planes over Rangoon. This phase of the campaign was ruinous, with the AVG covering a pell-mell retreat as the Japanese took Burma. The AVG gave American reporters a chance to inject a note of defiance into the campaign, as when *Collier's* described the group's heroics opposing much greater Japanese air strength.[706] Gregory Boyington, Marine aviator, got his first crack against the enemy then, starting the career which saw him become one of the celebrated aces of the war.[707] "Pappy" Boyington's Black Sheep Squadron drew more than a little inspiration from the unorthodox magic of the Flying Tigers. Ultimately, the loss of the Burma Road meant that aerial supply "over the hump" of the Himalayas became more important to Chiang's war effort, which kept the Flying Tigers busier than ever.

On the run in the Philippines

To most Americans, the main focus of the Asian war remained the Philippines. It was there that forces allied with locals faced off against the Japanese. Hopeful Americans wished to see the haughty invaders stopped. However, MacArthur's position became more vulnerable as Japanese landings took place around the archipelago. Slowly, he retreated around Manila Bay in a north-northwest zig-zag aimed at the Bataan Peninsula. On Bataan, his troops would take their stand, but in December, it was important to prevent Japanese General Homma from cutting off his route to better ground. MacArthur's tactics confounded Homma's attempts. Filipino-American troops were persistent in counterattacks, keeping the Japanese off-balance. They feinted, counterattacked, withdrew, redeployed, and repeated the process again.[708] Homma was aware that he faced the United States' most famous general and feared ruses. He grew concerned that his advance units might be cut off from the main body. Viewing the action, Carlos Romulo likened MacArthur's method to a boxer keeping an opponent on his heels, not letting them "get set for a punch."[709] "Filiamericans," as Romulo called his countrymen, had faith in MacArthur, fighting with whatever weapons they had at their disposal, including knives and bayonets.[710] Their loyalty during a retreat which doomed Manila spoke much about MacArthur's position in the country. Filipino culture emphasized reciprocal devotion strengthened by personal ties. *Utang na loob*, defined by observers as "an internal debt of gratitude," placed irresistible demands upon relationships, and those who broke them suffered accusations of anti-social shamelessness, or *walang hiya*.[711] These ideas were layered atop other cultural imperatives, such as the assumption by resident Americans of the former Spanish position of patron, or *compadre*, with concomitant obligations of protection. MacArthur knew all this in his bones.

Whatever the terminology, complexities were sometimes lost on American officers who watched MacArthur with a mixture of frustration and grudging admiration. "In many ways, MacArthur is as big a baby as ever. But we've got to keep him fighting," said Dwight Eisenhower that winter.[712] Eisenhower embodied the annoyance MacArthur's theatrics prompted, but also the truth that the General was an irreplaceable asset. News reports from Manila confirmed Eisenhower's instincts. Amidst a collapsing defense, CBS Manila correspondent Tom Wirthin made a point on December 20 of describing how popular the General remained with the populace.[713] MacArthur's favor with the American public was likewise no military secret. Americans would rather see the general as a hero than as a problem. The hasty 1941 attempts to reinvigorate American defenses there were inadequate to repairing decades of neglect. His defensive campaign was skillful, given the circumstances.

But the first three weeks of Japanese moves after Pearl Harbor sealed the first phase of their invasion. Their December 8 raid on Clark Field destroyed 18 B-17s, 53 P-40s, and assorted other aircraft; a grievous blow.[714] Japanese bombing continued nonstop through the 13th. In the air, at sea, and on land, all initiative lay with Japan. Their December 10 landings on Northern Luzon went smoothly. Imperial Army troops seized the airfields there, permitting air support when they landed at Lingayen Gulf on December 22. Some headlines still bragged about driving off invaders here and there. But these turned out to be incidents when nervous shore batteries fired into the empty sea.[715] When *Life* photo correspondent Carl Mydans investigated, he found no signs of Japanese activity in such areas.[716]

From Manila, Wirthin broadcasted with CBS-style local color. "This metropolis of the Far East, part Oriental, part European, and part a bustling center of international commerce, was snapped out of its diversified customs and habits overnight by the sound of distant falling bombs," he reported on December 20, adding that Filipino women had taken to wearing slacks, which they formerly wore "only to garden parties and at the beaches." The new, less formal look, Wirthin said, was "not unbecoming." He delivered more fashion updates, because, he explained, the capital of the Philippines was a stylish place. "Manila's men," he detailed, "well-known for the nattiness of their sartorial equipment, now go unshaven with impunity. Shirts and sportshirts are standard dress for the office." Wirthin continued: "There's a large fish market near my office, and for the first time since the first few days of the war, a lot of grumbling was to be heard around this market because of a shortage."[717] But as the battlefield approached the beleaguered city, Manila would no longer serve as a broadcast venue.

The main Lingayen Gulf landings came off well for the Japanese, who had 76 transports backed by a strong fleet.[718] CBS military affairs analyst Eliot was quick to lay out the strategic and tactical basics for his listeners. The Luzon landings he termed "the most dangerous of the Jap landings, closest to Manila, within reach of their communications."[719] He pointed the audience to their maps, showing Davao and Mindanao. "The Japanese are fighting with feverish energy, against time," he said, "We may be sure that no less energy is being expended to forestall their efforts."[720] The Japanese also landed at Legaspi, in southern Luzon, capturing the local railroad terminus as well as air bases.[721] Manila was without hope. MacArthur now intended to fight as long as possible, waiting for reinforcements. But not in Manila. Instead, American and Filipino defenders maneuvered around the inlet of Pampanga Bay to Bataan. By Christmas Eve, Manila was abandoned. MacArthur and Quezon went into conclave, agreeing to declare the capital an open city to prevent the devastation of street-to-street fighting. This was not a customary situation in World War II, although it emulated the French evacuation of Paris. In a prelude to another, soon-to-come embarkation, MacArthur left the city, shaking Romulo's hand and promising, "I'll be back."[722]

In Manila, Filipinos spent Christmas coping with twin shockers. First, their protector was gone, headed for a siege on the jungles ridges of Bataan. Second, the Japanese were almost there. In the United States, Americans were just as glum about MacArthur's position. To anyone with a map, the bad news was obvious. The map which ran in the *Baltimore Evening Sun* on December 22 carried fierce captions, such as "Jap landing at Davao meets fierce resistance from regular troops and from knife-wielding Moro tribesmen."[723] Leaving aside the question of how such tribesmen would fare against Japanese marines, the captions did not hide the fact that the entire archipelago was covered with arrows indicating Japanese movements. Also on the 22nd, the War Department communique admitted the Lingayen Gulf landings, putting Japanese strength at six divisions totaling 100,000 men. The report said landings met with "fierce resistance," which was not the same as saying they were repulsed.[724] Some reports still predicted an "all-out land, sea, and air battle" which would prove conclusive. But that ignored the superiority of the Japanese as well as the weakness of the United States Asiatic Fleet.[725] On Christmas Eve, *The New York Times* ran a story and map, which painted the "2-Way Drive on Philippine Capital."[726] When Americans awoke on Christmas morning, they had reason to be suspicious of cheerful headlines such as "Philippine Armies Check Jap Onslaught."[727] The accompanying story relied on an army spokesman who insisted that the outlook around Manila was "brightening," because "all reports were that they were giving better than they received from the reinforced invasion legions of Japan."[728] There was little substance to such a story. Romulo raced through Manila connecting with sources. He ushered in the New Year at the Manila Hotel, where his orders were to rustle up food for a dash to join MacArthur in the field nearer Bataan. The Filipino observed a few guests "trying to salvage a few reminscent hours of a doomed Manila that had been the gayest spot outside of prewar Paris."[729] "Their faces," he noted, "were masks of tragedy."[730] Well might they have worn the tragic mien. Despite its status as undefended, Manila had been bombed anyway, in raids MacArthur declared "completely violative of all the civilized processes of international law."[731] These raids, redolent of Japanese arrogance and a penchant for disrespecting norms of warfare, prompted Elmer Davis to comment.

It has killed forever the Japanese slogan, "Asia for Asiatics." he intoned.

The people suffering under these bombings are Asiatics, of course, just as are the many thousands of Chinese who have died under Japanese bombs in undefended cities. Yet, the Japs stick to it. . . . They mean only "Asia for the Japanese.[732]

CBS' Eliot made it clear that, try as he might, he could come up with no military rationale for bombing the open city other than "sheer unbridled savagery."[733] In that way, American news coverage shifted quickly from spinning hopeful tales of saving Manila to condemnation of Japanese conduct of the war. At the annual dinner of the New England Society of New York, held at the Plaza Hotel on December 22, Harvard President James Bryant Conant gave the intellectual seal of approval to the nation's fighting mood. "These are days of war," the scholarly Conant noted, adding that citizens were united and angry at the enemy's treachery. He looked beyond the current situation to a future which demanded American strength employed in service of global stability shored up by democratic values. "If freedom is to be protected once the Axis powers are beaten," Conant said, leaving the war's outcome in no doubt, "aggressors must be too weak to strike." What Conant proposed was a new idea born from current rage: the establishment of permanent American armed might in service of protecting democracy. "We have before us as a nation a twofold task: the winning of this war and the preservation of the American way of life. We cannot preserve our way of life unless we win this war."[734]

Newspaper readers were probably already convinced of Japanese perfidy, but headlines such as "Ruin Is Rained On An Open City: Merciless Attack Lasting Three Hours Destroys Many Old Landmarks,"[735] served to reinforce the consensus that Japan fought in ways beneath civilized decency. The story filed by United Press correspondent Frank Hewlett carried details, telling of planes roaring in waves over the ancient walled section of Manila, "wreaking fury on a helpless capital containing altogether 623,500 people," recounting stories that planes strafed fleeing civilians, and listing the damage caused by the resultant fires. "Hordes of half hysterical evacuees, worrying mostly for their children, scurried along with wailing babies in their arms, some carrying bundles, a few suitcases," delivered the latest iteration of an image that readers already associated with German assaults in Europe as well as Japanese attacks in China.[736] The helplessness which accompanied outrage prompted promises of future retribution, once the fortunes of war changed for the better. There was thus a great deal of talk warning the enemy that reckoning would come no matter how things were going at the moment. CBS carried a remark by Senator Alben Barkley (D-KY), which encapsulated the mood regarding the bombing of open Manila. "Think of Tokyo, with ten times as many inhabitants," he said, casting a gimlet eye on the future, "when the inevitable day of destruction comes, with our bombers swooping down from the sky."[737] While Americans comforted themselves by contemplating future revenge, they had to cope with news of current defeat. On January 2, 1942, front-page stories such as the *Detroit News'* "Manila Falls and Fleet Makes Escape: MacArthur Fights on North of City," were more informative than recent reports, as well as more depressing.[738]

Churchill comes to Washington—taking America by the hand at Christmas

There was not much to be found when I examined his heart. Indeed, the time I spent listening to his chest was given to some quick thinking. . . . The textbook treatment for this is at least six weeks in bed. That would mean publishing to the world—and the American newspapers would see to this—that the P.M. was an invalid with a crippled heart and a doubtful future. And this at a moment when America has just come into the war and there is no one but Winston to take her by the hand.

Sir Charles Wilson (Lord Moran), Churchill's personal physician, December 27, 1941, after examining the Prime Minister following a bout with angina[739]

You would have been quite proud of your husband on this trip. First, because he was ever so good natured. I didn't see him take anybody's head off, and he eats and drinks with his customary vigor, and still dislikes the same people. If he had half as good a time here as the President did having him about the White House, he surely will carry pleasant memories of the past three weeks.

Harry Hopkins, in a letter to Clementine Churchill[740]

Churchill and his retinue boarded *Duke of York* December 12 for the ten-day crossing. The battleship left its destroyer escort behind, so great was the hurry.[741] Churchill's fear that the United States might pursue a Pacific-only strategy was mollified so far. But it was still not implausible that pressures might reconstitute along Japan First lines. At sea, Churchill drafted documents roving over the world conflict, acknowledging the Russian–German battle as the war's "prime fact," but spending time on the need to get Americans fighting against Germany.[742] Churchill found out quickly enough that Roosevelt was sincere in his commitment to Germany First, and that the North Africa campaign would be mark an opportunity to get Americans into action against the Reich.[743] Churchill's trip to Washington provided him a chance to lobby Americans and to charm them.

Churchill was invited to stay at the White House. He accepted the offer. Cognizant of a guest's obligations, Lord Halifax wrote back, stressing that the P.M. would stay over with a reduced presence: "Only himself, his personal assistant Commander Thompson, his secretary Mr. Martin, his valet, and his two detectives."[744] So eager was Churchill to bend Roosevelt's ear that he requested Halifax to arrange air transport from Hampton Roads, Virginia. "I should like," he said, "to come on by aircraft to Washington Airfield reaching you in time for dinner."[745] Among the first orders of business for the Joint Washington ARCADIA Conference was setting up how the Anglo-American command structure would work. On December 22, Churchill's first night in Washington, the two Chiefs of Staff met, and agreed "that it was vital to forestall the Germans in North West Africa and in the Atlantic Islands."[746] General Marshall and Admiral Harold R. Stark spoke for the army and navy. "Our view remains that Germany is still the key to victory. Once Germany is defeated, the collapse of Italy and the defeat of Japan must follow."[747] Marshall was so fixated on Europe that he opposed the North Africa invasion as a distraction.[748] Roosevelt pointed out that North Africa offered the earliest possibility to hit the *Wehrmacht* with American land forces.[749] Marshall's vision of the joint command was that each war theater would have integrated command structure to avoid duplication or variance. Only Admiral Ernest King, Anglophobic and protective of his branch's independence, objected. Presidential support pushed the idea through. A sop to British sensibilities was the offer of command in the Western Pacific, where the US Navy knew that it would do most of the fighting no matter what any chart said.[750] Supervising much of the joint command activity would be the Combined Chiefs of Staff Committee. There was some discussion of other allies, such as the Soviets and Chinese, but there was no prospect of integrating their command structures. Problems with the Soviets included divergent strategic interests in the Pacific, where the Soviets hoped to avoid hostilities with Japan. Chungking was in no position to handle matters regarding the war as a whole, since only the China front was its concern.[751] One measure which gave Churchill satisfaction was agreement to send American divisions to Northern Ireland as soon as possible.[752] Having these soldiers in Ulster put American troops in the United Kingdom, bringing home the reality of American manpower. They took up positions in Ulster within a month, to great media attention. CBS covered their arrival, while London dailies yelled "The Yanks Are Here Once Again."[753]

Officials were selective about releasing the details of the Joint Command plan, but the direction of the talks was obvious. Enterprising reporters figured it out. Drew Pearson explained to *Washington Merry-Go-Round* readers that the first order of business between Roosevelt and Churchill was "a hard and fast Anglo-American alliance by which each country would agree to operate its army and navy in complete cooperation with the other."[754] The grand strategy was vague at that point. The year 1942 promised mostly defensive operations, with questions about the North African plan. The year 1943 might see a return to Europe via the Mediterranean. The need for a reactive spirit was emphasized by memoranda stressing that 1942 offered possibilities for "closing and tightening the ring around Germany," while staying "ready to take advantage of any opening . . . to conduct limited land offensives."[755] There was emphasis on production goals and the need for managed industrial performance, showing the seamlessness between economic and military considerations.[756] The Pacific theater received less attention, since it was predominately an American effort.

Churchill shared bad war news. Japan's landings across Luzon occurred then; so did the capitulation of Hong Kong. This created bonding which put both coteries together under common strain as they experienced disaster together. Solidarity was palpable during the afternoon of December 23, when Roosevelt and Churchill held a joint press conference. One reporter, noting the threat to Singapore, asked if that fortress was the "key to the whole situation" in the Far East. Churchill remonstrated with bellicose optimism. "The key to the whole situation," he insisted, "Is the resolute manner in which the British and American democracies are going to throw themselves into the conflict."[757] That was the key to Churchill's public performances in Washington. His assignment was to remind Americans that the Anglo-American alliance was an organic outcome of shared democratic values. The roomful of reporters ensured that his message got wide coverage. "When have newsmen in wartime ever before had such an opportunity? To fire questions at both the President of the United States and the Prime Minister of Great Britain," wondered a broadcaster. "They did it today, in the President's office at the White House. There was the President behind his desk. He always seems to enjoy press conferences, and today he was fully aware that he was offering something unusual."[758] Pearson was colorful: "When Churchill showed himself to the press, he seemed to be literally in the pink."[759] When news writers in the back of room asked Churchill to stand so that they could see him better, he climbed on a chair. "The effect was electric. Tough-crusted newsmen cheered. Then, they thrust their pencils in their teeth and applauded. Churchill had done something wholly American. The rest of the press conference was easy."[760]

On Christmas Eve, Churchill gave the first of the two command performances. The day was spent on ARCADIA business; the evening was when Yuletide magic unveiled itself. Sundown falls early in Washington in late December. The last beams slant eastward across the gray Potomac. The city, with no blackout, twinkled. In Washington, a popular habit was to go to the White House and cluster around the Christmas Tree, which federal power guaranteed would be tall, sparkling, and magnificent on the South Lawn.[761] The President would speak words of benediction. The gates to the South Lawn opened up, and 30,000 visitors passed through. Secret Service and White House police were there, although the atmosphere was quite open. Civilians headed to their favorite viewing spots. Some, familiar with the annual Easter Egg Rolls, which always took place near the portico, climbed a small knoll offering good vistas.[762] Pinkish gloaming provided a soothing backdrop, while crows called above. For visitors from London, it seemed like a peace-time atmosphere. At 4:30 p.m., the Marine Band started Christmas carols, switching to "Hail to the Chief" at 5:00 p.m. The Roosevelts and Churchills emerged on the portico and there went the "sunset gun" at Fort Meyer. People focused on the two democratic chiefs, flanked by Norwegian royals, Crown Prince Olaf, Crown Princess Martha, and their children.[763] As Albert Warner, narrating the scene for CBS put it, "As twilight came in Washington, they spoke from the South Portico of the White House, gazing over the heads of a distant crowd towards the slim spire which is the Washington Monument."[764]

Roosevelt threw the switch which lit the tree. Catholic University's rector, the Reverend Joseph Corrigan, delivered his ecumenical invocation: "Hear a united people, girded for battle, dedicate themselves to the peace of Christmas, nor find strangeness in our words," he began, going on to give thanks for the abundant American resources which could be put to effective use for the dread tasks ahead.[765] The President proclaimed New Year's Day to be a Day of Prayer for "our sons and brothers, who serve in our armed forces on land and sea, near and far—those who serve for us and endure for us."[766] Having lit the massive evergreen, he mentioned that "we light our Christmas candles now across this continent from one coast to the other," a reminder that, even at war, America remained a land alit.[767] Then, it was time for Churchill.

"I spend this anniversary and festival far from my country, far from my family," he observed, adding that he could not

truthfully say that I feel far from home. Whether it be the ties of blood on my mother's side, or the friendships I have developed here . . . or the commanding sentiment of comradeship in the common cause of great peoples who speak the same language, who kneel at the same altars, and to a very large extent, pursue the same ideals, I cannot feel myself a stranger here in the center of and at the summit of the United States.[768]

Having established his "right to sit at your firesides and share your Christmas joys,"[769] the Prime Minister moved on to talk about the holiday's meaning.

What he said captured democratic values put to fighting use on a wartime Christmas Eve. "This is a strange Christmas Eve," he noted. "Almost the whole world is locked in deadly struggle, and, with the most terrible weapons which science can devise, the nations advance upon each other." But their war was not brought about by "greed for the land or wealth of any other people, no vulgar ambition, no morbid lust for material gain at the expense of others." Without saying so, he left it clear that such motivations were for the enemy. Churchill saw the war, "raging and roaring over all the lands and seas," yet felt "here, amid all the tumult . . . the peace of the spirit in each cottage home and generous heart." It was a well-chosen phrase, for Americans saw themselves not as a nation made for war, but as a nation proficient at war while made for peace. War was not supposed to determine their character, even when it affected their lives. Churchill stressed that wartime should not preclude Christmas joys. "We may cast aside for this night at least, the cares and dangers which best us," he said, giving permission for merriment, "and make for the children an evening of happiness in a world of storm." Christmas would be an oasis amidst war's desolation that should be enjoyed. He continued—slipping in a nice touch of Anglophone solidarity which no doubt heartened his Canadian and Australian listeners as well—"each home in the English-speaking world should be a brightly-lit island of happiness and peace." This was a superb touch, since Americans liked to have fun even when at war. It let him link all Anglophone nations. Children, he continued, deserved "their night of fun and laughter. Let the gifts of Father Christmas delight their play," he went on, adding that "us grown-ups" should "share to the full their unstinted pleasures before we turn again to the stern task and the formidable years that lie before us."[770] Even the pleasures of Noel were conscripted to the great cause, cast as a necessary prelude to victory. With the celebrating children in mind, and the three Norwegian royal offspring at his side, he concluded that adults must be "resolved that, by our sacrifice and daring, these same children shall not be robbed of their inheritance or denied their right to live in a free and decent world."[771]

This was vintage stuff. In the White House later that evening, when Hopkins complimented him as an orator, Churchill brushed aside the idea with false modesty. "I don't know about oratory," he answered, "but I do know what is in people's minds and how to speak to them."[772] His physician, the future Lord Moran, overheard the exchange. He also observed Hopkins through a clinician's eye. "His lips are blanched as if he had been bleeding internally, his skin yellow like stretched parchment, and his eyelids contracted to a slit so that you can just see his eyes moving about restlessly, as if he was in pain," the doctor noted.[773] Infirm, Hopkins had a political appraiser's eye for a polished performance.

Christmas Day saw Churchill in church. Again, he sang at Roosevelt's side. Among the carols was "Oh Little Town of Bethlehem," which Churchill said was new to him. He liked the lines, "Yet in the dark streets shineth/The everlasting light;/The hopes and fears of all the years/Are met in thee tonight."[774] At the White House, he quoted Psalm 112, "He shall not be afraid of evil tidings: his heart is fixed, trusting in the Lord," much to Roosevelt's approbation. Dinner with the Roosevelts and guests concluded the quiet day. Roosevelt seemed "like a schoolboy, jolly and carefree," while Churchill was subdued.[775] Perhaps he was anticipating the most important address he ever gave to the American people. That was his Joint Session of Congress on December 26.

He grasped the podium with both hands, meeting the rapt gazes of members of the House of Representatives and Senate with a glint of amusement. Orating before legislators put Churchill in his element. The Prime Minister reminded all of his American ties. "I wish indeed that my mother, whose memory I cherish across the veil of years, could have been to see me. By the way," he added, "I cannot help reflecting that if my father had been American and my mother British instead of the other way around, I might have got here on my own."[776] Instantaneous laughter meant that he had them all; from that point on, Churchill was "one of the boys," as far as Congress was concerned.[777] He stroked the legislators' ample vanity by reminding them that he did "not feel quite like a fish out of water in a legislative assembly where English is spoken," explaining how he, like they, served at the pleasure of a voting public, which was the source of democratic legitimacy.[778]

Exuding fraternity, Churchill observed upon the public mood. "Anyone who did not understand the size and solidarity of the United States might easily have expected to find an excited, disturbed, self-centered atmosphere, with all minds fixed upon the novel, startling, and painful episodes of sudden war as it hit America," he said.[779] Instead, he was heartened to see "Olympian fortitude which, far from being based on complacency, is only the mask of an inflexible purpose and the proof of a sure, well-grounded confidence in the final outcome."[780] He, touched the nub of national attitudes, admitting recent shocks but also the determination to get back against the enemy. British people felt the same, he said. "We in Britain had the same feeling in our darkest days. We were sure that in the end all would be well."[781]

The enemy could not be bought off, but had to be destroyed. Churchill did not underestimate the Tripartite Pact nations, calling their forces "enormous," adding that they were "bitter" and "ruthless" on their "path of war and conquest" because "they know that they will be called to terrible account if they cannot beat down by force of arms the peoples they have assailed."[782] Churchill explained that "they will stop at nothing," that they had vast accumulations of war weaponry, that their armies, navies, and air forces were trained and disciplined, their designs long-planned. "We have therefore, without doubt, a time of tribulation before us," he admitted.[783]

Talking political philosophy, he limned the idea brought up on Christmas Eve that democracies could be mighty but were not warlike. Since the end of World War I, he said, "the youth of Britain and America have been taught that war was evil, which is true, and that it would never come again, which has been proved false." On the other hand, German, Japanese, and Italian youth were taught that aggressive war was their duty. "We have performed the duties and tasks of peace. They have plotted and planned for war." That, and only that explained the temporary advantages enjoyed by the Japanese in the Pacific. He led back to the truth that the war would be arduous. Churchill argued for honesty during crisis. "Our peoples would rather know the truth, somber though it be," he insisted, going on to call the tasks ahead the "noblest work in the world," because it meant "not only defending our hearths and homes but the cause of freedom in every land."[784]

What he described was a world war waged not for ideological reasons. Churchill stressed the point that Great Britain and the United States stood for freedom. He did not include the Soviet Union in that theme, although he did praise "the glorious defense of their native soil by the Russian armies and peoples." He ranged over the war fronts, including Libya, where "for the first time we have made the Hun feel the sharp edge of those tools with which he as enslaved Europe." He derided "boastful" Mussolini, claiming that he had "crumpled already." He covered the oceanic war, touching on the "life-line of supplies which joins our two nations across the ocean, without which all would fail." As far as good news, he said, the best development was that "The United States, united as never before, has drawn the sword for freedom and thrown away the scabbard." Any temporary disadvantages in the Pacific were exacerbated by the aid given "to us in munitions for the defense of the British Isles."[785] This was a friendly turn of phrase that might satisfy former isolationists while making interventionists feel virtuous.

Churchill then castigated. Twice in one generation, "the catastrophe of the world has fallen upon us. Twice in our lifetime has the long arm of fate reached out across the oceans to bring the United States into the forefront of battle." The reason was that London and Washington had allowed themselves to drift apart. "If we had kept together after the last war, if we had taken common measures for our safety, this renewal of the curse need never have fallen upon us." Churchill next spoke of the future, for he was already contemplating the shape of the postwar world and wanted to perpetuate the Anglo-American relationship. It was astonishing to realize that the Japanese were so imprudent, even insane, as to imagine that they could win a war against the United States and Great Britain. "What kind of a people do they think we are?" he demanded theatrically, thus uniting the British and Americans rhetorically at the most heated part of his speech. "IS it possible that they do not realize that we shall never cease to persevere against them until they have been taught a lesson which they and the world will never forget?"[786]

There were two main messages in Churchill's widely covered address. The first was that natural Anglo-American cooperation, due to shared democratic values, was a predicate for peace and freedom in the world. The second was that the war was not going well just then, but that final victory would be total, allowing the British and Americans to reassemble world conditions based upon the values he argued that they shared which he embodied. The linkage of himself to the shared heritage and ideology of both powers lent the speech its personal touch. The scope of the talk was global, the ramifications clear. The United States and Britain would collaborate, winning the war and rebuilding the world. Here, Churchill understood that he and Roosevelt—whose anti-colonial streak made him undevoted to the British Empire—might differ. But the broadness and depth of his speech's construction cushioned any potential disagreements. Congressmen stood and applauded, shouted their approval, waved papers and stamped their feet, cheering, cheering, cheering.[787]

Churchill had Congress. But so great was his nation's need for American cooperation that he was not sanguine. There were other Washington figures to win over. Cordell Hull was one he planned to pursue. Churchill was due in Ottawa, so he could not start his next round of lobbying right away. But he laid plans for Embassy dinners upon his return from Canada, so he could continue his PR campaign.[788] Roosevelt had such work of his own, such as sending a get-well message to Hugh Johnson, whose animosity melted.[789] Staying on top of the Washington heap required time and labor. With Churchill away, Roosevelt joked that he would at last have a few hours for work.

The press became Churchill's best American ally. Pearson cited his irrepressible appeal in the January 3 *Merry-Go-Round*. He reported a softball story, "Churchill's Peanuts." It described the Prime Minister's actions after "his smash-hit speech to Congress."[790] No dignitary could claim the honor of receiving Churchill first. Instead, went the story, "a messenger was sent to the sidewalk to buy a nickle bag of peanuts from 'Steve,' the Greek peanut vendor who holds forth outside the White House grounds at East Executive and Pennsylvania Avenues." Churchill then "walked out into the garden behind the executive mansion and fed the squirrels, for which, like Falla, the President's dog, the Prime Minister developed a great fondness."[791] More serious, if less fun, was Walter Lippmann, who monitored the trip and approved of what he saw. "No words can begin to express the debt which we, and all the people of the earth, owe to Winston Churchill and the British people," he told readers of "Today and Tomorrow" on Christmas Day. Lippmann knew that the figure "with us now in the hour of our peril" had earlier stood alone against Hitler, while Americans had not woken up to the fact that "the Pacific Ocean could not be protected by America from Hawaii alone, or even from the Philippines," until December 7. Wielding learnedness like a pike, Lippmann pronounced himself for the integration of American and British commands, in the spirit of Lucius Aemilius

Paulus, who, picked to wage war for Rome against Macedonia in 168 B.C., said that "commanders should be counseled, chiefly, by those especially who are skilled in the art of war and who have been taught by experience; and next by those who are present at the scene of the action, who see the enemy."[792]

The night following his Congressional triumph, Churchill sent for his doctor, who arrived at the White House by taxi. "I am glad you have come," Churchill told him, complaining that he felt overheated, with chest pains radiating down his left arm. Naturally alarmed but remembering his patient's "imaginative temperament of the feeling that his heart was affected," the dutiful physician took all vitals, fearing an onset of angina. Diagnosis was inconclusive, but the idea that Churchill might be ill was horrible. Lord Moran feared that ordering the Prime Minister to the hospital would undercut everything Churchill was trying to achieve in terms of publicity. "Your circulation is sluggish. It is nothing serious," said the doctor, before heading off to chat with Harry Hopkins.[793]

On December 31, Churchill addressed the Canadian Parliament. He also delivered another hit, reminding listeners of French General Maxime Weygand's 1940 prediction that England would "have her neck wrung like a chicken. Some chicken. Some neck!" Churchill riposted to a delighted assembly.[794] Churchill ushered in 1942 by flying back to Washington. A side trip to Florida with General Marshall gave him the opportunity to try out his material on new audiences. But it was soon back to Washington, hammering out the connection between his own Chiefs of Staff and their American counterparts. Not until January 15 did Churchill depart for Bermuda and home. Drew Pearson understood the value of Churchill's image-affirming visit. "Churchill did a public relations job which was worth more money in terms of British-American relations than the waning British exchequer could pay for today."[795]

3 JANUARY 1941

Two troublesome islands and the "United Nations"

This statement of twenty-six nations is destined to take its place among the immortal documents that are the milestones of human freedom. It means to Americans and to all the peoples of the world far more than a mere alliance against a common enemy, for more than a mere agreement to fight together without any thought of a separate peace until victory has been achieved. Its greatest significance is in the statement of the principles for which we fight. These are the great ideals of human liberty, the rights of the individual which government exists to protect and not to annul.

Henry Morgenthau, Jr., Secretary of the Treasury, commenting upon the Declaration By United Nations, January 2, 1942

On January 1, 1942, the Declaration of the wartime United Nations was signed by twenty-six governments, of whom we were not one. The strange, not to say troubling, nature of the attitude of the United States towards us was to be revealed, indeed, by an incident almost insignificant in itself but which was given serious importance by the official reaction of Washington.

Charles de Gaulle[1]

New Year's Day ushered the first full war year. It also marked the coming-out party for a term that shaped American understanding of why the war was being fought, as well as what the world would look like after war ended. The term was "United Nations," title appended to the so-called "Washington Declaration," signed by envoys from 26 countries. Besides the United States, Britain, the Soviet Union, and China, there were 22 others: Australia, Belgium, Canada, Costa Rica, Cuba, Czechoslovakia, the Dominican Republic, El Salvador, Greece, Guatemala, Haiti, Honduras, India, Luxembourg, the Netherlands, New Zealand, Nicaragua, Norway, Panama, Poland, South Africa, and Yugoslavia all signed.[2] Nine signatories were Central American and Caribbean nations. Eight were European nations occupied by Germany. Four were linked to Britain through the Commonwealth. India was intended to fit into this category, but that restive colony's disposition was up in the air. Thanks to the Vichy conundrum, France's signature was conspicuously absent.

These 26 countries formed a "United Nations" pledged not just to victory over Germany, Italy, and Japan, but to a reconstructed postwar world based upon "common program of purposes and principles."[3] The central plank of the platform was the promise not to seek a separate peace. The document extended Atlantic Charter principles. There was a hard dickering with the Soviets over points such as freedom of conscience, which Roosevelt sold to Moscow by through the Jeffersonian principle that religious freedom implied freedom not to have a religion.[4] There was more pressure on Soviet Foreign Minister Litvinov than on Churchill, who cheerfully agreed to the promise of military togetherness. The democratic principles embedded within were easily reconciled with the British. When the President showed the penultimate version to the Prime Minister, Churchill responded with lines from Lord Byron's *Childe Harold*: "Here, where the sword united nations drew/Our countrymen were warring on that day!"/ And this is much—and all—which will not pass away."[5]

Canny reporters, such as *Baltimore Sun* Washington Bureau Chief Dewey L. Fleming, guessed that "the document was carefully drawn so as not to put Russia in the position of being in direct war with Japan."[6] Instead, Fleming pointed out, the declaration bound nations only to fight to the finish against members of the Axis with which they were already at war. But the United Nations idea was instantly popular, whatever its limits in practice.[7] There was general media approval of the term, more impressive than "Allies," implying a global endeavor aimed at an improved postwar world. H.V. Kaltenborn was just one of the news figures who incorporated it as a replacement, as when he warned in a broadcast that "The German Armies still neutralize all the offensive strength of the United Nations."[8]

Military communiques immediately picked it up.[9] Secretary Hull saw the document as "living proof that law-abiding and peace-loving nations can unite in using the sword when necessary to preserve liberty and justice and the fundamental values of mankind."[10] Treasury Secretary Henry Morgenthau saw the United States joining 25 nations to serve as "the conscience of mankind," fighting against "the black shadow of oppression which has plunged nation after nation into darkness."[11] Senator Connally called the occasion "historic," and "significant."[12] The signing ceremony featured Roosevelt wondering if he should sign as "Commander-in-

Chief," being advised by a dry Hopkins, "President ought to do."[13] When T.V. Soong signed for China, Churchill murmured that "Four fifths of the human race" was bound by the declaration.[14] Soong was thrilled to occupy the same stage as the major leaders. No nation's position was more problematic than one not included. There was a gap in the alphabetical list between "El Salvador" and "Greece." That was the spot for France. De Gaulle noticed it: "On January 1, 1942, the Declaration of the wartime United Nations was signed by twenty-six governments, of whom we were not one."[15] He was galled by the absence of Free France. To De Gaulle, Free France was the legitimate claimant to French sovereignty and the proper authority over metropolitan France and overseas territories. That he was not in power in Paris was no impediment to this claim, went De Gaulle's reasoning, because his was a government-in-exile like that of the Netherlands or Norway. The Allies never considered recognizing collaborationist regimes in those nations, so why truckle with Vichy?

The decision to maintain diplomatic relations with the government in Vichy gave Washington direct contacts which Ambassador Leahy used to lobby against further French concessions to the Germans. This meant that while De Gaulle was assembling a fighting force and gaining support for his effort to re-inject an honorable French presence amongst the Allies, the United States and Vichy remained diplomatically connected. It was a sensitive issue that might have stayed a minor wartime curiosity, but for an unforeseen episode in the most obscure corner of North America.

* * *

They make the most unheard-of feature in North American political geography. Their archipelago is trifling, 93 square miles squatting off Newfoundland's southern coast. Low, sandy, long ago denuded of forest cover, there are two main islands. Miquelon is larger, shaped like a barbell, with the protuberances of Grande Miquelon on the north and Petite Miquelon to the south, connected by the skinny Langlade Isthumus. The southern tip of Petite Miquelon is Cap Coupe, also called Pointe de l'Oueste, across which sits the partner island of St. Pierre. St. Pierre is smaller,[16] but has more inhabitants, the main town with administrative, commercial, and legal headquarters as well as an apostolic prefecture. Given the islands' proximity to the Continental Shelf and St. Pierre Banks, the economy depended upon cod. Access to those fisheries led France to press Britain for sovereignty, finally granted by the 1814 Treaty of Paris. St. Pierre and Miquelon are the last French toehold in North America.[17] To France, the islands represent continued presence on the continent. To most Americans, the fact that there was still a French territory in North America was a surprise. Until January 1942, the islands made no impression on the American populace.

The Fall of France and the consequent struggle over governmental legitimacy made the islands more than an oddity. The commander was Admiral Georges Robert, Vichy's High Commissioner for the Antilles, Guyana, and St. Pierre,[18] stationed at Martinique.[19] The US Navy kept a wary eye on him to ensure that no German inroads occurred in the Caribbean. His minion in St. Pierre was the Baron de Bournat, who governed with Vichy authority. He suppressed expressions of Free French support.[20] As far as Washington was concerned, this was an internal French affair. Practically, it lent proximity to increasingly tense Franco-American ties. These were nerve-wracking since Joint Command plans for North Africa would put American and British troops ashore in Morocco and Algeria, where Vichy held control. Ideas such as pressuring Vichy for cooperation, backing a British attack to seize or destroy French naval bases, or dropping recognition of Vichy came from what Hull called "various sources outside the State Department."[21] Hull was doubly opposed to rupturing the Vichy connection; first, because his department had invested considerably in maintaining the Vichy ties, and second, because he hated Roosevelt's extra-departmental diplomacy. United States agents were negotiating with General Weygand, urging him to sneak out of Vichy and command a pro-Allied army in North Africa. Weygand refused, maintaining loyalty to Petain, whom he informed of the American advances, which included a secret letter from Roosevelt.[22] De Gaulle could not stomach Washington's canoodling with Vichy. He saw that the American President would affirm Vichy control over territories De Gaulle wanted for Free France.[23] Among these were St. Pierre and Miquelon.

There were British fears that the radio station on the island might send signals to German U-boats. Britain had a role because Newfoundland was not yet in confederation with Canada. Newfoundland answered to the United Kingdom. Canada signaled Washington on December 4 that London supported a Free French takeover of the islands, which Ottawa viewed as unnecessary.[24] De Gaulle's Naval Minister, Admiral Emile Muselier, who commanded vessels on the North Atlantic convoy routes, was prepared to move into the islands, but wanted permission from Ottawa and Washington. He was in the vicinity at the time, inspecting the corvettes which protected merchant ships.[25] Muselier asked De Gaulle to handle the British.[26]

But the Free French leader saw no reason to seek anyone's permission. The two islands were incontestably French, and Vichy was illegitimate. On December 18, he cabled Muselier, claiming that Canadians were preparing to destroy the radio transmitters. "I order you to carry out rallying of Miquelon Islands with means at your disposal and without saying anything to the foreigners," he wrote. "I assume complete responsibility for this operation, which has become indispensable in order to keep for France her possessions."[27] Meanwhile, the British and Canadians were arguing over the merits of a plan under which Ottawa would seize control of the islands. On Christmas Eve, Muselier sailed his Free French craft into St. Pierre.

That Christmas morning, the *New York Times* carried the heart-warming story of how happy the suffering islanders were to see their liberators. "A little less than half an hour after the first sailor had jumped ashore the islands had been secured in the military sense," ran the story. "Not a shot was fired; the Admiral's Chief of Staff was able to report with immense pride that not a drop of blood had been shed."[28] Displaying a canny knack for public relations—he allowed *Times* reporter Ira Wolfert to cover the occupation—Muselier announced plans for a plebiscite to ratify the locals' loyalty to Free France. As Wolfert put it, the election would be small but monumental in significance, since it would represent "the first free expression of opinion permitted Frenchmen who have been governed since the summer of 1940 by 'we, Henri Philippe Petain,' Chief of State of the Vichy regime."[29] Thrilled at the prospect of their democratic birthright restored to French citizens, Wolfert continued, "An extraordinary parable of the modern world at war comes on this obscure island on Christmas Day to the kind of climax for which the democratic world has been praying. A dictatorship that had been throttling the people was set aside temporarily by armed forces . . . until the people could speak and decide their fate."[30]

That rosy view was not shared by the Allies. The White House considered the affair an outrageous embarrassment. Hull's statement was categorical, referring to the landing by three "so-called Free French ships" as "an arbitrary action contrary to the agreement of all parties concerned and certainly without the prior knowledge or consent in any sense of the United States government."[31] That phrase "so-called" let Hull in for intense criticism. Americans applauded the occupation. "A special offensive was launched against us because of the word 'so-called'. . . . Our attackers thought that with this word we were questioning the existence of the Free French, or the fact that they were free, whereas by the phrase we simply meant: "three ships supposedly of the Free French," he explained.[32] Hull's plea for linguistic contingency was far-fetched.

Among Hull's complaints were that the landings upset arrangements already in place with Admiral Robert in Martinique; that Vichy would view the affair as evidence of American violations of French colonial sovereignty; and that it would spook Latin American nations, who opposed any transfers of sovereignty in the hemisphere.[33] The British reassured the American allies that it was not their idea. On Christmas, Anthony Eden telegraphed Lord Halifax, calling the incident "a complete surprise to us."[34] Halifax, however, showing the pragmatism of an experienced diplomat, argued that Britain, the United States, and Canada could complain, but should do nothing about it, leaving the Free French in place. Hull, who wanted a Free French departure, unloaded on Halifax. "According to you," he said,

We should ratify the unlawful act of the Free French, taken in absolute violation of their pledges . . . which means that the United States would have to throw over the entire problem of Vichy and French Africa which we've been nursing for a considerable period. If we hadn't been nursing this problem, Germany would probably be in occupation of North or West Africa, or both, now and during most of the past twelve months. Your government is perhaps more interested, if possible, in the Vichy angle of this matter than is the United States.[35]

Chastened or realistic, Halifax conceded "the force of this position."[36] At St. Pierre itself, the American consul was as irritated as his boss. He reported that even Admiral Muselier considered de Gaulle's high-handedness undemocratic. "He is convinced," said the diplomat, "that General de Gaulle's order was that of a dictator and that he is certain that the General did not even consult the National Committee of the Free French at London," adding that he would resign his post "as a protest against the unilateral order given to him by the General."[37]

De Gaulle was unrepentant. As he saw it, territory under Vichy's control meant French land under Nazi dominion, whereas Free French territories were liberated zones. Moreover, de Gaulle intuited the most dangerous implication of the new United Nations formulation for his country. If the United Nations aimed to win the war, make the peace, and forge the new world, then it was essential that France play a part. Nations on the outside would be non-belligerents or defeated enemies, and France must be treated as neither. Seeing France left out while governments-in-exile signed on behalf of occupied nations such as Luxembourg, the Netherlands, and Norway, was preposterous to the General. Washington wanted to protect the strange link to Petain and Pierre Laval for strategic reasons which did not help France's cause. Thus, France was excluded from the United Nations because of an American expedient, which put the French future in the hands of men like Cordell Hull. This constituted an arrogation of authority which de Gaulle opposed. It imperiled France's efforts for war redemption; it deprived France its rights as an Ally fighting the Axis. "One might have thought that this small operation, carried out so happily, would have been ratified by the American government without any shock," he wrote later. "The most to be normally expected was a little ill humor in the offices of the State Department. But no, it was a real storm that broke in the United States."[38]

At the White House, de Gaulle was now a full-fledged annoyance; an uncontrollable factor at a time calling for uniformity of action. It was now that the image of de Gaulle as problematic took hold in American power circles. From Roosevelt in the White House to Hull in the State Department to Eisenhower in the army, de Gaulle emerged as a pest. De Gaulle became represented as a factor in wartime equations which American leaders hated to deal with, but had to. They would try to ignore or circumvent him, but never could find a way around de Gaulle.

As far as American popular opinion was concerned, there was no controversy at all. To Americans and their media, de Gaulle was a hero for liberating the islands.

A public opinion survey taken in December showed that 75 percent of Americans did not believe that the Vichy government represented French independence. Sixty-five percent believed that it was only a matter of time before Petain handed over control of the French Navy to Hitler, as well as control of colonies.[39] Vichy represented Nazi interests as far as Americans were concerned, and Washington's Vichy experiment was a case of misguided diplomacy. When Churchill, speaking in Ottawa, heaped opprobrium upon Petain and Vichy, while praising de Gaulle and Free France, it seemed a cinch to the American press that St. Pierre and Miquelon would remain liberated.

"The men of Bordeaux, the men of Vichy—they lie prostrate at the foot of the conqueror," sneered the Prime Minister. "They fawn upon him. And what have they got out of it? The fragment of France which was left to them is just as powerless, just as hungry as, and even more miserable because divided than the occupied regions themselves."[40]

"If there was any longer any question about it," opined the *New York Times*, "the Prime Minister has certainly blown all question of St. Pierre-Miquelon and Washington's 'so-called Free French' through the dusty windows of the State Department."[41] The editorial noted that "to Mr. Churchill, there is nothing 'so-called' about the Free French," and that "truckling to the Vichy politicians" who fawned upon Hitler was beneath contempt. Concluding, the paper praised the idea that "in the grim psychology of war there are moments when the forthright and aggressive spirit, the boldness to demand as well as dicker, the capacity to grasp the emotional values of a situation, are more important than all the gains of deviousness and subtlety."[42] Meanwhile, the *New York Herald-Tribune* mocked Hull for being "so mad at Churchill because of his anti-Vichy speech in Canada."[43] At the White House, Robert Sherwood noticed that "the American people hailed this news joyfully." He understood why. The strange story represented a rare piece of good news, an example of derring-do aimed at those whom Americans saw as treacherous, as friends of Hitler.

The great majority of Americans had no idea who or what General de Gaulle was nor had they been acutely aware of the existence of islands named St. Pierre and Miquelon; all that matters is that some French sailors and marines who had been fighting in the Allied navies had gone off on their own to seize territory which belonged to their own country and had thereby snatched from Hitler's grasp a radio station which might have been used to help the Germans kill Americans.[44]

Irate, Hull wrote a memo to Roosevelt on December 31. He had, "carefully reviewed the record." He recapitulated it in detail, including negotiations between Ambassador Leahy, Marshall Petain, and Admiral Darlan pursuant to future arrangements in North Africa. "This is just the beginning of ominous and serious developments," Hull predicted. Disparagingly, he referred to "our British friends," who seemed,

> to believe that the body of the entire people of France is strongly behind de Gaulle, wheras according to all my information . . . 95 per cent of the entire French people are anti-Hitler whereas more than 95 per cent of this latter number are not de Gaullists and would not follow him.

Hull concluded with a nasty paragraph in which he hoped sarcastically that "Churchill would be disposed to talk with you, or rather to let you talk with him" about working out the matter.[45] Unfortunately for Hull's political numbers, the plebiscite at St. Pierre showed that, at least on the islands, virtually all the inhabitants wished to remain under Free French administration.[46]

At the time, Hull was determined to work out a formula whereby the Free French would depart, no matter the certain public outcry in the United States. He envisioned various face-saving devices, whereby the Canadians might wind up handling the islands in fact while leaving the question of sovereignty sufficiently open to palliate Vichy's wounded feelings. De Gaulle, he was convinced, was "a marplot acting directly contrary to the expressed wishes of Britain, Canada, and the United States," who should withdraw.[47] Churchill, propping up de Gaulle and hopeful as to his future utility, worried that relations with the Free French were ruined. Hull, working with the Vichy ambassador on the matter, was sufficiently exercised about the business to consider resignation. Quite aware of Hull's ire and hoping to stanch it, the Prime Minister listened as the Secretary of State lectured him directly. "This was led off by the incendiary speech of the British Prime Minister in Canada," the Secretary of State complained, "which gave trouble-making people a pretext to make it appear that the British were the only friends the Free French had, and, inferentially, that the United States was not their friend." Continuing on the theme of British perfidy, Hull added a menacing note.

> I wonder whether the British are more interested in a dozen or so Free Frenchmen, who seized these islands, and the capital they can make out of it primarily at the expense of the United States government, than they are in Singapore and in the World War situation itself.[48]

In the end, Hull did not demand radical rearrangements. He seemed as bitter over British sneakiness as de Gaulle's recklessness. There was discussion about involving the Free French in Canadian-American talks to quiet the fracas, but Sumner Welles objected, arguing that, after "moving heaven and earth to keep on close terms with the Vichy Government, in the hope that through such influence as we could exercise in Vichy and in North Africa, the French fleet would not get into German hands and North Africa would not be used as a base for military operations by the Germans," the United States would look feckless.[49] Halifax contented himself with requesting that Washington preserve the possibility of making common cause with de Gaulle in the future. Welles was polite, but chilly. "I was unable to see that the Free French movement at the present moment had anything very much to commend it from the practical standpoint" he observed. "I could not see that either General de Gaulle or his associates provided any rallying point for French patriotism."[50]

At the *New York Times*, percipient columnist Anne O'Hare McCormick understood the diplomatic saw that it was dangerous for smaller powers to play tricks on larger ones. She learned that through reporting from some of Europe's most remote troubled corners. In 1938, after the Munich Conference but before Hitler's march into Prague, McCormick traveled to Khust, capital of tiny Carpatho-Ukraine. This was the least-known portion of Czechoslovakia, home to Ukrainians and subject to counterclaims by Hungary. McCormick was determined to decipher one of Europe's most complex land disputes, and her reportage there and elsewhere established her as a brilliant correspondent.[51] As a columnist, she demonstrated the same commitment. On the subject of Vichy and de Gaulle, McCormick was willing to see how the conflict over policies played out. "Whether our policy toward France has been wise will be proved by events," she said, adding that Washington's tilt to Vichy was hardly impulsive. It was "a considered policy . . . patiently followed in the face of opposition, and fully understood by the Free French as well as the British." Speaking against what she saw as too-romantic interpretations of the St. Pierre incident, McCormick insisted that it could not be "considered apart from our policy toward France as a whole," which she likened to any theater of war. "The fact is that Washington has been fighting a delaying action in France as truly as General MacArthur has been playing for time in the Philippines," she contended. "And every week gained in the campaign against French collaboration with Germany is as important as any action in the field."[52] In sum, she argued, criticizing the State Department's approach without knowing all the facts was absurd.[53]

McCormick was the sort of news writer whose every word demanded respect. James "Scotty" Reston, another sterling *Times* reporter about to take up a post with the Office of War Information, and whose book *Prelude to Victory* was soon to appear, was effusive in his praise of his colleague. "Anne O'Hare McCormick was a great reporter in a special sense," he wrote.

> She had vitality, curiosity, intelligence, courage and all the other qualities a good reporter must have, but she had something more that gave to her reporting the dimension of wisdom and prophecy. This was a rare gift of sympathy for all sorts of people.[54]

In this case, "all sorts of people" included Hull, who came in for the highest dose of editorial bitterness from many news outlets. "In the weeks that followed," he recalled with bitterness, "The State Department, with myself as its chief, became the target of editorials, radio attacks, and representations from various organizations, although the President had given his full approval to our reaction."[55] So McCormick's measured advice to trust federal policy gave Hull a bit of high-profile support.

Other media coverage was unsympathetic to Washington's position. Eric Sevareid was at least clinical in his coverage. He saw how annoying De Gaulle's grab for the islands was to federal officials. As early as December 27 Sevareid termed the affair "an embarrassing muddle."[56] *The New Republic* made St. Pierre subject of the lead editorial in its January 5 edition. The magazine demonstrated concern over "the fatal weakness in the State Department's policy," which it saw as the department's "belief that Vichy can and must be appeased at all costs." *The New Republic* said that policy might alienate the Free French, calling Vichy appeasement "repulsive to all Americans who see in their country's contribution to the war something more than the perpetuation of corrupt regimes through power politics."[57] At *US News*, the hurt feelings of diplomats came up on January 9. "High State Department officials are somewhat upset by public reaction to the speed with which they acted to satisfy the Vichy Government . . . and to oppose the de Gaulle Free French forces which took over the two little French islands near Newfoundland," went the coverage in "Washington Whispers." "The official explanation now is that action was forced by the agreement with other nations of this hemisphere not to permit territorial changes without consultation."[58] More intense was I.F. Stone at the *Nation*. On January 3, his "Aid and Comfort to the Enemy" charged the State Department with being "the last stronghold of appeasement." American foreign policy looked like it was "being run in . . . half-wit fashion," he continued, going on to explain that he was in contact with Free French sources who were deeply rankled by their treatment, which supposedly undermined "the confidence of oppressed peoples everywhere." "I think some way should be found to let the world know in decisive fashion that the undemocratic little clique of decayed pseudo-aristocrats and backsliding liberals who dominate the State Department do not speak for the American people."[59] Stone charged that the State Department did the Vatican's bidding by supporting Vichy. This, he said, was driven by "the Vatican's old hatred—a hatred it shares with the Fascists—for 1789."[60] Stone's charges were iconoclastic, but revealed the passions which the Vichy issue could spark. His forthright connection between de Gaulle's Free French and the 1789 revolution made the issue one of values such as "Liberté, Egalité, Fraternité." These were emotional political reflexes unlikely to be assuaged by counsels to take a deep breath and trust the diplomats. The story of the tiny islands percolated for much of January. Adding to Hull's frustration was the fact that he came to personify the Vichy gamble. For example, on February 10, Pearson's *Washington Merry-Go-Round* cited progress on the Vichy issue, but attributed it to Sumner Welles and not the Secretary of State, whom the column termed "the staunchest policy of the appeasement policy with Vichy." Welles, claimed Pearson and Robert S. Allen, was able to improve the situation because Hull was "confined to his apartment with a cold."[61]

De Gaulle was aware of the furor, and realized that it was to his advantage. He resented Washington's "intimidation," as well as what he saw as the domineering attitude towards Canada and England.[62] He smilingly but firmly refused Hull's compromise formulae, promising Anthony Eden that, if American ships sailed into the St. Pierre harbor, his troops would "have to open fire." When Eden threw up his arms in dismay, De Gaulle, enjoying his moment of brinkmanship and aware of how damaging intra-Allied combat on North American soil would be, said with equal irony and defiance, "I have confidence in the democracies."[63] By his reckoning, the public relations cost to Washington of such a fiasco would be overwhelming. Reminding his boxed-in allies that his forces controlled other vital territories such as New Caledonia, de Gaulle watched with satisfaction as the State Department backed down. "The Americans soon saw the advantage which an understanding with us would present," he wrote.[64] But Hull, who came close to resigning but decided that other issues demanded his continued service as Secretary was not one to forget. "Our relations with De Gaulle's (*sic.*) movement were not helped by the incident," he noted.

> There was no doubt in the minds of the President or myself that De Gaulle was personally responsible for violating his commitment to Britain and for going directly contrary to the wishes of the United States and Canada. We regarded him as more ambitious for himself and less reliable than we had thought before.[65]

Meanwhile, Roosevelt, with customarily blitheness, enjoyed a distance from the entire controversy, as the State Department, but not the Oval Office, was the focus of editorial outcry. At the end of January, Hull made a relatively generous offer, in which a Free French administrator would remain as part of a consultative council which would run island affairs, while the troops in place would stay on, under the orders of the Free French National Committee. Seeing no reason to bargain, since he felt he had Washington, Ottawa, and London outmaneuvered, de Gaulle did not respond to the proposal.[66]

On February 2, Hull recommended to Roosevelt that the matter rest as it was, unsettled but non-violent, until the end of the war.[67] Four days later, newspapers ran a quiet little story. "Reach Pact on Miquelon, St. Pierre: De Gaulle and Britain Negotiate Agreement, Approved by US" was the headline in the *Chicago Sun*.[68]

According to the deal, a locally elected administrative council, dominated by Free French, would be in place, while Admiral Muselier would return his corvettes to sea duties. According to Frederick Kuh, London bureau chief of the *Sun*, "This favorable news is regarded as likely to dull the edge of renewed criticism in the United Nations against the recrudescence of United States appeasement measures toward Vichy."[69] De Gaulle's Free French retained de facto control of the islands, which slipped back into footnote status.

Listening to *vox populi*

War costs money. So far we have hardly even begun to pay for it.
Franklin Delano Roosevelt, State of the Union Speech, January 6, 1941[70]

In general, which do you think would be the better national policy for the duration of the emergency?
Attempts at curtailing consumer demands for goods in which shortages are likely to develop 59.1%
Rapid expansion of facilities, such as pipe lines, to meet both emergency and full normal civilian demands 39.2%
Both 1.7%
Fortune Poll, September 1941[71]

Americans learned most of the Arcadia details when President Roosevelt gave his State of the Union Message on January 6. Roosevelt not only prepared the way for rationing, shortages, and taxes, he also laid out production goals for industry. The year 1942 should see 60,000 new aircraft, 1943, 125,000. He wanted 45,000 tanks in 1942, 75,000 the next year. His listed goals for anti-aircraft guns, merchant ships, and "a multitude of other implements of war" were just as ambitious, all intended to "give the Japanese and the Nazis a little idea of just what they accomplished in the attack at Pearl Harbor."[72] Roosevelt used a favored rhetorical device, linking the Third Reich to the December 7 assault, fusing Japan and Germany in the public mind. He also made the production goals public to bait the enemy nations. "I rather hope that all these figures which I have given will become common knowledge in Germany and Japan," he taunted.[73] While Japanese and German leaders would no doubt toss off the speech as braggadocio, these production goals were met.[74] Largely the figures of his own imagination instead of the products of arithmetic, Roosevelt was cavalier when questioned whether his numbers were too high. "Oh, the production people can do it if they really try," he assured.[75]

Hitler was the main villain of the speech. According to this line of argument, Japan was on the march less because of its own imperial ambitions than because Hitler wanted his Asian ally to cut off supplies to Britain, Russia, and China.[76] As strategic interpretation, this was rubbish, but it served Roosevelt's purpose of situating Hitler at the center of the global tyranny operation. This supported the Germany First plan and had the added affect of disrespecting Japan. The purpose of the Pearl Harbor attack, he said, with a bit more clarity, was "to stun us, to terrify us to such an extent that we would divert our industrial and military strength to the Pacific area or even to our own continental defense. The plan has failed in its purpose. We have not been stunned. We have not been terrified or confused."[77] Roosevelt couched his defiance so that advocates of a Pacific-first approach were deemed to have fallen into an enemy trap.

There was a great deal of value-based discussion as to the war's meaning. Roosevelt called an end to days when "aggressors could attack and destroy their victims one by one," because "We of the United Nations will so dispose our forces that we can strike at the common enemy wherever the greatest damage can be done."[78] Thus was the United Nations collective defense idea formally introduced. Among the institutions Roosevelt promised to preserve were the "power of the British Commonwealth and of Russia and of China and of the Netherlands," which the enemy hoped to destroy before turning its attentions to "their ultimate goal, the conquest of the United States." At the root of the conflict, he explained, were incompatible world views. "They know that victory for us means victory for freedom. They know that victory for us means victory for the institution of democracy, the ideal of the family, the simple principles of common decency and humanity."[79]

Among the dangers ahead, he identified impatience and defeatism. "Many people ask 'When will this war end?'" he said.

There is only one answer to that. It will end just as soon as we make it end by our combined efforts, our combined strength, our combined determination to fight through and work through until the end, the end of militarism in Germany and Italy and Japan. Most certainly we shall not settle for less.

Roosevelt went on to deliver some bouquets for each ally. Churchill got a nod for his visit, which the President said cheered the entire nation. Also due for praise were "the Russian people, who have seen the Nazi hordes swarm up to the very gates of Moscow and who with almost superhuman will and courage have forced the invaders back into retreat." Stalin went unmentioned. The Chinese got their due, "those millions who for four-and-a-half long years have withstood bombs and starvation and have whipped the invaders time and again." There was no mention of France, merely a nod in the direction of "all the other governments in exile," an omission which de Gaulle certainly noticed. In a spiritual coda, Roosevelt ended by telling Congress that the ultimate purpose of the war was to be true to the divine heritage "which goes back through all the years to the first chapter of the Book of Genesis—'God created man in his own image.'"[80]

The State of the Union address was a combination of spiritual exhortation, brash production promises, and a manifesto for the United Nations. It marked Roosevelt's first formal enunciation of the term.[81] Roosevelt's careful phrasing designed to protect the Europe First approach from potential criticism revealed a president keenly aware that he sat astride his nation's power structure by virtue of the democratic process. Despite wartime unity, there was awareness that people's opinions needed to be catered to, and properly directed. Even at war, the United States remained a democracy operating according to the dictates of its democratic faith. It therefore came as no surprise that Public Opinion was much on the minds of professionals.

In December and January, the latest data from the Gallup, Roper, and AIPO polls, appeared in *Public Opinion Quarterly*. To the pollsters' credit, several of their questions posited an "emergency" in the near future, which would necessitate higher taxes for defense spending. It was clear that the public opinion business had been trying to look around the future's corner. But the figures only went up to September 1941. They provided an aggregate image of a nation preparing itself for a major trial. Defense-related questions were far-ranging, revealing broad majorities in favor of actions which isolationists would have considered needlessly provocative. AIPO found that 61 percent of Americans supported taking over defense of Iceland, while only 17 percent disapproved. In a question for *Fortune* readers, Roper pollsters divided the world into five areas, asking respondents whether they would be willing to support armed defense of each "if Germany or her allies tried to take it": 98.3 percent agreed that the continental United States needed to be defended with arms; 79.8 percent agreed that all of North America, plus Greenland, Hawaii, and the Panama Canal needed to; 67.4 percent supported fighting for South America. The majorities ceased, however, when only 37.7 percent felt that the Philippines, East Indies, and Australia were worth fighting for, and 42.5 percent felt that way about Great Britain.[82] Because of the lag between data collection, assessment, and publication, it would not be until Spring that researchers got their first statistical glimpse at American attitudes after December 7.

Asked before the attack whether or not Americans felt they would go to war with Japan soon, 52 percent of respondents said "yes." Pollsters also asked their subjects to agree or disagree with certain statements. More Americans (54%) agreed with statements indicating solidarity with England's fight than did those who expressed varying degrees of skepticism (40.2%). Asked just before the war began whether it was more important to avoid the conflict or to defeat Germany, 32 percent opted to stay out while 68 percent felt that German defeat was preferable to peace. On

December 23, asked which country was a greater threat, Germany or Japan, 64 percent chose Hitler's Reich and 15 percent selected Japan.[83] To a White House quite used to dissecting polling numbers, these figures had to be encouraging indeed, since they showed popular acceptance of the idea that the Third Reich represented the central focus of war danger.

The American people revealed realism about hardships ahead. Asked how long they thought the war would last, less than 1 percent foresaw a fast six months campaign, while only 4.6 percent predicted a one-year war; 14.5 percent thought the conflict would last two years, while 37.8 percent believed it would take two to five years, with an additional 9.7 percent picking five to ten years. As to the outcome, 72.5 percent believed the Allies would eventually prevail, however long it lasted, while 7 percent thought the Axis would win.[84]

There were queries about defense policy, postwar expectations and economic expectations. These were of interest to the administration, which knew it was about to unleash a host of restrictions. Drivers knew that the tires on their cars would have to last until the end of the war. Normal monthly tire consumption was 4 million; January's quota for civilians was a mere 356,974, meaning in practice that new tires were unobtainable, at least through legal channels.[85] The only loophole was that if a consumer bought a new car, it would come with new tires. But that lasted only a month, because on January 31, new car production stopped, except for a remnant of 200,000 to be built from already available parts. The market responded, meaning that bicycle sales soared, so bikes became hard to find.[86] Federal officials' main concern was to prevent black markets and profiteering, which meant instituting price controls on tires, cars, cigarettes, and other commodities. The OPM mandated a one-quarter reduction in civilian wool usage to preserve stocks for military uniforms.[87] Another question was whether or not Americans would accept these restrictions as necessary, or think them the result of poor foresight. The people seemed most concerned with fairness and effectiveness.

These affairs touched every American, but reporting on them presented a different challenge than reporting on battles. Among the leaders in covering the story of the move to wartime economics was Lippmann. On January 20, "Today and Tomorrow" gave a serious consideration of how the organizational schemes were going. What Lippmann feared was that the flurry of activity might be mistaken as sufficient unto itself. What Lippmann wanted was some sense that the economic policies and protocols would actually result in dollars-and-cents efficiencies supportive of war aims. He pointed to the push for price-controls, which necessarily brought about squabbling between different elements, including the Agriculture Department, which maneuvered to protect farm interests. Farm lobbyists wanted to remove agricultural prices from Henderson's OPA and place them under Agriculture Department control. Clucking his tongue editorially, Lippmann explained that such troubles had "arisen because of the fact that the

President could not put his mind on the problem, and no one else had the power to speak for him. The farm bloc got out of hand while Mr. Roosevelt was speaking with Mr. Churchill."[88] The solution, Lippmann insisted, was to bust open the one-man environment and to invest officials with real decision power, instead of waiting until a busy President could pay attention. Drew Pearson was also on the story. On January 5, his *Merry-Go-Round* charged the Farm Lobby with "log rolling" alongside labor elements. "The country may be at war, but the 'gimmie' boys are still riding the gravy train," he sneered.[89] Pearson's scapegoats were figures in Washington—lobbyists, union officials, or businessmen—who were selfishly working to protect their own interests. Charges of profiteering, such as those he leveled at the tin industry on January 11, were particularly inflammatory.[90] Another good target was any alleged bottleneck in the supply chain. On January 6, Pearson took on the slack pace of machine tools, arguing that Ford, Packard, and other companies were to blame for the shortage of aircraft not only because they dithered, but because they were inefficient at tooling up their plants. Pearson passed along OPM's four main recommendations, which were that machine tools should be registered, a government-run Machine Tools Board should assign tools where they were most needed, tooling plants needed to be put on a 168-hour per week schedule at once, and new programs to train workers properly should be put into effect.[91] Frequently these stories gave Pearson the chance to pass along the juicy tidbits which his audience liked. On January 18, describing a pow-wow between R.J. Thomas, United Autoworkers head, and Elliot Janeway, *Fortune* editor whom some called "Henry Luce's unofficial ambassador to the New Deal," Pearson said that Janeway wanted Tommy Corcoran to serve as head of a joint committee aimed at drawing up plans for converting the auto industry to wartime production. Corcoran was beloved by the union, Pearson claimed, but they felt he would never land the appointment, so they backed Federal Judge Jerry Frnak, former chairman of the Securities and Exchange Committee. This was opposed by Knudsen, who preferred Cyrus R. Ching, United States Rubber executive. The gist of Pearson's report was that unions and executives were not getting along smoothly despite calls for unity, and that there was potential for labor disputes even in the new wartime economy.[92] Somewhat frustrated at coverage of these supposed bottlenecks, inefficiencies, and disputes, Roosevelt said at a press conference that Washington was the worst rumor factory in the country; the source of more lies than any other place in the nation.[93] There was no diminution in the number of economic stories, however.

Humor was a wartime coping mechanism. A new lingo was heard in the corridors of Washington, where businessmen and officials were uncertain what to do where and where to go. *Air Force News* published a light-hearted glossary:

Under consideration: Never Heard of It

Under active consideration: Will have a shot at finding it in the files.

Have you any remarks?: Give me some idea of what it's all about.

The project is in the air: Am completely ignorant of the subject.

You will remember: You have forgotten, or never knew, because I don't.

Transmitted to you: You hold the bag awhile—I'm tired of it.

Concur, generally: Haven't read the document and don't want to be bound by anything I say.

Kindly expedite reply: For God's sake, try and find the papers.

Passed to higher authority: Pigeonholed in a more sumptuous office.

Appropriate action: Do you know what to do with it? We don't.

Giving him the picture: A long, confusing and inaccurate statement to a newcomer.[94]

So long as people were joking and the mood was understanding, these confusions did not pose a threat to the Administration's leadership. It was only once the complaints became bitter that problems might arise which could undermine authority. Pollsters asked voters their opinions on matters ranging from the propriety of wartime strikes to the diversion of goods and services to war purposes. Invariably, the responses showed that the main public concern were efficiency, shared sacrifice, and honesty in the system. Three weeks before Pearl Harbor, majorities ranging from 63 percent (unskilled workers) to 78 percent (farmers and businessmen) felt that, in the event of hostilities, strikes should be illegal.[95] At the same time, 55 percent of respondents to a Roper query laid blame at the feet of businessmen for "not more openly insisting on more efficient organization of government effort, even if it meant creation of dissension in Washington."[96] Data showed that neither labor nor management could count on public patience if people came to see either side as an impediment to the war effort. Resolving disputes and assuring efficiency was seen as the government's obligation. The White House knew that keeping the public's faith in wartime economic measures was part of mobilizing the nation. The administration took steps. On January 13, Roosevelt put Nelson atop yet another new agency, the War Production Board (WPB), which he invested with the power to make "final decisions."[97] This was a response to the sorts of concerns reporters and pundits expressed.

4 FEBRUARY 1942

Singapore—*not* "The Gibraltar of the East"

I expect every inch of ground to be defended, every scrap of material to be blown, and no question of surrender to be entertained until after protracted fighting among the ruins of Singapore City.

Winston Churchill to General Wavell, January 19, 1942[1]

By 0800 hours 9th February, hundreds of bedraggled Aussies were streaming down Bukit Timah Road on the way to the city. The Military Police attempted to check them but they were in no mood for homilies from "Red Caps." Some paused long enough to accept a cigarette, light it, and say, "Chum, to hell with Malaya and Singapore. Navy let us down, air force let us down. If the bungs (natives) won't fight for their bloody country, why pick on me?" There was more truth than discipline in the retort; we have no kodoism, no kempetai, and no bullet in the back for a straggler.

Captain David James, Australian Military Intelligence, February 1942[2]

By February, the direction of the war was in flux. In every belligerent capital, there was discussion over what to do next. For example, *Luftwaffe* Field Marshal Albert Kesselring, whose job was to win air supremacy over the Mediterranean and protect the maritime supply lines of Rommel's *Afrika Korps*, spent months agitating for a change of German strategic focus. Kesselring depended upon the Italian Navy, whose ships spread across a string of naval bases, from La Spezia, in northwest Italy to Taranto at the boot-heel, to Naples, Venice, and La Maddelena, in Sicily. Axis naval power could dominate parts of the Mediterranean. A victory over the British in the First Battle of Sirte in December 1941 was a morale-booster for the *Regia Marina*.[3]

But the British were effective with their submarines, which menaced Axis ships and planes. British submarines claimed 212,643 tons of German and Italian shipping against 10 lost subs in 1941, an impressive net ratio.[4] Capable during daylight hours but ill-equipped for night-fighting, Italian admirals were risk-averse.[5] The *Regia Marina* had successes and did manage to keep the supplies coming, but could never eliminate the British threat and was unable to win Kesselring the edge he needed. What Kesselring dreamed of was a Mediterranean free of British danger. The Field Marshal knew that the German effort in Libya and Egypt would be determined by supplies, which were unsafe as long as the British held Malta. While Hitler's inner circle lavished attention on the Russian front, Kesselring saw North Africa as decisive. He wanted German forces to smash through Egypt, grab the Suez Canal, and plunge into the Near East, capturing the oil fields. He imagined the shattered British retreating to India's gates, the consequent deprivation of Persian Gulf oil supplies, the relief of German forces in South Russia, and a threat to the entire Allied war plan. But Kesselring also felt threatened, because he intuited Allied interest in North Africa, an invasion pathway to Italy. As Rommel moved east, the *Luftwaffe* Field Marshal had a feeling that the Allies might move against him in Morocco and Algeria, where Vichy forces lent very doubtful protection.

Kesselring gained an audience at Hitler's General Headquarters in February. He argued to Goering and the *Fuhrer* that an invasion of Malta would stabilize Mediterranean supply lines and thus clinch Rommel's victory. Britain's naval strength in the theater was parlous, Kesselring knew: a handful of submarines, 4 cruisers and 15 destroyers against 4 battleships, 9 cruisers, and plenty of torpedo-boats and submarines which the Italians and Germans could send forth.[6] Malta was in real jeopardy, and the German air force marshal felt that a direct blow would give the Axis not just a victory but a strong point in the middle of the sea. Tantalized by triumph close at hand, Kesselring convinced Rommel to support his idea, but the only result of his long-sought meeting with Nazi leaders came when Hitler grabbed him by the arm and said, "Keep your shirt on, Field-Marshal Kesselring. I'm going to do it."[7]

Hitler was lying. Once again, the prospect of saltwater rendered his bravado hollow. Just as with Britain in 1940, Hitler decided on a bombing campaign. This did enormous damage; over the next few months, Axis planes dropped over 7,000 tons of bombs on the small island, especially on its ancient capital Valetta, with its still-functioning harbor.[8] But as before, Hitler's promise of victory through bombing failed to break the defenders in their island. Royal Air Force Hurricanes and Spitfires took a toll on the bomber fleets. Malta was called Britain's unsinkable aircraft carrier, and the island's endurance became an inspirational story. Rommel's already-stretched forces stopped near Gazala on February 7, along a line from Derna on the coast to Bir Hacheim in the south. They caught their breath before renewing the drive on Egypt after a rest. Eying Tobruk and the glories beyond, the Desert Fox called Hitler himself on February 17, echoing Kesselring and expounding on the potential importance of North Africa and the Middle East. Hitler would not turn his attentions away from Russia and refused to consider real reinforcements for Rommel. To quiet his most famous general, he grudgingly sent a single parachute brigade from Greece.[9]

By the end of January, northern and central Malaya were in Japanese hands. After the initially diffident reaction to Japan's landings at Kota Bharu,[10] Lieutenant-General A.E. Percival carefully moved his units southwards. These included Indian, Australian, and British elements, withdrawing one by one, covering each other's flanks, setting up new defensive lines along the way. The danger intensified as the Japanese took control of formerly Dutch-held Sumatra, across the Straits of Malacca. The challenge was to avoid being outflanked by Japanese amphibious landings which could cut off the Singapore-bound retreat.[11] The British sought to maintain order, fall back methodically, and prevent a rout. They needed to make Japan pay dearly for every inch of the peninsula before mounting a lasting defense at Singapore. The British withdrawal might have been considered a success until January. Then, the controlled nature of the pull-back deteriorated. At the Slim River, on January 7, catastrophic errors resulted in loss of field control, while audacious Japanese advances forced Percival to concede that central Malaya was lost.[12]

There were many British problems along the Slim River. These included exhausted troops and confused command. The Percival plan of staged withdrawals and delaying actions came apart. But the most dire problem was that the Japanese were well trained, their plans smart, and their command under the operational control of General Tomoyuki Yamashita. He had three divisions and over 200 tanks at his disposal; the British faced him with disparately mixed units, no armor and few antitank guns.[13] Yamashita had an aggressive style. Not for nothing was he nicknamed the "Tiger of Malaya." A fighter, he provided dash to a well equipped and highly trained attacking force that was justifiably confident. His numbers were not enormous, but by combining armor, infantry, and air support, the Japanese general emerged as his nation's most feared battlefield leader. Yamashita's charisma stemmed not just from competence, but derring-do. This was on display after blasting through a defensive line at Jitra which the British hoped to hold for months. Yamashita named the captured fuel and supply depots "The Churchill Ration," and the seized Alor Star air base "Churchill Airfield."[14] The British evacuated Kuala Lumpur, Malay capital city, on January 11. By January 19, the defenders lost the northern half of Johore Province, by January 29th, the southern half. On January 30, they withdrew from Johore Bahru across the Straits of Johore to Singapore island, leaving Malaya to Yamashita.[15] The British were not the only ones stunned by Yamashita's campaign.

It caused panic in Australia. There, Prime Minister John Curtin pressured London, demanding reinforcements and a renewed commitment to holding Singapore.[16] Hopes that the narrow Johore Straits might stem Yamashita were ridiculous. But in Canberra, the issue was as much psychological as strategic. Singapore was not just Britain's major base in Southeast Asia, it symbolized the Empire there.

"The Gibraltar of the East" was a stout link in a chain of bases from Southampton to Shanghai, or Sydney. Its strategic importance signaled when stingy London outfitted its docks to handle large Royal Navy warships, a project completed by 1938.[17] The loss of "Fortress Singapore" was unthinkable. It was where commerce, civil service, and the military operated amidst the tropes of colonial power and romance: cocktails under the ceiling fans at Raffles Hotel, Malays, Chinese, and Indians moving in the streets, whence wafted heady smells—spices, drying fish, flowers.[18] Godowns, small native boats, still plied the waters laden with cargo. The place was proof of the oceanic connections which Britain maintained. With the Americans under siege in the Philippines and Singapore imperiled, the possibilities for Australia were disorienting in their severity.

London was dazed. Commander Wavell cabled Churchill on January 21. "I am anxious that you should not have false impression of defenses of Singapore Island," he warned. "I did not realise myself until lately how entirely defences were planned against seaward attack only."[19] Wavell's point was hard to accept. Singapore was a naval fortress; its defenses facing Malaya lagged. This gave rise to the fable of cannons facing the wrong direction. The fact was that plans to defend the Johore side were last-minute adaptations. As damaging for Singapore's prospects was the fact that, as of mid-January, the requisite shells were not ordered, neither were anti-landing obstacles in place on the beaches or along the Causeway.[20]

Churchill admitted that Wavell's message gave "little hope for prolonged defense," which also included holding on to Burma. Still, the Prime Minister wanted Wavell to spell out for him the exact "value of Singapore above the many harbours in the Southwest Pacific if all naval and military demolitions are carried out?"[21] Across Britain, there was mounting awareness that something was wrong where the Empire had looked strongest. A cartoon in the *Guardian* entitled "Singapore's Needs" showed Colonel Blimp laid on the slab next to a sign reading "Inquest on Malaya Reverses."[22] This was accompanied by an editorial opining that,

> Americans, long before the war began, counted on the loss of the Philippines. . . . They did not expect to hold Guam. The Dutch knew well that they could not be sure of defending any of their main islands without help. . . . But the British had no doubts about their ability to hold Singapore.[23]

In Singapore, confidence collapsed at the end of January. Chinese grocers and storekeepers ceased accepting credit, a demoralizing shock for colonials used to paying with chits. Local authorities declared a siege, telling people to lay in supplies. That prompted a run on non-perishables.[24] Pessimism was proven correct on February 1, when Singapore's civilians learned that British forces had abandoned the mainland. Watching troops under orders destroy liquor stocks, suspicious residents wondered whether they were witnessing measures aimed at stopping defenders from drowning their sorrows or at preventing alcohol-crazed Japanese troops from marauding as they did after capturing Hong Kong.[25]

Coverage of the Malaya campaign in American media outlets stressed the resolute defense, the planned withdrawals, and the citadel-nature of Singapore. London-based Bob Trout did warn CBS listeners that statements such as "Singapore shall not fall," had a disquieting effect, since, he explained, "The British people had thought that there would be no need even to make such a statement."[26] While admitting that the Japanese were on the move, Cecil Brown spoke of high British spirits. "The Aussies have not yet engaged but are itching to get into it," Brown said, adding optimistically that "They are trained in jungle fighting." Asking rhetorically if the Japanese drive could be stopped, Brown quoted a British officer, "Of course it can. There isn't any doubt about that." Brown was a good reporter who could not be put off by positive statements. He mentioned seeing barbed wire strung across the downtown and harbor areas, concluding that "Singapore is getting ready for a Japanese landing attempt."[27] Raymond Gram Swing tried to sound upbeat. The usually astute radio commentator based his faith on two points: the fighting qualities of Australians, and the soothing words of Churchill. "Singapore is prepared to stand a siege," Swing asserted on February 2. "It is manned by courageous Australians, among the best fighters in the world."[28] Listening to London, he noted that "British leaders have spoken confidently about Singapore being able to stand a siege of months. To say this they must have known about defenses, and have been satisfied that Singapore could be held at the back-door as well as at the front."[29]

George Fielding Eliot was also tuned in to Singapore's peril. He interpreted the battles in Sumatra as an attempt to turn Singapore's flank, somehow finding a small element of solace in the rapidity of Yamashita's advance. Eliot pointed to "the furious desperation in the tempo of the whole Japanese effort" which he said "indicated they are aware they are working against time, and that unless they are able to make good their attack on Singapore and Luzon within time limits imposed upon them, they may find themselves in the most difficult, if not disastrous, position."[30] Eliot's intimation that Yamashita was overextended was wishful thinking.

That was the tone in the printed press. "British Hammer Enemy in Malaya: They Take Initiative for First Time but Are Unable to Attack in Force" was a confusing *New York Times* headline. The accompanying article went on to cite British sources which claimed that Japanese offensive pressure was "definitely dwindling."[31] At the same time, *Chicago Daily News* foreign correspondent George Weller filed a dispatch entitled "A Creeping, Stalking War," in which he accounted for Japanese advances but wrote colorfully of jungle tactics, "Nippon's clever officers," and the attempts of the attackers to outflank the defenders. "It would take the Japanese months to reach Johore Bahru, gateway to Singapore Island, by their present methods and at their present speed," he insisted, suggesting that Yamashita's army was really a decoy move preparatory to a naval landing at Singapore itself.[32] By the end of January, a hopeful *Times* headline read, "Resistance Stiffens at Western End of Line in Malaya,"[33] while an Associated Press article filed by correspondent C. Yates McDaniel spoke about "The British counteroffensive seventy miles above Singapore," which had presumably stopped Yamashita's invaders in their tracks.[34]

News from the Philippines diffused American attentions from Singapore in January and February. When the Japanese crossed the Johore Straits and the battle for the city began, it came as a surprise. Eliot still talked of what he called "the siege of Singapore."[35] He told listeners that the battle in store was a long fight over a stronghold with the defenders having advantages, including "well-emplaced heavy artillery" to take a toll on the exposed attackers.[36] "Can the defenders beat of Japanese bombers?" he asked. "Can they resupply their fighters?"[37] He laid open the possibility that nearby Dutch Indies bases could provide air cover for Singapore, correctly guessing for that reason that Sumatra was a likely invasion target itself. Eliot failed to encompass the reality of Singapore's situation. On January 27, Churchill told the House of Commons that "priority in modern aircraft, in tanks, in anti-aircraft and anti-tank artillery was accorded to the Nile Valley. . . . If we have not got large modern air forces and tanks in Burma and Malaya tonight, no one is more accountable than I."[38]

Eliot understood geography. Advising listeners to consult a map, he showed the straits of Malacca and Sunda, gateways to the Indian Ocean. Loss of this choke point could devastate the Empire. There were reasons for Americans to feel optimistic, Eliot argued. "The war in the Far East is still a race against time, with the Allied sea and air power slowly growing . . . while the Japanese smash desperately against Singapore and Manila Bay. After eight weeks, the Japanese have attained neither of their objects."[39] The problem with these hopes, which stemmed from prewar plans, was that they were obsolete.

That was a depressing way to see the battle underway. No commentator took up that view. On February 6, John Daly told CBS listeners that "Singapore stands firm, stronger than before," even suggesting that Japanese forces across the Johore causeway were being decimated by British heavy guns.[40] In the *New York Herald-Tribune*, optimism and pessimism mixed in a confusing headline on February 8: "Singapore Sinks Invasion Boats, Great Naval Base Now Vacated."[41] The article was written by Harold Guard, of United Press. It said that the $400 million base had been vacated under enemy fire and now stood vacant. "I went out to a giant graving dock and found myself entirely alone," wrote Guard. "After viewing the graving dock I climbed the stairway . . . I walked freely through offices which a few days before had been guarded by marines and bayoneted sentries."[42] By this time, Americans could understand that Singapore was not a mighty bastion, but a harried target. It was not until February 11 that the radio carried accounts from London admitting that city would fall soon.[43] From London that evening, Charles Collingwood told listeners that "the Japanese are driving on the city with armor and infantry;" that air-dropped leaflets demanded unconditional surrender; that there was no sign of British resistance in the air; that there was no optimism regarding an extended hold-out. "To be frank," reported Collingwood, "Most people think Singapore is doomed, and the British people are once more experiencing the heartache that comes from watching a hopeless defense. The British have been through that before and they like it less each time its repeated."[44] Four days later, Collingwood was just as downbeat. "The British nation is going through a black time," he said. "These days of unrelieved disaster have no bright glory of Dunkerque to lighten them." He called the loss of Singapore, "one of the Empire's greatest defeats, equivalent to the Fall of France."[45]

Mutual's Swing was demoralized. "The black pall, terrible, lies over the United Nations tonight. Singapore has not yet fallen, but . . . resistance might end tomorrow," he said. "If the Japanese timetable produces the fall of Singapore by tomorrow, one can understand if the indoctrinated Japanese believe that one day they will indeed be able to conquer and rule the whole world."[46] Swing noted that a major Japanese holiday coincided with the end of the Singapore battle, speculating that the Japanese would believe heaven was on its side. Swing forced himself—and his audience—to face further nasty facts. The Dutch were on the run in Celebes and Borneo, he said, which put the Japanese within easy bombing range of Java. And in Burma, the British were in full retreat; the news there was equally dismal.[47]

From Australia, where Cecil Brown moved his reportorial base, sentiments were no brighter. In Sydney, Brown said there were recriminations galore. The reporter editorialized. "Recriminations will not win this war. Once the mistakes are known, fault-finding deters the job of getting on to victory," he reminded listeners, in words which could apply equally to any post-Pearl Harbor or Manila complaints.[48] Brown's words had an ironic aspect. For months, he gained a reputation among the British as prickly and annoying because of his incessant complaints about censorship. He frequently tried to evade strictures and expose what he saw as the nakedness of Singapore's defenses.[49] This was in contrast to Murrow, who handled the Ministry of Information in London deftly, showing them how his stories would redound to Britain's benefit.[50] Brown was more abrasive, so for him to speak about the need to avoid complaints might have struck the British as rich.

Eliot was equally emphatic about the magnitude of the disaster. Singapore's fall overshadowed all other military news, he said. "It is impossible not to recall the words of Major General Sir Ian Hamilton, 20 years ago, who said, 'Let us take care that if we build a base at Singapore, we do not half-garrison it, as is our custom, and so make a present of it to the wrong people at the wrong moment."[51] Having located the apposite quote, Eliot explained to listeners that "The United Nations lost its major naval base in the Southwest Pacific."[52] Print sources were equally adamant. *Newsweek* was lurid, with "Fall of Singapore Puts Java in Jaws of Jap Nutcracker."[53] "The Singapore myth perished on February 15 at 7 p.m.," said the article.

> Japanese guns played the dirge for the "invulnerable" fortress. Smoke and flame from a hundred blazes swirled around the funeral pyre. Not even the direst prophets of gloom had foreseen the speed of the catastrophe . . . Crete had resisted the Germans for thirteen days. Hong Kong, bereft of Japanese support, had staved off the Japanese for sixteen. But Singapore, "City of Lions," and "the mightiest citadel in the world" toppled in exactly one week less four hours from the time invaders set foot on its shores.[54]

Mollie Panter-Downes could not have been more blunt. "This is one of the bad moments in English history," she observed, wondering if Singapore might prove so disastrous as to unseat Churchill, whom she said now wielded "more power here than any individual has since Cromwell." The problem for the Prime Minister, she explained, was that "his promises that Singapore would be defended haven't helped the public to view with equanimity the ignominious British retreats in Malaya and Libya." Panter-Downes did not see any immediate sign of a move that would topple Churchill's government, but she wondered if his earlier heroic reputation, forged in the May 1940 crisis and after, would remain intact, given recent failures.[55] Days after the surrender, on February 20, Panter-Downes' column had a lede both thunderous and depressing: "Although it had been regarded as inevitable," she wrote, "the fall of Singapore sounded to Britons something like an earth-shaking rehearsal for judgment day."[56]

There was plenty of misery ahead for Singapore. Percival was bullied by Yamashita at the surrender table. Some of the Japanese general's bluster was bluff, since Yamashita realized that his situation was not so dominant. "My attack on Singapore was a bluff," he admitted later. "I had 30,000 men and was outnumbered more than three to one. I knew that if I had been made to fight longer for Singapore I would have been beaten. That was why the surrender had to be immediate."[57] His bluff worked. Percival and defenders were destined for years of imprisonment in awful conditions at the hands of Japanese who viewed them as undeserving of decent treatment. Newsreels at movie theaters delivered "last, dramatic pictures" from Singapore on March 9, showing images of Japanese bombers raining destruction on civilian neighborhoods in the days prior to the fall. Americans received visual images of the disaster just weeks after the surrender.[58]

ABDA spells defeat: Americans and the stricken Dutch

If wars were won by feasting/Or victory by song/Or safety found, by sleeping sound/How England would be strong!/But honour and dominion/Are not maintained so,/They're only got by sword and shot/ And this the Dutchmen know!

Rudyard Kipling, "The Dutch in the Medway"[59]

One plane is worth two promises!

H.J. Van Mook, Governor-General of the Dutch East Indies, February 1942[60]

The Netherlands' position in the war was potentially ambiguous. The Dutch government's priority was to reduce that ambiguity. In some ways, Holland's situation was comparable to that of France. In other ways, it differed. Like France, the Netherlands lay under German occupation, with collaborators contending for legitimacy against a government-in-exile. Collaboration had some momentum, since there were Dutch who either shared National Socialist values or made their peace with the New Order. The Netherlands were neutral in World War I. Unlike France, the country did not have a long rivalry with Germany. Moreover, the Dutch were racially fine by Nazi standards. Thanks to Queen Wilhemina's escape to England, the international legitimacy of her government-in-exile was unequivocal, as was Anton Mussert's status as a Nazi puppet beholden to Arthur Seyss-Inquart, Reich Commissar. The irony which pained de Gaulle was that French strategic relevance kept the United States dealing with Vichy. In the case of the Netherlands, strategic power resided entirely with the government-in-exile, which held sway in Dutch possessions. The effect was that France had difficulty shedding its occupation identity. Not Holland. With colonial holdings in the New World and Pacific—Dutch Guyana, the Antilles, and the Netherlands East Indies—there was agreement that the Dutch were Allies in good standing.

Besides wishing to maintain their standing as a relevant power, the Netherlands had a political legacy of toleration and an equally proud military tradition. The defeat of the Spanish Hapsburgs by Maurice of Orange's army of the States-General in the 1590s capped off decades of revolts for Dutch independence, setting the stage for martial success and commercial opulence during Holland's era as a great power.[61] Wilhemina's government-in-exile was committed not only to reclaiming national honor, but perpetuating this legacy. That would afford the country its place among the Allies. It was during that seventeenth century Golden Age, contemporaneous with the American colonial period, that the Dutch claimed their Empire, thanks to affluence and a first-rate navy. Empire followed trade interests, for the Dutch anchored in profitable places: New Amsterdam, Indonesia, the Antilles, Japan, Formosa, Ceylon.[62] Profit required power to protect it. The Dutch Navy was powerful. Legend has it that, after winning 1652's Battle of Dungeness, Admiral Maarten Tromp tied a broom to his prow, taunting that he had swept the English Channel clean of British ships. In 1667, Admiral Michiel de Ruyter's fleet rampaged up the Thames in the Raid on the Medway, panicking Samuel Pepys to note that London was "in a very fearful stink for fear of the Dutch."[63] The impact of these achievements lasted long enough in the English mind to prompt Kipling's poem, "The Dutch in the Medway," a warning against peacetime parsimony, which concluded, "For, now De Ruyter's topsails/Off naked Chatham show,/We dare not meet them with our fleet –/And this the Dutchmen know!"[64] By World War II, those imperial holdings were all that remained from old days of armed might. The Netherlands hoped that the new war would bypass them. But the *Luftwaffe* insisted that Holland offered needed bases for air campaigns against Britain.[65] Its 200-mile frontier with Germany combined with its small size and flat terrain made the country impossible to defend, but the Dutch did have a plan. It called for a fighting withdrawal to "Fortress Holland," the area containing Amsterdam, Rotterdam, and the Hague, protected by the Maas River and Zuider Zee. There, the Dutch Army would hang on as long as possible, hoping for relief from an Allied counteroffensive. The German invasion, with its effective use of airborne drops behind Dutch lines and at strategic points like the Moerdijk bridges was too fast. It rendered water defenses ineffective. In a five-day assault lasting from May 10–15, 1940, German troops inundated the nation, obliterating resistance, terror-bombing Rotterdam and grabbing control. Only two things went right for the Dutch: the Queen and important officials evaded capture at the Hague, slipping off to Britain; so did the navy. General Henri Winkelmann sent Dutch warships to Britain before capitulating.[66]

These two circumventions proved crucial during the rest of the war. The Dutch were positioned to keep fighting as part of the United Nations coalition. This put the Netherlands in the ranks of conquered nations whose honor was intact. Neighboring Belgium's government-in-exile, by contrast, was put in the awkward position of having to disavow its own King Leopold, who surrendered to the Germans with his army still fighting. The escape of Wilhemina and her navy also obscured world awareness of Dutch support for Germany's *Neuropa* agenda that the Seyss-Inquart/Mussert regime—which raised thousands of volunteers for the SS—drummed up.[67] Close consultation with Dutch authorities in the East Indies buttressed the rationale of Allied cooperation. As Pacific tensions rose towards Pearl Harbor's zero hour, Netherlands officials kept Cordell Hull informed about Japanese moves in the area.[68] The United States, in turn, kept the Dutch—along with the Australians, British, and Chinese—informed about Japanese designs.[69]

In the United States, there were special ties which strengthened the Dutch connection. A.J. Drexel Biddle, Jr. served as Ambassador to the Netherlands government-in-exile, giving the Dutch a highly placed American contact.[70] Biddle brokered the deal whereby Americans helped to defend Aruba and Curacao. Roosevelt liked Wilhemina, writing to her graciously on January 2, 1942, assuaging concerns that American defense connections with Venezuela might result in loss of Dutch control of those islands.[71] The monarch visited family members summering in Massachusetts in June 1942,[72] when Roosevelt presented her, and the Dutch fleet, with a submarine pursuit craft. "From the earliest days of history, the people of the Netherlands—your people—have been willing to fight for their freedom and independence. They have won out in the face of great odds," said the President to the Queen at the ceremony. "We, too, are fighting for our freedom and it is natural and right that the Netherlands and the United States have joined hands in the common struggle."[73] Roosevelt praised Dutch heroism while Wilhelmina responded that the "excellent spirit of friendship which ever since the days of John Paul Jones has existed between our two navies" was alive and well.[74] She also addressed a Joint Session of Congress, and was presented at a press conference by Roosevelt, who made sure to remind all the reporters that "The Netherlands and this country have most of their ideals in common."[75]

Dutch diplomatic assets included Ambassador Alexander Loudon,[76] one of the most active members of Washington's diplomatic corps, determined to remind Americans that his nation remained part of the war and would help to make the peace. During the afternoon of December 7, 1941, he spoke with Undersecretary of State Welles, informing him that the Netherlands would immediately declare war against Japan. He confirmed the decision the next day, writing Welles to let him know that the Dutch Minister to Tokyo had delivered the war message.[77] Loudon wrote letters and articles and gave copious speeches to gatherings large and small, ranging from Washington cocktail parties to major events in distant states, such as dedication of the 67th Evacuation Hospital, at Fort Rodman, Massachusetts, in 1942.[78] When Churchill came to Washington, Loudon was received with the representatives from China and Australia, and assured by the Prime Minister that "Singapore was safe for a longer period than the public imagines."[79] Loudon was a frequent visitor to the offices of Assistant Secretary of State Breckinridge Long, Undersecretary Welles, and Secretary Hull, discussing a variety of matters. One issue in Spring 1942 was the legal position of a Dutch-flagged vessel, the *Wilhemina*, which escaped China to berth in Seattle, while diplomats figured out what to do with its Chinese crew. The Americans wanted to get the ship into war-related service, while the Dutch were concerned lest it be requisitioned, bruising their sovereignty.[80] The issue posed a legalistic problem, but it gave Loudon the chance to deal frequently with top State Department figures, underscoring his position. Alongside his wife, Loudon hosted frequent embassy events, including parties and professional receptions aimed at keeping the Dutch in the diplomatic conversation.[81] Loudon also worked assiduously with Leo T. Crowley, Foreign Economic Administrator at the Department of the Treasury, to keep open the lines of Lend-Lease. These took the form of generous loans of silver and friendly credit terms.[82]

Approval of the Dutch in the United States stemmed partly from shared ethnic and cultural traditions. There were plenty of Americans with Dutch roots, including the President. Relations had bloomed ever since the Pilgrims set off from Leiden. John Adams arrived in Holland in 1780, seeking funds for the American Revolution, enthusing, "One nation is a copy of the other."[83] When told that Frisians were especially fond of the American cause, Adams sagely noted that "Friesland is said to be a sure index of the national sense. The People of that Province have been ever famous for the spirit of liberty."[84] Dutch immigrants came in waves, from the Hudson Valley/New Amsterdam generation of the 1600s to the prairie settlers of the 1800s. The nineteenth century saw hundreds of thousands of land-hungry Dutch pioneers settle a Midwestern belt from western Michigan across to Iowa and Wisconsin. Towns with names like Holland, Zeeland, and Overisel, Michigan, or Pella and Orange City, Iowa, dotted the region. They had Dutch Reformed churches which kept the Calvinist faith, schools like Central, Northwestern, and Hope colleges, anchored in Dutch customs of mind, and newspapers like Henry Hospers' *Weekblad*, in Pella, or Charles L. Dyke's *Sioux County Capital*, in Orange City, publishing in Dutch and English.[85] Their towns decked themselves out in tulips every spring to celebrate ancestry and the end of another tiresome Midwestern winter. Civic expressions extolled the Dutch past and American present, as in "Transition: Holland-America," which appeared in the *Capital*: "We left a land we all do love,/'Twas wrested from the sea./It broke the power of haughty Spain/And won its liberty./There Rembrandt painted light and shade,/And law and learning true,/Gave freedom how to worship God,/Asylum to the Jew. . ."[86]

Democratic partnership between the Netherlands and the United States started "Holland Mania," an American fad for all things Dutch.[87] Theodore Roosevelt accentuated the enthusiasm. On his 1909 trip to Delft, he proudly evoked his heritage, saying, "I come from a great free Republic to the home of my forefathers, of which it may be said that they were among the very first to establish freedom as we now understand the word."[88] That was also the message in Mary Mapes Dodge's *Hans Brinker, or the Silver Skates*. Dodge described Holland as "one of the queerest countries under the sun," because of its watery orientation, canals, houseboats, windmills, peaked roofs with storks atop. She delivered one of the most influential pieces of Hollandiana; a portrait of a charming place whose enterprising inhabitants Americans should understand. The Dutch she called brave and placid; their nation "The Asylum of the world, for the oppressed of every nation have found there shelter and encouragement." According to Dodge, a tune familiar to Americans proved cultural ties: *Yankee didee dudel down/Didee dudel lawnter; Yankee viver, voover vown,/Botermelk and Tawnter!*" Dodge's story also contended that ethnicity was something Dutch and Americans shared, since "We Americans . . . after all are homeopathic preparations of Dutch stock."[89] In like vein, in 1903, Dutch-born *Ladies Home Journal* editor Edward Bok wrote "The Mother of America," an article which he credited the Netherlands with much that was worthwhile in American political and cultural life.[90]

The old country harbored reciprocal sentiments. The Holland-America steamship line published *With Roosevelt Through Holland*, by M.J. Brusse, in 1911. Brusse described Theodore Roosevelt's 1909 trip, calling the former president "our own distant cousin."[91] In the 1930s, a mania arose in the Netherlands as various provincial authorities claimed historical antecedents as the home town of the Roosevelts. The winner was Oud Vessemer, which found that Roosevelts lived there in the 1640s, before Klaes Martensen van Roosevelt headed for New Amsterdam. The President was proud of his Dutch roots.[92] Even as the bad war news flooded in during the months after Pearl Harbor, popular culture reinforced the American-Dutch connections, since pole-vaulter Cornelius "Dutch" Warmerdam was so often in the sports headlines. Using a bamboo pole, the Californian broke the 15-foot barrier 43 times between 1940 and 1944.[93] On February 18, 1942, as the Japanese attacked the Dutch Indies, superstar Warmerdam starred in a Universal Newsreel focusing on his latest 15 foot, 71/4 inch jump at a Boston meet. The film ran in theaters across the country, serving as another reminder of how deeply interwoven into American culture Dutch heritage truly was.[94]

But all this did not put Roosevelt in position to save the Netherlands East Indies in 1942. Unlike Holland, the colony had a low profile in American consciousness. Some knew it produced rubber and oil; the East Indies were a far-off place which only war brought to American attentions. Such notice as the region did attract was often arcane. This was the case when Margaret Mead graced the January 1942 issue of *The American Scholar*, Phi Betta Kappa's journal, with her short study, "Community Drama, Bali, and America."[95] Bali was a real enough place, between Java's east coast and the Lesser Sundas. But Mead's pre-December 7 analysis of Balinese community drama, and her hopes that American communities might emulate it, were overtaken by events.

The American Consul General in Batavia, writing to Hull on December 8, 1941, praised the purposeful spirit there. He approved of the round-up of local Japanese, who were placed in custody within an hour of the war announcement. It encouraged him that the locals remained calm.[96] The Japanese invaded on January 10.[97] Their first blows fell at Borneo and Celebes, where garrisons of Dutch and native troops resisted vigorously. Shore batteries at Tarakan, off Borneo, sank two of six Japanese destroyers in the invasion force, while Dutch planes destroyed two cruisers and two troop transports.[98] But the landings went off nevertheless. Winning their beachheads, Japanese troops moved inland.

J.J. Van Mook, Governor-General of the colonies, arrived in Washington to plea for immediate military supply, especially aircraft. He talked of stopping the Japanese advance before it claimed Java. Van Mook's brave front impressed his hosts. At a dinner given in his honor, he mentioned that he would return to the islands, where his family remained. The message was that the 200,000 Dutch in the Indies would never surrender. But there was little chance that van Mook's pleas for goods would succeed. The President made solicitous but vague references to reinforcement plans for the Philippines and Indies. A dolorous Van Mook replied, "One plane is worth two promises!"[99] Van Mook was correct that there were no plans to send much his way. But he was less accurate questioning American cooperation.

Roosevelt signed off on one of the most unusual attempts at coordination in the war. This was the ill-starred ABDA Command. The Dutch East Indies were Japan's most coveted prize. First of all, there was pro-independence unrest in the islands, which could mean support for an Asian campaign against colonialism. Second, there were many of the resources Japan needed. Third, the Indies looked easy to capture. Despite Dutch determination, the Japanese felt confident. There was little surprise in their invasion plan. The second wave of landings came on January 23, when invaders hit New Guinea, the Bismarck Archipelago, Rabaul, and Kavieng. Japanese power extended far enough east to menace Australia and eastern Java.

It was in these conditions that ABDA was born. The acronym stood for American, British, Dutch, and Australian elements under unified command. The idea was born on New Year's Day, when Admiral Thomas C. Hart, of the United States Asiatic Fleet, arrived on submarine USS Shark at the harbor of Surabaya, Dutch naval HQ. The plan brought together naval and army elements. Supreme Commander was Field Marshal Wavell, overseeing Hart, in naval command. Ground forces were led by Dutch Lieutenant General Hein ter Poorten, air units by Air Chief Marshal Sir Richard E.C. Peirse.[100] ABDA covered the East Indies, Burma, the Philippines, the South China Sea, the northeast Indian Ocean from Australia's Northwest Cape to the Torres Strait. ANZAC, which involved American, New Zealand, and Australian commands, covered the areas farther east and south.[101]

The lines joined perfectly and the map looked neat. In practice, ABDA was a last-minute arrangement put under pressure to meet a fast-moving enemy with the initiative. The Japanese were well-aware of its banged-together composition. The effort to blend Allied units into a single force did bear out the American commitment to the United Nations. The strategy for ABDA was basic. At issue was the Malay barrier to the Indian Ocean, and protection of territories proximate to Australia. Java was the crux. Protecting it from invasion meant keeping the Japanese away from Australia. The Dutch hoped to hold the Japanese to outer islands. The plan was determined by geographical necessity. With so many islands, the Indies were indefensible as a totality. Java was most important, so that was where the Dutch would make their stand. But each week drew the Japanese closer. The Malay campaign put them by the Macassar Straits, which doomed Sumatra. The Dutch practiced a scorched earth policy, demolishing the oil facilities at Palembang. By February 15, the oil installations were aflame, and the Japanese at the southern end of Sumatra. This put them at the Sunda Strait, across which lay Java's western end.[102] On February 20, Japanese troops moved into East Timor, ruled by the neutral Portuguese, in no position to eject them. Earlier, the Dutch and Australians proposed to occupy Timor as trustees, but the Portuguese threatened to fight if they came in.[103] Lisbon kept up its diplomatic protests against the Allies.[104]

The Dutch fought fiercely. On Java, they had resources at their disposal. Despite van Mook's complaint in Washington, they had many planes, mostly older American models such as the B-10 Martin, which the B-17 replaced in the American arsenal. The nucleus of their KNIL army was 30,000 Dutch soldiers, who fought alongside 100,000 native troops. Their navy consisted of 7 destroyers and 3 light cruisers, plus 15 submarines, and support ships.[105] This looked impressive, although the ships were old.[106] Dutch military preparedness was interrupted by World War II. Efforts had been split between strengthening the homeland and holding the world's third-largest empire.[107] Hart's Asiatic Fleet was a weaker element in the US Navy. Ground efforts on Java would clearly rest with the Dutch. The defense became truly frantic as Japan moved to Java. On February 19, Dutch and American vessels fired at troop transports, joined by Dutch bombers. This was major combat, which American media noticed.

"There's good news tonight!" became the trademark phrase for radio announcer Gabriel Heatter. He coined it after the Battle of Balikpapan. Heatter was a Mutual Radio commentator, whose positive on-air demeanor was hard to sustain against constantly bad war news. Heatter desperately wanted a story listeners could feel good about. He heard about Balikpapan. The engagement, the "Battle of the Macassar Strait," was a night action in which Dutch Brewster Buffaloes and submarines combined with American destroyers, *John D. Ford, Pope, Parrot,* and *John Paul Jones.* The Dutch planes destroyed the Balikpapan oil facilities, which burned brightly in the night, making silhouettes of the Japanese troop transports sliding by. Commander Paul Talbot took Hart's attack orders seriously. Using torpedoes, the American destroyers sank four transports. The battle was not decisive enough to stop the Japanese, but it did mark the US Navy's first surface engagement, delivering a tactical victory. That gave Heatter his opening. The trademark phrase became an aural morale booster. "Many calls came into the radio switchboard saying the same thing: they were happy to know that someone believed in American courage," Heatter recalled later.[108] So many approving callers expressed appreciation for the commentator's "good news tonight" line that Heatter kept it his signature. Soldiers wrote thanking him for boosting home front morale. "You have kept my mother going . . . with your broadcasts of hope and good news," went a typical letter.[109] Heatter's services connection went beyond clever phrasing. His son, Basil, was a navy officer wounded in combat.[110] "After you said good-night we could go home feeling better," wrote one of Heatter's listeners in a thank-you note, reaffirming the point made in a *Saturday Evening Post* article which explained, "Heatter was able to supply the bright crumb, which he customarily served up with a thick emotional frosting."[111]

On January 27, an Associated Press story passed along Dutch identification of a Japanese battleship lost in the fighting, which turned out to be false. "By now it has become clear that the heavy blows struck at the enemy certainly have upset his time table—and perhaps his future strategy," claimed Aneta, the Dutch East Indian news agency. "Tokyo now will realize how great are the risks of naval operations in this archipelago and may consider it necessary to revise plans."[112] The story ran under positive headlines such as "Jap Battleship Sunk, Dutch Report," in the *Baltimore Evening Sun*. Elsewhere, there was other media praise aimed at the Dutch efforts. *Newsweek* devoted its January 12 cover to a photograph of a Dutch submarine, with the cover caption: "Dutch Submarine: Star Performer in the Pacific."[113]

John Raleigh's commentaries for CBS painted the Indies as a strategic place run by planters. Raleigh moved to Sydney, but William J. Dunn continued in Batavia for CBS. On February 5, Dunn delivered an account which blended local color with the thrill of danger. He did this from his hotel room. Without news to report, Dunn used his storytelling ability to create a gripping story. "Java is on alert," he began, adding that the question was when the attack would start. Citing reports of Japanese bombers, he editorialized in a personal vein: "What a strange feeling, standing by, waiting for the first sound of bombs which you've been expecting for over two months, wondering, curiously, what your own reaction will be."[114] Some in Batavia were nervous, he admitted, but others Dunn described as "nonchalant, just as convinced that they've seen the worst that there is to see, and that they can go on, indefinitely, without personal fear." Returning to the first person, Dunn went on. "As you talk with these men," he said,

> You wonder just how you, yourself, are going to be classified when the long-expected showdown finally comes. In one year, you have visited Manila, Hong Kong, Chunking, Kunming, the Burma Road, Rangoon, Singapore, Surabaya, Balikpapan. All have been bombed, and many are in enemy hands since you last visited, some of them only a few hours after you left.

Keeping the personal element at the center of his dramatic narrative, Dunn put the listener in his place there in a city about to be attacked. "You realize that you can't go on in the midst of a war forever being lucky. When the time finally comes, you ask yourself, 'What will you do?' And you admit that you have to wait and see."[115]

Dunn evoked the Dutch colonial setting. "You look around the great silent room, in which you are alone," he went on.

A single light, carefully shielded from the outside world, shines down on your typewriter. As you look up, you see a portrait of the Governor General of the Indies, a rather human-looking person, replete with medals and epaulets. On the right wall is Princess Juliana and her two children, the same sort of youngsters you might see in Central Park on a Sunday afternoon.

Besides royal family members, Dunn described the portrait of Queen Wilhemina, "Who looks and is a Queen by any standard. It's quiet and peaceful," he added for emphasis, "It's hard to realize that the war is at your very doorstep."[116] With reports like these, Dunn revealed himself to be a talented wordsmith, a fitting member of the Murrow network. Using only his literary talents, seated in his room, Dunn broadcast a taut account devoid of action or even news value, which nonetheless conveyed the feel of a place on the edge.

Ten days later, on February 15, Dunn was still there. He described Palembang. "The Dutch have done everything in their power to prepare for such an attack as came 24 hours ago," he explained, adding that the loss of Palambang paralleled that of Singapore, the same day. Dunn added that additional airplanes might have saved the day, but were never delivered.[117] Here, Dunn played to the advantage of the Dutch. The angle bent around the point that the Dutch were not to be blamed. They were instead to be credited with steadfastness, and to be pitied because they had done all they could and been let down by reluctance to deliver them supplies. Neither Dunn nor other reporters overtly blamed Roosevelt, but the comparison to coverage of Singapore, where the British were taken to task for their failures, was stark. As far as the Indies were concerned, the Dutch were seen to have—as Dunn put it—"done everything in their power." That such efforts were insufficient to prevent defeat was presented more as a tragedy than an indictment. Dunn amplified that message on February 20, when he said that the Dutch on Java were still hoping for reinforcements, which—by virtue of their rugged fighting and heavy casualties—"they believe they have earned."[118]

By March 1, with Dunn on the move "somewhere in Java," it was left to Harry Marble, in New York, to describe the "heroic resistance of the Dutch" on Java, as well as to the equally stout "Allied naval forces against a three-pronged attack." Marble laid out the Battle of Java in a tone which made it sound as if that was the decisive action which could determine the war's outcome. But Java was doomed, and the Allies had already drawn a defensive perimeter around Australia. This meant that the Dutch Indies were written off. Dunn described "a glorious chapter in the history of the Dutch fleet," while, in Washington, Albert Warner opined that War Department officials were not confident about the outcome in Java but promised that there was more fighting in store there.[119] On March 8, Harry Marble cited Japanese and German news reports in his CBS account. The question was whether or not the Dutch had surrendered. Japan said they had, while the Dutch denied it, promising guerilla resistance.

This was an empty promise. The Netherlands could not count on the populace's loyalty. After three centuries, the Dutch no longer daunted their charges. Defeats stripped them of their mystique. The KNIL was more of a civil security force than a fighting army. This was codified by the Hague in a 1927 "Principles of Defense" document which named maintaining Dutch control against unrest from the "inland enemy"—the native peoples—as first priority.[120] It was consistent with many years of harsh administration, which did not endear the colonial regime to all of its peoples. The Dutch guessed that many Indonesians would welcome the Japanese as potential liberators, at least until the conqueror's own chauvinism and rapacity set in.[121]

American news observers never mentioned these points. Dutch suzerainty over the Indies was construed as a natural fact. Anti-colonial rhetoric was the purview of the Japanese. A pamphlet entitled "Read This Alone—And The War Can Be Won!" was distributed to Japanese soldiers. In it were appraisals of the injustice at the heart of the colonial system. Asking rhetorically, "The campaign area in South Asia—What is it like?" the answer began emphatically, "A treasure-house of the Far East, seized by the Americans, the French, and the Dutch." As for demography, a heading which read "A hundred million Asians tyrannized by three hundred thousand whites," made the numbers plain.

> Once you set foot on the enemy's territories you will see for yourselves, only too clearly, just what this oppression by the white man means. Imposing, splendid buildings look down from the summits of mountains or hills onto the tiny thatched huts of natives.[122]

Playing up the pan-Asian argument, the text continued, "Money squeezed from the blood of Asians maintains these small white minorities in their luxurious mode of life—or disappears to the respective home countries. These white people may expect, from the moment they issue from their mothers' wombs, to be allotted a score of natives as their personal slaves. Is this really God's will?"[123] Of course, the image of liberator was favorable to Japanese self-regard.

American commentary stressed Dutch patriotism. At CBS, Marble told listeners that Radio Bandeung signed off on March 7 with the final salute, "Good-bye until better times. God Save the Queen." He added that Queen Wilhemina—whom he referred to affectionately as "Queen Minnie"—promised that the Dutch flag would fly again over the Indies. The assumption was that this was the natural order of things. As in 1940, the Dutch were defeated, yet they remained in the Allied coalition. They were offered the consolation of respect due an ally which lost a battle but still planned to win the war.[124] De Gaulle could only wish for such charitable interpretations.

Van Mook was heard from again. H.R. Knickerbocker, the Pulitzer Prize-winning foreign correspondent for the *Chicago Sun*, reported from Batavia in a lengthy piece datelined February 23. The message was the same. There was still time to save Java, but only immediate resupply could do it. Van Mook argued that saving Java was not just in United Nations' interest. "From the purely military point of view," he explained, "holding Java would weaken the Japanese like nothing else. It would make an attack upon Australia impossible—not that I consider that the Japanese want to attack Australia. I don't."[125] He went on to term the threat to Australia "a palpable Japanese trick to scare the Allies into keeping their war materials at home rather than to send them where they are needed and could help defeat the enemy."[126]

Creatively, he suggested that keeping weaponry, planes, and reinforcements played into Japanese hands. Besides, he had been given assurances that resupply was forthcoming—yet he was still waiting. He put the battle into a world context, reminding Knickerbocker of Japan's Axis membership and arguing that Java's resources would benefit Hitler. Russia would be harmed, he said, since Japan could soon turn against them. The British would be tossed out of Asia because, while

No Asiatic loves the Japanese, their success here would be bound to influence every Asiatic against the white man, and this would be true above all in India—which is a fact the British ought to be thinking about at this moment.[127]

Not only the fate of the Dutch East Indies, but the war's outcome revolved around Java, he insisted. This was the pith of van Mook's case, and it might have had more purchase in the American mind if the notion of fighting a war to preserve European colonial assets was anywhere present in national discourse. But that was not an argument Americans cared much about. For his part, Knickerbocker admired the Governor, adding a pro-Dutch flourish of his own. "Van Mook spoke as plainly as a Dutchman can," said the reporter, "And that means as plainly as language can express thought."[128]

Preventing the invasion and loss of Java was ABDA's objective. Once Japan had the island, the quadripartite command was moot. ABDA always had an element of gimcrack, and was now a failure. Whether or not ABDA ever had a chance to save Java was questionable.[129] Under the strains of defeat and the need to reform under a better structure, the combined command system cracked up and fell apart.[130] The United States and Britain recognized the lost cause, moving to protect Australia.

The Dutch were left holding the bag. The geographical unity of the ABDA area was redivided. Burma was shifted to the India command, while MacArthur's imminent move to Australia showed that ABDA's hold on Philippine authority was pure phantasm. All that was left was a nominal command on Java itself. The Dutch, glad about ABDA's formation, now glumly saw its decimation. Vice Admiral Conrad E.L. Helfrich, last naval commander in the ABDA structure, understood that he no longer commanded a force capable of defending Dutch control of the Indies.[131] ABDA Command went defunct on February 25.[132] What was left to Helfrich and the last scraps of ABDA was heroic immolation. This happened at the Battle of the Java Sea, February 27.

This naval engagement consisted of the Dutch fleet, supported by American, Australian, and British ships, taking on a larger and better-organized Japanese fleet. The fighting took place off Surabaya, with the Allied task force of 5 cruisers and 11 destroyers challenging Japanese warships accompanying the troop transports.[133] The sortie was a last-ditch gambit to wreck the invasion. It was gallant but disarranged. Rear Admiral Karel W. Doorman commanded the Allied force, hampered by having no system for sharing codes between the Dutch, British, Australians, and Americans.[134] In the first large surface engagement since World War I's Battle of Jutland, Doorman's force fought to inhibit an invasion that was already underway. There was an edge in overall strength for the Japanese, but they benefitted most from seamlessness of command.[135] Aware of their own inferiority in numbers and speed, but especially in communications, torpedoes, and air cover for spotting and bombing,[136] the Allies fought aggressively if not smoothly. Doorman hunted out the enemy for a decisive action.

Japanese convoys were heading for both east and west sides of Java.

> I am afraid that the defense of the ABDA area has been broken down and that defense of Java cannot now last long. . . . Anything put into Java now can do little to prolong struggle. . . . I see little further usefulness for this HQ.

went Wavell's cable to Churchill.[137] The Eastern Attack Group, commanded by Rear Admiral Shoji Nishimura, had 41 troop transports, 2 heavy cruisers, 2 light cruisers, 18 destroyers, and assorted tenders. The Western Attack Group, led by Rear Admiral Takeo Kurita, boasted 56 transports, 4 heavy and 3 light cruisers, 1 aircraft carrier, 25 destroyers, and assorted supply ships. Sailing to intercept these flotillas was the divided ABDA armada. Helfrich's force included 3 British cruisers and 2 destroyers, sailing westward without air spotters, looking for an enemy they never found. Helfrich's ships put into Tjilatjap for resupply before steaming for Ceylon, since by then Java Sea was lost.[138]

There was tension between the Dutch and their allies as the situation deteriorated. When Royal Navy Admiral Sir Arthur Palliser informed his Dutch counterpart that he had instructions from the Admiralty to withdraw to Ceylon "when resistance will serve no further purpose," Helfrich was indignant. "Have you forgotten the enormous support I gave the British cause in Malaya?" he demanded.

All of my fighting fleet—my cruisers, my destroyers, my submarines, my air—all of it was placed at your disposal. And to our great loss. I did much more to defend Singapore than the British fleet has done to defend the Netherlands East Indies.[139]

But Palliser was firm, knowing the hopelessness of the situation. It was his duty to survive. Faced with the British Admiral's response, Helfrich turned to his American counterpart, Rear Admiral William A. Glassford. What were American intentions? Glassford felt that Palliser's take was accurate, but said, "My instructions are to report to you for duty. Any order you give me will be obeyed at once."[140] Touched by this display of martial honor and American respect for Dutch authority, Helfrich softened, gave Palliser permission to sail for Ceylon, and ordered the American ships to Australia.[141]

While Helfrich negotiated, Doorman intercepted the Japanese. He had 5 cruisers and 11 destroyers under his command. Not all were available for action. After some fruitless hunting, Doorman's impressively named Combined Striking Force headed for Surabaya. Before refueling was complete, Doorman heard that the Japanese were sighted off Bawean Island. Using voice commands by radio and signal flags, the brave Dutch Admiral ordered: FOLLOW ME THE ENEMY IS NINETY MILES AWAY.[142] British destroyers *Jupiter, Encounter,* and *Electra* formed the forward screen, followed by British cruiser *Exeter*, Dutch flagship *De Ruyter*, American cruiser *Houston*, with light cruisers *Perth*, flying Australia's flag, and Dutch *Java* next. Old "four-piper" destroyers, *John D. Edwards, Paul Jones, John D. Ford,* and *Alden* formed the rear.[143]

For each element of ABDA, there were different stakes. The Americans, British, and Australians had more fighting ahead of them. Doorman, however, had little need to preserve his assets. If Java was to be lost—which it was—then the Indies were lost, which meant his fleet was superfluous. He carried the action to the enemy and fought for hours, only to see his perforated force split up. Due partly to the graciousness of Helfrich, who saw no need for the British to pointlessly sacrifice themselves, most of the Royal Navy ships avoided destruction, as did most American vessels.[144] The United States lost *Houston* and, soon after in the Sunda Strait, destroyer *Pope*; the British lost heavy cruiser *Exeter*, famous for outfighting the German *Graf Spee* off Montevideo in 1939, now damaged in Java Sea and sunk with *Pope* in Sunda Strait; the Australians lost *Perth*.[145] Such losses were weighty, but not critical to the war effort. However, the Dutch lost their best cruisers, *Java* and *De Ruyter*. This meant destruction of the Royal Netherlands Navy.[146]

The loss of these ships was devastating symbolically and strategically. *De Ruyter*, built in 1935, was sleek and powerful, 560 feet in length, with a beam of 52 feet, a displacement of 7,548 tons fully loaded and a complement of 435 sailors. *Java*, built in 1921, was 509 feet, 53 feet at the beam, displaced 6,670 tons and carried a full complement of 504 sailors.[147] Afloat, they embodied Netherlands status as a world power. Doorman died with his flagship. Dutch defeat in Indonesia was absolute, and befitting their all-in commitment, they lost every major surface vessel except cruiser *Tromp*, which escaped, although heavily damaged by torpedoes. Lost also were eight submarines and several other ships, along with thousands of soldiers and sailors. No one could accuse the Netherlands of half-measures. Total defeat meant that there was no reason for the Americans and British to include the Dutch in the upcoming measures for defending Australia.[148] The Dutch kept a gritty reputation, but no future as a fighting ally in the Pacific.

Tactical details of the defeat in the Battle of the Java Sea were kept secret from the American public. But news of a major naval battle could not be suppressed for long. Axis news agencies gave the battle plenty of attention, so it was left for American outlets to explain. Matter-of-factness was the chosen approach. Readers of the *New York Herald-Tribune* on March 1 read the headline, "Java Landings Follow Heavy Naval Battle; Japanese Land at Three Points from Several 'Tens' of Transports; Americans, Dutch, Australians Resist."[149] The accompanying article, which utilized the "United Nations" label for ABDA, stressed the heaviness of the engagement, and the toll taken on the invaders, citing a navy communiqué whose modest claims were perhaps the best indicator of the gravity of the outcome. "None of our vessels suffered heavy damage in the initial phase of the battle for Java," said the announcement before adding, "and our forces are still intact, despite the overwhelming superiority in numbers of the enemy naval forces."[150] There were plenty of plaudits for tough Dutch resistance, and the references to headhunting natives assumed to oppose the Japanese out of loyalty to their European masters. Writing for Associated Press, Witt Hancock's dispatch from Bandoeng noted that the Japanese were using bicycles to great effect, just as in Malaya. Hancock also quoted Dutch admissions that large parts of the island were under Japanese control, although he stressed that fierce fighting continued.[151] By March 3, the *Baltimore Sun* carried the news that Wavell and Burma no longer figured in ABDA, and that the Dutch had control of whatever remnant of the command still existed.[152] As far as responding to Axis accounts of the Battle of the Java Sea, American articles debunked exaggerated claims from Tokyo that 23 warships were sunk against 1 Japanese mine sweeper.[153] Within the Japanese Navy, understanding of the Battle of the Java Sea was far more realistic. Admiral Matome Ugaki recorded qualified satisfaction in his diary. "Although I don't think much of it," he wrote, "I'm pleased that we have sent the main force of the Dutch East Indies to the bottom."[154]

The stakes were highest for the Dutch, which is the theme that came across in stories emphasizing the "End of A Dream" angle in the Indies. That was a headline in *Time* on March 2, which described life in a colonial capital where people clung as long as possible "to the forms of colonial pleasantry, to the ways and the life that were now like a passing dream."[155] The text described a dreamy and genteel circumstance brought to a rudely precipitate conclusion. A week later, dealing with the Java Sea battle, *Time* again said the loss was shattering for the Dutch. "Only to a Dutchman in the East Indies could the certainty that the Japs were coming mean what it did to Conrad Helfrich. For, if the Japs were coming to the Indies, they were coming to his home," went the text, stressing the local roots of Admiral Helfrich and other defenders of the colony.[156] The article was essentially a contextual biography of Helfrich, set against the backdrop of Dutch imperial and naval history, written with respect for the colonial legacy. Helfrich was portrayed as a son of the Indies and an heir to the tradition of Tromp and de Ruyter. He was shown to be loyal, dutiful, steadfast, and thoroughly at home whether in the Indies, the Netherlands, or the United Nations. Helfrich was a stand-in for every positive association any friendly American might carry for all things Dutch. He entirely eluded any negative verdict for recent defeats. In fact, the story argued, the war would not be so awful if certain parties—namely, the British—had listened to Helfrich when there was still time. The closest *Time* came to assigning blame was to quote Helfrich's reported words at a Singapore cocktail party before the war, at which he supposedly said that, when the Japanese attacked Malaya and the Indies, the British, Americans and Dutch would need to join forces. "Did you hear what the Dutchman said?" complained a nervous British official. The article implied that the "alarmist admiral" nearly had his career destroyed for "disturbing the peace of the Pacific."[157]

The moral seemed to be that the Dutch were an indomitable but small nation, and that their misfortunes were the fault of their allies, especially the British, who should have listened earlier. That negative image from the Neville Chamberlain years—England asleep—was dusted off in a Pacific context. After the Indies campaign, the British came off worse than the plucky Dutch in such American accounts.

Burma and India—defeat and the India question

The Burma Public Works Department had done a very fine job in constructing these all-weather airfields so rapidly and with such small mechanical resources, and it was not their fault that they had been told to put them in the wrong place.[158]

Field-Marshal Viscount Slim, leader of British forces in Burma

The British have one brigade east of Rangoon and one more on the way. That's what they thought sufficient to hold Burma. And the Supreme Commander, Wavell, refused Chiang K'ai-shek's offer of two corps. Didn't want the dirty Chinese in Burma.[159]

General Joseph Stillwell, January 24, 1942

In an empire full of exotic locales, Burma was one of the most outlying British colonies. Less famous than Singapore, less important than India, it was a mystery to most Britons and unknown in the United States. On the map, it showed long frontiers with India and China. It came to American attentions by virtue of the Flying Tigers, who provided air support to the fraying British effort to hold on to Burma. The first American planes fought there on December 23 against Japanese bombers heading for Rangoon and the Mingaladon airfields. Japan's plan was to pulverize these so that they could be seized when invaders arrived.[160] Then, the Japanese Army would move north along the Irawaddy River, flowing down from the Himalayas. This would put Japanese troops near China's Yunan Province, where the Tigers kept their main base at Kunming, and on the frontier of Assam, in India.

Late in January, General Stilwell was called by General Marshall to meet with Assistant War Secretary John McCloy. McCloy, fresh from conversations with T.V. Soong, passed along Chiang K'ai Shek's approval for making Stillwell the army's point man in the Burma theater. General Eisenhower and Secretary Stimson joined the discussions.[161] All these powerful figures wanted Vinegar Joe, no friend to the British, in Rangoon. In a letter to his wife, he was circumspect but nervous. "I am going where I believe you would want me to go," he wrote.

> A respectable job in a mixed sort of capacity. Now that the load is on me I can feel it and begin to have all sorts of doubts. Can I do anything worthwhile? Or will I ball it up? . . . Well, that will wear off, and anyway, I can only pitch in and try.[162]

He spent plenty of time reading the China and Burma files, "running around and finding nobody in and phoning vacant offices." He came across conflicting reports about the British. Earlier reports contended that Wavell was cavalier, even negative, about Chinese reinforcements. On February 8, Stilwell noted that "Archie now claims he never refused help. Said he'd take two [Chinese Divisions], and for the time being, leave the other where it was." At the same time, Stilwell noticed that Wavell and Chiang, whom the American already called "Peanut," were at odds. "Somebody is a liar," he wrote about the conflicting British and Chinese reports. "Archie missed Peanut at Lashio and now they are both sore, each thinking the other ducked out on him."[163] Stilwell apprised himself of the politicking for and against Chennault, whom the Chinese government wanted to keep in place. China hand Laughlin Currie poked into this argument, but Chiang and Soong prevailed upon Marshall, who explained to General Hap Arnold why his choice, Clayton Bissell, would not do. Currie and Chennault circled each other warily; Stilwell scornfully observed that "They are acting like a couple of kids, and they'll both have to behave."[164] Stimson asked Stilwell to weigh in "on the Jap situation on the coast."[165] After that, it was off to Rangoon. The journey, by way of Trinidad, Guyana, Liberia, Sudan, Egypt, Iran, Iraq, and India, took him from February 14–24. On the first leg, he flew with Clare Boothe Luce. "1942 will be a mess," he wrote in a letter to his wife. "But if we can keep it rolling for a year, we'll begin to hand it back."[166] Stilwell arrived ten days before Rangoon's capture by the Japanese.

One problem with the collapsing Burma theater was that it was more essential to China than to Britain. Although they were alarmed to see the Japanese approaching India, the British had many fronts to worry about. They felt that Assam could be defended if necessary. Chiang's government depended on maintaining its tenuous land link to the outside world. In India, Stilwell noticed that British leadership was jumpy, fearing that the population would not "stand bombing like the Chinese have." Such defenses as he saw he called "meager,"[167] and the specter of Indian discontent with British rule—which had the potential to destroy every assumption about defending India—was a sobering backdrop. Stilwell met in China with Wavell and Chennault on March 3. The former, he found downbeat. "They were shy of information, to say the least," he noted, adding to his anti-British grievance list. When he met Chennault, the two Americans got along well because Stilwell's practiced eye appreciated the obvious fighting qualities of AVG pilots, whom he reviewed. "They look damn good," he confided with pleasure to his diary.[168]

By then, the Burma campaign was in disarray. By February 9, the Japanese crossed the Salween River and headed for the Sittang River, beyond which lay a clear path to Rangoon. Soaring from Lashio air strip in a strenuous effort to hold off the advance, the Flying Tigers coped with unfamiliar terrain. Pilots used rivers as their only landmarks, which could be tricky. "The maps were Chinese maps and I couldn't read them too well and they were very small," recalled flier Bob Neale.

> The main physical aspects of the country were the Mekong and the Salween. . . . I called one fellow up and said, "That was the Mekong River we just went over, wasn't it?" He said, "No, that was the Salween . . ." I was getting into a little panic; why, the little old L field of Lashio showed up about 10 miles to the north.[169]

Those weeks were both costly and glorious for the flying group, which flew mission after mission—the skies over Rangoon, the Mouths of the Irawaddy, where the river flowed into the Andaman Sea, and the Gulf of Martarban. Some of the veteran flight leaders were killed, while harried ground crews battled mold, heat, rain, and fatigue. The Japanese had additional strength now that their planes were no longer needed over Singapore.[170]

The Burmese capital crammed with Indian reinforcements, but also with thousands of Indian civil servants, merchants, and other inhabitants. These formed much of the administrative and commercial backbone of the Burma colony—and they left, streaming towards the Indian border ahead of the fast-approaching Japanese.[171] On February 23, British Indian troops were shattered along the Sittang. Rangoon lay bereft of hope. Happening as it did at the same time as the Java Sea defeat and just after Singapore's fall, the news was too much for the normally unflappable Stilwell. Among his comments in those days were, the expostulation, "Christ, what the hell is the matter?" and the expression of amazement, "The world is crashing."[172]

There was no road system in Burma. Advancing across terrain meant passing through what the British themselves considered "the disease-ridden, jungle-covered mountain ranges." This wild landscape they considered an advantage for defense. The net result was that, as in Malaya, the Japanese benefited from jungle training which the British never considered.[173] As in their march to Singapore, the Japanese gained a reputation as terrific jungle fighters mainly because their opponents—British and Indians—never received similar training since the forest was considered impenetrable.

Britain's Burma Corps, Lieutenant-General Slim's new command, retreated across the Irawaddy on May 1, demolishing the bridge afterwards. Slim could not save Mandalay.[174] His 900-mile withdrawal did preserve his unit, however, which straggled intact across the Indian border to Imphal. "I stood on a bank beside the road and watched the rearguard march into India," he would write.

> All of them, British, Indian, and Gurkha, were gaunt and ragged as scarecrows. Yet, as they trudged behind their surviving officers in groups pitifully small, they still carried their arms and kept their ranks, they were still recognizable as fighting units. They might look like scarecrows, but they looked like soldiers, too.[175]

Chinese troops under Stilwell's command fell back after the Japanese captured Lashio, hell-bent for Myitkyina in the far northeast Burmese Triangle near the Yunnan border.[176] Wary of being cornered, realizing that his hungry, reduced ranks were in no state to fight, Stilwell traversed the ridges forming the Triangle, aiming for Imphal. He picked an obscure route, not just to evade the Japanese, but to avoid the refugee hordes. The desperate flight of more than 1 million civilians was turning into a death trek. Stilwell feared that his units might disintegrate amidst the misery. While his hard-working "Burma Surgeon," Lieutenant-Colonel Gordon Seagrave and a cadre of courageous nurses did their best to care for the soldiers, Stilwell drove everyone hard until they made Imphal on May 20.[177] There, he grumpily acknowledged his "nice welcome by the Limeys."[178] He also received a supportive message from General Marshall, passing along commendations from the President and War Department. Depressed, thinking that his Burma experience had reached its end in sad defeat, Stilwell responded to the congratulations with but a single vinegary word: "Why?"[179]

What neither Stilwell nor Slim envisioned was that their arduous withdrawals preserved military options that would result in reconquering Burma. Silm turned defeat into victory, reorganizing, mounting a guerilla campaign, and launching an offensive. Stilwell's war saw him become the leading American military figure in China, so important that he attended the 1943 Cairo Conference with Roosevelt, Churchill, and Chiang.[180] The retreats of Slim and Stilwell were overland Dunkerques, evacuations which salvaged Allied prospects at a dangerous juncture. But that angle of interpretation did not emerge in American media coverage of the campaign. Initial reports of Stilwell's retreat tried to convert it into a victory, as portrayed by headlines reading "Invading Jap Force Crushed by Stilwell," and "Stilwell's China Troops Trap Japs."[181] This kind of reportage, and the questions asked by scribes in Delhi, where he held May press conferences, aggravated the General. "I claim we got a hell of a beating," he stated with unyielding frankness. "We got run out of Burma and it is humiliating as hell. I think we ought to find out what caused it, go back and retake it."[182] Rather than shocking or demoralizing the reporters and public, however, Stilwell's candor—along with the bravery and skill that enabled him to make it to India—won them over. Vinegar Joe was emerging, not just as a stellar field commander, but as one of the war's memorable characters.

In the United States, the Burma battle ranked behind fighting in the Philippines, Singapore, and the Dutch Indies. But some press attention was paid because of the threat to China. *The Chicago Sun*, on February 21, published a map with a point-by-point explanation of the circumstances. "China will fight on even though she loses the Burma Road by receiving supplies from three alternate routes," the lesson began. The alternate routes listed were by ship to Bombay, then by rail to Calcutta, then north to the China border and aver the Assam Road to Chunking. Not mentioned was the fact that this "best route" traversed the highest mountain range in the world. The second route—the one which eventuated as the "Over the Hump" solution—was their air connection from Calcutta to Chungking. The third was an utterly impractical connection running from Alma Ata in the USSR, across Mongolia and Sinkiang, down to Chungking.[183] Here lay a problem with maps. They made lands appear more connected than they really were, and alliances look more cohesive. Land convoys were not going to have an easy time crossing the Gobi Desert or the Himalayas. The Soviet Union was not likely to permit such convoys in quantity.

On March 10, American papers reported the evacuation of Rangoon. "Rangoon City Abandoned by British Army," ran a headline in the *Baltimore Sun*. "Loss of All Southern Burma Indicated by Mandalay Dispatch."[184] The Associated Press cite Japanese claims. A British communiqué said dock works and factories were demolished before the city's capture. Smoke was rising 15,000 feet in the sky. Attentive readers mulled over reports that natives preyed upon the fleeing British. "The Dacoits, jungle murder gangs, stretched steel cables across the road, damaging many cars driving at high speed during the night. Snipers were active when cars not in convoy approached."[185]

On February 24, H.V. Kaltenborn lectured on the theater, concentrating on the China question.[186] Answering listener questions, Kaltenborn explained China could not help, "Because China hasn't got what it takes." "China has the man power but not the machine power. Modern war is mechanized war," he pointed out. Despite China's massive population, it "never had a war industry." Kaltenborn counseled understanding. "Don't forget that for nearly five years the Chinese have been holding the Japanese back with what little they have," he said. "Let us not underestimate China's outstanding contribution to the cause of the United Nations."[187] To keep China in the fight, Kaltenborn took up the question of air links over the Himalayas if Burma was lost. He talked about the importance of oil fields on March 17, concentrating on German-Italian threats to the Near East, putting Japanese moves to the Indian Ocean into the picture.[188]

The main American focus on Burma fell on Chennault and the Flying Tigers. The March 30 issue of *Life* featured a prominent photo spread by George Rodger, titled "Flying Tigers in Burma: Handful of American Pilots Shoot Down 300 Jap Warplanes in 90 Days." Its lede was blunt. "One shining hope has emerged from three catastrophic months of war. That is the American Volunteer Group of fighter pilots, the so-called "Flying Tigers," of Burma and southeast China, who paint the jaws of a shark on their Curtiss P-40s. Outnumbered often ten to one, they have so far shot down about 300 Jap planes, killed perhaps 800 Jap airmen."[189] The narrative credited the fliers with seizing air control over southern China and Burma away from the Japanese, and with conclusively proving "what was once only a Yankee belief: that one American flier is equal to two or three Japs."[190] Amplifying that point was an Australian-based American general who promised, "100 fighters to 200 Japs and I'll lick them every time." As if remembering who was winning the war at that point, the boastful American backed off just a bit: "I am not disparaging the Japs. They are good fighters."[191]

The article explained the success to date of the Flying Tigers by pointing to three assets. The first was experience, which gave them "an instinctive feel for what their machines will do." The second was that combat held no unknown terrors. The third was their aggression. "They are always looking for a fight."[192] What followed was a brief recapitulation of their earlier actions in December, and a general history of how the pilots were recruited "under hush-hush circumstances to avoid offending the Japs," and offered starting pay of $600 per month plus a $500 bonus for each Japanese plane downed. Claire Chennault emerged in the piece as "China's crack American air chief." The more than two dozen photographs which accompanied the text showed portraits with brief pilot biographies, mentioning home towns, schooling, and life stories. Included was Squadron Leader James H. Howard, "born in China, captured by Chinese bandits at 12 with his eminent doctor-father, Jim escaped. . . . He speaks Chinese;" and Flight Leader Edward F. Rector, "from a mountain farm outside Marshall, N.C., likes to grow tobacco and corn, went to Catawba College, learned to fly with the U.S. Navy. A quiet, hardworking country boy, he is well-liked by everybody." All of the stories were homespun, mentioning items such as the fact that Squadron Leader John V. Newkirk, Rensselear graduate, 'married a Lansing, Mich. girl,' or Pilot Robert Layher, a Colorado University alumni, who "married a Colorado University coed last September."[193]

Additional pictures included shots of fliers on duty waiting in a pilot tent along the airfield. Tom Cole, was killed soon after the photo was taken, shot as he parachuted out of his plane. "Those yellow so-and-so's had better write themselves off all the way down, now," promised an angry comrade. After a mission, a pilot talked over results. The caption mentioned that "Even in China, the AVG boys get American steak, ham and eggs, pie, hot and cold running water, see very ancient American movies. Most wear shoulder holsters."[194] Under a grove of mango trees which served to hold their chain-hoists, Chinese ground crewmen, not named, worked on the tail of a P-40: "With hand tools they can make any part of a plane's body work. They consider association with the AVG a high honor."[195] Other photographs showed turbaned Indians and native Burmese gazing at downed Japanese planes and dead pilots. The accompanying caption explained that enemy casualties were how the Tigers rated their performance. The performance of Japanese fighters was duly acknowledged. As if to balance this accurate account, the caption continued disingenuously, claiming that "The unoriginal Japs are, for the most part, flying American planes. Their bombers are home-made copies of ours, with modifications not always improvements."[196] This was false. More compelling was the claim that Japanese officers flew—and died—with their samurai swords. Among the more bellicose quotes was one from Chiang himself, who said, "Each of you has proved a match for 30 of more of the enemy. I hope to celebrate with you in Tokyo."[197]

The New Republic devoted much space to the commander in the March 2 issue, with the story "Claire Chennault: American Hero." Michael Straight's piece began,

We are living through terrible days. The loss of Singapore with its 60,000 veteran troops, the imminent loss of Java and of Rangoon, the threatened loss of India and the Indian Ocean, of Australia and New Zealand, have been heavy blows for the United Nations.

Here, Straight added locations not yet lost to the roster of defeats, making clear how astonishingly bad the war news was.

> It is good that from the Southern Pacific has come one shining story of venture and vision; the story of how a few American volunteers, flying side-by-side with the RAF, won victory after victory for the Chinese air force and rose to truly great heights of heroism.[198]

The story extrapolated on the events establishing the All Volunteer Group. Laughlin Currie's work with T.V. Soong formed part of the dramatic account. The former was portrayed as Roosevelt's intermediary, looking for a way to assist the Chinese and buck up the Nationalists in Chungking. The latter's initial efforts to buy planes centered on a cancelled export license to sell Sweden 100 P-40s. It was those planes, said Straight, which became Soong's focus and which the government figured out how to allot to China.[199] But Chennault and the intrepid volunteers were the stars, by Soong's own lights. "Not waiting to be called, this group went forward to meet the enemy in order that the democracies might save precious time, that freedom might live, that countless others might be saved."[200] Those words came in a letter written by Soong to the mother of a Tiger killed in combat.

The general emerged as a visionary working for his ideas against hidebound officialdom. "Part of success is due to our mobility," the writer quoted Chennault. "The Japanese never know where we are."[201] Even Rangoon failed to shake Straight's opinion that Chennault had turned things around. The article credited the Tigers with holding off the Japanese long enough for the best material in Rangoon to be taken away. Ultimately, Straight said, the value of the Flying Tigers was that they were serving to keep China in the war as an effective, connected ally. "When the Indian people were shaken by the threat of imminent invasion, it was not an English or an American statesman to whom we turned to keep the Indian people firm, it was Chiang Kai-Shek," he pointed out, adding that "the peoples of the Near East and the Far east hold the future of the war in their hands. China, hardened by warfare, knowing what a people's war really means, will become the bridge between our world and the world which we have oppressed, whose help we now so desperately need."[202]

The next page had an accompanying story, "Freedom for India."[203] Ralph Bates' article asked a question it deemed "once-fraudulent," namely, "whether this is an imperialist war." Bates was being intentionally provocative, pointing out that helping the British keep their grip on India was an odd pretext for the United States to endorse. Bates was grave in his predictions, reminding readers that Burma was the gateway to India. "There is no time for delay," he decided. "India must be given an immediate and inviolable assurance of independence."[204]

Bates made much of the contrast between China—where the Allies opposed Japanese imperial goals, and India—where Britain sought to perpetuate them. He scoffed at the coverage of the campaign in the Dutch Indies, warning readers:

> let us not condition our cup of bitterness with picturesque phrases, such as 'The Spice Islands gird for war.' We ought not to heed the military experts who once again are telling us that 'thanks to the wise colonial policy of Holland, the native army has an excellent morale.[205]

Here, *The New Republic* and its writer made an argument rarely heard in those days, that anti-colonialism might be a war-winning policy. He stated India deserved to be part of the free world, harkening back to support for Irish freedom, wondering why the United States seemed less committed to the anti-colonial principle. The closest Bates came to allaying British fears was suggesting that the promise of independence be made now but eventuated after the war, thus giving the Indian Congress Party reason to get behind the war effort rather than threatening to subvert it. At the core of Bates' argument was the nugget that colonies were enslaved regions whose bitterness made them unreliable during a war that needed all the moral and strategic certitudes it could find. That was why he brought up whether or not this was an imperialist war. "If we answer the question wrongly, not merely empires may change their name, but the world itself may be permanently enslaved," he wrote in a warning of defeat. "IF we are to win we must scrap the imperialist techniques which all the while have been cramping us and imprisoning our arms. That is the change demanded by the problem of Indian defense."[206]

The New Republic kept its attention on the Indian question. The March 16 cover ran the headline "The Hour of Decision." Stories included "The Crisis of the United Nations," "Nehru and the Future of India," and "Cripps for Prime Minister." Stafford Cripps' mission to India and a burp of parliamentary biliousness over Singapore and Burma raised his profile as a potential Churchill replacement. The magazine backed the idea, observing that "Britain has not yet won a really important victory," complaining that coal mine owners and businessmen in Britain were not taxed heavily enough, and that "Most of all, there is still India, as to which Churchill, at the beginning of this week, seemed determined to wait so long that his gesture to the Indian People would lose all its value." Boosting Cripps was the fact that he was a socialist; his elevation would mean that "we should have for the first time genuine New Deal governments simultaneously on both sides of the water."[207]

Other articles brought Jawaharlal Nehru to the fore. The Congress Party leader was the hero of "Nehru and India's Future," by contributor Anup Singh. It chronicled his career of independence activism, including years in British jails, where he wrote his autobiography, *Toward Freedom*. It described his international views, including his sorrow at Franco's triumph in Spain, and denunciations of

Hitler and Mussolini. Nehru, said the article, was once in favor of maintaining "the silken bonds of spirit" that bound Britain and its colony together, but came to the conclusion that structural inequalities in the relationship made parting ways mandatory. The United Nations gained his freedom, as Britain released its political prisoners, but the exclusion of India from the Atlantic Charter dismayed Nehru and lessened his faith in the Allies. Now, wrote Singh, was the time to win over this man of moment, who would assuredly be the man of tomorrow as well, by giving him what he wanted most: "the chance to do some solid, positive, and constructive work." Singh claimed that helping to win the war would enlist a rising statesman for the Allies. He pointed out that MacArthur's endurance at Bataan had much to do with Filipino loyalty to the United States, whereas Burma, Hong Kong, and Singapore natives showed no heart for the British Empire.[208]

Any hint that Britain must shed India under pressure from Japan raised Churchill's hackles. This issue of divergent colonial stances threatened the loyalty between Churchill and Roosevelt. The President saw Britain clinging to colonies as a retrograde impulse.[209] Nehru, who wrote articles appealing for American support in *Atlantic Monthly* and *Foreign Affairs*, intuited this. The Indian independence movement undertook a nonviolent campaign of non-cooperation with the British.[210] This did not stop Indian soldiers from fighting across several campaign theaters. Such thoughts were on Roosevelt's mind as he hosted Churchill, but the Prime Minister rebuffed attempts to broach decolonialization. "I reacted so strongly and at such length that he never raised it verbally again," Churchill related.[211]

Roosevelt, foxy as he was, thought the subject likely to become relevant as the war went on. "I have given much thought to the problem of India," he wrote to Churchill that March.

> As you can well realize, I have felt much diffidence in making any suggestion, and it is a subject which, of course, all of you good people know far more about than I do. . . . I have tried to approach the problem from the point of view of history and with a hope that the injection of a new thought to be used in India might be of assistance to you.[212]

He recalled the American revolution, the issue of sovereignty, and suggested "the setting up of what might be called a temporary government in India, headed by a small representative group, covering different castes, occupations, religions, and geographies," which could function during the war as a British dominion.[213]

There was much that Churchill wanted from the Roosevelt. But advice on how to shepherd India towards independence was not included. The part of Roosevelt's letter which Churchill paid closest attention to was the cordial disclaimer, "It is, strictly speaking, none of my business except insofar as it is a part and parcel of the successful fight you and I are making."[214] The Prime Minister considered Roosevelt out of his depths and wrote that any move towards the Nehru/Congress position would enrage Muslims, many of whom fought in the British ranks. He made it clear that detaching India was not part of the Anglo-American conversation.

Cripps' Mission in March stoked Indian hopes that change might be at hand. Thus, when Churchill squelched ideas about transferring responsibilities military and political to Delhi, there was an outpouring of anti-colonial anger. The most Churchill offered was Dominion status after the war, which was far from the near-independence desired at once by Nehru and Mahatma Gandhi. Protests erupted, including a "Quit India" campaign led by Gandhi. The British response included throwing Gandhi and other Congress leaders back in jail.[215] The world leader who reacted most strongly to this was Chiang, who wrote a letter to Roosevelt, describing Asian beliefs that the United Nations' integrity demanded extension of "their professed principle of ensuring freedom and justice for men of all races" to Asia.[216]

Kaltenborn took up issue on February 24, introducing his audience to Nehru, as well as identifying Gandhi as the leader of the "non-cooperation, non-violence movement." "India will soon play a larger role in the war," predicted the venerable pundit. "Out of an Indian population of some 370,000,000, only about 1,000,000 are under arms. Prime Minister Churchill's intimation that the Atlantic Charter does not apply to India discouraged Indian enthusiasm for a war effort. Now that was is coming very close to India, the situation may alter." Kaltenborn continued by taking a knock at Gandhi's "purely negative attitude of pacifism and non-cooperation."[217] Kaltenborn paid some attention to the role of Muslims. But to Raymond Gram Swing, that was the major issue regarding India, which not enough Americans understood. Swing said an Indian solution could be "just as good news as the fall of Singapore in its vast scope was bad news," but he admitted, "The solution may not be easy." Far more skeptical than *The New Republic*, Swing stressed that it was inaccurate to assume that Churchill was an impediment, or that a simple declaration of independence would unravel the Indian knot. "It doesn't depend on the British simply saying to Nehru, 'Go ahead and take over your independence,'" Swing warned. "It can't be done by giving the Congress party of Gandhi and Nehru the political control of all India."[218] The reason for his doubtfulness was that,

> the Indian Moslems, with their ninety millions, make up the world's largest minority, and they are not going to yield up to the Congress party the control over their destinies. If India is to be independent, they want either a disproportionate representation in the government, so as to safeguard their rights, or they want certain Moslem regions to be declared independent of Hindu India.[219]

Swing was always one of the most carefully insightful commentators on the air, and these broadcasts were no exception.

The issue of anti-colonialism did not fade away entirely. American principle was at variance with practice. When Sumner Welles delivered a 1942 Memorial Day address, he took up the theme. "If the war is in fact a war for the liberation of peoples it must assure the sovereign equality of peoples throughout the world," said the Undersecretary of State.

> Our victory must bring in its train the liberation of all peoples.. . . The age of imperialism is ended. . . . The principles of the Atlantic Charter must be guaranteed to the world as a whole—in all oceans and in all continents.[220]

Welles, whose close-lipped style commended itself to Pearson and Sevareid when they considered his performance at the Rio Conference, was not one to speak cavalierly when it came to American foreign policy principles and goals. So obviously, the issue of anti-imperialism remained alive in the American view of India. But just as obviously, the necessary measures for victory did not include fomenting disagreement with Britain at a sensitive and gloomy moment in the war.

The best chance for a major shift on India policy actually rested in Japanese hands. While Japan's army and navy squabbled over strategic imperatives, both agreed during the Spring of 1942 that the pace of victories required additional advances to break Allied ability to mount a counteroffensive.[221] A few options presented themselves: an attack on Australia, which could eliminate the place from which Americans planned their counterattack while crushing a white nation in the Pacific region. Another was a move through New Guinea and Rabaul, which would threaten Australia's north coast. Yet another was an attack on Hawaii, which would outdo the Pearl Harbor assault. Finally, some advocated a cross-Indian Ocean offensive, to seize French-held Madagascar, attack Ceylon, and menace India, capitalizing on unrest there.[222]

All of the proposals offered problems and tantalizing prospects. Australia was big and far. Taking it would require transferring troops from Manchuria. Rabaul would set up a barrier to American moves in Japan's direction. The Madagascar–Ceylon option sounded grandiose, but it had points to recommend it, especially if Rommel's drive on Egypt, Suez, and the Middle East succeeded. Then, the Suez Canal would be cut, and the entire Indian Ocean would be in flux, hurting Britain's chance to hold India and challenging access to the oil fields of Arabia, Iraq, and Iran.[223] Madagascar, under Vichy French control, was vulnerable. The Japanese advocated a joint German-Japanese operation there. Hitler had no eyes for such a distant percept.[224] As for Ceylon, any threat to that teardrop-shaped island, across the Palk Strait from Tamil Nadu, in India, would make the British position untenable. Berlin passed information to Tokyo about sites for amphibious landings, but it was clear that no German coordination could be expected.[225] The British lines of control were thin and widely stretched, based on their naval puissance, which Japan had already blasted. The scheme bid to knock Britain out of Asia.[226]

That was the optimistic assessment. There were many problems, such as diverting resources from the China campaign, which would anger the army. What the Americans might do while Japan's attentions were on India was another issue. Yamamoto judged that the trans-Indian Ocean plan might destroy Britain's war prospects, but that the operation would not harm the United States one bit. The Admiral never took his eyes off American intentions. A recent American air attack on Marcus Island, only 700 miles from Tokyo, disturbed Yamamoto despite its small scale. He expected the American counteroffensive, when it came, to move across the central Pacific. He thought in terms of major fleet actions, wanting to make the inevitable showdown determinative.[227] Yamamoto and others cut down the Indian Ocean operation. It resulted in the March 23 seizure of the Andaman Islands. These were technically part of India, but functioned for the Japanese as a defensive screen to protect gains in Burma, Sumatra, and Singapore. Five aircraft carriers sailed to Ceylon under Admiral Nagumo: *Akagi, Hiryu, Soryu, Shokaku, Zuikaku*, along with four battleships, *Haruna, Hiei, Kirishima, Kongo*, and cruisers and escorts. This task force left for the Bay of Bengal and Ceylon on March 26, where they rampaged along the coast, shelling Colombo on the West Coast, on April 5 and Trincomalee, on the East Coast, on April 5.[228] By appearances, the raids were successful, in that they shamed the British, showing up their weakness. Zeros outperformed Spitfires and Hurricanes, as the Japanese launched over 1,000 planes. Defenders braced for an amphibious landing which did not come.[229]

Ceylon generated speculation in the American media. Raymond Gram Swing saw its potential as early as February, when he broadcast warnings that the Fall of Singapore would allow Japan to hit Indian convoys and give the Axis "outflanking sea power" that could threaten the subcontinental position.[230] CBS covered it carefully. Cecil Brown, newly returned to the United States, analyzed the possibilities on April 5, seeing the Japanese attempt to control the Indian Ocean shipping lanes and praising the British for withdrawing their fleet. He connected the raids to the Cripps Mission, calling them a Japanese attempt to disrupt what he hoped would be India's evolution as an Allied nation.[231] From London, Bob Trout thought it significant that the battle opened in the air, not at sea. He cited anti-Japanese feelings among Muslim Indians as a reason not to panic about the subcontinent falling under Tokyo's sway.[232] Most blunt and bullish was George Fielding Eliot, who told CBS listeners that Ceylon was "a baited trap" for Japan. He predicted major air losses, saying only a seaborne invasion force could tackle India. What most excited Eliot were reports that Japanese carriers were at Ceylon, and therefore vulnerable. He predicted that the entire business was merely a large raid, and that "If they want to invade, they'll come back."[233]

Fearing disaster, the British were set to cut their losses. The Royal Navy, remembering *Repulse* and *Prince of Wales*, redeployed battleships to the safety of

East African waters. But in terms of effect, Nagumo's attack was no Pearl Harbor *redux*. It did not catch and destroy the British Indian Ocean fleet. It did not loosen Britain's hold on India or Ceylon, or encourage Indian opposition elements to revolt and support the Japanese. It was not a sustained operation.[234] No Japanese marines landed. That the raid went off at all showed that the idea of loosening India to wreck the British Empire was alive in Japanese minds. That it did not develop further showed that top leaders felt it was not the top priority. There were those in the Japanese Admiralty who believed in the eastward thrust; who dreamed of knocking Britain out of India and the war. Churchill's government survived the loss of Singapore, but losing India would have been worse. From Madagascar's east coast to the Arabian Sea, Japan's options might have been intriguing. Coupled with German advances into Egypt, Nagumo's foray could have proven a watershed. To imaginative planners, the operation might have been strategically crucial. What it was instead was a slap—deliberate and insulting, but not decisive. It caused the British loss of face, but did nothing to alter the situation in India.

It also exposed the limitations of the Tripartite Pact. The Germans and Japanese rarely knew what each other was up to. They had virtually no intra-staff cooperation and thus never coordinated operations. India fascinated Hitler, who saw it as the seat of Great Britain's imperial arrogance and thus the cause of the British superiority complex. But by Spring 1942, the persistent failure to take London out of the war, to make the British see the "sense" of a deal with Germany, had nudged the *fuhrer*'s attentions elsewhere. Hitler was less interested in Britain or the Middle East than in Russia. Despite *Barbarossa*'s shudder before Moscow the previous winter, he still convinced himself that the Soviet superstructure could be felled with a well-placed kick. Already, he dreamed of thrusts to the Caucasus Mountains, taking oilfields and securing his grip on fertile Ukraine. Rommel would never have the troops and resources he craved for his eastern Saharan offensive. Japan's Imperial Army had China foremost in mind and was skeptical of distractions, while powerful navy elements, including Yamamoto, remained more focused on the Pacific than the Indian Ocean. Berlin and Tokyo did not collude so much as operate contemporaneously. Secretive Hitler never liked to take even his own generals into confidence, much less the leadership from a far-off land he knew but poorly. Japan wanted closer cooperation, but none was offered. Berlin, Tokyo, and Rome never really opened up to each other. The contrast with the Anglo-American alliance, which represented true partnership despite inevitable abrading frictions, was obvious. It was harder to be a close ally than to operate on one's own, because it meant exposure to outsiders, which is anathema to dictatorships but possible, if not easy, for democracies. Thus, fantasies of Japanese warships steaming through a German-operated Suez Canal into the Mediterranean, of a German–Japanese meeting in the Near East, or of a revolutionary Indian movement collaborating with a Japanese subcontinental invasion, remained elusive.[235]

5 MARCH 1942

"A Prescribed Military Area from which Any or All Persons May be Excluded"— the Japanese-American plight in the western states

Our Chinese friends dislike to hear the Japanese referred to as "yellow," even when that adjective is followed by terms like "devils," "bandits," "snakes," or "bedbugs." They think of that word in its racial significance and remember that the yellow or Mongolian race includes many other peoples than the Japanese; the Koreans, for example, who hate the Japanese, and the Chinese themselves. So the Chinese, probably the Koreans, too, shiver at hearing a racial term that includes them used as one of opprobrium. The point is well-taken. And we do the Japanese too much honor by using for them a term which has been made honorable by the Chinese. Call them Japanazis if you please, or better still, Japaryans. That puts them where they belong, in Hitler's pocket, but call them nothing that puts them in association with the honorable people of the yellow race.

San Francisco Chronicle, January 7, 1942[1]

Whereas the successful prosecution of the war requires every possible protection against espionage and against sabotage to national-defense material, national-defense premises, and national-defense utilities. . . . Now, therefore, by virtue of the authority vested in me as President of the United States, and Commander in Chief of the army and navy, I hereby authorize and direct the secretary of war, and the military commanders whom he may from time to time designate, whenever he or any designated commander deems such actions necessary or desirable, to prescribe military areas in such places and of such extent as he or the appropriate military commanders may determine, from which any or all persons may be excluded, and with such respect to which, the right of any person to enter, remain in, or leave shall be subject to whatever restrictions the secretary of war or the appropriate military commander may impose in his discretion.

President Franklin D. Roosevelt, Executive Order No. 9066, February 19, 1942[2]

What frightened American authorities beyond reason was sabotage to pave the way for invasion, or to disrupt war operations. Stories of sabotage formed a part of war coverage. At first, these stories came from Europe, where fifth columnists presumably helped to open the way for Germany's rapid and surprising conquests. No less a savvy observer than Raymond Gram Swing told listeners in May 1940 that the Nazi *blitzkrieg* depended not only on careful coordination of air, armor, and infantry, but also on saboteurs.[3] Similar fears focused on Latin America, where it was thought that German spies might set up a network of subversion. So the idea that secret agents might infiltrate across sensitive United States areas was not primarily aimed at Japan before Pearl Harbor.

Of course, the attack in Hawaii changed the calculation, shining the harsh light of suspicion in places where its corrosive rays caused real damage to the American cultural tapestry. Even coverage intended to be balanced prompted negative impressions of Japanese-Americans. On January 25, the *Washington Merry-Go-Round* led off with a story about Hawaii's Congressional delegate, Samuel W. King (R-HI). The theme of the story was subversion, prompted by reports that agents in the territory were operating on behalf of Japan. "American citizens of Japanese ancestry in Hawaii are patriotic," insisted King. "Even the older, retired Japanese aliens are all right. Why, they think it's a real compliment for their citizen-children to be drafted in the United States armed forces. They usually throw a big party the night before a boy is inducted into the service."[4] But King's reasonable words, which also included the definitive statement that Japanese-American males made excellent soldiers and that charges that they were a latent fifth column were absurd, were undercut by the headline, "Delegate Reveals Arrest of 400 Agents in Hawaii," as well as congressional reaction—not for attribution—that derided King's views as "too optimistic."[5] Anti-Asian racism—which peaked in notorious legislation like California's 1920 Anti-Alien Land Law—was not new.[6] The attack on December 7 proved enough of a catalyst to revivify old impulses. Japanese-Americans were the unlucky recipients of unfair treatment, not just by angry neighbors, but by their own government.

One February 28 Associated Press article was headlined "Details of Japanese Plan for Conquest of America" when it ran in the *Baltimore Sun*.[7] The text detailed a plan uncovered by the Congress' Dies committee. The committee report revolved around a document supposedly written by a Japanese lieutenant. No one mentioned that the plan might be a contingency document. The story focused on

Japan's division of the war into four phases, which were (1) the capture of Hawaii; (2) the destruction of the American fleet and capture of the Panama Canal; (3) landings along the West Coast followed by attacks up to the Rocky Mountains; (4) a final advance to the East Coast. The report did state that only the first part of the plan was a reachable goal, adding that "Each period would probably last several years; the third and fourth periods would last the longest. Thus the war would last at least four or five years; it might even drag on to several score years."[8] Another such Associated Press article, headlined "Big Jap Spy Ring Revealed by Dies," dwelt upon espionage and anti-American training presumably underway through Japanese-American societies and language schools. "The Japanese Government has demonstrated a definite interest in the water supply system of the city of Los Angeles," it contended by way of example.[9]

Admiral Yamamoto did make a wisecrack about dictating peace terms at the White House. But the Japanese military was arguing over what to do after the conquest of the Dutch East Indies and Burma. Most assumed that, after the initial period of rapid advances, Japan's plan would be to hunker down behind a defensive perimeter. The prospect of amphibious landings from Seattle to San Diego was remote. The author of the so-called secret plan revealed by Dies emphasized that the first step was the most important, writing that, "We must, at all costs, even with the sacrifice of a few vessels, take possession of Hawaii," if any larger gains were to be realized.[10] The Dies Committee's bombshell did not impress everyone. At *The New Republic*, editors chose the moment to ask for Congress to break up the committee, which they accused of "breath-taking incompetence," including a "failure to warn the country about Japan."[11]

There was some military sense in the Dies Committee's document. The Panama Canal was a tempting target, and both the Germans and Japanese would have attacked it if they could. Any harm to the Canal would have hurt the United States' ability to wage a two-ocean war.

Also, it was true that Hawaii was the security key to the Pacific. That naval fact was why the United States annexed it. Hawaii put American maritime defenses into the western Pacific, rather than off the West Coast. Japanese naval planners understood this just as well, which was why, on December 9, 1941, Yamamoto ordered his staff to draw up invasion and occupation plans.[12] Yamamoto's own understanding of the United States led him to a comparatively modest ambition for Hawaiian occupation: he saw the island as a likely hostage to hold in negotiations when pressuring Washington for a peace settlement. The Admiral guessed that the prospect of 400,000 American citizens under Japanese occupation would prove a powerful inducement. More fulsome were the aspirations of Japanese civilian leaders and commentators. Spurred by a concatenation of the imperial spirit and hatred for the west, some made Hawaii an irredenta of the Yamato imagination. They claimed Hawaii as a corrective measure against American insolence and white arrogance. Journalists, authors, academics and government officials all speculated on the benefits accruing from Japanese Hawaii.[13]

Japanese awareness of the islands was accentuated by ethnic ties, since emigrants from Japan and their descendants constituted Hawaii's largest ethnic group.[14] American authorities knew this, too. White planting and commercial interests viewed Japanese-Hawaiians as a potential threat to American control. This was one reason for supporting annexation. Other reasons were strategic, explained by Mahan. In 1893, he wrote an article speculating that China might try to snatch control of the weak Hawaiian Kingdom, but after the Sino-Japanese War, he switched his suspicions to Japan. In 1897, he wrote to then Assistant Secretary of the Navy Theodore Roosevelt that the United States should "take the islands first and solve the problem [of Japan] later."[15] The winds of prejudice blew over Hawaii, which meant that the islands' fate was the subject of speculation from racial demagogues like Yellow Peril writer Homer Lea. Lea's early twentieth century fiction included accounts of how Japanese soldiers would infiltrate the archipelago as civilians before springing to revolt.[16] So overwrought were Lea's predictions of Japanese ascendancy that his works were translated in Japan and used for propaganda purposes.[17] Equally perfervid Japanese commentators ramped up, especially once war plans solidified.[18]

In Hawaii itself, while prejudice was not rare, there was sufficient socioeconomic development to permit a broadly prosperous environment in which opportunities were open to members of the ethnic groups which mingled there. The military presence lent stability, so that Hawaii was, by the 1940s, fixed in the geography of American imaginations. Its exotic charms formed the appeal of popular culture phenomena like the popular radio show, "Hawaii Calls," which featured slack-key guitar and drums laying out the mellow hula-hula sounds so perfect as backdrop for Bing Crosby and other crooners.

December 7 changed the entire feeling in Hawaii, which went under military control. Although some called for it, there was no legitimate prospect of sequestering the 90,000 Issei or 160,000 Nisei, too numerous and integrated into the Hawaiian economy.[19] But neither was there an absence of garden-variety bigotry and conflicted loyalties. Some Issei expressed satisfaction after the attack that Japan had pulled off such a feat. Others shot down expressions of glee, bothered by the treachery of the surprise raid and the realization that they were in an exposed position.[20] A more widespread reaction among younger Japanese-Americans was straightforward anger that their country had been attacked. Their country was the United States. Their patriotism manifested in the Varsity Victory Volunteers, formed from the ROTC students at the University of Hawaii, which became the only student military unit presented with the honor of a battle streamer because of its service record during the war. The VVV was the core of the Hawaiian Territorial Guard, then the 442nd Regimental Combat Team. Other VVV members served in sensitive military intelligence positions.[21]

The Pearl Harbor attack worsened tensions. Machine guns were emplaced in Kawaiaha's Church's tower, facing King Street, which seemed to locals like a measure against domestic revolt.[22] Martial Law was universal. The degree of invasion concern was revealed by the federal government's plan to withdraw regular currency from the islands and replace it with special banknotes, overprinted on old bills, which would become invalid should the Japanese take the islands.[23] One of the strangest Hawaiian episodes of the war occurred during and after the Pearl Harbor attack. This was the so-called "Niihau Incident."

Niihau was the mystery island of the Hawaiian chain, purchased from King Kamehameha IV by New Zealand immigrants in 1864. The family maintained control of Niihau and controlled access, allowing the 136 native Hawaiian inhabitants to live traditionally, speaking Hawaiian and living through old-fashioned practices.[24] But Aylmer Robison, the island's owner in 1941, had his own Japanese invasion fears, prompting him to plow up the largely flat dried lake bottoms which he felt might make good landing strips.[25] It was thought that Niihau was safe from aerial threats, but anti-aircraft fire damaged the Zero of Imperial Naval Airman First Class Shigenori Nishikaichi, necessitating a forced landing in a Niihau field on December 7. Meeting the plane, resident ranch hand Hawila (Howell) Kaleohano extracted the stupefied pilot, bringing him to the village after confiscating his sidearm and papers. The first person on Niihau who could communicate with Nishikaichi was Ishimatu Shintani, an Issei whose wife was Hawaiian. Shintani's position was emblematic of the legal netherworld in which Japanese-Americans resided. United States rules precluded him from citizenship and stripped his American-born wife's citizenship from her upon their marriage.[26] The pilot explained how he came to be there. Harada kept the news from his neighbors, setting the stage for a small and violent coda to the Pearl Harbor battle.[27]

Almost immediately, an agitated Nishikaichi began to demand his documents back. What he wanted to do was burn his secret papers to prevent their capture, then await rescue by minisub that was part of the briefing instructions given to pilots.[28] The Niihauans heard news of Pearl Harbor over their transistor radio. Aylmer Robison could not make his weekly visit, scheduled for December 8, because of the immediate ban on boat traffic. Pilot Nishikaichi was taken in by the two Nisei inhabitants, Yoshio and Irene Harada. Shintano offered Kaleohano cash for Nishikaichi's papers, meeting rebuff and making the Hawaiian suspicious. Yoshio Harada and the pilot then overpowered the guard at their house. Irene played records to cover the noise. They grabbed a shotgun and took a teenager hostage, heading to the downed Zero.[29] Once there, Nishikaichi started firing the 7.7 mm guns; islanders took cover. They decided to light a signal fire, and Kaleohano—who kept an eye on the Harada home and saw Harada, Nishikaichi, and their hostage running to the plane—resolved to paddle through the night to

Kauai, a ten-hour journey, to inform Robison. Kaleohano brought the documents with him. At Kauai, the first military officer to hear the amazing Niihau news was Lieutenant Jack Mizuha. Mizuha was Japanese-American himself; a product of the University of Hawaii's ROTC Program, he commanded the island's airfield.[30] Mizuha coordinated the response to the Niihau emergency, and his performance ought to have influenced official reactions.

The pilot and his conspirator set the plane on fire before returning to the village and taking Ben and Ella Kanahele hostage. Harada demanded to know Kaleohano's whereabouts, but was put off by evasive answers. The Kanaheles attacked their captors. Ben Kanahele was wounded but smashed the pilot against a wall, whereupon Ella Kanahele killed him by crushing his skull with a rock. The distraught Harada turned his gun on himself. Authorities arrived during the afternoon of December 13, arresting Irene Harada and Shintani.[31]

Kanahele and Kaleohana received credit for their courage. But authorities took note of the Haradas' and Shintani's assistance to Nishikaichi. Some officials concluded that Japanese-American loyalties were divided, and that ethnicity trumped citizenship.[32] An official navy report by Lieutenant C.B. Baldwin on January 26, 1942, saw significance in the fact that neither of the Haradas had ever shown loyalty to Japan, but helped still helped Nishikaichi. That, Baldwin told his superiors, indicated "likelihood that Japanese residents previously believed loyal to the United States may aid Japan if further Japanese attacks appear successful."[33] The story made it into the local and national press, with *Reader's Digest* concentrating on Kanahele in its story, "Never Shoot an Hawaiian More than Twice," which ran later in 1942. "They Couldn't Take Niihau Nohow" became a minor hit song.[34] It would be exaggeration to lay subsequent mistreatment of Japanese-Americans on the Niihau Incident, but the affair certainly provided some fodder for those already infected by an atmosphere of distrust against anyone connected to Japan by ancestry.

The islands were directly administered by military authorities. In the American West, the fear was that the absence of such administration might open the area to fifth columnists. Bogus reports of espionage cascaded after Pearl Harbor, helped along by Secretary Knox, who alluded to subversion as if only that could explain the Pearl Harbor debacle.

But war-awareness also sparked other emotions. Children in Washington, Oregon, California, and the other states gathered books, toys, wastepaper, rubber, fat, metal, and other scrap for war drives. Boy Scouts served as dispatch bearers, poster-hangers, and Civilian Defense boosters, while Girl Scouts worked as child-care and hospital aides. Both participated in aviation programs designed to raise awareness of various airplane silhouettes, friend or foe.[35] Perhaps the most high-profile early demonstration that war conditions meant a whole new way of doing things "out west" was the relocation of the 1942 Rose Bowl, slated as always for

New Year's Day in Pasadena. Large crowd events were banned along the entire West Coast, and the game would have been cancelled had not Durham, North Carolina—home to the Duke Blue Devils, one of the two teams invited—taken the game. It took three weeks, but Duke's stadium capacity was increased from 35,000 to 56,000. This allowed football fans to ring in 1942 by listening to the Rose Bowl, which saw the "home" team Oregon State Beavers stake themselves to an early lead and hold off the Blue Devils, 20-16.[36] Not only was America's favorite football game saved, but the Rose Bowl stadium was freed up for another use—as a rendezvous point for Japanese-Americans on their way to internment centers.[37] Another sports venue, Santa Anita Racetrack, also served.

At first, the question of what to do with people whom the war rendered security risks concentrated on the obscure issue of actual enemy aliens. The manager of the Greenbrier, West Virginia's famed resort, took a State Department call asking the hotel to receive a group of diplomats on December 17. This came in response to President Roosevelt's order to remove all enemy diplomats from the Washington metro area. On December 19, almost 200 German and Hungarian embassy personnel arrived; by March, the Greenbrier hosted 800, including Italians and Bulgarians. Four hundred Japanese diplomats and their dependents went to Virginia's Homestead, another vacation spot. Ultimately, over 1,000 diplomatic personnel were interned in the United States. At the same time, American diplomats were interned in Axis nations, including those at Bad Nauheim, led by George Kennan.[38] Negotiations through third countries and the Red Cross worked out exchange policies. This took until June to arrange. The entire business fell under protocols established by the Geneva Convention, and the treatment of their own nationals in enemy hands gave belligerents an inducement to follow the rules.[39]

The position of Americans of Japanese background, however, was not subject to well-established procedures. No laws allowed for treating an entire group of citizens as a security threat. The spike in anti-German prejudice during World War I was remembered as an embarrassment. There was to be no anti-German furor this time. But memories of 1917–1918 did not protect Japanese-Americans, who numbered approximately 100,000, mostly along the West Coast.[40]

The first measures came fast. On December 8, the Treasury Department froze assets owned by Japanese-Americans; on December 9, Japanese language schools closed. Those shuttered schools did not include the Military Intelligence Service classes in San Francisco, where Japanese-American men trained as interpreters. Their services would prove valuable.[41] On December 11, the FBI issued an alert for aliens using cameras or guns. Next, Attorney General Biddle ordered Japanese-Americans to turn in any shortwave radios, while California revoked Japanese-held liquor licenses.[42] By January, Japanese-Americans could not travel and had to surrender any weapons. On January 14, Roosevelt ordered "re-registration." Two weeks later, Los Angeles fired Japanese-Americans from civil service jobs. Prohibitions on practicing medicine and law followed. Biddle placed strategic places off-limits. Curfews began on February 4, and on Valentine's Day, Commanding General of the Western Defense Command, Lieutenant General J. De Witt, recommended to Stimson that "Japanese and other subversive persons" be removed from the West Coast. Roosevelt signed Executive Order Number 9066, setting up the internment process, on February 19. John McCloy worked up the plans to move all Japanese-Americans away from the coast.[43] De Witt became designated military commander of the affected areas, issuing Proclamation Number 1. This made the West Coast and part of Arizona a military zone. The army picked Manzanar, in California's Owens Valley, as the initial temporary detention center. Camp site selections began, and on March 21, Roosevelt signed the bill making resistance to the military commander a federal offense.[44]

Those were legal steps taken to implement the low point of American performance during the war. Legalism melded with fear resulted in the wholesale removal of 100,000 well-settled people of the "wrong" background.[45] There was remorse in later years. But as it unfolded, the broadly supported policy generated editorial commentary. No pundit was more significant on the topic than Lippmann. At the time, he was groping carefully towards the *realpolitik* enunciated in his 1943 *US Foreign Policy: Shield of the Republic*. The success of that bestseller underscored Lippmann's status as the voice of record interpreting international affairs.[46] After Pearl Harbor, Lippmann expressed worry over the American commitment to the Pacific. What he worried about was derogation of the Pacific's strategic importance. American leaders needed to bear in mind that what happened in Asia had vital effects on permanent American interests, he said. They should remind the citizenry of that fact. Roosevelt, wrote Lippmann on January 29, should,

> dispose of the poisonous impression that he and his advisers mean to wage a soft war in the Pacific. . . . If only he will say out loud what is unmistakably in his mind and his spirit, make it plain to all his subordinate commanders that the war in the Pacific is not to be conducted in the spirit of Pearl Harbor but in the spirit of MacArthur.[47]

Citing Dutch pilots and submarine crews in the Macassar Straits, he argued that the war had its own rhythm, and that the time for a stand was at that moment, "not a year hence, not when every bureaucrat's dream of perfection has been realized."[48] Plainly, Japan's unexpected advances unsettled the Georgetown sage. Also frustrating were inefficiencies of the command economy, as reflected in his impatience with price-freezing instead of rationing. Fixed pricing he termed "a mirage," deluding citizens into thinking they could dodge sacrifice.[49] Lippmann wanted the government in charge of the market as fast as possible, believing the crisis warranted a total rationing scheme as a matter of fairness and rational allocation. He saw Roosevelt failing to help Americans experience "their inalienable right to understand the war."[50]

As part of his discovery process, Lippmann left for the West Coast in February, interviewing military officials and observing the jittery public mood. The tenor of those views showed in comment of De Witt. "A Jap's a Jap," he said. "It makes no difference whether he's American or not."[51] "The ancient American rule is to assume that the allegiance of each citizen of a state is to the government of that state," Lippmann wrote on February 5.

> Thus, the citizens of an enemy state are, according to the rules, all of them enemy aliens. The citizens of an allied state are according to the rules all of them friendly aliens. The citizens of a neural state are all of them neutral aliens. The citizens of the United States are all of them loyal citizens.[52]

What troubled Lippmann was what happened when those rules no longer fit. He covered the Sudeten Germans, whose agitation undermined Czechoslovakia. Lippmann also analyzed the schism between Vichy and Free France. Lippmann pointed out how the map of Europe was dotted with irredentist hot spots and peoples whose national identity did not reflect their political status.

> The problem is extremely difficult and of much . . . importance. For it raises the question of whether a nation at war, as we now are, is to take the line that there is not necessarily a reward for helping us nor necessarily a penalty for fighting us.[53]

"A man can cross the continent as I have just done and see at first few outward signs of the American mobilization," wrote Lippman's on February 7.[54] He cited peaceable continuity as showing social power which the United States harnessed to the war effort. "So great are the American reserves that the effort itself has as yet wrought few visible changes in the outward aspects of civilian life."[55] Here was Lippmann's call for aggressive administrators to make the nation perform appropriately. "The immense scope and depth of the American reserves require leadership and administration and management of a much higher order than are needed to mobilize a smaller and poorer country."[56] Issues at hand included preparing the citizenry for the moments when "the real costs of war begin to bite," which was precisely the moment when "those of us who are behind the lines begin to put all our energy and all our weight into it."[57]

"A Report From Southern California" was the February 10 column. It began with his customary complaint that Washington seemed "too remote for efficiency" out there.[58] He informed readers that his clearance granted him access to "certain officers and their commands." A dab of humor emerged when he said that "the first time I used the credentials it turned out that the officer named in my papers had in fact been retired quite some time ago."[59] Wryly, Lippmann allowed that this might have been a clerical error. On the other hand, it might constitute a small example of inefficiency. "There is yet no solution in this vulnerable region to the problem of adequate authority and of unified command and of clearly fixed responsibility," he concluded.[60] His argument was America needed streamlined, comprehensive reorganization. "I do not know how it is to be done," he admitted. But it was a *sine qua non* if the United States was not to bungle the war. "It is certain, I believe," continued Lippmann, "That the full security of the Pacific region requires extraordinary measures and extraordinary powers, and that there is not now the necessary authority, the necessary organization of command and administration for doing what the situation requires."[61]

Two days later, he described the extraordinary measures needed. "The Fifth Column on the Coast" let readers know that subversion was on Lippmann's mind: "The enemy alien problem on the Pacific Coast, or, much more accurately, the fifth column problem, is very serious and it is very special."[62] There was no comparison to the situations in the East or inland areas. Only out West was there the chance of "a Japanese raid accompanied by enemy action inside American territory."[63] Officials with whom Lippmann spoke revealed fears of coordinated sabotage. Lippmann made a frightening claim, calling these "a sober statement of the situation, in fact, a report, based not on speculation but on what is known to have taken place and to be taking place in this area of the war."[64] Precisely what "area" Lippmann meant was unstated. But readers could assume that Lippmann referred to California. He certainly included Hawaii, and might have been referencing the Niihau Incident. The absence of espionage in the West was no indicator or of safety. Lippmann pulled in both Hawaiian and European precedents to argue that the very dearth of sabotage was sinister. "From what we know about Hawaii and about the fifth column in Europe, this is not, as some have liked to think, a sign that there is nothing to be feared. It is a sign that the blow is well-organized and that it is held back until it can be struck with maximum effect."[65] Lippmann gingerly pressed up against what was to be done. The army and navy bore responsibility for repelling any attack, but were "facing it with one hand tied down in Washington." Lippmann took up their case, he suggested.

> I am sure I understand fully and appreciate throughly the unwillingness of Washington to adopt a policy of mass evacuation and mass internment of all those who are technically enemy aliens. But I submit that Washington is not defining the problem on the Pacific Coast correctly.[66]

The danger encompassed American citizens, too. "It is certainly also a problem of native-born American citizens. There is the assumption that a citizen may not be interfered with unless he has committed an overt act, or at least unless there is strong evidence that he is about to commit an overt act." This was inadequate to the emergency, he argued. So was the assumption that "if the rights of a citizen are abridged anywhere, they have been abridged everywhere." The problem with these patterns of democratic thought, went the rationale, was that they precipitated "legalistic and logical arguments between the military authorities out here and the civil authorities in Washington, and between the aroused citizenry of the coast, and their fellow-countrymen of the interior."[67] These sorts of disjunctions aggravated Lippmann because he wanted a fusion of national energies into one formidable force.

Lippmann said that there was no need for disagreements. "A much simpler approach will . . . yield much more practical results." He elucidated, asking readers to "forget, for a moment, all about enemy aliens, dual citizenship, naturalized citizens, native citizens of alien enemy parentage." Instead, he wanted people to imagine "a warship in San Francisco Harbor, an airplant in Los Angeles, a General's headquarters at Oshokosh, an Admiral's at Podunk." Imagine also, he said, what would happen if a "lineal descendant . . . of George Washington . . . decided he would like to visit the warship, or take a walk into the airplane plant, or to drop in and photograph the general and the admiral." Mr. Washington would be stopped by the sentry, asked for identification and requested to explain his business. If he had good reasons, he might be accompanied by the sentries to his visit; if not, he would be asked to leave. In any case, no one could claim that "his constitutional rights have been abridged," nor that he had been "denied the dignity of the human person." To Lippmann, the case out west was similar, inasmuch as "The Pacific Coast is officially a combat zone: some part of it may at any moment be a battle zone."[68] By extension, the Japanese-Americans—to whom he referred only in the generic sense—were like the lineal descendant of George Washington. They needed to be escorted by sentries and sent on their way.

The west was "vital and vulnerable," Lippmann argued. There was no real issue of discrimination, since different rules always prevailed in a war zone. "By this system, the constitutional and international questions about aliens and citizens do not arise at the very place where they confuse the issues and prevent the taking of through measures of security." Instead, as Lippmann put it, "all persons are in principal treated alike. As a matter of national policy, there is no discrimination. But at the same time the authorities on the spot in the threatened region are able to act decisively and let the explanations and reparations come later" (Reparations would not come until 1990[69]). Declaring a war zone on the coast was a legalistic solution allowing removal. Another merit was that it would relieve the federal government from trying to find "a policy for dealing with all enemy aliens everywhere and all potential fifth columnists everywhere." This measure would be something more particular: a policy that would "recognize the Western combat zone as territory quite different from the rest of the country," just as had been done at Bataan, in Hawaii, in Alaska, and the Canal Zone.[70] Internment was thus framed as an act of hard-headed realism. Moralistic qualms could be subordinated to the legalistic measure of the war zone designation. Regulations were different in a war zone; moral judgments, too.

Lippmann was not the main force pressing for internment. He displayed guts in addressing the issue directly while other commentators dodged it. But his supporting argument was important, because it came from a deeply respected public intellectual. It was delivered as a rational measure appropriate to the moment. What Lippmann aimed at was rational steering of the economy and society by those who could make the best decisions. Internment he interpreted as part of that orientation. The paramount issue for him was security in the West. Everything else could be subordinated to that. There was no overt anti-Japanese racism in his language, which was dry and licit. Lippmann was no Westbrook Pegler, who wrote, "The Japanese in California should be under armed guard to the last man and woman right now—and to hell with *habeus corpus*."[71] But the policy he advocated was the same.

None other than Attorney General Biddle wrote Lippmann on February 19. "I wish you had talked to me or the Secretary of War, preferably both, before your recent column attacking our action to control the Japanese situation on the West Coat," Biddle complained. Biddle went on to cite his cooperation with the War Department. "I am in receipt of a telegram, dated February 16, from the Editor of one of the largest Southern California newspapers, which states 'Alien Japanese situation deteriorating rapidly. Lippmann's column and new newspaper attacks have started local citizens organizing some kind of irresponsible drive." Biddle concluded that the columnist should be more cooperative.[72] The Attorney General considered Lippmann's columns to be a warning to the government. That was a measure of how profound Lippmann's influence could be. Biddle worried that Lippmann might show the government as too soft on Japanese-Americans.

Biddle sounded hurt, but he was one of the columnist's friends. In the past, Lippmann had passed along friendly notes recommending promising young people for hire at the Department of Justice.[73] Upon returning east, Lippmann promptly dashed off a note. "I should, of course, like to have a talk with you about the situation," he told Biddle, adding that there was "a great gap between what you knew in Washington and what was known on the Pacific Coast." Having shown himself better-connected than the Attorney General, Lippmann added, "The irresponsible drives of which your editor speaks were clearly in the making when I was there, due to a grievous lack of communication between Washington and the Coast."[74]

Lippmann worked on other issues. Another correspondent was MacGeorge Bundy, "Harvey" to his friends, among whom the Special Assistant to the Secretary of War numbered the columnist. Lippmann wrote to the bright young man on

February 27, advising him on War Department matters.[75] The energetic columnist wrote again, passing along a letter by Major Stanley Washburn, an old friend and former World War I officer and Russian Front war correspondent. Washburn wanted to get back into useful war service. Lippmann requested Bundy to find him a position "at least as an adviser and continual consultant."[76] Also among Lippmann's epistolary contacts was Mary Astor—not the scandal-prone movie star, but Mary Cushing Astor, daughter of Johns Hopkins neurosurgeon Harvey Williams Cushing and wife of Vincent Astor. Art enthusiast, museum trustee, and society doyenne, Mary Cushing Astor was active in war-related philanthropy. She thanked Lippmann for supporting her navy relief fund-raiser by writing an article for the evening's program, read aloud by Loretta Young.[77] Veteran reporter George Britt, whom Lippmann knew from their 1920s days together at the *New York World* sent Lippmann a copy of a letter to Columbia University School of Journalism Dean Carl W. Ackerman, pushing Lippmann for a Pulitzer, "Because of his distinguished, farsighted, and courageous pieces from the year 1941, now justified beyond any possible contradiction since December 7."[78]

Internment was not the only issue on Lippman's mind that February. When Singapore fell, he advised the Allies that the time had come for "putting away the 'white man's burden' and purging themselves of the taint of an obsolete and obviously unworkable white man's imperialism"[79] This was a summons for the United States to embrace the United Nations declaration, and to extend it to the colonial peoples of the Far East.[80] Imperialism was dead, he argued, and a rational approach to the war by Americans would face the fact that there was no going back to the age of empires. The call for respecting nascent nationalisms in the Pacific was hardly the view of a figure blinded by anti-Asian racism. To some onlookers, his points in favor of internment and Asian self-determination might seem dissonant. But to Lippmann, they were complementary; both positions arrived at by facing facts clearly.

On imperialism, Lippmann was in synch with Pearl Buck, who spoke to the American Bookseller's Association at New York's Hotel Astor on February 10. *Dragon Seed*, her newest novel, dealing with Japanese occupation in Nanking, was newly released. Critics called it a fitting follow-up to *The Good Earth*. "The family with whom we live during the hours we are reading *Dragon Seed* . . . are in themselves much more interesting, familiar, and likable, even lovable, than the rough peasants of the *Good Earth*," enthused the *Book-of-the-Month-Club-News*.[81] Asked to speak about China, Buck demurred. "China is no more to be talked about as a separate entity in this world in which none of us is any more an individual or whole in himself. China," said the author, "has become a part of the world."[82] She spoke about United States influence across Asia, which she said frightened Japan. Buck contrasted this with Europe, where she said American influence was less important. Among Buck's concerns was overweening Anglophilia among

American intellectuals, who pushed for total integration of the United States with the British Empire. This alienated Asian independence activists and helped Japan. "We may as well present Japan with battleships and bombers as to go on with a union which denies democracy at the very start," she told the book merchants.

It was high time, Buck said, to embrace self-determination for Asians. She admitted that Americans, because of lingering racial prejudice, were leery about seeing the peoples of Asia and Africa step up to independence. That,was something United States needed to get past. The war offered the perfect opportunity for the country to dump its benighted racial past. "Today the colored peoples are still waiting, still watchful," she said, using the loaded term "colored," thus including Africans. They were weighing Japan, the United States, and Russia. The former talked up its pan-Asia stance, the latter was "justly proud of her freedom from race prejudices." But the United States had an ace neither rival could match—a commitment to the kind of democracy which Asians and Africans wanted. Laying aside racism was the first step to winning Asian support in a post-colonial world. "If we intend to persist blindly in our racial prejudices, then we are fighting on the wrong side in this war. We belong with Hitler. For the white man can no longer rule in this world unless he rules by totalitarian military force."[83]

Biddle, who sounded stung in his letters to Lippmann, did not content himself with missives. On February 1, he delivered a speech on CBS, "Let Us Not Persecute These People." His talk marked a process starting on February 2 to register Axis aliens older than 14. Biddle said that, in most cases, the "enemy" label was a mere technicality of war. His call was to be punctilious in dealing with such people. "I describe the identification programs as another part of the job of making America safe," he explained, adding that safety for the nation was accompanied by a desire to keep safe any aliens needing protection. "It is a big job," said the Attorney General. "It is a job that must be done with a minimum of understanding and with a maximum of accuracy and dispatch." He warned that "persecution of aliens— economic or social—can be a two-edged sword. Such persecution can easily drive people, now loyal to us, into fifth column activities." Biddle said that the name of the first American to disembark in Northern Ireland was Private van Henke, "son of a German immigrant who came to our country in search of freedom and opportunity."[84] Notably, this call for sensitive treatment of aliens avoided the Japanese-American issue.

He also wrote "Taking No Chances," defending internment, for the March 21 *Collier's*. The editors said it spelled out "the precautions the government is taking to separate out our alien sheep from the goats."[85] Running under a large photo captioned "A busload of Los Angeles Japanese," who displayed "a wide range of emotions after being picked up by the FBI a few hours after war was declared," the article explained the measures underway. Biddle described how his Justice Department moved swiftly after Pearl Harbor, rounding up 2,000 enemy aliens.

"We had sent representatives to England to study what had been done there," he explained. Mass arrests in 1939 "had caused only confusion and suffering, and had seemed a little silly when later suspects were properly classified and handled individually."[86] Humanitarianism accounted for the pokey federal pace on internment, said the Attorney General. The government had "made our classification beforehand, painstakingly, separating dangerous aliens from innocent ones," and that took time.[87] Here again, Biddle devoted energy to preempting complaints that the federal government was too slow to act against Japanese-Americans.

American values could be seen in the government's reluctance to overwhelm Review Boards with cases for preventive detention. "It was determined to be more in accordance with our American traditions, wiser, more humane, to hold only those who were dangerous to our safety, or who might become so," the Attorney General wrote. This fear of bureaucratic overload could be neutralized by the magic of the "war zone" designation, which would permit wholesale treatment without recourse to individual justice. Biddle reminded readers that Congress authorized registration of aliens in 1940. Thanks to that, the authorities had a good sense of where the 5 million registered aliens were. Arguing against prejudice aimed at the wrong ethnicity, Biddle told readers that he lived in Germantown, which antedated the Revolution, and "was founded by Germans whose solid qualities have built a generous civic life into the city . . . as thoroughly rooted in American life as any stock I know."[88] Seventeenth century German pietists were off the hook. Biddle praised American openness of heart, wishing that "we could find other words than 'alien enemies' to describe the men and women of these countries at war with us who share our loyalties and our lives." He referenced Arturo Toscanini.

As for Japanese out west, the main federal concern was their protection from angry citizens. Biddle predicted that the Issei and Nisei would "be the first to co-operate" with the federal government. The rest of his article was general. Biddle cited the need for broad presidential discretionary powers. He also mentioned race. Comparing the United States to England, he said, "Racially, we are not so completely integrated. We are not so attuned to a single race-habit of thinking. We can do it if we keep on insisting on freedom and order and fairness for everyone." Concentrating on expressions of unpopular thought, he cited a California man who heckled Roosevelt, "saying Hawaii was not ours, that we should never have defended it." When that pest was arrested, Biddle noted, "I ordered him released. He had committed no crime."[89] So it was that Biddle's article only in gentle and general terms touched on the circumstances Japanese-Americans were already facing. The Attorney-General blended together all issues related to war time dissent and delivered a one-size-fits-all explanation centering on the federal government's good will.

As if in answer to Lippmann's concerns, there was true efficiency to the interment operation that spring. In April came the first involuntary detentions in Los Angeles, Seattle, and Alaska. In May, the Western Defense Command established the first detention centers across the West. A civilian governmental agency, the War Relocation Authority, took over the camps during May.[90] Places like Manzanar, Tule Lake, Topaz, and Gila River, from Arkansas to eastern California, came to be synonymous with the experience.[91] Some resentful internees felt that their American loyalties were fruitless. At Manzanar, on December 6, 1942, there was protest aimed at members of the Japanese-American Citizen's League, which argued for patriotism and renewed American identity despite interment. But the Manzanar Riot was exceptional.[92] Far more common was a willingness to serve in the war, proving how wrong internment was from its outset. Twenty-five thousand Japanese-American men volunteered and fought with a valor all the more intrepid because their families lived out the war in camps. The 442nd Regimental Combat Team conducted swearing-in ceremonies at Manzanar.[93]

Not written in direct response to internment, but bearing upon the question of rights in wartime, was "Civil Liberties in the Present Crisis," by John Sparks, in the *Antioch Review*. Sparks' ire was raised, not by traducing civil rights in service of security concerns, but by those who raised the specter of the World War I experience of overly aggressive governmental controls. "I can never escape a sense of foreboding, amounting to alarm, whenever civil liberties begin to achieve any abnormal degree of popular prominence of official attention," he wrote provocatively.[94] Sparks attacked overly legalistic emphasis on civil rights. He outlined the ideas of Jose Ortega y Gasset, that without liberalism, civil rights themselves would perish. Sparks delivered quotes from the Spanish philosopher, such as, "Liberalism—it is well to recall this today—is the supreme form of generosity; it is the right which the majority concedes to minorities. . . . It announces the determination to share existence with the enemy; more than that, with an enemy who is weak."[95] Sparks then favorably reviewed *Censorship, 1917*, a scholarly book published in 1941 by James R. Mock, which countered the oft-recounted tale of a federal government suppressing dissent and tormenting the citizenry during World War I. What Mock—and Sparks—declared was that administration and legislation were not the dangers to civil liberties during war. The gravest threat was the public. The danger was that public opinion might come unmoored from liberal traditions and embrace the destruction of civil rights. Sparks warned that the threat lay in the hearts of Americans. But he was hopeful that widespread rights abuse was not in store. "At least, when we violate the civil rights of our fellow men, we have had a bad conscience," he observed. "This, I think, is a remarkable achievement."[96] It gave him hope that the Bill of Rights would survive what he expected to be "as grave a test as our civil liberties have faced in our history."[97]

Some Americans knew that internment was wrong. Photographer Dorothea Lange's picture, "Old Man," showed an elderly gentleman seated but erect in a crowd of deportees, his dignity a rebuke to the entire process.[98] The Universal Newsreel advertised during the last week of March carried powerful text which, while not written in protest, nevertheless made the power of the events clear. "Japanese by the hundreds are rooted from their homes and taken inland in a giant exodus," went the description, before adding that the measures were taken "to prevent possible sabotage."[99] In the Justice Department, Edward J. Ennis labeled internment dangerous and unfair, taking issue with Biddle, his boss.[100] The left-wing *People's World* editorialized against the policy, seeing "chauvinistic lynch incitement,"[101] and inveighing against those who profiteered off of internees as "sinister and unscrupulous."[102] More obliquely, Drew Pearson and Robert S. Allen led off the March 2 *Merry-Go-Round* with a sabotage story. March 2 was the day that De Witt designated the West Coast and Arizona as military zones. But instead of concentrating on West Coast scare stories, Pearson and Allen knocked the situation in New York: "Though Kept a Secret, Sabotage is Rampant in New York Harbor," read their headline. "Many Sly Tricks are Used to Delay and Damage Vital Shipping." The story went on to describe how saboteurs could destroy or damage British-bound cargo.[103] The point that the East Coast was vulnerable to sabotage, and *not* by persons of Japanese descent, was borne out during the Summer, when the FBI rolled up eight spies infiltrated by Germany as part of "Operation Pastorius." They were arrested before they could conduct operations. The military tribunal which tried these German agents wrapped up its proceedings by August, with six death sentences and two long prison terms, all to front-page press attention.[104] FBI Chief J. Edgar Hoover thought internment a bad idea, as did Socialist Norman Thomas and religious groups such as the Quakers.[105] Writing a letter to the editor which *Time* published on April 27, John L. Ulmer, of Toledo, expressed anger.

Can there be any greater atrocity in the annals of America history than the uprooting of the Japanese families from their homes on the Pacific coast? If these people were allowed to go about their business as honorable, law-abiding Americans, no doubt the majority of them would behave as such. Treat them as enemy aliens and you may expect anything. Why not transport all the native-born Italians and Germans and their American-born children to concentration camps in the Midwest?[106]

Another letter, by Lynn H. Skean, of Ary, Kentucky, compared the plight of the Japanese-Americans to that suffered by the Cherokee on the Trail of Tears: "History repeats itself."[107]

Writing for *The New Republic* on March 2, Carey McWilliams pointed to a Stockton riot after Pearl Harbor between residents of Filipino and Japanese backgrounds as an exception to Governor Cuthbert B. Olson's pleas for quietude. McWilliams was already controversial in California because of his record of defending of the downtrodden. He was an enemy of Earl Warren, who promised that if he became governor, he would fire muckraker McWilliams from his state job aiding farm laborers. McWilliams was the author of 1939s *Factories in the Fields*, a non-fiction counterpart to John Steinbeck's *Grapes of Wrath*. McWilliams' book, *Ill Fares the Land*, was a successor volume released in Spring 1942.[108] Using data culled from the Department of Agriculture and state farm experimental stations, the journalist indicted an agricultural business model bringing unsafe and unsanitary working and living conditions for farm workers, from black vegetable pickers near Lake Okeechobee to hops pickers in the Willamette Valley. The 1942 *Journal of Farm Economics* said that McWilliams looked "at conditions of farm workers through extremely dark glasses," but credited him with bringing up the possibility that bad conditions could hasten the exodus of agricultural labor into defense plant work, resulting in a wartime food crisis.[109]

McWilliams defended Japanese-Americans. He acknowledged the potential for civil unrest, but lambasted evacuation as a dangerous proposal. McWilliams expressed concern for the safety of Japanese-Americans. He warned against hysteria, recalling that many locals wondered darkly why 2,100 Japanese lived on Terminal Island in the Los Angeles Harbor District. "The answer is quite simple," McWilliams explained. "There are ten fish canneries located on the island, representing a capital investment of about $30,000,000. It has been the location of the canneries that has anchored the Japanese on the island as fishermen and cannery workers, particularly as there are few residential areas in Lost Angeles in which the Japanese are permitted to live."[110] McWilliams also said that these workers should not be permitted on Terminal Island. The government should move the canneries if worried about harbor security. McWilliams introduced *The New Republic* readers to the generational categories of Issei, Nisei, and Kibei, describing patterns of assimilation, reviewing anti-Asian codes in California. Among his objections to mass evacuation was the cost, as well as the danger that Japanese-Americans might be put into involuntary servitude as agricultural workers, which some westerners wanted.[111] Unlike Lippmann, who saw no linkage between democratic values and the policy so long as it was enacted in a war zone, McWilliams posited a direct link. "There is every reason to demonstrate the democratic objective of the war by fair treatment of the Japanese who are resident in California."[112] The article concluded with the call for an unbiased congressional committee which, McWilliams believed, "would recommend, after a first-hand investigation of the facts, against wholesale evacuation of the Japanese."[113] Left unanswered was why *The New Republic*, long a scourge of Congressman Dies and his committee, would trust a Congressional group. Also left unexamined was the propriety of faith in a federal government which was behind internment.

The Nation demonstrated concerns as well. Louis Fischer wrote "West Coast Perspective" for the March 7 issue. He demonstrated sympathy for the shivers he saw among the populace, commenting that "The majority of West Coast citizens lack the knowledge and perspective to keep themselves from falling into a slough of defeatism when the news from the battle area is black." Fischer detected a dearth of positive federal leadership. "They cannot be blamed for taking the fall of Singapore hard," he wrote, likening it to the shock felt by easterners when France fell in 1940. "They ought to have had guidance from the nation's capital," he concluded.[114] But his understanding did not prevent him from picking up vibrations of panic. He mentioned "the man-hunt on Japanese-born and American-born Japanese, who, it is alleged, might try to capture cities, shipyards, and plants during raids." Continuing in this vein, Fischer had "talked to women who were honestly afraid that the Japanese truck growers would poison their vegetables."[115] In Pasadena and Seattle, Fischer claimed, attitudes were more balanced, and the public did not seem spiteful or afraid. But such enclaves were exceptional, he suggested. Elsewhere,

> the reactionary press and the politicians are out for blood and wholesale internment. Jingoes are endeavoring, under the cover of war-time, flag-waving patriotism, to do what they always wanted to do in peacetime: get rid of the Japanese, harness labor, and frighten the liberals.[116]

Fischer's concern was that what he called "beautiful souls and progressive minds" who were "anxious and eager to set the world right"[117] would not prevail in what he saw as a liberal-conservative issue.

There was popular support for internment. Pollsters focused on the question more than once. A National Opinion Research Center query on March 28 found that 93 percent of respondents agreed with relocating aliens, while only 1 percent disagreed and 6 percent had no opinion. Fifty-nine percent supported moving native-born Japanese-American citizens to camps, while 25 percent did not. Once Japanese-Americans were in the camps, pollsters revealed 65 percent support for strict guard, with only 28 percent support for freedom of movement. Twenty-two percent thought prisoners should have some say over their activities, while 66 percent wanted them subject to orders. The only nod to equal treatment under the law came from 34 percent who felt Japanese-Americans put to forced labor deserved the same wages as their fellow Americans on the outside; 26 percent thought smaller wages fair, while 27 percent thought room and board was adequate compensation for whatever work they did. Seventy-four percent felt that anyone with a Japanese education was dangerous, while 70 percent thought that those born in the United States were less dangerous than those born in Japan.[118] Such inhospitable attitudes were not swiftly set aside. As late as April 1945, pollsters found only 6 percent of respondents agreeing with the statement that, when peace came, Japanese-Americans deserved as good a chance as anyone else to get a job; 56 percent thought that non-Japanese Americans deserved priority, while 34 percent wanted the internees shipped to Japan. Only victory and peace would start to reverse the odious trend. In May 1946, 50 percent told pollsters that they believed Japanese-Americans to be as loyal as everyone else in the country, with 25 percent considering them disloyal and 25 percent not sure.[119]

"Should I Sacrifice My Life to Live Half-American?" African-Americans and the Double-V

Like all true Americans, my greatest desire at this time . . . is for a complete victory over the forces of evil which threaten our existence today. Behind that desire is also a desire to serve this, my country, in the most advantageous way. Most of our leaders are suggesting that we sacrifice every other ambition to the paramount one, victory. With this I agree, but I also wonder if another victory could not be achieved at the same time . . .

James G. Thompson, Letter to the Editor,
Pittsburgh Courier, January 31, 1942[120]

Black Americans were no less patriotic than their white fellow citizens. But they saw the irony inherent in calls to fight against opponents whose crimes included racial injustice. P.B. Young, *Norfolk Journal and Guide* editor, wrote along these lines, "Help us get some of the blessings of democracy here at home before you jump on the 'free other peoples' bandwagon and tell us to go forth and die in a foreign land."[121] Some African-American leaders, such as W.E.B. DuBois, found the international situation challenging. DuBois thought that anti-Japanese racism was driving the United States towards war before December 7, 1941. His anti-colonial focus made him susceptible to Japanese rhetoric about ejecting white empires from Asia. Unfortunately for his reputation, he urged China to accept Japanese occupation in the interest of opposing western imperialism. The idea that China would sacrifice itself as an anti-western offering was bizarre. But Japanese violations of China worried DuBois less than European colonialism, his bugbear. "I believe in Japan," he argued. "It is not that I sympathize with China less but that I hate white European and American propaganda, theft, and insult more. I believe in Asia for the Asiatics and despite the hell of war and fascism of capital, I see in Japan the best agent for this end."[122]

But DuBois' intellectualism put him outside mainstream discourse. For black Americans, the war was largely a grass-roots experience, which meant that intellectuals were no vanguard. The Great Depression lingered longer for black Americans, since many lived beyond the reach of the preparedness economy. In 1940, black unemployment was 19 percent; poverty was the norm for most black families. "This nation cannot expect the colored people to feel that the US is worth defending if they continue to be treated as they are now," Eleanor Roosevelt said.[123] That race, war, and politics overlapped was demonstrated when Hamilton Fish (R-NY) introduced the 1940 Selective Service Act. Representing Roosevelt's Dutchess County home district, Fish was one of the President's most implacable critics. The White House energetically returned his disdain. But Fish was also a First World War veteran. He commanded the all-black combat regiment known as the "Harlem Hellfighters."[124] Intra-party debate over the draft bill had a racial context, with southern Democrats maneuvering to eliminate wording that might allow the President to move black conscripts into units needing manpower rather than segregated units. What emerged was a compromise that permitted black draftees, encouraged volunteers from both races, and discouraged discrimination in training. It left in place rules mandating race-specific units. Even the extreme national emergency was not enough to end military segregation.[125]

That was on the minds of A. Philip Randolph, Bayard Rustin, and A.J. Muste in 1941 when they staged a protest for desegregation of the armed forces. The idea for the march was part of Randolph's career organizing for equal treatment. It won support not just because of its fairness in a time of military crisis, but because it provided a new focal point for concerns that Washington's commitment to preparedness might reduce New Deal resource allocation vital to poor black citizens.[126] On June 18, 1941, Randolph, Rustin and Muste presented their petition at the White House meeting, claiming they could draw over 100,000 to Washington for the march. Roosevelt, erroneously supposing that he and Randolph were both Harvard graduates, was at his charming best. He held forth as a raconteur, in what was a small-scale filibuster. Randolph was "Phil," but he resisted the President's request to abandon calls for military integration and demanded some tangible move from the President. The negotiations took on the legal measures barring discrimination in war industry hiring.[127] The civil rights advocates left thinking they had a deal and were shocked when Press Secretary Early implied their agreement with the subsequent White House announcement ruling out military integration: "the policy of the War Department is not to intermingle the colored and white enlisted personnel."[128] The statement made it clear that the war would not knock down *Plessy v. Ferguson*. Early pointed to Executive Order 8802, the Fair Employment Act, which President Roosevelt signed into law later in June 1941. This disallowed racial discrimination in hiring by the defense industries. The OPM established the Committee on Fair Employment Practice to monitor compliance.[129]

The Fair Employment Act was a half-step forward, but did not place white and black citizens serving their country on an equal footing. Moreover, the Fair Employment Practice Committee ran into predictable resistance. In early 1942, it pointed at discrimination in war-related businesses across much of the North. It turned its attention to the South in June 1942. By then, Southern Democrats upholding the Roosevelt coalition made their opposition very plain. The administration decided not to push hard for compliance. War Manpower Commissioner Paul V. McNutt and Attorney General Biddle attempted to assuage the suspicions of civil rights leadership, but doubts about the administration's commitment were ineradicable. This proved a disillusionment for Randolph and civil rights leaders.[130]

Restriction to all-black regiments sometimes prompted recruiters to defer black enlistments:[131] 2.5 million black men registered for the draft, 909,000 served in uniform during the war, 125,000 went overseas.[132] The army took the largest number, 650,000, with 50,000 serving in combat.[133] They constituted some famous units, such as the 761st Tank Battalion, fighting under Patton, and the Tuskegee Airmen, commanded by Benjamin O. Davis, Jr., son of Benjamin O. Davis, Sr., promoted in 1940 as the army's first black General.[134] The first day of the war saw the first African-American fighting hero, Doris Miller. Miller was a *West Virginia* mess attendant who manned an anti-aircraft gun while his ship was under attack. He stayed at the gun while bombs and shipmates fell around him, "blazing away as though he had fired one all his life."[135] Admiral Nimitz pinned the navy cross on Miller's chest in May 1942.

Seismic shifts gathered as more black Americans entered the service branches. Changes were needed, given military racial history. World War I was traumatic for blacks in the service, not just because it was a brutal conflict, but because they were not respected by their own side. Black officers and enlisted personnel were subjected to demeaning treatment, while the Wilson administration looked away.[136] Since racism trumped solidarity even though the fighting qualities of African-Americans in World War I earned them the sobriquet, "hell soldiers," from awestruck Germans,[137] there was determination to avoid that in the new conflict. Honest onlookers knew that total commitment to victory meant utilizing all national resources without allowing race to prove a debilitating distraction. There was some institutional pressure in the direction of less racial friction in the services, but this did not include integration. Those who saw the senselessness of refusing to institute equal opportunity for blacks to serve were outmaneuvered by politicians determined to protect segregation even at the expense of meeting manpower needs.[138]

Stubborn defense of segregation was a revealing exception to the otherwise solid national consensus for maximum commitment to victory. One result was resistance to accepting black servicemen near southern military base. Heritages of racism and respect for military service collided, with racism proving powerful. In April 1941, Army Private Felix Hall was lynched near Fort Benning, Georgia. In July 1941, a Tampa city police officer shot a black soldier lying on the ground. In January 1942, a race riot ensued near Alexandria, Louisiana, after black soldiers were arrested by white Military Policemen.[139] Disturbances also took place in the north, at Fort Dix, New Jersey, and Camp Shenango, Pennsylvania.[140] After-the-fact investigations reflected the old canard that "Negro troops were troublesome, trained or not," as African-American Colonel Howard Donovan Queen bitterly recalled.[141] But despite violent outbreaks, changes were irresistible. World War II was proving prodigious enough to budge even inertia-bound American prejudice, one increment at a time. June 1942 saw the Marines enlist their first black members. Segregation outlasted the war, but the thrust of World War II pointed inexorably to its bankruptcy. Choosing segregation meant breaking faith with the emergent national consensus to do whatever victory required.

There were Americans who understood this. When James G. Thompson, a 26-year-old Wichita cafeteria worker, wrote to the popular black newspaper, the *Pittsburgh Courier*, on January 31, 1942, he expressed the conflict many African-Americans faced with the call to sacrifice for victory in a war for freedom. "Being an American of dark complexion," he wrote, "These questions flash through my mind: 'Should I sacrifice my life to live half American?' 'Will things be better for the next generation in the peace to follow?' 'Would it be demanding too much to demand full citizenship rights in exchange for the sacrificing of my life?'" Other queries included "Is the kind of America I know worth defending?" and "Will America be a true and pure democracy after the war?"[142] Thompson's heartfelt questions reflected not just sad incredulity but years of deprivation of inalienable rights. The questions were painful but apt. Response was prompt and widespread. Keenly attuned to readership interests, the *Courier* began the "Double V Campaign," for victory at home as well as abroad. Double V drawings appeared around the announcement of a national campaign, which by summer had 200,000 members.[143]

The black press had waited many years for something to break the logjam of segregation, *de jure* across the South, *de facto* elsewhere. The cartoon announcing the campaign was an American bald eagle between two V's. "Americans all are involved in a gigantic war effort to assure victory for the cause of freedom," said the ad copy. "We, as colored Americans, are determined to protect our country. . . . Therefore we adopted the Double V War Cry—victory over our enemies at home, and victory over our enemies on the battlefields abroad." Describing the two campaigns as part of a single fight for freedom, the paper promised "a two-pronged attack against our enslavers at home and those abroad who would enslave us . . .WE HAVE A STAKE IN THIS FIGHT! WE ARE AMERICANS, TOO!"[144]

Hesitant whites would be relieved at the patriotic impulses and imagery. At the same time, the campaign made plain that the fight for democracy was indissoluble, and could not be waged against Hitler while ignoring Jim Crow. Other campaign images included photographs of smiling African-Americans flashing the V-for-Victory sign made famous by Churchill. They used both hands. Such pictures appeared in black newspapers across the country. Occasionally, white people appeared alongside blacks in these photos, flashing the twin signs and smiling.[145]

The campaign attracted support from civil rights leaders, Randolph included. Governmental personnel spoke in favor.[146] Celebrities flashed the double-V, including Lionel Hampton, Jimmie Lunceford, Marian Anderson, Adam Clayton Powell, Jr., Roy Wilkins. UCLA basketball star Bill Terry was photographed jumping high—his legs and shadow made two V's.[147] Even DuBois supported it.[148] The campaign temporarily lightened the burden of doubt which so often weighed upon the academician as he wondered whether the United States could ever shed its burdensome racial legacy. Writing a letter-to-the-editor to *Fortune*, May 21, 1942, DuBois expressed no bitterness, instead expressing "large hopes for changing the world."[149] As he linked justice for black Americans with victory in the war, he was the subject of FBI scrutiny, thanks to his "socialistic tendencies" and earlier support for Japan.[150] While DuBois, in Atlanta, wrote to *Fortune*, a 10th grader at the city's Booker T. Washington High School headed into summer vacation. His name was Martin Luther King, Jr.[151]

Double-V howed potential for altering attitudes. It boasted famous white supporters. Wendell Willkie and Thomas Dewey boosted the campaign; Dorothy Thompson and Sinclair Lewis were supportive; Eddie Cantor, Gary Cooper, and Humphrey Bogart lent approval.[152] At *Harper's*, the editors solicited an article from Earl Brown, whom they called "One of the ablest Negro journalists," to explain how the war looked from a black perspective.[153] Brown explained the painful experiences of black volunteers, such as George Derrick, a graduate of Howard University with a degree in engineering and professional radio experience. The War Department offered him a janitorial position. Brown's article, "American Negroes and the War," introduced *Harper's* mostly white readership to the realities of military segregation, to the dust-up over hiring discrimination at defense plants, and to the story of Randolph's visit to Roosevelt. His conclusion was hard-hitting, but no less correct for that: "Morally speaking, nothing that is being done in the United States today gives the Axis Powers a better opportunity to condemn democracy than the treatment of our colored citizens."[154]

The Double-V was a peppy campaign. But it was inherently impermanent. Like so many other endeavors at the time, Double-V was subsumed by the immensity of the war. Despite initial momentum, the campaign wound down in 1942. But it was no failure. By the summer, when the campaign wrapped up, many thousands of black Americans were in the service. More Americans understood the implications of the war and the demands of victory. The Double-V was a send-off for those who realized that the liberty enshrined in texts like the United Nations announcement was needed at home. James Thompson's own story was symbolic. Soon after writing, he quit his job when denied a 5 cents raise. Interviewed at home by the *Courier* in April 1942, he was described as handsome, upstanding, and popular among his townsfolk, "The idol of Wichita's 6,000 Negro citizens."[155] In June, he became head of the *Courier* Double-V campaign. He worked in that capacity until joining up in February 1943.[156]

Blood spilled at sea: U-boats off the east coast

Our U-boats are operating close inshore along the coast of the United States of America, so that bathers and sometimes entire coastal cities are witnesses to the drama of war, whose visual climaxes are constituted by the red glorioles of blazing tankers.

Grossadmiral Karl Donitz[157]

The losses by submarines off our Atlantic seaboard and in the Caribbean now threaten our entire war effort.

General George C. Marshall, June 1942[158]

Hitler's meddling affected Donitz's plans. The *fuhrer* decided that submarines were needed near Gibraltar, so he limited Drumbeat to six U-boats. One of the submarines designated for *Paukenschlag* needed repair, so the great attack against the American east coast went ahead with five vessels.[159] On board the U-123, Captain Hardegen briefed his officers on December 27. His materials included a tourist guide to New York City, showing ports, bays, and channels. The likelihood is that the tourist guide was included by a rushed naval intelligence staff which had no time to collect operational charts.[160] U-123's orders called for the submarine to reach the American littoral and "attack unescorted independently sailing coastwise merchant traffic of any kind and nationality except vessels with clear neutral markings . . . south as far as Cape Hatteras."[161] The other four Drumbeat subs received similar orders. Noteworthy was the specification of "unescorted" traffic. Convoys afforded merchant ships the protection of accompanying destroyers and air cover. But lack of awareness along the East and Gulf coasts meant that ships continued sailing independently. Nor were those coastal waters under efficient air protection. The result was a rich target environment.

Hardegen was pleased when he read his orders. Now, he shocked his crew. By loudspeaker, he informed all aboard: "Men, I have opened our Operation Order and reviewed it with the officers. We are going against America. Our first destination is New York." He predicted success because "The element of surprise favors us. . . . The harbor at New York where we will begin is one of the busiest, if not the busiest, in the world. We should not lack for targets, and that will enable us to get even with the Americans," he added.[162] Much to everyone's delight on board U-123, radio signals came in loud and clear along the East Coast. Beacons and shore lights were bright, providing backlit night conditions, making ships easy to target. As they cruised, the U-boat crews enjoyed listening to American music.[163]

The American East Coast lay pregnable precisely when fears along the West Coast were intense. In the Pacific, Japanese submarines were part of the threat making civilians and the military nervous. Ships sailing between the mainland and the Philippines were sunk after December 7. The Imperial Sixth Fleet issued a directive before Pearl Harbor for nine submarines to "make reconnaissance of American fleet in Hawaii and West Coast area, and, by surprise attacks on shipping, destroy lines of communication."[164] These submarines reached American coastal waters on December 19 and operated for nearly two weeks, from San Diego up to Cape Flattery, Washington.[165]

Their performance was erratic. Only four hit shipping. Victims included SS *Emidio, Samoa, Larry Doheny,* and *Montebello,* all attacked off California, before Christmas.[166] *Emidio* and *Montebello,* were sunk, while the others escaped with damage. *Emidio,* owned and operated by the Socony-Vacuum Oil Company, went down on December 20, en route from Seattle to Ventura. Japanese sub I-17 spotted the ship in choppy seas during a squall. The hapless oiler tried outrunning the submarine, but the Japanese commander opened fire. The crew took to their boats. They were picked up by a lightship, and *Emidio* drifted onto rocks and was lost.[167] Given the proximity of the wreck to the shore, the story was no secret. The submarines returned to Kwajalein. Later, in February, two subs returned, patrolling from the Golden Gate up to Washington. One shelled oil installations at Santa Barbara. This was the occasion of the notorious February 24 "Battle of Los Angeles," in which fears sparked by the shelling mixed with concerns about Japanese-Americans, resulting in false alarms of incoming aircraft, prompting anti-aircraft fire.[168] Japan's sub campaign was intermittent and not very successful, but it attracted attention, intensifying fears that the West was exposed to enemy action.

Back east, somnolence reigned. On December 22, the North Atlantic Naval Coastal Frontier Commander warned the navy and coast guard that "should enemy submarines operate off this coast, this command has no force available to take adequate action against them, either offensive or defensive."[169] This was the weakness Hardegen and Donitz expected to exploit. Germans sank nearly 150 ships in 1942 alone.[170] The doctrine under which U-Boats operated was simple: reduce an enemy's merchant marine presence below the level required to maintain the war effort. This meant sinking sufficient American tonnage to affect the nation's economic health, and to disrupt trans-oceanic supplies to the British and Soviets.[171] In January 1942, the *Kriegsmarine* had 89 submarines in front line use.[172] The five devoted to Drumbeat were sufficient to do real damage, but far from the decisive force Donitz dreamed of. Hitler, preoccupied with the USSR and unconcerned about American potential, failed to deliver the needed support.[173]

In Britain, Bletchley Park built upon the work of Polish intelligence to figure out ENIGMA, the German cryptographic machine. Probably the outstanding intelligence achievement of the war, this project meant the Allies could understand the Reich's secret messages. The May 1941 capture of cipher materials from a German weather ship and a crippled U-boat put the keys to understanding *Kriegsmarine* communications in British hands.[174] Slowly, by cross-checking naval actions with intercepted communications, Britain learned German U-Boat strategy and tactics. London knew that five U-Boats had been pulled from convoy lanes and sent to the western Atlantic. "Be sure to keep the people in Washington informed," said Commander Rodger Winn, overseeing the Submarine Tracking Room on January 3, 1942.[175]

Unfortunately, the US Navy could not make good use of the information. One impediment was Admiral King's disdain for the British. Another was the poor shape of Naval Intelligence. The initial American naval mission to London arrived in July 1940. Another was sent in March 1941. The result was improved cooperation on convoy protection.[176] That kind of blue-water issue attracted the navy's closest scrutiny. But coastal defense was another matter. As of mid-January, few steps had been taken to institute anti-submarine measures along the seaboard.[177] The British had plenty to teach on this topic, but King did not see his navy needing tutelage from "a bunch of limeys."[178] King's gruffness amused his own daughter, who said, "He is the most even tempered man in the Navy. He is always in a rage."[179] King was no figurehead. He exuded competence, earning admiration from General Marshall and Roosevelt. King's willingness to think along new lines was admired by a fellow commander who opined that his ideas "were either so radical or so eccentric that they aroused universal opposition" from more traditionalist officers.[180] King's initial inability to see the submarine threat was a misstep in a successful tenure.

Naval Intelligence suffered from decentralization and turf squabbles.[181] Service in the Intelligence branch was long considered the second-rate domain of what Admiral Alan G. Kirk, who took over as Director of Naval Intelligence in March 1941, called the "striped pants, cookie-pusher" stereotype.[182] In his efforts to beef up Naval Intelligence, Kirk ran up against another of the navy's dominant figures, Rear Admiral Richmond "Kelly" Turner. Turner was Director of War Plans in Operations, loathe to cede prerogatives to his ambitious colleague.[183] Kelly's career illuminated the intermittent federal commitment to naval prowess during peacetime. Contingency planning made Congress nervous, which was why restrictions were imposed on the kinds of plans officers could work up.[184] But Kelly sailed nicely through naval bureaucracy. He spent years on board ship, serving as a Gunnery Officer in World War I and also working in Naval Aviation.

Turner took command of the heavy cruiser *Astoria* in 1938. His record was stellar enough that his ship performed a mission of honor, returning the body of deceased Japanese diplomat Hiroshi Saito—former ambassador and one of the best-informed sources on the United States in Japan's diplomatic corps, whose voice would be sorely missed as the militarists blundered their way to Pearl Harbor—back to Japan. The 1939 mission was a special assignment conceived by the State Department as a gesture of good will, so Turner's selection revealed trust.[185] Turner knew the doctrines animating the navy, writing in 1929 that "It is customary among Naval officers to consider it practically settled that the ORANGE [Japanese] forces in the case of an ORANGE-BLUE War will be landed on the shores of Lingayan Gulf. The existing ASIATIC FLEET operating plan covers this contingency in considerable detail."[186] The shape of the war by 1942 was not surprising to him. RAINBOW-FIVE was largely his own creation, as Admiral Royal E. Ingersoll knew. "Kelly Turner wrote RAINBOW-THREE and the first supporting draft for RAINBOW-FIVE," he said.[187]

Much of his effort was directed against reducing naval presence in the Pacific, which he felt would come from a too-enthusiastic interpretation of Germany-first. Turner accepted the emphasis on Germany. But he understood that defeating Germany was a task for ground and air forces ferried across the Atlantic by the navy. On the other hand, the navy, was likely to bear the fighting load in the Pacific. He admitted as much in wartime testimony regarding RAINBOW-FIVE. He explained:[188]

> While the Navy Department believed that our major military effort, considered as a whole, should initially be against Germany—that view I may add, was also held by the War Department—we were all in agreement that the principal naval effort should be in the Pacific . . . Our strongest concentration and naval effort ought to be in the Central Pacific.

So it was that Turner's concentration was firmly fixed on the Pacific and Japan. This did not alter after Pearl Harbor, when the second-guessing began. Turner refused to be a sacramental offering on the altar of blame. He took on investigators directly. He preserved his career, and never shied away from the fact that Pearl Harbor was a navy disaster.

> Why weren't I and a lot of others smarter than we were? I didn't put all the two's and two's together . . . to get four. Maybe I didn't before Pearl, but damned if I know just where. . . . If Noyes had only known that Kimmel couldn't read the diplomatic Magic. If Kimmel had only sent out a few search planes. If the words 'Pearl Harbor' had only survived the redrafting of the warning messages. . . . You find out and let me know.[189]

Turner was fixated on what went wrong and determined to avenge the attack. His emphasis would be preparing amphibious operations necessary for conquering Pacific islands. It was a long way to Long Island or Cape Hatteras. Turner was a dominant navy figure; Kirk lost out in his battle to control over Naval Intelligence. Frustrated, Kirk moved to a sea command. Rear Admiral Theodore "Ping" Wilson replaced him, just when collaboration with the Royal Navy might have helped efforts along the Atlantic coast. While naval cryptographers and translators accomplished major feats decoding Axis communications the top intelligence officers shuttling in and out lent an aura of disorder to the Intelligence division.[190] This did nothing to ensure an effective response to the U-boats. For this reason, some would blame Operations, not Intelligence, for the inert response to Drumbeat.[191]

On December 31, 1941, the North Atlantic Coastal Frontier's *War Diary* carried the information that fishermen off the Maine coast spotted a periscope. The next week, an army airplane, which had erroneously reported a mystery fleet (probably fishing vessels) and thus lost credibility, sighted a "large black submarine with a long conning tower and gun forward."[192] Defense measures in place then included the Temporary Reserve, under Coast Guard command. The Temporary Reserve was a strange conglomeration of vessels crewed by unpaid volunteers. On board sailboats, leisure craft, yachts, and fishing schooners, were teachers, business men, office clerks, and clergymen. They formed a picket line looking out for U-Boats.[193] These volunteers encapsulated the national determination to help with the war effort, and released many sailors for duty across the oceans. But reliance on the Temporary Reserve also epitomized the expedient nature of anti-submarine efforts. Rear Admiral Adolphus "Dolly" Andrews ran the North Atlantic Naval Coastal Frontier. Similar frontiers operated on the Gulf Coast. Andrews' ships included patrol cutters, wooden-hulled sub chasers from World War I, converted yachts and gunboats.[194] Coastal defense resources were tatterdemalion. Mines at the mouth of the Chesapeake sealed off that estuary, while booms and nets were installed at big harbors.[195] These protective measures were insufficient. Merchant ships were careless, showing smoke and light when they should have sailed dark. Air patrols were inadequate, convoy rendezvous were ignored. Few merchantmen were armed, save for Norwegian, Dutch, and British ships. Even these were rarely a match for submarines.[196]

Using his tourist map, Hardegen surfaced one January night in the Ambrose Channel, leading into New York Harbor. The skyline was a glowing nimbus lit by Manhattan's skyscrapers. Amazed, he watched cars driving with their lights on, the gleaming amusement rides at Coney Island, the red light atop WOR's tower.[197] The Germans were stunned by the casual attitude. For example, upon torpedoing the tanker *Norness* on the night of January 14 off the luminous Rhode Island coast, Hardegen was stunned when the ship broadcast a clear message stating that it had hit a mine. Incredulous, Hardegen exposulated: "A mine! Nobody seems to be expecting any German U-boats around here!" To his crew, Hardegen was more calm: "Listen to me, everyone," he announced, "We're here like a wolf in the middle of a flock of sheep . . . the Americans still haven't realized that there's a submarine in the area. So much the better for us. Let's take advantage of the situation."[198]

The first casualty of Drumbeat was *Cyclops*, a British steamer torpedoed by U-123 on January 12, 1942.[199] *Coimbra*, a British oiler went down, so did *Norness*. *Brazos, Malay, City of Atlanta, Allan Jackson, Frances Salman, Norvana, Venore, West Ivis, Francis E. Powell, Florence Luckenbach, Rochester* rounded out January's list. In February, Donitz sent a second wave of U-boats after Hardegen and comrades rotated back to Lorient. February saw *W. L. Steed, India Arrow, China Arrow, Major Wheeler, Arkansas, E.H. Blum, Mokihana, Lake Oswega, Pan Massachusetts, Del Plata, Aalea City, J.N. Pew, Republic, Cities Service Empire, W.D. Anderson, West Zeda, Liuhe, Sun, R.P Resor, Marore,* and *Oregon* lost.[200] The list was mind-numbing, the details depressingly familiar. The ships carried oil, manganese, sugar, iron ore, gasoline, diesel fuel, general cargo. Destinations, never reached, included Baltimore, Philadelphia, Carteret, New York, Iceland. Sometimes, their crews were spotted by Coast Guard planes, picked up by passing ships or fishing skiffs. Sometimes, the crews were lost, as the laconic report on the *Major Wheeler*, a sugar-carrying steamer en route from Puerto Rico to Philadelphia made clear: "None of the eight officers and 27 men survived."[201] Estimates held a sailor's prospects for survival in the event of sinking as about 50 percent. Unlike British merchant seamen, Americans were not equipped with devices like lifeboat pumps, lifejacket beacons, and survival clothing. Often, torpedo explosions wrecked hanging lifeboats.[202]

Precise details were kept as military secrets. But the prevalence of torpedoed ships was impossible to hide. Press accounts concentrated on the trials faced by the crews who were rescued and interviewed by enterprising reporters. "Tanker Torpedoed 60 Miles off Long Island: The Battle of the Atlantic Flared Within 150 Miles of New York City Yesterday" was a headline in the *New York Times* on January 15, 1942.[203] The *Baltimore Sun* headline was similar: "Panama Craft is Victim of U-Boat Attack, Scene 60 Miles South of Montauk Point . . . Navy Warns Danger from Submarines in Atlantic is Growing."[204] The text described a rescue from *Norness*, with one sailor missing and 39 plucked from the icy Atlantic. While the communique which formed the basis for this article "did not identify the nationality of the submerged attacker,"[205] there was no doubt about who sank the hapless Norwegian ship. The Associated Press story said the action was reminiscent of torpedo attacks from World War I. A hard-hitting Universal Newsreel on March 2 shouted: "U-Boat Kills 40 off New Jersey Coast!" The film claimed that a sailor on watch mistook the sub for a fishing boat.[206]

As the toll mounted, so did the headlines. Radio announcers broadcasted the reports. "Two Crewmen Killed In 14th Sinking Off East Coast" topped a story in the *Baltimore Evening Sun* on February 2, 1942. The story told the tale of the *San Gil*, a United Fruit Company freighter sunk off Lewes, Delaware en route from Honduras to Baltimore. The navy communique released the names of crewmen injured and killed.[207] On February 28, a story ran in the *Sun*. "Six Days of 'Freezing Hell' Described by U-Boat Victim," detailed travails of Wilfred G. Evans, an English sailor who endured a week in a lifeboat adrift in the Gulf Stream. The Third Naval District gave permission for Evans to speak with reporters while he convalesced at Long Island College Hospital. He attributed the rescue "to an ordinary ship's bucket and a stalwart fourth mate and chief engineer who roused the men with songs to keep them awake and cheerful." Chief Engineer S. Ernest Hall's repertoire included "My Bonnie Lies Over the Ocean." A Dutch freighter took them aboard.[208]

Not everything went the U-boats' way. *Malay*, which U-123 hit in January, failed to sink. At the end of the month, a Norwegian whaler commanded by Einar Gleditsch, whose personnel file called him "fearless," spied Hardegen's sub and tried to ram it. Hardegen barely outran the ship, and, fearful of air pursuit, counted U-123 lucky to survive.[209] That was the end of *Paukenschlag*. "YOU BEAT THE DRUM WELL" read his congratulatory telegram from Donitz, which Hardegen read on the way home.[210]

Once home, the German captain and crew received a heroes' welcome. U-123 had victory pennants flying, totals painted on its conning tower, and a pair of decorative shark fins mounted high on the fairwater.[211] The sub bobbed into its pen like a caparisoned pony prancing into its stall. Ashore, a marching band played bumptiously, while the sub crew stood at attention amid festive cheers. It was captured on film for the German Weekly Newsreel, the *Deutsche Wochenschau*, February 25, 1942. Donitz placed the Knight's Cross of the Iron Cross around Hardegen's neck; the crew received plaudits from sailors, soldiers and workers at the U-Boat base. Hardgen looked tired and triumphant as he accepted a wreath, reviewed the band and honor guard. Newsreel narrator Harry Giese explained Drumbeat's successes, touting up tonnage totals over a musical soundtrack. The newsreel recapitulated a U-Boat mission off New York, using footage of U-boat crews in action. Cinema attendees could see the U-boat men sleeping, reading in their hammocks, loading torpedoes, donning foul weather gear for watch duty atop the conning tower. There was footage of New York's nighttime skyline, of a sub diving when "Alarm!" went out, and of a smoking merchant vessel. Entitled *Unternehemen Paukehschlag*, the newsreel reminded viewers that all these events occurred "Off the coast of America."[212]

From Drumbeat through successor attacks, Donitz's U-Boats accounted for 303 ships and 2 million tons from January 15 through May.[213] He understood the stakes. "U-boat operations in the American area are . . . right from the point of view that the sinkings of the U-boat war are a race with merchant ship new construction," he explained to Hitler on May 14. "The American is the greatest enemy shipbuilder.

His shipbuilding industries lie in the eastern states. Shipbuilding and ancillary industries depend mainly on oil fuel."[214] That explained Donitz's eagerness to take the submarine campaign into the Gulf of Mexico. In those vulnerable waters were oil transports, from Venezuela to Texas. The *Galveston Daily News* became one of the newspapers whose beat included U-boat actions in the Caribbean and the Gulf. Stung by the disaster along the Atlantic coast, the navy organized the Gulf Sea Frontier on February 6.[215] In late April, U-507, commanded by Harro Schacht, became the first U-boat to hunt in the Gulf of Mexico.[216]

By then, the navy stirred. The rapacious U-boat offensives, the cost of the lost shipping, and the public amazement that German submarines operated with impunity just off the coast led to stiffening anti-sub measures. "The massacre enjoyed by the U-boats along our Atlantic Coast in 1942 was as much a national disaster as if saboteurs had destroyed half a dozen of our biggest war plants," admitted a training manual.[217] The infested waters off Cape Hatteras, where U-boats were particularly thick and only the Coast Guard Cutter *Dione* was in place to oppose them at the year's start, were called "Torpedo Junction."[218] Investigative reporters, especially Drew Pearson, covered the U-boat story. On February 13, his *Merry-Go-Round* column was emphatic. "The Navy is being more hush-hush than usual regarding the sinkings of oil tankers off the Atlantic Coast." He pointed to claims that smaller and older tankers fell victim, and that British accounts pointed to a rise in actions elsewhere, too. But Pearson also contended that heavy losses imperiled East Coast food supplies.[219] On March 3, Pearson cited suspicions from exiled French politicians, presumably Free French, that Vichy-governed Guadeloupe was a U-boat resupply haven.[220] Later that month, Pearson claimed unrest among merchant sailors who felt ill-protected by current navy policies. "Some very heroic stories have appeared in the newspapers recently telling how sailors have lived for days on rafts after their ships were sunk by Nazi submarines," he said. "What these stories do not tell, however, is the growing unrest among seamen because of the tremendous loss of life from these sinkings." And how did Pearson know? It was simple, he explained. "The exact number of men lost with each ship is published by the Navy daily. And all you have to do is take a paper and pencil to figure the total losses."[221] In this story, Pearson specifically cited British practices, such as the outfitting of British fishing trawlers with radios used to warn anti-sub patrols, as superior to American policies in place. "British fishermen equipped with radios have been the eyes of the British Navy in the North Sea," he wrote. "But not American fishermen. Meanwhile, we lose an average of more than one ship a day."[222]

It took three months, but eventually, military authorities forced local communities to dim their waterfront lights.[223] Improved Antisubmarine Warfare training resulted in better patrols. From the docile position during Drumbeat, with inefficient lookouts hoping to spot submarines, the emphasis shifted to a hunt-and-kill doctrine. This recognized that U-boats were most vulnerable when spotted and attacked by aircraft. In short, the US Navy began to implement measures that the British had learned many months before.[224] So obvious was the need to upgrade efforts that the navy even accepted direct assistance from the Royal Navy in the form of anti-sub trawlers and air patrol craft. The results were encouraging. While the famous "Sighted Sub, Sank Same" message from an eager patrol pilot proved too optimistic (the U-boat escaped), the first U-boats were sunk by anti-sub efforts in February and March, off Cape Race and Cape Hatteras.[225] More would follow. The Germans knew then they would be hunted, too. Stories of sunken U-boats were more enjoyable than tales of destroyed Allied merchant vessels.

Third Pan American conference: hemispheric diplomacy in Rio de Janeiro

On January 28, that dramatic last afternoon of the historic Pan-American conference in Rio, Brazil announced to the world that she was breaking all relations, diplomatic and commercial, with the Axis countries. Now she may find herself in actual war with these countries over the ship question.

Eric A. Sevareid, CBS Radio, March 7, 1942[226]

War lent a crisis atmosphere to the intra-American conference set for the end of January at Rio de Janeiro. St. Pierre and Miquelon showed that the hemisphere was not secluded. Latin American orientations were significant for US security. American reporters had been warning of Axis inroads into Argentina and Brazil for years. Ties of trade, ethnicity, and autocracy offered Berlin the chance to destabilize South America and conceivably threaten the United States. The Roosevelt administration prioritized hemispheric solidarity, dispatching Sumner Welles to the conference. The State Department wanted quietude, which meant keeping Argentina, and Chile from pro-Reich policies.

Media attention was heavy. Eric Sevareid traveled to Brazil to anchor CBS coverage. As he said, he barely knew who Simon Bolivar was, and "possessed but the vaguest notion of the material advancement of each South American land, their regimes and their aspirations." Sevareid's reckoning was that, "the stream of history . . . had passed them by."[227] He was disoriented by Brazil, "so vast, so tranquilly at east in her spaciousness upon the earth of crowded frontiers and shoving peoples."[228] Flying over, he gazed upon rainforest and plains, realizing that below him was a continent with a frontier settlement saga matching his own North Dakota remembrances. In Manaus, he saw the famous opera house, surrounded by jungle, and read the plaque announcing "Pavolva Danced Here." Sevareid wondered how his world view excluded South America. He still refracted things through the prism of war, learning how rubber seeds smuggled out of Brazil to Malaya broke South America's hold and gave rise to the rubber plantations now in Japanese hands. "It was a monumental example of the fatal anarchy that ruled the unplanned world of commercial license,"[229] decided Sevareid.

He compared Rio to Paris. Cariocas were slow warming up to strangers, but curious. Parisians he remembered as quick to interact, but incurious. The major difference struck him that Paris had a rich interior life. "The life of Rio is there, on the surface, simple, comfortable, and lazy, in one dimension, quite flat," he decided.[230] He admired the racial tolerance which struck him as an improvement over the American counterpart. Politically, he noted the dominance of Getulio Vargas, "a midget, kewpie doll of a man,"[231] whose dictatorship had benevolent, even cheerful aspects. Ultimately, Brazil struck the correspondent as Ruritanian— "Luxembourg City planted in a country bigger in extent than the United States."[232] But Sevareid realized that this image did not capture a rich country ruled by a dictator who seized power in a 1930 coup, smashed counter-coups, and played with his grandchildren in the presidential palace.

On January 22, Sevareid broadcasted an analysis of the conference, its stakes, and the negotiations. Argentina, he told listeners, was a stumbling block due to its friendship with Germany. Brazil, however was eager to play a positive hemispheric role. "Brazil is a long way from Germany," he observed, playing up an "enemy within" angle. "But the enemy is already at the gates of Brazil. Millions of Germans, Japanese, and Italians live here, if the Brazilian soldier fights, he may fight within his own borders." Besides the fifth column threat, which Brazil's Chief of Staff ridiculed, Sevareid mentioned the proximity between Brazil's easternmost reach, Recife, and Dakar, in French West Africa. "As one who has seen fifth column activity in Europe, the attitude of the Brazilian government seems to be one of complete serenity," he said, not without some nervousness. "I anticipated a hectic place, but all was quiet. The generals strolled in, we smiled and drank coffee and talked among other things of the three men whose pictures adorn the office wall: President Vargas, our own General Marshall, and Secretary Stimson."[233]

January 25, Sevareid described Rio Negro Palace, in the mountains 50 miles above Rio, where he saw Vargas in his element, including "his regular afternoon walk around this flower city." Sevareid described listening to colleague Charles Collingwood broadcasting from London. Vargas listened, too, dandling his one-year-old grandson and smoking a cigar, surrounded by impressionistic oil paintings from Brazil's cattle country.[234]

Later that day, Elmer Davis echoed Sevareid's opinions, particularly about Argentina. Chile was also a problem, due to "conservatives." "If conservatives are defeated in the Chilean elections a week from today, Chile may come aboard, too," said Davis. He said Buenos Aires seemed eager "not to act," due to outmoded pride about not following Washington.[235] In the end, American pressure delivered by Sumner Welles, with his "old school tie" and "Jacksonian integrity" persuaded the recalcitrant Argentines. "The unity of the Western Hemisphere has been preserved," the CBS correspondent reassured his audience.[236]

Sevareid came to the conclusion that Welles won a victory on "the South American front." "No North American in Rio could escape the deep realization that the attitude toward us of virtually a whole continent had been reversed," he declared on February 6. "It was only a few years ago that the United States headed the list of suspected and hated countries in that part of the world." Sevareid attributed the shift to "nine years of a new attitude in the White House," accompanied of slow diplomatic toil for which Welles deserved credit.[237] He concluded that South American representatives, "despite the very grave allied setbacks so far, despite the propaganda and threats poured upon these peoples each day by the Axis powers, are . . . strongly convinced that we shall win."[238]

Theodore "Dr. Suess" Geisel agreed in his January 15 cartoon for the newspaper *PM*. It showed a sombrero-wearing Hitler serenading Rio, only to be told off by a local, "Scram! We're listening to Sumner Welles!"[239] Columbia Journalism Dean Carl W. Ackerman made a speech to the Kiwanis Clubs of Doylestown, Pennsylvania and Lambertville, New Jersey, on March 31. He asked, "Will Our Southern Flank Become a Southern Front?" Ackerman wanted hemispheric defense cohesion. Just back from Latin America, he scathingly noted that movies constituted the only visible United States follow-up to the Rio Conference. "Orson Welles, the actor, has succeeded Sumner Welles, the statesman, as our spokesman in Brazil," complained the Dean. Ackerman wanted organization of South American resources, guarantees of rubber and minerals from Brazil, and meat and grain from Argentina—which, he noted with approval, supplied the Soviets.[240] Ackerman's complaint echoed earlier mockery in the *Washington Merry-Go-Round*. Pearson criticized "Young Nelson Rockefeller, who on the whole has done a good job for Pan-American cultural relations," but who "bogged down badly on films for our Pan-American neighbors." The column ripped into Rockefeller and the Museum of Modern Art for the film export scheme Ackerman derided. The movies were "utterly unsuited and without objective for South America."[241] Pearson was much more charitable towards Sumner Welles, whose performance in Rio he applauded as bravura, terming the Undersecretary of State "by far the most popular diplomat at the momentous parley."[242]

At the National Conference on of the Catholic Association for International Peace, Monsignor Donald A. MacLean, from Catholic University, addressed the need to "replace our long cherished neutrality by Christian conceptions of our fundamental social relations and our international responsibilities." MacLean supported Hoover's Good Neighbor Policy and Roosevelt's respect for South American sovereignty, suggesting that a new era should replace Washington's domination. He felt enthused by the performance to date of "the liberty loving republics of Central and South America," who "pledged their loyal and undivided forces to resist totalitarian, barbaric attacks on any front wherever freedom, democratic institutions, and Christian civilization may be imperiled." MacLean argued that defense of Christian Civilization did "not consist in drifting into World Wars and then barely winning them after a costly struggle," but rather meant setting up a world in which wars could not take place. He left little doubt that what he termed "Christian social solidarity" should play a major part in reconstructing postwar relations across the Americas.[243] In this conclusion, MacLean supported to the continued relevance of Pope Pius XII.

Wandering about the country: Murrow comes home

One month of wandering about our country from coast to coast has convinced me that we Americans are endowed with greater curiosity than any other people on earth. The questions asked of one back from three years in Europe are varied, and, in some cases, frightening.

Edward R. Murrow, February 1, 1942[244]

From the beginning of his European career, Edward R. Murrow interpreted the struggles he covered in a social sense. The war for Murrow was more than a case of rogue powers bullying weak democracies. It looked to him like an augury of future social improvement within democracies. If democracy survived, postwar political systems should be more receptive to the interests of the common folk whose stories were the mainstay of his London newscasts. Listeners took in the message that the people he described—taking refuge in tube stations, putting out fires, or fixing bomb-wrecked buildings—were fine because they maintained dignity and strength. Embedded was the message that, after the war, it would be necessary to heed these people and not merely to rule over them.[245]

When Murrow was on home tour during 1941–1942, Robert Sherwood approached him to work for the Office of War Information. Despite direct appeals from Hopkins, who cabled, "YOU SHOULD BE RELATED TO THE GOVERNMENT," and who informed Sherwood that he had "WIRED MURROW RECOMMENDING HE WORK WITH YOU," the star reporter declined. "AFTER MUCH SOUL-SEARCHING AM CONVINCED MY DUTY IS TO GO BACK TO LONDON. BELIEVE FIVE YEARS TRAINING THERE PLUS OPPORTUNITY DO SOME BROADCASTING FOR BBC MAKE SERVICES IN COMMON CAUSE MORE VALUABLE THERE THAN HERE AND THAT'S THE ONLY THING THAT INTERESTS ME."[246]

Those messages went back and forth in January 1942. Murrow could not get a Clipper berth back to England until April, which left him time to continue the travel and broadcasts he had been making since November. On February 1, Murrow gave a thoughtful monologue covering the American mood. People often asked him about Britain. "What are Britain's peace aims?" was one of the questions.

Some people were a little surprised to be told that is one of our problems, that there can be only joint peace aims, and that Mr. Churchill has said privately for many months that no peace aims could be formulated until America was in the war.[247]

Another question to Murrow was whether Britain would invade the continent. Murrow answered that any invasion could only come "when we are there in great strength to help them, and not before."[248] The point was that Allied forces needed more reinforcements, time, and training. Murrow answered those who inquiring whether Britain could "prevent communist-dominated control of Europe after the war?" "They certainly can't do it alone," he said. "The restoration of order, the feeding of a famished and impoverished continent of Europe will require American aid and plenty of it."[249]

Eyeing future intervention, Murrow explained that American power in Europe was indispensable for peace. "Now, we are the force that will determine the fate of free men everywhere. And it's probably only natural that some time should be required to adjust our thinking to change from spectator to participant. To realize that we are the dominant partner, that our decisions as to planning and strategy will be the decisions that count."[250] On the West Coast, he said, "Folks want to know about air raids. What's the safest place in a frame house? Is there anything that will prevent glass from shattering? What should be done if you're caught in the open during an air raid? How much light does London allow during the blackout?"[251] He said that British workers, who could buy only "23 cents worth of meat each week," were sacrificing for victory. He also said American workers could outproduce their German counterparts. Murrow said he "found no hysteria and no undue nervousness out on the West Coast. The absence of visitors in Southern California was noticeable, but the people out there maintain it's still a comfy place to be, and I agree with them."[252]

He addressed perceived lack of air raids on Berlin, explaining that distance, weather, and logistics made such attacks difficult. Moreover, he explained, the RAF was interested not just in hitting city targets, but in knocking down "Germany's industrial and transportation systems . . . shipyards, and factories."[253] Addressing British desires for revenge, he argued that "Human considerations play no part in this policy." Still, he admitted, strategic explanations would not satisfy everybody. "The little man in Britain would probably answer that by saying, "Bombing Berlin is a luxury we can't afford at the moment. We hope we will be able to do so later on!"[254]

One week later, Murrow spoke from Dallas. This time, he led off describing how unusual it was to sit and listen to his CBS colleagues from war theaters. The peacetime feel of the nation was on his mind. "Flying down from Chicago, over Kansas, Oklahoma, and Texas, it seemed to me that we, in this country, are not required to put up poles and other obstructions to prevent the landing of carrier-borne troops. I notice here in Texas that the fashion papers are more voluminous than are the entire newspapers in European capitals."[255] "I'd like to tell you something about this town of Dallas," he said, jocularly, "But in the first place I can't talk about the weather [due to security restrictions] and in the second place, if I tried to talk about the beauties of the city, most of you would think I'd been engaged by the Chamber of Commerce." He called Dallas "a delightful place to visit, with lovely homes stretching out the plains on every side of the city as these Texans are still searching for elbow room."[256]

Murrow returned to the slowness of Americans to shed the spectator's perspective on world affairs. He warned that this bred complacency. He was thinking of the tough times faced by Russians, and used the mission to Moscow of Britain's Sir Stafford Cripps to stress his point. Cripps warned that the crisis faced by the Soviets was severe. "He's one of Britain's most outspoken men, and its quite probable that his warning was directed at us, as well as at the British," Murrow explained, trying to show that battles in the Donets Basin and Crimea were intimately bound up with the war Americans were fighting in the Philippines or Java Sea. "I was in England when Russia entered the war," he recalled, "And it's quite clear that if Russia does not survive the Spring, the possibility of any sort of victory on the continent will greatly recede."[257] Here, Murrow gave a boost to CBS mate Larry LeSueur, on the eastern front. He suggested that listeners pay attention to Cripps' remark that the Soviets wanted "a declaration of American war aims," and that, in so doing, the British emissary had demonstrated and "admitted for the first time America's primary responsibility for the peace aims of the United Nations."[258]

"We must admit that most of the news is bad. That we and our allies are still on the defensive," he said. Noticing 'V-for-Victory' signs, he suggested that "putting up signs may have given some of us an illusion of accomplishment. They're certainly unlikely to frighten any of our enemies." He took issue with "Buy a Bomber" campaigns, whereby groups raised money for plane-building. These Murrow found too haphazard. "It's very unlikely that another million dollars of subscriptions would replace a single bomber," he scoffed, adding that, "if it did, there's something wrong with our whole production organization." Murrow, sounding a bit like Lippmann, wanted to see centralized, not individual efforts. "Private philanthropy is in the best Anglo-American tradition," he said, echoing

Toqueville over a century before.[259] But that hallowed tradition was insufficient to the present crisis. "It's just no way to finance and fight a war."[260]

One concern Murrow tackled head-on was complaints about the British reported by Bob Trout. Such criticism could be healthy, Murrow said,

> But so is humility and tolerance. Many of us may not admire British strategy. We may not believe that they have succeeded in producing at top speed. But statements that they are slothful and unaware of their responsibility can only be termed dangerous and downright irresponsible.[261]

Murrow likened disrespect for Britain to subversion. Critics were singing the same tune sung by those who "had some success in dividing France and Britain in 1940. We can't afford that the same thing should happen to us. We're not called upon to approve British production or politics," he said, "But before belaboring them too severely, we might look carefully at our own position."[262]

Here was a rhetorical cut against Anglophobia and shilling for a "Second Front Now." Bringing his broadcast to a close by returning to the light sacrificial load borne by Americans, he observed,

> It's sometimes easier to urge sacrifice upon others than to seek it for oneself. For so long, we've sat comfortable in our country and looked out at the uncomfortable Europeans, criticizing and sometimes pitying them. We've often failed to too look behind us, failed to observe what's been happening in our own country. We're now fighting for our existence, and the British are helping us as we're helping them. . . . Let's beware of shooting at too long range at the British, when there are more urgent problems that might be seen nearer home.

He concluded by warning against "needless bickering between the British and ourselves, which will probably, will undoubtedly, bring great pleasure to Berlin and Tokyo. But it won't shorten the war." Murrow wound up with a caution. "When one is engaged in fighting gangsters in a dark alley," he said,

> When one is on the defensive as we are, it may be unwise to inquire of the man who lends you a hand what kind of a tie he is wearing, whether he believes in meatless Sundays, before we decide to accept his aid and use it for all its worth.[263]

Murrow always took up for the people he covered on his London beat. When pollsters inquired about American attitudes towards their foremost ally, they found that Murrow's opinions were widely accepted by Americans. In 1938, when peace was a universal desire, the American Institute of Public Opinion found 39 percent of respondents agreeing with the idea of an Anglo-American alliance aimed at securing the peace, with 50 percent opposed.[264] In January 1940, 9.8 percent told *Fortune*'s Roper pollsters that "Great Britain had no greater claim upon our sympathy than any other nation because she has grown great by employing practically all the means of aggression, oppression, and secret diplomacy that we criticize in . . . Germany": 25.5 percent considered Britain "as decent as any nation is likely to be," but wished no alliance; 16.2 percent thought an alliance based on mutual interest without shared values made sense; while 38.3 percent thought that "The British do have a special claim on our sympathies because they are closest to ourselves by ties of blood and language, and because they too are defenders of democracy."[265]

As the war advanced, so did American acceptance of the London–Washington connection. Opinion never reached Murrow's level of love, but poll numbers showed willingness to consider Great Britain Ally Number One. While 24 percent agreed with a February 3, 1942 poll question implying that Britain was to blame for American involvement in the war, 60 percent disagreed. The same poll found 58 percent trusting the British to do their fair share of the fighting, while 32 percent expected them to evade their share and rely upon American efforts. The same question at the end of the month found 53 percent trusting the British to do their share and 29 percent expecting them to dodge it. On May 21, 57 percent trusted their ally to fight while 36 percent did not. In June, 1942, 36.5 percent of Americans favored treating Britain as a favored nation after victory, while 33.5 percent thought treating Britain the same as any other country would be proper. Smaller percentages had different answers—11.4 percent wanted British colonies awarded to the United States to cover aid costs, while 6.5 percent thought uniting into one country was advisable.[266]

6 APRIL 1942

"They Came From Shangri-La"— Doolittle's raid stuns Japan, stirs the United States

[If my plane is hit during the bomb run on Japan] I'm going to bail my crew out and then dive it, full throttle, into any target I can find where the crash will do the most good. I'm 46 years old and have lived a full life.

Army Air Corps Colonel James H. Doolittle, on board the
Hornet, April 17, 1942[1]

Enemy bombers appeared over Tokyo today shortly after noon for the first time in the current East Asia War. Heavy and telling damage was inflicted on schools and shipyards, and the population shows much indignation.

Japanese radio broadcast, April 18, 1942[2]

The President caught me off base when I went into his bedroom this morning. He said as usual, "What's the news?" Told him what he already knew, that the papers were full of speculation on the bombing of Japanese cities, concerning which no official confirmation has been forthcoming. He said: "You know, we have an airplane base in the Himalayas." That seemed to me, geographically, a prodigious distance from Tokyo. Then the Boss added: "The base is at Shangri-La." But I was unfamiliar with James Hilton's book Lost Horizon, and so was dumb enough until I sensed that he was kidding.

Bill Hassett, aide to President Roosevelt, April 19, 1942[3]

Radio silence was strict. Surprise alone could give them a chance. Japanese picket ships patrolled the western Pacific. On April 18, 650 miles northeast of Japan, an American reconnaissance pilot saw a lone vessel. When he found out, Admiral "Bull" Halsey, aboard *Enterprise*, swore and informed *Hornet*. Alarms sounded; sailors scrambled to their battle stations. The fate of the mission and the survival of Task Force 16's carriers looked compromised.

Whether or not the flier had been spotted became moot when *Nitto Maru*, a Japanese guard ship, spied the Task Force. "Three enemy carriers sighted. Position 650 nautical miles east of Inubo Saki," said the warning radioed to flagship *Kiso*.[4] His Wildcats strafed but could not sink *Nitto Maru*, so Halsey ordered *Nashille* to attack. The 10,000 ton light cruiser, with 15 six-inch and 8 five-inch guns,[5] should have sunk the converted fishing boat with dispatch, but *Nitto Maru* took half-an-hour to go down. Heavy seas and inexperienced gunners did not help.[6] The desultory performance was not what bothered Halsey, however. His concern was loss of surprise. All the training, all the complexities of a daring—harebrained?—endeavor, could be wasted. Halsey could call off the mission, or put the bombers below and sally forth for a naval engagement. He could continue, even though Task Force 16 was farther from Japan than the optimal 500 miles. At 0800, Halsey ordered B-25s into the air. A loudspeaker commanded: "Army pilots, man your planes!"[7] Army Air Corps Colonel Jimmy Doolittle moved decisively. "Come on, fellows, let's go," he ordered. To Doolittle and *Hornet* Captain Marc A. Mitscher, Halsey signaled: "To Col. Doolittle and Gallant Crew: Good Luck and God Bless You."[8]

Commander John Ford, Hollywood's famous director, captured the scene for the navy.[9] Swells made the takeoffs dangerous, but there was nothing ordinary about B-25 Mitchells taking off from a carrier. These twin-engine medium bombers were designed to fly from ground runways. Here they were, revving engines, lumbering down the deck, barely rising over the bow, timing liftoff with the upward pitch of the rolling sea.[10] The slightest miscalculation meant a plane in the ocean. Sailors cringed, then cheered. Doolittle took off first, heading straight for Tokyo since there was neither time nor fuel for formation. The other 12 Mitchells followed, and the most shocking air raid of the war since Pearl Harbor was underway.[11]

Doolittle's B-25s were going to bomb Japan. Since the war started, Roosevelt discussed such a raid with General Hap Arnold and Admiral King. Planning started in January, when it was decided that launching from China was impossible because the distances were unworkable.[12] What the army and navy worked out was a seaborne scheme requiring specialized training, since no bomber like a B-25 was ever launched from a carrier. Intelligence put Japanese patrols 300 miles off the home islands. That would give bombers the chance to take off and deliver their payloads, but not to return. The carriers would have hightailed it back to safety, anyway. Chosen to command was Doolittle, who picked volunteers. Their B-25s would have extra fuel. The bombers would hit Japan, then continue on to China, trying to reach friendly forces.[13]

In its wild improvization were elements of genius which Toqueville would have recognized as characteristically American. Doolittle was perfect for the impudent mission. He was born in San Francisco in 1896. His father joined the Alaska Gold Rush, finding prosperity because his carpentry skills made him useful. The Doolittle family came to Nome in 1900. It was an exciting environment; young Jimmy learned to hunt, fight, and lead a dog team.[14] At 11, he returned to the Lower 48 with his mother, settling down in Los Angeles. At 13, Doolittle watched an air race at Dominguez Field. Glenn Curtiss set a new speed record, flying 55 miles per hour with a passenger, while French pilot Louis Paulhan flew his Farman plane to the unheard-of altitude of 4,165 feet. Two Californians, Roy Knabenshue and Lincoln Beachey staged a dirigible race, and Arch Hoxey flew a Wright Brothers Flyer. Entranced, Doolittle fixed skyward, and two years later he tried to build a glider by following directions in the June 1909 issue of *Popular Mechanics*. His maiden voyage resulted in Doolittle being dragged along the street with no take-off.[15] During World War I, the aspiring pilot, by then a University of California student, enlisted in the Signal Enlisted Reserve Corps.[16] The end of World War I did not end his career. Doolittle stayed in the army as a flying instructor, accumulating experience, learning under Billy Mitchell and Hap Arnold. Doolittle's penchant for daredevilry marked him to critics as a "damn Chinese ace," because Chinese pilots were held in poor esteem. But the exuberance he showed endeared him to those willing to push boundaries in search of top performance.[17] By his own estimation, Doolittle was "free of spirit and a rebellious fighter pilot at heart."[18]

That rebelliousness prompted him to resign in 1930. He went to work as a test pilot for Shell Oil. The salary was higher, good news for his growing family, and the planes he flew were cutting-edge. He traveled the world, observing the state of aviation in other countries. These were halcyon days of fast and loose flying. The goal was to push planes past their limits, to establish just what the machines were capable of doing. It was dangerous and exhilarating. Doolittle joined the popular sport of air racing at the controls of one of the most dangerous airplanes in Depression-era skies, the notorious Granville Brothers Gee-Bee Model-R Sportster, the "Gee-BeeRacer."[19] Its nickname, the "Flying Silo," captured its aerodynamic capabilities. The stubby fuselage was mere housing for a mighty twin Pratt & Whitney Wasp 750 horsepower engines; wings and tail looked an afterthought.[20] The Gee-Bee Racer was famous for three things: weird looks, speed, and killing pilots. Doolittle considered it "perfect in every respect." He won the prestigious 1932 Thompson Trophy, and telling the *Springfield Union* that the Gee-Bee was "the sweetest ship I've ever flown."[21] In 1938, Doolittle visited Japan en route to Shanghai, strolling through Tokyo with his brother, Joe, lunching at the Imperial Hotel and enjoying Mount Fuji.[22] In 1940, he was elected President of the Institute of Aeronautical Sciences. Then, he left the reserves, going back on active service at the personal request of Ira C. Eaker, executive officer for General Arnold. Appropriately, Arnold made him liaison to aircraft manufacturers, where Doolittle could focus on how to better performance, and oversee the conversion of auto plants to aircraft production.[23] His approval of the Martin B-26 Marauder challenged critics who felt it was not durable enough to fly on one engine in the event of damage. To prove them wrong, Doolittle flew the plane with a dead engine, completed turning maneuvers deemed impossible, and proved the plane's capabilities. As per his recommendation, the Marauder stayed in production.[24]

Admiral King and others brainstormed ideas for hitting Japan during a January 10 meeting. Problems loomed so large that the gathering grew gloomy. China was too far, the Japanese too active. A carrier strike risked the flattops which escaped at Pearl Harbor because their planes had an operational limit of about 300 miles, meaning they would need to be launched close to Japan. It was Captain Francis Low who floated the concept of launching long-range army bombers from a carrier. Observing training at Norfolk, Low noticed bombers flying over the silhouette of a carrier deck painted on the tarmac. The picture was there so that flyers could learn carrier dimensions. But Low's imagination sparked.[25] Captain Donald "Wu" Duncan, King's ranking air officer, calculated the logistics involved, including whether bombers could take off from such a short runway, whether they could fly far enough with the requisite payload, where and how they could land. One point became clear quickly—the planes could not come back to the carriers. They would need to continue on to China or Vladivostok. Duncan fastened on the B-25, since its range, speed, and bomb-carrying capacity were within parameters. Doolittle would run the mission. Arnold briefed him, and training began at Florida's Eglin Field, where the crews learned to take off from a short 500 foot runway. They practiced bombing, night flying, celestial navigation, and carrier protocols. Theirs was a four-week secret cram course.[26] The crews figured that the mission was unusual because of plane alterations. The Norden bomb sight was removed from each Mitchell. "It's inevitable that some of the ships will fall into the enemy's hand," Doolittle explained as crews practiced dropping bombs from merely 1,500 feet.[27] Doolittle's trips to Washington prompted scuttlebutt that neither telephone nor telegraph was sufficiently secure for the conversations he was having.[28] In mid-March, Wu Duncan cabled King with go-ahead: "Tell Jimmy To Get On His Horse."[29] It was then that the "almost mythic ramifications of the mission", as Captain Ted Lawson put it, became plain.[30] *Hornet*, laid down by the Newport News Shipbuilding Company, and launched in December 1940,[31] loaded the B-25s on April Fool's Day at San Francisco.[32]

Discovery by *Nitto Maru* meant daytime instead of nighttime flying. The extra miles added to the mission meant that reaching the Chinese landing zones would be difficult. Task Force 16 turned around, sinking more picket vessels on its way home. The captain of one picket, sighting American carriers and realizing that his perimeter was breached, shot himself in shame, according to a captured Japanese sailor.[33] Halsey's crew listened to Radio Tokyo, relishing the rage Doolittle provoked. "The Japanese lose their heads completely when the unexpected happens," said one Captain. "They can make beautiful plans, but when something goes wrong, they can't improvise. If we get away without interception, and it looks like we shall, this little trip will have been worthwhile."[34] Doolittle's squadron winged towards Japan. Five flights made up the attack; three targeted Tokyo, one aimed at Yokohama and the Yokosuka Navy Base, the final would hit Nagoya, Osaka, or Kobe.[35] Targets included the Nippon Electric Company, Tokyo Gas and Electric Company, Ogura Oil Company, Mitsubishi Aircraft Works, and Kawasaki Aircraft Company.[36]

The planes and crews reflected their leader. "Whiskey Pete," "Ruptured Duck," "Whirling Dervish," and "Hari-Kari-er" were painted on the B-25 noses. All expected heavy flak and enemy interceptors. Bailing out over Japan was so unappealing that Doolittle said he would rather crash his plane into a target of opportunity.[37] But the squadron gained total surprise, and clear blue skies meant perfect bombing weather. Thirteen planes hit Tokyo targets, shooting down five pursuers and evading the rest of the Ki-27s, whose 7.7 millimeter ammunition simply ricocheted off the bombers.[38] Gratifying fire and smoke, observed by Doolittle, showed how ill-prepared Tokyo was for an attack. Hitting other cities caused the news to spread fast.[39]

Only one B-25 failed to crash before reaching the landing zones. One landed near Vladivostok, to be interned by the Soviets. Ten others crashed in Japanese-held China, while four ditched in the East China Sea.[40] Doolittle made contact with KMT forces, who smuggled crewmen to safety. Five men died in their parachutes, others were injured, hidden, and nursed back to health by sympathetic Chinese.[41] The Japanese manhunt lasted for months; maddened searchers executed 250,000 people.[42] The dragnet snared eight Americans, charged with inhuman acts. Their trial lasted 30 minutes; all were found guilty; five were sentenced to life in prison and three—Lieutenants Dean E. Hallmark, William G. Farrow, and Harold A. Spatz, were executed.[43]

The sham trial and bloody hunt showed the rampant Japanese phobia prompted by the raid. In tactical terms, the damage wrought by Doolittle's squadron was light. But Japanese leadership was appalled. The American blow represented a mortifying failure to protect the homeland and Emperor. Foreign Minister Togo, who had differences with the military, hammered at the army's bogus assurances that the capital was inviolable. The fact that bombs fell close to the Imperial Palace itself was humiliating.[44] Doolittle's raid cured "Victory Disease." For months, amazing triumphs neutralized war doubts. "Even people who had been against the war really became sort of for it," said Tokyo resident Paul Koroda. "That lasted for several months, I think, until the April 18, 1942 Tokyo raid by Colonel

Doolittle."[45] Noting the shamefaced silence in the press, Akira Kasahara observed that "Afterwards, not much was mentioned in the newspapers, but everyone was talking about the American planes and knew about the bombing."[46] One editorial in the newspaper *Nichi Nichi* laid the raid off on the inevitability of war. "What was unavoidable did happen," the paper admitted, adding that at all times, "The Imperial Household was absolutely safe." The piece added that someday, there might be a recurrence, even raids that were "more violent and on a larger scale." It ordered the populace to meet whatever happened with "calm and confidence."[47]

Suddenly, debates about where Japan should expect the next victories were displaced by anxiety about what else the Americans might try. The Indian Ocean fleet hustled back, and homeland defense became a concern.[48] The impact upon the Japanese military was dual. First, the shock gave impetus to demolishing the American ability to counterattack. Two weeks after Doolittle's raid, Yamamoto approved Operation MI, to invade the Aleutian Islands, drawing off US resources, and then to seize Midway Island.[49] The second reaction was the desire for vengeance strikes. This proved difficult. A scheme later in the war to launch balloon bombs saw 285 balloons reach the United States out of 6,000 launched.[50]

An equally dramatic effect was felt in the United States, where news of the first blow against Japan caused an effusion of joy. Initially, Washington was uncertain as to the attack's value. Doolittle wired through the American Embassy in Chunking, telling Arnold that the attack went off, but that crews were lost and scattered.[51] Arnold informed the President on April 21, "From the viewpoint of an Air Force operation, the raid was not a success, for no raid is a success in which losses exceed 10 percent and it now appears that probably all the planes were lost."[52] Arnold was with Roosevelt when the news came in that Tokyo had been bombed. They discussed what the news media should be told. "Mr President," said the General, "Do you remember the novel of James Hilton, *Lost Horizon*, telling of that wonderful timeless place known as Shangri-La? It was located in the trackless wastes of Tibet. Why not tell them that's where the planes came from? If you use a fictional place like that, it's a polite way of saying you do not intend to tell the enemy or anybody else where the planes really came from."[53] Roosevelt told Steve Early that, henceforth, Shangri-La was the launching point.

The news broke at home on April 17, when shortwave received Radio Tokyo's announcement. Newspapers, like the *New York Herald-Tribune*, published whatever relevant pictures they could, such as stock photographs of Tokyo, Yokohama, and Kobe, explaining that these were places "where bombs were reported to have fallen."[54] The *Baltimore Sun*, faced with official silence, resorted to printing announcements from Radio Tokyo. These described "schools, hospitals, and cultural establishments" as targets, called the attack "inhuman," and cited "widespread indignation" among Japanese citizens.[55] On April 19, the *Herald-Tribune* verified that Tokyo, Yokohama, Kobe, and Nagoya were hit. The paper mentioned that Japanese radio carried condolence notices.[56]

On April 21 at Roosevelt's Press Conference, he was asked "How about the story about the bombing of Tokyo?" Roosevelt gave the answer with evident pleasure. "Well, the only thing I can think of on that is this: you know occasionally I have a few people in to dinner, and generally, in the middle of dinner some—it isn't an individual, it's just a generic term—some 'sweet young thing' says, 'Mr. President, couldn't you tell us about so-and-so?" Roosevelt had the friendly White House Press Corps in hand. They waited for the rest. "Well, the other night this 'sweet young thing' in the middle of supper said, 'Mr. President, couldn't you tell us about that bombing? Where did those planes start from and go to?' And I said, 'Yes. I think the time has now come to tell you. They came from our new secret base at Shangri-La!' And she believed it!"[57]

The assembled reporters laughed before one pressed for details: "Mr. President, is this the same young lady you talked about—" Here, guffaws filled the room as Roosevelt protested, "This is a generic term. It happens to be a woman."[58] There was good-natured kidding about the mysterious young woman. Chortling, Roosevelt cut in, "Wait a minute, wait a minute—The President Admits—There's the headline!" Finally, a reporter asked about the raid again. "Would you care to go so far as to confirm the truth of the Japanese reports that Tokyo was bombed?" "No," answered the President. "I couldn't even do that. I am depending upon Japanese reports very largely," which started more laughter.[59]

Commentators were happy to speculate. On NBC, Kaltenborn was on the air frequently after the story came to light.[60] He answered a listener's question, "Why Jimmy Doolittle and his outfit were so chivalrous and did not bomb the Imperial Palace in Tokyo?"[61] Kaltenborn put that idea to rest. "It was not chivalry that led them to spare the palace. You can't always be chivalrous in dealing with Japan," he explained. "An enemy that uses peace-talks to conceal a long-planned treacherous attack neither deserves nor understands chivalry."[62] He added that he had stood before the Palace, Tokyo's most recognizable landmark. "Hence, Jimmy Doolittle missed on purpose. He missed it because he and his men were under orders to avoid it," surmised Kaltenborn.[63] He added that the United States did not target residential and civilian areas, because "we prefer to abide by international law because we are fighting for international law."[64]

He said the United States military chose not to anger 70,000,000 "with even greater hatred of everything American if we had attacked the revered home of the ruler they consider a divine descendant of the sun-god. Is it not possible," he asked, "that in their fury the Japanese might violate those remaining shreds of the laws of nations which require humane treatment of prisoners of war?"[65] The problem with Kaltenborn's logic was that Japan had already shredded such conventions. On firmer ground, he pointed out that "The time may come when, as a matter of necessary reprisals, we must violate the law of nations. War is a harsh, realistic business which sometimes requires an eye for an eye."[66] Kaltenborn credited Doolittle's men with chivalry, and hoped that American fighting men could retain such democratic impulses. But it was clear that the commentator envisioned a combat that would obviate such values.

John Gunther commented for Mutual. He said Tokyo radio had no reason to report a raid if one had not occurred. He called it a nice irony that "We hear of a remarkable United States achievement by virtue of the Axis radio." Noting the daylight hours, he emphasized "what a risk our pilots were willing to undergo."[67] Gunther admitted that nobody yet knew the details. China or Philippines were possible launch points, he said. Gunther showed the limits of official governmental silence when he guessed at another possibility. "The prevailing unofficial opinion in Washington is that small naval planes, based on a carrier or carriers, did the job."[68] If this was the case, it meant that the American fleet must have penetrated close to Japan. "No one need ask any more what our fleet is doing. Certainly, the Japanese were caught nicely napping." Only the previous week, Radio Tokyo joked about how Americans could never bomb Tokyo. "The people of Tokyo enjoy these quiet, peaceful, delightful spring days, observing the beautiful cherry blossoms," the Japanese report had said. Well, responded Gunther, "They had something else besides cherry blossoms to observe today."[69] Like Kaltenborn, Gunther was a globe-trotter. He recapitulated his own memories of the Imperial Palace.

> It's quite a building. There's a broad outer moat, iridescent green. Then comes and immense dark grayish wall, built of boulders, miles long, and interrupted by something like 40 gates and towers. Along are twisted pines and stunted trees. Inside are phenomena even more stunted and twisted. Sitting there in that palace is that small, unsmiling bespectacled man, the emperor, who claims descent from the sun god and whose only hobby is marine biology. Something else descended out of the sun at noon today; and marine biology now includes such specimens as an American aircraft carrier.[70]

At CBS, the story fell to Sevareid and Eliot. Sevareid led off on April 18 with the admission that no official confirmation was forthcoming. In fact, he said, if officialdom was the gauge, "There's not a shred of evidence available here to establish the fact that our forces did raid Japan." The navy refused to confirm it, as did the White House. "We have a rather amazing situation here tonight," he reported.

> Half the world is elated that the raid occurred and does not question Japanese statements that the raid occurred and was done by Americans. In Houston, they

dance in the streets, in Chicago, the British Foreign Minister issues a statement of praise and is very happy. But here, in the capital of the country supposedly responsible, the highest ranking officers here have no means of knowing if we have delivered one of the most sensational attacks of the war.[71]

Sevareid's excited tone made it pretty clear that he felt the attack was more than rumor. So, too, did Eliot's assessment. "It may or may not be true," said Eliot, "but one circumstance suggests it would be at least a logical development." Eliot speculated that Japanese air strength was "spread pretty thinly." "They can't concentrate strength everywhere," he went on, figuring that the best air units were off in various theaters, leaving the Japan denuded. "Japan is laying herself open to counteraction in the Pacific," he argued, claiming to see "signs of real United Nations strategy" there at last. "Carriers were probably responsible" for the planes, Eliot figured, "But they could have come from anywhere."[72]

Lowell Thomas chimed in. On April 20, his take was "that the damage was considerable, and that the consternation on the part of the Japanese was even more."[73] Thomas' disarming frankness was on display as he explained to listeners that they would have to be patient and wait for Washington's confirmation. "Whether Tokyo was bombed by American planes we won't know until our high command deems it militarily wise to publish the whole truth."[74] When Roosevelt used his Shangri-La line, Thomas explained it on April 21. His summary included sourcing the line to Hilton's novel and explaining the book's setting: "that beautiful utopia in a mythical Tibet, the paradise inhabited by monks who are forever young."[75] Perhaps it was then that Thomas fixed upon the Himalayan land which he would visit in the 1950s, becoming the seventh Americans ever in Lhasa.[76] It was on April 23 that Thomas added more analysis. "An American bomber landed in the Far Eastern territory of the Soviet Union yesterday," his report began.

It happened last Saturday, and that was the day Japan was bombed. This immediately raised the surmise that the American plane took part in the air attack on Tokyo. And the American pilot says he did. With a disabled American bomber landing in eastern Siberia, where did the Tokyo bombers take off, and where did the others go?[77]

Ultimately, the net effect of the Doolittle Raid was not measurable by the amount of damage it caused in Japanese cities. It mattered for three reasons. It affected the psyche of Japan's military leadership. It blossomed as an American news story, heartening the public. Most importantly, it showed what was to come. It took 26 months before American bombers returned to Japanese skies.[78] Their return marked the commencement of the campaign to pulverize Japan until submission, which reached its 1945 apogee with atomic fire.

Ares AND Calliope: war and letters

The little book was smuggled into the occupied countries. It was copied, mimeographed, printed on hand presses in cellars, and I have seen a copy laboriously hand written on scrap paper and tied together with twine. The Germans did not consider it unrealistic optimism. They made it a capital crime to possess it, and sadly to my knowledge this sentence was carried out a number of times. It seemed that the closer it got to action, the less romantic it seemed.

John Steinbeck, commenting on The Moon is Down[79]

Priests and Freudians will understand. In the throttling Papuan heat, even the rain is hot, even the rain carries the rot smell. Lying in mud or in soaked hammocks the soldiers stew and joke and empty their dead minds. Deprived of love and letters and the sight of woman, the dead mind rots. . . . Nearby, the natives make themselves strong by drinking sweat of warriors, eating fingernails coated with human blood. Priests and Freudians comprehend. And now I learn the missal prayers. I set up mental prayer wheels and spin them with whips of fear. Help me, Freudians and priests: when I say the proud Hail Mary the serpent takes me in the groin . . .

Karl Shapiro, from The Bourgeois Poet[80]

War stimulates poetry, but results vary when war god Ares consorts with poetic muse Calliope. Pocket Books started the paperback revolution in June 1939, so cheap reading material filled students' bookbags, soldiers' knapsacks, and sailors' duffles. The Pocket Book of Verse appeared in June 1940, neglecting the anti-war poetry sparked by World War I's waste of life in favor of Rupert Brooke.[81] Early on, war poetry in the United States reflected generalized unease and mournful disappointment. Intellectual anti-fascism, propelled along by the Spanish Civil war, continued.[82]

In 1939, W.H. Auden found himself, "Uncertain and afraid, in one of the dives/ On Fifty-Second Street," feeling "waves of anger and fear" over the earth.[83] John Ciardi, in "On a Photograph of a German Soldier Dead in Poland," mourned not just "the looted country . . . the raped country," but a nameless *Wehrmacht* infantryman.[84] In "9,19,1939," Robinson Jeffers was nervously impressed after a Hitler speech: "A man of genius . . . cored on a sick child's soul," was Jeffers' verdict, as he watched the "Blood-red moon droop slowly," and compared the day to a bleak ode, "with blood and barbaric symbols/Painful to excess, inhuman as a hawk's cry."[85] War seemed misdirected, a waste.[86] John Berryman wrote "The Moon and the Light and the Men," about Belgium: "On the night of the Belgian surrender the moon rose/Late, a delayed moon, and a violent moon," he began. Alluding to American, British, and French onlookers, he continued, "It was a cold night/ People put on their wraps, the troops were cold/No doubt, despite the calendar, no doubt/Numbers of refugees coughed, and the sight/Or sound of some killed others. A cold night." Henry Adams came to mind.

> History is approaching a horrible end/As Henry Adams said. Adams was right . . . The moon came up late and the night was cold/Many men died—although we know the fate/Of none, nor of anyone, and the war/Goes on, and the heart in the breast of man is cold.[87]

To show that new conditions required a new literary approach, William Everson planted a hoax poem in *Poetry*, under a pseudonym. He did it to mock literary obedience to the class-struggle theme.[88] Everson's point was that 1930s radicalism was inadequate for World War II. His prank matched Cowley's protest against supporting the Soviet invasion of Finland. Many progressive intellectuals reoriented themselves towards a pro-British, pro-American, anti-Nazi stance. Foremost among these Allied-identified intellectuals was Archibald MacLeish. He eviscerated generic anti-war platitudes in "The Irresponsibles," in the May 18, 1940 issue of *The Nation*. MacLeish then published the text as a book. He charged writers refusing to defend the West with being unfit legatees of its culture. American writers were sitting out the actual revolution heralded by the war, he said. The war was not, "The great Revolution of the Masses of which generous men once dreamed," but a "Revolution of negatives, a revolution of despair. . . . Created out of disorder by terror of disorder. A revolution of gangs, a revolution *against*."[89] MacLeish wanted to reclaim patriotism and pro-Western cultural confidence for the world of letters. For many intellectuals, this was hard to accept. Many *Nation* readers protested what they charged was war-mongering. But Frieda Kirchwey supported Britain and MacLeish. MacLeish was a public official, used to being the center of controversy. He had some prominent supporters. In 1940, he thanked James Jesus Angleton for praising, "America Was Promises," which attracted criticism for being jingoistic.[90] William L. Shirer wrote "The Poison Pen," which appeared in the May 1942 *Atlantic Monthly*, reiterating MacLeish's attack on writers hiding behind anti-war stances, not defending Western culture. Shirer also blasted uncooperative press magnates, including Robert McCormick, whom he stung as "ex-isolationists, ex-appeasers . . . now wrapped in the flag" trying to foment intra-Allied discord.[91] There was little to no respectable anti-war position, especially after Pearl Harbor.

One venue had foreign volunteers putting their voices into governmental service. Located on West 57th Street in midtown Manhattan, the Voice of America attracted foreign writers exiled from their homelands. Radio propaganda was a much-studied phenomenon which the United States government was eager to develop. Robert Sherwood helped to jump-start VOA upon joining William Donovan's Office of the Coordinator of Information in the summer of 1941. Operating synchronously with the Office of War Information's Overseas Branch, the VOA was in high gear by 1942.[92] Sherwood recruited a stable full of journalists, intellectuals, and native speakers to develop effective foreign-aimed broadcasts.[93]

Such was the case when Paul Tillich broadcasted into Germany. The Lutheran theologian served as a German Army chaplain in World War I, but had been in exile since 1936. Reconciling demands on people from faith, intellect, and society was a central theme of his work. To Tillich, the "Protestant Principle" meant that the justification of a person by faith should be applied to a wide range of experiences in each person's life. Tillich's exploration of this principle showed in his belief that cultural and political life required a constant process of affirmation and negation.[94] This demand for incessant self-examination put him at irreconcilable odds with National Socialism's demand for worship of the state and leader. He was rescued from the Reich by Reinhold Niebuhr, who invited him to join the faculty at New York's Union Theological Seminary. "Emigration at the age of 47 means that one belongs to two worlds: to the Old as well as to the New into which one has been fully received," Tillich wrote.[95] He missed his home region, with its "real European forests." Tillich struggled with "The American landscape that has been ravaged by technology and . . . from the forbidding wilderness to be found in many nonindustrial regions of America."[96]

Tillich was a part of Nazi Germany's discharge of Europe's brightest and freest intellectuals. Some, like Wanda Landowska, Marc Chagall, Max Ernst, Franz Werfel, Otto Meyerhoff, and Hannah Arendt, made it to the United States through the assistance of Varian Fry's Emergency Rescue Committee, which operated clandestinely in Vichy France.[97] The exiles made up a heterogeneous intellectual group. Some were Jewish, some not; some political, some not; but all were anathematized by the Nazi state. Tillich saw his key war job as working against the anti-Semitic and racial heresies promulgated by Hitler. His main radio theme was the impossibility of living as a Christian under Nazi dictates.

He wrote and delivered 112 broadcasts during the war.[98] Tillich began his declamations in March 1942, with "The Question of the Jewish People." He countered the Axis victory narrative by foretelling inevitable Allied victory. Tillich left little room for doubt that the Tripartite Pact was doomed. Japan's targeting of the United States he termed a grave error. He attributed Germany's inevitable defeat to its treatment of Jews. Hitler's prejudice was erroneous in practical and religious terms. Tillich identified the Jewish people as "the people of history, the people of the prophetic, future-judging spirit." Here, he hit at the central point of Hitler's entire system of thought. "This means," Tillich explained, "that we ourselves sin against the meaning of our own history if we bear guilt against the Jewish people. And the German people have become guilty."[99] Tillich told Germans that, by serving the Reich, they placed themselves, not just beyond the boundaries of polite international company, but beyond God:

> Wake up to the truth of your Christian—your human essence, and grasp what the persecution of the Jewish people means! Not only does it mean human misery, not only shame for all Germans—whether or not they want to feel it— not only a curse that redounds on those who have hurled it. Moreover, it means hostility against the spirit, against human dignity, and against God.[100]

Next came "The Death and Resurrection of Nations" and "Internal and External Freedom," during April; "Justice and Humanity," "Goethe on Reverence," and "The Ninth Anniversary of German Book Burning," during May, and "Guilt and Innocence" in June.[101] Tillich focused on Germany's misdeeds. His Holy Week message, "The Death and Resurrection of Nations," said that Germans should not consider Good Friday's message antiquated. "In Germany, despite many outward victories, people know what the Good Friday of a death of a nation, what the death of a world, means. Today, people in Germany know what death means," he said. "But do they also know what life is? They have learned the first part of the law of death and resurrection, death, but they have lost the second part, resurrection."[102] Only by disobeying Nazi leaders could Germany hope to find its way back to comprehending resurrection—of Christ and itself. Tillich effectively took a meme Nazis considered their own, the German spirit, and shattered it with systematic Christian thought.

In the United States, a counterpart in high-profile religious discussion was Peter Marshall, the Scottish-born Senior Pastor of New York Avenue Presbyterian Church, in Washington.[103] Naturalized in 1938, Marshall became Chaplain of the US Senate after the war.[104] His D.C. pulpit helped Marshall attract attention from government, media, and the public. His personality was attractive and his church a pillar of Washingtonian society. One of his most famous sermons, "Rendezvous in Samarra," came at the Naval Academy on December 7, 1941. All week prior, Marshall struggled with an inner feeling that his scheduled topic was not right. When it came time to preach—news of the attack was not yet public—he went with a message that many in attendance remembered as they fought in later months.[105] Marshall began with James 4:14—"For what is your life? It is even a vapor, that appeareth for a little time, and then vanisheth away."[106] He developed James' warning to "those who make great assumptions for the future with never a thought of God." Beware of making plans, he warned. "I shall go to such and such a city," "I shall be there for a year . . ." "These are our business plans."[107] "The issue of life and death is in the hands of God," the Reverend reminded the Midshipmen. Death was ever-present but rarely acknowledged, whether "a matter of seconds that was all between you and a crash out on the highway the other day," or "a tiny microbe—so small that your naked eye could not see it," which called many a man away from the broken toys of this life."[108] This sermon hit an encouraging note because Marshall freed the congregation from personal responsibility for their fate, reminding them that, in any case, "death is life's greatest, perhaps only certainty." The Christian heart of his message was that those who believed and lived in the right way were delivered from the need to fret about their death, since when Christ said "The meek shall inherit the earth," "He did not mean six feet in it—not a hole in the ground. The grave is not their final heritage. . . . Human personality will survive. It must survive or else God would be the capricious joker in the universe."[109] Marshall passed along the divine promise of life after death, and the argument that Love conquers Death. As he spoke, word began trickling in that Pearl Harbor was under attack.

His Sunday lessons constituted a regular series of faith-based interpretations of war news. "Why Does God Permit War?" came on May 3, 1942. Marshall reminded the congregation that answers in the midst of travails were not always what people expected. War's carnage did not augur meaninglessness. The universe was meaningful. The current war, with so much suffering, he analogized to Cavalry. A person's challenge was not to be driven away from God. "God may be permitting this war to lead us back to Him," Marshall speculated.[110]

While Tillich and Marshall worked to advance relevant religious positions, P.G. Wodehouse kept working on comedy related to war only by its timing. He billeted with a sympathetic noble family at their baronial estate at Degenerhausen, in the Harz Mountains, living "the life of a hermit, plugging away at my writing . . . right out of the world."[111] Ethel kept trying to arrange their exit,[112] while ensuring that Wodehouse gave no more ill-advised talks. This gratified the *Saturday Evening Post,* which wanted to protect its valuable property, *Money in the Bank.*[113] December 27, 1941 brought the final serialized chapter.

The finale resolved every complication. Anne Benedick sees past the oleaginous charms and silky mustache of Lionel Greene. Jeff Miller—disguised as a private eye and smuggling in a pork pie to Lionel, just to be near Anne—is her true love. Lord Uffenham digs up his money in the bank of the pond. American burglars, Soapy and Dolly, try to steal the loot, but wind up with a jar of tobacco by mistake. Still, they have each other. Uffenham returns, "And with a careless gesture he started spraying diamonds all over the desk."[114] It was a happy resolution designed to leave *Saturday Evening Post* readers wanting more of same.

To Americans, Wodehouse's stories were obviously notional; innocent of serious implications. By association, the author was, too. He was simply a genial goof for whom treachery would be ridiculous. His writing perfected chimeras of imagined England just at the time when Americans were finally committed to an alliance with the real thing. American readers liked to believe that Wodehouse's England, that Arcadia where humor was gentle and love conquered all, would transcend the fell clutches of war, just like the real Britain. The valuable *Post* asset was already at work on *Joy in the Morning*, which he promised the magazine would be "*the supremest Jeeves novel of all time.*"[115]

While Wodehouse trafficked in Anglo-American archetypes, other authors defended images of France. One was Pierre Cot, former member of France's Chamber of Deputies, delegate to the League of Nations, and cabinet minister in the Popular Front cabinet.[116] Cot wrote "The Immediate Future of France" for the Spring 1942 issue of *Antioch Review*. He argued against palliating Vichy. Cot contended the French Left, not De Gaulle's movement, best embodied the legacy of the French Revolution.[117] The same journal carried an article by Jacque LeFranc, pen name for a French academician. "French Literature Under the Nazi Heel" cautioned readers against trusting literature coming out of France because Paris was "no longer the center of the country; it is the resting place of German troops."[118]

The American-Scandinavian Review concentrated pro-Nordic sympathies. It delivered briefs for each Scandinavian nation. The journal had semi-official status, with ambassadors writing on behalf of their nations.[119] Some articles stressed strategic matters, such as the proximity of Danish Greenland: "Get into a plane at New Haven, Connecticut, take off and steer true North and without departing from your course you may land—and crash—on the Western point of Greenland."[120] Others recapitulated cultural events, such as the Christmas 1941 dinner given by the New York chapter of the American-Scandinavian Association, featuring Norway's Crown Prince Martha. Association President James Creese praised the devotion of Norwegian-Americans.[121] Spring 1942's issue featured "Norwegians at Dunkerque," telling about contributions by Norwegians to the evacuation flotilla. "Norway's Government-in-Exile," by Alva Myrdahl, assured that Norway's was the strongest and most important government-in-exile, thanks to the democratic spirit of the country, and the activities of the Royal Family.[122] Every issue reminded readers that Denmark and Norway resisted, that Swedish neutrality was sensible, that Finland merited understanding and not censure.

This pro-Scandinavian message was echoed in a Murrow broadcast from London on May 17, Norwegian Independence Day. The correspondent related a speech by King Haakon. "History will judge each of us for what he has suffered," the King said, "and for what he has contributed for the maintenance and honor of our ideals."[123] Murrow then recited an interview with a Norwegian businessman working for the resistance. These covered methods of sneaking to England via the North Sea; the food situation—"Rotten, what there was of it. No potatoes, no bread, if you could call it bread, no butter, and only margarine . . . meat is supposed to be rationed and before Christmas, we got a little of it once a fortnight, but since then, he hadn't seen it." Murrow said that Nazi censorship was total, but that the underground had

> illegal newspapers, just a typewritten page or two, mimeographed or sometimes copied out. . . . We knew that the Germans were on our track, so instead of being caught, we quit and hoped that somebody else would take up the good work. . . . The next day, by noon, four other papers had started.

Quisling had almost no support. Murrow concluded by declaring that resistance was proved by the fact that "they are fighting the Germans and giving them a licking."[124]

A scholarly article interpreting Europe's travails in historical context was Golo Mann's "Europe Under Napoleon: A Synopsis," in the Spring 1942 issue of *The American Scholar*. Mann explored how early nineteenth century Europe handled Napoleonic aggression, failing to produce an effective opposition coalition because leaders and intellectuals failed to grasp that the war was a revolutionary situation.[125] The same issue's main editorial took the world to task for failing to appreciate the irreducible incompatibility of Nazi Germany with civilization, for seeking a *modus vivendi* with the Third Reich. The problem, agreed the editors, was that "few of us can boast minds that are not in greater or less degree cluttered up with ideas that revolutionary totalitarianism has rendered obsolete."[126] Douglas and Elizabeth Rigby's "Dictators and the Gentle Art of Collecting" *The American Scholar* compared Hitler's approach to culture with that of Ashurbanipal, Sulla, and Shih Huang-ti, all book burners and thieves.[127] George Beiswanger heard proto-National Socialism in Richard Wagner, but not in Bach, Handel, Haydn, or Beethoven. Beiswanger analyzed Hitler's contention that "Whoever wants to understand National Socialistic Germany must know Wagner."[128] Jose Ortega y Gasset also tried to relate traditional German culture to current events, in "Kant and the Modern German Mind," running in the Spring issue of *Yale Review*.

> A Latin soul, contemplative by nature, cannot but listen in amazement when Kant instead of asking: How must I think in order that my thought may conform to reality? raises the opposite question: "What must reality be like in order that knowledge, that is, consciousness, that is, "I," may be possible?[129]

What bothered Ortega y Gasset was the way Kant privileged himself against reality. In this inversion, the Spaniard saw "the attitude of the intellect pass from humbleness to menace," and was reminded of ancient barbarians; of "the magnificent hordes of blond barbarians who once fell upon the radiant, gentle land south of the Alps," bringing to mind Plato's characterization of the Scythians, "a new type of men characterized . . . by their impetus."[130] The danger of subordinating reality to idealized aspirations was that "Viking philosophy" must inevitably result, with barbaric consequences. "Wherever we come upon an 'ought to be' in emphatic opposition to 'being' we suspect, hiding behind it, a human—all too human 'I will'."[131]

Flight to Arras, by Antoine de Saint-Exupery, appeared in the United States in February 1942. The book might have been a stirring tale of aerial war, but was instead a meditation on living with pain; a rumination by the pilot who flies back and forth through shells and *Luftwaffe* fighters. It was an American bestseller. Reviews were enthusiastic; book copies piled high on display in store windows.[132] In the *Atlantic*, reviewer Edward Weeks paired it with Churchill's addresses as "the best answer the democracies have found to *Mein Kampf*."[133] Writing in *Yale Review*, Andre Maurois found a hard appeal amidst the rambling prose. Comparing Saint-Exupery to Joseph Conrad, Maurois found that both authors reaffirmed faith in human nature not because "they describe any superhuman heroism. But, on the contrary, because they make heroism very human."[134] Maurois laid out the honesty of his compatriot's reaction to France's plight, as "the only one a Frenchman who has dignity and decency can take."[135] He quoted Saint-Exupery:

> Since I am one with the people of France, I shall never reject my people, whatever they may do. I shall never preach against them in the hearing of others. Whenever it is possible to take their defence, I shall defend them. If they cover me with shame, I shall lock up that shame in my heart and be silent. . . . I shall never bear witness against them. . . . I shall not divorce myself from a defeat which surely will often humiliate me. I am a part of France and France is a part of me.[136]

"Division breeds defeat," wrote Maurois. "Unity breeds victory."[137] Maurois hoped the book would be "a seed that will germinate in many an American mind and produce both admiration for the writer and respect for his country."[138]

One popular book provided literary support for the Naval Idea. Its author was already working at the military tasks which would enable him to write the finest American history of the war. *Admiral of the Ocean Sea: A Life of Christopher Columbus* was Samuel Eliot Morison's 1942 book. Morison was author of numerous respected tomes, including *The Growth of the American Republic*, the influential history text published in 1930, co-written with Henry Steele Commager.[139] *Admiral of the Ocean Sea* won the 1943 Pulitzer Prize for History. An advertisement by Little, Brown & Co. said,

> After four and a half centuries, the first time that the seaman-explorer has had a seaman-historian as a biographer. Mr. Morison not only sifted all the records; he sailed the same course Columbus sailed, sharing the same winds, the same weather, the same navigational problems.[140]

Morison's nautical skills infused the biography with salt air. No landlubber could have written his account of the famous October morning, 1492:

> Sun set under a clear horizon about 5:30, every man in the fleet watching for a silhouette of land against its red disk, but no land was there. . . . Anyone who has come onto the land under sail at night from an uncertain position knows how tense the atmosphere aboard ship can be. And this night of October 11–12 was one big with destiny for the human race, the most momentous ever experienced aboard any ship in any sea. . . . An hour before moon rise, at 10 p.m., it came. Columbus, standing on the sterncastle, thought he saw a light . . . "like a little wax candle rising and falling."[141]

Admiral of the Ocean Sea gave Morison a chance to write the vivid history he favored. It also was his last "civilian book." He was already Lieutenant Commander in the US Naval Reserve. Morison helped create the navy historical documentation program, which made possible his 15-volume *History of United States Naval Operations in World War II*.[142]

As war propelled Morison's career, it terminated a colleague's life. Stefan Zweig was an exiled Austrian-Jewish author, who epitomized the cosmopolitan Viennese world Hitler despised. Zweig's writing ranged from histories to plays, libretti to essays. He was a noted translator of French poetry. Intellectual history also set him apart, exposing him to American subjects. In *Mental Healers*, Zweig had analyzed Mary Baker Eddy alongside Sigmund Freud and Franz Mesmer. But it was his 1938 *Conqueror of the Seas: The Story of Magellan*, which gave American readers a nautical subject they appreciated. In better times, the Magellan story might have ushered in new popularity for an author banished from his continental home. Zweig conceived of the book en route to Brazilian exile, recounting its genesis.

> The sky was so unfailingly blue, and the blue waters were so unfailingly smooth," he wrote. "In my mood of exasperation the hours seemed to pass too slowly. I yearned for arrival in port. . . . Compare your present experiences with those of the valiant navigators who were the first to cross this ocean. . . . Are you not ashamed of yourself when you think of them? Try to picture how they set forth, on ships little larger than fishing-smacks, to explore the unknown, to sail they knew not whither. . .[143]

Zweig could not weather the storm of war. On February 25, 1942, with the Rio de Janeiro Conference in the news, he and his wife committed suicide at their house in Petropolis, north of Rio.[144]

The 1942 book which sparked the fiercest reaction was John Steinbeck's *The Moon is Down*. A short novel suited for stage adaptation, *The Moon is Down* described a small Norwegian town under German occupation. It was a product of Steinbeck's war work. Approached by Bill Donovan and Sherwood in October 1941, Steinbeck joined the literary migration into federal service.[145] At the Office of War Information, Donovan and Steinbeck discussed how literature might aid resistance movements in Europe.[146] At the OWI, Steinbeck met "escapees from occupied nations."[147] He listened to stories of "trying to help the underground organizations which kept a steady and heroic resistance to the occupying Germans," and he became fascinated with their experiences.[148] This drove him to explore, "The experiences of the victim nations, while they differed in some degree with national psychologies, had many things in common," Steinbeck recalled.

At the time of invasion there had been confusion; in some of the nations there were secret Nazi parties, there were spies and turncoats. Quisling has left his name as a synonym for traitor. Then there were collaborators, some moved by fear and others simply for advancement and profit. Finally, there were the restrictive measures of the Germans, their harsh demands and savage punishments.[149]

The Moon is Down was a spare volume with little action. The novel put forth the idea that together, the people could be strong; that individual courage needed collective support. Few readers knew that, after *The Moon is Down*, Steinbeck started on *Bombs Away*, a report for the Air Corps Training Program limning a "typical bomber training crew" without describing individuals at all. *Bombs Away*—which Steinbeck researched by following a crew through training in Texas—emphasized the teamwork that must become second nature to any successful bomber crew. There was no room for individualized action on board a bomber.[150]

"I'm going to write a book for the Air Corps on bombers and bomber crews," he explained in a letter. "I am going from one training camp to another and I'm going to live with the kids and find out what the air corps is about and then do a book with pictures in it."[151] Part of his "training" was traveling to Washington to meet Hap Arnold and other top brass. Their alcohol consumption impressed him. To his second wife, Gwyn, a shocked Steinbeck commented, "We drink, but not like that!"[152] The job entailed flying over the flat Texas landscape while the crews sharpened their skills. "I'm hot and tired and sunburned and lonesome," he complained in May 1942.[153] Roosevelt ordered Steinbeck to convert the report into a film: "Now, John, you are going to do what I want you to do—what I want you to do John." To son Oliver, Steinbeck recalled his response. "Then I found myself saying 'Yes, Mr. President, I am.'"[154] A piece of military propaganda, *Bombs Away* provided a glimpse into Steinbeck's attitude while writing *The Moon is Down*.

The novel was basic. The unnamed victim country is a snowy, mountainous nation with fjords and laconic inhabitants. The villainous attacker is a dictatorship run by "The Leader." Action centers on a small town, where occupier Colonel Lanser must simultaneously operate the local coal mine and break any resistance. A Quisling-equivalent, storekeeper George Corell, informs on the townspeople. Lanser commandeers the home of Mayor Orden as HQ. Sabotage is abetted by the British, who drop tiny dynamite charges for the locals to use. Lanser recognizes the futility of his orders, but obeys nevertheless. He takes Mayor Orden hostage along with Dr. Winter. Orden's wife, still professing democratic faith, protests: "But they can't arrest the mayor," she says to Orden. "No," he smiled, "They can't arrest the Mayor. The Mayor is an idea conceived by free men. It will escape arrest."[155] When Orden hears a distant explosion and realizes that a saboteur has detonated a bomb, he smiles with satisfaction on the way to execution. A refrain, "The flies have conquered the flypaper," repeats throughout the final scene. Orden's last soliloquy to Lanser is an address.

> You see sir, nothing can change it. You will be destroyed and driven out. . . .
> The people don't like to be conquered, sir, and so they will not be. Free men
> cannot start a war, but once it is started, they can fight on in defeat. Herd men,
> followers of a leader, cannot do that, and so it is always the herd men who win
> battles and the free men who win wars. You will find that is so, sir.[156]

Lanser does not disagree, although he responds that his orders are clear, making plain his own awareness that the war his nation started is immoral and hopeless.[157]

The Moon is Down runs at a chilly temperature, its logic blunt like the Socratic references Orden makes before being shot. Critics sprang, motivated by the novel's outstanding defect: it was not *The Grapes of Wrath, Part Two.* Some felt Steinbeck was too fatalistic.[158] This could mean that his social conscience was waning, especially since there was no class struggle in the novel.[159] Other critics found the device of delivering large insights by focusing on a small town contrived.[160] More than one reviewer stressed the slenderness of the volume, prompting Steinbeck to crack bitterly, "What should I write this time, a thin book or a thick one?"[161]

Leader of the critical assault was humorist James Thurber, who tackled *The Moon is Down* in the March 16 issue of *The New Republic,* with "What Price Conquest?"[162]

> There is, I regret to say, a kind of lamplight playing over the mood and style,
> the events and figures, of Mr. Steinbeck's new short novel. . . . I suspect that if a
> writer conceives of a war story in terms of a title like "The Moon is Down," he is
> likely to get himself into soft and dreamy trouble. Maybe a title like "Guts in the
> Mud" would have produced a more convincing reality. Anyway, this little book
> needs more guts and less moon.[163]

Thurber charged that Steinbeck "lovingly and gently brooded" upon the point that "there are no machines and no armies mighty enough to conquer the people" one too many times, citing Orden's speech as an example.[164] Also galling Thurber was the icy demeanor of the invaders. Thurber found primness inapposite for describing the Nazi occupiers. He wondered what the people of Poland would make of the scene in which British planes drop parachutes with chocolate and dynamite, stating that Steinbeck's gelid tale gave him the shivers.[165]

These were the weeks when *The New Republic* played up Stafford Cripps and insisted on a prompt second front to relieve the Red Army. Any suggestion that reactions to the war should be deliberate and rational had no place in the magazine. Thurber's review was of a piece with the editorial climate. Yet attacking *The Moon is Down* meant taking on the author who led the way in refracting Great Depression populism. Controversy was inevitable. Reaction came in the March 23 issue. Marshall Best, editor-in-chief at Viking, protested the review. He said Thurber misread the novel and was unfair to Steinbeck. Best called the review "A slap in the face for all the decent people who have been moved by the book's shining sincerity."[166] Thurber "apologized" for "the slap" by saying he meant to deliver a punch, but "didn't realize my hand was open." He stuck by his claims.[167]

Arguments in the Letters column prompted *The New Republic* to run an editorial, "Mr. Steinbeck, Friends and Foes," on March 30. Without disavowing Thurber, the editors explained that different readers read *The Moon is Down* differently. Their verdict was that "the book falls below the level of Steinbeck's best work." However, the editorial admitted that "many persons have read it and will read it, not as literature but as a comfort in an hour of desperate anxiety for the present and grim fear for the future." They suggested that, taken that way, the novel might have a palliative role for "American readers who, in their deep depression, are only too eager to be told that in the long run guns are not effective against the proud, inflexible love of liberty." But they objected to the "Hamlet-like Nazis" of Steinbeck's portrayal, and claimed that the novel's dynamite packets were ridiculous.[168]

An April 6 letter from Upton Sinclair sought to mediate between Thurber and Steinbeck. Sinclair's initial reaction upon reading *The Moon is Down* was to cable Viking: "Glory hallelujah, what a story! Sacrifice a cock for Steinbeck."[169] However, he admitted, Thurber's put-down caused him to reevaluate. Sinclair sought to placate both by defending Steinbeck's intention to write a dreamy novel: "He didn't want to write a realistic story about the invasion of Norway," explained the author of *The Jungle*. "Perhaps he has never been to Norway and doesn't know it well enough. . . . He tried to make his people like all people and his village like all villages."[170] Thurber needed to let Steinbeck be Steinbeck. Also, Sinclair suggested, Thurber "should write a story telling what he will do when the Nazis get *him!*"[171] The spat spilled into other publications, including *The Nation* and *Antioch Review*. In the latter, Lincoln R. Gibbs, Antioch College English professor, wrote "John Steinbeck, Moralist," defending Steinbeck. Gibbs saw in the arc of the novelist's previous work much prelude to *The Moon is Down*. The author was not evading political awareness, said the critic, but had "the heart of a rebel who hates cant and injustice."[172]

On May 18, *The New Republic* revisited the issue. "A few weeks ago we predicted that the controversy over John Steinbeck's new novel would be prolonged and bitter, but we didn't realize at the time that it was going to develop into all-out warfare on the literary front." So began "The Moon is Halfway Down," a sarcastic retrospective. The article credited Clifton Fadiman with "assuming command of the Blue, or anti-Steinbeck forces," and John Chamberlain with enlisting in "the Green army, so called by its opponent because it is defending Steinbeck's moon, which they insist is really green cheese."[173] Editors claimed amazement over a Lewis Gannett column in the *Herald-Tribune* charging them with "a totalitarian crusade." Among Gannett's charges were that *The New Republic* promulgated World War I-style anti-German bigotry, the prejudice that, "The whole German nation, even down to ten-year-old children, must be annihilated forever . . . a racialist philosophy in reverse . . . artistic totalitarianism."[174]

The New Republic laughed off Gannett's charges, but made a climb-down from their previous position. The proud weekly even claimed to have been "neutral" regarding *The Moon is Down*. They still sided with Thurber on the book's artistic demerits, stating that Gannett and others were overreacting.[175] The controversy dried up after that, but the novel had two more iterations. The first was as a 1943 film, with Cedric Hardwicke as Colonel Lanser, Henry Travers as Mayor Orden, and Lee J. Cobb Orden's friend, Dr. Winter. The first review in *The New York Times* recounted "the noisy and passionate controversy aroused by *The Moon is Down*," but assured moviegoers that "such traces of defeatism as were apparent in the book" were wrung out of the film.[176] The second elaboration came because Winston Churchill read the novel in May 1942. Impressed, he recommended it to Lord Selborne, Minister of Economic Warfare, with the observation that "it stresses, I think quite rightly, the importance of providing the conquered nations with simple weapons such as sticks of dynamite which could be easily concealed and are easy in operation."[177] The upshot was a secret plan, initially "The Moon Project," later renamed "Operation Braddock." The plan envisioned parachuting small attack packs to resistance fighters, maturing into a scheme whereby incendiary packets were dropped behind German lines for use by saboteurs. The packets contained flammable gel and a small timing fuse. The tiny device burst into flames 30 minutes after ignition. In what was an unusual tribute to Steinbeck's novel, Braddock II went into effect in September 1944.[178] Two decades later, the novelist received another indirect tribute when he received a battered manuscript published secretly by the Danish underground in 1942. The novel brought them great relief during the war's bleakest phase, said the senders. Steinbeck felt justified.

The little book was smuggled into the occupied countries. It was copied, mimeographed, printed on hand-presses in cellars, and . . . laboriously hand-written on scrap paper and tied together with twine. The Germans did not consider it unrealistic optimism. The made it a capital crime to possess it, and sadly . . . this sentence was carried out a number of times. It seemed that the closer it got to action, the less romantic it seemed.[179]

The revulsion against war-related romanticism of 1942 was strictly a highbrow reaction. Popular reactions to sentimental war writing were favorable. The paramount case was "High Flight," the poem by John Gillespie Magee, Jr. Magee was shot down and killed December 11, 1941, flying with the Royal Canadian Air Force. Both MacLeish and his predecessor as Library of Congress Poetry Consultant, Joseph Auslander, named the poem "classic," including it in "Poems of Faith and Freedom" an exhibit in February 1942.[180] The two did not agree on much (MacLeish once likened Auslander to "a masturbating monkey"),[181] so their mutual choice approval of the sonnet drew notice.

Magee was a China-born son of missionaries, his father American and his mother English. He left Yale in 1939, volunteering for the RCAF in September 1940.[182] "High Flight" became aviation's anthem. "Oh I have slipped the surly bonds of earth/And danced the skies on laughter-silvered wings," the young flier exulted. "Sunward I've climbed and joined the tumbling mirth/Of sun-split clouds—and done a hundred things/You have not dreamed of. . ."[183]

In the Library of Congress exhibit, Magee's poem ran alongside Rupert Brooke's "The Soldier," and John McCrae's "In Flanders Fields." Accompanying text explained that Magee's parents, living in Washington, gave permission for "High Flight" to be displayed at air-training posts across the British Empire. The text added that the young poet, a graduate of Avon Old Farms School who spent three years at England's Rugby School, freely chose the RCAF and martyrdom over Yale. Readers contemplating the end of his sonnet could believe it: "I've topped the wind-swept heights with easy grace/Where never lark, or even eagle flew;/And while with silent, lifting mind I've trod/The high untrespassed sanctity of space,/Put out my hand and touched the hand of God."[184] The fact that the young poet died made him immune to charges of romanticizing war.

Poetry in 1942 ran close to the beating heart of American culture, and verse was full of corpuscular vigor. Numerous poets staked their claim as emergent voices of the war. But of all these, one not yet well-known and already on duty in the South Pacific made the strongest claim. This was Karl Shapiro. Born in Baltimore in 1913, he graduated from City College, a prestigious public high school. He studied English poetry. "Living an imaginary English life meant living a phony life of the mind, for I was not English in any sense of the word," he recalled later.[185] "Nobody in the Oxford Book of English Verse was named Shapiro. In fact, nobody was named

Shapiro except tailors and junk dealers."[186] Shapiro flirted with changing his name, considering Carl Camden, after a Baltimore railroad station, but contented himself with altering his first name from "Carl" to "Karl:"[187]

> Poets are name-proud craftsmen; Greeks and Jews,/Chinese and Arabs out of time have penned/The symbols of their authorship against /Oblivion. One significant conceit/Of Tudor rime was that its pages were/Imperishable, and we choose to think our own/At least as durable.[188]

In Baltimore, he lived with the heritage of Edgar Allen Poe, for whom he developed sardonic appreciation.[189] More modernly, he confronted the legacy of Mencken, whom he termed "a kind of Nietzschean of the turn-of-the-century variety" who baited the "booboisie" and "retained also a vestigial Germanism, even with a flavor of militarism, though Mencken was no Junker."[190] Shapiro saw himself as Jewish and Southern. Here were the roots of a concept he explored—the Divided Self, a "sad duality" or "imperfect half."[191] In 1932, he attended the University of Virginia, loathing it and discerning the drive "to hurt the Negro and avoid the Jew."[192] Next, he won a scholarship at Johns Hopkins, thanks to the 1935 publication of his first book of poems. He studied to be a librarian at the city's Enoch Pratt Free Library. The timing was serendipitous. During the 1930s, practical visionary Joseph Wheeler led the Pratt. It was under his leadership that the library flourished as a cultural depot. Wheeler brought over from England six famous full-length oil portraits of each Lord Baltimore. Hanging in public view, these became local favorites. Under the countenances of these Cavaliers, Shapiro triangulated the English–Southern–Jewish combination that was his cultural matrix.[193] He was drafted into the army in March 1941.[194] He headed to the South Pacific in 1942, and the Medical Corps in New Guinea. He wrote "The Twins" on a transport sailing westward, analyzing the fraternal bond connecting twin brother soldiers: "Each is the other's soul and hears too much/The heartbeat of the other; each apprehends/The sad duality and the imperfect half . . . For they go emptily from face to face/Keeping the instinctive partnership of birth."[195]

Shapiro found New Guinea enormous and remote. The island makes a parallelogram, distended at the acute corners, running southeast to northwest, divided by the jagged Owen Stanley Mountains. The Papua region was Australian territory.[196] They would fight for it desperately.[197] Japanese military reports made the strategic value apparent:

> These possessions . . . form a natural barrier dividing the Pacific Ocean from north to south. . . . Possession of this territory would make it easy to obtain command of the air and sea in the Southwest Pacific and to acquire "stepping-stone" bases for operations against Australia.[198]

Japan wanted to render Australia's east coast dangerous all the way to Sydney, forcing ships clear down to the Great Australian Bight. Allied leaders, meanwhile, needed to protect Australia's northern coast.

In mid-1942, Japan controlled northern New Guinea. General Tomitaro Horii's men were supposed to traverse through heavy bush, cross the overgrown mountains by Kokoda Trail, and attack the capital, Port Moresby. Australians fought them in the jungly passes, while American landings threatened Horii's rear.[199] Into this campaign came the poet from Baltimore. It formed Shapiro's war world, which he translated with much care. He wrote about the battlefront, about wounded men, about missing home.

Full Moon: New Guinea," gave readers his experience. "These nights we fear the aspects of the moon,/Sleep lightly in the radiance falling clear/On palms and ferns and hills and us; for soon/The small burr of the bombers in our ear/Tickles our rest; we rise as from a nap/And take our helmets absently and meet,/Prepared for any spectacle or mishap,/At trenches fresh and narrow at our feet.[200]

Few poetry fans failed to appreciate the tropical exoticism, existential threat, intense fear, and dutiful bravery so omnipresent in 1942.

Look up, look up, and wait and breathe. These nights/We fear Orion and the Cross. The crowd/Of deadly insects caught in our long lights/Glitter and seek to burrow in a cloud/Soft-mined with high-explosive. Breathe and wait./The bombs are falling darkly for our fate.[201]

Nor could many readers have missed the physical agony and psychic pain which the wounded soldier feels and his medic feel in "The Leg."

Among the iodoform, in twilight sleep,/*What have I lost?* he first inquires,/Peers in the middle distance where a pain,/Ghost of a nurse, hastily moves . . . One day beside some flowers near his nose/He will be thinking *When will I look at it?*/And pain, still in the middle distance, will reply,/*At what?* And he will know it's gone,/O, where! And begin to tremble and cry./He will begin to cry as a child cries/Whose puppy is mangled under a screaming wheel.[202]

Fascinated by Catholicism's pitch and rhythm, the Jewish poet's verses delve into Christian sentimentality which wartime readers found comforting.[203] Shapiro described church services in the field, in "Sunday: New Guinea." "The bugle sounds the measured call to prayers,/The band starts bravely with a clarion hymn," it begins. But soon, the power of prayer loosens the collective feelings so barely suppressed among the congregation of citizen-soldiers.

And over the hill the guns bang like a door/And planes repeat their mission in the heights./The jungle outmaneuvers creeping war/And crawls within the circle of our sacred rites./I long for our dishevelled Sundays home,/Breakfast, the comics, news of latest crimes,/Talk without reference, and palindromes,/Sleep and the Philharmonic and the ponderous *Times*./I long for lounging in the afternoons/Of clean intelligent warmth, my brother's mind,/Books and thin plates and flowers and shining spoons,/And your love's presence, snowy, beautiful, and kind.[204]

Shapiro kept writing his poetry during and after the 1942 campaign. Allen Tate was particularly effusive in praising the works. The dean of Southern Fugitive poets singled out Shapiro's "special savagery of attack," using a quote from Hart Crane, "We have to slap all humanity in the face!"[205] Judges still living lives of "thin plates and flowers and silver spoons" voted *Person, Place, and Thing* the 1945 Pulitzer Prize. Upon his return to civilian life, Shapiro took up office in Washington, D.C., as the Library of Congress' Poetry Consultant, sitting in the same chair filled earlier by Auslander and MacLeish.

In a more popular vein, Marion Hargrove, Jr., explored similar literary ground. It was in May 1942 that *See Here, Private Hargrove*, Hargrove's send-up of a new soldier's transition to military life, was published by Henry Holt. Screenwriter and playwright Maxwell Anderson wrote the Introduction. Comprising chapters published previously in the *Charlotte News*, the novel was an immediate sensation. It sold out the first printing by July, running through 13 printings in 1942.[206] Hargrove was a sunny young American swept up into the citizen's army of the country he loved. His book afforded readers apolitical chuckles as they nodded in recognition over army training experiences. Anderson's Foreword set up the conceit that the stories were actual documents collected at Fort Bragg. The book's theme was the trials and triumphs of Hargrove, who frustrates his superiors while learning army dos-and-don'ts. The tone is embodied at the book's early observation about army lessons: "Most of what you are taught will impress you as utterly useless nonsense, but you'll learn it."[207] It describes the inevitable fate of "Kitchen Patrol."

> You'll be initiated into the mysteries of the kitchen police, probably before you've been in the Army for a week. Possibly two days later, you'll be sent on a ration detail to handle huge bags of groceries. You'll haul coal and trash and ashes. . . . You'll stoke fires, you'll mop floors, and you'll put a high polish on the windows. You'll wonder if you've been yanked out of civil life for This.[208]

Readers follow Hargrove through induction, monitor his progress as he learns to handle sergeants and other hazards at the base, suffers during a quarantine that restricts leave, and meets fellow soldiers from across the country. They could see how he and the army gradually shape each other, as he comes to grips with his duty. "Private Hargrove," I said to myself,

> You have been doing quite too much gallivanting lately. There have been too many movies, too many bull sessions, too many hours spent at the Service Club and too much time spent flirting with that cute little waitress at the delicatessen in Fayetteville. Tonight, Private Hargrove, you will take this interesting and improving book, read it until Lights Out, and go to bed promptly at nine o'clock.[209]

Only in the last chapter does the tale become a war story. Pearl Harbor is described as "stunning news. . . . It was startling and dreadful."[210] A major dispels rumors. "The main thing," says the officer, whom the soldiers suddenly heed respectfully,

> that has us worrying this afternoon is the very same thing we're being trained to protect. It's what they call the American Way—and they spell it with capitals. I have my own ideas about the American Way. I think the American Way is shown in you boys whose parents paid school taxes so that you could know what it was to cut hooky. It's shown in the men who pay two dollars to see a wrestling match, not to watch the wrestlers, but to boo the referee. It's the good old go-to-hell American spirit and you can't find it anywhere but here.[211]

Hargrove's novel showed readers how the go-to-hell American spirit could be adapted during war, accepting the provisional shape of army rules and regulations without losing all irreverence. For Hargrove, 1942s publishing success meant service on the editorial staff of *Yank*, the Army weekly. The movie version came out in 1944, starring Robert Walker, Donna Reed, and Keenan Wynne. The war added to the author's trove of material. Readers applauded when Private Hargrove earned promotion to Corporal. *What's Next, Corporal Hargrove?*, appeared in 1945.[212]

7 MAY 1942

Bataan and Corregidor—the "Indomitable Will To Win" transfigures defeat

THE DUTY AND THE NECESSITY OF RESISTING JAPANESE
AGGRESSION TO THE LAST TRANSCENDS IN IMPORTANCE ANY
OTHER OBLIGATION NOW FACING US IN THE PHILIPPINES . . . IT IS
MANDATORY THAT THERE BE ESTABLISHED ONCE AND FOR ALL
IN THE MINDS OF ALL PEOPLES COMPLETE EVIDENCE THAT THE
AMERICAN DETERMINATION AND INDOMITABLE WILL TO WIN
CARRIES ON DOWN TO THE LAST UNIT.

Franklin D. Roosevelt to Douglas MacArthur,
February 10, 1942[1]

We're the battling bastards of Bataan:
No mama, no papa, no Uncle Sam,
No aunts, no uncles, no nephews, no nieces,
No rifles, no planes, or artillery pieces,
And nobody gives a damn.

Soldier on Bataan, Spring 1942[2]

General Wainwright is a right guy and we are willing to go on for him, but shells were dropping all night, faster than hell. Damage terrific. Too much for guys to take. Enemy heavy cross-shelling and bombing. They have got us all around and from the skies . . . Corregidor used to be a nice place, but it's haunted now. Withstood a terrific pounding. . . . The jig is up. Everyone is bawling like a baby. They are piling dead and wounded in our tunnel. . . . I know how a mouse feels. Caught in a trap waiting for guys to come along and finish it up. Canned pineapple. Opening it up with Signal Corps knife . . ."

Corporal Irving Strobing, Radio Operator on Corregidor,
May 6, 1942[3]

Corregidor needs no comment from me. It has sounded its own story at the mouth of its guns. It has scrolled its own epitaph on enemy tablets. But through the bloody haze of its last reverberating shots, I shall always see a vision of grim, gaunt, ghastly men, still unafraid.

Douglas MacArthur, May 6, 1942[4]

Bataan's peninsula runs north to south, forming the western side of Manila Bay. Heavily forested, its ridges and valleys support defense. The sea on both sides protects defenders' flanks, while rugged terrain slows attackers. Corregidor was the stopper in the bottle, or, as one PT boat officer put it, "a hard little pill between two lips."[5] "The Rock" is the island off Bataan's southern tip, commanding the Bay. The Spanish made Corregidor a fortress which American servicemen improved. Artillery pieces atop ancient walls loomed impassively over ships steaming in and out of Cavite.[6] When MacArthur left Manila, it was to make a stand on Bataan; to wage a war of attrition until reinforcements arrived.

The Bataan campaign lasted from late December 1941 until the surrender of Corregidor on May 6, 1942. The Bataan Defense Force was established by the US Army Forces in the Far East on December 24, 1941; its mission peninsular defense.[7] Psychologically and strategically, the campaign ranked with the gravest US Army defeats, alongside Fredericksburg (1862), Little Big Horn (1876), Bladensburg (1814), or Brandywine (1777). There were reasons to rank Bataan/Corregidor as the army's worst loss ever. Americans comprehended the catastrophe's scale. Yet Bataan did not usher in defeatism. Instead, it prompted desires for revenge.

On January 5, 1942, Filipino fate hung on a steel strand—the Layac Bridge, leading into Bataan from Luzon. Eight thousand American and Filipino fighters on the north side covered 80,000 already across. At a signal from Major General Jonathan Wainwright, the rearguard 21st Philippine Army Division, under Brigadier General Mateo Capinpin, disengaged and rushed across the bridge. Wainwright delivered the order and the bridge blew up. Bataan was temporarily safe, shielded from aerial bombardment by tropical foliage. People there could breathe easier, but they were also trapped.[8]

Withdrawing to Bataan was part of War Plan Orange. USAFFE put Orange into effect on December 23, 1941.[9] Unfortunately, fighting a defensive campaign until relief arrived fell victim to the rapid Japanese advances and intense emphasis on the Germany-first policy. The navy and army did not always see eye to eye, but

General Marshall agreed that saving the Philippines was the wrong move.[10] Admiral King did not want to cede Pacific command to MacArthur.[11] Washington decided that Bataan would buy time, but the Philippines must be sacrificed. MacArthur disagreed vehemently.[12] "IF THE WESTERN PACIFIC IS TO BE SAVED IT WILL HAVE TO BE SAVED HERE AND NOW," he cabled to General Marshall.[13] But MacArthur's stance was at odds with the direction of American strategic thinking. For years, War Plan Orange had grown vaguer about relieving the Philippines.[14] MacArthur lashed the Orange plan as "defeatist," and "stereotyped." He invoked only at it the last minute, when Manila was beyond saving.[15] The concomitant effort to stock the depots and storerooms at Bataan needed more time.[16] Referring to Bataan as he spoke to Churchill and Roosevelt, Stimson was unsparing. "There are times when men have to die," said the Secretary.[17]

What MacArthur accomplished in getting his troops to the peninsula was a feat of sterling generalship. He kept a disparate force intact en route to better positions. Assisted by Wainwright, he had to move his units backward, leaving one as a covering force while shifting others back, setting up temporary defensive lines, then disengaging the rear guard. Over and over again, he kept the pieces separate enough to operate but united enough not to shatter, without allowing Homma to trap his men.[18] Elements of the plan were drawn up earlier by a Major with expertise in logistics and maneuvering large units, Dwight Eisenhower.[19] Eisenhower's methodical personality chafed under MacArthur's flash, so the Major obtained a transfer to Washington and promotion in 1939.[20] Colonel Eisenhower emerged there as a favorite of MacArthur's old nemesis, Drew Pearson. Eisenhower credited his next promotion to Brigadier General to this positive press.[21] Marshall asked him about relieving Bataan. Eisenhower was emphatic.

> It will be a long time before major reinforcements can go to the Philippines, longer than the garrison can hold out with any driblet assistance, if the enemy commits major forces to their reduction. Our base must be in Australia, and we must start at once to expand it and to secure our communications to it.[22]

Filipino-American defenders set up their initial defense line 10 miles below the Layac Bridge, at a banana plantation called Abucay. The Abucay Line went from the Bay, over volcanic mountains, to the South China Sea.[23] Homma, assuming that the defenders were on the verge of collapse, diverted crack troops to Java, replacing them with soldiers trained for occupation duty.[24] A forward attack ran into trouble immediately. Despite *Banzai* charges, the Japanese flailed against the Abucay Line for days. Homma realized with a jolt that his troops faced a well-organized defense which required a major offensive commitment.[25] Japanese plans were further disrupted by American PT boat crews, who ran their nimble craft against Japanese supply boats. Their exploits earned the PT boats and their Commander Lieutenant

John Bulkeley, immediate renown. *They Were Expendable* was rushed into print in 1942. Bulkeley's boats harassed Japanese movements, made nighttime submarine rendezvous to resupply the army, and removed Filipino gold reserves.

It was during a February PT Boat mission that first word of Bataan's fate seeped into the sealed off Bataan: "The subs had news. They said America was building a big Australian base—that supplies were rolling down there."[26] Contrasted with the episodic supply efforts along the peninsula, this ran counter to assumptions that a major influx was on the way. MacArthur blamed those false rumors on misunderstood radio messages, which were "published to the troops and aroused great enthusiasm."[27] The reality had a depressing effect. MacArthur believed that Roosevelt and Marshall led him on with false assurances. To Manuel Quezon, the American President's assurance that "every vessel available is bearing . . . the strength that will eventually crush the enemy," coupled with the pledge that the freedom of the people of the Philippines would be retained, meant that Bataan was not to be abandoned.[28] MacArthur, in hearing Marshall's words that streams of bombers were underway, that "our strength is being concentrated and it should exert a decisive effect on Japanese shipping and force a withdrawal northward," thought the same thing.[29] But neither the Filipino leader nor his American general paid enough attention to the watery vagueness of those messages.

The terrain was nigh impassable, described by one soldier:

> Cliffs are unscalable. Rivers are treacherous. Behind huge *nara* (mahogany) trees, eucalyptus trees, ipils, and tortured banyans, almost impenetrable screens are formed by tropical vines, creepers, and bamboo. Beneath these lie sharp coral outcroppings, fibrous undergrowth, and alang grass inhabited by pythons.[30]

It rained constantly. But, while they fell back from Abucay in late January, resistance continued. Information came from Carlos Romulo's radio Voice of Freedom. "You know these men," Romulo said in a broadcast aimed at occupied Manila.

> They are your sons, fathers, husbands, or sweethearts—all were your blood brothers in devotion and faith—they belong to you who are their kin and friends. But they have now become heroes of freedom and democracy—they belong to the entire world.[31]

Troops could also tune in American programs, including "Freedom for the Philippines," aired nightly from KGEI, in San Francisco.[32] This led to some over-the-air oddness. "Often, during a shelling or bombing, we would hear a swing number or a Xavier Cugat rumba blaring away between the explosions," Romulo wrote, "because in the dash for shelter no one thought to turn off the radio."[33]

Corregidor was the headquarters. MacArthur's landed the uncharitable tag, "Dugout Dug," because he spent so much time there. Filipino troops never lost their trust in him, but his American soldiers sang, "Dugout Doug MacArthur lies ashakin' on the Rock/Safe from all the bombers and from any sudden shock."[34] In fact, defense was alien to MacArthur's spirit. He preferred attack.[35] His conduct on the Rock was influenced by the presence of his wife and four-year-old son, who stayed in the Malinta Tunnel, which doubled as an air raid shelter and field hospital.[36] He and Quezon pored over communications from Washington, seeing in recommendations that the Filipino President head to Australia mounting evidence that no rescue was in store.[37] It was only when Roosevelt sent a message on February 10, demanding that the defense carry on "TO THE LAST UNIT" so as to embody "THE AMERICAN DETERMINATION AND INDOMITABLE WILL TO WIN" that the two leaders finally accepted this.[38] "I THEREFORE GIVE YOU THIS MOST DIFFICULT MISSION IN FULL UNDERSTANDING OF THE DESPERATE SITUATION TO WHICH YOU MAY SHORTLY BE REDUCED," wired Roosevelt, adding that the "TITANIC STRUGGLE" which the United States faced mandated that Bataan hold out.[39] Bataan/Corregidor was an Alamo, a last-stand delaying operation. MacArthur responded on February 11. "I HAVE NOT THE SLIGHTEST INTENTION IN THE WORLD OF SURRENDERING OR CAPITULATING THE FILIPINO ELEMENT OF MY COMMAND," he vowed. "THERE HAS NEVER BEEN THE SLIGHTEST WAVERING AMONG THE TROOPS."[40] MacArthur and his wife thought in terms of sharing the troops' fate. As for young Arthur, they said, "He is a soldier's son."[41] But MacArthur was too valuable to lose. The administration wanted him in Australia.

General Homma had problems, too. Crossing the abandoned Abucay line, Japanese ran into a new perimeter 10 miles south. Attempts to outflank it amphibiously came to grief thanks to PT heroics in the Battle of the Points. Then, Japanese units were surrounded in the Battle of the Pockets. "The battalion is about to die gloriously," read the message Homma received.[42] Now, instead of a swift victory, Homma faced a stalemate. His superiors were disgusted on February 8, when he asked for reinforcements. Homma was stymied by an enemy Tokyo considered beaten. It was a prestige blow which caused the miserable general to weep.[43] It became a matter of honor for the Japanese to take Bataan in battle, not as a result of blockade.[44] The problem was that the battle was not going according to Tokyo's plan. Tojo pressured Homma mercilessly, demanding not a sustained siege, but a decisive victory to rank alongside Singapore.

The battles of the Points and Pockets, lasting from January 28 to February 17, boosted Filipino-American morale. They showed that the Japanese could be bested. But sickness, starvation, and shortages were beginning to bite. During the last week of February, cavalryman Wainwright ordered the slaughter of horses and mules, since the native buffalo had all been eaten.[45] Half-rations were instituted on January 6. On March 15, these were halved again.[46] Rice and canned tuna or salmon were "staples," but rare.[47] Monkey meat supplemented rations, along with roots, snails, and birds.[48] Dispatch riders carried orders around the clock; a famous news photograph of a rider sleeping by his motorcycle, using an ammunition drum as a pillow, symbolized the fatigue all defenders felt.[49]

Bataan was malarial. Mosquitoes, leeches, and pests were unavoidable.[50] Now, with the men starving and stressed, the harried hospital staff coped not just with combat wounds but dysentery, beriberi, dengue fever, and other illnesses. Medical supplies dwindled.[51] The medical staff saved lives with blood plasma. When that ran out, they typed themselves; doctors and corpsmen made "donations on demand."[52] Without quinine, they coped with 500–700 new cases of malaria per day.[53] They ran a Japanese ward, where prisoners of war were shocked to receive treatment instead of being killed.[54] It was from these prisoners that the US Army began to accumulate valuable data about their enemy. The average weight of a prisoner was 125.8 pounds; the oldest was 31 and the youngest, 19. Average length of military service was 1 ½ years. Sixty-five percent were infantry, while 70 percent had a grammar school education, with 15 percent completing high school. In civilian life, 30 percent were farmers, mechanics and factory workers 25 percent, clerks 20 percent. All this information went to intelligence officials in Australia.[55] Interrogations yielded insights into the attitudes of the Japanese. They were amazed to find Americans and Filipinos fighting together, since they had been told that the natives considered Japan their liberator. Others mentioned the Tripartite Pact:

> I do not know who will win the war, America or Japan. I am not sure Japan will. I know it is mixed up with what happens to Germany. Germany has promised us assistance, but Germany has no navy so it is only moral assistance.[56]

Some addressed their nation's motivations: "Japan is fighting America because this is the time when Japan must either rise of fall."[57] The fact that they were prisoners weighed on these Japanese minds: "I have been told it is a disgrace to be captured and that I can never return home. However, after the war, I would like to go back to Japan, but that depends on you."[58]

Army nurse Juanita Redmond recalled false accounts of relief.

> Once our spirits soared sky-high. Convoys were on their way to Australia. Surely, surely, they would break through to us. . . . We hugged to ourselves each optimistic report: about the Russians, and the rising production at home; and the fighting anger of the English and their relief from the incessant bombing of the year before; we were avid for news from China, for China was fighting the enemy facing *us,* had been fighting him for many years and our sense of kinship was very strong.[59]

Amidst carnage and pressure, humor did poke through. On February 23, word came of the Japan's shelling of Santa Barbara. In the hospital, someone joked, "So MacArthur wired US officials that if they can hold out for thirty days we'll send 'em help."[60] As long as the paper supplies lasted, two corpsmen published a newspaper, *Jungle Journal*, for the diversion of the patients and troops, while others put on skits.[61]

On February 22, FDR ordered MacArthur to prepare for his evacuation.[62] This came the day before a presidential speech on Universal Newsreels, calling on Americans to commit to victory and denying that democracy was soft. "Tell it to the Marines," he said.[63] Probably irritating MacArthur. Official insistence wore down MacArthur's resistance, and on March 11, the family climbed aboard Bulkeley's PT-41, which shuttled them through Japanese-held waters to Mindanao. They continue on to Australia. "I want you to understand my position very plainly," MacArthur explained to Wainwright, left in command. "I'm leaving for Australia pursuant to repeated orders from the President."[64] He requested that Wainwright inform the command. "In the meantime you've got to hold."[65] "Good-bye, Jonathan," MacArthur said. "If you're still on Bataan when I get back, I'll make you a Lieutenant General." "I'll be on Bataan if I'm still alive," Wainwright responded.[66]

In Australia, MacArthur received a hero's welcome, vowing, "I shall return."[67] The specters of Bataan and Corregidor spooked the General ever after, but the experience taught him valuable lessons. One went into effect right away. Having felt himself at the mercy of planners whose visions did not mesh with his own, MacArthur and his staff made plans of their own, setting up an autonomous structure paralleling the Navy's.[68] The decision was made to establish Southwest Pacific headquarters in Australia, although there was already a Central Pacific HQ in Hawaii.[69] MacArthur's HQ never lost focus on fulfilling his promise to return to the Philippines. To his critics, MacArthur's emphasis on recapturing the Philippines was an ego-driven distraction from the Central Pacific thrust.[70] Handling MacArthur meant giving him enough of what he wanted without listening to outlandish demands such as stripping naval strength from the Atlantic and Indian Oceans before Midway and delivering the ships to him.[71] Obviously, such an idea ran afoul of navy thinking as well as Roosevelt's Germany First commitment.[72]

MacArthur's removal caused a crash in morale on Bataan. Filipinos took it hardest. Romulo, torn between deep loyalty to the commander and the desire to remain in his country at its moment of ruin, wanted to stay at Corregidor. "I knew you'd say that, Carlos," MacArthur said before overruling his subordinate. "The Voice of Freedom can't be stilled. It must go on. It's our voice."[73] The journalist-soldier was dispatched to talk with his fellow Filipinos at Bataan; to explain "That I had to do this and that they are to believe me when I say it's for the best."[74] For the first time, Romulo detected deep sadness in the General he revered. He accompanied MacArthur to Australia.[75]

In Washington, MacArthur was honored. In late February, the Library of Congress organized its bibliographical materials about him, an unprecedented honor for a living subject. The published version included 253 references, committing the living General to historical status by library fiat.[76] He was awarded the Congressional Medal of Honor, which Marshall said was sure to "meet with . . . popular approval both within and without the armed forces."[77] The citation mentioned "conspicuous leadership in preparing the Philippine Islands to resist conquest," as well as calm and inspirational decision-making.[78]

By April, Quezon was in Australia. American soldiers altered the words of their ditty. "Dugout Doug is ready in his Chris Craft for the flee/Over bounding billows and the wildly raging sea./For the Japs are pounding on the gates of old Bataan,/ And his troops go starving on."[79] One understood the implication of MacArthur's escape: "When MacArthur left and went to Australia, that's what I called doomsday for Bataan, because he issued orders to fight to the last man. And that's when we know what our fate was going to be."[80] On April Fool's Day, Wainwright received a surrender demand. He did not answer, but his situation was disintegrating fast. Out of the original 80,000 who crossed the Layac Bridge, only 27,000 remained "combat effective," and most of these were sick and hungry.[81] Homma had 15,000 reinforcements, heavy artillery and air support. Homma sent out 150 bomber sorties while his guns delivered a five-hour barrage in preparation for attack on April 3.[82] Filipino and American troops hung to their latest line, along Mount Samat, but Japanese pressure created a salient which no counterattack could erase. American artillery crews pushed their 155 mm guns off cliffs to prevent capture, while retreating soldiers dug in along the San Vincente River, the last defensible position before Corregidor.[83] By April 7, Japan's breakthrough was complete; retreat was underway to the port of Mariveles, where boats ferried fighters through shark-infested waters to Corregidor.[84] Three thousand five hundred Marines made it to the Rock.[85] On April 9, American officers still at Mariveles approached Japanese lines under a white flag. They met Homma's operations officer, Colonel Motoo Nakayama. Nakayama was direct when asked if surrendering men would be well-treated. "We are not barbarians," he assured them.[86] But these assurances proved premature. The Japanese, had suffered 60,000 casualties in a frustrating campaign.[87] They were exhausted and angry.[88]

For 28 days, the Japanese shelled and strafed the two square miles of Corregidor, two miles off Mariveles. The island had no way to respond. Inside the tunnel, air pumps gave out and water ran out; thousands of patients filled every space.[89] Among the worst barrages was that of April 29, a salvo in honor of Hirohito's birthday.[90] The Rock was a subterranean labyrinth of tunnels running throughout, its outside covered by machine gun emplacements. It could withstand direct bombardment.[91] Those underground suffered claustrophobically, amidst stink and darkness. Those aboveground envied their safety from shellfire, but those beneath wished for fresh air.[92] Cut off, low on supplies, and overcrowded, Corregidor was doomed and Wainwright knew it. Homma's men made amphibious landings May 5–6. On May 6, Roosevelt sent Wainwright a final message. "During recent weeks we have been following with growing admiration the day-by-day accounts of your heroic stand against the mounting intensity of bombardment," the President wrote, calling that stand "a shining example of patriotic fortitude and self-sacrifice. The American people," he added, "ask no finer example of tenacity, resourcefulness, and steadfast courage."[93] His concluding lines showed how the imminent defeat was being transfigured in the national psyche into something noble. "You and your devoted followers have become the living symbols of our war aims and the guarantee of victory," the President wrote the General.[94]

Wainwright certainly needed whatever succor such words provided. The distraught General recalled MacArthur's urgings to hold and make a last-ditch attack.[95] Homma's first request for surrender was ignored, but the prospect of Japanese ransacking through the tunnels made Wainwright realize that further slaughter was pointless.[96] He responded to Roosevelt: "With broken heart and head bowed in sadness but not in shame I report to your Excellency that today I must arrange terms for the surrender of the fortified islands of Manila Bay," he informed the Commander-in-Chief. "With profound regret and continued pride in my gallant troops, I go to meet the Japanese commander. There is a limit to human endurance and that limit has long since been passed."[97]

Corporal Irving Stroberg tapped out the last messages prior to capitulation.[98] His updates transfixed Hawaii HQ. The radio operator praised Wainwright. "General Wainwright is a right guy, and we are willing to go on for him. But shells were dropping all night, faster than hell."[99] Making a joke, Stroberg asked, "How about a chocolate soda?" mentioning that he had just downed the last canned pineapple. Most of his message was grim.

> I feel sick at my stomach. . . . I am really low down. They are around now smashing rifles. They bring in the wounded every minute. We will be waiting for you guys to help. . . . Everyone is bawling like a baby. They are piling up dead and wounded in our tunnel.[100]

The radio operator's last message was for his family.

> Get this to my mother, Mrs. Minnie Strobing, 605 Barbey Street, Brooklyn, NY. They are to get along OK. . . . Message, my love to Pa, Joe, Sue, Mac, Harry, Joy, and Paul. Also to all family and friends. God bless 'em all. Hope they be there when I come home. Tell Joe, wherever he is, to give 'em hell for us. . .[101]

Strobing went into captivity, surviving the war.

Wainwright went to treat with Homma. One American concern was that Corregidor would see a massacre unless remnant hold-outs across the Philippines obeyed surrender orders. Wainwright ordered General William Sharp, who had units elsewhere, that "General Homma has declined to accept my surrender unless it included the forces under your command."[102] He reiterated surrender orders by radio under guard once he was in enemy hands. "I now give a direct order to William Sharp. I repeat, those receiving it please notify General Sharp at once. Subject: Surrender!"[103] The problem for Homma was that once Wainwright was captured, the American general lost his power to command. Wainwright agreed to the broadcast to prevent the slaughter of 10,000 men stranded on Bataan and Corregidor.[104] On Mindanao, Sharp had to decide for himself. MacArthur sent a radiogram: "ORDERS EMANATING FROM GENERAL WAINWRIGHT HAVE NO VALIDITY. IF POSSIBLE SEPARATE YOUR FORCE INTO SMALL ELEMENTS AND INITIATE GUERILLA OPERATIONS."[105] Nor was Sharp the only one deciding what Wainwright's decision meant elsewhere in the Philippines. On Negros, where Roy Bell and his Silliman College colleagues saw no Japanese, a group of Filipino officers captured on Bataan and paroled to deliver surrender orders were locked up. An order from Sharp came in late May, advising authorities on Negros to give up. But Bell and others took to the jungles, starting a resistance movement that lasted throughout the war.[106] The overall guerilla campaign eventually included nearly 300,000 Filipinos.[107]

The last chapter of the Bataan campaign was the most notorious. This was the Death March. Its seeds were sewn when Homma's army failed to take the peninsula quickly enough to satisfy Tokyo. Weeks of hard fighting not only upset their logistical arrangements, it left them devoid of the triumphal spirit Imperial Army units elsewhere experienced. Homma's troops felt frustrated. Their code disdained surrender, so they considered captives contemptible. Standard protocol for dealing with prisoners started with shouting and beatings, proceeding from there.[108]

The sustained atrocity began before Corregidor's fall, on April 9, when Japanese troops gathered prisoners on Bataan, marshaling them together for a forced march northwards to permanent POW facilities. Given the contempt of the Japanese, and conditions after months of combat, prisoners were in a dangerous position. As they began to march, Captain Manny Lawton asked Colonel John Erwin what to expect. The Colonel was blunt. "You can anticipate the very worst, Lawton," he predicted. "It's going to be tough. These Japs are running around like crazy men. They are excitable and unreasonable under stress."[109] Seventy-six thousand men surrendered on Bataan—the largest capitulation in American history. Postwar reports at his war-crimes trial indicated that Homma expected less than half that number, so Japanese preparations were inadequate.[110] Additionally, as many as 26,000 Filipino refugees clustered around Mariveles. All had to be moved north.[111] The Japanese plan was to march everyone to Balanga, where they would board trucks and drive to a POW camp. But the trucks were nowhere in evidence, so the trip was made on foot. Survivors recalled awful incidents amidst a pattern of pointless cruelty. Hot dust rose from the road when Japanese troop trucks sped by, choking the shuffling prisoners. Imperial Army troops amused themselves by hitting the prisoners as they marched in the opposite direction. If anyone fell, they were likely to be bayoneted. There was neither water nor food; any civilians who offered sustenance to prisoners were chased away.[112] Beheadings with samurai swords, burial alive, shootings, and death from thirst and sickness cost up to 10,000 lives, of whom 2,300 were American.[113] In one awful incident, an aged captain could not continue marching and begged to be shot. Japanese soldiers plucked a GI from the ranks and ordered him to bury the officer alive. The younger soldier later committed suicide.[114] Deliberate mistreatment was traumatic to survivors, to say the least. What began as a logistics mistake degenerated into atrocity as the Japanese faced their logistical failure and the obvious inability of hard-pressed prisoners to obey brutal commands.[115] The bad treatment continued at Camp O'Donnell, which itself became the scene of squalid violence.[116] Homma would be executed after the war due to this episode.[117]

The general shape of what transpired at Bataan and Corregidor was known to Americans. But many details were sketchy, and there was misinformation, since reporters and the audience hoped that the battlefield disaster might be reversed. "MacArthur and Filipinos Spurn Jap Demands to Give Up Arms and Quit," said a *Baltimore Sun* headline on January 31.[118] The article described Japanese propaganda pamphlets, which told the defenders that no relief would save them. These leaflets drew no reaction but mirth.[119] In early February, reports that Japan tried to infiltrate Corregidor with a sneak raid described the killing of the amphibious team. Here, the Japanese seemed desperate, trying a hopeless attack "through the back door."[120] On February 2, Raymond Gram Swing honored MacArthur's performance. "It is true that General MacArthur continues to perform miracles on Bataan Peninsula," he said.[121] Swing's words revealed that Americans could understand the Philippine campaign. They knew that MacArthur was fighting a defensive campaign; a series of retreats. They did not expect a battlefield victory. But they could appreciate his accomplishments nonetheless. Swing understood that the men on Bataan were fighting for time.[122]

US News covered the campaign carefully. A lengthy article in the February 20 issue, "The Real Story Behind Gen. MacArthur's Stand: Hazards of Sending Relief Through Japanese-Dominated Approaches," located Bataan within the larger war. It explained how difficult resupply by sea was, since the Japanese had naval control and air supremacy. It held out hope that the ABDA Command might reverse this, but also argued that it was unwise to rush a convoy to Bataan. It explained withdrawal from Manila as preplanned, describing Bataan: "General MacArthur's little army is strongly placed on this mountainous thumb, with the China Sea at his left, Manila Bay at his right, and off the point guarding his rear, the heavily fortified island of Corregidor," it explained.

The streams of the Mariveles Mountains supply him with water. The rugged land makes hard going for tanks. The thick foliage screens troops from the prying eyes of Japanese fliers. . . . Backing slowly down the peninsula in the face of repeated assaults, the American and Philippine guns have extracted a terrible toll of the Japanese.

The article made MacArthur's position sound promising, and indeed it promised a powerful defense—with one major condition: "while his supplies last."[123]

On March 8, CBS announcer Albert Warner asked aloud whether rumors that Homma had committed hari-kari out of shame for his dilatory advance were really true.[124] In the same broadcast, Webb Edwards, from Honolulu, hinted at a relief effort. The atmosphere in Hawaii, he told listeners, was a "mass feeling, a state of mind, a growing tension, as with a football team before a big game." There was an inescapable sense, Edwards contended, "that the entire population of Hawaii is pointing towards something big. Just what it is, they're not quite sure. Let's say that they're pointing towards the big game."[125] He added that MacArthur's stand was an enormous inspiration. Warner was less encouraging, closing with a sober reminder: "When you lose a campaign, you don't necessarily lose a war."[126]

John Raleigh now reported from Australia. His March 12 broadcast told of American bombers flying with the Royal Australian Air Force.[127] The informational value here was not high, since rules against divulging operational details precluded mentioning the theater. The real story was that Raleigh and his colleagues were now someplace the Allies meant to protect. But Allied ripostes from Australia were then aimed at New Guinea, to assist the defense of Port Moresby. Another target was Rabaul, where Allies bombed Japan's air base to contest the skies over the Solomon Islands.[128] By the end of April, Allied air ascendancy in the theaters near Australia was established.[129] On March 16, the arrival of American troops in Australia was announced. Raleigh stressed the happiness of Aussies with their new partners, as well as the comic aspects of Americans adjusting to life down under.[130]

Raleigh shifted CBS coverage from Bataan to Australia. "The Japanese appear to be behaving like a circling dog in the north," he said on March 14, "Snapping here and there at the heels of Australia."[131] Harry Marble followed suit the next day, leading off with Japan's threat to Australia.[132] On March 16, Warner concentrated on Allied air success over Rabaul, praising the bravado of Australian ambassador Richard Casey, who swore resistance against any attack on his nation. "We will attack the enemy before he lands. We will continue to attack if by evil chance he succeeds in landing. If it should be necessary, we will destroy our homes, our crops, our herds, lay wasted to our towns, cripple the railway," promised the Minister, in Churchillian terms.[133] Warner noted approvingly that "The watchword throughout Australia truly is, work, fight, or perish."[134]

Then came the announcement that MacArthur, not the Japanese, had landed in Australia. Raleigh was present to welcome the General and cover his press conference. The CBS correspondent recounted the excitement MacArthur's arrival brought. "News of General MacArthur's appointment as head of ANZAC has been received with greatest enthusiasm, and that's putting it mildly," he stated. "This morning, the hotel clerk, who awakens me daily at the prosaic hour of 7:30, said happily over the phone that MacArthur was here, and had I heard of his arrival? As an afterthought, he told me the time."[135] Raleigh cited "complete delight" as the ubiquitous response. "Since I have been in Australia," he said, "no single event appears to have raised morale more than the General's assumption of command in this commonwealth."[136] He predicted smooth collaboration between MacArthur and the Australians, and closed with a colorful description of the Australian outback, including an anecdote of a lost pilot forced down in the desert who survived by eating frogs.[137] While the Philippines had not yet finally fallen, Americans were getting to know their Australian ally through the news, and being conditioned to think of that nation as the spot from which the eventual offensive would come.

That process continued on CBS throughout March and April. Accounts of aerial combat over New Guinea emphasized favorable loss ratios and the destruction of Japanese invasion plans.[138] American reporters even made a story out of MacArthur's treatment by the Australian press, describing with amusement the "press blitz" as Commander and his hosts got to know each other.[139] He was, said Raleigh, "polite, appreciative, but still a little dazed at the reception he's getting everywhere."[140] Another angle was the handsome shape of American troops in Australia. "The American soldiers I have seen have all been splendid sights," said Raleigh. "Their aim is to get into the fight and get it over with as quickly as possible. General MacArthur's presence has bucked up morale among many Aussies, too."[141] Australia emerged as a focus for reports from Europe, too. Albert Warner described a Pacific Council meeting in London, at which Australia and New Zealand made clear that they believed in "the necessity for first-hand contact with the United States. By appointing General MacArthur," Warner opined, "the President has himself initiated the offensive, but to destroy Japanese aggression, all the implements of war, especially aircraft, must be provided at once."[142]

Eric Sevareid delivered the most direct CBS commentary on Bataan. On March 21, he leveled with listeners. "An ominous message comes from General Wainwright tonight," he said. "He reports to the War Department that strong skirmishes occurred all along the Bataan front and added that the long-delayed Japanese offensive now appears to be coming."[143] What he and Wainwright were referring to was Homma's reinforcement-fueled attack against the last perimeters holding the peninsula's southern end. The newsman foreshadowed bad tidings to come. "The American government now joins the British in claiming to the world that the Japanese have committed atrocities upon their captives," he announced. "Our State Department confirms Anthony Eden's charges of atrocities in Hong Kong. . . . Other men here today had other things to say about the Japanese code of honor."[144] Sevareid added that Roosevelt was aware of numerous reports from the Philippines outlining mistreatment of military and civilian prisoners. Raleigh discussed Bataan by implication. Continuing the theme of MacArthur's hero's welcome in Australia, Raleigh discussed what he left behind. "Modern war requires something more than courage and willingness to die," explained the CBS correspondent. "It requires preparation. This means furnishing sufficient troops and sufficient materials to meet the known strength of the enemy."[145] Bataan/ Corregidor was being explained to the public, and the proper take-away points were underscored. The battle was a defeat, like Pearl Harbor. It resulted from the enemy's sneaky surprise, and from their preparations. It was too late to save the Philippines. But determination, planning, and production would set the stage for victory.

Sevareid anticipated the end of the Bataan campaign. He noted the demands for Wainwright to surrender, attributing them to Yamashita instead of Homma. The Tiger of Malaya was rumored as propping up Homma. "He'll have to fight, not give ultimata," Sevareid pointed out, adding that the fortified islands, including Corregidor, now faced unending fusillades.[146] Stressing the antipodeal season, William J. Dunn, in Melbourne, reported on Quezon's arrival. "On a crisp, March morning in autumn, the Philippine President arrives, after a long journey," he said. There was little direct mention of Bataan. Instead, Dunn concentrated on the weather in Australia, noting that surprised American troops were unhappy upon disembarking and discovering that, after late winter at home, they now faced early winter below the equator. Other points of confusion included traffic.

> Probably the first thing the Yank soldier notices in Australia is the movement of traffic along the left side of the street, or as they content, the wrong side. . . . When US soldiers explain to Aussies that we drive on the right, the Aussie replies, "Boy, you must have a lot of left-handed people in the States!"[147]

Dunn added that Yanks were surprised to see that cities down under resembled those at home, and that to see a kangaroo meant a trip to the outback. He stressed the "amazing and uniformly good" behavior of Americans. For a local touch, he read from the *Melbourne Times-Argus*. "It's a curious contrast, from 1917 to 1942. Perhaps memory is a cheat," went the article. "The US fighting man we see today seems quieter, more serious, more urbane. His manners would do credit to a diplomat. He is as frank and open as ever, but he shows no signs at all of the old tendency to tell the world. He sings less, shouts less, reads *Reader's Digest*, and likes to talk to people. He seems a much more mature person."[148] That mirrored the cheerful tone struck by the March 18 Universal Newsreel, which advertised MacArthur's arrival as "Good News from Australia!" On March 23, the newsreel stressed the resupply campaign in response to Australian appeals, while on March 25, the newsreel stress featured the potential for a Japanese invasion, the Darwin air raids, and defense preparations in Sydney. Universal delivered visual support for the shift of American awareness to Australia as the ally of the moment.[149]

Australia stories were good for morale. Stories dealing with the Philippines had to find a way not to be depressing. On April 15, William J. Dunn, from Melbourne, reported on a bombing run against Japanese positions in the Philippines, hinting that this was "the first fulfillment of MacArthur's promise to return."[150] His analysis was too optimistic, since the air campaign was concentrated on attacking Japanese shipping. But he emphasized that the attack was "distinctly offensive, and of the type that may ultimately succeed in blocking the air superiority of the enemy."[151] He recounted meetings with American troops extricated from the Philippines, and delivered a gentle version of the Bataan lament, "No mama, no papa, no Uncle Sam," wishing aloud that recent build-ups of strength in Australia had come earlier so as to help Bataan's defense.[152] Gently, subtly, Dunn delivered Bataan and Corregidor's eulogy.

When print media dealt with the story, analysis was the thrust. Maps made it hard to deny what was plain: Americans and Filipinos were clinging on, but Japanese lines kept advancing. "Philippine Reverse Jolts US but American Forces Hit Back," was how *Newsweek* introduced the Bataan campaign in mid-January. The magazine quoted War Department accounts portraying MacArthur's withdrawal as a major reversal for Japan.[153] In February, the campaign was set against the catastrophes of Singapore and Java, so Philippine news did not seem as bad. In March, *Newsweek* and other magazines carried false reports of Homma's suicide. On March 16, *Newsweek* mentioned that Yamashita was supposed to buck up Homma.[154]

"Defenses Crushed" was the April 10 *New York Times* headline announcing the fall of Bataan.[155] Copy attributed the defeat to "An overwhelming Japanese Army, aided by the allies of hunger, fatigue, and disease."[156] In contradistinction to the "overwhelming Japanese Army," the Filipino-American defenders were called "a mixed force," their numbers cited at 38, 853, "set against 200,000 Imperial troops supported by tanks, artillery, bombers, and attack planes in profusion."[157] Reporter Charles Hurd quoted Stimson praising the defenders, as well as claiming contention that shiploads of supplies had been sent in, "but for every ship that arrived safely, we lost nearly two."[158]

Corregidor's fall was assumed to be imminent. When it came, it was no surprise. By then, news of the naval battle in the Coral Sea nudged into the news lead. Corregidor seemed a sad but not decisive development. Uncertainty regarding the defenders' fate was plain, however, thanks to the Bataan aftermath. "Corregidor

Falls after 28-Day Siege; 7,000 are Believed Taken Prisoners," said *The Detroit New* on May 6.[159] The article stressed that hunger was the main reason for the surrender. Japanese radio reports formed the basis for stories on May 8, which cited Imperial Headquarters' claims to have captured The Rock. The stories mentioned Hirohito's satisfaction. "His Imperial Majesty graciously commended the brilliant success in the reduction of the last remaining American outpost in East Asia."[160] The Japanese added that "The fall of Corregidor has deprived the United States of its last basis of propaganda to hide American defeats in the Philippines."[161] "Manila Bay Forts Taken by the Japanese" was a *New York Times* headline on May 8, 1942. A large photograph of the Rock and nearby Ft. Drum Island accompanied the headline, "released yesterday from the secret files of the War Department."[162] The caption cited Corregidor as "focal point of the desperate last stand."[163]

Coral Sea—"Scratch One Flattop"

Scratch one flattop! Dixon to Carrier, Scratch one flattop!
Lieutenant Commander R.E. Dixon, May 7, 1942[164]

Certain truths were evident by April 1942. Western powers stood ejected from their colonies. From the Indian border to Rabaul, Japan was ascendant. Interpretations told much about Japanese and American visions of the war ahead. Japanese military leaders were at the acme of their victory phase. Particularly to the Imperial Army, the Allies looked disjointed. Their pre-war power looked like a rickety fraud. Dutch, British, and American forces were all destroyed. At Singapore, Java, and Bataan, Japan threw aside Allied defensive positions, registering prestigious triumphs. Victory looked complete to the Army General Staff, which recommended transferring soldiers back to China and Manchuria.[165]

Japan's navy was unconvinced. Australia remained an Allied redoubt, so the navy advocated invasion.[166] The army reacted sullenly. One compromise was to take all of New Guinea, use Rabaul as an offensive base, and grab New Caledonia, Fiji and Samoa, extending Japan's protective barrier to the International Date Line. Japan could then pressure Australia in the Coral and Tasman seas.[167] Yamamoto dreamed of invading Hawaii, carrying the war to the United States' West Coast. Victory, or at least a favorable settlement, would be the result, he felt.[168] But the army balked at overextending the defense perimeter. Some generals remained focused on China, some still foresaw combat with the Soviet Union. Yamamoto was hampered by army objections. He shifted his gaze to Midway, where he hoped to draw out the American fleet for a climactic battle.[169]

First, New Guinea—Rabaul and the Solomon approaches had to be stabilized. Australian defenses were building up; MacArthur's arrival showed a strong

Allied commitment there. Fighting on New Guinea was slow, Rabaul suffering frequent Allied air attacks. Looking at their maps, the Japanese spied Tulagi, in the Solomons. The Solomon Islands form the northern arc of the Coral Sea. Control there would strengthen Japan's chances in southern New Guinea, relieve Rabaul, and keep pressure on Australia's north and east coasts. The Tulagi invasion was set for May 3, covered by separate naval elements. The core was a carrier task force aiming for Port Moresby.[170] Unknown to Tokyo, parts of this plan were well-studied by American naval officers, since codebreakers at Pearl Harbor had cracked "JN-25," the Imperial Navy's operational code. The sleuths could not understand every communication, but they did appreciate patterns of messages, prompting Nimitz to dispatch his own carrier force to the Coral Sea.[171]

The centrality of aircraft to naval operations was now accepted. For Japan, the danger was spreading their forces too thinly, lessening their numerical advantage in a given spot.[172] Victory would let Japan use land-based craft and seaplanes to protect sea lanes within her defensive perimeter. Rabaul was crucial. American naval analysts paid close attention to concentrations of planes, supplies, and ships on Rabaul, adding information to the decrypted intercepts and figuring that Port Moresby was Japan's next objective. Nimitz decided to commit to a battle. He organized not just a force to disrupt landings in New Guinea, but a stronger flotilla that would include four carriers: *Lexington* and *Yorktown* at the nucleus, with *Hornet* and *Enterprise*, if they arrived in time.[173] *Hornet* and *Enterprise* faced a 3,500 mile trip from Pearl Harbor. Their potential arrival altered Japanese plans.[174] Nimitz was the guiding spirit, but Vice Admiral Frank J. Fletcher was the local commander, supported by Rear Admiral Aubrey W. Flitch.[175]

Japan's navy planned to support the amphibious attacks on Port Moresby and Tulagi Solomons with a striking force headed by aircraft carriers *Shokaku* and *Zuikaku*, along with two heavy cruisers and six destroyers. The two large carriers each displaced 20,000 tons, carried 60 planes, and slid down the ways in 1941.[176] The plan was intricate. A transport force would pick Japanese troops up from New Guinea's north shore and sail to Port Moresby, since they had not been able to fight their way. Other transports would head for Tulagi. That island would house an air base. Yet another invasion force would build more air bases on nearby Santa Isabel. These were to be supported by extra cruisers and support craft, and also by the light carrier *Shohu*.[177] Vice Admiral Shigeyoshi Inoue was overall commander in the area, tasked with capturing Port Moresby. Rear Admiral Takeo Takagi commanded the Coral Sea strike force. Rear Admiral Aritomo Goto commanded the cruiser squadron, and Rear Admiral Chuichi Hara led the carriers.[178]

Each side's aircraft turned out to be crucial. The American workhorse was the F4F Grumman Wildcat. Rugged, able to hit 330 mph, its climb rate did not match the Zero's, but its toughness and firepower lent it survivability. Airmen learned to handle it in appropriate formations such as the "Thatch Weave," named after the

Lieutenant who invented it. The Thatch Weave was a maneuver in which pairs of planes kept a gap between themselves. If any foe engaged one of the pair, the two pilots flew towards each other, closing the gap and allowing the wingman to rake his partner's pursuit.[179] Another important plane was the Douglas SBD Dauntless dive bomber. Stability was its hallmark, so vital for accurate targeting. Torpedo bombers included Douglas TBD Devastators, nearly obsolete.[180] On the Japanese side, the main planes were the Zero, fast but vulnerable with its non-sealing gas tank and lack of armor. Also well-known were the Aichi Val dive bomber and the Nakajima Kate torpedo plane.[181]

Both fleets entered the Coral Sea at the beginning of May. They scouted each other, hoping for the initial advantage. First blood was drawn when Japanese planes spotted and attacked a destroyer and tanker. They initially thought the ships were carriers.[182] Losing oiler *Neosho* meant that Fletcher had less time to win the battle, since fuel supplies were restricted.[183] American planes took off from *Yorktown* and *Lexington*, sinking *Shohu*. Alarmed, Inoue pulled back the invasion of Port Moresby, deciding instead to kill the American carriers. *Yorktown* also sent planes against Tulagi invasion. With the Port Moresby landings cancelled and the Tulagi invasion contested, Japanese calculations were thrown off.[184]

Japanese officers realized that victory for them meant success in each phase of their plan. For the Americans, merely blunting Japan's attack would mean success. Admiral Matome Ukagi noted the effective American timing. He did not know about the code breaking, but on May 4, he speculated that "The enemy seems to have attacked after detecting our situation fairly well."[185] May 5–6 saw each side reconnoitering. On May 7, Ukagi mourned the loss of *Shohu* and the effective American countermoves: "A dream of great success has been shattered. . . . There is an opponent in a war, so one cannot progress just as one wishes."[186] Ugaki took heart that there were still two American carriers at large. Action on May 7 was peripheral but significant. The Japanese launched planes from Rabaul against American cruisers and destroyers. The surface ships repulsed the bombers.[187] The carriers of each flotilla remained the main issue.

The fleets found each other on May 8. Carriers launched bombers and fighters. The result was the major naval battle of the war to date. *Shokaku* was hit, as was *Lexington*. *Yorktown* sustained light damage. *Zuikaku* lost planes. At the end of the day, the forces disengaged as Japanese officers worried about the arrival of *Enterprise* and *Hornet*. The United States task force split up and headed to New Caledonia and Tonga for repairs and resupply.[188] The end result just then was unclear. At first, it looked like "Lady Lex" would survive, but a fuel vapor buildup detonated in the ship's innards.[189] *Lexington* went down as destroyers picked up survivors. It was a painful loss: Lady Lex, her keel laid down in 1921, almost 900 feet long, was one of the best-loved and luckiest ships in the navy. All who served as captain reached flag rank. Her third captain was Ernest J. King. Many of the *Lexington's* crew were "plank owners"; serving since she first set sail.[190] In a demonstration of pragmatism, the crew ate up *Lexington's* ice cream stores before abandoning ship.[191]

Loss of *Lexington* made Coral Sea either a tactical draw or a defeat for the United States.[192] But Japan's "victory" was pyrrhic. The invasion of Port Moresby fell through, which meant no conquest of southern New Guinea. They took Tulagi, but ongoing fighting over Rabaul showed that their grip on the Solomons was insecure. Lost planes, pilots, and ground crews could not be easily replaced. Meanwhile, the US Navy learned a great deal. This was the first battle in which ships never fired at each other. Instead, they projected power through their planes. Emerging and encouraging was the fact that American planes could exploit Japanese weaknesses.[193] The American knack for adaptability contrasted with Japanese obedience to plans. In the final analysis, Coral Sea was a strategic achievement for the US Navy, which forced the Japanese to alter their carefully calibrated scheme for regional supremacy. Australia was safer, and the Japanese admiralty still had to stem rising American naval potential.

Battle details were not laid out during the fighting, but the news appeared soon thereafter. Reporters were on board *Lexington*, listening when the battle's most famous utterance, "Scratch one flattop! Dixon to carrier: Scratch one flattop!" came in from Robert E. Dixon, a lieutenant commander leading dive bombers against *Shohu*. The memorable line went into the war's lexicon, reported by Stanley Johnston, *Chicago Tribune* correspondent.[194] Maps and damage summaries appeared in the evening papers on May 8. Conflicting claims by Tokyo and Washington ran alongside each other in these stories, which said much about American expectations for news disclosure. Extravagant Japanese claims included two battleships, two carriers, and a cruiser, while Allied HQ made accurate claims.[195] The first articles stressed the battle's magnitude. A *Baltimore Evening Sun* headline was representative: "Fight is Called US Navy's Biggest Ever."[196]

The Associated Press story quoted Australian Prime Minister John Curtin. He cautioned that the result remained uncertain, but said that if the Allies lost, Australia faced "a sterner ordeal and greater responsibility."[197] Curtin spoke of imminent invasion dangers, so American readers would link the Coral Sea battle to an invasion of Australia. When that invasion failed to materialize, readers could extrapolate that the Japanese offensive was stopped. Reporters suggested other interpretations of the battle's stakes. "It was not immediately clear, however, whether the battle betokened an effort to cut off Australia's supply lines by smashing the Allied fleet, or whether it was the prelude to a new invasion thrust—aimed at Port Moresby, Allied outpost in southern New Guinea, or perhaps at the east Australian coast," read one caveat.[198] But Curtin was in the midst of stressing Australia's importance, cementing war-forged American ties. Americans had been told for weeks that Australia would be the foundation for Pacific victory. They had to be pleased when an invasion did not occur. The secrecy surrounding the Battle of the Coral Sea made it likely that readers believe that it prevented the invasion, as one headline, "Battle for Australia," suggested.[199]

"A naval engagement between our forces and those of the Japanese has been in continuous progress in the general area southward of Bismarck Archipelago, in the Coral Sea, since Monday, and there is no indication of a cessation," ran the laconic US Navy Communique on May 9.[200] Speculation about the battle was rampant; analysis was much in demand. "The great sea battle, uncertainty about which is keeping the whole country on tenterhooks, is taking place on the flank of the American supply line to Australia," explained an editorial. "If the Japanese succeed in weakening the defense of that supply line, our Pacific supply problem will be greater. If, on the other hand, the Japanese fleet it beaten back with grave losses, the problem will be made simpler."[201] As far as the result, the writer urged "calm as to the outcome," since even a defeat would not preclude withdrawal to defensible positions.[202] But the flow of information made it plain that, this time, there was no need to explain away a defeat. On May 9, at MacArthur's General Headquarters, Curtin briefed reporters on the battle's meaning. The main thing, he said, was that Japan's smooth path of conquest had been terminated. At Coral Sea, the Australian PM claimed, Australia was "saved from falling in Axis control."[203]

On May 11, CBS correspondent William J. Dunn quoted an Australian cabinet minister's view that the only way to follow up was to increase production. "The epic fight put up by brave Allied personnel in Coral Sea, successful as it was, should be a great stimulus upon all the peoples of the democracies," he said. "But if the efforts of the fighting men are not to be in vain, we must speed up air supplies."[204] From London, Murrow stated that Australian officials confided to him that they expected a Japanese attack on Midway to be the next Pacific challenge.[205]

The news magazines covered the battle in depth, since the details made public by the navy were delayed by a few days. The magazines concentrated on analysis. On May 4, *Time* Asia updates gave space to Australia and New Guinea. The Australian emphasis was of the "Yanks in a foreign land" variety, with anecdotes such as the American habit of playing baseball on Sundays, which upset Aussie Sabbatarians. But, the magazine noted, Sydney newspapers supported the GI's. The rest of the coverage was devoted to intensifying New Guinea combat.[206] This put *Time* in a good position to analyze the Coral Sea action. The May 11 issue came out too soon. But May 18 gave *Time* the chance to explain to readers why Coral Sea mattered. The story concentrated upon President Roosevelt's description, which claimed seven Japanese vessels sunk. Quoting the summary communique, *Time* termed the battle "very excellent news." *Time* admitted that Americans thirsted for battle news they did not need to minimize or explain away.

The nation, sore and grim over the fall of Corregidor, dared not be so sure. Nobody knew the US losses; commentators reserved comment; the public waited as they would wait patiently all this year for further news. . . . By week's end, their doubts were gone. . . . US losses were light: the Jap was in retreat. The Jap might be back, might win another battle, but this time the US had won.[207]

That was the approach taken by *The Nation.* "The communiques issued by both sides make it difficult to know exactly what the outcome was," said an editorial,

and as long as the enemy does not know, we can restrain our curiosity.; but as there have been no reports of further large-scale landings by Japanese forces, it seems reasonable to supposed that the Japanese foray was indeed set back. This is most encouraging news.[208]

For the first time, the magazine noted, the Japanese were not pressing their advantage; the Allies were not retreating. It was likely, the *Nation* decided, that there would be more fighting at sea, but the signs were not depressing. The editorial used Coral Sea as a counterpoint to Bataan and Corregidor, acknowledging the bravery of the doomed defenders. "Pearl Harbor and Wake Island may stand for incompetence," said the piece. "But Bataan and Corregidor will go down in history as symbols of the courage and determination of American and Filipino troops in the face of overwhelming odds."[209] At the same time, the Battle of Coral Sea, for all its opacity, showed *The Nation* that triumph and defeat could coincide in such a big war. *The New Republic* praised "the fleet of the United Nations," in a semantical gesture since the "Allies" were entirely represented by the US Navy. Taking note of censorship restrictions, the magazine still got to the battle's heart. "The importance of the Battle of the Coral Sea lies chiefly in the fact that it severely delayed the Japanese schedule at a moment when time is working on the side of the United Nations."[210]

8 JUNE 1942

Midway, Pacific sea change

The United States is withholding from the public all news of her uninterrupted series of military and naval disasters while spreading fictitious reports of victory in an attempt to maintain popular confidence. . . . It is but natural that dissatisfaction is bound to be voiced among the intellectual classes in the United States over the American Government which has despotically dragged the nation into an uncertain war with Japan without any chance of success, completely disregarding the welfare of the masses.

Japanese Foreign Minister Shigenori Togo, speaking to the Diet on 'Navy Day,' May 27, 1942, the 37th anniversary of the victory at Tsushima Straits, May 27[1]

The enemy who has had to suffer the ignominy of successive defeats is now concentrating his whole energy on rolling back the tide of war and on reinforcing its forces, and it is to be taken for granted that the enemy will resort to all conceivable means to counterattack us, and for this reason we should not, even for a moment, be off our guard.

Minister of the Navy Admiral Shigetaro Shimada, speaking to the Diet on Navy Day, May 27, 1942[2]

DEFENSES MIDWAY . . . X CONSIDER ISLAND AT PRESENT ABLE TO WITHSTAND MODERATE ATTACK BUT WOULD REQUIRE FLEET ASSISTANCE FORWARD AGAINST MAJOR ATTACK X AM MAKING INSPECTION ABOUT TWO MAY X WILL GIVE FULL CONSIDERATION TO SUCH STRENGTHENING AND DEVELOPMENT AS MAY BE PRACTICABLE.

Admiral Chester Nimitz to Admiral Ernest J. King, April 29, 1942[3]

If presence of Task Forces 16 and 17 remains unknown to enemy, we should be able to make surprise flank attacks on enemy carriers from position northeast of Midway. Further operations will be based on results of these attacks, damage inflicted by Midway forces, and information of enemy movements. The successful conclusion of the operation now commencing will be of great value to our country.

Admiral Raymond Spruance, signal communication, June 3, 1942[4]

There was a month between the battles of Coral Sea and Midway. During that time, American war news ranged widely. May 1942 gave Americans the chance to bone up on the fighting between the Soviet Union and the Reich. Spring put a stop to the Red Army counteroffensive. But the next German offensive had not yet commenced. Hitler would look south, to the Caucasus oilfields between the Black and Caspian seas. To cover this attack, the *Wehrmacht* advanced across the riparian plain lying between great Don bend and the Volga. Stalingrad was a self-evident target. Much American news coverage focused on the heavy fighting in the Crimea that May. On May 13, American papers said the long-awaited German offensive was underway. Typical reports that "Red infantrymen were said to have broken the first German lunge and to have sent the Nazis reeling back to their original positions on all but one sector . . ." accompanied explanations that the Crimea offered a pathway to the Caucasus.[5]

New Masses cared most about what happened to the Soviet Union. It began advertising a special June 22 issue: "Our Soviet Ally," with contributions, articles and statements by Pearl Buck, Corliss Lamont, Max Lerner, Lion Feuchtwanger, and others. It celebrated "One year of the Red Army's heroic battle, The developing collaboration with Russia, The agreement for a Second Front in 1942."[6] Another cause the magazine supported was springing CPUSA Secretary Earl Browder from prison, where he served a four-year sentence for passport fraud.[7] Browder's 51st birthday was May 20, the occasion for a rally by supporters and sympathizers at Madison Square Garden, which was advertised both in *New Masses* and *The New Republic*.[8] It turned into a celebration when President Roosevelt pardoned him on May 16, at the 14-month mark. That attracted the attention of Sevareid, who reported on it from Washington. "Earl Browder, the soft spoken man from Kansas, the leader of the Communist Party in the United States, is now a free man," Sevareid observed. "There is in today's action no question about Browder's guilt, but the President said he was being released in the interest of national unity, that his sentence had been longer than is usual for that offense."[9] The American hard left had reason to feel grateful to Roosevelt. He, in turn, had less reason to worry about their animosity breaching the national consensus, although the second front was not imminent.

The New Republic also supported relief for the Soviets, but was pessimistic about an immediate second front. The magazine cautioned against unrealistic expectations. "The air is suddenly filled with surmises that war may end in a victory for the United Nations in 1942," went one story, taking note of advances in production, bullishness on Wall Street, and a Soviet victory before Kharkov. "American production has reached extraordinary figures in a miraculously short time," the editorialists granted.

> We don't wish to seem needlessly pessimistic, but this sort of thing can be very dangerous. Overconfidence at this juncture might be fatal, and Hitler is entirely capable of turning out his propaganda to achieve that aim. We are not out of the woods by a long way. The Japanese have been stopped on only one battle front—Australia—and there only temporarily.[10]

The weekly overreached for good news. Gazing at Crimea, editorial writers said that the Germans "had not dared" to storm Sebastopol.[11] The city fell in June. Elsewhere, the magazine touted Red Army Marshall Timoshenko's pincer attacks in the Donets Basin: "For the first time in the course of the entire war the Red Army, with this offensive, has scored a blow in a direction of its own initiative and choice," one article enthused. "This is no longer a mere counter-offensive but the real thing. . . . The entire course of the war in Russia may depend on the outcome of this test."[12] Sometimes, Soviet officials delivered appeals for support, as when Foreign Minister Litvinov spoke to NBC on May 16, 1942, on the program *United Nations Speak*.[13]

On CBS, Eliot was realistic. "The Russians benefit from victory or stalemate, while the Germans need positive gains in this year before they bleed too much in 1943," he said. "It is apparent that the great trial of strength between the Russians and the Germans is still to come. . . . The Germans have great reserves of striking power which they have not yet thrown into the fight," he added, developing a theme that it was Hitler who needed to win in 1942. "The Germans stake all on victory in 1942. . . . Beyond purely military considerations, there are underlying psychological factors."[14] Eliot credited Joseph Harsch for observing that

> German morale stands on two legs: A lively anticipation of the possible fruits of victory, and an equally lively anticipation of the certain consequences of defeat. Every German believes that victory would bring him an easier and better life. But an increasing number of Germans are losing their belief in the possibility of such a victory, and all of them know very well that, if Germany is beaten, the Nazis have made themselves so hated throughout the surrounding countries of Europe that a beaten Germany is unlikely to escape without feeling the revenge of the insulted and injured.[15]

Eliot and Harsch understood what the Second Front Now advocates would not—time favored the Allies.

Other press concerns during May included the Free French, Britain's landings in Madagascar, and the efficacy of rationing and economic planning efforts. The war economy was changing life at home. The rubber shortage grew worse. Sugar was scarce. Citizens received War Ration Book Number 1 on May 4, 1942. Inside were coupons redeemable for a pound of sugar every two weeks.[16] In kitchens across the country, cooks figured out how to stretch, while children remembered candy.[17] Gasoline rationing hit on May 15. "A" card holders, with no war-relevant transportation needs, could pump three gallons per week, which made "B" and "X" cards coveted items. "B" cards were for commercial use, while "X" cards granted unlimited pumping privileges.[18] Dried up gas tax revenues hurt local budgets. More and more women poured into the service branches. On May 16, NBC and CBS reported Major Oveta Culp Hobby's commission as head of the Woman's Army Auxiliary Corps.[19]

Also on the press docket was the war's proper name. *The New Republic* announced in May that "The Second World War" was better than "The Survival War," "War of World Freedom," "Anti-Nazi War," or "War for Humanity." "It's the Second World War, officially, World War II for *Time* readers who insist upon a free man's right to have the salad before the soup and sprinkle it with sand," joked *The New Republic.* "The Second World War was what the people named it at the beginning."[20]

On May 26, Rommel attacked in the Libyan Sahara. German and Italian *panzers* headed for Bir Hacheim and Tobruk, grabbing coastal roads, and routing Britain's demoralized 8th Army. By June, Auchinleck told Churchill that it might be time to fall back to Egypt. The British garrison at Tobruk surrendered on 21 June. Military analysts considered this Rommel's most brilliant victory.[21] Churchill hurried to Cairo, dispatching Auchinleck to Iraq, replacing him with Harold Alexander. Bernard Law Montgomery would head the 8th Army. The British stopped Rommel at El Alamein, fighting battles there in June and November.[22] American media covered all the North African combat.

Topical American commentary on the desert war came via CBS, courtesy of Cairo-based correspondent Edward Chorlian. His work was supplemented from London by Bob Trout and Murrow. Chorlian was well-placed stringer who also worked for Egyptian state radio.[23] This meant that he had a feel for the medium, and access to British authorities. Chorlian's reports were in the CBS tradition—colorful, anecdote-laden, delivered with feeling. On May 24, he narrated the arrival of Polish officers in the Middle East, saying that the stage was set "for the next round of the Libyan Tournament." He discussed the heat, commended Rommel's genius during battle, and praised Allied efforts to interrupt the cross-Mediterranean supply of the fuel needed by German tanks. He described an interview with a British sub commander attacking Axis shipping, asking him "What does it feel like to have depth charges dropped on you?" The answer Chorlian passed along was, "Pretty grim. It sounds like the crack of doom and feels like an earthquake."[24]

Days later, Chorlian again discussed Rommel, describing him as "all in" for the Libyan gamble, attempting to settle Egypt's fate and change the war's strategic calculation in Germany's favor. Chorlian, like Eliot, said that if the Allies held on in 1942, 1943 would see the balance shift in their favor. "It's now or never" for Rommel and Germany, he insisted, likening the campaign through Egypt to the drive on the Caucasus; part of the Reich's desperate gambit for oil. Addressing the arrival of more exiled Allied troops—this time, Czechs—he explained that oppressed peoples made good commandoes. "In our country, all the people are commandoes," said one a Czech soldier.[25]

The shooting of Heydrich in Prague by British-trained Czech commandoes made the news just as the Battle of Midway kicked off. The *Reichsprotektor* was shot on May 27 and died June 3. Murrow discussed the assassination.

As you know, Heydrich is dead," he led off. "He died as he lived, ignobly. The two men who shot him somewhere outside Prague have not yet been caught. The Germans, in their reprisals, have executed about 175 people. They will probably kill more. It must be a long time since any man's death caused less regret. One evening newspaper [in London] prints an epitaph without a name, merely a quotation from *Richard III*: "'The bloody dog is dead."[26]

Murrow did not yet know the exact nature of German reprisals, which included liquidating the entire town of Lidice. "Lidice" soon served as shorthand for Nazi war crimes before the Final Solution—which Heydrich did so much to advance—made it into American news.

There was a palpable sense in the media that, while Coral Sea was positive, initiative in the war was still at stake. So far, Japan determined where and when fighting would occur. The Allies reacted. Murrow said in early May that Midway was the pivot on which the Pacific campaign would turn. An unprepossessing dot on the map, Midway looked insignificant. Devoid of tropical charms, this coral outcropping boasted two related attributes: gooney birds (the native albatross) and location. They look ungainly but nesting seabirds know where to find landfall. In 1935, Pan Am built a Midway airport and hotel for its Clippers.[27] Before Pan Am's lobbying, the atoll—two islands , Eastern and Sand—was obscure,[28] but once the navy gained jurisdiction in 1934, Midway's importance became more clear. Midway is near the center of the Pacific Ocean. The navy built an air station and the Marines set up a security detachment. They erected everything necessary for occupation, including fresh water storage facilities and fuel depots.[29] Midway became an important way station on the Air Ferry Route across the Pacific.[30]

Japan's naval brass spent May polishing Yamamoto's plan for capturing this westernmost extension of the Hawaiian chain. Yamamoto remained bothered by the Doolittle Raid, convinced that the United States represented Japan's major threat. Grudgingly, an April 5 Naval General Staff agreed to his Midway action plan, Operation MI. Doolittle's Raid lent Yamamoto's idea the air of inevitability.[31] Operation MI was part of the evolving Japanese strategy, which had four segments. First, the fleet would capture Midway and the western Aleutians. This would set back American naval capacities.[32] Second, battleships would sail back to home waters, while the Midway force attacked New Caledonia and Fiji.[33] Third, a carrier force under Nagumo would bomb Sydney and southern Australia. Finally, Nagumo would meet up with the New Caledonia-Fiji fleet and set forth against Johnston Island and Hawaii. The key to the entire enterprise was luring an outnumbered American fleet to Tsushima-style destruction. Yamamoto counted on his initiative, since he would choose the location and nature of the decisive battle.[34]

Each of these steps was inordinately ambitious. Some critics—such as Vice Admiral Nobutake Kondo—called the proposal crazy.[35] But Yamamoto's ideal was Hawaii in Japanese hands. Breaking the enemy's ability to counterattack, holding on to initial gains, and making those permanent through negotiations was the model for victory over Russia in 1904–1905. Portsmouth was as great a Japanese victory as Tsushima Straits, which Yamamoto understood. All of the moving gyres in Yamamoto's plan were designed to accomplish two goals: the ruin of the US Pacific Fleet, and the capture of Hawaii. However, Yamamoto's plan spread his forces across a wide ocean instead of concentrating all striking power at Midway, the crucial point.

Since spirit and faith were so important in the Imperial Navy, it was hard for Japanese leaders to assess their prospects rationally. Another factor working against Tokyo was the fact that the US Navy's OP-20-G, the Communication Security Station of the Office of Naval Communications, understood Japan's ciphered messages. Acquiring this understanding took years. From 1937 onwards, the navy manned listening posts across the Pacific, intercepting and logging Japanese communications for analysis at Pearl Harbor and Washington.[36] Cryptographers and supervisors had to manage a mass of minutiae without losing sight of the big picture. By April 1942, only a small overall percentage of coded Japanese communications could be broken and read. But April saw real breakthroughs. By May, much more of the code could be understood.[37] As the larger shape of Japanese intentions emerged through its veil, so did the centrality of Midway. A clever ruse saw Midway send a clear message detailing water problems. When Japanese intelligence commented on the water situation, American cryptographers could see that Midway was Yamanoto's focus. It became Nimitz' focus, too.

Yamamoto intended to draw American naval forces north by attacking the Aleutians. Attu and Kiska were the bait for this trap. The idea was to creep along the Kuriles, rush across the Bering Sea, then invade the islands. Presumably, the United States would rush ships in to deal with such effrontery. Attu and Kiska saw protracted fighting.[38] Dutch Harbor was bombed on June 3.[39] But the Aleutians never became the distraction Yamamoto hoped. Nimitz resisted any pressure to divert strength from Midway, convinced that the Aleutians attack was a feint.[40] But jabs come before the knockout punch. Japan did not realize how much American strength accumulated at Midway. Diverting ships to Alaska was moot.[41]

Admiral Nagumo's 21-ship flotilla left Hashirajima, on May 27. "Midway Island acts as a sentry for Hawaii," Nagumo wrote, so the importance of his objective warranted the power at his command.[42] It was a mighty force: four carriers, *Akagi, Kaga, Soryu,* and *Hiryu*; a battleship, *Kirishima,* cruisers *Mikuma, Chikuma, Tone,* and *Haruna,* along with support vessels.[43] The accompanying invasion force contained 5,000 marines in 12 transport ships, under protective escort from a pair of battleships and four heavy cruisers.[44] Six hundred miles behind, one day's sailing time, sailed Yamamoto with the rest of the force. This included battleship, *Yamato,* the 72,800 ton behemoth.[45] Including everything afloat on the Japanese side, there were 93 ships available for the Midway effort, 119 if the Aleutians contingent was included.[46] This was the most prodigious naval force in world history, commanded by leaders with recent, stunning victories. Yamamoto counted on outnumbering his foe. He was correct, since total American ships devoted to the Midway battle numbered 47, 69 counting the Aleutian campaign.[47]

The move against Midway was supposed to divide the American fleet and destroy it. Nimitz knew he faced a complex plan. On May 28, he dispatched Rear Admiral Raymond A. Spruance directly to Midway. Spruance was a replacement for Halsey, hospitalized with psoriasis. Spruance's Task Force 16 had flattops *Enterprise* and *Hornet,* heavy cruisers *Pensacola, Northampton, New Orleans, Minneapolis,* and *Vincennes,* light cruiser *Atlanta,* 11 destroyers, 2 tankers, and 19 submarines.[48] Task Force 17, under Fletcher, sailed on May 30, with *Yorktown,* the carrier, *Portland* and *Astoria,* heavy cruisers, and 6 destroyers.[49]

On May 31, the Imperial Navy noted the unusually heavy volume of "urgent" US Navy messages, concluding that the Midway attack might be anticipated. The possibility might have chilled a more cautious HQ, since Yamamoto depended upon surprise. Two days later, Spruance and Fletcher rendezvoused northeast of Midway.[50] On the evening of June 3, the Americans were 400 miles east from where Nagumo intended to launch his planes the following morning.[51]

"An attack for the purpose of capturing Midway is expected," went the signal from Spruance to ships under his command.

The attacking force may be composed of all combatant types including four of five carriers. . . . If presence of Task Forces 16 and 17 remains unknown to enemy, we should be able to make surprise flank attacks on enemy carriers from positions northeast of Midway. Further operations will be based on results of these attacks. . . . The successful conclusion of the operation now commencing will be of great value to our country.[52]

Unflappable, Spruance was a quiet man without that charisma which made other admirals into press heroes.[53] But he grasped the situation. On June 3, a plane spotted the Japanese landing force 700 miles west of Midway. B-17 Flying Fortresses from the Naval Air Station attacked these transports without much result. Catalina seaplanes hit a Japanese oiler.[54] Neither Spruance nor Fletcher gave credence to hasty claims that the transports were part of the carrier group. It was the carriers that interested them, so the Americans kept searching for Nagumo. Nagumo had an advantage. He knew the location of his main objective—the island itself. But he did not know the location of his opponents. Japanese submarines were supposed to have lain in wait at French Frigate Reef, fueling seaplanes to monitoring comings and goings from Pearl Harbor. But American patrols discovered them. Destroyers appeared, the subs left, and there was no seaplane observation. This occurred when the *Yorktown*, which the Japanese thought they sank at Coral Sea, returned for repair. Nagumo and Yamamoto were without important information about enemy strength.[55]

Nagumo sent planes aloft at 4:30 a.m. on June 4—108 Zero fighters and Val bombers headed for Midway, but an American seaplane spotted them and warned the air station, which sent up interceptors. The resultant aerial skirmish went Japan's way, but winning an air battle was not Nagumo's objective. The Japanese planes were supposed to annihilate Midway's defenses, which they could not do while dealing with American pursuit.[56] A Japanese destroyer sighted an approaching squadron of Marauders and Avengers. Its signal flags, "ENEMY PLANES IN SIGHT," presented Nagumo with fateful choices. He wanted to neutralize Midway, but his carrier force needed protection. He had to decide whether to equip his planes with torpedoes for use against carriers or bombs to hit Midway again. Yamamoto had ordered him to torpedo planes on standby, and to protect his own flattops.[57] But Nagumo also needed to pave the way for invasion of Midway. He hesitated, then ordered the switch from torpedoes to bombs.[58] This required lowering each plane from the flight deck into a hanger, where the payloads could be swapped.[59] He could not launch and receive planes at the same time.[60] The result was a flurry of flight deck work which made take-off and landings difficult, leaving *Akagi* and *Kaga* exposed when the Marauders and Avengers showed up. Flying through anti-aircraft fire, the American planes failed to do much damage, but by harrying *Akagi* and *Kaga*, they disrupted Nagumo's plans. The role of American torpedo planes in the battle was self-sacrifice. Fifty-one planes went after Japanese carriers; only seven escaped; 126 torpedo bomber crewmen set out, only 29 survived. Torpedoes were inaccurate, as well. That was overlooked for many years, since the sacrificial nature of the torpedo plane actions helped to win the battle.[61]

Nagumo still craved information about which target to hit first. If American carriers were close, then they would be first priority. If they were distant, then bombing Midway could proceed. He halted the rearming of the Kates to await solid information.[62] Mitsuo Fuchida and Masatake Okumiya, two of Japan's best naval aviators, saw that Nagumo was the victim of a plan allocating him two incompatible tactical objectives. The priority of amphibious assault on Midway on June 5 locked his ships into a position which cut their flexibility. That impinged on seeking and destroying the American flotilla.[63] Nagumo's hesitancy was a microcosm of his divided responsibilities.

It was then that American dive-bombers launched from *Enterprise, Hornet,* and *Yorktown.* Fletcher was tipped off by a Japanese message announcing sighting of Force 16. Spruance accepted the risk of faulty information and ordered the attack.[64] Observers pinpointed this stroke as a turning point.[65] Anti-aircraft fire and Zeroes took their toll, but the carrier-based bombers hit their targets.[66] Beneath the sea, submarine *Nautilus* fired away at the Japanese carriers, as well. Nagumo was under assault from above and below.[67] Planes from *Hiryu* bombed *Yorktown,* which remained afloat. Fletcher transferred to cruiser *Astoria,* and granted operational control to Spruance, promising to conform to his movements.[68] The Battle of Midway reached its highest pitch. Pilots made sightings, signal officers passed along information, commanders made decisions. Spruance kept his concentration doggedly fixed on Japan's carriers. The spree saw American planes strike *Akagi, Soryu,* and *Kaga.* By the end of June 4, one American and three Japanese carriers suffered serious damage. Having dared greatly all day, Spruance prudently disengaged, sailing east instead of chasing Nagumo's remnant. Running into the approach of Yamamoto's follow-up force might have led to Spruance's destruction.[69] Later critics of Spruance's sudden caution failed to imagine that the loss of his newly victorious carriers would have turned victory into defeat.[70] Late on June 4, Japanese intelligence remained flawed, for *Hiryu* Admiral Tamon Yamaguchi thought his planes had destroyed two different carriers, whereas they really hit *Yorktown* twice.[71] Midway never received the follow-up wave from Nagumo, since the Japanese task force found itself fighting for its life. Fuchida observed with astonishment, "Instead of the expected easy victory, the picture had suddenly become one of catastrophic defeat!"[72]

The next day, after damage assessment, Yamamoto abandoned *Akagi,* sinking it with torpedoes after its crew evacuated. Spruance's planes went after stragglers. *Hiryu* was hit by planes from *Enterprise* and sank.[73] Yamamoto still hoped that his own force, properly managed, might win yet.[74] He hoped that Spruance would launch a follow-up attack. But Spruance demurred, intending to keep his fleet intact. *Soryu* sank, as did *Kaga,* maimed by dive bombers from *Yorktown.* By June 6, Nagumo's carrier force was wrecked. Fuchida noted that Yamamoto was "too stunned to speak"; he "just groaned as he read the tragic words" of the report, while "the jubilant optimism of the staff changed instantly to black despair."[75] Yamamoto ordered a withdrawal and the two fleets broke contact. Spruance hunted Yamamoto for awhile, but was still careful, aware that coming under the range of Japanese planes operating from Wake Island might give the enemy a chance to accomplish what they failed to at Midway.[76] His third masterful decision was not to risk losing his victorious flotilla at this late stage.[77] The coda came on June 7, when Japanese sub *I-168* located and sank the damaged *Yorktown*, under tow on the way back to Pearl Harbor. This put American losses at a destroyer, a flattop, 150 aircraft and 307 pilots and sailors.[78] Total Japanese losses were 3,500 men, 4 aircraft carriers, and a cruiser. Three hundred and twenty-two planes and pilots were lost, along with maintenance crews.[79] The Imperial Navy never recovered, seeing its naval air capability—that striking arm which began its war at Pearl Harbor—severely degraded.[80]

Yamamoto accepted blame, and Ukagi wrote,

> We can't help concluding that the main cause for the defeat was that we had become conceited with past success and lacked studies of what to do in case an enemy air force appears on a flank while we are launching a concentrated attack.[81]

At the same time, dizzied by the downfall, Tokyo suppressed the news. Ukagi thought this wise: "Except for those made public by the General Staff, nothing should be revealed about Midway and the Aleutian operation inside as well as outside of the Navy."[82] Within the navy, it was admitted only that *Kaga* was lost. Japanese newspapers published drawings of American carriers being sunk by Japanese planes. A *Japan Times* headline ran, "Navy Scores Another Epochal Victory." The article proclaimed "American hopes of conducting guerilla war on Japan by means of planes from aircraft carriers" now dashed, claiming two carriers sunk at Midway, adding that only two more remained from a pre-December 7 total of seven. The Aleutians and Midway were added to the list of great Imperial Navy victories.[83] The navy unloaded its casualties onto a hospital ship at Hashirajima under cover of night, keeping the wounded under tight security with no family contact.[84] Soon, the propensity for secrecy—intimately connected to the shame impulse—resulted in quashing the on-air claims of Tokyo rose and other propaganda outlets, which made their usual boasts about the magnitude of the victory for two days, but whose quick silence showed a Japanese taboo draped over Midway.[85]

American headlines were accurate and upbeat. "They Wanted to Know, 'Where's the US Pacific Fleet?' Did They? Admiral Nimitz had the Answer and it Has been Delivered at Midway!"[86] So enthused the *The Honolulu Star-Bulletin*. "US Strives for KO Blow in Pacific in Biggest Sea Battle Since Jutland," exulted the June 8 *Detroit News*.[87] The *News* added: "8 to 16 Japanese Warships Damaged in Crushing Defeat in Mid-Pacific."[88] The Associated Press text could not go beyond the navy communique, but pointed out that transports were included in the official message, indicating that a Midway invasion had been stopped. There was understanding of key battle elements. "If Japan hoped to catch by surprise the Midway defenders . . . the surprise worked in reverse," went one observation.[89] "Midway's outpost is poised like a dagger over Japan's Marshall Islands to the southwest, and the enemy's big gamble, its first with such heavy and costly armament . . . was indicative of its determination to knock out the possible stepping stone to a western resurgence of the United States in the Pacific" went another.[90]

"Japs Raid Honolulu, Rome Radio Reports"[91] might have caused panic earlier, but when the headline ran on June 6, derision was the reaction. "Jap People Being Prepared for Bad Sea News" crowed the *Baltimore Evening Sun* on June 9, drawn from Berlin broadcasts. German radio quoted a philosophical Japanese Admiral, "One cannot always expect victories but must also be able to stand losses," the unnamed figure was supposed to have said.[92] The article noted Radio Tokyo's unbroken silence as speaking volumes.[93] By June 11, details began to appear. AP's Clark Lee described the shape of the Japanese fleet, divided between transports for invasion and a battle force. He gave accurate dates, covering the defense of Midway Island and actions of American ships. "Part of the epic story of the battle of Midway was told today by the American Army pilots, who, with navy and marine flyers, smashed Admiral Yamamoto's fleet and saved the Hawaiian Islands from invasion," he wrote. "It is a story of cool courage and firm determination—of the unbeatable combination of American men and machines."[94] Lee's beat within the fleet gave him an insider's view. He followed up his news stories with a book on the 1942 actions, *They Call it Pacific: An Eye-Witness Story of our War Against Japan from Bataan to the Solomons.*

Reporters had waited a long time to write copy like this; the US Navy had waited just as long to give such news to the press. It was only on June 12 that the navy released the fullest account of the Coral Sea Battle, along with pictures. These made better reading with the early news of Midway.[95] The careful delivery masked a potentially explosive scoop obtained by McCormick's *Chicago Tribune*. Thanks to Stanley Johnston, well-connected reporter at the Coral Sea with good navy contacts, the paper had advance word. It knew that the US Navy considered the Aleutians attack a diversion from Midway.[96] This was combustible, for Johnston's information implied to the secret of Japan's broken naval code. "Navy Had Word of Jap Plans To Strike at Sea, Knew Dutch Harbor Was a Feint," shouted the *Tribune*. "Jap Fleet Smashed by US, 2 Carriers Sunk at Midway."[97] Thankfully, amidst the hullaballoo, these stories were not seized upon by Axis intelligence. But the navy was livid with Johnston. Admiral King took steps to exclude *Tribune* reporters from press conferences; some officials wanted McCormick hauled up on treason charges. A grand jury investigated.[98] In the end, probably to avoid drawing further attention, the matter lapsed.

With his admirable grasp of strategy, Raymond Gram Swing was one of the most forthright commentators. On June 6, he was direct. "The greatest air and sea battle of the war was still being fought in the Midway Island area today, but already it looms as a certain and imposing American victory," he said, adding with surprising accuracy the details that "The Japanese have lost two airplane carriers and possibly a third, with all their planes." He went on, "Without waiting for details, it is clear that Japan's effective striking power on its colossal assignment of conquest in the Pacific has been cut almost in half so far as aircraft carriers go."[99] Swing reminded Mutual listeners that there was still no final word on the exact damage at Pearl Harbor, and so totals from Midway should be taken as tentative. Nimitz's HQ still described the battle as an invasion forestalled. Instead of concentrating on elusive battle details, Swing filled in gaps with analysis.

> Whether the Japanese attack on Dutch Harbor was a diversion to distract attention from an attempt to conquer Midway Island, or whether both . . . were to be diversions to cover some other attack elsewhere is not known.

he explained.

> The simplest interpretation of the known facts is that the Japanese expected to take Midway Island. They arrived there in force and with troops. . . . It may also be that the Japanese were . . . hoping to suck into this area heavy naval forces which could be struck by still heavier naval forces of their own.[100]

CBS News led off on June 5 declaring that

> Somewhere in the Pacific, within striking distance of Midway Island, a great naval battle may be raging tonight. It's a battle in which the Japanese were severely pounded in the first round of their latest attack on our sturdy little Pacific outpost.[101]

This made Midway sound like Wake Island—an outpost defending against Japanese attack. It took days before the different nature of the Midway battle emerged. Initial accounts overplayed the role played by island-based planes to such an extent that navy aviators were disenfranchised from many news accounts.[102] Stories like "Army Fliers Blasted Two Fleets Off Midway," from the June 12 *New York Times*, perpetuated this misunderstanding.[103] The navy still needed to figure out how to publicize its fliers without revealing too much about operations.

On June 5, Alfred Warner discussed Washington's silence on naval matters. Nimitz controlled the news flow, he said. "But the impression in naval circles here is that Japan may have launched an all-out attack on Midway," he added, showing that official silence was not enough to stop informed speculation.[104] Within three days, CBS discussion revolved around the extent of Japanese losses. "Very heavy damage indeed," was the summation of June 6, with the addenda that "the Japanese seem to be withdrawing, our fleet is still pressing the attack," and the grace note from Admiral King that the US Navy would "continue to make the enemy realize that war is hell."[105]

Sevareid observed that the Pacific Fleet was now in better shape than before Pearl Harbor, let Midway wipe away six months of horrible news. "There is not much doubt that the fighting around Midway Island was of first-class proportions, and that the enemy has suffered a first-class defeat," he added.

> And what were the Japanese trying to do? The best opinion in Washington today is that this was an all-out attempt to smash and occupy Midway, permanently. If they had been successful in doing that, Pearl Harbor would have been in constant peril, also the Johnston Island lifeline to Australia.[106]

Sevareid concluded that,

> Midway is of extreme importance. As Navy men put it, Midway is to Hawaii what Hawaii is to the continental United States.... With Midway gone, the Japs might have some chance to take Hawaii itself. And it goes without saying that if that should happen, America's chances of winning this war with the Japanese would not be very imposing.[107]

John Daley observed that "this was a day in which communications and statements by Allied leaders took on a marked literary and inspirational character. Some of them are worthy of being remembered," he said from the CBS news desk, quoting Nimitz: "On every occasion when we have met the enemy, our officers and men have been superlative in their offensive spirit and complete lack of fear. Our country can feel safe with personnel such as this."[108]

By June 7, Harry Marble said, "The news from the Pacific is the most encouraging since the war began."[109] From Honolulu, Webley Edwards remembered where he was "six months ago, December 7. Pearl Harbor wasn't a pretty sight," he recollected. "This morning, six months later to the day and almost to the minute, I drove out again, and what a change. Uncle Sam's great Pacific Naval base, flanked by the Army and Marines, was in smooth working action this morning." Edwards described Nimitz as quiet, friendly, and smiling, and Japanese losses as disastrous. "This observer is able to put the picture together, and any way you put it together, it's a mighty good picture," Edwards summed up.[110] Eliot was no less positive. "It is obvious that naval command of the Pacific must soon pass, perhaps has already passed, into the hands of the United States fleet," he said, stressing that Japanese losses from Coral Sea and Midway were beyond any fleet's ability to withstand. "The destruction of the enemy's floating war power and the loss of many ships is bound to make a tremendous difference and may well permit us to pass definitely to a continuous series of offensive operations of increasing importance and result."[111]

The Battle of Midway brought no intimations that the war would end soon. However, the six months of Axis initiative were over. Henceforth, instead of chronicling Allied defeats, it was time to report on victories. In July, the British took their stand at El Alamein; Operation TORCH saw Anglo-American landings in Morocco and Algeria that November. By January 1943, the *Afrika Korps* retreated to Tunisia. In August, Hitler resolved to capture Stalingrad; *Wehrmacht* troops pressed into the Volga city by September. The Red Army counterattack cutting off the German VI Army came in November, and the Germans surrendered in February 1943. Such victories were bought with many lives. Americans and their Allies died at places like Guadalcanal, Kursk, Monte Cassino, Normandy, Leyte Gulf, and Okinawa. Millions of civilians across Europe, Asia, and Africa were killed. But each campaign, though bloody, meant an Allied victory. Every victory brought peace closer, and with it, the chance to build a better world. The first victory came at Midway in June 1942.

NOTES

Chapter 1

1. John Toland, *Infamy: Pearl Harbor and its Aftermath* (Garden City, NY: Doubleday, 1982), 11.
2. Mitsuo Fuchida & Masatake Okumiya, *Midway: The Battle That Doomed Japan, The Japanese Navy's Story* (Annapolis: Naval Institute Press, Bluejacket Books, 1992 c1955), 52.
3. Fuchida & Okumiya, *The Battle That Doomed Japan*, 51.
4. Gordon W. Prange, *At Dawn We Slept: The Untold Story of Pearl Harbor* (New York: McGraw-Hill, 1981), 499.
5. Daniel Madsen, *Resurrection: Salvaging the Battle Fleet at Pearl Harbor* (Annapolis: Naval Institute Press, 2003), 6.
6. Cesar Salmaggi & Alfredo Pallavisini, *2194 Days of War: An Illustrated Chronology of the Second World War* (New York: Barnes & Noble Books, 1993), 177.
7. *The Picture History of World War II* (formerly Collier's Photographic History of World War II) (New York: Grossett & Dunlap, 1971 c1946), 60.
8. Salmaggi & Pallavisini, *2194 Days of War,* 176.
9. *The Picture History of World War II*, 64.
10. Madsen, *Salvaging the Battle Fleet at Pearl Harbor*, 6–12.
11. Linda Lotridge Levin, *The Making of FDR: The Story of Stephen T. Early, America's First Modern Press Secretary* (Amherst, NY: Prometheus Books, 2008), 257.
12. James MacGregor Burns, *Roosevelt 1940–1945: The Soldier of Freedom* (New York: Harcourt, Brace, Jovanovitch, 1970), 162.
13. Kenneth S. Davis, *FDR: The War President, 1940–1943, A History* (New York: Random House, 2000), 339.
14. Robert E. Sherwood, *Roosevelt and Hopkins, An Intimate History* (New York: Enigma Books, 2008 c1948), 331.
15. Levin, *The Making of FDR*, 251.
16. Ibid., 252.
17. Ibid.
18. Ibid., 252–61.
19. Robert A. Divine, *Roosevelt and World War II* (New York: Penguin Books, 1983), 16.
20. Divine, *Roosevelt and World War II*, 16–18.
21. Melvin G. Holli, *The Wisard of Washington: Emil Hurja, Franklin Roosevelt, and the Birth of Public Opinion Polling* (New York: Palgrave, 2002), 54–5.

22. Charles A. Lindbergh, "America and the War," Radio Speech, April 23, 1941. From Richard A. Hofstadter, ed., *Great Issues in American History: From Reconstruction to the Present Day, 1864–1969* (New York: Vintage, 1969), 404.
23. Levin, *The Making of FDR*, 248.
24. George Washington, "Farewell Address," September 17, 1796. From Richard Hofstadter, ed., *Great Issues in American History: From the Revolution to the Civil War, 1765–1865* (New York: Vintage Books, 1958), 219.
25. Nicholas John Cull, *Selling War: The British Propaganda Campaign Against American "Neutrality" in World War II* (New York: Oxford University Press, 1995), 31, 63–5.
26. Charles Kupfer, *We Felt the Flames: Hitler's Blitzkrieg, America's Story* (Carlisle, PA: Sergeant Kirkland's Press, 2004), 204.
27. Anne Morrow Lindbergh, *The Wave of the Future: A Confession of Faith* (New York: Harcourt, Brace, 1940), 19.
28. Anne Morrow Lindbergh, *War Within and Without: Diaries and Letters, 1939–1944* (New York: Harcourt, Brace, Jovanovich, 1980), 143.
29. Clare Boothe Luce, Book Review. *Current History*, November 7, 1940.
30. Anne Morrow Lindbergh, 152–3.
31. Walter L. Hixson, *Charles A. Lindbergh: Lone Eagle* (New York: Pearson-Longman, 2007), 115.
32. Anne Morrow Lindbergh, 146.
33. Charles A. Beard, *President Roosevelt and the Coming of the War 1941* (New York: Archon Books, 1968 c1948), 210–11.
34. Ronald H. Bailey, *The Home Front: USA* (New York: Time/Life, 1977), 23.
35. Robert A. Divine, *The Illusion of Neutrality: Franklin D. Roosevelt and the Struggle over the Arms Embargo* (Chicago: Quadrangle Books, 1968), 229–335.
36. Patrick Renshaw, *Franklin D. Roosevelt* (Harlow, UK: Pearson-Longman, 2004), 45.
37. Renshaw, Franklin D. Roosevelt, 45.
38. Richard M. Ketchum, *The Borrowed Years: 1938–1941, America on the Way to War* (New York: Random House, 1989), 375, 434–5, 528.
39. Kupfer, *We Felt the Flames*, 1.
40. Robert E. Herzstein, *Roosevelt and Hitler: Prelude to War* (New York: John Wiley & Sons, 1994), 94–5.
41. A.M. Sperber, *Murrow: His Life and Times* (New York: Bantam, 1986), 204.
42. Kupfer, *We Felt the Flames*, 11–21 & passim.
43. Cpt. Alfred H. Miles, USN, "Anchors Aweigh" (original lyrics), 1905. Available at: www.usna.edu./USNABand/FAQ/Lyrics/htm
44. Rev. William Whiting & Rev. John B. Dykes, "Eternal Father Strong to Save: 'The Navy Hymn.'" Available at: www.usna.edu/USNABand/FAQ/Lyrics.htm
45. Kenneth Wimmel, *Theodore Roosevelt and the Great White Fleet: American Sea Power Comes of Age* (Dulles, VA: Brassey's, 1998), 48.
46. "A British Tar," *H.M.S. Pinafore* W. S. Gilbert & Arthur Sullivan, 1878. "The 1930 D'Oyly Care Recording" (London: Romaphone, 1996).
47. A. J. Langguth, *Patriots: The Men Who Started the American Revolution* (New York: Simon & Schuster, 1988), 338.
48. *Encyclopedia Brittanica*, 15th edn, s.v. "Mahan, Alfred Thayer," vol. 6, 498–9.
49. Alfred Thayer Mahan, *The Influence of Sea Power Upon History, 1660–1783* (Boston: Little, Brown, 1898), 1.

50. John L. Gaddis, *The Long Peace: Inquiries into the History of the Cold War* (New York: Oxford University Press, 1987), 22–5.

51. Edward S. Miller, *War Plan Orange: The US Strategy to Defeat Japan, 1897–1945* (Annapolis: Naval Institute Press, 1991), 37.

52. Emily S. Rosenberg, *Spreading the American Dream: American Economic and Cultural Expansion, 1890–1945* (New York: Hill and Wang, 1982), 230.

53. H. P. Wilmott, *The Barrier and the Javelin: Japanese and Allied Pacific Strategies, February to June 1942* (Annapolis: Naval Institute Press, 1983), 7, 18–19.

54. Miller, War Plan Orange, 37.

55. Vincent P. O'Hara, *The U.S. Navy Against the Axis: Surface Combat 1941–1945* (Annapolis: Naval Institute Press, 2007), 1.

56. Arthur Herman, *To Rule the Waves: How the British Navy Shaped the Modern World* (New York: Harper Perennial, 2004), 466.

57. "Famous Navy Quotes: Who Said Them and When." From "Naval History & Heritage Command." Available at: www.history.navy.mil/trivia/trivia02.htm

58. William S. Dudley. ed., *The Naval War of 1812: A Documentary History*, vol. 2 (Washington, DC: Naval Historical Center, 1992), 553.

59. Chester G. Hearn, *Admiral David Glasgow Farragut: The Civil War Years* (Annapolis: Naval Institute Press, 1988), 263.

60. George Dewey, *Autobiography of George Dewey, Admiral of the Navy* (New York: Charles Scribner & Sons, 1913), 214. From "Naval History & Heritage Command." Available at: www.history.navy.mil/trivia02.htm

61. Theodore Roosevelt, "Second Annual Message to Congress," December 2, 1902. From "Naval History & Heritage Command." Available at: www.history.navy.mil/trivia/trivia02.htm

62. Wimmel, *Theodore Roosevelt and the Great White Fleet*, 48.

63. Joseph Alsop, with Adam Platt, *I've Seen the Best of It: Memoirs* (Mount Jackson, VA: Axios Press, 1992), 12.

64. President Woodrow Wilson, December 8, 1914, Annual Message to Congress. From Arthur S. Link, ed., *The Papers of Woodrow Wilson*, vol. 31 (Princeton: Princeton University Press, 1979), 423.

65. Gaddis, *The Long Peace*, 22.

66. Wimmel, *Theodore Roosevelt and the Great White Fleet*, 60–1.

67. Ralph Henry Gabriel, *The Course of American Democratic Thought* (New York: Ronald Press, 1943), H 347.

68. Gabriel, *The Course of American Democratic Thought*, 349.

69. Ibid.

70. Gaddis, *The Long Peace*, 22.

71. Ibid., 22–3.

72. Arthur Link, *Wilson the Diplomatist: A Look at his Major Foreign Policies* (New York: New Viewpoints, 1974), 12–13.

73. Link, *Wilson the Diplomatist*, 13–14.

74. Ibid., 102–05.

75. Ibid., 105.

76. Lorena A. Hickok, *The Road to the White House, FDR: the Pre-Presidential Years* (Chilton/Scholastic: New York, 1963), 34–5, 105–16.

77. Donald Cameron Watt, *How War Came: The Immediate Origins of the Second World War, 1938–1939* (New York: Pantheon Books, 1989), 125.

78. Watt, *How War Came*, 125–7.
79. John Toland, *But Not In Shame: The Six Months After Pearl Harbor* (New York: Random House, 1961), 40.
80. Toland, *But Not In Shame,* 39.
81. Cecil V. Crabb, Jr. & Pat M. Holt, *Invitation to Struggle: Congress, the President, and Foreign Policy* (Washington, DC: Congressional Quarterly, 1989), 30–1.
82. Barry Rubin, *Secrets of State: The State Department and the Struggle over US Foreign Policy* (New York: Oxford University Press, 1987), 24–6.
83. Dean Acheson, *Present at the Creation: My Years in the State Department* (New York: W.W. Norton, 1969), 11.
84. Acheson, *My Years in the State Department,* 12–13.
85. Rubin, *Secrets of State,* 26.
86. Prange, *At Dawn We Slept,* 6–7.
87. Sherwood, *Roosevelt and Hopkins,* 336.
88. Cordell Hull, *The Memoirs of Cordell Hull* (New York: Macmillan, 1948), 1095.
89. Davis, *FDR: The War President,* 339.
90. Ibid.
91. Hull, *The Memoirs of Cordell Hull,* 1096.
92. Ibid., 1097.
93. Ibid., 1096.
94. Davis, *FDR: The War President,* 340.
95. Hull, *The Memoirs of Cordell Hull,* 1098.
96. Levin, *The Making of FDR,* 261–2.
97. Davis, *FDR: The War President,* 340.
98. Hull, *The Memoirs of Cordell Hull,* 1100.
99. Sherwood, *Roosevelt and Hopkins,* 338.
100. Burns, *Roosevelt 1940–1945,* 164.
101. Ibid.
102. Francis Biddle, "The Power of Democracy: It Can Meet All Conditions," *Vital Speeches of the Day,* October 15, 1941, 5–9.
103. Burns, *Roosevelt 1940–1945,* 164–5.
104. Ibid., 164.
105. Davis, *FDR: The War President,* 340.
106. Burns, *Roosevelt 1940–1945,* 165.
107. Eric Sevareid, *Not so Wild a Dream* (Columbia, MO: University of Missouri Press, 1995 c1946), 205.
108. Sperber, *Murrow,* 206.
109. Davis, *FDR: The War President,* 342.
110. Sperber, *Murrow,* 206.
111. Philip Seib, *Broadcasts from the Blitz: How Edward R. Murrow Helped Lead America into War* (Washington, DC: Potomac Books, 2007), 158.
112. Seib, *Broadcasts from the Blitz,* 158–9.
113. Peter Kurth, *American Cassandra: The Life of Dorothy Thompson* (Boston: Little, Brown, 1990), 321.
114. Sperber, *Murrow,* 206.
115. Ibid.
116. Davis, *FDR: The War President,* 342.
117. Graham J. White, *FDR and the Press* (Chicago: University of Chicago Press, 1979), 9–10, 162.

118. Sperber, *Murrow*, 206–07.
119. Ibid., 207–08.
120. Henry H. Adams, *1942: The Year that Doomed the Axis* (New York: Paperback Library, 1967), 42–3.
121. *The Picture History of World War II*, 65.
122. U.S. Department of State, *Papers Relating to the Foreign Relations of the United States, Japan: 1931–1941* (Washington, DC: Government Printing Office, 1943), 793.
123. Julia Ward Howe, "Battle-Hymn of the Republic," *The Golden Treasury of Poetry* (New York: Golden Press, 1968), 311.
124. William H. Goetzmann, *Beyond the Revolution: A History of American Thought from Paine to Pragmatism* (New York: Basic Books, 2009), 382.
125. Goetzmann, *Beyond the Revolution*, 3.
126. State Department Papers, *Japan: 1931–1941*, 794.
127. Sherwood, *Roosevelt and Hopkins*, 342.
128. Ibid.
129. H.W. Brands, *Traitor to his Class: The Privileged Life and Radical Presidency of Franklin Delano Roosevelt* (New York: Anchor Books, 2009), 633.
130. Gabriel, *The Course of American Democratic Thought*, v.
131. "Demetia Praecox," from *The Freeman*, June 21, 1922; from Loren Baritz, *The Culture of the Twenties* (Indianapolis: Bobbs-Merrill, 1978), 29.
132. Veblen from Baritz, 35.
133. Henry Steele Commager, *The American Mind: An Interpretation of American Thought and Character since the 1880s* (New Haven: Yale University Press, 1950), 242.
134. Justus D. Doenecke, ed., In *Danger Undaunted: The Anti-Interventionist Movement of 1940–1941* as revealed in the Papers of the America First Committee (Palo Alto: Hoover Institution Press, 1990), 5.
135. H. D. Mencken, *The Diary of H.L. Mencken* (New York: Alfred A. Knopf, 1989), 149.
136. Robert M. Crunden, *American Salons: Encounters with European Modernism, 1885–1917* (New York: Oxford University Press, 1993), 164–5.
137. Watt, *How War Came*, 127.
138. Kupfer, *We Felt the Flames*, 183.
139. Hugh S. Johnson, "Defend America First: We Must Rely on our own Strength." NBC Radio, September 5, 1940. From *Vital Speeches of the Day*, October 1, 1940, 763.
140. Irving Fang, *Those Radio Commentators!* (Ames, IA: Iowa State University Press, 1977).
141. Walter L. Hixson, *Charles A. Lindbergh: Lone Eagle* (New York: Pearson-Longman, 2007), 111.
142. Hixson, *Lone Eagle*, 121.
143. Ibid., 123.
144. Kupfer, *We Felt the Flames*, 184–6.
145. Cull, *Selling War*, 33–153, passim.
146. Justus Donecke, In *Danger Undaunted: The Anti-Interventionist Movement of 1940–1941* as revealed in the Papers of the America First Committee (Palo Alto: Hoover Institution Press, 1990) 6.
147. William R. Castle to R. Douglas Stuart, Jr. December 8, 1942. Document 143. Donecke, 453–4.
148. Adams, *The Year that Doomed the Axis*, 44.
149. State Department Papers, *Japan: 1931–1941*, 795.

150. Martin V. Melosi, *The Shadow of Pearl Harbor: Political Controversy over the Surprise Attack, 1941–1946* (College Station, TX: Texas A&M University Press, 1977), 3.

151. Melosi, *The Shadow of Pearl Harbor*, 3.

152. E. B. White, "One Man's Meat," *Harper's*, January 1942, 329.

153. White, "One Man's Meat," 329.

154. Donald Dewey & Nicholas Acocella, *Total Ballclubs: The Ultimate Book of Baseball Teams* (Toronto: Sport Classic Books, 2005), 557–8.

155. Joseph L. Reichler, ed., *The Baseball Encyclopedia: The Complete and Official Record of Major League Baseball* (New York: Macmillan, 1982), 355–7.

156. Lawrence S. Ritter, *Lost Ballparks: A Celebration of Baseball's Legendary Fields* (New York: Viking Studio Books, 1992), 73–8, 197.

157. James Edward Miller, *The Baseball Business: Pursuing Pennants and Profits in Baltimore* (Chapel Hill: University of North Carolina Press, 1990), 23.

158. Dewey & Acocella, *Total Ballclubs*, 557–8.

159. William B. Mead, *Even the Browns: Baseball During World War II* (New York: Dover Press, 2010) pp. 186–203.

160. George Robinson & Charles Salzburg, *On a Clear Day They Could See Seventh Place: Baseball's Worst Teams* (New York: Dell Trade, 1991), 153.

161. Brands, *Traitor to his Class*, 633.

162. Peter T. Rohrbach, "Radio in World War II: News and Entertainment," *Performing Arts Broadcasting* (Washington, DC: Library of Congress/Government Printing Office, 2002), 125.

163. Franklin Delano Roosevelt, *Fireside Chats* (New York: Penguin, 1995), 64.

164. Roosevelt, *Fireside Chats*, 64–5.

165. Ibid., 65.

166. Ibid., 66.

167. Kupfer, *We Felt the Flames*, 116–40.

168. Roosevelt, *Fireside Chats*, 68–9.

169. Ibid., 68–75.

170. Rohrbach, "Radio in World War II: News and Entertainment," 125.

171. Brands, *Traitor to his Class*, 635.

172. Ibid., 635.

173. Adams, *The Year that Doomed the Axis*, 53.

174. Ibid., 55.

175. Ibid.

176. Ibid.

177. Roosevelt, 12/9/41, 75.

178. Peter Bulkeley, "New England and Her Covenant," 1646, from William H. Goetzmann, ed., *The Colonial Horizon: America in the Sixteenth and Seventeenth Centuries* (Reading, MA: Addison-Wesley, 1969), 178.

179. Alfred W. Crosby, *Ecological Imperialism: The Biological Expansion of Europe, 900–1900* (New York: Cambridge, 1989), 208.

180. William H. Goetzmann, *When the Eagle Screamed: The Romantic Horizon in American Diplomacy, 1800–1860* (New York: John Wiley & Sons, 1966), xii–xvii.

181. James Kirke Paulding, *The Diverting History of John Bull and Brother Jonathan*, (Philadelphia: R. Desilver), 1827, c1812. From Googlebooks, available at: www.books.google.com/books

182. Lawrence W. Levine, *Highbrow, Lowbrow: The Emergence of Cultural Hierarchy in America* (Cambridge, MA: Harvard University Press, 1988), 145.

183. Winston S. Churchill, *The Grand Alliance* (Boston: Houghton-Mifflin, 1951), 606.

184. Sabine Baring-Gould & Arthur S. Sullivan, "Onward Christian Soldiers," *Service Book and Hymnal* (Minneapolis: Augsburg Publishing House, 1958), 560.

185. Warren F. Kimball, *Forged in War: Roosevelt, Churchill, and the Second World War* (Chicago: Ivan R. Dee, 2003), 15.

186. John Colville, *The Fringes of Power* (Guilford, CT: Lyons Press, 1985), 136.

187. "James Kirk Paulding," from Wikipedia, www.wikipedia.org.

188. Paulding, *Diverting History of John Bull and Brother Jonathan*.

189. Levine, *Highbrow, Lowbrow*, 20.

190. Ibid., 17.

191. Ibid., 17–18.

192. Ibid., 39.

193. Sacvan Bercovitch, *The American Jeremiad* (Madison: University of Wisconsin Press, 1978), 117.

194. Mark Twain, *A Connecticut Yankee in King Arthur's Court* (New York: Washington Square Press, 1973 c1889), 341.

195. William H. Goetzmann, with Dickon Pratt *The American Hegelians: An Intellectual Episode in the History of Western America* (New York: Alfred A. Knopf, 1973), 4.

196. Goetzmann, Ibid., 9.

197. Ibid., 9.

198. George P. Soule & Vincent Carosso, *American Economic History* (New York: Holt, Rinehart, & Winston, 1957), 191.

199. Harvey S. Perloff, Edgar S. Dunn, Jr, Eric E. Lampard, and Richard F. Muth, *Regions, Resources, and Economic Growth* (Lincoln: University of Nebraska Press, 1960), 197.

200. Clark G. Spence, *British Investments in the American Mining Frontier, 1869–1901* (Ithaca, NY: Cornell University Press for the American Historical Association, 1958), 2–3.

201. Spence, *British Investments in the American Mining Frontier*, 241–60.

202. Levine, *Highbrow, Lowbrow*, 145.

203. David M. Kennedy, *Over Here: The First World War and American Society* (New York: Oxford University Press, 1980), 215–26.

204. Barbara Tuchman, *The Proud Tower: A Portrait of the World Before the War, 1890–1914* (New York: Ballantine Books, 1996), 139.

205. Matthias Maass, "Catalyst for the Roosevelt Corollary: Arbitrating the 1902–1903 Venezuela Crisis and its Impact on the Development of the Roosevelt Corollary to the Monroe Doctrine," from *Diplomacy & Statecraft* (London: Routledge, Taylor & Francis, 2009), 383–402.

206. David Dimbleby & David Reynolds, *An Ocean Apart: The Relationship Between Britain and America in the Twentieth Century* (New York: Random House, 1988), 48.

207. Tuchman, *The Proud Tower*, 134–67.

208. Kenneth McNaught, *The Pelican History of Canada* (New York: Penguin, 1982), 208–09.

209. Bradley Smith, *Japan: A History in Art* (Tokyo: Gemini Incorporated, 1964), 230.

210. Dimbleby & Reynolds, *An Ocean Apart*, 48.

211. Ibid.

212. William Woodruff, *America's Impact on the World: A Study of the Role of the United States in the World Economy, 1750–1970* (New York: John Wiley & Sons, 1975), 45.

213. Woodruff, *America's Impact on the World*, 45.
214. "J. Russell to Palmerston," September 17, 1862. "Russell and Palmerston Discuss Intervention," from Henry Steele Commager, ed., *The Blue and The Gray: The Nomination of Lincoln to the Eve of Gettsyburg* (New York: Mentor, 1973), 532.
215. William Eward Gladstone, "An Error, Most Singular and Palapable," from Commager, ed., 535.
216. *The Times*, October 7, 1862. "The English Press Condemns the Emancipation Proclamation," from Commager, ed., 537–40.
217. "Manchester Workingmen to President Abraham Lincoln," December 31, 1862. "We Are Truly One People," from Commager, ed., 540–1.
218. "President Abraham Lincoln to the Workingmen of Manchester," January 19, 1863, "An Instance of Sublime Christian Heroism," from Commuter, ed., 542–4.
219. Dimbleby & Reynolds, *An Ocean Apart*, 46.
220. Alfred North Whitehead, *Dialogues of Alfred North Whitehead, as Recorded by Lucien Price* (New York: Mentor Book, 1954), 40.
221. Whitehead, *Dialogues of Alfred North Whitehead*, 41.
222. Ibid.
223. "Darwin in the New World," *Wall Street Journal Online*, available at: online.wsj.com/article/SB123146367064466617.html
224. Henry Adams, *The Education of Henry Adams* (New York: Heritage Press, 1942), 354.
225. Levine, *Highbrow, Lowbrow*, 172.
226. Henry Adams, *The Degradation of the Democratic Dogma* (New York: Macmillan, 1947), 261–305.
227. Brooks Adams, *The Law of Civilization and Decay: An Essay of History* (University of Michigan Library, HathiTrust Digitized Archives), 1895, *passim*.
228. Tuchman, *The Proud Tower*, 139.
229. William Graham Sumner, "What Social Classes Owe to Each Other," from Michael B. Levy, ed., *Political Thought in America: An Anthology* (Prospect Heights, IL: Waveland Press, 1992), 325.
230. Sumner, "What Social Classes Owe to Each Other," 327.
231. Leon Edel, *Henry James: A Life* (New York: Harper & Row, 1985), 206–07.
232. David Simpson, *The Politics of American English: 1776–1850* (New York: Oxford University Press, 1986), 125.
233. Booth Tarkington, *Penrod: His Complete Story* (Garden City, NY: Doubleday, 1931 c1913), 197.
234. Commager, *The American Mind*, 243.
235. Barbara Tuchman, *The Proud Tower: A Portrait of the World Before the War, 1890–1914* (New York: Ballantine Books, 1996), 15–16.
236. "Hugh Lowther, 5th Earl of Lonsdale," Wikipedia, http://en.wikipedia.org/wiki/Hugh_Lowther
237. Robert Sobel & David P. Sicilia, *The Entrepreneurs: An American Adventure* (Boston: Houghton-Mifflin, 1986), 114.
238. Sobel & Sicilia, *The Entrepreneurs*, 116–17.
239. "Harry Bensley," Wikipedia, http://en.wikipedia.org/wiki/Harry_Bensley
240. Alan Moorehead, *The White Nile* (New York: Harper & Row, 1971), 121.
241. Moorehead, *The White Nile*, 113–34.
242. J. Valerie Fifer, *American Progress: The Growth of the Transport, Tourist, and Information Industries in the 19th Century West* (Chester, CT: Globe-Pequot, 1988), 207.

243. Richard Usborne, *Plum Sauce: A P.G. Wodehouse Companion* (London: Ebury Press, 2002), 49.

244. P. G. Wodehouse, "One Touch of Nature," *The Man With Two Left Feet and Other Stories* (Woodstock, NY: Overlook Press, 2009, c1917, London: Methuen), 167–8.

245. Robert McCrum, *Wodehouse* (New York: W.W. Norton, 2004), 127–59.

246. Andrew Kohut & Bruce Stokes, *America Against the World: How We Are Different, and Why We Are Disliked* (New York: Holt Paperbacks, 2007), 22–3.

247. R. W. B. Lewis, *The American Adam: Innocence, Tragedy, and Tradition in the Nineteenth Century* (Chicago: University of Chicago Press, 1955), 99.

248. James Fenimore Cooper, *Homeward Bound, or, The Chase: A Tale of the Sea* (Philadelphia: Carey, Lea & Blanchard, 1838), 340. Available at: http://books.google.com/books

249. Cooper, *Homeward Bound*, 339.

250. Lord James Bryce, *The American Commonwealth* (New York: Putnam/Capricorn Books, 1959), 1.

251. Bryce, *The American Commonwealth*, 1, 302.

252. Christopher Morley, "In Memoriam Sherlock Holmes," from Arthur Conan Doyle, *The Complete Sherlock Holmes* (New York: Doubleday, 1940), xiii.

253. Morley, "In Memoriam Sherlock Holmes," xii–xiii.

254. *Encyclopedia Brittanica*, 15th edn, s.v. "Kipling, Rudyard," vol. 10, 486.

255. Frederic F. Van Der Water, *Rudyard Kipling's Vermont Feud* (Weston, VT: Countryman Press, 1937), 35.

256. Rudyard Kipling, *Letters of Travel* (New York: Macmillan, 1920), available at: http://en.wikipedia.org/wiki/Kipling_rudyard

257. *Encyclopedia Brittanica*, 15th edn, s.v. "Kipling, Rudyard," vol. 10, 486.

258. David Gilmour, *The Long Recessional: The Imperial Life of Rudyard Kipling* (New York: Farrar, Straus, and Giroux, 2002). Available at: http://en.wikipedia.org/wiki/Kipling_rudyard

259. Ralph Waldo Emerson, "Journals and Letters," Sept.–Nov. 1843. From *Selected Writings of Ralph Waldo Emerson* (New York: Signet, 1965), 117.

260. Calton Younger, *Ireland's Civil War* (Glasgow: Fontana Press, 1986), 34–5.

261. T. W. Moody & F.X. Martin, *The Course of Irish History* (Cork: Mercier, 1984) 306–12.

262. Alsop, *I've Seen the Best of It*, 13.

263. Ibid., 25.

264. R. H. Tawney, *Religion and the Rise of Capitalism* (New York: 1926), 22. From Perry Miller, *Errand into the Wilderness* (New York: Harper TorchBooks, 1964), 133.

265. John W. Derbyshire, "Bliss Was It . . ." *National Review* October 4, 2010, "Books, Arts & Manners," 42.

266. F. Scott Fitzgerald, *The Great Gatsby*, available at: http://ebooks.adelaide.edu.au/f/fitzgerald/f_scott/gatsby/Chapter4.html

267. C. David Heymann, *The Georgetown Ladies' Social Club: Power, Passion, and Politics in the Nation's Capital* (New York: Atria Books, 2003), 298–9.

268. Averell Harriman, "Recollection," December 6, 1941. From Martin Gilbert, ed., *The Churchill War Papers: The Ever-Widening War, Volume 3, 1941* (New York: W.W. Norton, 2000), 1571.

269. Heymann, *The Georgetown Ladies' Social Club*, 298.

270. Ibid.

271. Gilbert, *The Churchill War Papers*, 1571.

272. Rudy Abramson, *Spanning the Century: The Life of W. Averell Harriman, 1891–1986* (New York: William Morrow, 1992), 312–13.

273. Alsop, *I've Seen the Best of It*, 477.

274. Heymann, *The Georgetown Ladies' Social Club*, 299.

275. Abramson, *Spanning the Century*, 316.

276. Ibid., 316–18.

277. Heymann, *The Georgetown Ladies' Social Club*, 309–10.

278. Edward R. Murrow, *This is London* (New York: Shocken Books, 1985), 163.

279. Kupfer, *We Felt the Flames*, 127–8.

280. Sevareid, *Not so Wild a Dream*, 170.

281. Ralph Waldo Emerson, "Journals and Letters, March 14, 1848." From *Selected Writings of Ralph Waldo Emerson* (New York: Boston, 1965), 136.

282. Churchill, *The Grand Alliance*, 605.

283. Jonathan Clements, *Mannerheim: President, Soldier, Spy* (London: Haus Publishing, 2009), 264–5.

284. William Manchester, *Winston Spencer Churchill: The Last Lion, Visions of Glory 1874–1932* (New York: Laurel Trade, 1989), 99–104.

285. Manchester, *Winston Spencer Churchill*, 106–07.

286. Churchill, *The Grand Alliance*, 605.

287. Ibid., 605.

288. Ibid.

289. Cable C-138x; from Warren F. Kimball, ed., Churchill and Roosevelt: The Complete Correspondence, I. Alliance Emerging, October 1933–November 1942 (Princeton: Princeton University Press, 1984), 283.

290. Cable C-138x, from Kimball, 283.

291. Churchill, *The Grand Alliance*, 611.

292. Ibid.

293. Ibid.

294. Ibid.

295. Winston S. Churchill to Eamon de Valera, 8 December 1941. Churchill papers 20/46. From Gilbert, *Churchill War Papers, vol. 3*, 1579.

296. Winston S. Churchill to King George VI, 8 December 1941. Churchill papers 20/20. From Gilbert, *Churchill War Papers, vol. 3*, 1585.

297. King George VI to Winston S. Churchill, 10 December 1941. Churchill papers 20/20. From Gilbert, *Churchill War Papers, vol. 3*, 1596.

298. Winston S. Churchill: Speech to House of Commons, 11 December 1941. From Gilbert, *Churchill War Papers, vol. 3*, 1607.

Chapter 2

1. Quetin Reynolds, "The Man Who Didn't Quit," *Collier's*, August 10, 1940.

2. William L. Shirer, *20th Century Journey, A Memoir of the Life and Times—The Start: 1904–1930* (New York: Bantam, 1985), 201.

3. "The Last Time I Saw Paris," Oscar Hammerstein & Jerome Kern. Sung by Kate Smith.

4. Charles Kupfer, *We Felt the Flames: Hitler's Blitzkrieg, America's Story* (Carlisle, PA: Sergeant Kirkland's Press, 2004), 32–45.

5. William L. Langer, *Our Vichy Gamble* (New York: W.W. Norton, 1966 c1947), 118 & *passim*.
6. Scott Donaldson & R.H. Winick, *Archibald MacLeish: An American Life* (Boston: Houghton Mifflin, 1992), 329–30.
7. A. J. Liebling, "Letter from Paris," *The New Yorker*, June 1, 1940.
8. Kupfer, *We Felt the Flames*, 84–8.
9. Charles De Gaulle, *The Speeches of General De Gaulle* (New York: Oxford University Press, 1944), 1.
10. Reynolds, "The Man Who Didn't Quit."
11. De Gaulle, *The Speeches of General De Gaulle*, 90.
12. Ibid., 94–5.
13. Ibid., 99.
14. Ibid., 107.
15. Ibid., 112.
16. Ibid.
17. Ibid.
18. Ibid.
19. Adolf Hitler, *Mein Kampf* (New York: Hurst and Blackett, 1942), 162.
20. Joseph Goebbels, Diary entry August 19, 1941. From Richard J. Evans, *The Third Reich at War* (New York: Penguin, 2009), 247.
21. Hitler, *Mein Kampf,* 92.
22. Ibid., 173.
23. Timothy Snyder, *Bloodlands: Europe Between Hitler and Stalin* (New York: Basic Books, 2010), 15.
24. Carl N. Degler, *In Search of Human Nature: The Decline and Revival of Darwinism in American Social Thought* (New York: Oxford University Press, 1991), 15.
25. Degler, *In Search of Human Nature*, 15.
26. Jonathan Lewis, Hugh Strachan, Corina Sturner, et al. "Shackled to a Corpse," (episode), *The First World War: The Complete Series* (documentary) Image Entertainment, 2005.
27. Snyder, *Europe Between Hitler and Stalin*, 3–10.
28. Hitler, *Mein Kampf,* 13.
29. Robert T. Elson, *Prelude to War* (New York: Time/Life Books, 1976), 85.
30. Iulian-Nicusor, ISAC. "The United States of Greater Austria: A Step Toward European Union?" available at: www.centralgafencu.ro/user/image/12isac.pdf
31. Alan Bullock, *Hitler: A Study in Tyranny* (New York: Harper, 1971), 11–16.
32. Bullock, *A Study in Tyranny*, 14.
33. Elson, *Prelude to War*, 85.
34. Robert A. Kann, *A History of the Hapsburg Empire 1526–1918* (Vienna, 1977), 464. From Paul Lendvai, *The Hungarians: A Thousand Years of Victory in Defeat* (Princeton: Princeton University, 2003), 359.
35. Hitler, *Mein Kampf,* 163.
36. Ibid. 87.
37. Norman Rich, *Hitler's War Aims: Ideology, the Nazi State, and the Course of Expansion* (New York: W.W. Norton, 1992), 238.
38. Hitler, *Mein Kampf,* 87.
39. Ibid. 247.
40. "Hitler's Zweites Buch PDF." Available at: http://en.wikipedia.org/wiki/Zweites_Buch
41. *Encyclopedia Brittanica*, 15th edn. s.v. "Karl Haushofer," vol. 4, 952.

42. Kenneth Wimmel, *Theodore Roosevelt and the Great White Fleet: American Sea Power Comes of Age* (Dulles, VA: Brassey's, 2000), 60–1.
43. *Encyclopedia Brittanica*, "Karl Haushofer."
44. Gerry Kearns, *Geopolitics and Empire: The Legacy of Halford Mackinder* (New York: Oxford University Press, 2009), 15.
45. Edouard Calic, *Reinhard Heydrich: The Chilling Story of the Man Who Masterminded the Nazi Death Camps* (William Morrow: New York, 1985), 231–2.
46. Kearns, *Geopolitics and Empire*, 15.
47. Brian W. Blouet, "Halford Mackinder and the Pivotal Heartland." From Brian W. Blouet, ed. *Global Geostrategy: Mackinder and the Defense of the West* (New York: Frank Cass, 2005), 1.
48. Halford J. Mackinder, *Democratic Ideals and Reality: A Study in the Politics of Reconstruction* (London: Constable, 1919), 194.
49. Blouet, "Halford Mackinder and the Pivotal Heartland," 1–2.
50. Richard J. Evans, *The Third Reich at War* (New York: Penguin Press, 2009), 167.
51. Blouet, "Halford Mackinder and the Pivotal Heartland," 3–4.
52. A.B.C. Whipple, *The Mediterranean* (New York: Time Life Books, 1981), 88.
53. Albert Speer, *Inside the Third Reich: Memoirs* (New York: Collier Books, 1970), 107.
54. Speer, *Inside the Third Reich*, 121.
55. Ibid.
56. Rich, *Hitler's War Aims*, 241.
57. James V. Compton, *The Swastika and the Eagle: Hitler, the United States, and the Origins of World War II* (Boston: Houghton-Mifflin, 1967), 14.
58. David Brinkley, *Washington Goes to War: The Extraordinary Transformation of a City and a Nation* (New York: Alfred A. Knopf, 1988).
59. Compton, *The Swastika and the Eagle*, 85–104.
60. Ibid., 105.
61. Brinkley, *Washington Goes to War*, 37.
62. Charles Kupfer, "We Felt the Flames: American Reactions to the Blitzkrieg of Summer, 1940" (Ph.D. dissertation, University of Texas, 1998), 765–808.
63. *Fortune Magazine*, "Fortune Survey XXXII—The War." July 1940.
64. Hadley Cantril, "American Faces the War: A Study in Public Opinion," *Public Opinion Quarterly*, September 1940, 387.
65. Rich, *Hitler's War Aims*, 245.
66. Meirion Harries & Susie Harries, *Soldiers of the Sun: The Rise and Fall of the Imperial Japanese Army* (New York: Random House, 1991), 377.
67. Kenneth S. Davis, *FDR: The War President, 1940–1943, a History* (New York: Random House, 2000), 350.
68. Davis, *FDR: The War President*, 351.
69. Ibid., 351.
70. Richard Overy & Andrew Wheatcroft. *The Road to War: The Origins of World War II* (London: Macmillan, 1989), 295.
71. James MacGregor Burns, *Roosevelt 1940–1945: The Soldier of Freedom* (New York Harcourt, Brace, Jovanovitch, 1970), 173–4.
72. Michael Gannon, *Operation Drumbeat: The Dramatic True Story of Germany's First U-Boat Attacks Along the American Coast in World War II* (Annapolis: Naval Institute Press, 1990), 93–4.
73. Richard Norton Smith, *The Colonel: The Life and Legend of Robert R. McCormick* (New York: Houghton-Mifflin, 1997), 417.

74. Smith, *The Colonel,* 417.

75. Ibid., 416–17.

76. Rich, *Hitler's War Aims,* 246.

77. Ibid., 246.

78. Sidney A. Freifeld, "Nazi Press Agentry and the American Press," *Public Opinion Quarterly,* Summer 1942, 227.

79. Burns, *Roosevelt 1940–1945,* 174.

80. Ibid., 174.

81. Ibid.

82. Ibid.

83. "Hitler's War Speech," *Baltimore Sun,* December 12, 1941. From archival collection, J.A.H. Hopkins (compiler) "*Diary of World Events*" (Baltimore: National Bureau of Information and Education, National Advertising Company, 1942), vol. XV.

84. "Hitler's War Speech," *Baltimore Sun,* December 12, 1941.

85. Ibid.

86. Burns, *Roosevelt 1940–1945,* 174.

87. Ibid.

88. Ibid., 174–5.

89. Ian Kershaw, *The "Hitler Myth:" Image and Reality in the Third Reich* (New York: Oxford University Press), 230.

90. Christian Gerlach, "The Wannsee Conference, the Fate of German Jews, and Hitler's Decision in Principle to Exterminate all European Jews," *Journal of Modern History,* December 1998, 759–812.

91. Christopher Browning with Jurgen Matthaus, *The Origins of the Final Solution: The Evolution of Nazi Jewish Policy, September 1939–March 1942* (Lincoln and Jerusalem: University of Nebraska Press and Yad Vashem, 2004), 408.

92. Browning, *The Origins of the Final Solution,* 408.

93. Ibid., 408–09.

94. Ibid., 408.

95. Ibid., 410.

96. Ibid.

97. Ibid., 404.

98. Ibid.

99. Ibid.

100. Hugh Trevor-Roper, ed., *Hitler's Table-Talk, 1941–1944: His Private Conversations* (New York: Enigma Books, 2000), 144.

101. Trevor-Roper, *Hitler's Table-Talk,* 151.

102. Ibid., 150.

103. Ibid., 159.

104. Ibid., 159.

105. Michael Gannon, *Operation Drumbeat: The Dramatic True Story of Germany's First U-Boat Attacks Along the American Coast in World War II* (Annapolis: Naval Institute Press, 1990), 97–8.

106. "U-Boat Lied," from "World War II Songs," Available at: www.ingeb.org

107. John Lamberton Harper, American Visions of Europe: Franklin D. Roosevelt, George F. Kennan, and Dean G. Acheson (New York: Cambridge University Press, 1994), 72.

108. Gannon, *Operation Drumbeat,* 64.

109. Ibid.

110. Ibid., 65.
111. Ibid., 69.
112. Ibid.
113. Ibid., 68–71.
114. Ibid., 70.
115. Ibid.
116. Ibid., xvi.
117. Ibid., 75–7.
118. Peter Padfield, *Donitz: The Last Fuhrer* (London: Panther, 1985), 94.
119. Padfield, *The Last Fuhrer,* 267.
120. Gannon, *Operation Drumbeat*, 81.
121. War Plans Division paper, sub: "Immediate Mil Measures," 21 December 1941, "Notes on Agenda Proposed by Gt Brit, Folder-Bk 2, Exec. 4." From Richard M. Leighton and Robert W. Coakley, *The War Department: Global Logistics and Strategy 1940–1943* (Washington, DC: Office of the Chief of Military History, Department of the Army, 1955), 196.
122. Omar N. Bradley & Clay Blair, *A General's Life: An Autobiography* (New York: Simon & Schuster, 1983), 99.
123. Bradley & Blair, *A General's Life,* 102.
124. Ibid., 101–05.
125. Ibid., 104–06.
126. Ibid., 105–06.
127. Ibid., 106.
128. Ibid.
129. John Toland, *But Not in Shame: The Six Months After Pearl Harbor* (New York: Random House, 1961), 19.
130. Forrest G. Pogue, *George Marshall: Statesman, 1945–1959* (New York, Penguin, 1987), 9.
131. Pogue, *George Marshall*, 9–10.
132. Ibid., 11.
133. Leighton & Coakley, *The War Department,* 196.
134. Ibid., 196.
135. Ibid.
136. Ibid.
137. Ibid.
138. Walter LaFeber, *The Clash: U.S.–Japanese Relations Throughout History* (New York: W.W. Norton, 1997), 129.
139. Sidney Tyler, *The Japan–Russia War: An Illustrated History of the War in the Far East* (Philadelphia: P.W. Ziegler, 1905), 561.
140. Jonathan Clements, *Mannerheim: President, Soldier,* Spy (London: Haus Publishing, 2009), 40–78.
141. Edward S. Miller, *War Plan Orange: The U.S. Strategy to Defeat Japan, 1897–1945* (Annapolis: Naval Institute Press, 1991), 23.
142. Miller, *War Plan Orange*, 24.
143. Louis Morton, *The United States Army in World War II: The War in the Pacific – Strategy and Command, the First Two Years* (Washington, DC: Department of the Army, 1962), 24.
144. Morton, *The United States Army in World War II*, 25.
145. Ibid., 25.

146. H. P. Wilmott, *Empires in the Balance: Japanese and Allied Pacific Strategies to April 1942* (Annapolis: Naval Institute Press, 1989), 32.

147. Wilmott, *Empires in the Balance*, 34–7.

148. Akira Iriye, *The Origins of the Second World War in Asia and the Pacific* (London: Longman, 1987), 2–5.

149. Wilmott, *Empires in the Balance*, 36.

150. Ibid., 36.

151. Iriye, *The Origins of the Second World War*, 11.

152. Wilmott, *Empires in the Balance*, 37.

153. Ibid., 35.

154. Ibid., 48–9.

155. Merrion Harries & Susie Harries, *Soldiers of the Sun,* 141–5.

156. Iriye, *The Origins of the Second World War*, 1.

157. Elson, *Prelude to War*, 136.

158. Harries & Harries, *Soldiers of the Sun,* 183–93.

159. Wilmott, *Empires in the Balance*, 50–1.

160. Morton, *The United States Army in World War II*, 27.

161. Ibid.

162. Ibid.

163. Ibid.

164. Miller, *War Plan Orange*, 26.

165. Ibid., 26.

166. Ibid.

167. Ibid., 27.

168. Ibid.

169. Ibid., 27–9.

170. Ibid., 223–4.

171. Ibid., 224.

172. Ibid.

173. Ibid, 225.

174. Ibid., 226.

175. Ibid., 29.

176. Roland H. Worth, Jr, *No Choice But War: The United States Embargo Against Japan and the Eruption of War in the Pacific* (Jefferson, NC: McFarland, 1995), 147.

177. Saburo Ienaga, *The Pacific War: 1931–1945, A Critical Perspective on Japan's Role in World War II* (New York: Pantheon Books, 1978), 142.

178. Harries & Harries, *Soldiers of the Sun,* 253.

179. Ibid., 210–13.

180. Ibid., 210–39.

181. Elson, *Prelude to War*, 136.

182. Ibid., 137.

183. Ienaga, *The Pacific War,* 97–128.

184. Smith, *The Colonel,* 194.

185. Ibid., 231.

186. Carl Vincent, *No Reason Why: The Canadian Hong Kong Tragedy – an Examination* (Stittsville, Ontario: Canada's Wings, 1981), 17.

187. Paul S. Dull, *A Battle History of the Imperial Japanese Navy, 1941–1945* (Annapolis: Naval Institute Press, 1978), 4–5.

188. Nobutaka Ike, ed., *Japan's Decision for War: Records of the 1941 Policy Conferences* (Palo Alto: Stanford University Press, 1967), 208.

189. Ike, *Japan's Decision for War*, 236.

190. Ibid., 236.

191. Ibid., 236–7.

192. Matthias Maass, "Problems of Perception in Spanish-American Diplomatic Communication – Prelude to the War of 1898" (M.A. Thesis, Freidrich-Meinecke Institute, Free University of Berlin, 1996), 4–13.

193. Ike, *Japan's Decision for War*, 237

194. Ibid., 238.

195. Ibid.

196. Akira Iriye, *Power and Culture: The Japanese-American War, 1941–1945* (Cambridge, MA: Harvard, 1981), 119.

197. Iriye, *Power and Culture*, 119.

198. Ike, *Japan's Decision for War*, 248.

199. Ibid., 248.

200. Walter LaFeber, *Clash: U.S.–Japanese Relations Throughout History* (New York: W.W. Norton, 1997), 208.

201. LaFeber, *U.S.–Japanese Relations Throughout History*, 209–10.

202. Ronald H. Spector, *Eagle Against the Sun: The American War with Japan* (New York: Vintage Books, 1985), 267–9.

203. Spector, *Eagle Against the Sun*, 271.

204. Ibid., 270–1.

205. LaFeber, *U.S.–Japanese Relations Throughout History*, 210–11.

206. Worth, *No Choice But War*, 211.

207. Spector, *Eagle Against the Sun*, 271.

208. Raymond Gram Swing radio script, December 10, 1941. From the Raymond Gram Swing Papers, Library of Congress.

209. Drew Pearson & Robert Kittner, "Washington Merry-Go-Round," December 10–11, 1941. From the Papers of Drew Pearson, American University Library.

210. Ronald Steel, *Walter Lippmann and the American Century* (New York: Vintage Books, 1980), 74.

211. Letter, Walter Lippmann to Viscountess Astor, December 3, 1941. From the Walter Lippmann Papers, Sterling Library, Yale University.

212. C. David Heymann, *The Georgetown Ladies' Social Club: Power, Passion, and Politics in the Nation's Capital* (New York: Atria Books, 2003), 41–61.

213. Lippmann to Astor, December 3, 1941.

214. Ibid.

215. S. L. Price, "The Second World War Kicks Off," *Sports Illustrated*, November 29, 1999. Available at: http://sportsillustrated.cnn.com/vault/article/magazine/MAG1017830/index.htm

216. Brinkley, *Washington Goes to War*, 88.

217. Ibid., 88.

218. Price, "The Second World War Kicks Off."

219. Brinkley, *Washington Goes to War*, 88.

220. Price, "The Second World War Kicks Off."

221. Giraud Chester, Garnet Garrison, & Edgar Willis, *Television and Radio* (New York: Appleton-Century-Crofts, 1971), 38.

222. Frank Luther Mott, *American Journalism: A History, 1690–1960* (New York: Macmillan, 1962), 680.
223. Mott, *American Journalism*, 680–1.
224. Edward W. Chester, *Radio, Television, and American Politics* (New York: Sheed & Ward, 1969), 4.
225. Chester, Garrison, & Willis, *Television and Radio*, 38.
226. Kenneth Bilby, *The General: David Sarnoff and the Rise of the Communications Industry* (New York: Harper & Row, 1986), 244.
227. Robert Metz, *CBS: Reflections in a Bloodshot Eye* (New York: Playboy Press, 1975), 4.
228. Bilby, *The General*, 244.
229. Giraud, Chester, & Willis, *Television and Radio*, 30.
230. *BBC Radio Handbook* (London: British Broadcasting Company, 1941), 58.
231. Kupfer, *We Felt the Flames*, 155–66.
232. Charles J. Rolo, *Radio Goes to War: The 'Fourth Front'* (New York: G.P. Putnam's, 1942), 88, 170.
233. Harold Lavine & James Wechsler, *War Propaganda and the United States* (New Haven: Yale University Press, Institute for Propaganda Analysis, 1940), 268.
234. George Gallup, "Public Opinion in a Democracy:" The Stafford Little Lectures (Princeton University Press, 1939), 4.
235. Edward A. Grunwald, ed., *Variety Radio Directory 1940–1941* (New York: Variety, 1940), 458–65.
236. NBC Radio Index Card Catalogue, WJZ Blue Network/WEAF Red Network, December 7, 1941, NBC Collections, Recorded Sound Section, Library of Congress.
237. CBS Radio, December 8, 1941. From Milo C. Ryan Collection, reel #2004, National Archives II Annex, College Park, MD (Unless otherwise indicated, all CBS broadcasts cited come from this Collection, henceforth referred to here as "MCR," with accompanying reel number.).
238. "Books: Democratic War," *Time Magazine*, November 28, 1938. Available at: www.time.com/time/magazine/article/0,9171,771252,00.html
239. CBS Radio, December 8, 1941, MCR, reel #2004.
240. Ibid.
241. Ibid., MCR reel #2005.
242. Ibid., MCR reel #2005.
243. Raymond Clapper, *Watching the World* (New York: McGraw-Hill, 1944), 287.
244. CBS Radio, December 9, 1941, MCR reel #2005.
245. Ibid., MCR reel #2006.
246. Ibid.
247. Ibid.
248. Ibid.
249. CBS Radio, March 29, 1942, MCR reel #2131.
250. CBS Radio, December 9, 1941, MCR reel #2006.
251. Stanley Cloud & Lynne Olson, *The Murrow Boys: Pioneers on the Front Lines of Broadcast Journalism* (Boston: Houghton-Mifflin, 1996), 16.
252. CBS Radio, December 9, 1941, MCR reel #2006.
253. Eric A. Sevareid, *Not So Wild a Dream* (Columbia, MO: University of Missouri Press, 1995 c1946), 169–70.
254. Sevareid, *Not So Wild a Dream*, 184.
255. Ibid., 195.

256. CBS Radio, December 10, 1941, MCR reel #2006.

257. Ibid., MCR reel #2008.

258. Ibid., MCR reel # 2009.

259. Ibid., MCR reel #2010.

260. Gregory J. W. Urwin, *Facing Fearful Odds: The Siege of Wake Island* (Lincoln: University of Nebraska Press, 1997), 8.

261. CBS Radio, December 12, 1941, MCR reel #2008.

262. John Wukovits, *Pacific Alamo: The Battle for Wake Island* (New York: New American Library, 2003), 15.

263. CBS Radio, December 14, 1941, MCR reel # 2010.

264. Ibid.

265. Ibid.

266. H. V. Kaltenborn, *Kaltenborn Edits the War News* (New York: E.P. Dutton, 1942), 2.

267. Irving E. Fang, *Those Radio Commentators!* (Ames: Iowa State University Press, 1977), 76.

268. Hilmar Robert Baukhage used only his last name on-air.

269. NBC Radio Index Cards, December 7–15, 1941. From NBC Collections, Recorded Sound Reference Center, Library of Congress.

270. A. M. Sperber, *Murrow: His Life and Times* (New York: Bantam, 1986), 186.

271. Frederick S. Voss, *Reporting the War: The Journalistic Coverage of World War II* (Washington, DC: Smithsonian Institution Press for the National Portrait Gallery, 1994), 13–16.

272. *Variety Radio Directory* (New York: Variety, 1940), 472–3.

273. Fang, *Those Radio Commentators!,* 275–6.

274. Ibid., 277.

275. Ibid.

276. "Biographical Sketch," The H.V. Kaltenborn Collection, Mass Communications History Center of the State Historical Society of Wisconsin, 34.

277. "Biographical Sketch," H.V. Kaltenborn Collection, 4.

278. Fang, *Those Radio Commentators!,* 25–35.

279. "Biographical Sketch," H.V. Kaltenborn Collection, 34.

280. Kupfer, *We Felt the Flames*, 59.

281. Kaltenborn, *Kaltenborn Edits the War News*, 14.

282. Ibid., 14.

283. Ibid., 65.

284. Ibid.

285. Ibid., 64.

286. Ibid., 65.

287. Ibid.

288. Ibid., 75.

289. Ibid.

290. Fang, *Those Radio Commentators!* 72.

291. H.M. Beville, Jr, "The ABCDs of Radio Audiences," *Public Opinion Quarterly*, June, 1940, 202.

292. Wiliam Paley, "Foreword," in Lowell Thomas, *History as You Heard It* (Garden City, NY: Doubleday), 1957, p. vii.

293. Lowell Thomas, *From Cripple Creek to Samarkand* (New York: Morrow, 1976), 311–12.

294. Lowell Thomas & Burton Braley, *Stand Fast for Freedom* (Philadelphia: John C. Winston, 1940), 281.
295. Lowell Thomas, *History as You Heard It* (Garden City, NY: Doubleday, 1957), 183.
296. Thomas, *History as You Heard It*, 183–4.
297. Ibid., 184.
298. Ibid.
299. Ibid.
300. Ibid.
301. Raymond Gram Swing, *Preview of History* (Garden City, NY: Doubleday, Doran, 1943), 27.
302. "Radio: Find," *Time*, January 8, 1940. Available at: www.time.com/time/magazine/article/0,9171,763171,00.html
303. "Radio: Find," *Time*, January 8, 1940.
304. Charles J. Rollo, *Radio Goes to War: The "Fourth Front"* (New York: G.P. Putnam's, 1942), 184.
305. *BBC Radio Handbook 1941* (London: British Broadcasting Corporation, 1941), 58.
306. "Radio: Find," *Time*, January 8, 1940.
307. Ibid.
308. Fang, *Those Radio Commentators!* 151.
309. Ibid., 159–60.
310. Ibid., 161.
311. Raymond Gram Swing, Radio Script, December 8, 1941. From the Papers of Raymond Gram Swing, Library of Congress, Washington, DC Hereafter all Swing scripts cited as "Swing Radio Script," followed by date.
312. Swing Radio Script, December 8, 1941.
313. Ibid.
314. Ibid.
315. Ibid.
316. Swing Radio Script, December 10, 1941.
317. Ibid.
318. Ibid.
319. Ibid.
320. Ibid.
321. Ibid.
322. Ibid.
323. Ibid.
324. Ibid.
325. Ibid.
326. Swing Radio Script, December 17, 1941.
327. Swing Radio Script, December 31, 1941.
328. Sevareid, *Not So Wild A Dream*, 205.
329. Sperber, *Murrow*, 204.
330. Ibid., 205.
331. Eric A. Sevareid, Radio Script, December 8, 1941. From the Papers of Eric A. Sevareid, Library of Congress, Washington, DC Hereafter referred to as EAS Radio Script, with date.
332. EAS Script, December 8, 1941.
333. Ibid.

334. Ibid.
335. Ibid.
336. EAS Script, December 10, 1941.
337. Ibid.
338. Ibid.
339. Ibid.
340. Raymond A. Schroth, *The American Journey of Eric Sevareid* (South Royalton, VT: Steerforth Press, 1995), 197.
341. EAS Script, December 14, 1941.
342. Ibid.
343. Letter, Eduard Benes to Walter Lippmann, January 14, 1936. From the Papers of Walter Lippmann, Beinecke Library, Yale University. Microfilm Series III, Unit 1, Reels 40–46, HM254. Hereafter all Lippmann correspondence referred to by signatory, addressee, date, "Walter Lippmann Papers."
344. Letter, Eve Curie to Walter Lippmann, August 21, 1941. Walter Lippmann Papers.
345. Letter, Nevile Butler to Walter Lippmann, December 19, 1941. Walter Lippmann Papers.
346. John Earl Haynes & Harvey Klehr, *Venona: Decoding Soviet Espionage in America* (New Haven: Yale Nota Bene, 2000) 93–6, 97–100.
347. Haynes & Klehr, *Decoding Soviet Espionage in America*, 241.
348. H. V. Kaltenborn, *Fifty Fabulous Years*, quoted in Francine Curro Cary, *The Influence of War on Walter Lippmann, 1914–1944* (Madison: State Historical Society of Wisconsin for University of Wisconsin, 1967), 3.
349. Cary, *The Influence of War on Walter Lippmann*, 4.
350. Steel, *Walter Lippmann and the American Century*, 195.
351. Cary, *The Influence of War on Walter Lippmann*, 24.
352. Ibid., 24.
353. D. Steven Blum, *Walter Lippmann: Cosmopolitanism in the Century of Total War* (Ithaca: Cornell University Press, 1984), 40–3.
354. Blum, *Walter Lippmann*, 43.
355. Ibid., 43.
356. Ibid.
357. Thomas C. Leonard, *News for All: America's Coming-of-Age With the Press* (New York: Oxford University Press, 1995), 221.
358. Leonard, *News for All*, 221.
359. Cable draft, Walter Lippmann to Ambassador William Bullitt, (no date), 1940. From the Papers of Walter Lippmann, Beinecke Library, Yale University. Microfilm Series III, Unit 1, Reels 40-46 HM257. Hereafter referred to as "Walter Lippmann Papers."
360. Letter, William Henry Chamberlin to Walter Lippmann, May 13, 1941. Letter, Walter Lippmann to William Henry Chamberlin, May 15, 1941. Walter Lippmann Papers.
361. Letter, Alistair Cooke to Walter Lippmann, October 17, 1941. Walter Lippmann Papers.
362. Letter, Bernard Baruch to Walter Lippmann, April 30, 1940. Walter Lippmann Papers.
363. Letter, Van Wyck Brooks to Walter Lippmann, August 21, 1941.
364. Letter, Max Ascoli to Walter Lippmann, July 3, 1941. Walter Lippmann Papers.
365. Letter, James Byrne to Al Smith, August 28, 1941. Walter Lippmann Papers.
366. Letter, Eve Curie to Walter Lippmann, August 21, 1941. Walter Lippmann Papers.

367. Official German Radio Digest, Transcript of German Short Wave Broadcasts from Berlin, August 14, 1941. Walter Lippmann Papers.

368. Letter, Walter Lippmann to Gaillard Lapsley, September 12, 1941. Walter Lippmann Papers.

369. Letter, Walter Lippmann to Paul Sachs, November 9, 1942. Walter Lippmann Papers.

370. Letter, Bruce Barton to Walter Lippmann, September 22, 1941. Walter Lippmann Papers.

371. Letter, Noel Coward to Walter Lippmann, September 20, 1941. Walter Lippmann Papers.

372. Letter, Walter Lippmann to Giiti Imai, December 5, 1941. Walter Lippmann Papers.

373. Letter, Mark W. Clark to Walter Lippmann, December 6, 1941. Walter Lippmann Papers.

374. Letter, William H. Chadbourne to Walter Lippmann, December 10, 1941. Walter Lippman Papers.

375. "Today and Tomorrow: On Rising to the Occasion," by Walter Lippmann, *New York Herald-Tribune*, December 11, 1941. Hereafter, all Lippmann columns referred to as "T&T: Title, *NYHT*, Date."

376. "T&T: On Rising to the Occasion," *NYHT*, December 11, 1941.

377. "T&T: Some Necessary Measures," *NYHT*, December 13, 1941.

378. Ibid.

379. "T&T: Some Necessary Measures," *NYHT*, December 13, 1941.

380. "T&T: Mayor LaGuardia and Mrs. Roosevelt," *NYHT*, December 16, 1941.

381. "T&T: Mayor Laguardia & Mrs. Roosevelt," *NYHT*, December 16, 1941.

382. "T&T: For American Intervention in Europe," *NYHT*, December 23, 1941.

383. "T&T: The Main Obstacles Here at Home," *NYHT*, December 27, 1941.

384. Ibid.

385. Ibid.

386. "T&T: Dislocation is Necessary," *NYHT*, December 30, 1941.

387. Oliver Pilat, *Drew Pearson: An Unauthorized Biography* (New York: Pocket Books, 1973), 188.

388. Fang, *Those Radio Commentators!* 216.

389. Ibid., 217.

390. Ibid.

391. Ibid.

392. Ibid., 218.

393. Ibid., 218–20.

394. Pilat, *Drew Pearson,* 87–8.

395. Fang, *Those Radio Commentators!* 220–1.

396. Pilat, *Drew Pearson,* 85–6.

397. Ibid., 103.

398. Fang, *Those Radio Commentators!* 220.

399. Pilat, *Drew Pearson,* 103–08.

400. Ibid., 168–9.

401. Fang, *Those Radio Commentators!* 222.

402. Ibid., 221.

403. Pilat, *Drew Pearson,* 169.

404. Ibid., 157.

405. Ibid., 156.

406. Ibid., 157.

407. Ibid., 157–61.

408. William Manchester, *American Caesar: Douglas MacArthur, 1880–1964* (Boston: Little, Brown, 1978), 144.

409. Manchester, *American Caesar,* 144.

410. Ibid., 144.

411. Ibid., 145.

412. Pilat, *Drew Pearson,* 161.

413. Ibid., 162–3.

414. Ibid., 164.

415. Ibid.

416. Ibid., 186.

417. United Feature Syndicate, "To Editors," December 10, 1941. From the Drew Pearson Papers, American University. Hereafter all "Washington Merry-Go-Round" columns listed by date, followed by "DPP."

418. "To Editors," December 10, 1941, DPP.

419. Ibid.

420. "The Washington Merry-Go-Round," December 10, 1941, DPP.

421. Ibid.

422. Ibid.

423. Ibid.

424. "The Washington Merry-Go-Round," December 11, 1941, DPP.

425. Ibid.

426. "The Washington Merry-Go-Round," December 13, 1941, DPP.

427. Ibid.

428. Ibid.

429. "The Washington-Merry-Go-Round," December 16, 1941, DPP.

430. Ibid.

431. Ibid.

432. "The Washington Merry-Go-Round," December 15, 1941, DPP.

433. "The Washington Merry-Go-Round," December 13, 1941, DPP.

434. Ibid.

435. "The Washington Merry-Go-Round," December 16, 1941, DPP.

436. "The Washington Merry-Go-Round," December 15, 1941, DPP.

437. "The Washington Merry-Go-Round," December 17, 1941, DPP.

438. Ibid.

439. Ibid.

440. Ibid.

441. William S. Knickerbocker, "Asides and Soliliquies," *Sewanee Review* vol. XLX no. 1, January–March, 1942, 2.

442. "The Press: Censorship in Action," *Time,* December 22, 1941. Available at: www.time.com/time/printout/0,8816,932013,00.html

443. Len Deighton, *Blitzkrieg: From the Rise of Hitler to the Fall of Dunkirk* (London: Jonathan Cape, 1979), 262.

444. "WAR NEWS," advertisement, *U.S. News,* December 19, 1941.

445. "WAR NEWS," *U.S. News,* December 19, 1941.

446. Ibid.

447. "Newsgram," *U.S. News,* December 19, 1941, 7.

448. Ibid.

449. Ibid.

450. "Plus and Minus: Trend of American Business," *U.S. News*, December 19, 1941, 41.

451. Ibid.

452. "The U.S. at War: Tragedy at Honolulu," *Time*, December 15, 1941. Available at: www.time.com/time/magazine/article/0,9171,772807,00.html

453. "The U.S. at War: Tragedy at Honolulu," *Time*, December 15, 1941.

454. "The U.S. at War: Japan Runs Amuck," *Time*, December 15, 1941. Available at: www.time.com/time/magazine/article/0,9171,772814,00.html

455. "The U.S. at War: Japan Runs Amuck," *Time*, December 15, 1941.

456. "State of the Nation: Last Week of Peace," *Time*, December 15, 1941. Available at: www.time.com/time/magazine/article/0,9171,772815,00.html

457. "Litvinoff" *Time*, December 15, 1941. Available at: www.time.com/time/magazine/article/0,9171,772815,00.html

458. "Table of Contents," *Time*, December 22, 1941. Available at: www.time.com/time/magazine/0.9263,7601411222,00.html

459. "Havoc in Honolulu," *Time*, December 22, 1941.

460. "The U.S. at War, Full Blast," *Time*, December 22, 1941.

461. Ibid.

462. Ibid.

463. "The Press: Censorship in Action," *Time*, December 22, 1941.

464. Ibid.

465. Ibid.

466. Ibid.

467. "The U.S. at War: To the Last Ounce," *Time*, December 22, 1941. Available at: www.time.com/time/printout/0,8816,931946,00.html

468. "The U.S. at War: To the Last Ounce," *Time*, December 22, 1941.

469. Ibid.

470. "World Battlefronts: The Way to Singapore," *Time*, December 22, 1941. Available at: www.time/com/time/printout/0,8816,931962,00.html

471. "World Battlefronts: The Way to Singapore," *Time*, December 22, 1941.

472. Ibid.

473. Ibid.

474. Samuel Eliot Morrison, *History of United States Naval Operations in World War II, Volume 3: The Rising Sun in the Pacific: 1931–April 1942* (Boston: Little, Brown, 1988 c1948), 292.

475. H. P. Wilmott, *Empires in the Balance*, 93.

476. Ibid., 93.

477. Field Marshal Viscount William Slim, *Defeat into Victory: Battle Japan in Burma and India, 1942–1945* (New York: Cooper Square Press, 2000 c1956), 28–9.

478. Wilmott, *Empires in the Balance*, 130.

479. "Home Affairs: Hot to Tell Your Friends from the Japs," *Time*, December 22, 1941. Available at: www.time/com/time/printout/0,8816,932034,00.html

480. "Home Affairs: How to Tell Your Friends from the Japs," *Time*, December 22, 1941.

481. Ibid.

482. Ibid.

483. Ibid.

484. Thomas Doherty, *Projections of War: Hollywood, American Culture, and World War II* (New York: Columbia University Press, 1993), 135.

485. "Always After Time: Collecting Newsweek Magazine from 1933 to the 1960's & Beyond," Magazines.things-and-other-stuff.com, www.things-and-other-stuff.com/magazines/newsweek-magazine.html

486. John Tebbel & Mary Ellen Zuckerman, *The Magazine in America: 1741–1990* (New York: Oxford University Press, 1991), 173.

487. "Always After Time: Collecting Newsweek Magazine from 1933 to the 1960s & Beyond."

488. *Newsweek*, December 15, 1941.

489. "Blitz Chronology: Swift Stroke by Japanese Caught U.S. Forces Unawares," *Newsweek*, December 15, 1941.

490. "Nation's Full Might Mustered for All-Out War," "Washington Banks on Long-Term Strategy," *Newsweek*, December 15, 1941.

491. "Initial Reverse Stirs Demand for Investigation," *Newsweek*, December 15, 1941.

492. "Our War," *The New Republic*, December 15, 1941.

493. Ibid.

494. William Harlan Hale, "After Pearl Harbor," *The New Republic*, December 15, 1941.

495. Ibid.

496. Cesar Salmaggi & Alfredo Pallavisini, *2194 Days of War: An Illustrated Chronology of the Second World War* (New York: Barnes & Noble Books, 199378–81.

497. William Harlan Hale, "Trouble for Admirals," *The New Republic*, December 22, 1941.

498. Ibid.

499. Nathaniel Peffer, "China's Future—and Our Own," *The New Republic*, December 22, 1941.

500. T.A. Bisson, "Japan's Strategy—and Resources," *The New Republic*, December 22, 1941.

501. Max Werner, "Moscow and Pearl Harbor," *The New Republic*, December 29, 1941.

502. Max Werner, "Moscow and Pearl Harbor," *The New Republic*, December 19, 1941.

503. Malcolm Cowley, *And I Worked at the Writer's Trade* (New York: Viking, 1978), 156.

504. Samuel Sillen, *New Masses*, October 8, 1940, 4–8.

505. "Biography;" Finding Aid, Frieda Kirchwey Papers, 1871–1972, Harvard University, Available at: www.oasis.lib.harvard.edu/oasis/deliver/deepling?_collection=oasis&uniqueId=sch00306

506. "Biography," Finding Aid, Frieda Kirchwey Papers.

507. Archibald MacLeish, "The Irresponsibles," *The Nation*, May 18, 1940, 618.

508. MacLeish, "The Irresponsbiles."

509. Frieda Kirchwey, "Help Britain Win!" *The Nation*, August 10, 1940, 105.

510. I.F. Stone, *Business as Usual: The First Year of Defense* (New York: Modern Age Books, 1941).

511. The Website of I.F. Stone; "Writings by I.F. Stone, 'Business as Usual,' Advance Comments." Available at: www.ifstone.org/business_as_usual.php

512. I.F. Stone, "Rumors for Russia," *The Nation*, December 20, 1941, 631–2.

513. Frieda Kirchwey, "Is Latin America Safe?" *The Nation*, December 20, 1941, 630–1.

514. Donald W. Mitchell, "What the Navy Can Do," *The Nation*, December 20, 1941, 633.

515. Donald W. Mitchell, "The Outlook in the Pacific," *The Nation*, December 27, 1941, 661.

516. I.F. Stone, "The Shake-up We Need," *The Nation*, December 27, 1941, 659.

517. I.F. Stone, "The Shake-up We Need," 659.

518. Ibid., 660.

519. Frieda Kirchwey, "Partners in Guilt," *The Nation*, December 27, 1941, 656–7.
520. "Acknowledgements/Photographic Credits," *Collier's Photographic History of the Second World War* (New York: Grosset & Dunlap, 1945), 273.
521. *Collier's Photographic History of the Second World War*, 273.
522. George H. Roeder, Jr, *The Censored War: American Visual Experience During World War II* (New Haven: Yale University Press, 1993), 4–5.
523. Roeder, *The Censored War*, 8.
524. *Baltimore Evening Sun*, December 16, 1941.
525. Ibid.
526. Ernest O. Hauser, "America's 150,000 Japanese," *American Mercury*, December 1941, 689.
527. Hauser, "America's 150,000 Japanese," 693.
528. Ibid., 697.
529. "Personal and Otherwise: New Chapter," *Harper's*, December 1941.
530. Peter Drucker, "We Must Accept Rationing: Why it is a Political and Economic Necessity," *Harper's*, December 1941, 3.
531. Drucker, "We Must Accept Rationing," 8.
532. Ibid., 8.
533. James Barbour & Fred Warner, eds, *Liebling at the New Yorker* (Albuquerque: University of New Mexico Press, 1994), ix–x.
534. A. J. Liebling, "Letter from Paris," *The New Yorker*, March 16, 1940.
535. Ibid., April 13, 1940.
536. Ibid., June 8, 1940.
537. Mollie Panter-Downes, *London War Notes 1939–1945* (New York: Farrar, Straus & Giroux, 1971), 60.
538. Panter-Downes, *London War Notes 1939–1945*, 184.
539. Ibid., 185.
540. Ibid.
541. Ibid.
542. Ibid., 186.
543. Ibid., 188.
544. Ibid., 189.
545. Ibid.
546. "The Saturday Evening Post," Wikipedia, available at: www.en.wikipedia.org/wiki/The_Saturday_Evening_Post
547. "The Art of Fiction – P.G. Wodehouse," *The Paris Review*, Available at: www.theparisreview.com/media/Wodehouse.pdf
548. Frances Donaldson, *P.G. Wodehouse: A Biography* (London: Prion, 1982), 103.
549. Richard Usborne, *Plum Sauce: A P.G. Wodehouse Companion* (London: Ebury Press, 2002), 174.
550. Usborne, *Plum Sauce*, 174.
551. P.G. Wodehouse, *The Code of the Woosters* (New York: Vintage, 2005 c1938), 46.
552. Geoffrey Jaggard, *Wooster's World: A Companion to the Wooster-Jeeves Cycle of P.G. Wodehouse* (London: MacDonald, 1967), 154.
553. Wodehouse, *The Code of the Woosters*, 20.
554. Ibid., 138.
555. Jaggard, *Wooster's World*, 155.
556. Robert McCrum, *Wodehouse* (New York: W.W. Norton, 2004), 255.

557. McCrum, *Wodehouse*, 259–61.

558. Donaldson, *P.G. Wodehouse*, 140–6.

559. McCrum, *Wodehouse*, 249.

560. Donaldson, *P.G. Wodehouse*, 153.

561. Ibid., 152.

562. Ibid.

563. McCrum, *Wodehouse*, 270–3.

564. Iain Sproat, *Wodehouse at War: The Extraordinary Truth about P.G. Wodehouse's Broadcasts on Nazi Radio* (New York: Ticknor & Fields, 1981), 10–11.

565. Sproat, *Wodehouse at War*, 107–28.

566. McCrum, *Wodehouse,*285.

567. Ibid., 310.

568. Sproat, *Wodehouse at War*, 55–6.

569. Ibid., 56.

570. Ibid., 12–13.

571. Ibid., 13.

572. Ibid., 30–3.

573. Ibid., 33.

574. Donaldson, *P.G. Wodehouse*, 233.

575. Ibid., 233.

576. McCrum, *Wodehouse*, 322.

577. Ibid., 322–3.

578. McCrum, *Wodehouse*, 322.

579. Sproat, *Wodehouse at War*, 28.

580. *Saturday Evening Post,* December 20, 1941. Table of Contents. From "magawiki," Available at: www.magawiki.com/2822/saturday-evening-post/1941-12-20/

581. Curt Riess, ed., *They Were There: The Story of World War II and How it Came About, by America's Foremost Correspondents* (Garden City, NY: Garden City Publishing Company, 1945), 654.

582. Otto Tolischus, "Tokyo: December 7th," from Riess, ed., 400.

583. Riess, *They Were There*, 654.

584. Walter Bernstein, "Juke Joint," from Hyes, et al., 289.

585. Bernstein, "Juke Joint," 289.

586. Ibid., 297.

587. *Detroit News*, December 10, 1941. From War . . . In Headlines from the Detroit News, 1939–1945 (Detroit: The Detroit News, 1945).

588. *Detroit News*, December 22, 1941.

589. *Detroit News*, December 11, 1941.

590. *Detroit News*, December 25, 1941.

591. *Baltimore Sun*, December 17, 1941.

592. Ibid.

593. Ibid.

594. Ibid.

595. Ibid.

596. Ibid.

597. Cecil V. Crabb, Jr, and Pat M. Holt, *Invitation to Struggle: Congress, the President, and Foreign Policy* (Washington, DC: Congressional Quarterly, 1989), vii.

598. "Diary of Admiral Kichisaburo Nomura," December 16, 1941. From Donald M. Goldstein & Katherine V. Dillon, *The Pacific War Papers: Japanese Documents of World War II* (Washington, DC: Potomac Books, 2004), 215.

599. *New York Times*, December 18, 1941.

600. Samuel Eliot Morrison, *The Rising Sun in the Pacific: 1931–April 1942; History of United States Naval Operations in World War II, Vol. III* (Botson: Little, Brown, 1988 c1948), 220–54.

601. CINCPAC = "Commander-in-Chief, Pacific"

602. Urwin, Gregory J. W., *Facing Fearful Odds: The Siege of Wake Island* (Lincoln: University of Nebraska Press, 1997), 514.

603. John B. Toland, *The Flying Tigers* (New York: Random House, 1963), 37.

604. Richard M. Gordon (with Benjamin S. Llamzon), *Horyo: Memoirs of an American P. O. W.* (St. Paul, MN: Paragon House, 1999), 57.

605. Gordon, 57.

606. Carlos P. Romulo, *I Saw the Fall of the Philippines* (Garden City, NY: Doubleday, Doran, 1943), 30.

607. Maass, 37–46.

608. Frank Friedel, *The Splendid Little War* (Boston: Little, Brown, 1958), 13.

609. John Hersey, *Men on Bataan* (New York: Alfred A. Knopf, 1943), 42.

610. John M. Fitzgerald, *Family in Crisis: The United States, the Philippines, and the Second World War* (Bloomington, IN: First Books, 2002), xxiii.

611. Fitzgerald, xxiv.

612. Rafael Steinberg, *Return to the Philippines* (New York: Time-Life Books, 1979), 36.

613. Steinberg, 36–7.

614. "Thomasites," Available at: http://en.wikipedia.org/wiki/thomasites

615. Scott A. Mills, *Stranded in the Philippines: Professor Bell's Private War Against the Japanese* (Annapolis: Naval Institute Press, 2009), vii–xii, 1–10.

616. Fitzgerald, xxvi.

617. Elinor Chamberlain, *The Far Command* (New York: Ballantine Books, 1952), 245.

618. Glen M. Williford, *Racing the Sunrise: Reinforcing America's Pacific Outposts, 1941–1942* (Annapolis: Naval Institute Press, 2010), 1.

619. Manchester, *American Caesar,* 161.

620. Steinberg, *Return to the Philippines,* 41.

621. Ibid.

622. Harries & Harries, *Soldiers of the Sun,* 314.

623. Ibid.

624. Williford, *Racing the Sunrise,* 4.

625. Ibid., xiv.

626. Ibid., 35–91.

627. Ibid., 66.

628. Celedondo A. Ancheta, ed., *Historical Documents of World War II in the Philippines, The Wainwright Papers, vol. 1* "Report of Operations of USAFFE and USFIP in the Philippine Islands 1941–1942" (Quezon City, Philippines: New Day Publications, 1979), 3.

629. Ancheta, *Wainwright Papers, vol. 1*, 11.

630. Celedondo A. Ancheta, ed., *Historical Documents of World War II in the Philippines, The Wainwright Papers, vol. 2,* "Report of Operations on the Harbor Defenses of Manila and Subic Bays 14 February 1941–1946 May 1942" (Quezon City, Philippines: New Day Publications, 1980), 15.

631. Steinberg, *Return to the Philippines,* 44.

632. Henry H. Adams, *1942: The Year That Doomed the Axis*, 40.

633. Manchester, *American Caesar,* 205.

634. Douglas MacArthur, *Reminiscences* (New York: The Great Commanders/Collectors Reprints, 1997 c1964), 109–10.

635. MacArthur, *Reminiscences,* 110–11.

636. Ibid., 113.

637. Manchester, *American Caesar,* 198.

638. MacArthur, *Reminiscences,* 120.

639. Adams, 40.

640. MacArthur, *Reminiscences,* 120.

641. William Manchester, *Goodbye, Darkness: A Memoir of the Pacific War* (Boston: Little, Brown, 1980), 57.

642. MacArthur, *Reminiscences,* 121.

643. Harries & Harries, *Soldiers of the Sun,* 314.

644. Carlos Romulo, *I Saw the Fall of the Philippines* (Garden City, NY: Doubleday, Doran, 1943), 28.

645. Romulo, *I Saw the Fall of the Philippines* 30.

646. Ibid., 31.

647. Ibid., 33.

648. Ibid., 43.

649. Ibid., 44.

650. Arthur R. Poindexter, "Wake Island: America's First Victory," *Leatherneck: Magazine of the Marines,* December 1991. Available at: www.mca-marines.org/leatherneck/wake-island-america's-first-victory

651. Poindexter, "Wake Island: America's First Victory."

652. Bill Sloan, *Given Up for Dead: America's Heroic Stand at Wake Island* (New York: Bantam Books, 2003), 74.

653. Urwin, 137.

654. Ibid., 138.

655. Poindexter, "Wake Island: America's First Victory."

656. Ibid.

657. Urwin, 310.

658. Ibid., 311.

659. R.R. Keene, "The Corps Raised its Name to Honor and Fame," *Leatherneck: Magazine of the Marines,* December 2001. Available at: www.mca-marines.org/leatherneck/wake-island

660. Sloan, *Given Up for Dead,* 147.

661. Urwin, 141.

662. Keene, "The Corps Raised its Name to Honor and Fame."

663. John Wukovits, *Pacific Alamo: The Battle for Wake Island* (New York: New American Library, 2003) 140–77.

664. Wukovits, *Pacific Alamo,* 177.

665. Ibid., 191.

666. *Collier's Photographic History of the Second World War,* 76.

667. *Collier's Photographic History of the Second World War,* 76.

668. Hanson W. Baldwin, "The Saga of Wake," *The Virginia Quarterly Review,* Summer 1942, vol. 18, no. 3, 314–445.

669. John Rogers Haddad, *The Romance of China: Excursions to China in U.S. Culture, 1776–1876* (New York: Columbia University Press, 2008), 1. Available at: www.gutenberg-e.org/haj01/frames/fhaj02.html

670. Hannah Pakula, *The Last Empress: Madame Chiang Kai-Shek and the Birth of Modern China* (New York: Simon & Schuster, 2009), 5.

671. Pakula, *The Last Empress*, 10–17.

672. Ibid., 181–2.

673. Ibid., 60–1.

674. John Toland, *The Flying Tigers* (New York: Random House, 1963), 6.

675. Barbara W. Tuchman, *Stilwell and the American Experience in China 1911–1945* (New York: Macmillan, 1971), 220.

676. Tuchman, *Stilwell and the American Experience in China,* 220.

677. Alan Brinkley, *The Publisher: Henry Luce and his American Century* (New York: Alfred A. Knopf, 2010), 293–4.

678. Tuchman, *Stilwell and the American Experience in China,* 230.

679. Joseph W. Stilwell, Theodore H. White, ed., *The Stilwell Papers* (New York: Da Capo Press, 1991 c1948), 1–30.

680. Toland, *The Flying Tigers,* 7.

681. Daniel Ford, *Flying Tigers: Claire Chennault and his American Volunteers, 1941–1942* (New York: Harper Collins/Smithsonian Books, 2007), 31.

682. Ford, *Flying Tigers,* 31.

683. Toland, *The Flying Tigers,* 6.

684. Ford, *Flying Tigers,* 1–4.

685. Giulio Douhet, *The Command of the Air* (Norwalk, CT: Easton Press, 1994 c1921), 3–4.

686. Douhet, *The Command of the Air,* 5.

687. Daniel Ford, "Flying Tigers Bite Back!" America in World War II: The Magazine of a People at War 1941–1945, December 2010, 30.

688. Anna Chennault, *Chennault and the Flying Tigers* (New York: Paul S. Eriksson, 1963), 49–50.

689. Ford, "Flying Tigers Bite Back!" 31.

690. Toland, *The Flying Tigers,* 16–17, 26–9.

691. Ford, *Flying Tigers,* 84.

692. Ibid., 85.

693. Toland, *The Flying Tigers,* 34–5.

694. Ford, *Flying Tigers,* 85.

695. Ibid., 85.

696. Ibid.

697. Toland, *The Flying Tigers,* 37.

698. Ford, "Flying Tigers Bite Back!" 32.

699. Toland, *The Flying Tigers,* 43.

700. Ford, "Flying Tigers Bite Back!" 33.

701. Ibid. 37.

702. "Japanese Claim Hong Kong Isle, Colony is Cut Off," *New York Times,* December 20, 1941.

703. "Japanese Lose 30,000 in a Day, China Reports," *Baltimore Sun,* January 5, 1942.

704. "American Officers Take Charge of Burma Road," *Baltimore Evening Sun,* January 19, 1942.

705. Slim, *Defeat into Victory*, 5.
706. *Collier's Photographic History of World War II*, 71.
707. Toland, *The Flying Tigers*, 78–9.
708. Romulo, *I Saw the Fall of the Philippines*, 58–9.
709. Ibid., 59.
710. Ibid.
711. Carol Morris Petillo, *Douglas MacArthur: The Philippine Years* (Bloomington: Indiana University Press, 1981), 210.
712. Petillo, *Douglas MacArthur*, 211.
713. CBS Radio, December 20, 1941. MCR Collection, Tape # 2018.
714. Fitzgerald, *Family in Crisis*, 18–19.
715. Adams, 59.
716. Ibid.
717. CBS Radio, December 20, 1941. MCR Collection, Tape # 2018.
718. Adams, 59.
719. CBS Radio, December 21, 1941. MCR Collection, Tape # 2019.
720. Ibid.
721. Fitzgerald, *Family in Crisis*, 19.
722. Romulo, *I Saw the Fall of the Philippines*, 62.
723. "Invasion of the Philippines," *Baltimore Evening Sun*, December 22, 1941. From J.A.H. Hopkins, *Diary of World Events*, vol. XV.
724. "War Department Communique," *Baltimore Evening Sun*, December 22, 1941. From J.A.H. Hopkins, *Diary of World Events*, vol. XV.
725. "Heavy Fighting Rages on Gulf of Lingayen," *Baltimore Evening Sun*, December 22, 1941. From J.A.H. Hopkins, *Diary of World Events*, vol. XV.
726. "New Landing Indicates 2-Way Drive on Philippine Capital," *The New York Times*, December 24, 1941. From J.A.H. Hopkins, *Diary of World Events*, vol. XV.
727. "Philippine Armies Check Jap Onslaught," *The Detroit News*, December 25, 1941. From *War . . . In the Headlines from the Detroit News 1939–1945* (Detroit: The Detroit News, 1945).
728. "Submarine Victories Reported," *The Detroit News*, December 25, 1941.
729. Romulo, *I Saw the Fall of the Philippines*, 85–8.
730. Ibid., 88.
731. Ibid., 81.
732. CBS Radio, December 28, 1941. MCR Tape #2027.
733. Ibid.
734. James Bryant Conant, "What Victory Requires: Our Heritage Can be Preserved Only by Fighting," From *Vital Speeches of the Day*, January 15, 1941, 199–202.
735. "Ruin Is Rained on an Open City," *Newark Evening News*, December 27, 1941.
736. "Ruin Is Rained on an Open City."
737. CBS News, December 29, 1941. MCR tape #2028.
738. "Manila Falls and Fleet Makes Escape," *The Detroit News*, December 25, 1941. From *War . . . In the Headlines from The Detroit News 1939–1945* (Detroit: The Detroit News), 1945.
739. Lord Moran, *Churchill at War 1940–1945* (New York: Carrol & Graf, 2002 c1966, *The Struggle for Survival*), 17.
740. Scott Hart, *Washington at War: 1941–1945* (Englewood Cliffs, NJ: Prentice-Hall, 1970), 61.

741. Warren F. Kimball, *Forged in War: Roosevelt, Churchill, and the Second World War* (Chicago: Ivan R. Dee, 2003), 127.

742. Kimball, *Forged in War*, 127.

743. Ibid., 126–9.

744. Document C-143 x. Halifax to Roosevelt, December 18, 1941. From Kimball, ed., *Churchill and Roosevelt: The Complete Correspondence, I. Alliance Emerging* (Princeton: Princeton University Press, 1984), 290.

745. Document C-144x. Prime Minister to Halifax, December 21, 1941. From *Churchill and Roosevelt: The Complete Correspondence*, 293.

746. Martin Gilbert, *Churchill and America* (New York: Free Press, 1995), 247.

747. Gilbert, *Churchill and America*, 247.

748. Kimball, *Forged in War*, 128–9.

749. "The First Washington Conference (ARCADIA)" From *Churchill and Roosevelt: The Complete Correspondence*, 292.

750. "The First Washington Conference (ARCADIA)" From *Churchill and Roosevelt: The Complete Correspondence*, 292–3.

751. "The First Washington Conference (ARCADIA)" From *Churchill and Roosevelt: The Complete Correspondence*, 293.

752. Lord Moran, *Churchill at War 1940–1945*, 11.

753. *London News Chronicle*, January 27, 1941. From J.A.H. Hopkins, *Diary of World Events*, Vol. XVII.

754. Drew Pearson & Robert S. Allen, "Washington Merry-Go-Round," December 26, 1941. Drew Pearson Papers.

755. Richard Leighton & Robert Coakley, *United States Army in World War II: Global Logistics and Strategy, 1940–1943* (Washington, DC: Office of the Chief of Military History, Department of the Army, 1968), 196.

756. Leighton & Coakley, *United States Army in World War II*, 197–212.

757. Gilbert, *Churchill and America*, 248.

758. CBS Radio, December 23, 1941. MCR Tape # 2022.

759. Drew Pearson & Robert S. Allen, "Washington Merry-Go-Round," December 27, 1941. Drew Pears Papers.

760. Drew Pearson & Robert S. Allen, "Washington Merry-Go-Round," December 27, 1941. Drew Pearson Papers.

761. Hart, *Washington at War: 1941–1945*, 50.

762. Ibid.

763. Ibid., 51–2.

764. CBS Radio, December 24, 1941. MCR Collection, Tape # 2023.

765. Hart, *Washington at War: 1941–1945*, 52.

766. Ibid., 52–3.

767. Ibid., 53.

768. Ibid.,

769. Ibid.

770. Ibid., 54.

771. Ibid.

772. Moran, *Churchill at War 1940–1945*, 12.

773. Ibid., 12.

774. Adams, 63.

775. Moran, *Churchill at War 1940–1945*, 13–15.

776. Winston S. Churchill, "Here We Are Together, Defending all that to Free Men is Dear," From *Vital Speeches of the Day*, January 15, 1942, 197.

777. Adams, 62.

778. Churchill, "Here We Are Together," 197.

779. Ibid.

780. Ibid.

781. Ibid.

782. Ibid.

783. Ibid.

784. Ibid., 198.

785. Ibid.

786. Ibid., 199.

787. Moran, *Churchill at War 1940–1945*, 16.

788. Ibid., 16–17.

789. John Kennedy Ohl, *Hugh S. Johnson and the New Deal* (DeKalb, IL: Northern Illinois University Press, 1985), 305.

790. Drew Pearson & Robert S. Allen, "Washington Merry-Go-Round," January 3, 1942. Drew Pearson Papers.

791. Drew Pearson & Robert S. Allen, "Washington Merry-Go-Round," January 3, 1942. Drew Pearson Papers.

792. Walter Lippmann, "Today and Tomorrow," *New York Herald-Tribune*, December 25, 1941.

793. Moran, *Churchill at War 1940–1945*, 17–18.

794. Ibid., 20–1.

795. Drew Pearson & Robert S. Allen, "Washington Merry-Go-Round," December 27, 1941. Drew Pearson Papers.

Chapter 3

1. Charles De Gaulle, *The Call to Honour, 1940–1942* (New York: Viking Press, 1955), 213–14.

2. "26 Nations Vow War to the End on Axis, Pledge All Resources," *Baltimore Sun*, January 3, 1942.

3. "26 Nations Vow War . . ."

4. James MacGregor Burns, *Roosevelt 1940–1945: The Soldier of Freedom* (New York: Harcourt, Brace, Jovanovitch, 1970), 184.

5. Burns, *Roosevelt 1940–1945*, 184.

6. "26 Nations Vow War . . ."

7. Dan Plesch, *America, Hitler, and the U.N.: How the Allies Won World War II and Forged a Peace* (New York: I.B. Tauris, 2011), 1.

8. H.V. Kaltenborn, *Kaltenborn Edits the War News* (New York: E.P. Dutton, 1942), 62.

9. Plesch, *America, Hitler, and the U.N.*, 40.

10. "26 Nations Vow War. . ."

11. "26 Nations Vow War. . ."

12. "26 Nations Vow War. . ."

13. "26 Nations Vow War. . ."

14. Burns, *Roosevelt 1940–1945*, 185.
15. De Gaulle, *The Call to Honour*, 213–14.
16. Melville Bell Grosvenor (editor-in-chief), *National Geographic Atlas of the World* (Washington, D.C.: National Geographic Society, 1970), "Eastern Canada" (map) 59.
17. "St. Pierre and Miquelon," *Encyclopedia Brittanica*, vol. VIII (Chicago: Encyclopedia Brittanica, 1974), 794–5.
18. De Gaulle, *The Call to Honour*, 214.
19. William L. Langer, *Our Vichy Gamble* (New York: W.W. Norton, 1947), 212.
20. Langer, *Our Vichy Gamble*, 212.
21. Cordell Hull, *The Memoirs of Cordell Hull* (New York: Macmillan, 1948), 1127.
22. Hull, *The Memoirs of Cordell Hull*, 1127.
23. De Gaulle, *The Call to Honour*, 214–15.
24. Langer, *Our Vichy Gamble*, 213–14.
25. Robert Sherwood, *Roosevelt and Hopkins, an Intimate History* (New York: Enigma, 2008), 376–7.
26. Langer, *Our Vichy Gamble*, 214.
27. Sherwood, *Roosevelt and Hopkins*, 377.
28. Ibid., 377.
29. Ibid., 378.
30. Ibid.
31. Hull, *The Memoirs of Cordell Hull*, 1130.
32. Ibid., 1130–1.
33. Ibid., 1130.
34. Sherwood, *Roosevelt and Hopkins*, 378.
35. Ibid., 1131.
36. Ibid., 1131.
37. Langer, *Our Vichy Gamble*, 216.
38. De Gaulle, *The Call to Honour*, 215.
39. Langer, *Our Vichy Gamble*, 217.
40. Ibid., 219.
41. Sherwood, *Roosevelt and Hopkins*, 379.
42. Ibid., 379.
43. Ibid., 380.
44. Ibid., 378.
45. Ibid., 381.
46. Ibid.
47. Hull, *The Memoirs of Cordell Hull*, 1132.
48. Ibid., 1136.
49. Langer, *Our Vichy Gamble*, 222.
50. Ibid., 223.
51. Vincent Shandor, *Carpatho-Ukraine in the 20th Century* (Cambridge, MA: Ukrainian Research Institute, Harvard University Press, 1997), 86.
52. *New York Times*, January 7, 1942.
53. Ibid.
54. "Introduction," James B. Reston. From Anne O'Hare McCormick, *The World at Home: Selections from the Writings of Anne O'Hare McCormick* (New York: Alfred A. Knopf, 1956), v.
55. Hull, *The Memoirs of Cordell Hull*, 1130.

56. Eric A. Sevareid, Radio Script, December 27, 1941, from the Papers of EAS, Library of Congress.
57. "St. Pierre and Miquelon," *The New Republic*, January 5, 1942, 3.
58. "Washington Whispers," *U.S. News*, January 9, 1942, 44.
59. I.F. Stone, "Aid and Comfort to the Enemy," *The Nation*, January 3, 1942, 6.
60. Stone, "Aid and Comfort to the Enemy," *The Nation*, January 3, 1942, 7.
61. Drew Pearson & Robert S. Allen, "Washington Merry-Go-Round," February 10, 1942. From the Papers of Drew Pearson.
62. De Gaulle, *The Call to Honour*, 216.
63. Ibid., 217.
64. Ibid.
65. Hull, *The Memoirs of Cordell Hull*, 1137.
66. Ibid., 1136.
67. Ibid., 1137.
68. *Chicago Sun*, February 6, 1942.
69. Ibid.
70. Henry H. Adams, *1942: The Year That Doomed the Axis*, 67.
71. "Gallup and Fortune Polls," *Public Opinion Quarterly*, Winter 1941, 685.
72. Franklin Delano Roosevelt, "The State of the Union," *Vital Speeches of the Day*, January 15, 1942, 195.
73. Roosevelt, "The State of the Union," *Vital Speeches of the Day*, January 15, 1942, 195.
74. Adams, 67.
75. Ibid.
76. Roosevelt, "The State of the Union," *Vital Speeches of the Day*, January 15, 1942, 194.
77. Ibid.
78. Ibid., 195.
79. Ibid., 196.
80. Ibid., 197.
81. Plesch, *America, Hitler, and the U.N*, 2.
82. "Gallup and Fortune Polls," *Public Opinion Quarterly*, Winter 1941, 684–6.
83. "Gallup and Fortune Polls: The War in Europe and the Far East," *Public Opinion Quarterly*, Spring 1942, 149–65.
84. Ibid., 153.
85. Adams, 68.
86. Adams, 68.
87. Adams, 68–9.
88. Walter Lippmann, "Today and Tomorrow," *New York Herald-Tribune*, January 20, 1942.
89. Drew Pearson & Robert S. Allen, "The Washington Merry-Go-Round," January 5, 1942. Papers of Drew Pearson.
90. Ibid., January 11, 1942.
91. Ibid., January 6, 1942.
92. Ibid., January 18, 1942.
93. Helen Lombard, *While They Fought: Behind the Scenes in Washington, 1941–1946* (New York: Scribner's, 1947), 53.
94. Adams, 70.
95. "Gallup and Fortune Polls," *Public Opinion Quarterly*, Spring 1942, 167.
96. Ibid., 169.
97. Adams, 70.

Chapter 4

1. Karl Hack & Kevin Blackburn, *Did Singapore Have to Fall? Churchill and the Impregnable Fortress* (New York: RoutledgeCurzon, 2004), v.
2. Peter Elphick, *Singapore: The Pregnable Fortress* (London: Hodder & Stoughton, 1995), 304–5.
3. Vincent P. O'Hara, W. David Dickson, & Richard Worth, *On Seas Contested: The Seven Great Navies of the Second World War* (Annapolis: Naval Institute Press, 2010), 146–51.
4. O'Hara, Dickson, & Worth, *On Seas Contested,* 151.
5. Ibid., 153–6.
6. Cesar Salmaggi &Alfredo Pallavisini, *2194 Days of War: An Illustrated Chronology of the Second World War* (New York: Barnes & Noble, 1993), 223.
7. Albert Kesselring, *Kesselring: A Soldier's Record* (Norwalk, CT: The Easton Press, 1994 c1953), 124.
8. Salmaggi & Pallavisini, *2194 Days of War,* 223, 226.
9. Ibid., 212–13.
10. Meirion Harries & Susie Harries, *Soldiers of the Sun: The Rise and Fall of the Imperial Japanese Army* (New York: Random House, 1991), 305.
11. H.P. Wilmott, *Empires in the Balance: Japanese and Allied Pacific Strategies to April 1942* (Annapolis: Naval Institute Press, 1982), 218–54.
12. Wilmott, *Empires in the Balance,* 252–53.
13. Alan J. Levine, *The Pacific War: Japan Versus the Allies* (Westport, CT: Praeger, 1995), 44.
14. Harries, *Soldiers of the Sun,* 306.
15. *Pictorial History of the Second World War, Volume II* (New York: Wm. H. Wise & Co., 1944), 611, 621.
16. Levine, *The Pacific War,* 45–6.
17. Hack & Blackburn, *Did Singapore Have to Fall?* 22–3.
18. Ibid., 25–8.
19. Winston S. Churchill, *The Second World War: The Hinge of Fate* (Boston: Houghton-Mifflin, 1950), 55.
20. Hack & Blackburn, *Did Singapore Have to Fall?* 110–31.
21. Churchill, *The Second World War,* 56.
22. Kate Caffrey, *Out in the Midday Sun: Singapore 1941–1945 – The End of an Empire* (New York: Stein and Day, 1973), 125.
23. Caffrey, *Out in the Midday Sun,* 127.
24. Ibid., 125.
25. Elphick, *Singapore,* 278–79.
26. CBS Radio, December 17, 1941. MCR Collection, Tape # 2015.
27. Ibid., Tape #2016.
28. Raymond Gram Swing radio script, February 2, 1942. Raymond Gram Swing Papers, Library of Congress.
29. Raymond Gram Swing radio script, February 2, 1942.
30. CBS Radio, December 28, 1941. MCR Collection, Tape #2027.
31. "British Hammer Enemy in Malaya," *New York Times,* January 1, 1942.
32. "Malaya Combat – A Creeping, Stalking War," *Baltimore Evening Sun,* January 1, 1942.

33. "Resistance Stiffens at Western End of Line in Malaya," *New York Times*, January 22, 1942.
34. "Counter-Move Made 70 Miles Above Big Base," *Baltimore Sun*, January 23, 1942.
35. CBS Radio, February 4, 1942. MCR Tape #2075.
36. Ibid.
37. Ibid.
38. Hack & Blackburn, *Did Singapore Have to Fall?* 46.
39. CBS Radio, February 4, 1942. MCR Tape #2075.
40. Ibid., Tape #2077.
41. *New York Herald-Tribune*, February 8, 1942.
42. Harold Guard, "$400,000,000 Singapore Base Vacated Under Japanese Fire," *New York Herald-Tribune*, February 8, 1942.
43. CBS Radio, February 11, 1942. MCR Tape #2083.
44. Ibid.
45. Ibid., Tape #2086.
46. Raymond Gram Swing radio script, February 14, 1942. From Raymond Gram Swing Papers, Library of Congress.
47. Raymond Gram Swing radio script, February 14, 1942.
48. CBS Radio, February 15, 1942. MCR Tape #2086.
49. Stanley Cloud & Lynne Olson, *The Murrow Boys: Pioneers on the Front Lines of Broadcast Journalism* (Boston: Houghton Mifflin, 1996), 150–3.
50. Charles Kupfer, *We Felt the Flames: Hitler's Blitzkrieg, America's Story* (Carlisle, PA: Sergeant Kirkland's Press, 2004), 48.
51. CBS Radio, February 15, 1942. MCR Tape #2086.
52. Ibid.
53. "Fall of Singapore Puts Java in Jaws of Jap Nutcracker," *Newsweek*, February 23, 1942.
54. Ibid.
55. Panter-Downes, *London War Notes*, 204–7.
56. Ibid., 207–8.
57. Karen Farrington, *Handbook of World War II: An Illustrated Chronicle of the Struggle for Victory* (New York: Abbeydale Press/Barnes & Noble, 2008), 43–4.
58. Universal Newsreels. Newsreel advertisement catalogue, March 9, 1942. From Motion Picture, Sound, & Video Branch, National Archives Annex, College Park, MD/
59. Rudyard Kipling, "The Dutch in the Medway," available at: www.kipling.org/poems_dutchmedway.htm
60. Helen Lombard, *While They Fought: Behind the Scenes in Washington, 1941–1946* (New York: Scribner's, 1947), 52.
61. Geoffrey Parker, *The Dutch Revolt* (London: Pelican Books, 1985), 13–17, 228–9.
62. Luigi Barzini, *The Europeans* (New York: Simon & Schuster, 1983), 208.
63. Samuel Pepys, *The Diary of Samuel Pepys*, July 10, 1667, available at: www.pepysdiary.com
64. Kipling, "The Dutch in the Medway."
65. Len Deighton, *Blitzkrieg: From the Rise of Hitler to the Fall of Dunkirk* (London: Jonathan Cape, 1979), 215–16.
66. Telford Taylor, *The March of Conquest: The German Victories in Western Europe, 1940* (New York: Simon & Schuster, 1958), 187–205.
67. Gordon Williamson. *Loyalty is My Honor: Personal Accounts from the Waffen-SS* (Osceola, WI: Motorbooks International, 1995) 24, 34–7, 153–4.

68. Cordell Hull, *Memoirs of Cordell Hull* (New York: Macmillan, 1948), 909–12, 1071.

69. Hull, *Memoirs,* 1073.

70. "Arrangements for Sending American Military Forces to the Netherlands Islands of Curacao and Aruba to Assist in their Defense," Department of State, *Foreign Relations of the United States: Diplomatic Papers 1942, Europe* (Washington, DC: Government Printing Office, 1961), 49.

71. "Arrangements for Sending American Military Forces to the Netherlands Islands of Curacao and Aruba to Assist in their Defense," 49.

72. Cynthia Koch, "Franklin Roosevelt's 'Dutchness:' At Home in the Hudson Valley, from Roger Panetta (ed.), *Dutch New York: The Roots of Hudson Valley Culture* (New York: Hudson Valley Museum/Fordham University Press, 2009), 357.

73. "Remarks of the President on the Presentation of a Submarine-Chaser to Queen Wilhelmina for the Dutch Navy, August 6, 1942," Rosenman, Samuel I. (ed.), *The Public Papers and Addresses of Franklin D. Roosevelt, 1942 Volume* (New York: Harper & Brothers, 1950), 322.

74. "Remarks of the President on the Presentation of a Submarine-Chaser. . ." Rosenman, 323.

75. "The Eight Hundred and Fortieth Press Conference—The Press is Presented to Queen Wilhelmina, August 7, 1942," Rosenman, 324.

76. Hull, *Memoirs,* 712, 765.

77. "Netherlands Minister to Under Secretary of State," December 8, 1941. From Department of State, *Foreign Relations of the United States, 1941, Volume IV: The Far East* (Washington, DC: GPO, 1956), 733–44.

78. "Annual Report of the Activities of the 67th Evacuation Hospital," January 1, 1943. From the Office of Medical History—67th Evacuation Hospital, available at: www history. amedd.army.mil/booksdocs/wwii/67thEVACHOSP/67thEH1942.htm

79. Helen C. Lombard, *While they Fought: Behind the Scenes in Washington 1941–1946* (New York: Scribner's, 1947), 22.

80. Department of State, *Foreign Relations of the United States: Diplomatic Papers 1942, Vol. III Europe* (Washington, DC: Government Printing Office, 1961), 40–9.

81. Lombard, *While they Fought,* 74.

82. United Nations Treaty Series, Number 4220. "Netherlands and the United States of America: Exchange of Notes constituting an agreement concerning the return of silver supplied to the Government of the Kingdom of the Netherlands under lend-lease. Washington, 30 March and 25 May 1955."

83. Nina Ascoly & Bart Plantenga, "The Dutch Door to America," *American Heritage Magazine*, April 1999, Volume 50, Issue 2. Available at: www.americanheritage.com/ articles/magazine/ah/1999/2/1999_2_1-2.shtml

84. Ascoly & Plantenga, "The Dutch Door to America." The author's great-grandfather.

85. Olin G. Reiniger, "Transition, Holland-America," from Charles Libbe Dyke, *The Story of Sioux County* (Sioux County Capital: Orange City, IA, 1942), 399.

86. Annette Stott, Holland Mania: *The Unknown Dutch Period in American Art and Culture* (Woodstock, NY: Overlook Press, 1998), *passim.*

87. Koch, *Dutch New York,* 347.

88. Mary Mapes Dodge, *Hans Brinker, or the Silver Skates* (Garden City, NY: Junior Deluxe Editions, 1954), 14–18.

89. Firth Haring Fabend, "The Reformed Dutch Church and the Persistence of Dutchness in New York and New Jersey," from Panetta (ed.), 155.

90. Laura Vookles, "Return in Glory: The Holland Society Visits 'The Fatherland,'" from Panetta (ed.), 269.
91. Ascoly & Plantenga, "The Dutch Door to America."
92. Bill Mazer, *The Answer Book of Sports: Answers to Hundreds of Questions about the World of Sports* (New York: Grosset & Dunlap, 1969), 134–5.
93. Universal Newsreels, February 18, 1942, newsreel advertising catalogue, Motion Picture, Sound & Video Branch, National Archives Annex, College Park, MD.
94. Margaret Mead, "Community Drama, Bali, and America," *The American Scholar*, January 1942, 79–88.
95. "Consul General at Batavia (Foote) to the Secretary of State," December 8, 1941. From *Foreign Relations of the United States, Volume IV*, 735.
96. "The Dutch East Indies is Lost Forever," Available at: www.dutch-east-indies.com/sotry/page23.php
97. Edgar McInnis, *The War: Third Year* (New York: Oxford University Press, 1945), 128.
98. Lombard, *While they Fought*, 52–3.
99. Morrison, *History of United States Naval Operations in the Pacific, Volume III: The Rising Sun in the Pacific* (Boston: Little, Brown, 1948), 271–7.
100. Morrison, *History of United States Naval Operations in the Pacific*, 278–9.
101. McInnis, 129–32.
102. "Ambassador to the Netherlands Government in Exile to the Secretary of State," December 17, 1941. From *Foreign Relations of the United States, Volume IV*, 757.
103. McInnis, *The War,* 132.
104. H.W. Wilmott, *Empires in the Balance: Japanese and Allied Pacific Strategies to April 1942* (Annapolis: Naval Institute Press, 1982), 264.
105. McInnis, 125.
106. Wilmott, 265–6.
107. Gabriel Heatter, *There's Good News Tonight* (Garden City, NY: Doubleday, 1960), 122.
108. Irving E. Fang, *Those Radio Commenators!* (Ames, IA: Iowa State University Press, 1977), 292–3.
109. Fang, *Those Radio Commenators!* 293.
110. Ibid., 293.
111. "Jap Battleship Sunk, Dutch Report," *Baltimore Evening Sun*, January 27, 1942. From J.A.H. Hopkins, vol. XVII, #3586.
112. *Newsweek,* January 12, 1942.
113. CBS Radio, February 5, 1942. MCR Tape #2076.
114. Ibid.
115. Ibid.,
116. Ibid., Tape #2085.
117. Ibid., Tape # 2091.
118. Ibid., Tape #2100.
119. H. P. Wilmott, *Empires in the Balance: Japanese and Allied Pacific Strategies to April 1942* (Annapolis: Naval Institute Press, 1982), 265–6.
120. Wilmott, *Empires in the Balance*, 363.
121. Masanobu Tsuji, *Singapore: The Japanese Version* (New York: St. Martin's Press, 1960), 295–01.
122. Tsuji, *Singapore, 301–02.*
123. CBS Radio, March 8, 1942. MCR Tape #2107.
124. H.R. Knickerbocker, "Planes, Men, Send them Quickly," *Chicago Sun*, February 24, 1942. From J.A.H. Hopkins, vol. XVIII, #3740.

125. Knickerbocker, *Chicago Sun*, February 24, 1942.
126. Ibid.
127. Ibid.
128. Willmott, *Empires in the Balance*, 336–7.
129. Morison, *History of United States Naval Operations in the Pacific, Volume III, The Rising Sun in the Pacific*, 332.
130. Wilmott, *Empires in the Balance*, 343.
131. Ibid., *Empires in the Balance*, 337–9.
132. Cesar Salmaggi & Alfredo Pallavisini, *2194 Days of War: An Illustrated Chronology of the Second World War* (New York: Barnes & Noble Books, 1993), 215–16.
133. Morrison, 342–3.
134. Paul S. Dull, *A Battle History of the Imperial Japanese Navy, 1941–1945* (Annapolis: Naval Institute Press, 1978), 87.
135. Morrison, 358.
136. John Toland, *But Not in Shame: The Six Months After Pearl Harbor* (New York: Random House, 1961), 240.
137. Henry H. Adams, *1942: The Year that Doomed the Axis* (New York: Paperback Library, 1967), 88–9.
138. Toland, *But Not in Shame*, 275.
139. Ibid.
140. Ibid.
141. Adams, 89.
142. Adams, 89–90.
143. Wilmott, *Empires in the Balance*, 345.
144. Paul S. Dull, *A Battle History of the Imperial Japanese Navy, 1941–1945* (Annapolis: Naval Institute Press, 1978), 68–88.
145. Salmaggi & Pallavisini, 216.
146. *Jane's Fighting Ships of World War II* (London: Studio Editions, 1989), 208.
147. Wilmott, 267.
148. *New York Herald-Tribune*, March 1, 1942. From J.A.H. Hopkins, vol. XVIII, #3768.
149. Ibid.
150. *Baltimore Sun*, March 2, 1942.
151. "Wavell Out, Dutch Taking Over in Indies," *Baltimore Sun*, March 3, 1942. From J.A.H. Hopkins, vol. XVIII, #3777.
152. "Tokyo Claims 23 Warships Sunk in 3 Days," *Baltimore Evening Sun*, March 3, 1942. From J.A.H. Hopkins, vol. XVIII, #3777.
153. Donald M. Goldstein & Katherine V. Dillon, eds, *Fading Victory: The Diary of Admiral Matome Ugaki, 1941–1945* (Annapolis: Naval Institute Press, 1991), 87.
154. "Battle of the Pacific: End of a Dream," *Time*, March 2, 1942, 16.
155. "Home is the Sailor," *Time*, March 9, 1942, 18.
156. Ibid., 19.
157. Field Marshal Viscount William Slim, *Defeat Into Victory: Battling Japan in Burma and India, 1942–1945* (New York: Cooper Square Press, 2000 c1956), 6.
158. Joseph Stilwell, *The Stilwell Papers* (New York: Da Capo, 1991), 31.
159. Toland, *The Flying Tigers*, 55.
160. Stilwell, *The Stilwell Papers*, 30–1.
161. Ibid., 33.
162. Ibid., 35.
163. Ibid., 37–8.

164. Ibid., 35.
165. Tuchman, *Stilwell and the American Experience in China, 1911–1945*, 254–5.
166. Stilwell, *The Stilwell Papers,* 47.
167. Ibid., 49.
168. Daniel Ford, *Flying Tigers: Claire Chennault and his American Volunteers 1941–1942* (New York: Harper Collins, 2007), 154.
169. Anna Chenault, *Chennault and the Flying Tigers* (New York: Paul S. Erikson, 1963), 128–9.
170. Tuchman, *Stilwell and the American Experience in China,* 253.
171. Ibid., 254.
172. Ibid., 257.
173. John Pimlott, *The Atlas of World War II* (Philadelphia: Courage Books, 2006), 94.
174. Viscount William Slim, *Defeat into Victory: Battle Japan in Burma and India, 1942–1945* (New York: Cooper Square Press, 2000 c1956), 109–10.
175. Pimlott, *The Atlas of World War II,* 95.
176. Tuchman, *Stilwell and the American Experience in China,* 296–8.
177. Stilwell, *The Stilwell Papers,* 104.
178. Tuchman, *Stilwell and the American Experience in China,* 298.
179. Ibid., 396–407.
180. Ibid., 300.
181. Ibid.
182. *Chicago Sun*, February 21, 1942. From J.A.H. Hopkins, vol. XVII, # 3717.
183. *Baltimore Sun,* March 10, 1942. From J.A.H. Hopkins, vol. XVIII, #3808.
184. Ibid.
185. H.V. Kaltenborn, *Kaltenborn Edits the War News* (New York: E.P. Dutton, 1942), 48.
186. Kaltenborn, *Kaltenborn Edits the War News* 50.
187. Ibid., 24.
188. "Flying Tigers in Burma," *Life*, March 30, 1942. Available at: http://cbi-theater-1.home.comcast/net/~cbi-theater-1/flyingtigers/flying_tigers.html
189. *Life*, March 30, 1942.
190. Ibid.
191. Ibid.
192. Ibid.
193. Ibid.
194. Ibid.
195. Ibid.
196. Ibid.
197. Michael Straight, "Claire Chennault: American Hero," *The New Republic*, March 2, 1942, 288.
198. Straight, "Claire Chennault: American Hero," 289.
199. Ibid., 288.
200. Ibid.
201. Ibid., 290.
202. Ralph Bates, "Freedom for India," *The New Republic*, March 2, 1942, 290.
203. Bates, "Freedom for India," 291.
204. Ibid., 291.
205. Ibid., 290.
206. "Cripps for Prime Minister," *The New Republic*, March 16, 1942, 348.
207. Anup Singh, "Nehru and India's Future," *The New Republic*, March 16, 1942, 359–61.
208. Brands, 661.

209. Ibid., 661.

210. Ibid., 662.

211. Ibid., 663.

212. Ibid.

213. Ibid., 663–4.

214. Salmaggi & Pallavisini, 221.

215. Brands, 664.

216. Kaltenborn, 48.

217. Raymond Gram Swing, *Preview of History*, 58.

218. Swing, *Preview of History*, 59.

219. Gary R. Hess, "U.S. Influence in Southeast Asia," from Akira Iriye & Warren Cohen, eds, *American, Chinese, and Japanese Perspectives on Wartime Asia, 1931–1949* (Wilmington, DC: Scholarly Resources, 1990), 196.

220. Eric M. Bergerud, *Fire in the Sky: The Air War in the South Pacific* (Boulder, CO: Westview, 2001), 29.

221. Bergerud, *Fire in the Sky*, 25–35.

222. Ibid.

223. H. P. Wilmott, *The War With Japan: The Period of Balance, May 1942–October 1943* (Wilmington: SR Books, 2002), 11.

224. Wilmott, *The War With Japan: The Period of Balance, May 1942-October 1943*, 11.

225. Wilmott, *Empires in the Balance*, 437–40.

226. Ibid., 438–9.

227. Ibid., 441–5.

228. Karen Farrington, *Handbook of World War II: An Illustrated Chronicle of the Struggle for Victory* (New York: Abbeydale Press, 2008), 45.

229. Raymond Gram Swing Radio Script, February 2, 1942. From Raymond Gram Swing Papers, Library of Congress.

230. CBS Radio, April 5, 1942. MCR Collection, Tape #2140.

231. Ibid.

232. Ibid.

233. Wilmott, 445.

234. Herman Wouk, *War and Remembrance* (Boston: Little, Brown 1985), 282–3.

Chapter 5

1. Lawson Fusao Inada (ed.), *Only What We Could Carry: The Japanese-American Internment Experience* (Berkeley: Heyday Books, 2000), 13–14.

2. Inada, *Only What We Could Carry*, 401–2.

3. Charles Kupfer, *We Felt the Flames: Hitler's Blitzkrieg, America's Story* (Carlisle, PA: Sergeant Kirkland's Press, 2004), 59.

4. Drew Pearson & Robert S. Allen, "Washington Merry-Go-Round," January 25, 1942. From the Drew Pearson Papers.

5. Ibid.

6. Inada, *Only What We Could Carry*, 402–06.

7. "Details of Japanese Plan for Conquest of America," *Baltimore Sun*, February 28, 1942. From J.A.H. Hopkins, vol. XVIII, #3763.

8. *Baltimore Sun*, February 28, 1942.

9. "Big Jap Spy Ring Revealed by Dies," *Baltimore Sun*, February 28, 1942.

10. *Baltimore Sun*, February 28, 1942.

11. "The Failure of Mr. Dies," *The New Republic*, February 23, 1942, 253.

12. John J. Stephan, *Hawaii Under the Rising Sun: Japan's Plans for Conquest After Pearl Harbor* (Honolulu: University of Hawaii Press, 1984), 1–2.

13. Stephan, *Hawaii Under the Rising Sun*, 2–3.

14. Ibid., 11.

15. Ibid., 55–6.

16. Ibid., 56.

17. John W. Dower, *War Without Mercy: Race and Power in the Pacific War* (New York: Pantheon, 1986), 113–14.

18. Stephan, *Hawaii Under the Rising Sun*, 69.

19. Clark G. Reynolds, *America at War 1941–1945: The Home Front* (New York: Gallery Books, 1990), 99.

20. Franklin Odo, *No Sword to Bury: Japanese-Americans in Hawaii During World War II* (Philadelphia: Temple University Press, 2004), 104.

21. Odo, *No Sword to Bury,* 1–4, 101–06, 263.

22. Ibid., 103.

23. Stan Cohen, *V for Victory: America's Home Front During World War II* (Missoula: Pictorial Histories Publishing Company, 1991), 207.

24. Nick D'Alto, "The Niihau Zero: Pieces of Pearl Harbor's Lone Surviving Zero Tell of a Violent Clash of Cultures and a Race for Technology," *Air & Space Magazine*, July 1, 2007. Available at: www.airspacemag.com/military-aviation/Zero.html

25. "Ni'ihau Zero: The Rest of the Story," *Pacific Aviation Museum Pearl Harbor Newsletter*, Fall 2007. Available at: www.pacificaviaionmuseum.org

26. Allan Beekman, *The Niihau Incident: The True Story of the Japanese Fighter Pilot who, after the Pearl Harbor Attack, Crash-Landed on the Hawaiian Island of Niihau and Terrorized the Residents* (Honolulu: Heritage Press of the Pacific, 1990 c1982), 41.

27. "Niihau Incident," Wikipedia, available at: http://en.wikipedia.org/wiki/Niihau_Incident

28. Nick D'Alto, "The Niihau Zero."

29. "Niihau Incident," Wikipedia.

30. Beekman, 72–9.

31. "Niihau Incident," Wikipedia.

32. Gordon Prange, December 7, 1941: The Day the Japanese Attacked Pearl Harbor (New York: McGraw-Hill, 1962), 375–7.

33. Beekman, *The Niihau Incident*, 111–12.

34. Ibid., 103.

35. Stan Cohen, *V for Victory: America's Home Front During World War II* (Missoula: Pictorial Histories Publishing Company, 1991), 221–31.

36. Anthony C. DiMarco, *The Big Bowl Football Guide: A Game-by-Game History of College Football's Major Bowl Contests* (New York: G.P. Putnam's Sons, 1976), 29–30.

37. Reynolds, *America at War 1941–1945,* 100.

38. Cohen, *V for Victory,* 239–40.

39. Ibid., 239–40.

40. Ibid., 246.

41. Inada, *Only What We Could Carry*, 348.

42. Ibid., 413.
43. Steel, *Walter Lippmann and the American Century*, 393–4.
44. Inada, *Only What We Could Carry*, 413–14.
45. Reynolds, *America at War 1941–1945,* 100.
46. Steel, 406.
47. "Today and Tomorrow," *New York Herald-Tribune*, January 29, 1942.
48. Ibid.,
49. Ibid., January 31, 1942.
50. Ibid., February 3, 1942.
51. Steel, 393.
52. "Today and Tomorrow," *New York Herald-Tribune*, February 5, 1942.
53. Ibid., 1942.
54. "Today and Tomorrow," *New York Herald-Tribune*, February 7, 1942.
55. Ibid., 1942.
56. Ibid., 1942.
57. Ibid., 1942.
58. "Today and Tomorrow," *New York Herald-Tribune*, February 10, 1942.
59. Ibid., 1942.
60. Ibid., 1942.
61. Ibid., 1942.
62. "Today and Tomorrow," *New York Herald-Tribune*, February 12, 1942.
63. Ibid.
64. Ibid.
65. Ibid.
66. Ibid.
67. Ibid.
68. Ibid.
69. Inada, *Only What We Could Carry*, 412.
70. "Today and Tomorrow," *New York Herald-Tribune*, February 12, 1942.
71. "A More Perfect Union: Japanese-Americans and the U.S. Constitution," Smithsonian Institution touring exhibit; Available at: www.americanhistory.si.edu/perfectunion/resources/touring/html
72. Letter, Attorney General Francis Biddle to Walter Lippmann, February 19, 1942. From the Papers of Walter Lippmann, Beinecke Library, Yale University.
73. Letter, Walter Lippmann to Francis Biddle, November 25, 1940. From the Papers of Walter Lippmann, Beinecke Library, Yale University.
74. Letter, Walter Lippmann to Francis Biddle, February 20, 1942. From the Papers of Walter Lippmann, Beinecke Library, Yale University.
75. Letter, Walter Lippmann to Harvey Bundy, February 27, 1942. From the Papers of Walter Lippmann, Beinecke Library, Yale University.
76. Letter, Walter Lippmann to Harvey Bundy, March 9, 1942. From the Papers of Walter Lippmann, Beinecke Library, Yale University.
77. Letter, Mary Cushing Astor to Walter Lippmann, March 18, 1942. Letter, Walter Lippmann to March Cushing Astor, March 20, 1942. Letter, Mary Cushing Astor to Walter Lippmann, March 25, 1942. From the Papers of Walter Lippmann, Beinecke Library, Yale University.
78. Letter, George Britt to Walter Lippmann, February 9, 1941. Letter, George Britt to Carl W. Ackerman, February 9, 1941. From the Papers of Walter Lippmann, Beinecke Library, Yale University.

79. Iriye, 75.

80. Iriye, 75–6.

81. Advertisement, *Harper's*, January 1942, 223.

82. Pearl Buck, "The Asiatic Problem: The Colored People Are Still Waiting, Still Watchful," Available at: *Vital Speeches of the Day*, March 1, 1942, 303.

83. Pearl Buck, "The Asiatic Problem: The Colored People Are Still Waiting, Still Watchful."

84. Francis Biddle, "Identification of Alien Enemies: Let Us Not Persecute These People," available at: *Vital Speeches of the Day*, February 15, 1942, 279–80.

85. "Taking No Chances," *Collier's*, March 21, 1942, 21.

86. Francis Biddle, "Taking No Chances, *Collier's*, March 21, 1942, 21.

87. Biddle, "Taking No Chances."

88. Ibid.

89. Ibid.

90. Lon Kurashige, *Japanese-American Celebration and Conflict: A History of Ethnic Identity and Festival in Los Angeles, 1934–1990* (Berkeley: University of California Press, 2002), 85.

91. Inada, *Only What We Could Carry*, 414–15.

92. Kurashige, *Japanese-American Celebration and Conflict*, 75–7.

93. Inada, *Only What We Could Carry*, 349.

94. John Sparks, "Civil Liberties in the Present Crisis," *Antioch Review*, Spring (March) 1942, 129.

95. Sparks, "Civil Liberties in the Present Crisis," 130.

96. Ibid., 136.

97. Ibid., 136.

98. Dorothea Lange, "Old Man," Bancroft Library #1967.014

99. Universal Newsreels, March 23, 1942. Newsreel Advertisements, Motion Picture, Sound & Video Branch, National Archives Annex, College Park, MD.

100. "A More Perfect Union: Japanese-Americans and the U.S. Constitution."

101. *People's World*, January 9, 1942, From Inada, 16.

102. *People's World*, February 2, 1942.

103. Drew Pearson & Robert S. Allen, "Washington Merry-Go-Round," March 2, 1942.

104. *Pictorial History of World War II*, 99.

105. "A More Perfect Union: Japanese-Americans and the U.S. Constitution."

106. "Letters to the Editor," *Time*, April 27, 1942, 7.

107. Ibid.

108. "Contributors: Carey McWilliams," *Antioch Review*, June 1942, 152.

109. "Book Reviews," *Journal of Farm Economics*, 1942, 901.

110. Carey McWilliams, "California and the Japanese," *The New Republic*, March 2, 1942, 297.

111. Carey McWilliams, "California and the Japanese."

112. Ibid.

113. Ibid.

114. Louis Fischer, "West Coast Perspective," *The Nation*, March 7, 1942, 277.

115. Fischer, "West Coast Perspective," 277.

116. Ibid.

117. Ibid.

118. Hadley Cantril, ed., *Public Opinion, 1935–1946* (Princeton: Princeton University Press, 1951), 380–1.

119. Cantril, *Public Opinion,* 381.
120. Pat Washburn, "The *Pittsburgh Courier*'s Double V Campaign in 1942," Paper presented at Annual Meeting of the Association for Education in Journalism (64th, East Lansing, 1981), Available at: www.eric.ed.gov:80/ERICWebPortal
121. "Turning Point: World War II," *The Civil Rights Movement in Virginia,* Museum Exhibition, Virginia Historical Society, Online Exhibitions, Available at: www. vahistorical.org/civilrights/ww2/htm
122. Gerald Horne, *Black and Red: W.E.B. DuBois and the Afro-American Response to the Cold War, 1944–1963* (Albany: SUNY Press, 1986), 10.
123. "Turning Point: World War II," The Civil Rights Movement in Virginia.
124. Maggi M. Morehouse, *Fighting Jim Crow: Black Men and Women Remember World War II* (Lanham, MD: Roman & Littlefield, 2000), 4.
125. Morehouse, *Fighting Jim Crow,* 5.
126. Cornelius L. Bynum, *A. Philip Randolph and the Struggle for Civil Rights* (Urbana: University of Illinois Press, 2010), 165.
127. Jervis Anderson, *A. Philip Randolph: A Biographical Portrait* (New York: Harcourt, Brace, Jovanovich, 1973), 256–8.
128. David Levering Lewis, *W.E.B. DuBois: The Fight for Equality and the American Century* (New York: Owl Books, 2001), 469.
129. Executive Order Number 8022, Available at: www.archive.eeoc.gov
130. Bynum, *A. Philip Randolph and the Struggle for Civil Rights,* 178.
131. Morehouse, *Fighting Jim Crow,* 5.
132. "African-American Military History," Available at: http://lwfaam.net
133. Morehouse, *Fighting Jim Crow,* 5.
134. "African-Americans in World War 2," Aavailable at: www.historyplace.com/unitedstates/aframerwar/index
135. Prange, *At Dawn We Slept,* 514–15.
136. Mary Penick Motley, *The Invisible Soldier: The Experience of the Black Soldier, World War II* (Detroit, Wayne State University Press, 1975), 11.
137. Motley, *The Invisible Soldier,* 14.
138. Ibid., 25.
139. Kareem Abdul Jabbar & Anthony Walton, *Brothers-in-Arms: The Epic Story of the 761st Tank Battalion, World War Two's Forgotten Heroes* (New York: Broadway, 2005), 26–8.
140. Motley, *The Invisible Soldier,* 39–40.
141. Ibid., 40.
142. Washburn, "The *Pittsburgh Courier*'s Double V Campaign in 1942," 1.
143. Ibid., 1.
144. Ibid., 3.
145. Ibid., 3–6.
146. Morehouse, *Fighting Jim Crow,* 9.
147. Washburn, "The *Pittsburgh Courier*'s Double V Campaign in 1942," 13.
148. Horne, *Black and Red,* 10.
149. Ibid., 10.
150. Lewis, *W.E.B. DuBois,* 470.
151. Taylor Branch, *Parting the Waters: America in the King Years, 1954–1963* (New York: Simon & Schuster, 1988), 52–3, 58.
152. Washburn, 5.

153. Earl Brown, "American Negroes and the War," *Harper's*, March 1942, 545–52.

154. Brown, 552.

155. Washburn, "The *Pittsburgh Courier's* Double V Campaign in 1942," 15.

156. Ibid., 16.

157. Michael Gannon, *Operation Drumbeat: The Dramatic True Story of Germany's First U-Boat Attacks Along the Atlantic Coast In World War II* (Annapolis: Naval Institute Press, 1990), vii.

158. Gannon, *Operation Drumbeat*, vii.

159. Gudmundur Helagson, "Operation Drumbeat," available at: Uboat.Net, www.uboat.net/ops/drumbeat/htm

160. Gannon, *Operation Drumbeat*, 137.

161. Ibid., 138.

162. Ibid., 141.

163. Ibid., 143.

164. Edwin C. Bearss, "War on the Pacific Coast: Japanese Submarines Cruise the Pacific Coast," from Cohen, 196.

165. Bearss, "War on the Pacific Coast: Japanese Submarines Cruise the Pacific Coast,"196.

166. Ibid., 196.

167. Robert M. Browning, Jr. *U.S. Merchant Vessel War Casualties of World War II* (Annapolis: U.S. Naval Institute Press, 1996), 9–10.

168. Bearss, "War on the Pacific Coast: Japanese Submarines Cruise the Pacific Coast," 197.

169. Cohen, 200.

170. Ibid.

171. Vincent P. O'Hara, W. D. Dickson, Richard Worth, *On Seas Contested: The Seven Great Navies of the Second World War* (Annapolis: Naval Institute Press, 2010), 49.

172. Ibid., 74.

173. Ibid., 77.

174. Gannon, *Operation Drumbeat*, 149–53.

175. Ibid., 154–60.

176. Peter Padfield, *Donitz: The Last Fuhrer* (London: Panther, 1985), 267.

177. Padfield, *Donitz*, 267.

178. Patrick Beesley, *Very Special Intelligence* (London: Hamish Hamilton, 1977), 107.

179. Eric Larabee, *Commander in Chief: Franklin Delano Roosevelt, His Lieutenants, and Their War* (New York: Harper & Row, 1987), 155.

180. Larabee, *Commander in Chief*, 157.

181. Padfield, *Donitz*, 268.

182. Gannon, *Operation Drumbeat*, 160.

183. Ibid., 160.

184. Vice Admiral George Carrol Dyer, *The Amphibians Came to Conquer: The Story of Admiral Richmond Kelly Turner* (Washington DC: Department of the Navy/United States Marine Corps Fleet Marine Reference Publications, 1991 c1969), 153.

185. Dyer, *The Amphibians Came to Conquer*, 19, 107–41.

186. Ibid., 101.

187. Ibid., 165.

188. Ibid.

189. Ibid., 193.

190. Gannon, *Operation Drumbeat*, 161.

191. Ibid., 163–4.

192. Homer Hickam, Jr, *Torpedo Junction* (Annapolis: Naval Institute Press, 1989), 5–6.

193. Eugene Rachlis, *The Story of the U.S. Coast Guard* (New York: Random House, 1961), 148–9.
194. Gannon, *Operation Drumbeat*, 171–6.
195. Samuel Eliot Morrison, *History of United States Naval Operations In World War II: The Battle of the Atlantic, September 1939-May 1943* (Boston: Little, Brown, 1989 c1947), 126.
196. Morrison, *Battle of the Atlantic*, 126–7.
197. Gannon, *Operation Drumbeat*, 231–2.
198. Hickam, *Torpedo Junction*, 9.
199. Morrison, *Battle of the Atlantic*, 130.
200. Browning, *U.S. Merchant Vessel War Casualties of World War II*, 13–37.
201. Ibid., 22.
202. Gannon, *Operation Drumbeat*, 273–4.
203. Ibid., 221.
204. *Baltimore Sun*, January 15, 1942. From J.A.H. Hopkins, vol. XV, #3507.
205. *Baltimore Sun*, January 15, 1942.
206. Universal Newsreels, March 2, 1942. Newsreel advertising catalogue, Motion Picture, Sound, & Video Branch, National Archives Annex, College Park, MD.
207. *Baltimore Evening Sun*, February 4, 1942. From J.A.H. Hopkins, vol. XVI, #3634.
208. *Baltimore Sun*, February 28, 1942. From J.A.H. Hopkins, vol. XVII, #3763.
209. Gannon, *Operation Drumbeat*, 277–9.
210. Ibid., 280.
211. Ibid., 299.
212. "Unternhemen Paukenschlag," *Die Deutsche Wochenschau*, #599, February 25, 1942. Available at: www.youtube.com
213. Padfield, *Donitz*, 271.
214. Ibid., 271.
215. Morrison, *Battle of the Atlantic*, 135.
216. Melanie Wiggins, *Torpedoes in the Gulf: Galveston and the U-Boats, 1942–1943* (College Station: Texas A&M University Press, 2004 c1995), 16–22.
217. Gannon, *Operation Drumbeat*, 380.
218. Hickam, *Torpedo Junction*, 25, 82.
219. Drew Pearson & Robert S. Allen, "Washington Merry-Go-Round," February 13, 1942.
220. Ibid., March 3, 1942.
221. Ibid., March 20, 1942.
222. *Washington Merry-Go Round*, March 20, 1942.
223. Wiggins, *Torpedoes in the Gulf*, 20.
224. Gannon, *Operation Drumbeat*, 380.
225. Morrison, *Battle of the Atlantic*, 154.
226. Eric A. Sevareid, Radio Script, March 7, 1941. From the Papers of Eric A. Sevareid, Library of Congress.
227. Sevareid, *Not So Wild a Dream*, 206.
228. Ibid., 206.
229. Ibid., 206.
230. Ibid., 207.
231. Raymond A. Schroth, *The American Journey of Eric Sevareid* (South Royalton, VT: Steerforth Press, 1995), 198.
232. Sevareid, *Not so wild a Dream* 209.
233. CBS Radio, January 22, 1942. MCR Tape #2059.

234. CBS Radio, January 25, 1942. MCR Tape #2063.
235. Ibid., Tape #2063.
236. CBS Radio, January 26, 1942. MCR Tape #2064.
237. Eric A. Sevareid Radio Script, February 6, 1942. From the Papers of Eric A. Sevareid, Library of Congress.
238. Ibid.
239. Andre Schiffin, Dr. Suess & Co. *Go to War: The World War II Editorial Cartoons of America's Leading Comic Artists* (New York: The New Press, 2009), 126.
240. Carl W. Ackerman, "Will Our Southern Flank Become a Southern Front: Performance and Not Propaganda Counts," from *Vital Speeches of the Day*, April 15, 1942, 402–03.
241. Drew Pearson & Robert S. Allen, "Washington Merry-Go-Round," January 22, 1942.
242. Ibid., January 25, 1942.
243. Rt. Rev. Mgr. Donald A. MacLean, "The Americas in the World Crisis," from *Vital Speeches of the Day*, May 1, 1942, 429–33.
244. CBS Radio, February 1, 1942. MCR Tape # 2070. National Archives Annex, College Park, MD.
245. Kupfer, *We Felt the Flames,* 128.
246. Sperber, 210.
247. CBS Radio, February 1, 1942. MCR Tape #2070.
248. Ibid.
249. Ibid.
250. Ibid.
251. Ibid.
252. Ibid.
253. Ibid.
254. Ibid.
255. CBS Radio, February 8, 1942. MCR Tape #2080.
256. Ibid.
257. Ibid.
258. Ibid.
259. Alexis de Tocqueville, *Democracy in America & Two Essays on America* (London: Penguin Books, 2003), 590–612.
260. CBS Radio, February 8, 1942. MCR Tape #2080.
261. Ibid.
262. Ibid.
263. Ibid.
264. Cantril (ed.), 955.
265. Ibid.
266. Ibid.

Chapter 6

1. Howard J. Langer, ed., *World War II: An Encyclopedia of Quotations* (Westport, CT: Greenwood Press, 1999), 205–06.
2. Clayton K.S. Chun, *The Doolittle Raid, 1942: America's First Strike Back at Japan* (New York: Osprey Publishing, 2006), 81–2.

3. William D. Hassett, *Off the Record With FDR: 1942–1943* (New Brunswick, NJ: Rutgers University Press, 1958), 40–1.
4. Chun, *The Doolittle Raid, 1942,* 43.
5. Jane's Fighting Ships of World War II, 278.
6. Chun, *The Doolittle Raid, 1942,* 45.
7. Toland, *But Not in Shame: The Six Months After Pearl Harbor* (New York: Random House, 1961), 360.
8. Chun, 45.
9. Toland, *But Not in Shame,* 359.
10. Ibid., 360.
11. Ibid., 360.
12. "Letter, H.H. Arnold to Samuel I. Rosenman, April 25, 1949," from Rosenman, 214.
13. "Letter, H.H. Arnold to Samuel I. Rosenman, April 25, 1949," from Rosenman, 215.
14. James H. Doolittle, with Carrol V. Gines, *I Could Never Be So Lucky Again: An Autobiography by General James H. 'Jimmy' Doolittle* (New York: Bantam, 1992), 13–23.
15. Doolittle, *I Could Never Be So Lucky Again,* 23–5.
16. Ibid., 36–7.
17. Ibid., 45–61.
18. Ibid., 47.
19. Ibid., 150–63.
20. "Gee Bee Racer," *The History of Flight* (Sausalito, CA: Portal Publications, undated).
21. "Gee Bee Model R," Wikipedia, available at: www.en.wikipedia.org/wiki/Gee_Bee_Model_R
22. Doolittle, *I Could Never Be So Lucky Again,* 179.
23. Ibid., 197.
24. Ibid., 211.
25. Missions that Changed the War: The Doolittle Raid, part I. The Military Network, 2010.
26. Adams, 126–9.
27. Ted W. Lawson & Robert Considine, *Thirty Seconds Over Tokyo* (New York: Fall River Press, 2007 c1942), 26–7.
28. Lawson & Considine, *Thirty Seconds Over Tokyo,* 27.
29. Doolittle, *I Could Never Be So Lucky Again,* 231.
30. Lawson & Considine, *Thirty Seconds Over Tokyo,* 27.
31. Jane's Fighting Ships of World War II, 267.
32. Adams, 130.
33. Ibid., 134.
34. Foster Hailey, *Pacific Battle Line* (New York: The Macmillan, 139.
35. Chun, *The Doolittle Raid, 1942,* 51.
36. Ibid., 51.
37. Ibid., 53.
38. Ibid., 54–6.
39. Ibid., 74–5.
40. Ibid., 83.
41. Toland, *But Not in Shame,* 361.
42. Chun, *The Doolittle Raid, 1942,* 83.
43. Toland, *But Not in Shame,* 361.

44. Ibid., 361.

45. Rex Allan Smith & Gerald A. Meehl, *Pacific War Stories: In the Words of Those Who Survived* (New York: Abbeville Press, 2004), 407.

46. Smith & Meehl, *Pacific War Stories*, 410.

47. Gordon W. Prange, with Donald M. Goldstein and Katharine V. Dillon, *Miracle at Midway* (New York: McGraw-Hill, 1982), 25.

48. Chun, *The Doolittle Raid, 1942*, 88.

49. Carroll V. Glines, *The Doolittle Raid: America's Daring First Strike Against Japan* (New York: Jove Books, 1988), 218.

50. Glines, *The Doolittle Raid*, 219.

51. Doolittle, *I Could Never Be So Lucky Again*, 256.

52. Chun, *The Doolittle Raid, 1942*, 84.

53. "H. H. Arnold to Samuel I. Rosenman, April 25, 1949," Rosenman, 216.

54. *New York Herald-Tribune*, April 19, 1942. From J.A.H. Hopkins, Diary of World Events, vol. XIX, 3999.

55. *Baltimore Sun*, April 18, 1942. From Hopkins, vol. XIX, 3991.

56. *New York Herald-Tribune*, April 18, 1942. From Hopkins, vol. XIX, 3996.

57. Rosenman, Public Addresses and Papers of Franklin D. Roosevelt, 1942, 213–14.

58. Ibid., 214.

59. Ibid.

60. NBC Radio Index Cards of Programming, April 19–22, 1942, record numbers 22948–22956. Recorded Sound Section, Library of Congress, Washington, D.C.

61. Kaltenborn, *Kaltenborn Edits the War News* (New York: E.P. Dutton, 1942), 50.

62. Ibid., 51.

63. Ibid.

64. Ibid., 50–1.

65. Ibid., 51.

66. Ibid.

67. John Gunther Radio Script, April 17, 1942, from the Raymond Gram Swing Papers, Library of Congress, Washington, DC.

68. Gunther, April 17, 1942.

69. Ibid.

70. Ibid.

71. CBS Radio, April 18, 1942. MCR Collection, Tape # 2155.

72. Ibid.

73. Thomas, *History as You Heard It*, 197.

74. Ibid., 197.

75. Ibid., 198.

76. Fang, *Those Radio Commentators!* (Ames, IA: Iowa State University Press, 1977), 75.

77. Thomas, *History as You Heard It*, 198.

78. Glines, *The Doolittle Raid*, ix.

79. Jackson J. Benson, *The True Adventures of John Steinbeck, Writer* (New York: Viking Press, 1984), 499.

80. Karl Shapiro, *The Bourgeois Poet* (New York: Random House, 1964), 61–2.

81. Paul Fussell, *Wartime: Understanding and Behavior in the Second World War* (New York: Oxford University Press, 1989), 241.

82. Allen Guttmann, *The Wound in the Heart: America and the Spanish Civil War* (New York: Free Press, 1962), 126–9.

83. W.H. Auden, "September 1, 1939," Oscar Williams, ed., *The New Pocket Anthology of American Verse* (New York: Pocket Books, 1977), 17.

84. John Ciardi, "On the Photograph of a German Soldier Dead in Poland," *Poetry*, June 1940, 182.

85. Robinson Jeffers, "Five Poems," *Poetry*, December 1940, 171–2.

86. Warren French, *John Steinbeck* (New York: Twayne Publishers, 1961), 119.

87. John Berryman, "The Moon, The Night, and The Men," 1940. www.blueridgejournal.com/poems/jb2-moon.htm.

88. *Poetry*, May 1940, 108–09.

89. Archibald MacLeish, "The Irresponsibles," *The Nation*, May 18, 1940, 620.

90. Letter, Archibald MacLeish to James Angleton, January 26, 1940. From the Archibald MacLeish Papers, Yale University, Beinecke Rare Books Library.

91. William L. Shirer, "The Poison Pen," *Atlantic Monthly*, May 1942, 549–50.

92. Holly Cowan Shulman, *The Voice of America: Propaganda and Democracy, 1941–1945* (Madison: University of Wisconsin Press, 1990), 1–16.

93. Shulman, *The Voice of America*, 18.

94. *Encyclopedia Brittanica*, 15th Edition, s.v. "Paul Tillich."

95. Jerald C. Brauer, "Introduction," Tillich, Paul, *My Travel Diary*, edited by Jerald C. Brauer (New York: Holt & Rinehart, 1970), Available at: www.scribd.com.doc6935385/Paul-Tillich-My-Travel-Diary-1936-Between-Two-Worlds

96. Brauer, "Introduction."

97. Varian Fry, *Assignment: Rescue* (New York: Scholastic, 1968 c1945), 3, 82, 182.

98. Ronald H. Stone & Matthew Lon Weaver, eds, *Against the Grain: Paul Tillich's Wartime Radio Broadcasts into Germany* (Louisville: Westminster John Knox Press, 1998), 1.

99. Paul Tillich, "The Question of the Jewish People," March 31, 1942, Stone & Weaver, 14–15.

100. Tillich, "The Question of the Jewish People," Stone & Weaver, 16.

101. Stone & Weaver, *Against the Grain*, v.

102. Tillich, "Death and Resurrection of Nations," April 20, 1942, Stone & Weaver, 18.

103. Dr. Peter J. Marshall, "Foreword," from Catherine Marshall, *A Man Called Peter: The Story of Peter Marshall* (Grand Rapids: Chosen Books, 2002 c1951), 7.

104. Catherine Marshall, *A Man Called Peter*, 121.

105. Rev. Peter J. Marshall, ed., *The Wartime Sermons of Dr. Peter Marshall* (Dallas: Clarion Call Marketing, 2005), 39.

106. Peter J. Marshall, *The Wartime Sermons of Dr. Peter Marshall*, 41.

107. Ibid., 41.

108. Ibid., 42.

109. Ibid., 51.

110. Ibid., 73.

111. Frances Donaldson, P. G. *Wodehouse: A Biography* (London: Prion, 1982), 256.

112. Ibid., 256.

113. Robert McCrum, *Wodehouse* (New York: W.W. Norton, 2004), 326.

114. P.G. Wodehouse, Money in the Bank (Overlook: New York, 2007 c1941), 301.

115. McCrum, 329.

116. "Contributors," *Antioch Review*, March 1942, 151.

117. Pierre Cot, "The Immediate Future of France," *Antioch Review*, March 1942, 27–39.

118. Jacque LeFranc, "French Literature Under the Nazi Heel," March 1942, 137–42.

119. Henrik de Kauffmann, "A Message from the Minister of Denmark," *The American-Scandinavian Review*, September 1940, 306.

120. Rockwell Kent, "Greenland: An Obligation," *The American-Scandinavian Review,* Spring 1941, 204.

121. James Creese, "A Message from the Foundation," *The American-Scandinavian Review,* Winter 1941, 63.

122. "Norwegians at Dunkerque," & "Norway's Government-in-Exile," *American-Scandinavian Review,* Spring 1942, 160–5.

123. CBS Radio, May 17, 1942. MCR Collection, Tape #2188.

124. Ibid.

125. Golo Mann, "Europe Under Napoleon: A Synopsis," *The American Scholar,* March 1942, 133–48.

126. "Editorial," *The American Scholar,* March 1942, 131–2.

127. Douglas & Elizabeth Rigby, "Dictators and the Gentle Art of Collecting," *The American Scholar,* March 1942, 168–80.

128. George Beiswanger, "Richard Wagner: Oracle of National Socialism," *The American Scholar,* 228–42.

129. Jose Ortega y Gasset, "Kant and the Modern German Mind," *The Yale Review,* September 1941.

130. Ortega y Gasset, "Kant and the Modern German Mind," 115.

131. Ibid.

132. Stacy Schiff, *Saint-Exupery: A Biography* (New York: Henry Holt, 1994), 360–3.

133. Schiff, *Saint-Exupery,* 363.

134. Andre Maurois, "New Books in Review: Meditations of a French Aviator," *Yale Review,* March 1942, 819.

135. Maurois, "New Books in Review: Meditations of a French Aviator," 820.

136. Ibid., 820.

137. Ibid., 820.

138. Ibid., 821.

139. "Bibliography of Morison's Writings," www.history.navy.mil/library/guides/morison_bib.htm> from "Official United States Navy Biography," Available at: www.history.navy.mil.bios/morison_s.htm

140. Advertisement: "Books of Enduring Value from Beacon Hill," *Yale Review,* March 1942, ix.

141. Samuel Eliot Morison, *Admiral of the Ocean Sea: A Life of Christopher Columbus* (Boston: Little, Brown, 1942), 221–5.

142. "Naval History & Heritage Command," Available at: www.history.navy.mil/bios/morison_s.htm

143. Stefan Zweig, *Conqueror of the Seas: The Story of Magellan* (New York: Viking Press, 1938), xi–xiii.

144. Salmaggi & Pallavisini, 217.

145. Benson, 487.

146. Howard Levant, *The Novels of John Steinbeck: A Critical Study* (Columbia: University of Missouri Press, 1974), 145.

147. Benson, 487.

148. Ibid.

149. Ibid., 488.

150. Levant, *The Novels of John Steinbeck,* 146.

151. Benson, 504.

152. Ibid., 505.

153. Ibid., 506.
154. Ibid., 508.
155. John Steinbeck, *The Moon is Down* (New York: Viking Press, 1942), 186.
156. Steinbeck, *The Moon is Down,* 185–6.
157. Levant, *The Novels of John Steinbeck,* 149.
158. Warren French, *John Steinbeck* (New York: Twayne Publishers, 1961), 114–15.
159. Benson, 497.
160. French, *John Steinbeck,* 114.
161. Benson, 497.
162. Ibid., 498.
163. James Thurber, "What Price Conquest?" "Books in Review," *The New Republic,* March 16, 1942, 370.
164. Thurber, "What Price Conquest?" 370.
165. Ibid., 370.
166. Benson, 498.
167. Ibid., 498.
168. "Mr. Steinbeck, Friends and Foes," *The New Republic,* March 30, 1942, 413.
169. Upton Sinclair, "More Moon," "Correspondence," *The New Republic,* April 6, 1942, 463.
170. Sinclair, "More Moon," 463.
171. Ibid., 463.
172. Lincoln R. Gibbs, "John Steinbeck, Moralist," in E.W. Tedlock, Jr. and C.V. Wicker, *Steinbeck and His Critics: A Record of Twenty-Five Years* (Albuquerque: University of New Mexico Press, 1957), 95.
173. "The Moon is Halfway Down," *The New Republic,* May 18, 1942, 657.
174. "The Moon is Halfway Down," 657.
175. Ibid.
176. Bosley Crowther, "The Screen: 'The Moon is Down," *The New York Times,* March 27, 1942, Available at: www.movies/nytimes.com/movie/review?res=9C06ED7143FE33B BC4F51DFB566838859EDE
177. Lee Richards, "Operation Braddock," from *Black Propaganda,* Available at: www. psywar.org/braddock/php
178. Braddock, "Operation Braddock."
179. Benson, 499.
180. "Poem by US Flyer, Killed at 19, Hailed as First Classic of War," *New York Herald-Tribune,* February 8, 1942. From J.A.H. Hopkins, *Diary of World Events,* vol. XVII, #3652.
181. Scott Donaldson, *Archibald MacLeish: An American Life* (Boston: Houghton Mifflin, 1992), 326–7.
182. Kupfer, We Felt the Flames: American Reactions to the Blitzkrieg of Summer, 1940 (Ph.D. Dissertation, University of Texas, 1998), 676.
183. John Gillespie Magee, Jr. "High Flight," *New York Herald-Tribune,* February 8, 1942.
184. Magee, Jr. "High Flight."
185. Karl Shapiro, "The Decolonization of American Literature," from *To Abolish Children and Other Essays* (Chicago: Quadrangle Books, 1968), 33.
186. Shapiro, "The Decolonization of American Literature," 33.
187. "In Memory of Karl Shapiro," Available at: www.departments.bucknell.edu/stadler_ center/shapiro/
188. Karl Shapiro, *Essay on Rime* (Cornwall, NY: Cornwall Press, 1945), 32.

189. Karl Shapiro, "Is Poetry an American Art?" from *To Abolish Children and Other Essays*, 50.

190. Karl Shapiro, "A Malebolge of Fourteen Hundred Books," from *To Abolish Children and Other Essays*, 235.

191. Joseph Reino, *Karl Shapiro* (Boston: Twayne Publishers, 1981), 9.

192. "In Memory of Karl Shapiro," Available at: www.departments.bucknell.edu/stadler_center/shapiro/

193. Francis F. Beirne, *The Amiable Baltimoreans* (Baltimore: Johns Hopkins University Press, 1984 c1951), 13.

194. Karl Shapiro, "The Poetry Wreck," from *The Poetry Wreck: Selected Essays, 1950–1970* (New York: Random House, 1975), 353.

195. Karl Jay Shapiro, "The Twins," *Person, Place and Thing*, 27.

196. Wilmott, *The Barrier and the Javelin*, 141.

197. Eric M. Bergerund, *Fire in the Sky: The Air War in the Pacific* (Boulder, CO: Westview Press, 2000), 27–8.

198. Ibid., 27.

199. Pimlott, 128.

200. Karl Shapiro, "Full Moon: New Guinea," (New York: Reynal & Hitchcock, 1944), 35.

201. Karl Shapiro, "Full Moon: New Guinea," 35.

202. Karl Shapiro, "The Leg," *Person, Place, and Thing*, 38.

203. Reino, *Karl Shapiro*, 25.

204. Karl Shapiro, "Sunday: New Guinea," *Person, Place and Thing*, 13.

205. Reino, *Karl Shapiro*, 23.

206. Marion Hargrove, *See Here, Private Hargrove* (New York: Henry Holt, 1942), copyright page.

207. Hargrove, *See Here, Private Hargrove*, 3.

208. Ibid., 3.

209. Ibid., 111.

210. Ibid., 203.

211. Ibid., 205.

212. "The Home Front: Veterans Stories, Marion Lawton Hargrove, Jr." *The Charlotte-Mecklenburg Story*.

Chapter 7

1. Toland, *But Not in Shame: The Six Months After Pearl Harbor* (New York: Random House, 1961), 205.

2. William Manchester, *Goodbye, Darkness: A Memoir of the Pacific War* (Boston: Little, Brown, 1980), 60.

3. Robert McG. Thomas, Jr. "Irving Strobing, Radio Operator on Corregidor, Dies at 77," *The New York Times*, July 24, 1977, Available at: www.nytimes.com/1997/07/24/nyregion/irving-stroging-radio-operate-on-corregidor-dies-at-77.html?

4. Robert Conroy, *The Battle of Bataan: America's Greatest Military Defeat* (New York: Macmillan, 1969), 75.

5. William L. White, *They Were Expendable* (New York: Harcourt, Brace, 1942), 7.

6. Hugh Ambrose, *The Pacific* (New York: NAL Caliber, 2010), 11.

7. W. Victor Madej, ed., *U.S. Army and Marine Corps Order of Battle, Pacific Theater of Operations, 1941–1945, Volume I* (Allentown, PA: Game Publishing Company, 1984), 5.

8. Conroy, *The Battle of Bataan*, 1–6.

9. Madej, *U.S. Army and Marine Corps Order of Battle*, 5.

10. Manchester, *American Caesar: Douglas MacArthur, 1880–1964* (Boston: Little, Brown, 1978), 241.

11. Wilmott, *The Barrier and the Javelin*, 165.

12. Eric Bergerud, *Touched With Fire: The Land War in the South Pacific* (New York: Penguin, 1996), 5.

13. Manchester, *American Caesar*, 213.

14. Chris Henry, *Battle of the Coral Sea* (Annapolis: Naval Institute Press, 2003), 12.

15. Manchester, *American Caesar*, 215.

16. Joseph C. Harsch, *At the Hinge of History: A Reporter's Story* (Athens, GA: University of Georgia, 1993), 93.

17. Manchester, *American Caesar*, 241.

18. Manchester, *American Caesar*, 218.

19. Harsch, *At the Hinge of History*, 67.

20. D. Clayton James, ed., *South to Bataan, North to Mukden: The Prison Diary of Brigadier General W.E. Brougher* (Athens, GA: University of Georgia Press, 1971), 5.

21. Harsch, *At the Hinge of History*, 67.

22. Manchester, *American Caesar*, 242.

23. Conroy, *The Battle of Bataan*, 23.

24. Ibid., 23.

25. Ibid., 23–30.

26. White, *They Were Expendable*, 87.

27. Douglas MacArthur, *Reminiscences* (New York: The Great Commanders Collectors Reprints, 1994 c1964), 133.

28. Manchester, *Goodbye, Darkness*, 58.

29. Ibid., 59.

30. Ibid., 59–60.

31. Carlos P. Romulo. *I Saw the Fall of the Philippines* (Garden City, NY: Doubleday, Doran, 1943), 115.

32. James, ed., *South to Bataan*, 30.

33. Romulo, *I Saw the Fall of the Philippines*, 116.

34. Manchester, *Goodbye, Darkness*, 60.

35. Clark Lee, *They Call it Pacific: An Eye-Witness Story of our War Against Japan from Bataan to the Solomon Islands* (New York: Viking Press, 1943), 234.

36. Carol Morris Petillo,. *Douglas MacArthur: The Philippine Years* (Bloomington: Indiana University Press, 1981), 203.

37. Petillo, *Douglas MacArthur* 203.

38. Conroy, *The Battle of Bataan*, 39.

39. Toland, *But Not in Shame*, 205.

40. Ibid., 206.

41. Lee, *They Call it Pacific*, 234.

42. Conroy, *The Battle of Bataan*, 30–4.

43. Ibid., 37.

44. Gordon, *Horyo: Memoirs of an American POW*, 69.

45. Conroy, *The Battle of Bataan*, 40.

46. Gordon, *Horyo: Memoirs of an American POW*, 69.
47. Ibid., 69.
48. James, ed., *South to Bataan*, 28.
49. *The Picture History of World War II*, 78.
50. Gordon, *Horyo: Memoirs of an American POW* 69.
51. Conroy, *The Battle of Bataan*, 40.
52. Juanita Redmond, *I Served on Bataan* (New York: Garland Publishing, 1984 c1943), 48.
53. James, ed., *South to Bataan*, 28.
54. Redmond, *I Served on Bataan*, 49.
55. John Hersey, *Men on Bataan* (New York: Alfred A. Knopf, 1943), 294.
56. Hersey, *Men on Bataan*, 295.
57. Ibid., 295.
58. Ibid., 295.
59. Redmond, *I Served on Bataan*, 6.
60. Ibid., 86.
61. Hersey, *Men on Bataan,* 284.
62. Meirion Harries & Susie Harries, *Soldiers of the Sun: The Rise and Fall of the Imperial Japanese Army* (New York: Random House, 1991), 315.
63. Universal Newsreels, February 23, 1942. From National Archives Annex, College Park, Motion Picture, Sound, & Video Branch.
64. Alan Schom, *The Eagle and the Rising Sun: the Japanese-American War 1941–1943, Pearl Harbor Through Guadalcanal* (New York: W.W. Norton, 2004), 235.
65. Schom, *The Eagle and the Rising Sun*, 235.
66. Conroy, *The Battle of Bataan*, 41–2.
67. "MacArthur Vows 'I Shall Return,' Universal Newsreels 5245, Available at: www.youtube.com/watch?v=C2QyfnUSahc&feature=return
68. Miller, 272.
69. Stephen F. Ambrose, *Rise to Globalism: American Foreign Policy Since 1938* (New York: Penguin Books, 1988), 42.
70. Michael Schaller, "General Douglas MacArthur and the Politics of the Pacific War," from Gunter Bischof and Robert L. Dupont, eds, *The Pacific War Revisited* (Baton Rouge: Louisiana State University Press, 1997), 27–8.
71. Schaller, "General Douglas MacArthur and the Politics of the Pacific War," 28.
72. Ibid., 28.
73. Romulo, *I Saw the Fall of the Philippines*, 225.
74. Ibid., 226.
75. Ibid., 226–7.
76. Hersey, *Men on Bataan*, 1.
77. Schom, *The Eagle and the Rising Sun*, 247.
78. Ibid., 247.
79. Conroy, *The Battle of Bataan*, 44.
80. Julia Ward Howe, "Battle-Hymn of the Republic," *The Golden Treasury of Poetry* (New York: Golden Press, 1968), 38.
81. Conroy, *The Battle of Bataan*, 44.
82. John M. Fitzgerald, *Family in Crisis: The United States, the Philippines, and the Second World War* (Bloomington, IN: First Books, 2002), 35.
83. Conroy, *The Battle of Bataan*, 49.
84. Romulo, *I Saw the Fall of the Philippines*, 136.
85. *The Picture History of World War II*, 658–9.

86. Conroy, *The Battle of Bataan,* 54.
87. *The Picture History of World War II,* 659.
88. Harries & Harries, *Soldiers of the Sun,* 315.
89. Schom, *The Eagle and the Rising Sun,* 237.
90. Conroy, *The Battle of Bataan,* 67.
91. Ibid., 57.
92. Conroy, *The Battle of Bataan,* 69–70.
93. Schom, *The Eagle and the Rising Sun,* 238.
94. Ibid., 238.
95. Toland, *But Not in Shame,* 322.
96. Schom, *The Eagle and the Rising Sun,* 238.
97. Ibid., 238.
98. Robert McG. Thomas, Jr. "Irving Strobing, Radio Operator. . ."
99. Irving Strobing, "Last Broadcast from Corregidor," Available at: www.youtube.com
100. "Irving Strobing, Radio Operator. . ."
101. Ibid.
102. Toland, *But Not in Shame,* 380.
103. Ibid., 383.
104. Scott A. Mills, *Stranded in the Philippines: Professor Bell's Private War against the Japanese* (Annapolis: Naval Institute Press, 2009), 32.
105. Toland, *But Not in Shame,* 385.
106. Mills, *Stranded in the Philippines,* 32–3.
107. Saburo Ienaga, *The Pacific War: 1931–1945, A Critical Perspective on Japan's Role in World War II* (New York: Pantheon Books, 1978), 172.
108. Richard M. Gordon, with Benjamin S. Llamzon, *Horyo: Memoirs of an American POW* (St. Paul, MN: Paragon House, 1999), 84.
109. Manny Lawton, *Some Survived: An Eyewitness Account of the Bataan Death March and the Men who Lived Through It* (Chapel Hill: Algonquin Books, 2004), 17.
110. Conroy, *The Battle of Bataan,* 58.
111. Ibid., 60.
112. Gordon, 87–102.
113. Conroy, *The Battle of Bataan,* 62–5.
114. Harries & Harries, *Soldiers of the Sun,* 315.
115. Ibid., 315–16.
116. Ibid., 316.
117. Ibid., 340.
118. *Baltimore Sun,* January 31, 1942. From J.A.H. Hopkins, vol. XVII, #3619.
119. *Baltimore Sun,* January, 31, 1942.
120. *Baltimore Sun,* February 2, 1942. Hopkins, #3623.
121. Raymond Gram Swing Radio Script, February 2, 1942, from the Raymond Gram Swing Papers, Library of Congress.
122. Raymond Gram Swing Radio Script, February 2, 1942.
123. "The Real Story Behind Gen. MacArthur's Stand," *U.S. News,* February 20, 1942, 13.
124. CBS Radio, March 8, 1942. MCR Collection, Tape #2107.
125. Ibid.
126. CBS Radio, March 8, 1942. MCR Collection, Tape #2107.
127. CBS Radio, March 12, 1942. MCR Collection, Tape #2111.
128. Edgar McInnis, *The War: Third Year* (New York: Oxford University Press, 1945), 140–1.
129. McInnis, *The War,* 144.

130. Ibid.

131. CBS Radio, March 14, 1942, MCR Collection, Tape #2113.

132. CBS Radio, March 15, 1942, MCR Collection, Tape #2114.

133. CBS Radio, March 16, 1942. MCR Collection, Tape #2116.

134. Ibid.

135. Ibid.

136. Ibid.

137. Ibid.

138. CBS Radio, March 18, 1942. MCR Collection, Tape #2118.

139. CBS Radio, March 19, 1942. MCR Collection, Tape #2119.

140. Ibid.

141. Ibid.

142. CBS Radio, March 20, 1942. MCR Collection, Tape #2120.

143. CBS Radio March 21, 1942. MCR Collection, Tape #2121.

144. Ibid.

145. Ibid.

146. CBS Radio, March 22, 1942. MCR Collectoin, Tape #2123.

147. CBS Radio, March 29, 1942. MCR Collection, Tape #2131.

148. Ibid.

149. Universal Newsreels. Newsreel advertisement catalogue, March 18, 23, 25, 1942. From Motion Picture, Sound, Video Branch, National Archives Annex, College Park, MD.

150. CBS Radio, April 15, 1942. MCR Collection, Tape #2152.

151. Ibid.

152. Ibid.

153. "Fighting Fronts: Philippine Reverse Jolts US, but American Forces Hit Back," *Newsweek*, January 12, 1942, 13–14.

154. "Luzon Blow," *Newsweek*, March 16, 1942, 21.

155. *The New York Times*, April 10, 1942. From J.A.H. Hopkins, vol XIX, #3952.

156. Ibid.

157. Ibid.

158. Ibid.

159. *The Detroit News*, May 6, 1942. From War Headlines from the Detroit News.

160. *The New York Times*, May 8, 1942. From J.A.H. Hopkins, vol. XX, #4094.

161. Ibid.

162. *The New York Ti*mes, Mary 8, 1942. From J.A.H. Hopkins, vol. XX, #4097.

163. Ibid.

164. Samuel Eliot Morison, *History of United States Naval Operations in World War II, Vol. IV, Coral Sea, Midway, and Submarine Actions May 1942–August 1942* (Boston: Little, Brown, 1988 c1949), 42.

165. Harries & Harries, *Soldiers of the Sun,* 316.

166. Alan J. Levine, *The Pacific War: Japan Versus the Allies* (Westport, CT: Prager, 1995), 53.

167. Ibid.

168. Ibid, 54.

169. Ibid.

170. Ibid, 61.

171. Ibid.

172. Henry, *Battle of the Coral Sea,* 8–11.

173. Ibid., 15.

174. Ibid., 15.
175. Ibid., 16–17.
176. *Jane's Fighting Ships of World War II*, 187.
177. Henry, *Battle of the Coral Sea,* 14–15.
178. Ibid., 18–19.
179. Ibid., 34.
180. Ibid., 34–7.
181. Ibid.
182. Goldstein & Dillon, *Fading Victory*, 122.
183. Wilmott, *The Barrier and the Javelin*, 240.
184. Ibid., 228–9.
185. Goldstein & Dillon, *Fading Victory*, 120.
186. Ibid., 122.
187. Henry, *Battle of the Coral Sea,* 76.
188. Ibid., 84.
189. Wilmott, *The Barrier and the Javelin*, 279.
190. Adams, 150–1.
191. Jane & Michael Stern, *Square Meals* (New York: Alfred A. Knopf, 1985), 232.
192. Levine, 62.
193. Henry, *Battle of the Coral Sea,* 90.
194. "Admiral Robert E. Dixon, Hero of a Naval Battle," *The New York Times*, October 24, 1981. Available at: www.nytimes.com/1981/10/24/obituaries/adm-robert-e-dixon-hero-of-a-naval-battle.html?
195. Associated Press, "Summary of Sinkings," *Baltimore Evening Sun*, May 8, 1941. From J.A.H. Hopkins, vol. XX, #4100.
196. *Baltimore Evening Sun*, May 8, 1942.
197. Ibid.
198. Ibid.
199. "Battle for Australia," *Baltimore Evening Sun*, May 8, 1942.
200. *Baltimore Sun*, May 9, 1942. From J.A.H. Hopkins, vol. XX, #4105.
201. *Baltimore Sun*, May 9, 1942. From J.A.H. Hopkins, vol. XX, #4106.
202. *Baltimore Sun*, May 9, 1942.
203. *Baltimore Sun*, May 9, 1942. From J.A.H. Hopkins, vol. XX, #4105.
204. CBS Radio, May 11, 1942. MCR Collection, Tape #2182.
205. Ibid.
206. "World Battlefronts," *Time*, May 4, 1942, 18-19.
207. "US at War: Realization," *Time*, May 18, 1942, 13.
208. "The Shape of Things," *The Nation*, May 16, 1942, 558.
209. "The Shape of Things," 558.
210. "Victory in the Coral Sea," *The New Republic*, May19, 1942, 651.

Chapter 8

1. Prange, Goldstein & Dillon, *Miracle at Midway*, 91–2.
2. Prange, Goldtstein & Dillon, *Miracle at Midway,* 93.
3. Prange, Goldstein & Dillon, *Miracle at Midway*, 29.

4. Toland, *But Not in Shame*, 408.
5. "Nazis Renew In Crimea After Lull," *Baltimore Sun*, May 13, 1942. From J.A.H. Hopkins, vol. XX, # 4123.
6. *New Masses*, June 22, 1942.
7. CBS Radio, May 16, 1941. MCR Collection, Tape #2187.
8. "Free Browder Rally," advertisement, *The New Republic*, May 18, 1942, 679.
9. CBS Radio, May 17, 1941. MCR Collection, Tape #2187.
10. "Victory this Year?" *The New Republic*, May 25, 1942, 717.
11. "Crisis in German Strategy," *The New Republic*, May 25, 1942, 719.
12. Ibid., 720.
13. NBC Radio, Index Card May 16, 1942, Record #23208. From Recorded Sound Section, Library of Congress.
14. CBS Radio, May 24, 1942. MCR Collection, Tape #2196.
15. Ibid.
16. Henry H. Adams, *1942: The Year that Doomed the Axis*, 158.
17. Ibid., 158.
18. Adams, 159.
19. NBC Radio, May 16, 1942. Index Card, Record #23027. Recorded Sound Section, Library of Congress.
20. "Our Baby's Name," *The New Republic*, May 25, 1942, 718.
21. Matthew Bennett, "The Battle of Gazala: Rommel's Masterpiece," from Stephen Badsey, *Atlas of World War II Battle Plans, Before and After* (New York: Barnes & Noble, 2000), 30–41.
22. Salmaggi & Pallavisini, 240–86.
23. Edward Bliss, *Now the News: The Story of Broadcast Journalism* (New York: Columbia University Press, 1991), 120.
24. CBS Radio, May 24, 1942. MCR Collection, Tape #2196.
25. CBS Radio, May 29, 1942. MCR Collection, Tape #2201.
26. CBS Radio, June 4, 1942. MCR Collection, Tape #2208.
27. Adams, 191.
28. Paul S. Dull, *A Battle History of the Imperial Japanese Navy, 1941–1945* (Annapolis: Naval Institute Press, 1978), 133.
29. Glen M. Williford, *Racing the Sunrise: Reinforcing America's Pacific Outposts, 1941–1942* (Annapolis: Naval Institute Press, 2010), 133.
30. Glen M Williford, *Racing the Sunrise: Reinforcing America's Pacific Outposts, 1941–1942* (Annapolis: Naval Institute Press, 2010), 31–3, 106–19.
31. Mitsuo Fuchida & Masatake Okumiya, *Midway: The Battle That Doomed Japan, the Japanese Navy's Story* (Annapolis: Naval Institute Press, Bluejacket Books, 1992 c1955), 97.
32. Prange, *Miracle at Midway*, 30–1.
33. Ibid., 31.
34. Dull, *A Battle History of the Imperial Japanese Navy*, 133.
35. Prange, *Miracle at Midway*, 30.
36. Wilmott, *The War with Japan: The Period of Balance, May 1942–October 1943*, 21–9.
37. Ibid., 21–2.
38. Samuel Eliot Morison, *History of United States Naval Operations in World War II: Vol. VII, Aleutians, Gilberts, and Marshalls, June 1942–April 1944* (Boston: Little, Brown, 1984 c1951), 3–21.
39. Toland, *But Not in Shame*, 407.
40. Adams, 193.

41. Wilmott, *The War with Japan*, 389.
42. Adams, 191.
43. Cesar Salmaggi & Alfredo Pallavisini, *2194 Days of War: An Illustrated Chronology of the Second World War* (New York: Barnes & Noble Books, 1993), 248.
44. Salmaggi & Pallavisini, *2194 Days of War,* 248.
45. Ibid., 248.
46. Adams, 193.
47. Ibid.
48. Salmaggi & Pallavisini, *2194 Days of War,* 249.
49. Ibid.
50. Ibid., 250.
51. Toland, *But Not in Shame*, 407.
52. Ibid., 408.
53. Adams, 195.
54. Ibid, 203.
55. Paul S. Dull, *A Battle History of the Imperial Japanese Navy, 1941–1945* (Annapolis: Naval Institute Press, 1978), 134–6.
56. Salmaggi & Pallavisini, *2194 Days of War,* 250.
57. Wilmott, *The War with Japan*, 385.
58. Ibid., 385–6.
59. Toland, *But Not in Shame*, 411.
60. Wilmott, *The War with Japan*, 385.
61. Alvin Kernan, *The Unknown Battle of Midway: The Destruction of the American Torpedo Squadrons* (New Haven: Yale University Press), 76–122, 145–54.
62. Wilmott, *The War with Japan*, 388–9.
63. Fuchida & Okumiya, *Midway,* 157.
64. Herman Wouk, *War and Remembrance* (Boston: Little, Brown, 1985), 422–3.
65. Wilmott, *The War with Japan*, 386–7.
66. John Pimlott, *The Atlas of World War II* (Philadelphia: Courage Books, 2006), 125.
67. Salmaggi & Pallavisini, *2194 Days of War,* 251–2.
68. Toland, *But Not in Shame*, 424.
69. Levine, 66.
70. Morison, History of United States Naval Operations in World War II: Vol. IV, Coral Sea, Midway, and Submarine Actions, May 1942–August 1942, 142.
71. Toland, *But Not in Shame*, 425.
72. Fuchida & Okumiya, *Midway,* 243.
73. Salmaggi & Pallavisini, *2194 Days of War,* 250–1.
74. Toland, *But Not in Shame*, 412–24.
75. Fuchida & Okumiya, *Midway,* 243.
76. Goldstein & Dillon, eds, *Fading Victory: The Diary of Admiral Matome Ugaki, 1941–1945* (Annapolis, MD: Naval Institute Press, 1991), 156.
77. Wouk, *War and Remembrance,* 428.
78. Salmaggi & Pallavisini, *2194 Days of War,* 253.
79. Ibid.
80. Jonathan Parshall & Anthony Tully, *Shattered Sword: The Untold Story of the Battle of Midway* (Dulles, VA: Potomac Books, 2007), 391.
81. Gordon W. Prange, with Donald M. Goldstein and Katharine V. Dillon, *Miracle at Midway* (New York: McGraw-Hill, 1982), 359.

82. Ibid., 361.

83. Ibid., 361–2.

84. Ibid., 361–3.

85. Morison, Coral Sea, Midway, & Submarine Actions, 158–9.

86. Prange, 363.

87. *The Detroit News*, May 8, 1942. From War Headlines in the Detroit News, 1939–1945.

88. *The Detroit News*, May 9, 1942. From War Headlines in the Detroit News, 1939–1945.

89. The Detroit News, May 9, 1942.

90. Ibid.

91. Ibid.

92. *Baltimore Evening Sun*, June 9, 1942. From J.A.H. Hopkins, vol. XXI, #4236.

93. Baltimore Evening Sun, June 9, 1942.

94. *Baltimore Evening Sun*, June 11, 1942. From J.A.H. Hopkins, vol. XXI, #4246.

95. "Full Story of Coral Sea: Text of Naval Communique," *Baltimore Evening Sun*, June 12, 1942. From J.A.H. Hopkins, vol. XXI, #4257.

96. Rex Allan Smith and Gerald A. Meehl, *Pacific War Stories: In the Words of Those Who Survived* (New York: Abbeville Press, 2004), 428–30.

97. Smith and Meehl, 431.

98. Smith, 430–7.

99. Raymond Gram Swing radio script, June 6, 1942. From Raymond Gram Swing Collection, Library of Congress.

100. Swing radio script, June 6, 1942.

101. CBS Radio, June 5, 1942. MCR Collection, Tape #2209.

102. Morison, Coral Sea, Midway, & Submarine Actions, 159.

103. Morison, 159.

104. CBS Radio, June 5, 1942. MCR Collection, Tape # 2209.

105. CBS Radio, June 6, 1942. MCR Collection, Tape #2210.

106. Ibid.

107. CBS Radio, June 6, 1942. MCR Collection, Tape #2210.

108. Ibid.

109. CBS Radio, June 7, 1942. MCR Collection, Tape #2211.

110. Ibid.

111. Ibid.

BIBLIOGRAPHY

Books

Abramson, Rudy. *Spanning the Century: The Life of W. Averell Harriman, 1891–1986* (New York: William Morrow, 1992).

Adams, Brooks. *The Law of Civilization and Decay: An Essay of History* (University of Michigan Library, HathiTrust Digitized Archives, c1895).

Adams, Henry. *The Education of Henry Adams* (New York: Heritage Press, 1942).

—*The Degradation of the Democratic Dogma* (New York: Macmillan, 1947).

Adams, Henry H. *1942: The Year that Doomed the Axis* (New York: Paperback Library, 1967).

Acheson, Dean. *Present at the Creation: My Years in the State Department* (New York: W.W. Norton, 1969).

Alsop, Joseph and Adam Platt. *I've Seen the Best of It: Memoirs* (Mount Jackson, VA: Axios Press, 1992)

Ambrose, Hugh. *The Pacific* (New York: NAL Caliber, 2010).

Ambrose, Stephen F. *Rise to Globalism: American Foreign Policy Since 1938* (New York: Penguin Books, 1988).

Ancheta, Celedondo A. ed., Historical Documents of World War II in the Philippines, The Wainwright Papers, vol. 1, "Report of Operations of USAFFE and USFIP in the Philippine Islands 1941–1942" (Quezon City, Philippines: New Day Publications, 1979).

—etc ed., Historical Documents of World War II in the Philippines, The Wainwright Papers, vol. 2, "Report of Operations on the Harbor Defenses of Manila and Subic Bays 14 February 1941–1916 May 1942" (Quezon City, Philippines: New Day Publications, 1980).

Anderson, Jervis. *A. Philip Randolph: A Biographical Portrait* (New York: Harcourt, Brace, Jovanovich, 1973).

Atkinson, Rick. *An Army at Dawn: The War in Africa, 1942–1943* (New York: Henry Hold, 2001).

Auden, W. H. "September 1, 1939," Oscar Williams, ed., *The New Pocket Anthology of American Verse* (New York: Pocket Books, 1977).

Bailey, Ronald H. *The Home Front: USA* (New York: Time/Life, 1977).

Barbour, James and Fred Warner. eds, *Liebling at the New Yorker* (Albuquerque: University of New Mexico Press, 1994).

Barzini, Luigi. *The Europeans* (New York: Simon & Schuster, 1983).

BBC Radio Handbook (London: British Broadcasting Company, 1941).

Beard, Charles A. *President Roosevelt and the Coming of the War 1941* (New York: Archon Books, 1968 c1948).

Beekman, Allan. *The Niihau Incident: The True Story of the Japanese Fighter Pilot who, after the Pearl Harbor Attack, Crash-Landed on the Hawaiian Island of Niihau and Terrorized the Residents* (Honolulu: Heritage Press of the Pacific, 1990, c1982).

Beesley, Patrick. *Very Special Intelligence* (London: Hamish Hamilton, 1977).

Beirne, Francis F. *The Amiable Baltimoreans* (Baltimore: Johns Hopkins University Press, 1984, c1951).

Bennett, Matthew. "The Battle of Gazala: Rommel's Masterpiece," from Stephen Badsey, *Atlas of World War II Battle Plans, Before and After* (New York: Barnes & Noble, 2000).

Benson, Jackson J. *The True Adventures of John Steinbeck, Writer* (New York: Viking Press, 1984).

Bercovitch, Sacvan. *The American Jeremiad* (Madison: University of Wisconsin Press, 1978).

Bergerud, Eric M. *Touched With Fire: The Land War in the South Pacific* (New York: Penguin, 1996).

—*Fire in the Sky: The Air War in the South Pacific* (Boulder, CO: Westview, 2000).

Bilby, Kenneth. *The General: David Sarnoff and the Rise of the Communications Industry* (New York: Harper & Row, 1986).

Bischof, Gunter and Dupont, Robert L. eds, *The Pacific War Revisited* (Baton Rouge: Louisiana State University Press, 1997).

Bliss, Edward. *Now the News: The Story of Broadcast Journalism* (New York: Columbia University Press, 1991).

Blouet, Brian W., ed. *Global Geostrategy: Mackinder and the Defense of the West* (New York: Frank Cass, 2005).

Blum, D. Steven. *Walter Lippmann: Cosmopolitanism in the Century of Total War* (Ithaca, NY: Cornell University Press, 1984).

Bradley, Omar N and Blair, Clay. *A General's Life: An Autobiography* (New York: Simon & Schuster, 1983).

Branch, Taylor. *Parting the Waters: America in the King Years, 1954–1963* (New York: Simon & Schuster, 1988).

Brinkley, Alan. *The Publisher: Henry Luce and his American Century* (New York: Alfred A. Knopf, 2010).

Brinkley, David. *Washington Goes to War: The Extraordinary Transformation of a City and a Nation* (New York: Alfred A. Knopf, 1988).

Browning, Christopher and Matthaus, Jurgen. *The Origins of the Final Solution: The Evolution of Nazi Jewish Policy, September 1939–March 1942* (Lincoln and Jerusalem: University of Nebraska Press and Yad Vashem, 2004).

Browning, Robert M. Jr. *U.S. Merchant Vessel War Casualties of World War II* (Annapolis: U.S. Naval Institute Press, 1996).

Bryce, Lord James. *The American Commonwealth* (New York: Putnam/Capricorn Books, 1959).

Bullock, Alan. *Hitler: A Study in Tyranny* (New York: Harper, 1971).

Burns, James MacGregor. *Roosevelt 1940–1945: The Soldier of Freedom* (New York: Harcourt, Brace, Jovanovitch, 1970).

Bynum, Cornelius L. *A. Philip Randolph and the Struggle for Civil Rights* (Urbana: University of Illinois Press, 2010).

Caffrey, Kate. *Out in the Midday Sun: Singapore 1941–1945 – The End of an Empire* (New York: Stein and Day, 1973).

Calic, Edouard. *Reinhard Heydrich: The Chilling Story of the Man Who Masterminded the Nazi Death Camps* (William Morrow: New York, 1985).

Cantril, Hadley. ed., *Public Opinion, 1935–1946* (Princeton, NJ: Princeton University Press, 1951).

Cary, Francine Curro. *The Influence of War on Walter Lippmann, 1914–1944* (Madison: State Historical Society of Wisconsin for University of Wisconsin, 1967).

Chamberlain, Elinor. *The Far Command* (New York: Ballantine Books, 1952).

Chennault, Anna. *Chennault and the Flying Tigers* (New York: Paul S. Eriksson, 1963).

Chester, Edward W. *Radio, Television, and American Politics* (New York: Sheed & Ward, 1969).

Chester, Giraud, Garnet Garrison, and Edgar Willis. *Television and Radio* (New York: Appleton-Century-Crofts, 1971).

Chun, Clayton K. S. *The Doolittle Raid, 1942: America's First Strike Back at Japan* (New York: Osprey Publishing, 2006).

Churchill, Winston S. *The Second World War: The Hinge of Fate* (Boston: Houghton-Mifflin, 1950).

—*The Grand Alliance* (Boston: Houghton-Mifflin, 1951).

Clapper, Raymond. *Watching the World* (New York: McGraw-Hill, 1944).

Clements, Jonathan. *Mannerheim: President, Soldier, Spy* (London: Haus Publishing, 2009).

Cohen, Stan. *V for Victory: America's Home Front During World War II* (Missoula: Pictorial Histories Publishing Company, 1991).

Collier's Photographic History of the Second World War (New York: Grosset & Dunlap, 1945).

Colville, John. *The Fringes of Power* (Guilford, CT: Lyons Press, 1985).

Commager, Henry Steele. *The American Mind: An Interpretation of American Thought and Character since the 1880s* (New Haven: Yale University Press, 1950).

—ed., *The Blue and The Gray: The Nomination of Lincoln to the Eve of Gettsyburg* (New York: Mentor, 1973).

Compton, James V. *The Swastika and the Eagle: Hitler, the United States, and the Origins of World War II* (Boston: Houghton-Mifflin, 1967).

Conroy, Robert. *The Battle of Bataan: America's Greatest Military Defeat* (New York: Macmillan, 1969).

Cooper, James Fenimore. *Homeward Bound, or, The Chase: A Tale of the Sea* (Philadelphia: Carey, Lea & Blanchard, 1838).

Cowley, Malcolm. *And I Worked at the Writer's Trade* (New York: Viking, 1978).

Crabb, Cecil V. Jr. and Pat M. Holt, *Invitation to Struggle: Congress, the President, and Foreign Policy* (Washington, DC: Congressional Quarterly, 1989).

Craye, Florence. *Spindrift* (London: Worplesdon & Gorringe, 1925).

Crosby, Alfred W. *Ecological Imperialism: The Biological Expansion of Europe, 900–1900* (New York: Cambridge, 1989).

Crunden, Robert M. *American Salons: Encounters with European Modernism, 1885–1917* (New York: Oxford University Press, 1993).

Cull, Nicholas John. *Selling War: The British Propaganda Campaign against American "Neutrality" in World War II* (New York: Oxford University Press, 1995).

Davis, Kenneth S. *FDR: The War President, 1940–1943, a History* (New York: Random House, 2000).

Degler, Carl N. *In Search of Human Nature: The Decline and Revival of Darwinism in American Social Thought* (New York: Oxford University Press, 1991).

Deighton, Len. *Blitzkrieg: From the Rise of Hitler to the Fall of Dunkirk* (London: Jonathan Cape, 1979).

DePastio, Todd. *Bill Mauldin: A Life Up Front* (New York: W.W. Norton, 1998).

Dewey, Donald and Nicholas Acocella. *Total Ballclubs: The Ultimate Book of Baseball Teams* (Toronto: Sport Classic Books, 2005).

Dewey, George. *Autobiography of George Dewey, Admiral of the Navy* (New York: Charles Scribner & Sons, 1913), 214. From "Naval History & Heritage Command," available at: www.history.navy.mil/trivia02.htm

DiMarco, Anthony C. *The Big Bowl Football Guide: A Game-by-Game History of College Football's Major Bowl Contests* (New York: G.P. Putnam's Sons, 1976).

Dimbleby, David and David Reynolds. *An Ocean Apart: The Relationship between Britain and America in the Twentieth Century* (New York: Random House, 1988).

Divine, Robert A. *The Illusion of Neutrality: Franklin D. Roosevelt and the Struggle over the Arms Embargo* (Chicago: Quadrangle Books, 1968).

—*Roosevelt and World War II* (New York: Penguin Books, 1983).

Documents on German Foreign Policy, 1918–1945; Series D (1937–1945) (Washington, DC: GPO/Department of State Publication 6312, 1956).

Dodge, Mary Mapes. *Hans Brinker, or the Silver Skates* (Garden City, NY: Junior Deluxe Editions, 1954).

Doenecke, Justus D. ed., *In Danger Undaunted: The Anti-Interventionist Movement of 1940–1941 as Revealed in the Papers of the America First Committee* (Palo Alto: Hoover Institution Press, 1990).

Doherty, Thomas. *Projections of War: Hollywood, American Culture, and World War II* (New York: Columbia University Press, 1993).

Doolittle, James H. and Carrol V. Gines, *I Could Never Be So Lucky Again: An Autobiography by General James H. "Jimmy" Doolittle* (New York: Bantam, 1992).

Donaldson, Frances. *P.G. Wodehouse: A Biography* (London: Prion, 1982).

Donaldson, Scott and R. H. Winick. *Archibald MacLeish: An American Life* (Boston: Houghton Mifflin, 1992).

Douhet, Giulio. *The Command of the Air* (Norwalk, CT: Easton Press, 1994 c1921).

Dower, John W. *War Without Mercy: Race and Power in the Pacific War* (New York: Pantheon, 1986).

Doyle, Arthur Conan. *The Complete Sherlock Holmes* (New York: Doubleday, 1940).

Dudley, William S. ed., *The Naval War of 1812: A Documentary History*, vol. 2 (Washington, DC: Naval Historical Center, 1992).

Dull, Paul S. *A Battle History of the Imperial Japanese Navy, 1941–1945* (Annapolis: Naval Institute Press, 1978).

Dyer, George Carrol. *The Amphibians Came to Conquer: The Story of Admiral Richmond Kelly Turner* (Washington DC: Department of the Navy/United States Marine Corps Fleet Marine Reference Publications, 1991 c1969).

Dyke, Charles Libbe. *The Story of Sioux County* (Orange City, IA: Sioux County Capital, 1942).

Edel, Leon. *Henry James: A Life* (New York: Harper & Row, 1985).

Elphick, Peter. *Singapore: The Pregnable Fortress* (London: Hodder & Stoughton, 1995).

Elson, Robert T. *Prelude to War* (New York: Time/Life Books, 1976).

Encyclopedia Brittanica, 15th edition (New York: Encyclopedia Brittanica, 1974).

Evans, Richard J. *The Third Reich at War* (New York: Penguin Press, 2009).

Fang, Irving E. *Those Radio Commentators!* (Ames, IA: Iowa State University Press, 1977).

Farrington, Karen. *Handbook of World War II: An Illustrated Chronicle of the Struggle for Victory* (New York: Abbeydale Press/Barnes & Noble, 2008).

Fifer, J. Valerie. *American Progress: The Growth of the Transport, Tourist, and Information Industries in the 19th Century West* (Chester, CT: Globe-Pequot, 1988).

Fitzgerald, F. Scott. *The Great Gatsby*, available at: http://ebooks.adelaide.edu.au/f/fitzgerald/f_scott/gatsby/Chapter4.html, c1925

Fitzgerald, John M. *Family in Crisis: The United States, the Philippines, and the Second World War* (Bloomington, IN: First Books, 2002).

Ford, Daniel. *Flying Tigers: Claire Chennault and his American Volunteers, 1941–1942* (New York: Harper Collins/Smithsonian Books, 2007).

— "Flying Tigers Bite Back!" America in World War II: The Magazine of a People at War 1941–1945 (December 2010).

Foreign Relations of the United States, 1941 Volumes I–VII, 1941 (Washington, DC: Department of State, 1958–1962).

Foreign Relations of the United States, 1942 Volumes I–VI, 1942 (Washington, DC: Department of State, 1960–1963).

French, Warren. *John Steinbeck* (New York: Twayne Publishers, 1961).

Friedel, Frank. *The Splendid Little War* (Boston: Little Brown, 1958).

Fry, Varian. *Assignment: Rescue* (New York: Scholastic Books, 1968 c1945).

Fuchida, Mitsuo and Masatake Okumiya, *Midway: The Battle That Doomed Japan, the Japanese Navy's Story* (Annapolis: Naval Institute Press, Bluejacket Books, 1992 c1955).

Fussell, Paul. *Wartime: Understanding and Behavior in the Second World War* (New York: Oxford University Press, 1989).

Gabriel, Ralph Henry. *The Course of American Democratic Thought* (New York: Ronald Press, 1943).

Gaddis, John L. *The Long Peace: Inquiries into the History of the Cold War* (New York: Oxford University Press, 1987).

Gallup, George. *"Public Opinion in a Democracy:" The Stafford Little Lectures* (Princeton University Press, 1939).

Gannon, Michael. *Operation Drumbeat: The Dramatic True Story of Germany's First U-Boat Attacks Along the American Coast in World War II* (Annapolis, MD: Naval Institute Press, 1990).

Gaulle, Charles De. *The Speeches of General De Gaulle* (New York: Oxford University Press, 1944).

— *The Call to Honour, 1940–1942* (New York: Viking Press, 1955).

Gilbert, Martin. *Churchill and America* (New York: Free Press, 1995).

— ed., *The Churchill War Papers, Volume II: Never Surrender* (New York: W.W. Norton, 1995).

—Global ed., *The Churchill War Papers, Volume III: The Ever-Widening War* (New York: W.W. Norton, 2001).

Gilmour, David. *The Long Recessional: The Imperial Life of Rudyard Kipling* (New York: Farrar, Straus, and Giroux, 2002).

Glines, Carroll V. *The Doolittle Raid: America's Daring First Strike against Japan* (New York: Jove Books, 1988).

Goetzmann, William H. *When the Eagle Screamed: The Romantic Horizon in American Diplomacy, 1800–1860* (New York: John Wiley & Sons, 1966).

—ed., *The Colonial Horizon: America in the Sixteenth and Seventeenth Centuries* (Reading, MA: Addison-Wesley, 1969).

—*Beyond the Revolution: A History of American Thought from Paine to Pragmatism* (New York: Basic Books, 2009).

Goldstein, Donald M. and Katherine V. Dillon, eds, *Fading Victory: The Diary of Admiral Matome Ugaki, 1941–1945* (Annapolis, MD: Naval Institute Press, 1991).

—*The Pacific War Papers: Japanese Documents of World War II* (Washington, DC: Potomac Books, 2004).

Gordon, Richard M. (with Benjamin S. Llamzon), *Horyo: Memoirs of an American P.O.W.* (St. Paul, MN: Paragon House, 1999).

Grosvenor, Melville Bell (editor-in-chief), *National Geographic Atlas of the World* (Washington, DC: National Geographic Society, 1970).

Grunwald, Edward A. ed., *Variety Radio Directory 1940–1941* (New York: Variety, 1940).

Gunther, John. *Inside Asia* (New York: Harper & Bros., 1939).

Guttmann, Allen. *The Wound in the Heart: America and the Spanish Civil War* (New York: Free Press, 1962).

Hack, Karl and Kevin Blackburn. *Did Singapore Have to Fall? Churchill and the Impregnable Fortress* (New York: RoutledgeCurzon, 2004).

Haddad, John Rogers. *The Romance of China: Excursions to China in U.S. Culture, 1776–1876* (New York: Columbia University Press, 2008), available at: www.gutenberg-e.org/haj01/frames/fhaj02.html

Hailey, Foster. *Pacific Battle Line* (New York: Macmillan, 1944).

Hargrove, Marion. *See Here, Private Hargrove* (New York: Henry Holt, 1942).

Harper, John Lamberton. *American Visions of Europe: Franklin D. Roosevelt, George F. Kennan, and Dean G. Acheson* (New York: Cambridge University Press, 1994).

Harries, Meirion and Susie Harries. *Soldiers of the Sun: The Rise and Fall of the Imperial Japanese Army* (New York: Random House, 1991).

Harsch, Joseph C. *At the Hinge of History: A Reporter's Story* (Athens, GA: University of Georgia, 1993).

Hart, Scott. *Washington at War: 1941–1945* (Englewood Cliffs, NY: Prentice-Hall, 1970).

Hassett, William D. *Off the Record With FDR: 1942–1943* (New Brunswick, NJ: Rutgers University Press, 1958).

Haynes, John Earl and Harvey Klehr. *Venona: Decoding Soviet Espionage in America* (New Haven: Yale Nota Bene, 2000).

Hearn, Chester G. *Admiral David Glasgow Farragut: The Civil War Years* (Annapolis: Naval Institute Press, 1988).

Heatter, Gabriel. *There's Good News Tonight* (Garden City, NY: Doubleday, 1960).

Henry, Chris. *Battle of the Coral Sea* (Annapolis: Naval Institute Press, 2003).

Herman, Arthur. *To Rule the Waves: How the British Navy Shaped the Modern World* (New York: Harper Perennial, 2004).

Hersey, John. *Men on Bataan* (New York: Alfred A. Knopf, 1943).

Herzstein, Robert E. *Roosevelt and Hitler: Prelude to War* (New York: John Wiley & Sons, 1994).

Heymann, C. David. *The Georgetown Ladies' Social Club: Power, Passion, and Politics in the Nation's Capital* (New York: Atria Books, 2003).

Hickam, Homer, Jr. *Torpedo Junction* (Annapolis: Naval Institute Press, 1989).

Hickok, Lorena A. *The Road to the White House, FDR: the Pre-Presidential Years* (Chilton/Scholastic: New York, 1963).

Hitler, Adolf. *Mein Kampf* (New York: Hurst and Blackett, 1942).

Hixson, Walter L. *Charles A. Lindbergh: Lone Eagle* (New York: PearsonLongman, 2007).

Hofstadter, Richard, ed., *Great Issues in American History: From the Revolution to the Civil War, 1765–1865* (New York: Vintage Books, 1958).

— ed., *Great Issues in American History: From Reconstruction to the Present Day, 1864–1969* (New York: Vintage, 1969).

Melvin G. Holli, *The Wisard of Washington: Emil Hurja, Franklin Roosevelt, and the Birth of Public Opinion Polling* (New York: Palgrave, 2002).

Hopkins, J.A.H. ed., *Diary of World Events, vols. XV–XXII* (Baltimore: National Advertising Company, 1942).

Horne, Gerald. *Black and Red: W.E.B. DuBois and the Afro-American Response to the Cold War, 1944–1963* (Albany: SUNY Press, 1986).

Howe, Julia Ward. "Battle-Hymn of the Republic," *The Golden Treasury of Poetry* (New York: Golden Press, 1968).

Hull, Cordell. *The Memoirs of Cordell Hull* (New York: Macmillan, 1948).

Ienaga, Saburo. *The Pacific War: 1931–1945, A Critical Perspective on Japan's Role in World War II* (New York: Pantheon Books, 1978).

Ike, Nobutaka. ed., *Japan's Decision for War: Records of the 1941 Policy Conferences* (Palo Alto: Stanford University Press, 1967).

Inada, Lawson Fusao. ed., *Only What We Could Carry: The Japanese–American Internment Experience* (Berkeley: Heyday Books, 2000).

Iriye, Akira. *The Origins of the Second World War in Asia and the Pacific* (London: Longman, 1987).

— *Power and Culture: The Japanese–American War, 1941–1945* (Cambridge, MA: Harvard, 1981).

Iriye, Akira and Warren Cohen. eds, *American, Chinese, and Japanese Perspectives on Wartime Asia, 1931–1949* (Wilmington, DC: Scholarly Resources, 1990).

Jabbar, Kareem Abdul and Anthony Walton. *Brothers-in-Arms: The Epic Story of the 761st Tank Battalion, World War Two's Forgotten Heroes* (New York: Broadway, 2005).

Jaggard, Geoffrey. *Wooster's World: A Companion to the Wooster-Jeeves Cycle of P.G. Wodehouse* (London: MacDonald, 1967).

James, D. Clayton. ed., *South to Bataan, North to Mukden: The Prison Diary of Brigadier General W.E. Brougher* (Athens, GA: University of Georgia Press, 1971).

Jane's Fighting Ships of World War II (London: Studio Editions, 1989).

Kaltenborn, H.V. *Kaltenborn Edits the War News* (New York: E.P. Dutton, 1942).

Kearns, Gerry. *Geopolitics and Empire: The Legacy of Halford Mackinder* (New York: Oxford University Press, 2009).

Kennedy, David M. *Over Here: The First World War and American Society* (New York: Oxford University Press, 1980).

Kernan, Alvin. *The Unknown Battle of Midway: The Destruction of the American Torpedo Squadrons* (New Haven: Yale University Press, 2005).

Kershaw, Ian. *The "Hitler Myth": Image and Reality in the Third Reich* (New York: Oxford University Press, 1987).

— *The Nazi Dictatorship: Problems of Perspective and Interpretation* (London: Edward Arnold, 1989).

Ketchum, Richard M. *The Borrowed Years: 1938–1941, America on the Way to War* (New York: Random House, 1989).

Kesselring, Albert. *Kesselring: A Soldier's Record,* (Norwalk, CT: The Easton Press, 1994 c1953).

Kimball, Warren F. *Forged in War: Roosevelt, Churchill, and the Second World War* (Chicago: Ivan R. Dee, 2003).

Kipling, Rudyard. *Letters of Travel* (New York: Macmillan, 1920).

Kohut, Andrew and Bruce Stokes. *America against the World: How We Are Different, and Why We Are Disliked* (New York: Holt Paperbacks, 2007).

Kupfer, Charles. We Felt the Flames: American Reactions to the Blitzkrieg of Summer, 1940 (Ph.D. dissertation, University of Texas, 1998).

—*We Felt the Flames: Hitler's Blitzkrieg, America's Story* (Carlisle, PA: Sergeant Kirkland's Press, 2004).

Kurashige, Lon. *Japanese–American Celebration and Conflict: A History of Ethnic Identity and Festival in Los Angeles, 1934–1990* (Berkeley, CA: University of California Press, 2002).

Kurth, Peter. *American Cassandra: The Life of Dorothy Thompson* (Boston: Little, Brown, 1990).

LaFeber, Walter. *The Clash: U.S.–Japanese Relations Throughout History* (New York: W.W. Norton, 1997).

Langer, Howard J. ed., *World War II: An Encyclopedia of Quotations* (Westport, CT: Greenwood Press, 1999).

Langer, William L. *Our Vichy Gamble* (New York: W.W. Norton, 1966 c1947).

Langguth, A.J. *Patriots: The Men who Started the American Revolution* (New York: Simon & Schuster, 1988).

Larabee, Eric. *Commander in Chief: Franklin Delano Roosevelt, His Lieutenants, and Their War* (New York: Harper & Row, 1987).

Lavine, Harold and James Wechsler. *War Propaganda and the United States* (New Haven: Yale University Press, Institute for Propaganda Analysis, 1940).

Lawton, Manny. *Some Survived: An Eyewitness Account of the Bataan Death March and the Men who Lived Through It* (Chapel Hill: Algonquin Books, 2004).

Lawson, Ted W. and Robert Considine. *Thirty Seconds Over Tokyo* (New York: Fall River Press, 2007 c1942).

Lee, Clark. *They Call it Pacific: An Eye-Witness Story of our War Against Japan from Bataan to the Solomon Islands* (New York: Viking Press, 1943).

Leighton, Richard and Robert Coakley. *United States Army in World War II: Global Logistics and Strategy, 1940–1943* (Washington, DC: Office of the Chief of Military History, Department of the Army, 1968).

Leonard, Thomas C. *News for All: America's Coming-of-Age With the Press* (New York: Oxford University Press, 1995).

Lendvai, Paul. *The Hungarians: A Thousand Years of Victory in Defeat* (Princeton: Princeton University, 2003).

Levine, Alan J. *The Pacific War: Japan Versus the Allies* (Westport, CT: Praeger, 1995).

Levant, Howard. *The Novels of John Steinbeck: A Critical Study* (Columbia: University of Missouri Press, 1974).

Levine, Lawrence W. *Highbrow, Lowbrow: The Emergence of Cultural Hierarchy in America* (Cambridge, MA: Harvard University Press, 1988).

Levin, Linda Lotridge. *The Making of FDR: The Story of Stephen T. Early, America's First Modern Press Secretary* (Amherst, NY: Prometheus Books, 2008).

Lewis, David Levering. *W.E.B. DuBois: The Fight for Equality and the American Century* (New York: Owl Books, 2001).

Lewis, R.W. B. *The American Adam: Innocence, Tragedy, and Tradition in the Nineteenth Century* (Chicago: University of Chicago Press, 1955).

Lindbergh, Anne Morrow. *The Wave of the Future: A Confession of Faith* (New York: Harcourt, Brace, 1940).

— *War Within and Without: Diaries and Letters, 1939–1944* (New York: Harcourt, Brace, Jovanovich, 1980).

Link, Arthur. *Wilson the Diplomatist: A Look at his Major Foreign Policies* (New York: New Viewpoints, 1974).

— ed., *The Papers of Woodrow Wilson, Vol. 31* (Princeton: Princeton University Press, 1979).

Liska, George. *The Ways of Power: Pattern and Meaning in World Politics* (Oxford: Basil Blackwell Ltd, 1990).

Lombard, Helen. *While They Fought: Behind the Scenes in Washington, 1941–1946* (New York: Scribner's, 1947).

Maass, Matthias. *Problems of Perception in Spanish-American Diplomatic Communication – Prelude to the War of 1898* (M.A. Thesis, Freidrich-Meinecke Institute, Free University of Berlin, 1996).

MacArthur, Douglas. *Reminiscences* (New York: The Great Commanders/Collectors Reprints, 1997 c1964).

Mackinder, Halford J. *Democratic Ideals and Reality: A Study in the Politics of Reconstruction* (London: Constable, 1919).

Madej, W. Victor. ed., *U.S. Army and Marine Corps Order of Battle, Pacific Theater of Operations, 1941–1945, Volume I* (Allentown, PA: Game Publishing Company, 1984).

Madsen, Daniel. *Resurrection: Salvaging the Battle Fleet at Pearl Harbor* (Annapolis: Naval Institute Press, 2003).

Mahan, Alfred Thayer. *The Influence of Sea Power Upon History, 1660–1783* (Boston: Little, Brown, 1898).

Manchester, William. *American Caesar: Douglas MacArthur, 1880–1964* (Boston: Little, Brown, 1978).

— *Goodbye, Darkness: A Memoir of the Pacific War* (Boston: Little, Brown, 1980).

— *Winston Spencer Churchill: The Last Lion, Visions of Glory 1874–1932* (New York: Laurel Trade, 1989).

Marshall, Catherine. *A Man Called Peter: The Story of Peter Marshall* (Grand Rapids: Chosen Books, 2002 c1951).

Marshall. Peter J. ed., *The Wartime Sermons of Dr. Peter Marshall* (Dallas: Clarion Call Marketing, 2005).

Mazer, Bill. *The Answer Book of Sports: Answers to Hundreds of Questions about the World of Sports* (New York: Grosset & Dunlap, 1969).

McCormick, Anne O'Hare. *The World at Home: Selections from the Writings of Anne O'Hare McCormick* (New York: Alfred A. Knopf, 1956).

McCrum, Robert. *Wodehouse* (New York: W.W. Norton, 2004).

McInnis, Edgar. *The War: Third Year* (New York: Oxford University Press, 1945).

McNaught, Kenneth. *The Pelican History of Canada* (New York: Penguin, 1982).

Melosi, Martin V. *The Shadow of Pearl Harbor: Political Controversy over the Surprise Attack, 1941–1946* (College Station, TX: Texas A&M University Press, 1977).

Mencken, H. D. *The Diary of H.L. Mencken* (New York: Alfred A. Knopf, 1989).

Metz, Robert. *CBS: Reflections in a Bloodshot Eye* (New York: Playboy Press, 1975).

Miller, Edward S. *War Plan Orange: The US Strategy to Defeat Japan, 1897–1945* (Annapolis: Naval Institute Press, 1991).

Miller, James Edward. *The Baseball Business: Pursuing Pennants and Profits in Baltimore* (Chapel Hill: University of North Carolina Press, 1990).

Miller, Perry. *The Raven and the Whale: Poe, Melville, and the New York Literary Scene* (Baltimore: Johns Hopkins University Press, 1997, c1956).

—*Errand into the Wilderness* (New York: Harper TorchBooks, 1964).

Mills, Scott A. *Stranded in the Philippines: Professor Bell's Private War against the Japanese* (Annapolis: Naval Institute Press, 2009).

Moody, T. W. and F. X. Martin. *The Course of Irish History* (Cork: Mercier, 1984).

Moorehead, Alan. *The White Nile* (New York: Harper & Row, 1971).

Moran, Lord. *Churchill at War 1940–1945* (New York: Carrol & Graf, 2002, c1966, *The Struggle for Survival*).

Morehouse, Maggi M. *Fighting Jim Crow: Black Men and Women Remember World War II* (Lanham, MD: Roman & Littlefield, 2000).

Morison, Samuel Eliot. *Admiral of the Ocean Sea: A Life of Christopher Columbus* (Boston: Little, Brown, 1942).

—*History of United States Naval Operations in World War II: The Battle of the Atlantic, September 1939–May 1943* (Boston: Little, Brown, 1989, c1947).

—*History of United States Naval Operations in World War II, Vol. III: The Rising Sun in the Pacific: 1931–April 1942* (Boston: Little, Brown, 1988, c1948).

—*History of United States Naval Operations in World War II, Vol. IV, Coral Sea, Midway, and Submarine Actions, May 1942–August 1942* (Boston: Little, Brown, 1955).

—*History of United States Naval Operations in World War II, Vol. VII, Aleutians, Gilberts, and Marshalls, June 1942–April 1944* (Boston: Little, Brown, 1984 c1951).

Morton, Louis. *The United States Army in World War II: The War in the Pacific – Strategy and Command, the First Two Years* (Washington, DC: Department of the Army, 1962).

Motley, Mary Penick. *The Invisible Soldier: The Experience of the Black Soldier, World War II* (Detroit: Wayne State University Press, 1975).

Mott, Frank Luther. *American Journalism: A History, 1690–1960* (New York: Macmillan, 1962).

Murrow, Edward R. *This is London* (New York: Shocken Books, 1985).

Odo, Franklin. *No Sword to Bury: Japanese–Americans in Hawaii During World War II* (Philadelphia: Temple University Press, 2004).

O'Hara, Vincent P. *The U.S. Navy Against the Axis: Surface Combat 1941–1945* (Annapolis: Naval Institute Press, 2007).

O'Hara, Vincent P., W. David Dickson, and Richard Worth. *On Seas Contested: The Seven Great Navies of the Second World War* (Annapolis: Naval Institute Press, 2010).

Ohl, John Kennedy. *Hugh S. Johnson and the New Deal* (DeKalb, IL: Northern Illinois University Press, 1985).

Overy, Richard and Andrew Wheatcroft. *The Road to War: The Origins of World War II* (London: Macmillan London, 1989).

Padfield, Peter. *Donitz: The Last Fuhrer* (London: Panther, 1985).

Papers Relating to the Foreign Relations of the United States, Japan: 1931–1941 (Washington, DC: GPO/Department of State, 1943).

Pakula, Hannah. *The Last Empress: Madame Chiang Kai-Shek and the Birth of Modern China* (New York: Simon & Schuster, 2009).

Paley, William. "Foreword," in Lowell Thomas, *History as You Heard It* (Garden City, NY: Doubleday, 1957).

Panetta, Roger. ed., *Dutch New York: The Roots of Hudson Valley Culture* (New York: Hudson Valley Museum/Fordham University Press, 2009).

Panter-Downes, Mollie. *London War Notes 1939–1945* (New York: Farrar, Straus & Giroux, 1971).

Parker, Geoffrey. *The Dutch Revolt* (London: Pelican Books, 1985).

Parshall, Jonathan and Anthony Tully. *Shattered Sword: The Untold Story of the Battle of Midway* (Dulles, VA: Potomac Books, 2007).

Paulding, James Kirke. *The Diverting History of John Bull and Brother Jonathan* (Philadelphia: R. Desilver, 1827, c1812), available at: Googlebooks, www.books.google.com/books

Pepys, Samuel. *The Diary of Samuel Pepys*, available at: www.pepysdiary.com

Perloff, Harvey S., Edgar S. Dunn, Jr., Eric E. Lampard, and Richard F. Muth. *Regions, Resources, and Economic Growth* (Lincoln: University of Nebraska Press, 1960).

Petillo, Carol Morris. *Douglas MacArthur: The Philippine Years* (Bloomington: Indiana University Press, 1981).

The Picture History of World War II (formerly Collier's Photographic History of World War II) (New York: Grossett & Dunlap, 1971, c1946).

Pilat, Oliver. *Drew Pearson: An Unauthorized Biography* (New York: Pocket Books, 1973).

Pimlott, John. *The Atlas of World War II* (Philadelphia: Courage Books, 2006).

Plesch, Dan. *America, Hitler, and the U.N.: How the Allies Won World War II and Forged a Peace* (New York: I.B. Tauris, 2011).

Pogue, Forrest G. *George Marshall: Statesman, 1945–1959* (New York, Penguin, 1987).

Prange, Gordon W. *December 7, 1941: The Day the Japanese Attacked Pearl Harbor* (New York: McGraw-Hill, 1962).

—*At Dawn We Slept: The Untold Story of Pearl Harbor* (New York: McGraw-Hill, 1981).

Prange, Gordon W. with Donald M. Goldstein & Katharine V. Dillon, *Miracle at Midway* (New York: McGraw-Hill, 1982).

Pusey, Merlo. *The Way We Go To War* (Boston: Houghton-Mifflin, 1969).

Rachlis, Eugene. *The Story of the U.S. Coast Guard* (New York: Random House, 1961).

Redmond, Juanita. *I Served on Bataan* (New York: Garland Publishing, 1984, c1943).

Reichler, Joseph L. ed., *The Baseball Encyclopedia: The Complete and Official Record of Major League Baseball* (New York: Macmillan, 1982).

Reino, Joseph. *Karl Shapiro* (Boston: Twayne Publishers, 1981).

Renshaw, Patrick. *Franklin D. Roosevelt* (Harlow, UK: Pearson-Longman, 2004).

Reynolds, Clark G. *America at War 1941–1945: The Home Front* (New York: Gallery Books, 1990).

Rich, Norman. *Hitler's War Aims: Ideology, the Nazi State, and the Course of Expansion* (New York: W.W. Norton, 1992).

Riess, Curt. ed., *They Were There: The Story of World War II and How it Came About, by America's Foremost Correspondents* (Garden City, NY: Garden City Publishing Company, 1945).

Ritter, Lawrence S. *Lost Ballparks: A Celebration of Baseball's Legendary Fields* (New York: Viking Studio Books, 1992).

Robinson, George and Salzburg, Charles. *On a Clear Day They Could See Seventh Place: Baseball's Worst Teams* (New York: Dell Trade, 1991).

Roeder, George H. Jr. *The Censored War: American Visual Experience During World War II* (New Haven: Yale University Press, 1993).

Rohrbach, Peter T. "Radio in World War II: News and Entertainment," *Performing Arts Broadcasting* (Washington, DC: Library of Congress/Government Printing Office, 2002).

Rolo, Charles J. *Radio Goes to War: The "Fourth Front"* (New York: G.P. Putnam's, 1942).

Romulo, Carlos P. *I Saw the Fall of the Philippines* (Garden City, NY: Doubleday, Doran, 1943).

Roosevelt, Franklin Delano. *Fireside Chats* (New York: Penguin, 1995).

Rosenberg, Emily S. *Spreading the American Dream: American Economic and Cultural Expansion, 1890–1945* (New York: Hill and Wang, 1982).

Rosenman, Samuel I. ed., *The Public Papers and Addresses of Franklin D. Roosevelt, 1942 Volume* (New York: Harper & Brothers, 1950).

Rubin, Barry. *Secrets of State: The State Department and the Struggle Over US Foreign Policy* (New York: Oxford University Press, 1987).

Salmaggi, Cesar and Alfredo Pallavisini. *2194 Days of War: An Illustrated Chronology of the Second World War* (New York: Barnes & Noble Books, 1993).

Schom, Alan. *The Eagle and the Rising Sun: the Japanese-American War 1941–1943, Pearl Harbor Through Guadalcanal* (New York: W.W. Norton, 2004).

Schroth, Raymond A. *The American Journey of Eric Sevareid* (South Royalton, VT: Steerforth Press, 1995).

Seib, Philip. *Broadcasts from the Blitz: How Edward R. Murrow Helped Lead America into War* (Washington, DC: Potomac Books, 2007).

Sevareid, Eric. *Not so Wild a Dream* (Columbia, MO: University of Missouri Press, 1995 c1946).

Service Book and Hymnal (Minneapolis: Augsburg Publishing House, 1958).

Schiff, Stacy. *Saint-Exupery: A Biography* (New York: Henry Holt, 1994).

Schiffin, Andre. *Dr. Suess & Co. Go to War: The World War II Editorial Cartoons of America's Leading Comic Artists* (New York: The New Press, 2009).

Shandor, Vincent. *Carpatho-Ukraine in the 20th Century* (Cambridge, MA: Ukrainian Research Institute, Harvard University Press, 1997).

Shapiro, Karl. *Person, Place and Thing,* (New York: Reynal & Hitchcock, 1944).

— *Essay on Rime* (Cornwall, NY: Cornwall Press, 1945).

— *Person, Place and Thing* (New York: Reynal & Hitchcock, 1944).

— *The Bourgeois Poet* (New York: Random House, 1964).

— *To Abolish Children and Other Essays* (Chicago: Quadrangle Books, 1968).

— *The Poetry Wreck: Selected Essays, 1950–1970* (New York: Random House, 1975).

Sherwood, Robert E. *Roosevelt and Hopkins, An Intimate History* (New York: Enigma Books, 2008, c1948).

Sherwood, Robert E. with Wilson Miscamble & Irwin Gellman, *Roosevelt and Hopkins: An Intimate History* (New York: Enigma, 2008 c1949).

Shirer, William L. *20th Century Journey, A Memoir of the Life and Times – The Start: 1904–1930* (New York: Bantam, 1985).

Shulman, Holly Cowan. *The Voice of America: Propaganda and Democracy, 1941–1945* (Madison: University of Wisconsin Press, 1990).

Simpson, David. *The Politics of American English: 1776–1850* (New York: Oxford University Press, 1986).

Slim, Viscount William. *Defeat into Victory: Battle Japan in Burma and India, 1942–1945* (New York: Cooper Square Press, 2000 c1956).

Sloan, Bill. *Given Up for Dead: America's Heroic Stand at Wake Island* (New York: Bantam Books, 2003).

Smith, Bradley. *Japan: A History in Art* (Tokyo: Gemini Incorporated, 1964).

Smith, Rex Allan and Gerald A. Meehl, *Pacific War Stories: In the Words of Those Who Survived* (New York: Abbeville Press, 2004).

Smith, Richard Norton. *The Colonel: The Life and Legend of Robert R. McCormick* (New York: Houghton-Mifflin, 1997).

Snyder, Timothy. *Bloodlands: Europe Between Hitler and Stalin* (New York: Basic Books, 2010).

Sobel, Robert and David P. Sicilia, *The Entrepreneurs: An American Adventure* (Boston: Houghton-Mifflin, 1986).

Solzenhitsyn, Alexander. *The Red Wheel: November 1916* (New York: Farar, Straus & Giroux, 2000).

Soule, George P. and Vincent Carosso. *American Economic History* (New York: Holt, Rinehart, & Winston, 1957).

Spector, Ronald. *Eagle Against the Sun: The American War with Japan* (New York: Vintage, 1985).

Speer, Albert. *Inside the Third Reich: Memoirs* (New York: Collier Books, 1970).

Spence, Clark G. *British Investments in the American Mining Frontier, 1869–1901* (Ithaca, NY: Cornell University Press for the American Historical Association, 1958).

Sperber, A. M. *Murrow: His Life and Times* (New York: Bantam, 1986).

Sproat, Iain. *Wodehouse at War: The Extraordinary Truth about P.G. Wodehouse;s Broadcasts on Nazi Radio* (New York: Ticknor & Fields, 1981).

Stanley, Cloud and Olson, Lynne. *The Murrow Boys: Pioneers on the Front Lines of Broadcast Journalism* (Boston: Houghton-Mifflin, 1996).

Steel, Ronald. *Walter Lippmann and the American Century* (New York: Vintage Books, 1980).

Steinbeck, John. *The Moon is Down* (New York: Viking Press, 1942).

Steinberg, Rafael. *Return to the Philippines* (New York: Time-Life Books, 1979).

Stephan, John J. *Hawaii Under the Rising Sun: Japan's Plans for Conquest After Pearl Harbor* (Honolulu: University of Hawaii Press, 1984).

Stern, Jane and Michael Stern. *Square Meals* (New York: Alfred A. Knopf, 1985).

Stilwell, Joseph W. *The Stilwell Papers,* Theodore H. White, ed. (New York: Da Capo Press, 1991 c1948).

Stone, I.F. *Business as Usual: The First Year of Defense* (New York: Modern Age Books, 1941).

Stone, Ronald H. and Matthew Lon Weaver. eds, *Against the Grain: Paul Tillich's Wartime Radio Broadcasts into Germany* (Louisville: Westminster John Knox Press, 1998).

Stott, Annette. *Holland Mania: The Unknown Dutch Period in American Art and Culture* (Woodstock, NY: Overlook Press, 1998).

Strachan, Hew. *The First World War* (New York: Penguin, 2003).

Sumner, William Graham. "What Social Classes Owe to Each Other," in Michael B. Levy, ed., *Political Thought in America: An Anthology* (Prospect Heights, IL: Waveland Press, 1992).

Swing, Raymond Gram. *Preview of History* (Garden City, NY: Doubleday, Doran, 1943).

Tarkington, Booth. *Penrod: His Complete Story* (Garden City, NY: Doubleday, 1931, c1913).

Tawney, R.H. *Religion and the Rise of Capitalism* (New York: 1926).

Taylor, Telford. *The March of Conquest: The German Victories in Western Europe, 1940* (New York: Simon & Schuster, 1958).

Tebbel, John and Mary Ellen Zuckerman. *The Magazine in America: 1741–1990* (New York: Oxford University Press, 1991).

Tedlock, E.W. Jr. and C.V. Wicker. *Steinbeck and His Critics: A Record of Twenty-Five Years* (Albuquerque: University of New Mexico Press, 1957).

Ten Broek, Jacobus., Edward Beinhart, and Floyd Matson. *Prejudice, War and the Constitution* (Berkeley: University of California Press, 1968).

Thomas, Lowell. *History as You Heard It* (Garden City, NY: Doubleday, 1957).

— *From Cripple Creek to Samarkand* (New York: Morrow, 1976).

Thomas, Lowell and Burton Braley. *Stand Fast for Freedom* (Philadelphia: John C. Winston, 1940).

Thurber, James. *A Thurber Carnival* (New York: Harper & Bros. 1949).

Tillich, Paul. *My Travel Diary*, edited by Jerald C. Brauer (New York: Holt & Rinehart, 1970), available at: www.scribd.com.doc6935385/Paul-Tillich-My-Travel-Diary-1936-Between-Two-Worlds

Tobin, James. *Ernie Pyle's War* (New York: Free Press, 2006).

Tocqueville, Alexis de. *Democracy in America & Two Essays on America* (London: Penguin Books, 2003).

Toland, John. *But Not In Shame: The Six Months After Pearl Harbor* (New York: Random House, 1961).

—*Infamy: Pearl Harbor and its Aftermath* (Garden City, NY: Doubleday, 1982).

Toland, John B. *The Flying Tigers* (New York: Random House, 1963).

Trevor-Roper, Hugh. ed., *Hitler's Table-Talk, 1941–1944: His Private Conversations* (New York: Enigma Books, 2000).

Tsuji, Masanobu. *Singapore: The Japanese Version* (New York: St. Martin's Press, 1960).

Tuchman, Barbara. *The Proud Tower: A Portrait of the World Before the War, 1890–1914* (New York: Ballantine Books, 1996).

Tuchman, Barbara W. *Stilwell and the American Experience in China 1911–1945* (New York: Macmillan, 1971).

Tyler, Sidney. *The Japan–Russia War: An Illustrated History of the War in the Far East* (Philadelphia: P.W. Ziegler, 1905).

Urwin, Gregory J. W. *Facing Fearful Odds: The Siege of Wake Island* (Lincoln: University of Nebraska Press, 1997).

Usborne, Richard. *Plum Sauce: A P.G. Wodehouse Companion* (London: Ebury Press, 2002).

Van Der Water, Frederic F. *Rudyard Kipling's Vermont Feud* (Weston, VT: Countryman Press, 1937).

Variety Radio Directory (New York: Variety, 1940).

Veblen, Thorstein. "Demetia Praecox," in *The Freeman*, June 21, 1922; in Loren Baritz, ed., *The Culture of the Twenties* (Indianapolis: Bobbs-Merrill, 1978).

Vincent, Carl. *No Reason Why: The Canadian Hong Kong Tragedy – an Examination* (Stittsville, Ontario: Canada's Wings, 1981).

Volkogonov, Dmitri. *Stalin: Triumph and Tragedy* (New York: Gene Weideinfeld, 1991).

Voss, Frederick S. *Reporting the War: The Journalistic Coverage of World War II* (Washington, DC: Smithsonian Institution Press for the National Portrait Gallery, 1994).

Watt, Donald Cameron. *How War Came: The Immediate Origins of the Second World War, 1938–1939* (New York: Pantheon Books, 1989).

Wegener, Peter P. *The Pennemunde Wind Tunnels: A Memoir* (New Haven: Yale University Press, 1996).

Whipple, A. B. C. *The Mediterranean* (New York: Time Life Books, 1981).

White, Graham J. *FDR and the Press* (Chicago: University of Chicago Press, 1979).

White, William L. *They Were Expendable* (New York: Harcourt, Brace, 1942).

Whitehead, Alfred North. *Dialogues of Alfred North Whitehead, as Recorded by Lucien Price* (New York: Mentor Book, 1954).

Wiggins, Melanie. *Torpedoes in the Gulf: Galveston and the U-Boats, 1942–1943* (College Station: Texas A&M University Press, 2004, c1995).

Williamson, Gordon. *Loyalty is My Honor: Personal Accounts from the Waffen-SS* (Osceola, WI: Motorbooks International, 1995).

Williford, Glen M. *Racing the Sunrise: Reinforcing America's Pacific Outposts, 1941–1942* (Annapolis: Naval Institute Press, 2010).

Wilmott, H. P. *Empires in the Balance: Japanese and Allied Pacific Strategies to April 1942* (Annapolis: Naval Institute Press, 1982).

— *The Barrier and the Javelin: Japanese and Allied Pacific Strategies, February to June 1942* (Annapolis: Naval Institute Press, 1983).

— *Empires in the Balance: Japanese and Allied Pacific Strategies to April 1942* (Annapolis: Naval Institute Press, 1989).

— *The War With Japan: The Period of Balance, May 1942–October 1943* (Wilmington: SR Books, 2002).

Wimmel, Kenneth. *Theodore Roosevelt and the Great White Fleet: American Sea Power Comes of Age* (Dulles, VA: Brassey's, 1998).

— *Theodore Roosevelt and the Great White Fleet: American Sea Power Comes of Age* (Dulles, VA: Brassey's, 2000).

Wodehouse, P. G. "One Touch of Nature," *The Man With Two Left Feet and Other Stories* (Woodstock, NY: Overlook Press, 2009, c1917, London: Methuen)

— *The Code of the Woosters* (New York: Vintage, 2005, c1938).

— *Money in the Bank* (New York: Overlook Hardcover, 2007 c1940)

Woodruff, William. *America's Impact on the World: A Study of the Role of the United States in the World Economy, 1750–1970* (New York: John Wiley & Sons, 1975).

Worth, Roland H. Jr. *No Choice But War: The United States Embargo Against Japan and the Eruption of War in the Pacific* (Jefferson, NC: McFarland, 1995).

Wouk, Herman. *War and Remembrance* (Boston: Little, Brown, 1985).

Wukovits, John. *Pacific Alamo: The Battle for Wake Island* (New York: New American Library, 2003).

Wyman, David S. *The Abandonment of the Jews: American and the Holocaust, 1941–1945* (New York: Pantheon, 1983).

Younger, Calton. *Ireland's Civil War* (Glasgow: Fontana Press, 1986).

Zweig, Stefan. *Conqueror of the Seas: The Story of Magellan* (New York: Viking Press, 1938).

Newspapers

Baltimore Sun
Baltimore Evening Sun
Chicago Sun
Chicago Tribune
Detroit News
Honolulu Advertiser
Los Angeles Times
London News Chronicle
Newark Evening News
New York Herald-Tribune
New York Times
Pittsburgh Courier
Wall Street Journal

Periodicals

Air & Space Magazine
American Heritage Magazine
American Mercury
America in World War II
Atlantic Monthly
American-Scandinavian Review
American Scholar
Antioch Review
Collier's
Current History
Fortune
Harper's
History of Flight
Journal of Modern History
Leatherneck: Magazine of the Marines
Life
The Nation
National Review
New Masses
The New Republic
The New Yorker
Paris Review
People's World
Poetry
Public Opinion Quarterly
Saturday Evening Post
Sewanee Review
Time
US News
Virginia Quarterly Review
Vital Speeches of the Day
Yale Review

Archival Collections

From Library of Congress, Washington, DC:

Papers of Eric A. Sevareid
Papers of Raymond Gram Swing
NBC Recordings; Broadcast Index & Card Catalogue, WJZ Blue Network/WEAF Red Network; December 1941–August 1942, Motion Picture, Broadcasting & Recorded Sound Reference Center
From National Archives, Motion Picture, Sound & Video Branch, College Park, MD Annex.
Milo C. Ryan Collection, CBS Recordings, December 1941–August 1942

Universal Newsreels & Newsreel Advertising Catalogues
From Sterling Memorial Library, Yale University, New Haven, CT.
Papers of Walter Lippmann
From American University, Washington, DC.
Papers of Drew Pearson
From Mass Communications History Center, State Historical Society of Wisconsin, Madison
H.V. Kaltenborn Papers & Collection

Television Programs

Lewis, Jonathan, Hugh Strachan, Corina Sturner, et al. "Shackled to a Corpse" (episode), *The First World War: The Complete Series* (documentary) Image Entertainment, 2005.
Missions that Changed the War: The Doolittle Raid, part I. The Military Network, 2010.

Museum Exhibitions

"A More Perfect Union: Japanese-Americans and the U.S. Constitution," Smithsonian Institution touring exhibit; available at: www.americanhistory.si.edu/perfectunion/resources/touring/html
"Turning Point: World War II," The Civil Rights Movement in Virginia, Museum Exhibition, Virginia Historical Society, Online Exhibitions, available at: www.vahistorical.org/civilrights/ww2/htm

Music

Miles, Alfred H. *USN, "Anchors Aweigh" (original lyrics), 1905.* Available at: www.usna.edu./USNABand/FAQ/Lyrics/htm
"U-Boat Lied," from "World War II Songs," available at: www.ingeb.org
Whiting, William and John B. Dykes, *"Eternal Father Strong to Save: 'The Navy Hymn.'"* Available at: www.usna.edu/USNABand/FAQ/Lyrics.htm

Government Documents Online

"Annual Report of the Activities of the 67th Evacuation Hospital," January 1, 1943. From the Office of Medical History – 67th Evacuation Hospital, available at: www.history.amedd.army.mil/booksdocs/wwii/67thEVACHOSP/67thEH1942.htm
"Bibliography of Morison's Writings," available at: www.history.navy.mil/library/guides/morison_bib.htm; *"Official United States Navy Biography,"* available at: www.history.navy.mil.bios/morison_s.htm

Executive Order Number 8022, available at: www.archive.eeoc.gov

Roosevelt, Theodore. *"Second Annual Message to Congress,"* December 2, 1902. From *"Naval History & Heritage Command,"* available at: www.history.navy.mil/trivia/trivia02.htm

United Nations Treaty Series, Number 4220. *"Netherlands and the United States of America: Exchange of Notes constituting an agreement concerning the return of silver supplied to the Government of the Kingdom of the Netherlands under lend-lease. Washington, 30 March and 25 May 1955."*

War Plans Division paper, sub: *"Immediate Mil Measures,"* December 21, 1941, *"Notes on Agenda Proposed by Gt Brit, Folder-Bk 2, Exec. 4."*

Miscellaneous and Online Sources

"African-American Military History," available at: http://lwfaam.net

"Harry Bensley," Wikipedia, available at: http://en.wikipedia.org/wiki/Harry_Bensley

"The Dutch East Indies is Lost Forever," available at: www.dutch-east-indies.com/sotry/page23.php

"Famous Navy Quotes: Who Said Them and When." From *"Naval History & Heritage Command,"* available at: www.history.navy.mil/trivia/trivia02.htm

"Gee Bee Model R," Wikipedia, available at: www.en.wikipedia.org/wiki/Gee_Bee_Model_R

"Gee Bee Racer," The History of Flight (poster) (Sausalito, CA: Portal Publications, undated)

Gudmundur Helagson, "Operation Drumbeat," from Uboat.Net, available at: www.uboat.net/ops/drumbeat/htm

"Hitler's Zweites Buch PDF," available at: http://en.wikipedia.org/wiki/Zweites_Buch

"Hugh Lowther, 5th Earl of Lonsdale," Wikipedia http://en/wikipedia.org/wiki/Hugh_Lowther

"In Memory of Karl Shapiro," available at: www.departments.bucknell.edu/stadler_center/shapiro/

Kipling, Rudyard. *The Dutch in the Medway.* Available at: www.kipling.org/poems_dutchmedway.htm

"MacArthur Vows 'I Shall Return,'" Universal Newsreels 5245, available at: www.youtube.com/watch?v=C2QyfnUSahc&feature=return

"Naval History & Heritage Command," available at: www.history.navy.mil/bios/morison_s.htm

"Ni'ihau Zero: The Rest of the Story," Pacific Aviation Museum Pearl Harbor Newsletter, Fall 2007. Available at: www.pacificaviaionmuseum.org

Richards, Lee. *"Operation Braddock,"* from Black Propaganda, available at: www.psywar.org/braddock/php

Roosevelt, Theodore. *"Second Annual Message to Congress,"* December 2, 1902. From *"Naval History & Heritage Command,"* available at: www.history.navy.mil/trivia/trivia02.htm
The Website of I.F. Stone; *"Writings by I.F. Stone, Business as Usual,' Advance Comments."* available at: www.ifstone.org/business_as_usual.php

Strobing, Irving. "Last Broadcast from Corregidor," available at: www.youtube.com

"*Unternhemen Paukenschlag*," Die Deutsche Wochenschau, #599, February 25, 1942. Available at: www.youtube.com

Washburn, Pat. "*The Pittsburgh Courier's Double V Campaign in 1942.*" Paper presented at Annual Meeting of the Association for Education in Journalism (64th, East Lansing, 1981), available at: www.eric.ed.gov:80/ERICWebPortalStrobing, Irving. "Last Broadcast from Corregidor," available at: www.youtube.com

INDEX

anti-Semitism 29, 64, 65, 74, 284
ANZAC 210
Arendt, Hannah 284
Argentina 136, 265, 266, 267
Arkansas 262
Arnold, Hap 104, 221, 275, 276, 278, 291
Ascoli, Max 116, 356n. 364
Ascoly, Nina 373nn. 83–4, 374n. 91
Ashahi Shimbun 116
Ashley, Brett 59
Asiatic Fleet 210, 211
Associated Press 96, 149, 202, 212, 218,
    224, 234, 235, 262, 319, 332, 395n. 195
Astor, Mary Cushing 245, 379n. 77
Astor, Nancy 95
Astor, Vincent 245
Astoria 260, 329, 331
Atlanta 329
Atlantic, the 289
Atlantic Charter 21, 39, 57, 92, 180, 228,
    229, 230
Atlantic Monthly 228, 283
Auchinleck, Claude 58, 326
Auden, W.H. 282, 387n. 83
Auslander, Joseph 295
Australia 84, 93, 94, 95, 97, 100, 180, 192,
    199, 200, 201, 203, 206, 207, 210, 211,
    213, 215, 216, 217, 218, 224, 225, 230,
    296–7, 303, 305, 306, 307, 308, 312,
    313, 314, 315, 316, 319–20, 335
Austria 66
Autry, Gene 31

Bailey, Ronald H. 338n. 34
Baldwin, C.B. 238
Baldwin, Hanson W. 364n. 668
Balestier, Carrie 52
*Baltimore Evening Su*n 138, 168, 212, 263,
    319, 333, 361nn. 524–5, 383n. 207,
    395nn. 196–9, 398nn. 92–5
Baltimore Sun 119, 180, 218, 224, 234, 262,
    278, 311, 362nn. 591–6, 375n. 150,
    376nn. 183–4, 378nn. 8, 10, 383nn.
    204–5, 208, 386n. 55, 393nn. 118–20,
    395nn. 200–3
Bancroft, George 41
Bankhead, Tallulah 106
Barbarossa 136, 232

Barbour, James 361n. 533
Baring-Gould, Sabine 343n. 184
Barkley, Alben 20, 170
Barnes, Donald 30–1
Barrymore, Lionel 52, 54
Barton, Bruce 116, 357n. 370
Baruch, Bernard 116, 356n. 362
Barzini, Luigi 372n. 62
Bataan and Corregidor 301–16
Bataan Defense Force 302
Batavia 89, 99, 102, 209, 212, 215
Bate, Fred 103
Bates, Ralph 226–7, 376nn. 202–5
Baukhage, Hilmar Robert 103, 354n. 268
BBC 97, 146
BBC Radio Handbook 353n. 230, 355n. 305
Beachey, Lincoln 275
Beard, Charles 8, 23, 338n. 33
Bearss, Edwin C. 382nn. 164–6, 168
Beekman, Allan 378nn. 26, 30, 33–4
Beer Hall Putsch 68
Beesley, Patrick 382n. 178
Beirne, Francis F. 390n. 193
Beiswanger, George 288, 388n. 128
Belgium 10, 84, 126, 180, 206
Bell, Edna 153
Bell, Roy 153, 310
Belloc, Hilaire 144
Benedick, Anne 286
Benes, Eduard 113, 141, 356n. 343
Bennet, James Gordon 49
Bennett, Matthew 396n. 21
Benny, Jack 96
Bensley, Harry 49, 344n. 239
Benson, Jackson J. 386n. 79, 388nn. 145,
    147–9, 151–2, 389nn. 153–4, 159,
    161–2, 166–7, 179
Bentley, Elizabeth 114
Bercovitch, Sacvan 343n. 193
Berenson, Bernard 116
Bergerud, Eric M. 377nn. 220–2, 390nn.
    197–8, 391n. 12
Bernstein, Walter 149, 362nn. 584–6
Berryman, John 282, 387n. 87
Best, Marshall 293
Beveridge, Albert 44
Beville, H.M., Jr. 354n. 291
Biddle, A.J. Drexel, Jr. 207

Elson, Robert T. 347nn. 29, 32, 351nn. 157, 181–2
Emancipation Proclamation 45
Emergency Rescue Committee 284
Emerson, Ralph Waldo 53, 56, 345n. 259, 346n. 281
Empress of China 160
Encounter 217
England *see* Britain
ENIGMA project 259
Ennis, Edward J. 249
Enterprise 274, 317, 318, 329, 331
Ernst, Max 284
Erwin, John 310
Ethiopia 33, 62
Eurasia 15, 68, 69
Evans, Richard J. 348n. 50
Evans, Walter 21
Evans, Wilfred G. 263
Everson, William
    Poetry 283
Exeter 217

Fabend, Firth Haring 373n. 89
Fadiman, Clifton 294
Fair Employment Act (1941) 253
Fair Employment Practice
    Committee 253–4
Fall of France 59, 67, 71, 140, 182, 203
Fang, Irving 341n. 140, 354nn. 267, 273–5, 278, 290, 355nn. 308–10, 357nn. 388–93, 395, 398, 401–2, 374nn. 108–10, 386n. 76
Farragut, David Glasgow 13
Farrington, Karen 372n. 57, 377n. 228
Farrow, William G. 277
Feuchtwanger, Lion 324
Fichte, Johann Gottlieb 41
Field, Gilmore 31
Fifer, J. Valerie 344nn. 242
Final Solution 74, 75
Finland 33, 56, 135, 136, 287
Fireside Chat 9, 32, 33, 35, 36, 38
Fireside Chats 9
Fischer, Louis 250–1, 380nn. 114–17
Fish, Hamilton 253
Fitzgerald, F. Scott 54, 345n. 266
Fitzgerald, John M. 363nn. 610–11, 616, 366n. 714, 721, 392n. 82

Flannery, Harry 145
    Assignment to Berlin 145
Fleming, Dewey L. 180
Fletcher, Frank J. 317, 318, 329, 331
Flitch, Aubrey W. 317
Florence Luckenbach 262
Flying Tigers 88, 162, 163, 166, 220, 224, 226
Ford, Daniel 365nn. 680–2, 684, 687, 689, 691, 694–6, 698, 700–1, 376n. 168
Ford, Gerald 29
Ford, John 274
Foreign Affairs 228
Fortune 192, 194, 256, 272, 348n. 63
Four-Power Treaty 84
France 10, 14, 32, 33, 39, 40, 41, 42, 59, 60–1, 62, 82, 84, 100, 110, 124, 125, 127, 129, 140, 141, 144, 181, 184, 187, 191, 205, 251, 271, 284, 287
Frances Salman 262
Francis E. Powell 262
Frank, Hans 75
Frank, Waldo 135
Frankfurter, Felix 106
Franklin, Benjamin 142
Freedom 159
Freifeld, Sidney A. 349n. 78
French, Warren 387n. 86, 389nn. 158, 160
French Guyana 60
Freud, Sigmund 290
Friedel, Frank 363n. 608
Frnak, Jerry 194
Fry, Varian 284, 387n. 97
Fuchida, Mitsuo 1, 2, 330, 337nn. 2–3, 396n. 31, 397nn. 63, 72, 75
Fuhrer 39, 63, 72, 76, 105, 198, 232, 257
    see also Hitler, Adolf
fuhrerprizip 63
Fussell, Paul 386n. 81

Gabriel, Ralph Henry 26, 339nn. 67–9, 341n. 130
    The Course of American Democratic Thought 14
Gaddis, John L. 339nn. 50, 65, 70–1
Gallup, George 5, 97, 115, 353n. 234
Galveston Daily News 264
Gamelin, Maurice 27, 140

Jones, John Paul 13, 207
Jones Act (1916) 85
Journal of Farm Economics 250
Journal of Speculative Philosophy 41
Jungle Journal 307
Jupiter 217

Kaga 329, 330, 331, 332
Kajioka, Sadamichi 158, 159
Kaleohano, Hawila (Howell) 237, 238
Kaltenborn, H.V. 102, 103–5, 114, 180, 224,
    229, 279–80, 354nn. 266, 281–9, 356n.
    348, 368n. 8, 376nn. 185–7, 377n. 216,
    386nn. 61–6
Kanahele, Ben 238
Kanahele, Ella 238
Kann, Robert A. 347n. 34
Kant, Immanuel 41, 288
Kasahara, Akira 278
Kauffmann, Henrik de 387n. 119
Kearns, Gerry 348nn. 44, 46
Keene, R.R. 364nn. 659, 662
Kellogg-Briand Pact 83–4
Kelly, Colin 105
Kennan, George 239
Kennedy, David M. 343n. 203
Kennedy, Joseph 7, 39
Kent, Rockwell 388n. 120
Kerker, Wayne 59
Kern, Jerome 60
Kershaw, Ian 349n. 89
Kesselring, Albert 197, 198, 199, 371n. 7
Ketchum, Richard M. 338n. 38
KGMB 97
Kido Butai 2
Kimball, Warren F. 343n. 185, 346nn.
    289–90, 367nn. 741–3, 748
Kimmel, Husband 20, 113, 127, 141, 150,
    155, 260
King, Ernest J. 81, 150, 171, 259, 276, 303,
    319, 333, 335
King, Martin Luther, Jr. 256
King, Samuel W. 234
Kipling, Rudyard 12, 52, 107, 152, 205,
    345n. 256, 372nn. 59, 64
Kirchwey, Frieda 135–6, 137, 283, 360nn.
    509, 513, 361n. 519
Kirishima 231, 329

Kirk, Alan G. 259, 261
Kiso 274
Kittner, Robert 94, 352n. 209
Kjellen, Rudolf 68
Klehr, Harvey 356nn. 346–7
Knabenshue, Roy 275
Knickerbocker, H.R. 215, 374n. 124,
    375nn. 125–7
Knickerbocker, William S. 125,
    358n. 441
KNIL army 211, 214
Knortz, Karl 40
Knox, Frank 4, 19, 22, 71, 112, 123, 137,
    150, 238
Knudsen, Otto 136, 139, 194
Knudsen, William S. 35, 118
Koch, Cynthia 373nn. 72, 87
Kohut, Andrew 345n. 246
Kondo, Nobutake 328
Kongo 231
Konoe, Fumimaro 94
Korea 233
Koroda, Paul 277
Kriegsmarine 70, 258, 259
Kristallnacht 70
Kuh, Frederick 190
Kung, H.H. 161
Kupfer, Charles 338nn. 26, 39, 42,
    341n. 138, 144, 342n. 167, 346n. 279,
    346n. 4, 347n. 8, 348n. 62, 353n. 231,
    354n. 280, 372n. 50, 377n. 3, 384n.
    245, 389n. 182
Kurashige, Lon 380nn. 90, 92
Kurita, Takeo 216
Kurth, Peter 340n. 113
Kurusu, Saboro 18, 19, 122, 128
Kusaka, Ryunosuke 1
Kwei-tseng, Ni 161

Ladies Home Journal 209
LaFeber, Walter 350n. 138, 352nn. 200–1,
    205
La France Libre 140
LaGuardia, Fiorello 117
Lake Oswega 262
Lamont, Corliss 324
Lampard, Eric E. 343n. 199
Landowska, Wanda 284

MacArthur, Douglass 20, 85, 98, 111, 120, 121, 125, 129, 130, 153, 154–6, 166–7, 168, 169, 187, 228, 240, 302, 303, 304, 305, 307–8, 309, 311, 312, 313, 315, 364nn. 634–6, 638, 640, 642, 391n. 27
MacCracken, Henry Noble 7
Machine Tools Board 194
Mackinder, Halford 12, 68–9, 348n. 48
  Democratic Ideals and Reality 69
MacLean, Donald A. 267–8
MacLean, Donald A. 384n. 243
MacLeish, Archibald 10, 60, 110, 135, 283, 295, 360nn. 507–8, 387nn. 89–90
Madagascar 230, 232, 326
Madej, W. Victor 391nn. 7, 9
Madsen, Daniel 337nn. 5, 9
Magazine of Fantasy and Science Fiction 138
magazines 126–48
Magee, John Gillespie, Jr. 295, 389nn. 183–4
Magellan, Ferdinand 152
Maguire, Matthew 124
Mahan, Alfred Thayer 11–14, 43, 68, 86, 338n. 49
  The Influence of Sea Power Upon History, 1660–1783 12, 13
  The Interest of America in Sea Power, Present and Future 12
Major Wheeler 262
Malay 262, 263
Malaya 24, 57, 86, 105, 130, 141, 155, 197, 199, 200, 202, 204, 210, 217, 218, 219, 222, 266
Malta 198
Manchester, William 346nn. 284–5, 358nn. 408–11, 363n. 619, 364nn. 633, 637, 641, 390n. 2, 391nn. 10, 13, 15, 17–18, 22, 391nn. 28–30, 34
Mann, Golo 288
Mann, Golo 388n. 125
Marble, Harry 213, 214, 335
Marore 262
Marshall, Catherine 397n. 104
Marshall, George C. 19, 80, 129–30, 150, 162, 165, 171, 178, 221, 223, 257, 259, 266, 303, 308
Marshall, George Preston 96

Marshall, Peter J. 285–6, 397nn. 103, 105–10
Martin, F.X. 345n. 261
Martin, Frederick L. 150
Martin, Joseph 20
Martin B-26 Marauder 276
Martyn, Thomas J.C. 132
Marx, Karl 135
Matthaus, Jurgen 349n. 92
Maurois, Andre 289, 388nn. 134–8
Mazer, Bill 374n. 92
MBS 96, 97, 106–9
McCloy, John 220, 240
McCormick, Anne O'Hare 187, 188, 369n. 54
McCormick, Robert 23, 36, 72, 119, 283, 333
McCoy, Frank R. 149
McCrae, John 295
McCrum, Robert 345n. 245, 361n. 556, 362nn. 557, 559, 563, 566–7, 576–8, 387nn. 113, 115
McDaniel, C. Yates 202
McInnis, Edgar 374nn. 97, 101, 103, 105, 393nn. 128–9, 394n. 130
McKinley, William L. 152
McNarney, Joseph T. 150
McNaught, Kenneth 343n. 208
McNutt, Paul V. 254
McWilliams, Carey 249–50, 380nn. 110–13
  Factories in the Fields 250
  Ill Fares the Land 250
Mead, Margaret 209, 374n. 94
Mead, William B. 342n. 159
Meehl, Gerald A. 386nn. 45–6
Meet the Press 138
Melbourne Times-Argus 314
Melosi, Martin V. 342nn. 150–1
Mencken, H. D. 341n. 135
Mencken, H.L 27–8, 42, 296
Merry-Go-Round 120, 121, 122, 123, 124, 125, 177, 194, 249, 264
Mesmer, Franz 290
Metz, Robert 353n. 227
Meyerhoff, Otto 284
Midway 24, 33, 98, 133, 157, 278, 316, 320, 323–4, 327–36
Mikuma 329

Paulding, James Kirke 38, 342n. 181,
    343nn. 187–8
  *The Diverting History of John Bull and
    Brother Jonathan* 40
Paulhan, Louis 275
Paul Jones 217
Pearson, Drew 94, 118–25, 172, 178, 230,
    249, 264, 303, 352n. 209, 367nn. 754,
    759–60, 368nn. 790–1, 795, 370nn. 61,
    89–92, 377nn. 4–5, 380n. 103, 383nn.
    219–21, 384nn. 241–2
  Washington Merry-Go-Round 120, 172,
    189, 234, 267, 383n. 222
Pearson, Luvie 120
Peffer, Nathaniel 134, 360n. 499
Pegler, Westbrook 244
Peirce, Charles Sanders 41
Peirse, Richard E.C. 210
Penang 141
Pensacola 329
People's World 249, 380nn. 101–2
Pepys, Samuel 206
Pepys, Samuel 372n. 63
Percival, A.E. 130, 199, 204
Perloff, Harvey S. 343n. 199
Perry, Matthew Calbraith 43, 148
Perry, Oliver Hazard 13, 32
Pershing, John J. 59, 129
Perth 217
Petain, Henri-Philippe 60, 182, 183,
    184, 185
Petillo, Carol Morris 366nn. 711–12,
    391nn. 36–7
Philippines 13, 14, 20, 24, 37, 81, 83, 86,
    90, 98, 105, 106, 121, 125, 127, 129,
    130, 131, 149, 151, 152–7, 166–70,
    187, 192, 200, 202, 210, 216, 223, 258,
    270, 280, 303, 307, 308, 310, 313, 314,
    315, 316
Pilat, Oliver 357nn. 387, 394, 396–7,
    399–400, 403–5, 358nn. 406–7, 412–16
Pimlott, John 376nn. 173, 175, 390n. 199,
    397n. 66
Pittsburgh Courier 255, 256
Plantenga, Bart 373nn. 83–4, 374n. 91
Plesch, Dan 368nn. 7, 9, 370n. 81
Plessy v. Ferguson 253
PM 267

Poe, Edgar Allen 296
Pogue, Forrest G. 350nn. 130–2
Poindexter, Arthur R. 364nn. 650–1, 655–6
Poland 10, 33, 65, 75, 103, 180, 293
Poorten, Hein ter 210
Pope 211, 217
Popular Mechanics 275
Portland 329
Portugal 84, 211
Post 96
Powell, Adam Clayton, Jr. 256
Powell, William 31
Prange, Gordon W. 337n. 4, 340n. 86, 378n.
    32, 381n. 135, 386n. 47, 395nn. 1–3,
    396nn. 32–3, 35, 397nn. 81–2, 398nn.
    83–4, 86
Pravda 135
Price, Lucien 45
Price, Mary 113, 114
Price, S.L. 352nn. 215, 218, 220
Priestley, J.B. 97
Prince of Wales 58, 72, 101, 102, 104, 108,
    112, 133, 141, 149, 231
Public Opinion Quarterly 192

Quantril, Hadley 5
Queen, Howard Donovan 255
Quezon, Manuel 153, 154, 168, 208, 304,
    305, 314

Rachlis, Eugene 383n. 193
racism 254–5
Radio Tokyo 277, 278, 280
Raft, George 31
Rainbow Five Plan 87, 98, 154, 260
Raleigh, John M. 99–100, 102, 212, 312,
    313, 314
Randolph, A. Philip 253, 254, 256
Rankin, Jeanette 26, 29, 35
Ratzell, Friedrich 68
Rayburn, Sam 20, 24
Reader's Digest 138, 238, 314
Reb, Johnny 37
Rector, Edward F. 225
Redmond, Juanita 306, 392nn. 52, 54,
    59–60
Reed, Donna 299
Reed, John 114

Wilson, Woodrow 13, 15–16, 24, 37, 67, 69, 73, 83, 115, 117, 339n. 64
Wimmel, Kenneth 338n. 45, 339nn. 62, 66, 348n. 42
Winant, John G. 39, 56, 57
Winchell, Walter 120
Winick, R.H. 347n. 7
Winkelmann, Henri 206
Winn, Rodger 259
Winter, William 99
Winthrop, Jonathan 36, 37
Wirthin, Tom 167
W. L. Steed 262
Wodehouse, Ethel 144, 146, 286
Wodehouse, P.G 50–1, 142–8, 286, 345n. 244, 361nn. 551, 553–4, 387n. 114
  The Code of the Woosters 143–4
  Eggs, Beans, and Crumpets 144
  Joy in the Morning 287
  Money in the Bank 143, 144, 146, 147, 286
  Quick Service 144
  Something New 142
  Uncle Fred in the Springtime 144
Wolfert, Ira 183
Wood, Leonard 85
Woodring, Harry H. 86
Woodruff, William 343n. 212, 344n. 213
Worth, Richard 371nn. 3–5, 382nn. 171–3
Worth, Roland H. 351n. 176, 352n. 206
Wouk, Herman 377n. 234, 397nn. 64, 77
Wu Duncan, Donald 276

Wukovits, John 354n. 262, 364nn. 663–5
Wynne, Keenan 299
Yale Review 288

Yamamoto, Isoruku 93, 94, 128, 231, 232, 235, 278, 316, 327–9, 331, 332, 333
Yamashita, Tomoyuki 105, 199–200, 201, 202, 204, 314, 315
Yamato 329
Yank 299
Yank at Eton, A 54
Yank at Oxford, A 54
Yarnell, Harry E. 83
Yat-Sen, Sun 161
Yeats, William Butler 60
York, Alvin C. 80
Yorktown 317, 318, 329, 330, 331, 332
Young, Loretta 245
Young, P.B. 252
Young, Stark 132
Younger, Calton 345n. 260
Yubari 158
Yugoslavia 33, 180

Zhukov, Georgi 33
Zuckerman, Mary Ellen 360n. 486
Zuikaku 231, 317, 318
Zweig, Stefan 388n. 143
  Conqueror of the Seas: The Story of Magellan 290
  Mental Healers 290